T5-AFS-501

NEW TESTAMENT COMMENTARY

# NEW TESTAMENT COMMENTARY

*By*

WILLIAM HENDRIKSEN

*Exposition*

*of*

*Galatians*

(Ephesians starts after
p. 260)

BAKER BOOK HOUSE
GRAND RAPIDS, MICHIGAN

Originally published in separate volumes:

*Galatians*, Copyright 1968 by William Hendriksen
ISBN: 0-8010-4028-0
Library of Congress Catalog Card Number: 54-924

*Ephesians*, Copyright 1967 by William Hendriksen
ISBN: 0-8010-4010-8
Library of Congress Catalog Card Number: 67-18179

Combination volume issued 1979
ISBN: 0-8010-4211-9

*First printing, July 1979*
*Second printing, March 1981*
*Third printing, October 1982*
*Fourth printing, February 1984*



PHOTOLITHOPRINTED BY CUSHING - MALLOY, INC.
ANN ARBOR, MICHIGAN, UNITED STATES OF AMERICA

# TABLE OF CONTENTS

# LIST OF ABBREVIATIONS

The letters in book-abbreviations are followed by periods. Those in periodical-abbreviations omit the periods and are in italics. Thus one can see at a glance whether the abbreviation refers to a book or to a periodical.

A. *Book Abbreviations*

| | |
|---|---|
| A.R.V. | American Standard Revised Version |
| A.V. | Authorized Version (King James) |
| Gram.N.T. | A. T. Robertson, *Grammar of the Greek New Testament in the Light of Historical Research* |
| Gram.N.T. (Bl.-Debr) | F. Blass and A. Debrunner, *A Greek Grammar of the New Testament and Other Early Christian Literature* |
| Grk.N.T. (A—B—M—W) | *The Greek New Testament,* edited by Kurt Aland, Matthew Black, Bruce M. Metzger, and Allen Wikgren, 1966 edition. |
| I.S.B.E. | *International Standard Bible Encyclopedia* |
| L.N.T. (Th.) | Thayer's *Greek-English Lexicon of the New Testament* |
| L.N.T. (A. and G.) | W. F. Arndt and F. W. Gingrich, *A Greek-English Lexicon of the New Testament and Other Early Christian Literature* |
| M.M. | *The Vocabulary of the Greek New Testament Illustrated from the Papyri and Other Non-Literary Sources,* by James Hope Moulton and George Milligan (edition Grand Rapids, 1952) |
| N.A.S.B. (N.T.) | New American Standard Bible (New Testament) |
| N.N. | *Novum Testamentum Graece,* edited by D. Eberhard Nestle, revised by Erwin Nestle and Kurt Aland, 25th edition, 1963 |
| N.E.B. | New English Bible |
| N.T.C. | W. Hendriksen, *New Testament Commentary* |
| R.S.V. | Revised Standard Version |
| S.H.E.R.K. | *The New Schaff-Herzog Encyclopedia of Religious Knowledge* |
| Th.W.N.T. | *Theologisches Wörterbuch zum Neuen Testament* (edited by G. Kittel) |
| W.D.B. | *Westminster Dictionary of the Bible* |

### B. *Periodical Abbreviations*

| | |
|---|---|
| *ABR* | *Australian Biblical Review* |
| *BA* | *Biblical Archaeologist* |
| *BW* | *Biblical World* |
| *CTM* | *Concordia Theological Monthly* |
| *EQ* | *Evangelical Quarterly* |
| *ET* | *Expository Times* |
| *Exp* | *The Expositor* |
| *GTT* | *Gereformeerd theologisch tijdschrift* |
| *Int* | *Interpretation* |
| *JBL* | *Journal of Biblical Literature* |
| *TT* | *Theologisch tijdschrift* |

*Please Note*

In order to differentiate between the second person plural (see Gal. 6:1: "y o u who are spiritual") and the second person singular (same verse: "lest you also be tempted"), the letters in "y o u pl." are spaced; those in "you sing." are not.

# Introduction

# to

# The Epistle to the Galatians

# I. Why Is This Epistle Important?

"The epistle to the Galatians is my epistle. To it I am as it were in wedlock. It is my Katherine." Thus spoke Luther, who considered Galatians the best of all the books in the Bible. It has been called "the battle-cry of the Reformation," "the great charter of religious freedom," "the Christian declaration of independence," etc.

It is important because *in any age* it answers the basic question asked by the human heart: "How can I find true happiness?" "How can I obtain peace, tranquility, freedom from fear?"

In his own strength and by his own wisdom man is totally unable to discover the answer. The slogan that has appeared in various forms, one of them being: "No Christ for a gift God gave us, Mankind alone must save us," fails completely. It fails in each of its manifestations, be it ritualism in obedience to the law of Moses—that was the snare in which the Galatians of Paul's day were becoming entangled (3:10; 5:2-4) —, rigorous asceticism, the affliction of the body, works of supererogation, the self-righteous deeds of "the moral man," strict obedience to "the laws of Nature," confidence in Science (these two here purposely spelled with a capital letter), or, lastly, the leaning either on oneself, as the captain of one's fate and the master of one's soul, or on this or that political Führer or false religious Messiah.

At times the attempt to satisfy man's deepest yearning takes an entirely different, even *opposite,* direction. *Legalism yields to license.* It is as if men were saying, "Since *obedience* to law—whether of Nature, of Moses, of the demagogue, or even of unenlightened conscience—has not brought the desired result, let us try *dis*obedience to law. Let us break their bonds asunder, And cast away their cords from us. Away with every restraint!" However, those who have sown the wind of (what *they* are pleased to call) "personal liberty"—in reality it is unbridled license!—with its emphasis on such things as sex and sadism, robbery and rioting (cf. 5:19-21), are reaping the whirlwind of intellectual impoverishment, moral decay, and spiritual bankruptcy. The solution, clearly, does not lie in this direction.

For all those who are willing to take God at his word Galatians shows the way to true freedom (5:1). That genuine liberty is neither legalism nor license. It is the freedom of "bondage to Christ." It consists in becoming a captive in his train, that is, surrendering oneself to God Triune as he has revealed himself in Jesus Christ unto salvation. It is discovered when one is willing to desist from every attempt to save oneself, and to accept Christ

Jesus as his Lord and Savior, glorying in his cross alone (6:14) and trusting in him as the fulfiller of the law (3:13). For all those who have by God's sovereign grace been led to do this the law ceases forevermore to be the means of attaining happiness now or the ticket to heaven when death arrives (2:16). Guided by Christ's Spirit, the redeemed, out of gratitude for the salvation which they have thus received as a gift, begin to adorn their lives with "the fruit of the Spirit: love, joy, peace, longsuffering, kindness, goodness, faithfulness, meekness, and self-control" (5:22, 23). Now fear has fled. Lust has vanished as a guiding principle (5:24). The prison-door has been opened. The air is exhilarating, invigorating. True freedom at last has been found. The sinner has been reconciled to his God. He is walking by the Spirit (5:16). Not only has he *found* the blessing, but he has also *become* a blessing, for it is through him that God blesses *the world.*

This last observation deserves emphasis. In Paul's day neither *legalism* nor *libertinism* (licentiousness) was winning any victories, real and lasting. It was exactly the gospel of *liberty in and through Christ* which was going forth conquering and to conquer. Had Paul surrendered to *legalism* Christianity would have become known as nothing more than a modified Judaism, which in no sense whatever could have conquered the world. The Gentiles would have rejected it. Had he compromised with *libertinism* after the example of those who had adopted the slogan, "Let us continue in sin that grace may abound" (cf. Rom. 6:1), the hearts of men chosen to eternal life would never have been satisfied. Sooner or later the falsity of "the new religion" would have been exposed. But because, by God's sovereign power, he succumbed to neither but proclaimed the riches of God's pardoning *and transforming* (!) grace, Christianity became—not just *a* but—*the* great world-religion, the religion destined to invade the hearts of all those whom God from eternity had chosen "out of *every* tribe and tongue and people and nation" (Rev. 5:9). *Legalism, libertinism,* or *true liberty,* that was the question then. It is the question also today.

## II. To Whom Was It Addressed?

About the year 278 B.C. a large body of Gauls or Kelts, who had previously invaded and ravaged Greece, Macedonia, and Thrace, crossed over into Asia Minor. Their coming was not—at least not altogether—an unwarranted intrusion, for they arrived as a result of an invitation that had been extended to them by Nicomedes, king of Bithynia. So, here they were, with their wives and children, occupying the very heart-land of Asia Minor, a broad belt extending northward from the center (see accompanying sketch).

They belonged to three tribes: the Trochmi, Tectosages, and Tolisbogii, with whom are associated the cities, respectively, of Tavium, Ancyra, and

Pessinus. All three of these tribes were *Galli,* that is, Gauls ("warriors"), also called *Galatae,* that is, Galatians ("nobles"). They rapidly gained the mastery over the native population of "Phrygians," of mixed ancestry, devotees of the ancient and impressive religion of Cybele. For a long time, due to constant raids into adjacent districts, the boundaries of the Gallic domain remained fluid, but the newcomers were finally forced by the Romans to live in peace with their neighbors and to remain within the limits of their own territory. In course of time, as happens often in such cases, the Gauls amalgamated with the earlier population, adopted their religion, but in most other respects remained the dominant strain.

Since the Gallic rulers were gifted with shrewdness they generally allied themselves with whoever happened to be "on top" in Rome. The latter reciprocated by allowing the former to be treated more as an ally than as a conquered nation. They were considered a "kingdom." During the reign of their last king, Amyntas IV, their realm was even extended southward. Upon the death of Amyntas (25 B.C.) the Romans fell heir to this already somewhat enlarged kingdom and converted it into the Roman "province of Galatia," which soon comprised, in addition to the *central and northern* territory, *to the south:* parts of Phrygia, Lycaonia, Pisidia, and Isauria (see the sketch).

It is understandable that the terms *Galatia* and *Galatians* could now be used in a twofold sense, as indicating either *a. Galatia proper* with its Gallic population, or *b. the larger Roman province,* inhabited not only by the Gauls as the dominant race in the central and north, but also by others farther south. When the term *Galatians* was used in the former sense, it naturally could not refer to those to whom the gospel had been proclaimed in the course of Paul's first missionary journey. The churches of Antioch (Pisidia), Iconium (Phrygia), Lystra and Derbe (cities of Lycaonia),[1] would then be excluded. On the other hand, when it was used in the latter sense it could very well refer to these early converts to the Christian faith about whom we read in Acts 13 and 14.

All of this leads to the question: "To whom was Galatians addressed: to the churches of Pessinus, Ancyra, Tavium and surroundings, or to those in Antioch (Pisidian), Iconium, Lystra, Derbe, and vincinity? Did the apostle use the term *Galatians* (3:1; cf. 1:2) in the racial (ethnic) or in the political sense? Was he thinking of people in the north or of those in the south?"[2]

---

[1] Ancient writers do not always link these cities with the districts as here indicated. There is much confusion, brought about to some extent by the individual author's point of departure, whether it be geographical or political. Moreover, boundaries shifted. See, however, Acts 13:14; 14:6.

[2] The great distance between the cities of the north and those of the south and also certain specific incidents mentioned in the letter (4:12-16) make it impossible to believe that he was addressing the churches of *both* North and South Galatia. Either the one or the other must be true.

For well-nigh two centuries there has been a sharp division of opinion with respect to this subject. Both camps of advocates have their great scholars as well as their lesser lights. For a representative defense of the North Galatian theory see J. B. Lightfoot, *The Epistle of St. Paul to the Galatians,* reprint,

## WHO WERE THE GALATIANS?

ASIA, GALATIA, etc.: Roman Provinces
*Mysia*, *Galatia*, etc.: Geographic Regions
— — — — — — — — — — — : Beginning of second Miss. Journey: Antioch (Syria) to Troas; and of third: Antioch (Syria) to Ephesus

Grand Rapids, no date, pp. 1–35; for the South Galatian view see W. M. Ramsay, *The Church in the Roman Empire,* London, 1893, pp. 3–112; *St. Paul the Traveler and the Roman Citizen,* reprint, Grand Rapids, 1949, pp. 89–151; and *A Historical Commentary on St. Paul's Epistle to the Galatians,* reprint, Grand Rapids, 1965, pp. 1–234.[3]

---

[3] Among those favoring the North Galatian theory are also the following (for titles of their works see the Bibliography): Calvin, Coneybeare and Howson, Erdman,

Excellent summaries of arguments and counter-arguments, logically arranged, can be found in several commentaries. In order to avoid duplication and, if possible, increase the interest in this subject, which is not wholly devoid of significance for the proper interpretation of certain Galatian passages, I shall follow a new approach, and present the matter in the form of a brief imaginary debate between a defender of the North Galatian theory and an advocate of the opposite view.

*Resolved: That Galatians is addressed to the churches in North Galatia.*

### A. *Affirmative*

Mr. chairman, honorable judges, worthy opponent, and all other friends of biblical investigation:

In the days of the apostle Paul there existed in central and northern Asia Minor a people known as *Gauls* or *Galatians.* They were Gauls or Galatians by blood and descent. Even long before they had crossed over from Europe into Asia Minor they were known thus. The new kingdom which they established in Asia Minor was consequently a Gallic or Galatian kingdom. It is true that when this kingdom was converted into a Roman province, named Galatia, a few small districts were added, inhabited by people of a different nationality, who, in a remote or definitely secondary sense, were able, from that moment on, to call themselves Galatians. However, it cannot be denied that the primary meaning of this word *Galatians* is not "inhabitants of the province of Galatia," but *Gauls,* nothing else. When, therefore, a letter is addressed "To the Galatians," convincing proof to the contrary would be needed before it would be possible to interpret this address in any other way than in harmony with the long established connotation of the word.

Such convincing proof, however, is completely absent. Ask the ancient interpreters, the men who lived much nearer to the time when this letter was written, how *they* interpreted the term *Galatians* as used in Gal. 3:1, cf. 1:2. With one voice they will tell you that it refers to the Gauls of Galatia *proper,* and not to just anyone who, due to some political maneuvering, happened to be living within the Roman province of Galatia. Now this testimony of the ancients should be given its proper due. In all other disputes—for example, touching such matters as the origin of Infant Baptism or of the religious observance of the first day of the week—we are always asking,

Findlay, Greijdanus, Kerr, Moffatt, Schaff, and Schmoller. Kirsopp Lake's criticism of the South Galatian view (in *The Beginnings of Christianity,* Part I, London, 1933, pp. 224–240) "has tended to keep minds open on this issue," remarks Sherman E. Johnson, "Early Christianity in Asia Minor," *JBL,* 77 (March 1958), p. 9. For the defense of the South Galatian theory see (in addition to Ramsay's works) Berkhof, *New Testament Introduction,* p. 179 ff.; Bruce, *Commentary on Acts,* p. 300, Burton, Cole, Ellis, Emmet, Goodspeed, Jones, Rendall, Ridderbos, Ropes, Scott, Stamm, Tenney, Thiessen, Van Leeuwen, and Zahn.

"What does early tradition say about this?" Why should we ignore such unanimous tradition in *this* particular instance?

Besides, careful study of the contents of the epistle strengthens the proposition which I am defending. We note that those addressed are pictured as *fickle*. When the apostle arrived in their midst and preached to them the glorious gospel, they accepted it at once. Yes, they even welcomed him as they would have welcomed an angel or Jesus Christ himself, and had it been necessary, they would even have plucked out their very eyes and given them to Paul (Gal. 4:14, 15). Soon afterward, however, due to the arrival in their midst of some false teachers who slandered the apostle and belittled his preaching, they turn right around, so that they are now at the point of rejecting both Paul and his message (Gal 3:1-4). Now has not instability of character always been the outstanding trait of *Gauls,* yes, and even of their descendants to this present day? Do we not read in Caesar's *Gallic War* IV.5: "Caesar was informed of these events; and fearing the fickleness of the Gauls . . . decided that no confidence could be reposed in them"? These Galatians whom Paul addressed in his epistle were typical Gauls, therefore.

Moreover, when with Luke's account of the first missionary journey, during which the gospel was proclaimed to the people of Antioch (Pisidian), Iconium, Lystra, and Derbe, we compare the apostle's own account of his reception by the *Galatians* and his work among them (Gal. 4:13, 14), do we not see immediately that these two are completely different? This difference is not because one is true and the other false. Rather, it is because the two accounts deal with two entirely different subjects, two different missions. Thus, the apostle tells the Gauls or Galatians: "It was because of an infirmity of the flesh that I preached to y o u the gospel on that former occasion" (Gal. 4:13). Now compare this remark with Luke's review of Paul's work in Antioch, Iconium, Lystra, and Derbe (Acts 13 and 14). In that account is there even the least hint that it was because of infirmity that the apostle either *began* his work in these more southern cities or *continued* it for a longer period than he had at first intended? Of course not, for these are different people. They cannot be identified with Paul's *Galatians.*

Besides, when does Luke first mention the word *Galatia?* Not until he has reached the point in his story where Paul, on his *second* missionary journey, has left behind the more southern cities of Derbe, Lystra, etc., and is turning *northward* (Acts 16:6; cf. 18:23; 19:1). It is very clear, then, that when Paul's close friend and frequent companion, Luke, whom the apostle calls "the beloved physician," now finally speaks about *Galatia,* he cannot have been thinking of the cities of the south that had but recently been added[4]

[4] His opponent might have challenged this bit of information, as these people had been "Galatians" for at least 75 years. But in a debate you cannot delve into every minor point!

to the province of Galatia. His eyes are now turned toward the north. And if that was true with respect to Luke, why should it not hold for Paul? Why should we assume that the latter uses the terms *Galatia* and *Galatians* in any sense different than the ethnic?

There is one additional reason that makes it well-nigh impossible to identify the people of the more southern part of the Roman province of Galatia with the *Galatians* whom Paul addresses in his letter. It is clear from the entire contents of this epistle that those addressed were—either exclusively or at least almost exclusively—converts from the Gentile world (Gal. 4:8-11; 6:12). They were people who had never been circumcised (Gal. 5:2; 6:12), but were now in danger of accepting the rite of circumcision. They could not have been Jews, therefore, for the Jews were circumcised, and were even called "the circumcision." On the other hand, the churches established in the southern part of the Roman province of Galatia consisted of both Jews and Gentiles, perhaps in equal proportion. The Jews may even have predominated. In fact, in Antioch of Pisidia there were "*many* Jews" who turned to Christ (Acts 13:43). In Antioch and in Iconium there were found synagogues of Jews. Into these synagogues the apostle entered and preached. At Iconium "a great multitude both of Jews and of Greeks believed" (Acts 14:1). This decided difference between the constituency of the southern churches, described in the book of Acts, and the Gentile converts whom Paul addresses in his letter to the Galatians, proves that this letter cannot have been written to South and must have been intended for North Galatia.

### B. *Negative*

Mr. president, noble referees, friendly adversary, and all those interested in scriptural research:

First of all I wish to remind y o u of the proposition which my worthy opponent was supposed to defend. It was this: "Resolved: That Galatians is addressed to the churches in North Galatia." Permit me to underscore the word *churches*. At what point in his argument did he ever give us a clear conception of these churches? All he told us was that at some point in the second missionary journey and also later Paul turned "to the north." He evidently wanted us to draw the conclusion that since Paul's letter was addressed to the Gauls, and since the more southern churches did not consist of Gauls, the apostle must have labored for a considerable time among the Gauls of the north, long enough to establish churches there. Am I being unfair when I state that his conclusion is drawn from a false premise? Fact is that when Paul says *Galatians* he does not necessarily mean *Gauls*. Rather, in distinction from Luke, he, Paul, in making mention of the churches under his care, and grouping them, uses the names of *Roman provinces* rather than those of races or nationalities. Thus, for example, in I Cor. 16:5 the apostle speaks of *Macedonia;* in the fifteenth verse of the same chapter he refers to

*Achaia,* and in the nineteenth verse to *Asia.* Now all of these were *Roman provinces.* Therefore, when in the opening of the chapter (I Cor. 16:1) he mentions "the churches of *Galatia,*" is it not logical to assume that here, too, as well as in the other three cases, he refers to it as *a Roman province?* And if in I Cor. 16:1 the meaning must be "the churches of the Roman province of Galatia," why should the identical phrase in Gal. 1:2 have a diffierent meaning?[5] We see, therefore, that it is far better to say that the epistle of Paul which figures in this debate was addressed to "churches in the Roman province of Galatia" than to argue that this letter must have been intended for churches in *North* Galatia.

My opponent made much of the fact that it was in the old ethnic sense that the Church Fathers interpreted the terms *Galatia* and *Galatians.* He omitted to mention the reason for this patristic error. That reason was that in the days of these fathers the province of Galatia had again been restricted to virtually its old dimensions, so that for *them* "the territory inhabited by the Gauls" and "the province of Galatia" coincided. Hence, without further investigation they concluded that Paul, in addressing the churches of Galatia, was speaking to the people who had come from across the sea, the Gauls. But, as has been shown, this opinion of the fathers is not in harmony with Paul's use of political terms.

It somewhat amazes me that my beloved adversary, in the defense of his proposition, even resorts to the now seldom heard argument based on the *instability* of the Gauls. But is it ever fair and honest for us, who do not possess the gift of infallible inspiration, to characterize an entire nation as being fickle? Is instability a *national* characteristic? Is it not rather a weakness that pertains to unregenerate human nature in general? Let it be granted that the Galatians whom the apostle addressed in his letter were fickle in that they so quickly abandoned their initial enthusiasm with respect to Paul and the message he had brought. Of whom does this instability remind us? Does it not immediately recall the scene at Lystra, a city of Lycaonia in the *southern* part of the province of Galatia, whose inhabitants, after having first welcomed Paul and Barnabas, shouting, "The gods have come down to us," shortly afterward stoned the apostle almost to death? Truly, to be fickle one does not have to be a Gaul! Besides, strictly speaking, is it even correct to imply that at this late date, the first century A.D., the northern tribes were exclusively *Gauls?* Granted that the Gallic strain was dominant, is it not true that many tributaries had poured their water into the stream of their composite nationality?

[5] Moreover, I Cor. 16:1 speaks about the collection for the Judean saints, which had been recommended to "the churches of Galatia" (among others). According to Acts 20:4, among the delegates who carry this gift to Jerusalem were Gaius of Derbe and Timothy (of Lystra, Acts 16:1), both, therefore, of *South* Galatia. Not a single delegate from *North* Galatia is mentioned. Though there are ways to circumvent the force of this argument, it may, nevertheless, carry some weight.

My opponent also appeals to the fact that the book of Acts does not speak of physical infirmity (cf. Gal. 4:13) as a reason why Paul either began or prolonged his mission in South Galatia. But, first of all, this difference between the two accounts can be removed by a different interpretation of Gal. 4:13, according to which it would not read *"because of"* but *"amid"* physical infirmity, which would fully harmonize with Acts 13:50; 14:5, 6, 19; cf. II Tim. 3:11. And secondly, even if we retain "because of," and assume a real difference between Gal. 4:13 and the account in Acts, let it be remembered that of those many afflictions which the apostle himself enumerates in II Cor. 11:23-33 Luke mentions only a few. Is it safe, then, to conclude that Paul never endured those which Luke does not record?

As to the Jew versus Gentile difference between Acts and Galatians, diligent study of Acts 13 and 14 leaves the impression that wherever there was a synagogue Paul entered it and proclaimed the gospel, reaching both Jews *and Gentiles,* proselytes (Acts 13:43; 14:1). Though Jews as well as Gentiles accepted the gospel, the former, on the whole, rejected it, causing the apostle to remark, "Since y o u thrust it from y o u, we turn to the Gentiles." Moreover, in some of the places visited, Jews were so few in numbers that there was not even a synagogue. This tallies with the situation as pictured in Paul's epistle. And as concerns the latter, the apostle assumes that those addressed have sufficient knowledge of the Old Testament to follow his reasoning, even including that of Gal. 4:21-31. Does not this fact rather point in the direction of the presence of at least some Jews among the addressed and of considerable Jewish influence even in these predominantly Gentile congregations?

I conclude by saying that my opponent has failed to show that *Galatians* is addressed to the churches of *North* Galatia. Of the founding and existence in Paul's day of such churches the book of Acts does not with certainty say anything at all, neither in 16:6 nor in 18:23; 19:1. And, on the other hand, of the establishment of churches in *South* Galatia it has given us a detailed account.

### *C. Rebuttal for the Affirmative*

As to my opponent's contention that, in referring to groups of churches, Paul classifies them according to the Roman provinces in which they were located, and that, consequently, the term "the churches of Galatia" must refer to churches in the *province* of Galatia, that rule has its exceptions. Thus, it cannot be proved that the apostle is using political terminology when he speaks of Cilicia (Gal. 1:21), of Judea (Gal 1:22), and of Arabia (Gal. 4:25).

As for the rest, I must express my profound admiration for my opponent's cleverness. He can turn an argument from silence in either direction, to suit his purpose. It makes me think of what a child will at times say to his playmate to determine who will receive the biggest slice of the apple: "Let's flip a coin. Heads I win; tails you lose." When I called attention to the silence of the book of Acts with respect to any infirmity on Paul's part on his first missionary journey, during which he founded the churches of South Galatia, my opponent told us that such silence, if it were a fact, would mean nothing at all. Nevertheless, he was certain that when that same book of Acts fails to say in so many words that *churches* were established in North Galatia, this silence speaks volumes, and must mean that no churches were established there, churches to which Paul might have addressed his epistle. He maintains this in spite of the fact that Acts 18:23 states that the apostle went through this northern region "establishing *all* the disciples." Does not the word *all* indicate that there were *many?* Does not this imply that these many disciples must have organized themselves into churches? And does not the fact that on this third missionary journey Paul *established* or *strengthened* all these disciples indicate that these several churches must have been founded previously, a fact to which Acts 16:6 would seem to call our attention? Moreover, does not Acts 19:1 say that Paul, *having passed through the upper country,* came to Ephesus? What else can this "upper country" mean but North Galatia, with its cities of Tavium, Ancyra, and Pessinus? It is true that Luke does not tell us in so many words that churches were established in these cities, but neither does he tell us that a church was ever established in Colosse. Yet Paul wrote a letter to the Colossians. Luke does not even tell us anything about the founding of the church in Rome. Yet we know that a church was established there and that Paul wrote a letter to that church.

I conclude my summary, therefore, by stating once more that it is my firm belief that there were churches in North Galatia, and that it was to these genuinely *Galatian* churches that Paul addressed his letter.

### D. *Rebuttal for the Negative*

It is clear, is it not, that my opponent has not succeeded to overthrow my contention that wherever in Paul's epistles we are in a position to determine with certainty the location and extent of any group of churches the apostle uses *political* terminology to describe it. He uses the names of Roman provinces.

As to these silences of the book of Acts, here my opponent fails to distinguish between expected and unexpected silences. When Luke presumably fails to mention Paul's infirmity, this *silence* is more or less *expected.* At least it cannot mean that there was no such infirmity, for by comparing Luke's account with Paul's own catalogue of sufferings (II Cor. 11:23-33) we learn that Luke is not in the habit of particularizing Paul's sufferings. Rather, he recounts Christ's work on earth, establishing a church here, a church there, and welding them into an organic unity. So when, while narrating a journey in which churches were being established, Luke omits any reference to the establishment of churches in a district covered on that journey or to Paul's preaching there, this would be an *unexpected silence,* unless nothing of importance happened in that district.

My opponent emphasized Acts 16:6; 18:23; 19:1, as if these three passages described Paul's work in the cities of *North* Galatia. Now in Acts 16:6-8 (second missionary journey), since God intended to send Paul to Europe via Troas, the route may well have touched the western edge of the more northerly part of the Roman province of Galatia. But this passage in Acts says nothing about establishing churches or even preaching there. As to Acts 18:23; 19:1 (third missionary journey), a look at the map suffices to show that the route from Antioch (in *Syria*) to Ephesus was probably not over Tavium, Ancyra, and Pessinus! The more southerly part of this same Roman province of Galatia is indicated.[6] And the words "establishing all the disciples" probably mean "in *South* Galatia." Cf. Acts 14:20-23; 16:1-5.

It is also significant that, as the last reference indicates, it was to the churches of *South* Galatia that the regulations of the Jerusalem Council were delivered, showing that it was exactly there that Judaism was a live issue, the very Judaism against which Paul contends in his letter. I believe, therefore, that Paul used the term *Galatians* in the political sense, as did also Peter (I Peter 1:1). It is hard to believe that the Judaistic errorists, with their sinister propaganda, would have bypassed *South* Galatia on their way to *North* Galatia. Moreover, Barnabas, mentioned three times in Galatians (2:1, 9, 13), had worked with Paul in *South* Galatia. And it was only with respect to the *South* Galatian churches, established on the *first* missionary journey, that Paul, at the time of the Jerusalem Council, could say, " (I did not yield to the infiltrators) in order that the truth of the gospel *might continue* with y o u" (Gal. 2:5).

I conclude, therefore, in stressing once again that the proposition according to which Paul's letter was meant for *North* Galatia is to be rejected.

Report of *one* of the judges (the author of this book. The readers are the other judges): I believe that both speakers have done justice to their assignment. Nevertheless, the speaker for the negative deserves a slight reprimand for having saved a few of his minor arguments to the very last, so that his opponent lacked any opportunity to answer him. Had the latter been given this opportunity, he would, no doubt, have somewhat diminished the force of these arguments. He would have shown, for example, that Barnabas is mentioned not only in Galatians but also elsewhere (I Cor. 9:6; Col. 4:10). Nevertheless, all things considered, I cast my ballot in favor of the negative and of the South Galatian theory. To believe that the South Galatian churches, so dear to Paul because of his blessed experiences among them

[6] See sketch; also N.T.C. on Colossians and Philemon, pp. 6–9.

(Acts 13:33, 44, 48; 14:1, 3, 20-23), and so vividly impinged upon his memory because of the persecutions which he had endured while laboring in their cities (Acts 13:50; 14:2, 5, 19; cf. II Tim. 3:11), would have played virtually no part in his correspondence and would have disappeared almost completely from sacred history, is difficult. And if the apostle did write to them, as I believe the speaker for the negative has proved, by what common name could he have addressed them better than by that of *Galatians?*

# III. When, Where, and Why Was It Written?

## A. *When and Where?*

On this subject there is a great diversity of opinion. Some accept as the *date* the close of the first missionary journey (about A.D. 50), and as the *place* of composition: Antioch. There are also those, at the other extreme, who assign this letter to the apostle's Roman imprisonment (A.D. 60 and afterward). While the former date once enjoyed great popularity and is still being favored by certain eminent scholars, the latter is now seldom met.[7] Various intermediate dates have gained large followings. Naturally, as a rule, the advocates of the *North* Galatian theory accept a rather late date because the apostle did not enter those parts until he was on his second missionary journey. As they see it, Paul revisited North Galatia during his third journey. And so, quite generally they hold that Galatians was written on the third missionary journey at Ephesus (Greijdanus), or, more precisely, at Ephesus a few weeks before I Corinthians (Warfield), or after I and II Corinthians but before Romans, and then either: *a.* on the journey from Macedonia to Achaia (Lightfoot) or *b.* at Corinth (Robertson). We who have adopted the South Galatian theory (see chapter II) arrive at an earlier date because during his three missionary journeys Paul labored in South Galatia earlier than in any other group of churches. Is it possible to be more specific? The following items may be of some help, though certainty cannot be attained:

1. Galatians was written *after the Jerusalem Council,* for it describes Paul's relation to the other leaders at that great meeting. The journey to Jerusalem mentioned in Gal. 2:1 must be identified with the one indicated in Acts 15:1-4. For proof see on Gal. 2:1.

2. It was written *after two previous visits to South Galatia,* the first of

---

[7] In addition to the various commentaries see the following articles all of which bear the identical title, "The Date of the Epistle to the Galatians": F. F. Bruce, *ET,* 51 (1939–1940), pp. 157, 158; Maurice Jones, *Exp,* 8th series, 6 (1913), pp. 192–208; D. B. Knox, *EQ,* 13 (1941), pp. 262–268; and B. B. Warfield, *JBL* (June and December, 1884), pp. 50–64.

which is indicated in Acts 13 and 14, the second in Acts 15:40-16:5. This is the most natural interpretation of Gal. 4:13 (see on that verse).

3. It was composed *not long after the conversion of the Galatians*—hence also: not long after Paul's two visits—, for Paul is amazed that the Galatians are "so quickly" moving away from God who had called them (see on 1:6).

4. It may well have been written, therefore, *on the second missionary journey, at Corinth, before the arrival of Timothy and Silas.*[8] This would explain the omission of greetings from these two men, both of whom occupied a special place in the hearts and memories of the South Galatian churches (Acts 15:40; 16:1-3). Contrast Gal. 1:1, 2, where these two names are omitted, with I Thess. 1:1; II Thess. 1:1, which mention both, the probable reason for the omission and the inclusion being that when Galatians was composed Timothy and Silas were still absent, but when the letters to the Thessalonians were written these two fellow-workers had arrived in Corinth and were again in Paul's company. This would fix the date of composition somewhere near the middle of the period A.D. 50-53 (second missionary journey), just previous to the writing of I Thessalonians.

Galatians, then, may well be the very first or oldest of all the letters of Paul that have been preserved. It has been objected that it is improbable that Paul, during his early Corinthian ministry, would dispatch in close succession letters as diverse in general theme as Galatians, on the one hand, and I and II Thessalonians, on the other. To the Galatians Paul writes: "A man is not justified by law-works but only through faith in Jesus Christ" (Gal. 2:16); while to the Thessalonians he writes: "For they [people everywhere] are reporting about us, what kind of entering in we had among y o u and how y o u turned to God from those idols (of y o u r s), to serve God, the living and real One, and to await his Son out of the heavens" (I Thess. 1:9, 10). The following, however, should be borne in mind:

1. The subject matter of Paul's epistles was determined not so much by the apostle's gradual mental development as by specific needs arising from concrete situations in the various churches. The Galatians needed to be reminded about the doctrine of salvation by grace through faith only. The Thessalonians needed encouragement in connection with their dramatic conversion and with respect to the return of Christ. *Each group receives what it needs!*

2. The Galatians and the Thessalonians lived in different continents, *amid different surroundings.*

3. The two differed also in their *degree of loyalty to the truth.*

4. Even so, the difference between the two situations is not nearly as radical as it is sometimes made to appear. For example, the doctrine of conver-

[8] In general this is also the position taken by Zahn, Berkhof, Hiebert, Lenski, Ridderbos, etc.

sion to the living God from dead idols was proclaimed among both (cf. Acts 14:15 with I Thess. 1:9). And as to the difference in content between the letters themselves: though it is true that the doctrine of the last things is stressed in Thessalonians far more than in Galatians, it is not absent from the latter (Gal. 5:21). Moreover, does *faith* working through *love* occupy a place of prominence in Galatians (Gal. 5:6)? It does also in I Thess. 1:3; 3:6; 5:8. Was Paul concerned lest he might have labored in vain among the Galatians (Gal. 3:4)? Before Silas and Timothy rejoined him he had entertained somewhat similar fears with respect to the Thessalonians (I Thess. 3:5). Cf. also Gal. 1:4; and 5:5 with I Thess. 1:10; and II Thess. 3:2; Gal. 5:3 with I Thess. 2:12; Gal. 5:13, 16, 19 with I Thess. 4:3; Gal. 5:21 with II Thess 2:5; Gal. 6:6 with I Thess. 5:12; and see footnote 129 on p. 175.

I can see no reason, therefore, to deny that the epistle to the Galatians was followed soon afterward by I Thessalonians, which, in quick succession, was followed by II Thessalonians, all three having been written from Corinth about the year A.D. 52.

## B. *Why?*

### *Occasion and Purpose*

In harmony with all that has been established, in this and in the preceding chapter, touching the identity of the Galatians, the time when, and the place from which Paul wrote his letter, the latter's historical background and purpose will appear from the following account:

In the church of Syrian Antioch there was great joy, for, after an eventful and perilous journey, Paul and Barnabas, who had been ordained for missionary work, and had been sent forth by the Holy Spirit and by a dedicated congregation committed to the grace of God, had returned in safety, with a wonderful story to tell (Acts 13:1-3; 14:25-27). "They rehearsed all things that God had done with them, and how he had opened a door of faith to the Gentiles," we read. The two then spent "not a little time" with the church at Antioch.

Now Antioch, "the queen of the east," was cosmopolitan in outlook. There was a colony of Jews here, to be sure (Acts 11:19), but the Christian community, which has been called "the cradle of Gentile Christianity and missionary endeavor," refused to be hemmed in within the narrow limits of Jewry. It was in Antioch that it had been most clearly discerned that the followers of Jesus were not just another Jewish sect but had a religion that was unique among all the religions of the empire. It was here that the disciples were first called "Christians." Hence, if anything were to occur that would tend to impede the worldwide progress of Christianity, the church of Antioch could be counted on to do something about it.

And something of this nature did indeed occur, for Antioch's joy because of the return of the missionaries and the tidings which they had brought, about multitudes of people, especially *Gentiles,* having embraced Christ and salvation in him, did not remain a secret. It spread far and wide. Jerusalem, too, heard about it. Also there, we may well believe, the church rejoiced. But this joy was not universal. In this Judean city among those who heard the news there were also some nominal converts from the sect of the Pharisees (Acts 15:5). In common with the disciples of the Lord, *all* Pharisees believed in the resurrection from the dead. In addition, the Pharisees mentioned here in Acts 15:5 may have been impressed by the strength of the evidence for *Christ's* resurrection, and by the indisputable grandeur of his miracles, and may for these reasons have joined the followers of the Nazarene. But at heart they had remained Jewish legalists. They were convinced that it took more than simple faith in Jesus to be saved; and that strict observance of Jewish ceremonies, particularly circumcision, was also necessary.

So, when news of the conversion of the Gentiles *apart from the work of the law, and especially apart from the necessity of receiving circumcision,* reached the ears of these men, off to Antioch they went, with a protest in their hearts and an ultimatum on their lips. Arrived in the city, they hesitated not a moment to announce to the startled, mostly Gentile, congregation, "Unless y o u are circumcised according to the custom of Moses, y o u cannot be saved" (Acts 15:1). This stern pronouncement, whereby the majority of the congregation was relegated to the limbo of the lost, must have caused considerable consternation and alarm.

The church, however, decided to do something about it, encouraged no doubt by the growing and well-founded suspicion that these trouble-makers had not been authorized to deliver this scare-fomenting message (cf. Acts 15:24). And so it was agreed to refer this matter to a General Conference at Jerusalem, that is, to "the apostles and elders" (Acts 15:2) together with "the whole church at that place" (Acts 15:22). Paul, Barnabas, and certain other men were selected to go to Jerusalem in order to represent the church of Antioch (and, in a sense, every uncircumcised Gentile convert everywhere) with respect to this matter. As had been true when Paul was commissioned to go on his first missionary journey, so also now, the decision of the Antioch church and Paul's compliance with it were no merely human matters. God himself had a hand in it: the apostle went up to Jerusalem "by revelation" (Gal. 2:2).

In the company of men going to Jerusalem was also Titus, of heathen extraction both on his father's and on his mother's side, *a test case,* therefore, a manifest challenge to the Judaizers. The decision to place the entire matter, with reference to uncircumcised Titus and every Gentile convert, before the Jerusalem Council by no means implied that Paul was thereby abdicating his authority as an apostle or that the validity of his gospel ministry among the Gentiles was left in doubt until the mother church would come forth with an official answer to the question: "Must Gentiles be circumcised in order to be saved?" Paul, "an apostle not from men nor through man but through Jesus Christ and God the Father" (Gal. 1:1), knew that the divine approval rested on him and his work. But on a matter as important as this the church must not be divided, for this would hurt the great cause of evangelizing the Gentiles. The leaders, moreover, must speak clearly and unequivocally to the people, so that all may know what is the truth. Solutions must also be reached to problems which, though not basic, deal with temporary arrangements whereby in mixed churches Jews and Gentiles can dwell together in harmony (cf. Acts 15:29). For these various reasons and others, no doubt, the convocation of this General Council or Conference was entirely in order.

*The Council,* described in Acts 15, was, in all probability, preceded by *a private interview* of the leaders, to which Gal. 2:2-10 refers. Paul says, "I set before them the gospel which I am accustomed to preach among the Gentiles; but (I did this) privately, to 'those of repute,' to make sure that I was not running or had not run in vain" (Gal. 2:2). Complete agreement was evident on every point: Titus must not receive circumcision; the basic doctrine of salvation for Gentiles as well as for Jews by faith in Jesus Christ, apart from the works of the law, must be courageously upheld before the entire church; there must be a division (probably geographical) of labor, so that James, Cephas, and John will preach the gospel to the Jews, Paul and Barnabas to the Gentiles; the poor must be remembered. At the close of the interview the Jerusalem "pillars" give to Paul and to Barnabas "the right hand of fellowship."

At the meeting of the General Council the Judaists avail themselves of the opportunity to defend their position (Acts 15:5). However, when ample time has been allowed for this "questioning," *Peter* arises and in well-chosen words defends the perfect *parity* of Jew and Gentile: "God made no distinction between us and them." He points out that the way of salvation is exactly the same for both groups (15:7-11). After a respectful pause *Paul* and *Barnabas* take the floor and rehearse to the assembled multitude the *phenomenal blessings* which God had showered upon the Gentiles, "the signs and wonders" by means of which he had placed the seal of his approval on the work of his ambassadors (15:12). *James* then gives his *judgment.* Moved by the fact that what was happening in the Gentile world was a clear fulfilment of prophecy (Amos 9:11, 12), he states, "Wherefore my judgment is that we do not trouble those who from the Gentiles turn to God." Without in any way injuring the doctrine of justification by faith alone, apart from the works of the law, James, who is a very practical individual, suggests the adoption of certain regulations which, in this period of transition, would make it possible for Jewish and Gentile Christians to live together in peace and harmony (Acts 15:20, 21).

The apostles and elders, together with "the whole church," reach a consensus, and decide to embody the decision in a written decree, a Charter of Freedom, as it were, which is to be brought to Antioch by Paul, Barnabas, and two other leaders (15:22-29). The arrival of these men and the message which they convey bring general rejoicing (15:31).

The decision of the Conference was made known in Antioch and Syria and Cilicia (15:23), and also in the cities of South Galatia (16:1-4). "So the churches were strengthened in faith, and increased in number daily" (16:5).

The Judaizers, however, are not about to give up the fight. They follow Paul at his heels in order to destroy the results of his labors. In Antioch they are partly to blame for Peter's reprehensible conduct (Gal. 2:11, 12). They traverse Galatia, insisting that the Gentiles be circumcised as a means unto salvation (Gal. 5:2, 3; 6:12). They do not deny that faith in Christ is necessary, but they loudly proclaim that circumcision and obedience to certain additional legal requirements are also necessary (4:9, 10). Yet, with amazing inconsistency, they do not insist on obedience to the whole law (5:3). In order to bolster their cause they cast suspicion on Paul. They attempt to discredit him, claiming that his apostleship is not from God but from men, and that his gospel is second-hand, therefore (Gal. 1:1; cf. I Cor. 9:1 ff.); that he is simply striving to win the favor of men (Gal. 1:10), and that when it suits him he himself preaches circumcision (Gal. 5:11).

Paul knew that these trouble-makers were Christians in name only. They were insincere and inconsistent, for while trying to force others to observe the law, they themselves failed to keep it (Gal. 6:13). Their aim was: *a.* to escape persecution from the side of the Jews, and *b.* out of personal ambition to glory in the flesh of their followers; that is, to be able to point with pride at those Gentiles who, due to *their* (the Judaizers') urging, had received circumcision (4:17; 6:13). "But far be it from me to glory except in the cross of our Lord Jesus Christ," says Paul (6:14).

Strange to say, *many* of the Galatians listen attentively to these usurpers. They are on the point of exchanging bread for a stone, a fish for a serpent. Big-hearted, solicitous Paul is filled with sadness when he hears that in Galatia the doctrine of Christian freedom is in danger. Guided by the Spirit and under the latter's direction, he decides to write a letter to these people who are so dear to his heart. Are they not among the first fruits of his labors as an *ordained* foreign missionary? To them the doctrine of sovereign grace in all its simplicity and glory must be set forth once again.

Yet, while glorying in the cross, the apostle knew that it was necessary to warn the Galatians against a perversion of this doctrine of grace, as if this new Christian liberty were tantamount to license. He emphasizes that if a person really walks by the Spirit, the Spirit of *freedom,* he will not fulfil the desire of the flesh but will instead bear fruit, even the fruit of the Spirit (Gal. 5:16-26).

Briefly, therefore, *the occasion* which prompted Paul to write this letter was the sinister and, to some extent, successful influence which Judaistic trouble-makers were exerting upon the churches of South Galatia. And *the purpose* was to counteract this dangerous error by re-emphasizing the glorious gospel of free grace in Christ Jesus: justification by faith alone, apart from the works of the law, and to urge those addressed to adorn their faith and prove its genuine character by means of a life in which the fruit of the Spirit would abound. Thus the cause of truth would be advanced, and sectionalism, caused in part by the sinister propaganda of the Judaizers, with which *many* agreed but others were undoubtedly not so ready to agree, would cease. By heeding Paul's—that is, the Holy Spirit's—admonitions the Galatian churches would be enabled to present a united testimony to the world.

## IV. Who Wrote It?

Since the Pauline authorship of Galatians is almost universally acknowledged today, little need be said about it. In the middle of the nineteenth century under the influence of F. C. Baur, the Tübingen School, proceeding from the premise that only those writings can be ascribed to Paul in which he appears *prepared for combat,* denied the authenticity of all the letters passing under the apostle's name *except* Galatians, I and II Corinthians and Romans. Bruno Bauer, in his extreme radicalism, considered even these four epistles as products not of Paul but of the second century. In this rejection of the Pauline authorship of Galatians, etc. he was followed by the radical Dutch School: Loman, Pierson, Naber, and Van Manen. They held that the sharp clash between Pauline and Judaistic Christianity pictured in Gal. 2:11-21 (as interpreted by them), could not have developed as early as the days of the apostle Paul, and that the Christology of Galatians was far too lofty. All of this rests on purely subjective reasoning and is not worthy of further comment.

Eusebius, writing at the beginning of the fourth century, includes Galatians in the list of Paul's letters (*Eccl. History* III.iii. 4, 5). Origen, Tertullian, Clement of Alexander, and Irenaeus, in their respective writings, quote this epistle again and again. The Muratorian Fragment (about 180–200) places it second among Paul's epistles. The canon of the heretic Marcion is the first to mention the epistle by name (about the year 144), and places it first in the list of ten Pauline letters. It is found in the Old Syriac and in the Old Latin Versions. Polycarp (martyred 155) in his *Epistle to the Philippians* V.1 quotes Gal. 6:7, "God is not mocked." About the year 100 Clement of Rome writes, "Y o u kept his sufferings before y o u r eyes" (I Clement II.1), which reminds one of Gal. 3:1. And at about the same time Ignatius writes about a "ministry neither from himself nor through men, but in the love of God the Father and the Lord Jesus Christ" (*To the Philadelphians* III.1), in which there may be an allusion to Gal. 1:1. Barnabas, Hermas, Justin Martyr, *the Epistle to Diognetus* are among the other writings of very early date which contain passages which are viewed by many as allusions to Galatians.

But more important is the fact that as soon as this epistle was ascribed to anyone, it was ascribed to Paul. That has been the belief of the church throughout the centuries and is its conviction today. No argument of any merit has ever been presented to show that this view is in error. And the compromise theories, which are propounded every now and then up to the very present, according to which Galatians contains a Pauline core around which in post-apostolic times a pseudo-Pauline shell fastened itself, break down under the weight of their self-contradictions.

The author tells us that his name is Paul (1:1; 5:2). The letter is clearly a unit. It pictures a condition true to the times in which Paul lived (cf. Acts 15:1; I Cor. 7:19). It is, moreover, very personal, and reveals throughout "a man in Christ." Here is a mind so broad that it has room for both sovereign grace and human responsibility, a heart so loving that it administers stern rebuke just because it loves so deeply! The Paul of Gal. 1:15, 16; 2:20; 3:1; 4:19, 20 is clearly also the Paul of Rom. 9:2; I Cor. 9:22; 10:33; II Cor. 11:28; 12:15; Eph. 4:1; and Phil. 3:18, 19. It is Paul of Tarsus.

## V. What Is Its Theme? Its Outline?

It has become clear that the apostle's chief concern was that the Galatians should not lose their hold on the only true gospel. It is significant how often the word *gospel,* either as a noun or as a component element of a verb, occurs in this small epistle: 1:6, 7, 8, 9, 11, 16, 23; 2:2, 5, 7, 14; 3:8; 4:13. The essence or content of this gospel is also affirmed and reaffirmed: "A man is not justified by law-works but only through faith in Jesus Christ" (2:16; cf. 2:21; 3:9, 11; 4:2-6; 5:2-6; 6:14-16).

Now *justification by faith apart from law-works* is also the theme of Romans. There is a close resemblance between the larger and the smaller epistle. Gen. 15:6: "Abraham believed God, and it was reckoned to him for righteousness" is quoted in both letters (Rom. 4:3; Gal. 3:6). Among other verbal resemblances are especially the following: Rom. 6:6-8 and Gal. 2:20; Rom. 8:14-17 and Gal. 4:5-7; Rom. 13:13, 14 and Gal. 5:16, 17. Nevertheless, there is a striking difference between the two. Romans sets forth calmly and majestically that for every sinner, whether he be a Jew or a Gentile, there is salavation full and free through faith in Christ, apart from law-works. Galatians, in a tone that is not nearly as calm and at times becomes fiery, defends this glorious gospel over against its detractors. Against the latter its denunciations are withering (1:8, 9; 5:12). With respect to those addressed, with whom there was a tendency to lend a listening ear to the impostors, the apostle's reprimands (1:6; 3:1-4) are as sharp as are the contrasts which characterize this epistle.[9]

The reason why Paul reprimands the Galatians so sharply and warns them so sternly is that he loves them with a love that is genuine, tender, and deep: "My dear children, for whom I am again suffering birth-pangs until Christ be formed in y o u, I could wish to be present with y o u now and to change my tone of voice, for I am perplexed about y o u" (4:19, 20).

The theme of Galatians, then, is:

*The Gospel of Justification by Faith apart from Law-works Defended against Its Detractors*

Now in the first two chapters, by a selection of events from his life, the apostle defends himself against the charge, expressed or implied, that he had never received a divine commission and that his gospel was, accordingly, not to be trusted. This section is described at times as Paul's Self-defense. It is more than this, however. Calvin aptly expresses this by saying, "Let us remember, then, that in the person of Paul the truth of the gospel was assailed." The assailants attacked Paul in order thereby to destroy his gospel. They reasoned that if Paul's so-called apostleship was of merely human origin, then his gospel was also a merely human invention. Hence, at bottom it is *the gospel* with which we are dealing in Chapters 1 and 2 as well as in the rest of the epistle. Briefly, then, Galatians may be divided as follows:

| | | |
|---|---|---|
| ch. 1 and 2 | I. | This Gospel's Origination: it is not of human but of divine origin, hence, is independent. |
| ch. 3 and 4 | II. | Its Vindication: both Scripture—i.e., the Old Testament—and life (experience, past history) bear testimony to its truth. |
| ch. 5 and 6 | III. | Its Application: it produces true liberty. Let the Galatians stand firm, therefore, as does Paul, who glories in in the cross of Christ. |

[9]

| | | | |
|---|---|---|---|
| only true gospel | versus | no gospel at all | (1:6-9) |
| grace or promise | versus | law | (2:21; 3:18) |
| faith | versus | law-works | (2:16; 3:2, 5, 10-14) |
| flesh | versus | Spirit | (3:3; 5:16; 6:8) |
| slave-woman | versus | free-woman | (4:21 ff.) |
| Jerusalem of today | versus | Jerusalem that is above | (4:25, 26) |
| freedom | versus | slavery | (5:1) |
| to love | versus | to bite and devour | (5:14, 15) |
| circumcision | versus | new creation | (6:15) |

*Chapter 6*

E. Restore the fallen in a spirit of gentleness. Bear one another's burdens. Share all good things with y o u r instructor. Bear in mind that a man will reap what he sows. Let us do good to everybody, and especially to those who are of the household of the faith.

F. The Letter's End: Paul's "huge letters." Final warning against the disturbers and exposure of their motives: ease, honor. Concluding testimony: Far be it from me to glory except in the cross of our Lord Jesus Christ. Last plea: From now on let no one cause trouble for me, etc. Closing benediction.

# Commentary

on

# The Epistle to the Galatians

# Chapter 1

Verses 1-5

Theme: *The Gospel of Justification by Faith apart from Law-works Defended against Its Detractors*

I. *This Gospel's Origination: it is not of human but of divine origin*

A. Introduction which really introduces!

Name of addressor, of the addressed; opening salutation.

# CHAPTER I

**GALATIANS**

1 1 Paul, an apostle—not from men nor through man but through Jesus
Christ and God the Father, who raised him from the dead—2 and all the
brothers who are with me, to the churches of Galatia; 3 grace to y o u and peace from
God our Father and the Lord Jesus Christ; 4 who gave himself for our sins, that he
might rescue us out of this present world dominated by evil; (having thus given
himself) according to the will of our God and Father, 5 to whom (be) the glory
forever and ever. Amen.

---

1:1-5

A. *Introduction*

The spiritual atmosphere is charged. It is sultry, sweltering. A storm is threatening. The sky is darkening. In the distance one can see flashes of lightning; one can hear faint muttering sounds. When each line of verses 1-5 is read in the light of the letter's occasion and purpose (see Introduction III B, pp. 16–19) the atmospheric turbulence is immediately detected. The apostle, though in perfect control of himself, for he is writing under the guidance of the Holy Spirit, is greatly agitated, deeply moved. His heart and mind are filled with a medley of emotions. For the perverters there is withering denunciation springing from holy indignation. For the addressed there is marked disapproval and an earnest desire to restore. For the One who has called him there is profound reverence and humble gratitude.

Now in these opening lines there is, to be sure, a measure of restraint. The most vivid flashes of lightning and the most deafening peals of thunder are reserved for later (1:6-9; 3:1, 10; 5:4, 12; 6:12, 13). Nevertheless, even now the storm is definitely approaching. This will be shown in connection with each element of this Introduction: *a.* the manner in which *the addressor* describes himself, *b.* the way in which he designates *the addressed,* and *c.* the qualifying clause by means of which he enlarges on his *opening salutation.*

**1. Paul, an apostle.** He is a *sent,* a *commissioned* one (cf. John 20:21), an *apostle* in the deepest, richest sense, fully clothed with the authority of the One who sent him. His apostleship is equal to that of the Twelve. Hence, we speak of "the Twelve and Paul." Elsewhere he even stresses the fact that the risen and exalted Savior had appeared to *him* just as truly as to Cephas (I Cor. 15:5, 8; cf. 9:1). The Savior had assigned to him a task so broad and universal that his entire life was henceforth to be occupied with it.

To the words "Paul, an apostle" the writer adds a very significant modifier, one which immediately points to the theme of the entire letter. Among uninspired men introductions do not always introduce. In fact, at times they may even confuse. But here is an Introduction which really introduces, for the words **not from men nor through man but through Jesus Christ and God the Father** can only mean: "My apostleship is genuine; hence, so is *the gospel* which I proclaim, no matter what the Judaizers who disturb y o u may say! I am a divinely appointed emissary." As was pointed out previously, Paul's opponents had infiltrated the South Galatian churches, and were casting slurs on his apostleship, in order to show that his gospel was not from God. They charged—or at least insinuated—that *Paul's apostolic office or commission was either not derived from God but merely from men,* from the church of Syrian Antioch perhaps, as if this church had acted without divine guidance and authorization (Acts 13:2); *or else,* though derived originally from God, *had been transmitted to him through this or that man* (Ananias or an apostle?), with the implication that in the process of transmission it had been substantially modified, adulterated.

Paul's answer is an unequivocal and double denial. Not only had he received his office *from* the historical Jesus, who is at the same time the Anointed One, but that very Jesus Christ *in person* had invested him with this high distinction. Hence, Paul is an apostle *through*—not only *from*—Jesus Christ. Moreover, since Jesus Christ, in turn, as Son is one in essence with the Father (John 1:1; 10:30), and as Mediator always performs his Father's will (John 4:34; 5:30, etc.), hence Paul's apostleship is *through*[10] Jesus Christ and God the Father.

The implication is clear: since Paul and his message are backed by divine authority, those who reject him and his gospel are rejectors of Christ, hence also of the Father who sent him and **who raised him from the dead.** The detractors *oppose* the very One whom the Father had *honored;* the very One upon whose work of redemption the Father, by the act of raising him from the dead, had placed the seal of his approval, thereby designating him as the complete and perfect Savior, whose work does not need to be, and cannot be, supplemented; the very One who from his exalted position in heaven had called Paul to be an apostle!

The divine source of Paul's mission, to which he here bears witness, is confirmed by the book of Acts, which shows that it was Christ *himself* who had appeared to Paul (9:1-5; 22:1-9). True, it was Ananias who encouraged Paul concerning his *commission* (Acts 22:15), but either *a.* Ananias con-

---

[10] *One* preposition διά governs both appellatives.

veyed that commission to Paul *so exactly* that the latter was able afterward to merge the words of Jesus and those of Ananias as if all had been spoken by Christ himself, or (better perhaps) *b. the commission itself* also had *first of all* been uttered directly by Christ, not by Ananias. When Acts 26:12-18 is interpreted either way, Gal. 1:1a remains true. See also on Gal. 1:16.

**2.** Paul adds, **and all the brothers who are with me.** Of these words there are three main interpretations: *a.* "all fellow-believers at the place from which I am writing this letter." Those who favor this view stress the fact that "brothers" is a very common term that is often used to indicate Christians in general (I Thess. 1:4; 2:1; I Cor. 5:11; 6:5-8; 8:12; etc.). Some also add that if it be true that this letter was written from Corinth in the early days of the work there, a *church* may not yet have been organized, though there were already some *believers* or *brothers.* Interpretation *b.* is: "all those mentioned under *a.* (above) plus all the members of the Galatian delegation that is with me." The adherents of this view point out that Paul must have received his information about the situation in the South Galatian churches from some reliable source (cf. I Cor. 1:11), perhaps from a delegation sent to him by the officials of these churches, who wanted him to know what was going on and who desired to benefit by his advice. Theory *c.:* "all my fellow-workers who are with me here." Those who favor this interpretation point to a similar phrase in Phil. 4:21, where it refers to the apostle's assistants in Rome, in distinction from "all the saints," namely, all of Rome's resident Christians, mentioned in the next verse. They are of the opinion, moreover, that a traveling missionary like Paul, one who stays in a place for a while and then moves on again, would hardly refer to the place's *residents* as "all the brothers who are *with me.*" A closer look as this argument, however, shows that it is not as strong as it may at first appear to be. The distinction drawn in Phil. 4:21, 22 between Paul's assistants and all of Rome's resident Christians is altogether natural in a city (Rome) where there was a numerically strong church that had been established long before the apostle's arrival. But in Corinth from which, probably on his second missionary journey, the apostle wrote Galatians (see our Introduction, pp. 14–16), and where the work had just begun and the number of believers may still have been rather small, the apostle could very well have referred to this small company as "all the brothers who are *with me.*" The word *all,* moreover, stresses unanimity of sentiment rather than numerical immensity. Even if there were only ten or twenty converts, as long as there was no disagreement among them the apostle would still be justified in writing in the name of "*all* the brothers who are with me." Also, as to the several fellow-workers who, according to theory *c.* were with Paul, I answer that if the time and place of the letter's composition was as has been surmised, their presence in any considerable quantity would seem rather doubtful. On his second missionary journey only one assistant accompanied the apostle from the start: Silas; a little later also Timothy (Acts 15:40-16:3). Luke was with them for a little while, but soon left again (16:10-17). He was no longer present when Paul reached Corinth and did not rejoin him until the latter, returning from his third missionary journey, had reached Troas (20:5). As has been indicated previously, when Galatians was written even Silvanus and Timothy were probably not in Paul's company. All things considered, therefore, the true meaning of the words "and all the brothers who are with me" would seem to lie in the direction of theory *a.* or possibly *b.* rather than in that of theory *c.* Certainty on this point, is, however, unattainable.

What is often forgotten, however, is *the main lesson.* That lesson would seem to be this, that even though it is true that Paul alone—not Paul plus these brothers who are with him—authored this letter (note constant recurrence of first person sing.: Gal. 1:6, 10-17, etc.), nevertheless, before composing and sending it he thoroughly discussed *with all the brothers* the matter with which it was to deal. So unanimous was their agreement with Paul's proposed method of handling this difficult situation that the apostle writes in the name of all. Moral: when it becomes necessary to send someone a letter of sharp reproof, discuss the matter with others who also have the welfare of Zion at heart, if such can be done without violating any confidences or of coming into conflict with the principles established in Matt. 18. Were this rule always observed, what a difference it would make in the end-product! It is true that Paul was writing under the infallible guidance of the Holy Spirit. Even so, however, this work of inspiration makes use of means. It operates organically, not mechanically. Besides, Paul's loving heart, filled with intense yearning to reclaim the Galatians, makes use of every legitimate means to attain this end, one of these means being to impress upon the addressed that his own apprehensions concerning the course which they are now beginning to pursue is being shared by *all* the brothers who are *with*[11] him.

Those whom Paul addresses are designated as follows: **to the churches of Galatia.** Every commendatory modifier—for example, "beloved of God" (cf. Rom. 1:7), "sanctified in Christ Jesus" (cf. I Cor. 1:2), "saints and believers" (Eph. 1:1)—is lacking here. The apostle loves, but does not believe in flattery. The atmosphere remains tense.

Note: church*es* both here and in 1:22. Paul recognizes the autonomy of the local church. Nevertheless, he is also fully aware of the fact that all believers everywhere constitute *one* body of Christ, *one* church (1:13). He

[11] The flexibility or wide variety of connotations adhering to the preposition σύν makes it impossible for me to join those exegetes who are of the opinion that it must here mean "*supporting* (me)," in distinction from μετά, which would simply have meant "in (my) company." Is not the *support* already clearly implied?

keeps perfect balance, a lesson for all time! That these churches were in all probability located in the southern part of the Roman province of Galatia has been established (Introduction, Chapter II).

**3.** The opening salutation proper is as in Rom. 1:7; I Cor. 1:3; II Cor. 1:2; Eph. 1:2; and Phil. 1:2: **grace to you and peace from God our Father and the Lord Jesus Christ.** Although it is true that the apostle finds little to praise, much to deplore, in the churches of Galatia, this does not mean that he has given them up as being hopeless. Far from it. See on 5:10a; cf. 4:19, 20. Though he is "perplexed" about them, he still regards them as Christian communities, upon whom, accordingly, he is fully justified in pronouncing this salutation. *Grace,* as here used, is God's spontaneous, unmerited favor in action, his freely bestowed lovingkindness in operation, bestowing salvation upon guilt-laden sinners who turn to him for refuge. It is, as it were, the rainbow round about the very throne out of which proceed flashes of lightning, rumblings, and peals of thunder (Rev. 4:3, 5). We think of the Judge who not only remits the penalty but also cancels the guilt of the offender and even adopts him as his own son. Grace brings *peace.* The latter is both a *state,* that of reconciliation with God, and a *condition,* the inner conviction that consequently all is well. It is the great blessing which Christ by his atoning sacrifice bestowed upon the church (John 14:27), and it surpasses all understanding (Phil. 4:7). It is not the reflection of an unclouded sky in the tranquil waters of a picturesque lake, but rather the cleft of the rock in which the Lord hides his children when the storm is raging (think of the theme of Zephaniah's prophecy); or, to change the figure somewhat but with retention of the main thought, it is the hiding place under the wings, to which the hen gathers her brood, so that the little chicks are safe while the storm bursts loose in all its fury upon herself.

Now this grace and this peace have their origin in God *our* (precious word of appropriation and inclusion!) Father, and have been merited for believers by him who is the great Master-Owner-Conqueror ("Lord"), Savior ("Jesus"), and Office-Bearer ("Christ"), and who, because of his threefold anointing "is able to save to the uttermost them that draw near to God through him" (Heb. 7:25).[12]

For further details about certain aspects of Paul's opening salutations see N.T.C. on I and II Thessalonians, pp. 37–45; on Philippians, pp. 43–49; and on I and II Timothy and Titus, pp. 49–56; 339–344.

**4.** Everywhere else the opening salutation proper is very brief. Having read the words "from God our Father and the Lord Jesus Christ," the addition *here* of a modifier to the title of the second person of the Holy

---

[12] The *one* preposition *from* introduces the entire expression "God our Father and the Lord Jesus Christ," showing that these two Persons are placed on the level of complete equality.

Trinity comes as somewhat of a surprise. Clearly, in keeping with the occasion and purpose of the letter, there must be a reason why Paul *here* adds: **who gave himself for our sins, that he might rescue us out of this present world dominated by evil.** The reason is that the atmosphere continues to be loaded. The greatness and magnanimity of Christ's act of self-surrender is stressed in order to underscore the grievous nature of the sin of those who teach that this supreme sacrifice must be supplemented by law-works. Christ surrendered himself to sorrow and scorn, to the curse of eternal death during his entire sojourn on earth but especially at Gethsemane, Gabbatha, and Golgotha. He laid down his life for his sheep. No one took it from him, but he laid it down of his own accord, voluntarily (John 10:11, 17, 18). He did this motivated by love incomprehensible; hence, "for our sins," that is, to deliver us from the pollution, guilt, and punishment adhering to the many ways in which, by inner disposition, thought, word, and deed, we *miss the mark* of existing and living to the glory of God Triune.

Note: "He gave himself . . . that [meaning: that in so doing] he might rescue us." The word *rescue* is very descriptive. It presupposes that those to whom it applies are in great danger from which they are unable to extricate themselves. Thus Joseph *was rescued* out of all his afflictions (Acts 7:10), Israel out of Egypt's house of bondage (Acts 7:34), Peter out of Herod's hand (Acts 12:11), and thus also Paul would one day be delivered or rescued out of the hands of Jews and Gentiles (Acts 23:27; 26:17). The rescue described here in Gal. 1:4 is all the more glorious because: *a.* it concerns those who by nature are enemies of the Rescuer, and *b.* it was accomplished by means of the voluntary death (in this case *eternal* death) of the Rescuer. One is reminded of a swimmer who plunges into the fast moving current in order to rescue the child that has fallen into the stream and is about to be pitched over the cliff of the cataract to its death. In the act of seizing the youngster and hurling him to the side where loving arms reach out and catch him, he himself is swept over the precipice to his death. All comparisons fall short, however, since in the case of Christ the sacrifice was great beyond all comprehension, and the beneficiaries were thoroughly unworthy of such love!

Paul states that Christ gave himself that he might rescue us out of this present world dominated by evil.[13] For *world* Paul uses the term *aeon*. It denotes *the world in motion* in contrast with *cosmos* which, though used in a variety of senses, indicates *the world at rest*. The *aeon,* then, refers to the world viewed from the standpoint of time and change. This is especially true when the adjective *present* is added, as here. It is the world or transitory

[13] The position of the adjective πονηροῦ gives it special emphasis, which accounts for my translation "this present world dominated by evil" instead of simply "this present evil world."

era which is hastening to its close and in which, in spite of all its pleasures and treasures, there is nothing of *abiding* value. Over against *this present world or age* is *the coming world,* the glory-age, that will be ushered in at the consummation of all things (cf. Eph. 1:21; I Tim. 6:17; II Tim. 4:10; Titus 2:12).

The *rescue* from this present world dominated by evil, though not complete until the last trumpet has sounded, is progressive in character. It is being accomplished whenever a sinner is brought out of the darkness into the light and whenever a saint gains a victory in his struggle against sin.

It is not sufficient, however, to bow in adoration before *the Son,* as if he alone were deserving of thanksgiving and honor because of his marvelous, self-sacrificing, work of redemption. On the contrary, the Son gave himself for our sins, that he might rescue us, etc. (**having thus given himself**) **according to the will of our God and Father.**[14] The son gave himself; the Father—yes, *our* (see on 1:3) God and Father—"spared not his own Son, but delivered him up for us all" (Rom. 8:32). In fact, in the very act of the Son's self-sacrifice the Father's *will*—his decree as revealed *in time,* his *desire*—was being accomplished. Therefore the Father loved the Son! (John 10:17, 18; cf. 4:34; 6:38).—Let the trouble-makers bear in mind, therefore, that when they belittle the work of the Son, they make light of the Father also!

**5.** When the apostle contemplates the Father's marvelous love revealed in delivering up his own dear Son, the Only-begotten, for our salvation, his soul is lost in wonder, love, and praise, so that he exclaims: **to whom be**[15] **the glory**[16] **forever and ever. Amen.** When the wicked infiltrators *minimize* God's work of redemption, Paul will *magnify* it, calling upon all men to do this with him. So marvelous is this work that it is worthy of *never-ending* praise; hence, "to whom be the glory *forever and ever,*" literally: to the ages of the ages. With a solemn "Amen" he reaffirms his personal gratitude as again and again he ponders God's great undying love, the unfathomable depth of his grace and mercy in Jesus Christ.

[14] This modifier ("according to," etc.) belongs to verse 4 in its entirety, as brought out in the translation.

[15] Though the verb is missing, so that one could either insert ἐστιν, *is* (Rom. 1:25; I Peter 4:11) or εἰή *be* (Ps. 113:2; LXX:112:2), the resultant meaning would be about the same, for if his *is* the glory then glory should certainly *be* ascribed to him.

[16] On the concept *glory* see N.T.C. on Philippians, pp. 62, 63, footnote 43.

# Chapter 1

Verses 6-10

Theme: *The Gospel of Justification by Faith apart from Law-works Defended against Its Detractors*

I. *This Gospel's Origination: it is not of human but of divine origin*

B. I am amazed that y o u are so quickly moving to a different gospel. There is only one true gospel. Let him be accursed who preaches another. There! Is it the favor of men that I am now seeking to win or of God?

6 I am amazed that y o u are so quickly moving away from him who called y o u (and turning) to a different gospel, 7 which (in reality) is not (even) another; but (the fact is that) certain individuals are throwing y o u into confusion and are trying to pervert the gospel of Christ. 8 But even though we ourselves or an angel from heaven were to preach to y o u any gospel other than the one which we preached to y o u, let him be accursed! 9 As we have said before, so now I say again, If anyone is preaching to y o u any gospel other than that which y o u have received, let him be accursed! 10 There! Is it the favor of men that I am now seeking to win or of God? Or is it men whom I am seeking to please? If I were still trying to please men, I would not be a servant of Christ.

1:6-10

B. *There is only one true gospel*

**6, 7.** We have reached the place in the letter where ordinarily, according to the custom of the day, words of thanksgiving would be found. It stands to reason that in Paul's epistles this expression of gratitude would be addressed to the one true God and not, as among the Gentiles, to this or that pagan divinity. For the apostle, then, it was generally a grateful acknowledgment of divine grace bestowed upon the addressed, whereby they had been enabled to make progress in knowledge, faith, love, etc. It was an expression of inner satisfaction and was frequently accompanied by a prayer that the advance already made might continue on and on (Rom. 1:8 ff.; I Cor. 1:4-9; Phil. 1:3-11; Col. 1:3 ff.; I Thess. 1:2 ff.; II Thess. 1:3 ff.). Sometimes the thanksgiving was in the form of a doxology (II Cor. 1:3 ff.; Eph. 1:3 ff.).

In Galatians, however, we are confronted with the very opposite. What we find *here* is not satisfaction but stupefaction: overwhelming amazement, painful perplexity. Says Paul: **I am amazed that y o u are so quickly moving away from him who called y o u (and turning) to a different gospel, which (in reality) is not (even) another.** Paul could be stern.[17] He was no flatterer. To be sure, he was very tactful. It was his custom to *commend* before he began to *condemn,* to use words of praise and encouragement before using words of criticism and warning. He does this even in I Corinthians, addressed to a church not lacking in failings both common and uncommon. But in Galatians *the very essence of the gospel* is at stake. Had this not been the case Paul would have been very tolerant, as Phil. 1:15-18 proves. But when the issue is momentous—God's glory and man's salvation—tolerance has its

[17] In the original the abruptness of this outburst is heightened by the absence of any introductory particle.

limits. In view of the occasion and purpose of Galatians, as previously explained, the unceremonious and uncompromising character of 1:6-10 is not surprising. Now this does not mean that in connection with those whom he addresses the apostle was unaware of anything whatever that he might be able to acknowledge with gratitude. In the present circumstances, however, such acknowledgment must bide its time (3:3; 4:12-15; 5:7).

But although 1:6-10 is in the nature of an outburst, nevertheless, *as far as the Galatians themselves are concerned* it is not an outburst of anger. There is consternation rather than indignation, amazement rather than resentment. Though Paul reproaches, he does not reject. Even now he is convinced that in the end everything will turn out favorably (5:10). The apostle is amazed or astonished to hear that the addressed are *in the process of changing their position.* The verb used can have either a favorable or an unfavorable sense; here obviously the latter. Moreover, the Galatians are transferring their loyalty *so quickly,* that is, so soon after their conversion (4:12-15; 5:7); hence also: so soon after the evangelistic labor that had been performed in their midst by Paul and his companions. And it is they themselves who are turning (themselves) away; they are not just being turned away.[18] Neither is it merely a theological position from which they are swerving. On the contrary, they are in the process of transferring their loyalty from the One who in his grace and mercy had called them—that is, from *God* (Rom. 4:17; 8:30; 9:11, 24; Gal. 1:15; Eph. 1:18; 4:1, 4; Phil. 3:14; I Thess. 2:12; 4:7; II Thess. 1:11; II Tim. 1:9)—to a different gospel. The *call* to which reference is made, is here, as everywhere in Paul, the internal or effectual calling: that act of the Holy Spirit whereby he savingly applies the gospel-invitation to the heart and life of certain definite individuals among all of those to whom, in the course of history, that invitation is extended. It is a call to salvation, full and free, via the avenue of sanctification. Speaking by and large, the apostle is convinced that the Galatians whom he here addresses had received *that* effectual call.

If it be argued that surely in the case of the Galatians the call cannot have been effectual since they were in the process of turning away from the God who had called them, the answer is that this position can be maintained only if it could be demonstrated that these people, after having first accepted the gospel by a true and living faith, afterward rejected it and died in that condition, not having given heed to Paul's admonition contained in this letter or to subsequent warnings. As has been pointed out, Paul himself is far more optimistic (5:10). It must ever be borne in mind that divine sovereignty does not abrogate human responsibility, and that

[18] It is true that the form of the verb can be interpreted either as a middle or as a passive, but passages like 3:1 ff.; 5:7 show that the apostle is definitely blaming the Galatians for lending a listening ear to the trouble-makers' false teaching.

God, accordingly, carries out his eternal purpose by so operating through his Spirit in the hearts of backsliders that they give heed to the earnest appeals that are made to them. Individuals who until their last breath persist in their disobedience prove that they had never embraced Christ with a true and living faith, even though they may have been church-members outwardly. The fact that the internal call results in salvation, in other words, that God's grace is irresistible, in the sense that it cannot be resisted effectively to the very end, is clear from such passages as John 4:14; 10:28; Rom. 8:28-39; 11:29; I Cor. 1:9; and Phil. 1:6. In the chain of means whereby this calling is made effectual, and this grade irresistible, earnest warnings and obedience to these warnings are important links. No one can ever afford to take his ultimate salvation for granted. Everyone must *strive* to enter in. "And as it has pleased God, by the preaching of the gospel to begin his work in us, so he preserves, continues, and perfects it by the hearing and reading of his Word, by meditation thereon, and by the exhortations, threatenings, and promises thereof, and by the use of the sacraments" (Canons of Dort, v. 14). Note *the threatenings and the warnings!*

In their present condition, then, the Galatians are turning to a *different* gospel, that is, to a gospel that differs radically from the one which they had received from Paul. The latter gospel was: "that a man is not justified by law-works but only through faith in Jesus Christ" (2:16; cf. Rom. 3:24; Eph. 2:8; Titus 3:4-7). That gospel the Galatians were abandoning in favor of a different gospel, one which proclaimed *faith plus law-works* as the way to salvation. It stands to reason that the substitute to which the addressed were turning was a gospel only in name, not in reality. It was really no gospel at all, exactly as Paul here declares: "a different gospel, which (in reality) is not (even) another." Much has been written about the combination *"different . . . not another."*[19] The translation which I favor and which, in one way or another, is also favored by A.R.V., N.E.B., N.A.S.B., (N.T.), Williams, Goodspeed, Weymouth, etc. (contrast A.V.), has been sharply criticized, even ridiculed at times! Some have arrived at the conclusion that Paul is saying that the Galatians are turning away to another gospel which in reality is not essentially different! But the context is clear and decisive: the gospel (?) to which the Galatians are in the process of turning is the perversion of the true gospel (verse 7); it is a gospel (?) different in quality from the one which Paul and his assistants had preached to the Galatians (verse 8), and which the latter had embraced (verse 9);

[19] On ἕτερος as compared with ἄλλος see, among many references that could be listed, M.M., p. 257. It should be obvious that the attempt at a consistent distinction between these two words, applicable in all cases, must fail, especially in Koine Greek. In the New Testament, for example, the two are sometimes used interchangeably (I Cor. 12:9, 10; II Cor. 11:4). For the rest, the rule "ἄλλος adds, while ἕτερος distinguishes" is often helpful.

it is a gospel (?) so bad that a curse is invoked upon him who *might*—and also upon him who actually *does*—proclaim it (respectively verses 8 and 9).

With disdain for such a perversion of the true gospel the apostle continues: **but (the fact is that) certain individuals are throwing y o u into confusion and are trying to pervert the gospel of Christ.** The reference is clearly to the extreme rightists, the Judean Judaizers (cf. Acts 15:1), who, though in a very general sense "coming from James" (Gal. 2:12), do not truly represent James at all (Acts 15:24). Very descriptively the apostle says that these "certain individuals"—they are not nearly as important as they assume themselves to be!—*are throwing y o u into confusion. Literally* this verb means *to shake, stir up, trouble, agitate,* as when Egypt's king is said to resemble a monster that *troubles the waters with its feet,* thereby contaminating the rivers (Ezek. 32:2). *Figuratively,* as here, it has reference to *upsetting* the mind and/or heart. Thus Herod was shaken, deeply disturbed, when he heard about the birth of a king of the Jews (Matt. 2:3); the disciples were troubled when they imagined that they were looking at a ghost (Matt. 14:26); and Zechariah when he saw an angel (Luke 1:12). Another unforgettable illustration of the meaning of the word is found in John 14:1, where Jesus, in the night of his betrayal, says to his disciples, who are gathered with him in the upper room, "Let not y o u r hearts any longer be troubled" (see N.T.C. on the Gospel according to John, Vol. II, pp. 262, 263).

The Galatians, then, were being thrown into confusion by men who were wishing and attempting *to turn upside down* the gospel which centers about Christ and glories in him, the Christ-gospel. Surely, a teaching according to which men are saved *through faith plus law-works* is a perversion of the true gospel which proclaims the glad tidings of salvation (by grace) *through faith alone.*

**8.** Paul continues: **But even though we ourselves or an angel from heaven were to preach to y o u any gospel other than the one which we preached to y o u, let him be accursed**; that is, "Even though we, God's human representatives (I, Paul, and my assistants[20]), or a good angel, one who descends out of heaven in the radiant blaze of his consummate holiness, should begin to preach to y o u any good news other than—hence, contrary to[21]—the gospel which we previously (on the first missionary journeys and on the first leg

[20] The fact that in the very next verse the author clearly distinguishes between "we" and "I," mentioning them in one breath, makes it quite clear that even in verse 8 his "we" is not a literary plural. On this subject see N.T.C. on I and II Thessalonians, p. 82, footnote 65.

[21] For this meaning of παρά see also Acts 18:13; Rom. 1:26; 4:18; 11:24; 16:17. The root idea of this preposition is *beside, alongside;* Cf. the English *parallel.* One can place things *side by side* for the sake of comparison. This easily shifts into that of *opposition;* for example, the worship of a false god *besides* the true God is carried on in opposition to—contrary to the will of—the true God.

of this second missionary journey) preached to y o u, let him (I myself in that case, any of my assistants, that angel) *be doomed.*[22] So far the *hypothetical* case. There follows *reality,*[23] *verse* **9. As we have said before, so now I say again, If anyone is preaching to y o u any gospel other than that which y o u have received, let him be accursed.** The truth expressed in the first conditional sentence (verse 8) greatly strengthens that expressed in the second (verse 9). We have here the reasoning: if even, then all the more. In effect, Paul is saying, "If even we (I, or a fellow-worker) or a holy angel must be the object of God's righteous curse, were any of us ever to preach a gospel contrary to the one we humans previously preached to y o u, then *all the more* the divine wrath must be poured out upon those self-appointed nobodies who are now making themselves guilty of this crime." Here the storm is unleashed in all its fury. Paul's "Let him be anathema" is not a mere wish, but an effective invocation. The apostle, as Christ's fully authorized representative, is pronouncing the curse upon the Judaizers, who are committing the terrible crime of calling the true gospel *false,* and of substituting the false and ruinously dangerous gospel for the true and saving one.

But this word of severe condemnation for the trouble-makers is at the same time one of earnest remonstrance and warning for the Galatians, who were in the process of allowing themselves to be misled, and were actually moving away from the One who, in his love and mercy, had called them. That the addressed deserved this rebuke is clear *first of all* from the fact that they had been forewarned, and "forewarned is forearmed," that is, *if* one heeds the warning. When Paul says, "As we have said before," he probably means that immediately after the Jerusalem Council the apostle and Silas, fully realizing that the Judaizers were not at all satisfied with the decisions of this council and would do all in their power to render them ineffective, had plainly told the Galatians, "There is every possibility that soon after we, y o u r true shepherds, have left y o u, wolves will arrive and

---

[22] According to H. L. Strack and P. Billerbeck, *Kommentar zum Neuen Testament aus Talmud und Midrasch,* Vol. III, p. 260, in the terminology of the Septuagint the word ἀνάθεμα indicates anything which by God or in God's name has been devoted to destruction and ruin. The rabbinical *"ḥerem"* is a broader concept, inasmuch as it comprises *whatever* is devoted to God, not only that which is devoted to him for destruction. The same distinction is carried over into the New Testament, where the noun ἀνάθημα (Luke 21:5, according to the best reading) means that which has been devoted to God as a votive offering, naturally with no curse implications; while ἀνάθεμα (used here in Gal. 1:8, 9, and also in Acts 23:14; Rom. 9:3; I Cor. 12:3; 16:22) refers to that which is devoted to God without hope of being redeemed; hence, that which, or he who, is doomed to destruction, accursed. See also the entries ἀνάθεμα and ἀνάθημα in L.N.T. (Th.) and L.N.T. (A. and G.).

[23] The first conditional sentence (verse 8) has ἐάν and the aorist middle subjunctive in the protasis, and is, accordingly, *future more vivid* or *third class.* The second (verse 9) has εἰ and the present middle indicative, and is *simple, first class.* It *assumes* that the condition is true to fact. In the present case we know that it is also *actually* true to fact. The apodosis, in both cases, uses the present imperative.

will try to destroy y o u, by substituting the false gospel of salvation by law-works for the true gospel of salvation by grace through faith. Be on y o u r guard against these destroyers." It is even possible that already on the first missionary journey similar warnings had been issued, but certainly on the second. Paul adds, "So now I say again,"[24] etc. He now says "I" and not "we" because he alone is the author of this epistle, he himself is *the apostle,* clothed with full authority, and his former associates are absent at this moment. Also later on in life Paul would continue to warn those entrusted to his care about impending dangers (Acts 20:29 ff.; cf. II Tim. 3:1-5; 4:1-5). In this, as in so many other respects, he was following the example of his Master (John 16:1, 4, 33). Since the Galatians had disregarded the earlier warning, they had earned the reprimand.

*Secondly,* they had merited this reproof because not only had the gospel been previously preached to them (verse 8), but they had also accepted it (verse 9). In this respect verse 9 says more than verse 8. By the power of the Holy Spirit the external message had been translated into an inward conviction. They should have guarded the deposit that had been entrusted to them.

The question might be asked, "But was not Paul too severe in his denunciation and in his rebuke? Is it not true that even now the Judaizers believed in Jesus Christ for salvation, the only difference between Paul and those who differed with him being that to this required faith the latter *added* strict obedience to certain Mosaic regulations?" The answer is that the "addition" was in the nature of a complete repudiation of the all-sufficiency of Christ's redemption. Read Gal. 5:2. A beverage may be very healthful and refreshing, but when a drop of poison is *added* to it, it becomes deadly. Christ, too, used severe language in condemning the hypocrites of his day (Matt. 23, especially verses 15 and 33). Pharisees and Judaizers had much in common, were in fact closely related (Acts 15:5; Luke 11:46; cf. Gal. 6:12, 13).

Moreover, Paul and the gospel were friends. To him that gospel was the good news of salvation which God addresses to a world lost in sin. He considered it indispensable for salvation (Rom. 10:14, 15), and was so enthused about it that affectionately he called it *"my* gospel" (Rom. 2:16; cf. Rom. 1:16; I Cor. 1:17; 9:16; II Cor. 4:4; Phil. 1:17; I Tim. 1:11). On the concept *gospel* and *preaching the gospel* see N.T.C. on Philippians, pp. 81–85.

Paul's sharp distinction between the true and the false gospel has a present day application. Illustrations:

---

[24] He cannot have meant, "I now repeat what I just said" (in verse 8), for there is too much difference in content between the two statements, as has been, and will be, indicated.

*a*. At a church service *hymns* are sung which set forth salvation by grace. The *sermon*, however, proclaims an entirely different "gospel" (?).

*b*. The pastor calls on a family and enquires about the absent daughter. The parents exultantly inform him that she is about to marry "a very nice young man, a member of a church which our daughter, too, will soon join." Are these parents blissfully unaware of the fact that in that church the true gospel is not being proclaimed; or does this not matter?

*c*. At a "crusade" many people sign decision-cards. They begin to attend various churches, from some of which the "crusader's" gospel is banned!

**10.** Paul has used forceful language. That gives him an opportunity to answer a charge of the opponents. He writes: **There!**[25] **Is it the favor of men that I am now seeking to win or of God? Or is it men whom I am seeking to please?** Here one detects an echo of the opponents' accusations and insinuations, on this order: "Paul is trying to win human, rather than divine, favor. He tries to please everybody, so that everybody may follow him. Among his own people he preaches circumcision (Gal. 5:11; cf. Acts 16:3), for he knows that they believe in it. But he withholds this rite from the Gentiles because they welcome exemption from it."

Paul answers: "Would a popularity-seeker hurl anathemas at people? Is it not clear that it is not men's but God's approval in which I am interested, and that I am seeking to please my Lord?" Continued: **If I were still trying to please men, I would not be a servant of Christ.**[26] Two misinterpretations:

*a*. "I *never* yield to human customs and traditions."

Total indifference on this score would not have been like Paul. It would bring Gal. 1:10 into conflict with I Cor. 9:22. Tactfulness is not a vice but a virtue when paired with honesty and truth. The apostle desired to be "all things to all men, in order in one way or another to save some." Hence, among the Jews he was willing, during this transition period, to observe certain traditions (Acts 16:3; 21:17-26; cf. 18:18), as long as these were not considered *means unto salvation*, for on *that* issue he was adament. When Judaizers tried to force circumcision upon Gentiles, declaring that otherwise salvation could not be obtained, the apostle invoked God's curse on these distorters. In Paul's religion there was room for flexibility, but ever *within* the limits prescribed by the gospel.

*b*. "If I were still, *as formerly*, trying to please men," etc.

This supposed reference to the apostle's unconverted state is out of line with the present context.

---

[25] By no means does γάρ always mean *for* or *because*. It can also be strongly confirmatory or exclamatory: Yes, indeed! Certainly! There! What! Why! (cf. Matt. 27:23; John 7:41; Acts 8:31; I Cor. 9:10; 11:22; Phil. 1:18).

[26] This is a *contrary to fact* or *second class* conditional sentence: with εἰ and the imperfect indicative in the protasis; and the imperfect indicative with ἄν in the apodosis.

The true interpretation is this: "If, *in spite of* my claim that I am Christ's servant, I were *still,* or *nevertheless,* attempting to please men, my claim would be false." One who trims his sails to every breeze of opinion and bias, cannot be a *servant*[27] of Christ. Paul, on the contrary, is such a servant, for he joyfully acknowledges Jesus as his Redeemer, Owner, and Lord, and is fully surrendered to him. It was this very Christ who said, "No man can serve two masters" (Matt. 6:24). Paul realizes that for himself this life of complete loyalty means persecution (Gal. 5:1), but he glories in such affliction. Not Paul but his opponents are trying to avoid persecution (Gal. 6:12). *They* are the men-pleasers (Gal. 6:13), a type of conduct reprehensible even in slaves (Eph. 6:6; Col. 3:22). *Paul's* chief concern is God's glory.

[27] For the implications of the term *servant* see N.T.C. on Philippians, pp. 44, 109, 110.

# Chapter 1

Verses 11-17

Theme: *The Gospel of Justification by Faith apart from Law-works Defended against Its Detractors*

I. *This Gospel's Origination: it is not of human but of divine origin*

C. The gospel I preach is not a human invention. I received it through the revelation of Jesus Christ. Rescued by God's grace from intense Judaism, I did not immediately go to Jerusalem to seek men's advice, but went to Arabia, and again I returned to Damascus.

11 For I make known to y o u, brothers, with respect to the gospel that was
preached by me, that it is not a human invention; 12 for as concerns myself, I did
not receive it from men nor was I taught it; on the contrary (I received it) through
the revelation of Jesus Christ. 13 For y o u have heard of my former manner of life
when I practiced the Jewish religion, how beyond all bounds I was persecuting the
church of God and was trying to destroy it; 14 and I advanced in the Jewish
religion more than many of my contemporaries among my people, and was a more
ardent enthusiast for the traditions of my fathers. 15 But when it pleased him, who
separated me from my mother's womb and called me through his grace, 16 to
reveal his Son in me, in order that I might preach his gospel among the Gentiles,
I did not at once confer with flesh and blood, 17 nor did I go up to Jerusalem to
those who were apostles before me, but I went away to Arabia; and again I returned
to Damascus.

---

## 1:11-17

### C. *This gospel originated in God, as shown by Paul's experiences before, during, and shortly after his conversion*

11. Paul continues to show that the gospel which he proclaims is the only one worthy of the name, being of divine origin. He writes, **For I make known to y o u, brothers, with respect to the gospel that was preached by me, that it is not a human invention.** In connection with the present context "for" must mean something like "In justification of the facts which I have stated, namely, that my gospel is of divine origin and is the only true gospel, so that anyone who distorts it is accursed, note the following corroborative facts selected from the story of my life."

In the verses which follow, the apostle is not trying to present a complete autobiography. He chooses from his career only those events which support his main contention with reference to the source of his calling as an apostle and of the message which he proclaims. Hence, when he omits an event mentioned elsewhere—for example, in Acts or in Paul's letters to the Corinthians—this must not be charged against him, as if he were purposely suppressing certain facts in order to win the argument against the Judaizers. On the contrary, he is deeply conscious of telling the truth (Gal. 1:20). The omitted incidents are left unmentioned for the simple reason that they have nothing to do with the point which Paul is trying to prove.

The beginning of the sentence is rather striking: "For I make known to y o u," as if they did not already know. But they must have known many of the facts which Paul is going to relate. However, they were acting as if they did not know them. Otherwise they would not be lending a listening ear to the distorters of the true and only gospel of salvation. And for this reason the apostle must remind them again of the truth with reference to himself and the gospel he proclaims. He does this in a very tactful and tender manner, calling them "brothers," for even now, in spite of their deviation, he regards them as members of the same spiritual family to which he, too, belongs, "the Father's Family" (Eph. 3:14). The subject to which he calls their attention is "the gospel that was preached by me," *preached;* hence, they have heard it and are responsible for what they have heard; *by me,* never mind what enemies have been proclaiming; *the gospel,* for, as stated previously, the apostle's defense of himself is in reality a defense of the one and only gospel. He makes known to them that this good news is "not a human invention." This rendering, adopted also by Phillips and by N.E.B.,[28] is well-founded. Literally Paul writes, "not in accordance with man." This might leave the impression that he is simply saying that his gospel is not "in human style." But though, to be sure, this is implied and is even basic, yet the next verse clearly shows that what Paul has in mind is that the gospel which the Galatians have heard from his lips differs not only in *character* and *content* from any human "gospel" (?), but also—and for that very reason—in *origin:* it is not the *result* of human ingenuity or devising.[29] Continued: **12. for as concerns myself, I did not receive it from men nor was I taught it,** probably meaning: "As far as I myself am concerned (note emphatic "I"), in no way whatever did it reach me from any human source. It was not transmitted to me by means of *tradition* from father to son (or from one generation to the next), nor by means of *instruction* from teacher to pupil."[30] Continued: **on the contrary (I received it) through the revelation of Jesus Christ.** Paul here declares that he had received the gospel by a direct revelation of Jesus Christ concerning himself, exactly as the other apostles had also received it (see also on Gal. 1:15, 16; cf. I Cor. 9:1; 15:8).

This introduces a problem. The question might be asked, "But were there not ever so many human agents that had taken part, at one time or another, in supplying Paul with the materials for his gospel? How then can he affirm, repeatedly and with great emphasis, that he had received his gospel from Christ, from him alone, and not at all from men?" Leaving out of consideration many speculative theories concerning contacts which Saul of Tarsus may have had with Jesus during the latter's sojourn on earth, when the future apostle was in Jerusalem, where as a young man he

---

[28] Similarly Williams "not a human message," and Beck "not a human idea."
[29] With the accusative κατά has this merging quality; see N.T.L. (A. and G.), p. 408: the meaning "in accordance with" merges with "the result of."
[30] Others, interpreting παρέλαβον differently, and emphasizing the role of oral tradition especially as employed in the rabbinical schools, believe that Paul meant, "I did not receive it by tradition from men, that is, I was not taught it."

was brought up as a pupil of Gamaliel (Acts 22:3), speculative theories for which it is hard to find solid support in II Cor. 5:16 or anywhere else, it remains true that even before his conversion Paul must have received a great deal of information about Jesus. If he had not known what believers were saying about Jesus, why would he have persecuted *them*—hence *him* (Acts 9:4)—so bitterly? The persecutor must have heard many a ringing testimony from the quivering lips of martyrs, uttered while, with *his* approval, they were being put in chains, dragged off to prison, and at times even put to death. He had been present when Stephen was being stoned, and had heard *his* testimony (Acts 7:58). It is safe to assume, therefore, that even before his conversion Paul must have been fairly well acquainted with many of the historical facts and happenings regarding Jesus. In his epistles he gives evidence of a vast amount of historical knowledge (Rom. 1:3; 9:5; I Cor. 1:23; 15:1 ff.; Phil. 2:5 ff.; I Tim. 3:16; and see also on Gal. 3:1), which he must have gathered little by little, much of it even before Christ had met *him,* Saul the persecutor, as he approached the ancient city of Damascus.

Moreover, these *historical facts* are important. Apart from these *events*—Christ's birth, suffering, death, resurrection, etc.—there is no basis for salvation. How is it, then, that Paul can say that he had received his gospel from Christ, and not from men? The answer is that no matter how detailed Paul's knowledge of these events may have been, their totality does not as yet constitute "the gospel." For, first of all, the persecutor rejected forthwith the fact of Christ's resurrection from the grave and that of his ascension to heaven. And secondly, as to the other facts and events of which he had been apprised, he failed to see them in their true significance. He was constantly giving the wrong answer to such questions as these: Was this Jesus merely born or had he come from heaven? Was his birth a mere happenstance, or had he been born with a purpose? Was he merely human, or divine and human in one person? Was he a dreadful danger to true religion, or a great blessing? Was he a tool of Satan, or the Son of God? Were his life and death a mere vapor that vanishes quickly, or were they of abiding and universal significance? When he died on the cross, was he merely a victim, or was he Victor?

It was when the light from heaven had suddenly descended upon him and had engulfed him, and when he had heard a voice saying to him, "Saul, Saul, why are you persecuting me? . . . I am Jesus whom you are persecuting," etc., it was *then* that *everything changed.* It was here, close to Damascus, that in principle the radical turnabout was accomplished, and Paul received his *gospel.* He now saw the Christ as the really risen and exalted One, full of majesty and power, but also . . . full of incomprehensible love, love so marvelous and condescending that it had sought and found this ruthless, mordacious foe in order to make of him an ardent and kind-hearted friend. He now saw Christ as Victor, full of mercy and grace, reaching out his loving arms to embrace both Jew and Gentile, yes *all* those who would place their (God-given) trust in him. The experience, therefore, on the way to Damascus shed a flood of light on all the information which had been reaching Paul. It changed vehement denial into rapturous conviction, vague outward awareness into marvelous insight.

**13.** Paul now briefly touches upon the three important facts of *a.* his life as a persecutor, *b.* his conversion, and *c.* his activity immediately and shortly after his conversion, in order to show with reference to each of these items that the gospel had not been given to him by any human agency but was a gift from heaven. He writes: **For y o u have heard of my former manner of life when I practiced the Jewish religion.** Yes, the Galatians have heard, probably both from Paul himself and from others, about the manner in which he had conducted himself when his life was still being regulated by the principles which governed the lives of the Jews, unconverted to Christ. Continued: **how beyond all bounds I was persecuting the church of God and was trying to destroy[31] it.** For his present purpose it was not necessary that Paul make mention of all the horrid details of this persecuting activity: that it concerned women as well as men, that the victims were bound with chains, imprisoned, urged to blaspheme, sometimes even put to death (see Acts 8:3; 9:1, 13, 14; 22:4, 5; 26:10, 11). What he does say here in Galatians speaks volumes, showing that the persecution of which Paul had been guilty was *a.* extremely violent ("beyond all bounds"), *b.* directed against God's peculiar treasure, the church (as Paul *now,* after his conversion, sees it), the body of those whom God had *called out* from among all the children of men, to be his very own; and *c.* most sinister in its purpose, namely, utterly to destroy this church. Note that the word "church" as here used is a universal concept (other than in 1:2, 22), and that as such it embraces both Gentiles and Jews, also both dispensations, as is made clear in this very epistle (3:7-9, 13, 14, 29; 4:27; cf. Gen. 22:18; Isa. 54:1-3; Amos 9:11 ff.; Matt. 21:33 ff.; Rom. 11:15-24; Eph. 2:14; I Peter 2:9; and Rev. 21:12, 14).

**14.** The activity of persecution has been described, though in general terms. And now the *drive* or *impetus* behind it is indicated. For Paul this incentive was supplied by the progress which he had made in Pharisaic Judaism, a religion of *works and bondage,* and by his recognition of the fact that this was the very opposite of the Christian religion of *grace and freedom.* He thoroughly understood that Judaism and Christianity were irreconcilable enemies. Moreover, lukewarmness was not in his blood. He

[31] The imperfect tenses make this summary very vivid; thus not "persecuted" but "was persecuting" and "was destroying" or "was trying to destroy." As to the second verb, this can be rendered either way: *a.* "was destroying," for Paul's efforts were partially successful; *b.* "was trying to destroy," for these efforts fell far short of their goal. God took care of that!

was not at all the kind of person who, in a mood of relative indifference, afflicts others because he has been ordered to do this. On the contrary, the man from Tarsus was *himself* bent on oppression and destruction, and he put his whole soul into it. He was a fully convinced persecutor, believing with all his heart that what he was setting out to do *must* be done (Acts 26:9). It is in this light that we should understand him when he now writes: **and I advanced in the Jewish religion more than many of my contemporaries among my people, and was a more ardent enthusiast for the traditions of my fathers.** Paul here pictures himself in his pre-conversion state as a dedicated enthusiast (cf. Phil. 3:6), filled with Pharisaic zeal. In fact, in the original the word "enthusiast" is literally "zealot." Elsewhere Paul describes himself as persecuting "this Way unto death" (Acts 22:4), and as being "exceedingly mad" against the saints (Acts 26:11). Luke writes that Saul of Tarsus "was breathing murderous threats against the disciples of the Lord" (Acts 9:1).

This is not surprising, for, as he tells us here in Gal. 1:14, he had been "chopping ahead" *in the Jewish religion,* "hewing out a path" as a pioneer who is cutting his way through a forest, destroying every obstacle in order to advance.

This Jewish religion (literally, "the Judaism") was not that of Old Testament revelation, whose lines—historical, typological, psychological, and prophetical—converge at Bethlehem, Calvary, Olivet.[32] No, the Jewish religion in which Paul had been pushing his way forward was that in which God's holy law was being buried under a load of human traditions, which Paul calls "the traditions of my fathers," the entire *"halakah"* or body of Jewish oral law which supplemented the written law. In such passages as Matt. 5:21 ff.; 15:3, 6; 23:2 ff., Jesus states his opinion about some of these oral traditions. According to one of them God's commandment, "You shall love your neighbor as yourself" (Lev. 19:18; cf. Exod. 23:4, 5; Prov. 25:21, 22) really meant, "You shall love your neighbor *and hate your enemy"* (Matt. 5:43); and according to another, the exhortation to honor father and mother (Exod. 20:12; Deut. 5:16) was similarly emasculated (Matt. 15:1-6). By means of obedience to the entire Mosaic law as interpreted by all these traditions, many of them trivial and at times even directly contrary to the very intention of the commandment as originally given, the Jews, including Paul before his conversion, tried *to work their way* into "the kingdom of heaven." And according to Paul's own testimony as here given, he had advanced in this Jewish religion more than many of his own age among his people. And as he made progress in the *Jewish* religion, he naturally also advanced in hatred against the *Christian* religion. In fact, he had been going ahead with such frightful fanaticism and terrorism that in this area,

---

[32] See W. Hendriksen, *Bible Survey,* p. 92 ff.

at least, he had already surpassed his own teacher, Gamaliel (Acts 5:33-39).

The apostle's purpose in reminding the Galatians of this sad episode in his life must be borne in mind in order to grasp what he is trying to convey. He is saying that no human persuasion would ever have been able to impart *the gospel* to such a confirmed and ferocious persecutor. His purpose is to show that his gospel is *from God,* not from men.

**15, 16a.** It is with this same purpose in mind that he now continues: **But when it pleased him,[33] who separated me from my mother's womb and called me through his grace, to reveal his Son in me, in order that I might preach his gospel among the Gentiles. . . .** Here Paul's conversion story is told "from the inside." To be sure, there was also the outward or physical side. Paul's conversion was not the product of mere subjective imagination. What he had seen was no hallucination. With his physical eyes he had really beheld the ascended Christ. With his physical ears he had actually heard his voice. But the outward and physical would never have sufficed. What Paul had seen and heard had to be applied to his heart. That story is told here. "But when it *pleased* him . . . to reveal his Son in me" can also be rendered, "But when in his *good pleasure* he . . . revealed his Son in me." Though, according to what is probably the best text, the name "God" is here not mentioned, the reference to him is clear. When God's name, attitude, or activity is clearly implied, he is not always mentioned by name. In fact, *not* mentioning his name but merely saying *"he who"* (or, as here, *"him who"*) places the emphasis on God's gracious deeds and attributes. Another striking instance of this type of omission is found in Phil. 1:6: "he who began a good work in y o u." (See N.T.C. on that passage.) The words "who separated me . . . and called me through his grace" form a combination in which both God's sovereign good pleasure and his marvelous love to one so undeserving are stressed. The expression "separated me from my mother's womb" refers to far more than the divine providential activity revealed in Paul's physical birth. It indicates that God did not, as it were, wait until Paul had first proved his worth before appointing him to an important function in his kingdom. No, from his very birth Paul had already been designed for his specific mission, that design being itself the expression of God's plan from eternity (Eph. 1:11). Hence, the verb *separated,* as here used, means nothing less than "set (me) aside," "consecrated" (me), "marked (me) off from the rest of mankind." Similarly, "called me through his grace" refers here not only to the effectual call to salvation through sanctification (see on verse 6), but also to the assignment unto

[33] Though the textual evidence for "God" is not too strong, it is clear that *God* is meant. In the original, with the verb εὐδοκέω and the cognate noun εὐδοκία, the name of God is not always expressed (Luke 2:14; Col. 1:19; Phil. 2:13). However, the reference to God is clear from the context; thus also in Eph. 1:5, 9; see 1:3.

plenary apostleship. There is a rather clear allusion here to Jer. 1:5: "Before I formed you in your mother's body I knew you; and before you came out of the womb I sanctified you; a prophet to the nations I ordained you." Cf. Luke 1:15. How wonderful this grace operated in the calling of Paul. It changed a man who was breathing *murderous threats* against Christ's church into one who breathed *doxologies* whenever he reflected on this marvelous redeeming love which had been shown to him, yes to *him so* undeserving! In fact, Paul's career as a relentless persecutor, and whatever intervened between his birth and his entrance upon his work as an effective missionary for Christ, made grace stand out all the more brilliantly!

The immediate purpose of this separation and calling is here said to have been "to reveal his Son in me." To *reveal,* that is, "to remove the scales from the eyes of my heart, as the scales were removed from my physical eyes" (Acts 9:18). Moreover, Paul does not say "Jesus" or "Christ Jesus," but "his Son," for God wanted him to see that the Jesus whom in his disciples Paul had been persecuting, was indeed God's only Son, partaker of God's very essence, himself *God!* Yet, the words "to reveal his Son *in me*"[34] mean vastly more than "to my intellect." The phrase has reference to *illumining* grace ("to reveal") which is at the same time *transforming.* Cf. II Cor. 3:18. The more Paul sees that it was this very Son of God whom he had been persecuting but who, nevertheless, had taken pity on him, and in his infinite and tender love had sought him, had stopped him in his tracks, and had changed him into an enthusiastic ambassador of the mysteries of grace, so much the more he also loves and adores this Christ! And the more he adores him, so much the more his own mind, his inner disposition, is patterned after that of his Savior (cf. Phil. 2:5). It is thus that God's Son "was revealed" in Paul!

Now just as the *separation* and the *calling* had as its purpose "to reveal his Son in me," so, in turn, this revelation whereby, as just indicated, the image of Christ was engraved upon the very heart of Paul, had as *its* purpose: "in order that I might preach his gospel among the Gentiles"; literally, "in order that I might gospel him among the Gentiles." It should be obvious, therefore, that indirectly the "call" or "calling" was not just unto salvation but definitely also unto the office of "apostle to the Gentiles." In Paul's case these two cannot be separated. And in this connection one might well ask, "Is it ever possible to separate calling unto salvation from calling unto a task in God's kingdom?" Does not everyone who is called

[34] The phrase ἐν ἐμοί has given rise to much discussion. It has been rendered "to me," "through me," "in connection with me," "in my case," and simply "in (or *within*) me." Though there are parallels for each of these uses, the inward look of the present epistle—cf. "Christ lives in me" (2:20); "until Christ be formed in you" (4:19)—has convinced me that "*in* or *within* me" is correct.

have a duty "to show forth the excellencies of the One who called him out of the darkness into his marvelous light"? (I Peter 2:9).

Throughout his apostolic career Paul remained very conscious of the fact that even though he had been called to be an apostle *to Jews and Gentiles* alike (Acts 9:15; 26:20, 23), yet he had been *especially* selected as God's ambassador to the latter (Acts 13:47; 15:12; 18:6; 22:21; 26:17; 28:28; Rom. 11:13; Gal. 2:2, 8; Eph. 3:1, 6, 8; I Tim. 2:7; II Tim. 1:11; 4:17). But was this purpose made clear to Paul *directly by Christ himself* or *indirectly through the mediation of Ananias or anyone else?* This question has already been touched upon in the discussion of verse 1, but requires a more detailed answer here. Now in connection with Paul's dramatic experience on the way to Damascus it must be admitted that either alternative makes sense. As long as Ananias was, as it were, "the mouth" of Christ, Paul's unshakable conviction that he had been called by Christ and had received his gospel from him, and not *"from* men," nor even *"through* man" in the sense that somehow it had lost its purity through this human intervention, was altogether justified. Nevertheless, if a choice must be made, I would favor the former alternative.[35] According to Acts 26:15-18, in answer to Paul's question, "Who art thou, Lord?" the Lord answers, "I am Jesus, whom you are persecuting. But arise and stand upon your feet because for this purpose have I appeared to you: to appoint you a minister and a witness not only to the things which you have seen but also to the things in connection with which I will appear to you; delivering you from the [Jewish] people and from the Gentiles, to whom I am sending you, to open their eyes so that they may turn from darkness to light and from the dominion of Satan to God, in order that they may receive forgiveness of sins and an inheritance among those who have been sanctified by faith in me." This account certainly leaves the impression that not only the words, "I am Jesus whom you are persecuting," reported in all three accounts (Acts 9:5; 22:8; 26:15), but also the call to apostleship among the Gentiles had come directly from the lips of Christ! And do not even the words of 22:15, where Ananias is saying to Paul, "You will be a witness for him to all men concerning the things which you have seen *and heard,"* imply that Paul had already heard *many things* from the lips of Christ? Is it not probable, therefore, that the accounts which we have in Acts 9 and 22 were never intended to reproduce *in full* the words which Jesus addressed to Paul?

To this should be added Paul's experience while he was praying in the temple at Jerusalem, "three years" after his conversion, and long before he wrote Galatians. While Paul had fallen into a trance it was the Savior

---

[35] This is also the view of S. Greijdanus, *Is Hand. 9 (met 22 en 26) in tegenspraak met Gal. 1 en 2?*, Kampen, 1935, p. 40.

who had said to him, "Depart, for I will send you far away to the Gentiles" (Acts 22:21).

It is clear, therefore, that not only in connection with Paul's experience before his conversion (Gal. 1:13, 14) but also in connection with his conversion itself the point has been established that the gospel which he received and the call to proclaim it originated not in man but in God.

**16b, 17.** This holds also with respect to the apostle's experience, immediately and shortly *after* his conversion, for he continues: **I did not at once confer with flesh and blood, nor did I go up to Jerusalem to those who were apostles before me, but I went to Arabia; and again I returned to Damascus.** Having been led by the hand to Damascus (Acts 9:8), Paul never gave anyone an opportunity to impose his subjective ideas upon him. To be sure, Ananias, at the direction of the Lord, had visited the former persecutor, had laid his hands upon him, had restored his sight, had baptized him, and had told him that he, Paul, would be a witness to all men (Acts 9:10-18; 22:12-16). But all of this had been done at Christ's own command. In fact, Ananias, having heard so many distressing reports with respect to Saul the persecutor, had been reluctant to carry out the order he received. His reluctance had to be overcome (Acts 9:13, 14).

Moreover, it is not at all strange that the Lord had told Ananias to speak to Paul about the latter's mission to "all men." After all, Paul's experience had been so sudden and had occasioned such a complete turnabout in his thinking, and such a radical reversal in his aiming, that a full discussion of its meaning under calmer circumstances was altogether natural and required. Kind-hearted Ananias was the right man for this task. But inasmuch as the message which the latter conveyed to Paul was not his own, Paul here in Galatians is fully justified in omitting any reference to this disciple of the Lord and his mission, since it did not in any way affect the point which he, Paul, is trying to establish, namely, that his gospel and his calling to proclaim it came from above, not from below.

Having spent a number of days in Damascus, Paul, instead of going to Jerusalem in order to receive from the other apostles—whom he fully acknowledges as such!—instruction in the contents of the gospel, at once decided *not* to go there. The words, "I did not at once confer with flesh and blood" do not mean "not at once but later," but rather "I immediately decided not to confer *with flesh and blood";* that is, I decided not to consult mere man, man in all his weakness, over against God the Omnipotent (cf. Matt. 16:17; Heb. 2:14; and see N.T.C. on Eph. 6:12). So, Paul did not at that time go to Jerusalem. Literally he writes, "I did not at once *put myself upon* those who were apostles before me," seeking their advice or approval. He knew very well that, having seen the Lord and having already received the gospel and the call to proclaim it from *him,* he was on fully equal terms with the other apostles. So, instead of going to Jerusalem, he had gone *to*

*Arabia!* The fact that Luke does not make mention of this trip is not strange. Neither Luke nor Paul is trying to give us a complete biography of Paul. Paul's purpose has been stated more than once. And as to Luke, he is interested in setting forth the great works which Jesus, from his heavenly home, continued to do on earth in the establishment of his church (cf. Acts 1:1), mainly through the preaching of the Word. Since Paul, in all probability, did not carry out any preaching mission in sparsely settled "Arabia"—probably referring to the northern part of the large peninsula of Arabia, the part that extends almost to the very border of Damascus[36]—, it is not surprising that Luke omits mention of Paul's visit to that largely desert region. Surely, no one, not even the most confirmed Judaizer, would dare to claim that *in Arabia* Paul had received his gospel either *from* men or *through* man! And, on the other hand, the thought suggests itself that withdrawing to Arabia for rest, prayer, and meditation was exactly what Paul needed, so that his mind, violently shaken, would have time and opportunity to ponder the implications of the words which the Lord had spoken to him at the moment of his unforgettable experience. "And again I returned to Damascus," writes Paul. Note that he still does not go to Jerusalem to confer with the other apostles. Instead, having returned to Damascus, he begins to preach Christ in all his fulness. He does this not in this or that private dwelling (cf. Acts 18:7) or even in a school (cf. Acts 19:9), but *at once* in the synagogues (Acts 9:20). What courage! It reminds us of the "boldness" that characterized the other apostles when, shortly after Christ's resurrection, they addressed the people in the very courts of the temple (Acts 4:1). In both cases the reason for this lack of fear is to be sought in the conviction on the part of these men that they had seen *the risen Lord,* were proclaiming *his gospel,* and were discharging *the commission with which he himself had entrusted them.*

[36] See *Westminster Historical Atlas to the Bible,* Philadelphia, 1945, p. 87 and Plate XV.

# Chapter 1

Verses 18-24

Theme: *The Gospel of Justification by Faith apart from Law-works Defended against Its Detractors*

I. *This Gospel's Origination: it is not of human but of divine origin*

D. Not until three years later did I go up to Jerusalem to visit Cephas, for fifteen days. I saw none of the other apostles, only James. Then I went to Syria and Cilicia, but remained unknown by sight to the Christian churches of Judea. For the change wrought in me they glorified God.

18 Then after three years I went up to Jerusalem to become acquainted with Cephas, and I remained with him fifteen days; 19 but none of the other apostles did I see, only James the Lord's brother. 20 Now take note: with respect to the things which I am writing to y o u, in the presence of God (I affirm) that I am not lying. 21 Then I came to the districts of Syria and Cilicia. 22 But I was still unknown by sight to the Christian churches of Judea. 23 They simply kept hearing, "He who formerly persecuted us is now preaching the gospel of the faith which he formerly was trying to destroy." 24 And they were glorifying God on my account.

---

1:18-24

D. *This gospel originated in God, as shown by Paul's experiences shortly after his conversion* (continued)

**18. Then after three years I went up to Jerusalem to become acquainted with Cephas.** Having spent some time in Arabia and in Damascus, Paul afterward went up to Jerusalem. This trip took place "after three years," this intervening period being figured from the main event mentioned in verses 15 and 16: Paul's dramatic conversion. What portion of this "three years" was spent in Arabia, what portion in Damascus, is not indicated. We do not even know whether these "three years" were three full years, or two full years and part of another year, or only one full year and fractions of two other years. The main point is this, that not immediately after his conversion but now at last, "after three years" Paul leaves Damascus for Jerusalem. It is evident that he does not go to Jerusalem in order to receive a mandate to preach the gospel, nor in order to discover the latter's contents. He has *already* received his commission and also the gospel, namely, from the Lord himself. Moreover, according to Acts 9:20 he has *already* been *effectively* preaching the gospel in the synagogues of Damascus. In fact, it was that very preaching of the gospel which stirred up the Jews, so that they took counsel to kill the preacher. Somehow—by means of slandering Paul, describing him as a dangerous person, and perhaps offering a bribe?—they persuaded the ethnarch of Damascus to assist them in their plot to kill Paul. The result: Paul's enemies guarded the city's gates, thinking that thus they would certainly get the apostle in their trap. However, Paul got wind of this scheme, and, by means of a large basket in which he was lowered to the ground from a window of a disciple's house built on the city-wall, he found safety and freedom (Acts 9:23-25; II Cor. 11:32, 33).

Southward he then wended his way, probably proceeding through the darkness all by himself. But why did he turn his face toward the south, that is, toward Jerusalem? The answer, given here in Gal. 1:18, is that he wanted to *visit* or *become acquainted with*[37] Cephas (= Peter, John 1:42). He may have learned from traveling disciples that right at this moment Cephas was staying in Jerusalem.

Paul reached the place where Cephas was staying. He continues his report: **and I remained with him fifteen days.** Again, we cannot be certain whether the period was equal to our fifteen days or more nearly to our fourteen days (cf. the expression "three years" at the beginning of this verse, in connection with which we experience a similar difficulty). What was the purpose of this meeting, and what took place between these two men? One can only guess. It would seem probable that from Peter the escapee gained valuable information about the life of Jesus while still on earth, about the present state of the church in Jerusalem, and about plans for the future; while, in all likelihood Peter gained first hand knowledge concerning Paul's unforgettable experience as he drew near to Damascus, concerning the state of religion in that city and concerning the clever—and providential!—manner in which the plot of the Jews had been foiled. But whatever may have been the topics of discussion, one fact requires emphasis: the two men were meeting on a footing of perfect equality. Neither received his commission or his gospel from the other!

Paul's candid reporting of this visit with Cephas proves his honesty and historical objectivity. Had he been lacking in these qualities he would, no doubt, have left this incident unmentioned, for fear that the Judaizers would take advantage of it in support of their theory that Paul had received his gospel not from God but from men; particularly, in this case, from Peter. Paul, however, is not trying to hide anything that might be construed as being pertinent, one way or the other, to this basic point of contention (the gospel's origin). Besides, he must have been thoroughly convinced that, in the final analysis, the Judaizers in reality would derive little comfort from a visit so late in the day—that is, so long a time after the apostle's conversion—of such short duration, and for such a purpose ("to become acquainted"). Was it not altogether natural that Paul, an apostle of Jesus Christ, should wish to learn more about Peter, another apostle, commissioned by the same Lord, and should avail himself of the opportunity that presented itself?

**19.** Continued: **but none of the other apostles did I see.** The reason for this cannot have been that in Jerusalem Paul, out of fear, kept himself in hiding.

---

[37] The verb ἱστορέω (cf. the noun ἵστωρ, ἵστωρ) is from the stem ϝιδ; cf. εἴδω, οἶδα (*see, know*). From this same stem are derived the English *visit* (cf. *vision, wit*); A. S. *witan;* Dutch *weten,* and similar words in German, Danish, Swedish, etc. Hence, in Koine Greek the meaning of the verb under discussion is: *to visit with the purpose of getting to know, to become acquainted with.*

Lack of courage was not at all characteristic of this man (see Acts 14:19-21; 19:30; 20:24; 21:12-14; 27:21-26; I Cor. 4:9-13; II Cor. 11:22-33; Phil. 1:12-14; and I Thess. 2:2). For the "boldness" of the other apostles, displayed by them after Christ's resurrection, see Acts 4:29; 5:41. The real reason why Paul did not see the other apostles was probably the latters' absence from Jerusalem at this time. It is true that, according to Acts 8:1, immediately after Stephen's death the apostles had not joined in the flight of believers from that city. But do not Acts 11:30 and 12:1, 2 suggest that they, except Peter and James (the latter being John's brother whom Herod killed with the sword), did leave afterward? We are not told how long before the events reported in these two passages they had left. Besides, by this time there must have been many Christian communities scattered throughout the country that was inhabited by the Jews, communities in need of leadership. This guidance was provided, we may well assume, by the apostles. The point which Paul is making is that he did not deem it necessary to visit all these communities and meet all these apostles in order to be "approved" by them and receive instruction from them in the essence of the gospel. So he, already an apostle, had seen only Cephas, and this merely for the purpose of getting acquainted with him. None of the other apostles had he seen, **only** [or **except**] **James, the Lord's brother.** Does this mean that, after all, Paul had seen two apostles, namely, Peter, who, being one of the Twelve, was an apostle in the plenary sense of that term, and James, an apostle in a more general sense? Though from the point of view of grammar this possibility must be allowed, yet from the aspect of logic the alternative explanation would appear to be more reasonable, namely, "In addition to Cephas, the only apostle whom I saw in Jerusalem, I also saw one other person of special importance, James, the Lord's brother." This does not mean that Paul had seen no other *believers* in Jerusalem; only, that he saw no other individuals of special prominence in the kingdom, *Christian leaders.*[38]

Paul calls James "the Lord's brother." This distinguishes him from James, the brother of John (these two brothers being the sons of Zebedee), and from James, the son of Alphaeus (Matt. 10:2, 3). That James, the Lord's brother, was a man of prominence in the early church, particularly in Jerusalem, is clear from Acts 12:17; 15:13-29; 21:18; and Gal. 2:9, 12. In the days of Christ's earthly sojourn James and his brothers had remained unbelievers (John 7:5). But after the resurrected Christ had appeared to

---

[38] Accordingly, the charge that Gal. 1:19 and Acts 9:26-29 are in hopeless conflict is unfounded. Even Luke's statement that Paul was brought "to the apostles" is not necessarily in conflict with Paul's own declaration in the passage under discussion. The Praesidium of the Jerusalem church consisted originally of "the apostles," the Twelve. When, due to their absence, other men had to replace them—such as James, the Lord's brother, and certain "elders"—this governing body could very well continue to bear the name "the apostles." In Acts 14:14 Luke calls Barnabas an "apostle."

him (I Cor. 15:7), James and the other brothers of Jesus had become believers (Acts 1:14). Of all of Christ's brothers James occupied a leading role in the early history of the church. He was a person of special gifts and wide sympathies. Objects of his tender affection were both the Jews (Acts 15:21; 21:17 ff.) and the Gentiles (Acts 15:13-19). The endearing phrase "our beloved Barnabas and Paul" may well have come from him (Acts 15:25). He was a moderate, a man of peace, eager to weld Jew and Gentile into a single Christian fellowship. He wisely accepted the position that it was possible for believers of diverse origin and background to live together harmoniously, even though in non-essentials the forms of religious expression might not be exactly identical. In predominantly Jewish communities—for example, in Jerusalem—he favored, for the period of transition, the retention of the ancestral customs handed down from Moses, but never as a substitute for (or supplement of) faith in Christ. He was definitely opposed to burdening the Gentiles with the rite of circumcision and other Jewish ordinances, but tactfully proposed that in mixed communities certain practices offensive to Jews be avoided (Acts 15:13-29). Whether at times (cf. Acts 21:17-26), in pursuing his policy of conciliation he may have bent backward too far in his attempt to satisfy, as far as possible, those from the Jews who, like himself, had turned to the Lord, is a question that need not concern us here.

That James is here called "the Lord's brother" because he sprang from the same womb as did Jesus, according to the latter's human nature, would seem to follow naturally from such passages as Matt. 13:55, 56; Mark 6:3, where the names of the other brothers are also mentioned, and the presence of sisters is also indicated. The burden of proof rests entirely on those who defend the idea that "brother," as used here, means *step-brother* (son of Joseph by an earlier marriage) or *cousin*.[39]

For Paul, on his visit to Jerusalem, to have ignored a man of such prominence as James, would have been unthinkable. However, the apostle's testimony here in Gal. 1:19 is in line with his main contention, namely, that he did not receive his gospel or his call to proclaim it from any man, but from Christ. While Paul remained at the home of Cephas for a period of two weeks, he only *saw*—in *this* connection meaning perhaps "briefly contacted"—James. And there is not a hint of a clash between Paul and James.

**20.** Since the apostle is well aware of the fact that his own representation of the facts is going to be challenged by the enemies, he adds: **Now take note: with respect to the things which I am writing to y o u, in the presence of God (I affirm) that I am not lying.** Here *he solemnly affirms,* with an appeal to God's own presence and omniscience, that what he says is true.

---

[39] On this see F. F. Bruce, *Commentary on the Book of Acts,* pp. 44, 45.

In reading Paul's epistles it is striking how often the apostle's awareness of the presence of God shines through his lines, as it were (Rom. 1:8, 9, 25; 6:17; 7:25; 8:35-39; 9:1, 5; 10:1; 11:33-36; 15:13, 32; 16:25-27; Eph. 1:3 ff.; 1:15 ff.; 3:14-21; and in all the other epistles). He was filled with a genuine and overpowering consciousness of living "in the very presence of God," the God whom he loved and, what is even more meaningful, who loved him. A good rule for each person to follow is, therefore, this one:

"When you think, when you speak, when you read, when you write,
When you sing, when you walk, when you seek for delight,—
To be kept from all wrong both at home and abroad,
Live always as under the eye of your God."

(First lines of a poem
of anonymous authorship)

21. Paul continues: **Then I came to the districts of Syria and Cilicia.** Luke states that it was because of another plot against Paul's life that the brothers in Jerusalem, having become aware of it, decided that he should leave the city. Paul agreed, for, as he himself reports, the Lord appeared to him and told him to depart quickly, adding the encouraging words, "I will send you far away to the Gentiles" (Acts 9:30; 22:17-21). So Paul was conducted on his way to Caesarea, and from there sent to his home-town, Tarsus, the chief city of Cilicia, from which, probably after a period of several years, Barnabas, overtaxed with evangelistic activity, brought him to Antioch in Syria to join in the work there.

Now this sequence of events raises the question, "If Paul first made his abode in Cilicia, afterward in Syria, why does he, in making his own report, reverse this order; in other words, why "Syria and Cilicia" instead of "Cilicia and Syria"? Some answers are: *a.* because Syria adjoins Palestine, so that, traveling by land, one would reach Syria before entering Cilicia; *b.* because in Cilicia the apostle remained inactive, but he worked in Syria; and *c.* because Cilicia, though a Roman province, was rather weak and under the jurisdiction of Syria. Whatever may be the truth as to this question, the main point which Paul is trying to stress must not be lost sight of. He is saying, as it were, "Then I left Jerusalem and went to places so remote that the possibility of contact with the Twelve, to receive the gospel from them or to be seriously influenced by them, was excluded."

22, 23. Continued: **But I was still unknown by sight to the Christian churches of Judea.** The apostle was fully justified in making this statement, for in former days his persecution activity, as far as it had been carried on in the southern part of Palestine, had been largely confined to Jerusalem; and as a convert and apostle he, having spent a fortnight with Cephas, had not entered any of the surrounding territory.[40] Thus personally he was still unknown in these country churches, probably implying "and thus unknown also to the apostles who were serving them" (see on verse 19).

For various reasons the Christians in the outlying districts were used to making trips to Jerusalem. On these visits they would call on some of their fellow-believers. Also, those dwelling in Jerusalem would visit those outside the city. In both of these cases those of Jerusalem would joyfully and vividly impart to their friends and relatives the news about *the persecutor turned gospeler.* As a result **They,** that is, the members of the Christian churches of *Judea,* **simply kept hearing, "He who formerly persecuted us is now preaching the gospel of the faith[41] which he formerly was trying to destroy."** The underlying implication of this exuberant exclamation must not escape us. It is evident that the reporters, men and women of simple faith in Christ, approved of the gospel as preached by Paul! They recognized it as being the very same good news which they had accepted from the start, having heard it from the lips of Christ and his disciples. It was *that* gospel which at one time Paul had been trying to destroy. It was *that same gospel* which he was now preaching! What a crushing argument against the Judaizers, who were slandering the apostle for proclaiming the wrong kind of gospel, one that would not reach quite far enough to save people. What the church's "pillars" are reported to have done later on, namely, give expression to their conviction that the gospel as preached by Paul (and Barnabas, Gal. 2:6-10) was the true gospel, the Jerusalem saints were *shouting* even now, and their Judaean fellow-believers, who were constantly *hearing* it, were in glad accord with them. **24.** Paul concludes: **And they**—all of them together—**were glorifying[42] God on my account.** They were not *suspicious,* as those of Jerusalem had been at one time (Acts 9:26), nor *indifferent* (cf. Rev. 3:16), nor *unforgiving,* nor even *merely happy.* On the contrary, fully realizing that whatever comes from God must be returned to him in the form of praise and thanksgiving, and that this circle must never be broken, they declared the glorious character of God's marvelous attributes: power, sovereignty, wisdom, grace, mercy, etc., shown in saving a wretch, a relentless persecutor, and transforming him into a flame-tongued

[40] For use of the term "Judea" for the region round about Jerusalem, but excluding the latter, see also John 3:22. That here in Gal. 1:22 Jerusalem is indeed excluded follows naturally from verse 23, where the Jerusalem saints are introduced as referring to Paul's former activity as a persecutor in their midst. Certainly, if he had persecuted them, then *to them,* at least, he cannot have been unknown. It is impossible, however, to determine the exact boundaries of "Judea" as the term is employed here in verse 22. We do know, however, that from Jerusalem as a center the cause of the Lord had been spreading (Acts 8:4 ff.), so that the term "the churches of Judea in Christ" (thus literally) must not be taken in too narrow a sense.

[41] In this context the objective sense of the word *faith* surely predominates; that is, it is the *religion* or *doctrine* that is meant. See also on 6:10.

[42] On the cognate noun δόξα see N.T.C. on Philippians, pp. 62–64.

herald of the gospel! What depth of feeling must have overwhelmed Paul's soul as he wrote these last words: "They were glorifying God *on my account* (literally "in me") !"

*Summary of Chapter 1*

This chapter consists of four short paragraphs: verses 1-5; 6-10; 11-17; and 18-24. In the first of these subdivisions Paul's painful distress reveals itself in the manner in which he describes himself and the addressed, and in the qualifying clause by means of which he enlarges on his opening salutation. In that clause he clearly implies that to the sacrifice of Christ for sinners to purchase their salvation nothing can be added.

In the second paragraph Paul gives expression to his shocked amazement about those whom he addresses, because of their disloyalty to the God who had called them, and their readiness to accept a different gospel, which really was no gospel at all but a dangerous distortion. He pronounces God's curse upon anyone who might proclaim—or is actually proclaiming—a gospel other than the one which had been preached to the Galatians and had been accepted by them.

In this connection two facts must be borne in mind:

(1) Paul's anathemas have relevancy in every age. Anyone who teaches that God's grace and human endeavor are twin sources of salvation, that is, that *to a certain extent* men are able to lift themselves into heaven by the lobes of their ears, is here condemned. Implication: then would not this curse rest at least as heavily upon those who proclaim that salvation can be achieved apart *entirely* from divine help ("Mankind *alone* must save us") ?

(2) These anathemas are aimed at those who are leading the Galatians astray, not at the Galatians themselves. With the latter the apostle is sorely displeased. Nevertheless, in his love and patience he still regards them as *his* and *God's* children, grievously erring children though they be—a lesson for all pastors, parents, and leaders of men.

In verses 11-17 Paul proves that the charge of the opponents, namely, that he is not a true apostle and that his gospel had been imparted to him not by God but by men, and is accordingly a merely human invention, is false. He bolsters his argument by briefly setting forth certain relevant events from the story of his life. As to receiving the gospel from men, particularly from other apostles, he shows that *before his conversion* this would have been *psychologically impossible* for such a bitter persecutor; that *at the time of his conversion* it would have been *wholly unnecessary,* for Christ himself revealed the gospel to him by appearing to him and addressing him directly; and that *immediately after his conversion* it would, in addition, have been *geographically unthinkable,* for in Damascus and in Arabia, the places to which he wended his way, there were no apostles who could have imparted the gospel to him.

The same line of argumentation is continued in the closing paragraph. Paul shows that his first post-conversion visit to Jerusalem was of very short duration, had as its purpose "to become acquainted with Cephas (Peter)," *not* to receive the gospel from him, and was not followed by visits to the other apostles (though James, the brother of the Lord, was also briefly contacted). The writer had remained unknown to "the Christian churches of Judea," outside Jerusalem. Accordingly, when the wonderful news of his conversion began to spread, those who heard it did not begin to praise Peter or the rest of the apostles but "were glorifying *God*" on Paul's account, for it was from God—from Christ himself—that the former persecutor had received the glorious gospel of salvation full and free for Gentiles as well as for Jews.

Implication: since, then, this gospel is divine in origin and essence, no attempt must be made to distort it. It is the only good news whereby men are saved, enabled to be a blessing to their neighbors, and equipped to live to God's glory.

# Chapter 2

Verses 1-10

Theme: *The Gospel of Justification by Faith apart from Law-works Defended against Its Detractors*

I. *This Gospel's Origination: it is not of human but of divine origin; hence, is independent*

E. Then, on a visit to Jerusalem with Barnabas and Titus, its "pillars" in a private interview imparted nothing to me, but gave us the right hand of fellowship. Titus, a Greek, was not compelled to be circumcised. Thus, there was no yielding to infiltrators but continuation of blessing for y o u. A division of missionary labor was agreed on. The poor were to be remembered.

# CHAPTER II

**GALATIANS**

2 1 Then, after an interval of fourteen years, I went up again to Jerusalem
with Barnabas, also taking Titus with me. 2 I went up, moreover, as a result
of a revelation, and I set before them the gospel which I am accustomed to preach
among the Gentiles; but (I did this) privately to "those of repute," to make sure
that I was not running or had not run in vain. 3 Yet even Titus who was with me,
Greek though he is, was not compelled to be circumcised; 4 (in fact, the suggestion
would never have arisen) but for the uninvited sham brothers, who had infiltrated
our ranks to spy on our liberty which we have in Christ Jesus, and thus to reduce
us to slavery; 5 to whom not even for a moment did we yield submission, in order
that the truth of the gospel might continue with y o u. 6 Well, from those "who were
reputed" to be something—whatever they once were makes no difference to me;
God accepts no man's person—to me "those of repute" imparted nothing; 7 on the
contrary, when they saw that I had been entrusted with the gospel to the uncircumcised just as Peter (with that) to the circumcised 8 —for he who was at work
through Peter in apostolic mission activity for the circumcised was also at work in
me for the Gentiles—, 9 and when they perceived the grace that was given to me,
James and Cephas and John, "those who were reputed" to be pillars, gave to me
and Barnabas the right hand of fellowship, that we should (go) to the Gentiles, and
they to the circumcised. 10 Only, we were to continue to remember the poor, the
very thing which I was also eager to do.

---

2:1-10

E. *The Validity of the gospel as proclaimed by Paul acknowledged by Jerusalem's "pillars"; the work divided; the poor to be remembered*

In Chapter 1 the apostle has shown that he had received his gospel directly from Christ, not *from* men nor *through* this or that man. He now proceeds to show that, because of this very fact, *this gospel which he proclaims is independent of men's evaluation.* A God-given gospel does not need human validation. It can "stand on its own feet." And for this very reason, as soon as Jerusalem's "pillars" see that Paul and Barnabas had been thus divinely entrusted with the gospel, they extend to them the right hand of fellowship and agree to divide the work. James, Cephas, and John recognize *God's* hand when they see it!

1. The paragraph begins as follows: **Then, after an interval of fourteen years, I went up again to Jerusalem with Barnabas, also taking Titus with me.**

In 1:15, 16 Paul, in touching language, has spoken about his conversion. In verse 18 of that same chapter he has related how three years afterward he had gone to Jerusalem to become acquainted with Cephas. Leaving Jerusalem he had spent some time in Syria and Cilicia (verse 21). When he now continues by saying, "Then, after an interval of fourteen years, I went up again to Jerusalem," it is natural to interpret this statement as meaning that the trip to Jerusalem which he here introduces occurred fourteen years after that other visit to this city described in 1:18, *not* fourteen years after his conversion. If Paul's conversion occurred in A.D. 34, then the first trip to Jerusalem "after three years" took place *circa* A.D. 37. Nevertheless, as already indicated, it is impossible to be precise, since these "three years" may not have amounted to a full three years as we now count them. Thus, the real date may have been A.D. 36. Similarly, all we can safely affirm about the expression "after an interval of fourteen years" is that it probably means that the trip to Jerusalem described here in Gal. 2 took place *about* the year A.D. 50.[43]

Between the trip to Jerusalem indicated in Gal. 1:18 and the one here in 2:1 Paul had been in Tarsus, had labored with Barnabas in Antioch (Syria), about the time of the death of Herod Agrippa I (A.D. 44) had accompanied Barnabas on a relief mission to Jerusalem, had gone back to Antioch, and, together with Barnabas, had made his first missionary journey. It is from Antioch, to which they have again returned, that Paul and Barnabas now—after these fourteen years—make their trip to Jerusalem. They are sent to Jerusalem in order to assure *Gentile freedom over against the insistent demand of the Judaizers that the Gentiles be circumcised* (Acts 15:1, 2; Gal. 5:1). On this issue the minds of Paul and Barnabas are made up, but they are going to prove to the entire assembly, if such proof be required, that their own view and the course which they have been following is the only right one.

It is evident that, along with ever so many interpreters,[44] I accept the

---

[43] For a justification of this chronology which, with respect to several of its dates, cannot be more than *approximately* correct, see W. Hendriksen, *Bible Survey,* pp. 62–64, 70.

[44] For example, Berkhof, Erdman, Findlay, Greijdanus, Grosheide, Lightfoot, Rendall, Robertson. As I see it, the best and most detailed argument in favor of the view that the visit of Gal. 2 must be identified with that of Acts 15 is that of S. Greijdanus, *Is Hand. 9 (met 22 en 26) en 15 in tegenspraak met Gal. 1 en 2?,* Kampen, 1935. Ramsay, who did not commit himself to any fixed theory, states, "There is practically universal agreement among critics and commentators of every shade of opinion that the visit described as the third in Acts 15 is the one that Paul describes as the second in Gal. 2:1-10. Scholars who agree in regard to scarcely any other point of early Christian history are at one on this" (*St. Paul the Traveler and the Roman Citizen,* p. 154). I take exception to the phrase "as the second." P. Parker also links Acts 15 with Gal. 2, regrettably at the expense of Acts 9:26-30: "Once More, Acts and Galatians," *JBL,* 86 (June 1967), pp. 175–182.

identification of the Gal. 2 trip with that of Acts 15. My reasons are:

(1) The *big* question in both accounts amounts to this: "Is Christ sufficient unto salvation?" Phrased differently, this question may be expressed in these words, "Is it necessary to require of the Gentiles who have embraced Christ by a living faith that, for the sake of their salvation, they, in addition, observe the Mosaic ordinances?" Specifically, "Is it necessary that they be circumcised?" (cf. Acts 15:1-3, 10, with Gal. 2:3; 4:10; 5:2-4; 6:12, 13).

(2) Acts mentions the main speakers, namely, Peter, Barnabas, Paul, and James (15:7, 12, 13). These four are also mentioned in Galatians, as being, along with John, those who supply the leadership (2:7, 9).

(3) According to Acts, Barnabas and Paul relate before the whole assembly "what signs and wonders God had performed through them among the Gentiles" (15:12). And in Galatians Paul reports, "I set before them the gospel which I am accustomed to preach among the Gentiles." Also, "And he [God] was . . . at work in me for the Gentiles" (2:2a, 8).

(4) According to Acts "some of those who belonged to the party of the Pharisees" tell the assembly that for the Gentiles, too, circumcision is a necessity (15:5). The voices of these Judaizers are also heard in Galatians (2:4, 5).

(5) In Luke's account there is never any yielding to the expressed opinions and wishes of the Judaists or Judaizers (Acts 15:8-19). This is forcefully expressed in 15:10. The statement in Galatians is just as emphatic: "to whom [that is, *to the sham brothers*] not even for a moment did we yield submission" (2:5).

(6) From the start and throughout, according to Acts, there is perfect harmony among the leaders (15:8-29). This, according to the most reasonable interpretation, is also the case in Galatians: James and Cephas and John extend the right hand of fellowship to Paul and Barnabas (2:5, 9).

For the arguments which have, nevertheless, been advanced against this identification, see the footnote.[45]

---

[45] These arguments are as follows:

(1) If the visit of Gal. 2 must be identified with that of Acts 15, then very soon after this important Jerusalem Council, *in which Peter had taken a leading part,* he would have made himself guilty of conduct in direct conflict with its most important decision. This is inconceivable.

*Answer.* This objection is answered in some detail in the explanation of 2:11 ff.

(2) If it were true that Galatians was written soon after the Jerusalem Council, Paul would simply have referred the addressed to the decision of that Council.

*Answer.* Paul had *already* delivered to the Galatians the decrees of that assembly (Acts 16:4). The point is that *the Judaizers* had not been convinced, and, in turn, had succeeded to a certain extent in undermining the confidence of the Galatians in the wisdom of these decrees. Even today decisions of synods or general assemblies seldom convince those who, like the Judaizers, from the start have taken an opposite stand, or those who are influenced by them. Hence, in order to persuade the Galatians it was necessary for Paul to present arguments derived directly from

Scripture and—in close connection with this—from Christian experience. This he does in Galatians.

(3) Acts 15 deals with a *public* conference (verses 2 and 22); Galatians 2 with a *private* interview of the leaders (verse 2). Therefore, these two cannot refer to the same trip and the same meeting.

*Answer.* Galatians 2 leaves room for both. For the *public* conference see *especially* verse 2a (though some of the later verses may also refer to it). For the *private* interview see *especially* verse 2b. There is, accordingly, no conflict here.

(4) According to Galatians (2:2) Paul goes up to Jerusalem "as a result of a *revelation";* but according to Acts the church of Antioch *delegates* Paul and Barnabas to go to Jerusalem.

*Answer.* This twofold description of whatever it was that induced Paul to go to Jerusalem raises no conflict at all. One possibility is that he was at first rather reluctant to accept the assignment given to him by the church of Antioch; fearing, perhaps, that by placing before the "apostles and elders" at Jerusalem the question with respect to the circumcision of the Gentiles, he might endanger his standing as an apostle, the independence of the gospel which he had been proclaiming, and thus also the cause—so dear to himself—of mission activity among the Gentiles. If he actually harbored that reluctance, it is understandable that a divine revelation was necessary to send him on his way. But even aside from this, the present merging of a human factor and a divine in bringing about Paul's departure from one city to go to another is not at all exceptional; see also Acts 13:1, 2; and compare Acts 9:30 with 22:17-21.

(5) According to Galatians (2:1) when Paul and Barnabas go to Jerusalem, Titus is also in their company. Acts 15, however, does not name Titus. In fact, in the entire book of Acts Titus is never even mentioned.

*Answer.* From other passages—besides Gal. 2:1, 3—we know that Titus became one of Paul's beloved companions (II Cor. 2:13; 7:6, 13, 14; 8:6, 16, 23; 12:18; II Tim. 4:10; and, of course, Titus 1:4). It is not strange, therefore, to learn from Galatians that, *on Paul's initiative,* Titus is taken along to Jerusalem. Moreover, though it is true that, for an unknown reason, Titus is not mentioned by name in Acts 15, neither is his presence excluded. In fact, room is provided for him when it is stated that not only Paul and Barnabas but also "some other persons" were appointed to go up to Jerusalem (15:2). Hence, here, too, Galatians and Acts are not necessarily in conflict.

(6) The regulations mentioned in Acts 15:20 are not found in Gal. 2.

*Answer.* These regulations do not touch the main issue on which Paul rivets the attention in Gal. 2. Besides, it is not even certain that Gal. 2 does not contain a veiled reference to these regulations (see on verse 6).

(7) According to the book of Acts Paul's Jerusalem visit mentioned in Chapter 15 was his *third* (after his conversion); the first being recorded in 9:26, and the second in 11:27-30; 12:25. But according to Paul's own account, the visit to which Gal. 2:1 makes reference was only his *second;* the first trip being mentioned in 1:18. Therefore, the visit described in Gal. 2 cannot be identified with that of Acts 15, but must have occurred earlier. Far more probable, therefore, is the identification of Paul's visit mentioned in Gal. 2 with that described in Acts 11:27-30; 12:25. In both cases this would be the *second* visit. The view according to which in Galatians Paul simply skips the Acts 11:27-30; 12:25 visit, so that the Gal. 2 visit must be identified with that recorded in Acts 15, is unsound. Reason: in Gal. 2 (as well as in Gal. 1) the apostle is trying to prove that on none of his post-conversion trips to Jerusalem could he have received his gospel from *men,* that is, from the leaders of the Jerusalem church. Had Paul failed to include even *one* visit, he would have exposed himself to the charge of misrepresenting the facts, for in that case his enemies would have been able to say, "You have been in Jerusalem more often than you are now admitting. Hence, you had abundant opportunity to receive your gospel *from men.*"

*Answer.* It is not true that Gal. 2:1 must be interpreted to mean that the trip

There are some[46] who prefer to identify the Gal. 2 visit with that of Acts 11:27-30; 12:25. Their reasons for doing this may be gathered from footnote 45; see especially item (7).

With due respect for the scholarliness of the eminent men who favor this theory and for the many valuable works which they, as well as those who disagree with them, have produced, I here state the reasons for my inability to concur with their opinion:

(1) *The two accounts differ in their main theme.* Galatians 2 deals with the question whether or not the Gentiles who turn to Christ must be circumcised; Acts 11, 12 describes a relief mission, and (in the section referred to) says nothing about circumcision.

(2) In Acts 11:27-30; 12:25 it is Barnabas who takes the lead (note "Barnabas and Saul" in 11:30 and 12:25). In Gal. 2 Barnabas has no such priority (see verses 2:1, 6, 8, 9).[47]

(3) If the visit recorded in Gal. 2:1-10 is that of Acts 11:27-30; 12:25, then the question whether or not the Gentiles should receive circumcision was officially settled long before the time of the Council of Jerusalem described in Acts 15. On that supposition would not the latter meeting have been superfluous?

(4) Acts 11:30 makes mention only of "elders" ("sending it to the elders"). No "apostles" are referred to, either as a group or individually. Also in this respect Gal. 2 (see verse 9) resembles Acts 15 (see verses 7, 12, 22) far more closely than it does Acts 11:27-30; 12:25.

(5) Chronologically the identification of the Gal. 2 visit with the relief mission described in Acts 11:27-30; 12:25, which occurred at about the time of the death of Herod Agrippa I—hence, about A.D. 44—, presents difficulties that are well-nigh insurmountable. It would mean that the apostle's first post-conversion visit to Jerusalem—fourteen years earlier—took place around A.D. 30 or 31, and the conversion itself "three years" earlier than that; that is, during Christ's earthly ministry. Only by a very unnatural explanation of Gal. 2:1 is it possible to avoid that conclusion. Perhaps Lenski's remark is not too strong, "The supposition that [in Gal. 2:1-10] Paul is speaking of the visit which he and Barnabas paid to Jerusalem to bring relief . . . (Acts 11:27-30; 12:25) is chronologically impossible" (*op. cit.*, p. 68).

---

here mentioned was Paul's *second* post-conversion visit to that city. The word *again*—in the clause, "I went up again to Jerusalem"—does not necessarily mean *for the second time*. Also, it is not true that in Gal. 2 the apostle is still trying to prove that he had received his gospel not from men but from God. On both of these points see the explanation of 2:1.

[46] For example, Bruce (in his *Commentary on the Book of the Acts*, pp. 244, 298–301), Calvin, Duncan, Ellis, Emmet, Hoerber, Knox.

[47] Nor does he have this priority in Acts 15, which has both "Barnabas and Paul" (verses 12 and 25) and "Paul and Barnabas" (verses 2 and 22).

Now when Paul declares that after an interval of fourteen years he went up *again* to Jerusalem, this word *again* does not necessarily mean "for the second time."[48] It can just as well mean "once again," without indicating how many previous trips to Jerusalem there had been.[49] Moreover, it is not at all strange that here in *the second chapter* of Galatians Paul says not a word about the relief mission recorded in Acts 11:27-30; 12:25. The simple fact is that he is no longer talking *per se* about the source of his gospel but rather about the *implication* of the fact that he had obtained it directly from God; that implication being that this gospel is independent, does not need to stand, hat in hand, begging human approval for its existence and proper functioning.

It must be borne in mind that whatever happened in the year A.D. 44—whether it were a mission of relief or anything else—could have had no bearing whatever on the question how the gospel had *originally* been given to Paul, for by that time he had already been an apostle for some *ten years!* He had been preaching the gospel not only in Damascus and Jerusalem but also in (Tarsus? and) Antioch of Syria. It is exactly as Greijdanus says: "The question whether Paul in obtaining his gospel ministry had been dependent on the other apostles could have reference only to the early period of that ministry."[50] It is not even strictly necessary to argue that on this relief mission Paul and Barnabas had contacted only "elders" and not "apostles" in Jerusalem, for even if everyone of the apostles had been in the welcoming committee and if Paul had remained with them for an entire year, they could not have *given* him the gospel which he already *had,* and which he had been proclaiming for such a long period! This is the answer to objection (7), footnote 45.

Among the men who went up to Jerusalem three are definitely indicated here in Gal. 2:1: Paul, Barnabas, and Titus.

*Paul* was a man of boundless energy, steadfast determination, earnest devotion to his Lord, zeal for the work of winning souls, and resolute unwillingness that the great cause of the evangelization of the Gentiles be hindered in any way. He was not only an intellectual giant but also *deeply emotional* and *expertly tactful.* However, since this has been set forth in

---

48 The word πάλιν is more indefinite than δεύτερον, as in John 3:4, where Nicodemus literally says, "He cannot *a second time* enter into his mother's womb and be born, can he?" or as in Rev. 19:3, "And *a second time* they cried, 'Hallelujah.'" Though the meaning of II Cor. 13:2 is a matter of sharp controversy, that difference of interpretation does not really affect the word δεύτερον, which also there means *second time.*

49 If the trip of Gal. 2 was that of Acts 15, then, according to the latter's count, it was the third; just as the word πάλιν in John 18:27 refers not to the second but to the *third* denial, as the context indicates. See N.T.C. on the Gospel according to John, Vol. II, p. 389.

50 *Is Handelingen 9 (met 22 en 26) en 15 in tegenspraak met Galaten 1 en 2?,* p. 66.

some detail in other commentaries of this series, it is not necessary to repeat it here. See N.T.C. on Philippians, p. 181; and on Colossians and Philemon, pp. 231, 232. Paul was truly "a man in Christ," and for all these reasons the proper person to be sent to Jerusalem for the purpose that has been indicated.

Most of these characteristics applied also to *Barnabas,* the Levite from the island of Cyprus. By means of the many biblical references to him—approximately thirty—we are given a rather complete picture. He was "a good man, and full of the Holy Spirit and of faith" (Acts 11:24). The very name, Barnabas, that is, "son of prophecy" (Acts 4:36), hence "of consolation" (A.V.) or "exhortation" (A.R.V.; N.E.B.) or "encouragement" (R.S.V.; Williams), had been appropriately substituted for the one that had been given to him at birth, namely, Joses or Joseph. He was a spiritually eloquent man. When he is first mentioned (Acts 4:36, 37) he has moved from Cyprus to Jerusalem, where he has bought some property. When he realizes that many of the saints in that city and surroundings are poor, to which condition not only a famine but also their conversion to faith in Jesus may well have contributed, he, being himself also a believer and filled with generosity, sells a field and lays the proceeds at the apostles' feet. That same spirit of generosity, now coupled with pleasing trustfulness, also manifested itself in a totally different way. It caused him to dispel the suspicions of the disciples when Saul of Tarsus, known as the most bitter persecutor of the church, suddenly entered the city of Jerusalem, and claimed that he had experienced a dramatic conversion. When nobody else believed this story, it was Barnabas who stood by the side of the convert, and secured his admission into the disciples' fellowship (Acts 9:26-28). To these traits of *eloquence, generosity,* and *trustfulness* should be added that of *mission-mindedness,* which is *broadmindedness* in the best sense of that term. He entertained no scruples about allowing Gentiles to enter the church on the basis of simple faith in Christ, "without the works of the law." Accordingly, when, in Antioch (Syria), due to the preaching of his own countrymen and others, a great number of Greeks "turned to the Lord," it was Barnabas who by the church of Jerusalem was sent to this new Christian community to give direction and leadership to it (Acts 11:19-22). Touchingly beautiful, in this connection, is the description of this warm-hearted missionary's reaction to the mighty work of the Lord that was taking place in Antioch: "When he came and saw the grace of God, he rejoiced; and he encouraged them all to remain faithful to the Lord with steadfast hearts" (Acts 11:23). What a picture of genuine, fatherly *sympathy!* Add also *wisdom,* a wisdom in one respect exceeding even that of Moses (see Exod. 18; Num. 11:17). While Moses overloaded himself with work and had to be advised to share responsibility with others, Barnabas, confronted with a similar situation, immediately went into action *of his own accord,* and secured the help of Paul, whom he sought and found in Tarsus. Thus, the two men worked side by side for an entire year in this flourishing field (Acts 11:25, 26). And the Lord blessed their labors. Together also they are sent to Jerusalem with gifts for the needy (Acts 11:27-30; 12:25). And, having returned to Antioch, they are together ordained as missionaries and proceed on the trip that has become known as Paul's "First Missionary Journey" (Acts 13:1 ff.). At this point another virtue, of which Barnabas had so many, begins to stand out, namely, that of marked *humility;* for, though the man (Paul) who at the beginning was the *assistant* of Barnabas gradually becomes the *leader,* "the son of encouragement" (Barnabas) never shows the least resentment on that score. And to top it all, add unwearying *patience,* the willingness to give a deserter another chance. This characteristic was to manifest itself shortly after the Jerusalem Conference, to which Gal. 2 refers, but is mentioned here to fill out the picture. The deserter was John Mark, who, having started out with Paul and Barnabas on the first missionary journey, had left during its course and had returned to his home. Because of this act of disloyalty and cowardice Paul, after the close of the Conference, was going to turn down the suggestion of Barnabas that Mark be taken along on the second journey. Between the two leaders there was going to arise "a sharp contention" (Acts 15:36-41). But Barnabas was going to stand by John Mark, even though it would mean parting company with Paul. And his patience was gloriously rewarded, for this same Mark at a later time becomes "a comfort" to Paul (Col. 4:10b, 11), "very useful" to him for kingdom work (II Tim. 4:11), and the writer of the second Gospel!

The purpose of the description just given is not at all to exalt Barnabas above Paul, as if the former were the better of the two. As concerns Mark, did he not stand in need of *Paul's* stern discipline as well as of *Barnabas'* untiring patience . . . and, besides, of *Peter's* fatherly oversight? See N.T.C. on Colossians and Philemon, pp. 188, 189. Moreover, the fact that Barnabas, too, had his moments of weakness is clear from Gal. 2:13. And as to *leadership* qualities, *penetrating insight* into redemptive truth, and *consistency* in applying this truth to the conditions of everyday living, was there anyone in the days of the apostles who surpassed Paul? No one, not even Barnabas! The real purpose, therefore, of the descriptions of Paul and Barnabas was to show how eminently fit *both* of these big-hearted men were for accomplishing their task of making certain at Jerusalem that those who had already been gathered into Christ's fold from the Gentile world should not lose their freedom, that others, Gentile as well as Jew, should be added to the multitude of the saved, and that the glory of Christ as all-sufficient Savior should not be debilitated.

And then there was *Titus,* who was taken along on Paul's initiative, as verse 1 clearly implies: "also taking Titus with me." For a delineation of his character see N.T.C. on I and II Timothy and Titus, pp. 36, 37. From that description it will be evident that the apostle could not have taken along a better brother in the Lord, one who was more willing and eager to co-operate in every way, and who, being by race a Gentile of unmixed extraction, and thus *uncircumcised,* was *a test case,* a definite challenge to the Judaizers, as has already been explained. See p. 17.

2. Paul continues: **I went up, moreover, as a result of a revelation.** Whatever hesitancy there may have been on Paul's part when he and others were delegated by the Antiochian church to go to Jerusalem for the purpose already indicated, was removed by this divine revelation. See footnote 45, point (4). The Lord knew that the contemplated conference to be held in that city would prove to be of great value not only for Paul, Barnabas, Titus, etc., but also for James, Cephas, and John; and, in fact, for all the assembled brothers; yes, even for the entire church on earth both then and in the ages to follow. Continued: **and I set before them the gospel which I am accustomed to preach among the Gentiles.** For a commentary on this see Acts 15:4, 12. With enthusiasm and candor Paul and Barnabas related to the entire assembly the course which had been followed in proclaiming to the Gentiles the gospel of free grace, untrammeled by any ceremonial ordinances. They took special delight in rehearsing how astonishingly the Lord, by means of conversions, signs and wonders, had placed the stamp of his approval on this work.

In addition to the meeting which was attended by "the apostles and the elders and the whole church" (Acts 15:22), there had also been a private interview, a meeting of the *leaders:* Paul, Barnabas, James, Cephas, and John. Borrowing a term used with fondness by the Judaizers with respect to the last three of this list of five men, namely, the appellation "those of repute," Paul continues: **but (I did this) privately to "those of repute."** Exactly when this interview occurred, or whether these leaders met privately only once or more often, is of no great importance. It seems reasonable, however, to believe that upon arrival in Jerusalem the delegation from Antioch *first of all* went into conference with the local church leaders. Since the term "those of repute" occurs not only once but, in one form or another, no less than four times (2:2, 6a, 6b, 9), it is safe to assume that the apostle is here quoting the phraseology of the opponents. He is, however, not trying to belittle the men of prominence in the church at Jerusalem. He does not use the term "those of repute" to heap scorn upon them or to ridicule them. True, the language he uses here implies a degree of resentment, but the latter is not directed at James, Cephas, and John, but at the legalists who have made it a habit to exalt these three at the expense of Paul, a man altogether insignificant in their eyes, a merely second-hand apostle, not even worthy to be called "apostle." And be it always borne in mind that basic to their attack on Paul was their attack on *the gospel* which he proclaimed!

It is the worthiness and independence of this gospel that Paul is here defending.

Continued: **to make sure that I was not running or had not run in vain;** or, somewhat more literally, "lest by any means I should be running or had run in vain."[51] If, while Paul was preaching the gospel of justification by faith, *without the works of the law,* the other apostles, though in principle agreeing with him, would have been "soft" in their attitude toward those who seriously questioned the rightness of his convictions and of his preaching, the cause of mission work among the Gentiles would have been seriously undermined. The effectiveness of that which Paul had been doing in the past and was still doing would have been decisively weakened.

**3-5.** Any fears, however, which Paul may have entertained on this score were quickly dispelled. He writes: **Yet even Titus who was with me, Greek though he is, was not compelled to be circumcised; (in fact, the suggestion would never have arisen) but for the uninvited sham brothers.**[52] Even Titus! If

---

[51] It is probably correct to say that μή πως expresses negative purpose (cf. Robertson, *Word Pictures,* Vol. IV, p. 283). In such a construction τρέχω (probably subjunctive) followed by ἔδραμον (aorist indicative) is not unusual in Greek. See also N.T.C. on I and II Thessalonians, p. 85, footnote 68. The interpretation according to which Paul is here saying that he submitted to the Jerusalem pillars *the question* whether or not he were running or had run in vain seems unnatural and out of keeping with the apostle's strong convictions on this matter.

[52] The construction of διὰ δὲ τοὺς παρεισάκτους ψευδαδέλφους is difficult. It may well have been perfectly intelligible to the Galatians, Paul's contemporaries, who were better acquainted with the historical background and with the apostle's manner of speaking than we are today (see, however, II Peter 3:16). Ever so many translations have been proposed. A.V. has: "and that because of false brethren unawares brought in" (see also A.R.V. text). Interpreting δέ (which should be retained) adversatively, A.R.V., margin, has "*but* it was *because of*" (cf. R.S.V.). On either basis it is difficult to discover the connection of these words with the preceding clause. As I see it, Lenski's explanation on the basis of his translation—"even on account of the pseudo-brethren"—fails to do justice to what Paul says elsewhere about the reason for rejecting Gentile circumcision. See (2) below. The adversative rendering in R.S.V. yields no intelligible sense: Paul begins to say something but never finishes it: "But because of false brethren secretly brought in, who slipped in . . . that they might bring us into bondage—to them we did not yield submission," etc.

It is for this reason that the theory according to which certain words must be supplied is probably the best. Abbreviated expression is, after all, a characteristic of all living language. See N.T.C. on the Gospel according to John, Vol. I, p. 206. I, therefore, offer the rendering: "Yet even Titus . . . was not compelled to be circumcised; (in fact, the suggestion would never have arisen) but for the uninvited sham brothers." Another possibility would be: "Yet even Titus . . . was not compelled to be circumcised, (not even) on account of the uninvited sham brothers." If δέ is merely transitional and not to be translated, Beck's rendering has something to say in its favor: "But nobody forced him to be circumcised to please the false Christians." These last three possibilities are basically the same, since in each case the pseudo-Christians are considered to have been the only ones who demanded the circumcision of Titus, and also since in each case the demand was refused. As I see it, to be rejected are the following:

(1) Burton's suggestion that there were actually three parties in the situation: *a.* Paul and Barnabas, who favored receiving Gentiles as Christians without re-

a Christian of unalloyed Gentile extraction, though present here in the very heartland of the *Jews,* and in an assembly in which *Jewish* Christian leaders filled an influential role, was not compelled to be circumcised, then surely there could be no objection to waiving this requirement in the case of other non-Jewish converts who were living in a partly or wholly Gentile environment. From the very outset the leaders at Jerusalem agreed with the position of Paul and Barnabas anent the question of the circumcision of the Gentiles who accepted Christ. Was it not Peter who (in the plenary session of the assembly) uttered these emphatic words: "Now therefore why do y o u put God to the test by putting on the disciples a yoke which neither our fathers nor we have been able to bear?" (Acts 15:10). And did not James immediately endorse that position by adding that those who from among the Gentiles turn to God should not be troubled? (15:19). Not that everything went smoothly in the public gathering. It is implied both in Acts 15:5, 7 and in Gal. 2:4, 5 that the Judaizers voiced their opinions in no uncertain terms. But the point is: according to *both* accounts *the leaders* never wavered! The very suggestion that Titus be circumcised would never even have been broached had not the Judaizers

---

quiring them to be circumcised; *b.* the pseudo-brothers who insisted that such Gentiles be circumcised; and *c.* the "pillars," who urged Paul to yield to the wishes of the Judaizers, but finally agreed to Paul's point of view. His *translation* naturally harmonizes with that *explanation* (*op. cit.,* pp. 67, 77, 78). See also N.E.B. for similar view.

*Objections.* Nowhere else (either in Gal. 2 or in Acts 15) does Paul give any hint that the "pillars" urged the circumcision of Titus. Moreover, Gal. 2:5 indicates that it was to the false brothers that Paul had not yielded, showing that they were the ones who had done the urging, *they* and not the "pillars."

(2) Lenski's explanation that "what set everybody against circumcising Titus for any reason was the attitude of the 'pseudo-brethren.'" Again, "Even on account of these men . . . Titus was not compelled to be circumcised." (*op. cit.,* pp. 78, 79).

*Objection.* The non-circumcision of Titus was a matter of principle; hence, not dependent on the strength of the Judaizers' demand. See Gal. 2:15 ff.; 5:2, 3.

(3) Zahn's solution that οἷς οὐδέ at the beginning of verse 5 should be omitted, not being original, and that the true meaning is, accordingly, "For the sake of the false brothers we gave ground for a moment, namely, in consenting to go to Jerusalem" (*Der Brief des Paulus an die Galater,* 1922, p. 89 ff.).

*Objections.* The omission of οἷς οὐδέ has weak textural support. This method of connecting the thought of verse 5 with that of verses 1 and 2 is unnatural. Gal. 2:2 declares that Paul went up to Jerusalem not because of the false brothers but as a result of a revelation.

(4) The theory that οὐδέ at the beginning of verse 5 should be omitted, so that Titus, after all, was circumcised. Paul "yielded on the issue of the submission demanded." Cf. B. W. Bacon, "The Reading οἷς οὐδέ in Gal. 2:5," *J.B.L.,* Vol. 42 (1923), pp. 69–80; also N.E.B., footnote, "I yielded to their demand for the moment."

*Objection.* The textual support for the omission of οὐδέ is weak. The non-circumcision of Titus was a matter of principle with Paul, on which he certainly would not have yielded; especially in view of what he says in 2:15 ff.; 5:2, 3. (The omission of οἷς *only* would not change the sense of the passage. Nevertheless, there is no sufficient textual support for this omission.)

brought it up. They—they *alone*—were the ones who had started all the trouble. They, these uninvited guests, these intruders, *who had wormed their way into the assembly from the sidelines,*[53] were the ones, says Paul, **who had infiltrated our ranks to spy on our liberty which we have in Christ Jesus.** The interlopers mingled among the true believers with the purpose of *spying,* that is, discovering the strategic situation of those whom they opposed—their strong and their weak points—specifically, their *liberty,* that is, their freedom from the curse of the law, from the law as a way to salvation, and from the ceremonial observances which that law demands. This is the freedom which believers enjoy "in Christ," for had it not been for his atonement they would have been deprived of it (see on Gal. 3:13). Continued: **and thus to reduce us to slavery.** The word *slavery,* as used here, is none too strong, for the demands of the law constituted an unbearable yoke, as not only Peter put it (Acts 15:10) but Paul also (Gal. 5:1). The effort to comply with these demands amounted to a "bleeding to climb to God" in one's own strength, a tremendous effort to attain salvation by law-works, only to discover that this effort is hopeless, and that, like the fly in the spider's web, the more one struggles, the more he also imprisons himself.

With respect, then, to these pseudo-brothers, these infiltrators, the apostle continues: **to whom not even**[54] **for a moment**[55] **did we yield submission.** The meaning is clear and simple: not at any time during the Conference—whether in the private interview or at the public meeting; whether at the beginning, in the middle, or at the close—was there any yielding to the wishes of the enemies of the one and only true gospel. It was one and the same gospel, whether proclaimed by Paul or Barnabas; by Cephas, James, or John. It was not dependent on anything men might say about it. They were able neither to subtract from it nor to add to it. Neither did they wish to do so: **in order that the truth of the gospel**—that is, the gospel in all its purity—**might continue with y o u.** Those who oppose the South Galatian theory at times interpret this to mean, "that the truth of the gospel might continue with y o u, *believers (in general) from the Gentiles.*" It should be apparent, however, that in a letter written specifically to the Galatians, a missive with so much local color, the alternative explanation, namely, "that the truth of the gospel might continue *with y o u Galatians*" is more

---

[53] Greek *παρεισάκτους.* This harmonizes with *παρεισῆλθον,* which again stresses the idea of coming in from the side, "over the wall," as it were, and not "through the door." Cf. John 10:1, 2.

[54] On *οἷς οὐδέ* see footnote 52.

[55] Greek *ὥρα (ν)*; literally "hour," but it is rather apparent that this is to be taken in a figurative sense, so that "not [or: not even] for an hour" (A.V., A.R.V.; cf. German *Stunde,* Dutch Statenvertaling *uur,* Spanish *hora*) is equivalent to English "not for a moment" (Beck, Berkeley, Goodspeed, N.E.B., R.S.V., Williams; cf. Dutch, new version, *ogenblik,* Swedish *ögenblick,* French *moment,* and Latin *momentum*).

natural. The Galatians had already been evangelized, namely, on Paul's first journey. Soon afterward the trouble had started: the Judaizers had tried to substitute their "gospel" (?) of *salvation by grace-plus-works* (with emphasis probably on the latter) for Paul's gospel of salvation *solely by grace through faith.* Which view was to prevail? The unyielding stand of Paul and Barnabas, supported from start to finish by Jerusalem's "pillars," had as its purpose that from now on the Judaizers would never be able to say to the Galatians, "Paul has deceived y o u. The really 'prominent leaders' of the mother church in Jerusalem agree with us, not with him." Thus, the inflexible stand taken at Jerusalem would contribute significantly to the perpetuation of the true gospel among the Galatians.

Here is a lesson for all time. Paul was by no means a stubborn, inflexible individual. On the contrary, he was ready to accommodate himself and his message to any situation, becoming a Jew to the Jews, a Gentile to the Gentiles (I Cor. 9:19-23). Striking instances of this are reported in Acts 16:3; 21:17-26. But he was not willing to put any obstacle in the way of the gospel of Christ (I Cor. 9:12). In fact, rightly viewed, it was his inflexibility with respect to doing everything in his power to promote the simple gospel of God's grace in all its immaculate purity that made him so flexible in all relatively minor matters.

6. Returning now to "those of repute" (for the meaning see on verse 2) Paul continues: **Well, from those "who were reputed" to be something—whatever they once were makes no difference to me; God accepts no man's person—to me "those of repute" imparted nothing.** The break in grammatical sequence ("anacoluthon") is clear: when Paul starts out by saying, "Well, from those 'who were reputed' to be something," we expect him to conclude the sentence by adding, "I received nothing." Instead of this he interrupts himself. The thoroughly unfair comparison which his opponents are constantly drawing between himself and "those of repute," as if he and his gospel were definitely inferior, causes him to insert a parenthetical comment with respect to these vaunted leaders, the Jerusalem "pillars," not out of disrespect for *them* but from disapproval of *the comparison.* He then returns to the subject, but instead of completing the sentence by means of a predicate, he comes up with another independent clause in which the words "those of repute" constitute the subject: "to me those of repute imparted nothing." *Essentially* this disruption of grammatical sequence makes very little difference in meaning. *If* there be any difference at all it may possibly be indicated thus: "Not only did *I,* on my part, not receive or accept any new doctrine or regulation from these men of prominence, but I wish to emphasize that *they,* on their part, did not try to impose any dictates upon me." The main point to be emphasized in this connection is, however, the fact that the anacoluthon, coupled with parenthesis, reveals strong emotion. It shows how deeply Paul was affected

by any attempt to downgrade his divine commission and/or his gospel. Hence, he stresses the fact that the Jerusalem leaders did not try in any way to propose any changes in the gospel (of salvation solely by grace through faith) which he had been proclaiming. Specifically, they did not advise Paul that he must tell the Gentiles that in addition to believing in Jesus Christ they must be circumcised. It is possible that the apostle also implies that these leaders did not urge him to impose upon *Gentile* believers any new rules of conduct. To help them to live in peace with *Jewish* believers, the Council of Jerusalem asked the converts from paganism to observe the rules mentioned in Acts 15:20, 28, 29: avoiding meats sacrificed to idols or from which the blood had not been properly drained, and avoiding marriage within the degrees of affinity or consanguinity offensive to Jews and contrary to the regulations laid down in Lev. 18. But Paul did not regard such rules as bothersome novelties, *impositions* either upon himself or upon Gentile believers. In fact, as is clearly indicated in Rom. 12:18; 14:1 ff.; I Cor. 8:1 ff.; 9:19 ff.; 10:14 ff.; 10:23 ff., Paul was in the habit of insisting that for the sake of peace and harmony, as also to promote the spread of the gospel, Christians should, of their own accord, deny themselves certain privileges. As remarked earlier, though entirely inflexible in matters of principle (see Gal. 1:6-9), in all other matters the apostle was ready to yield and conform to the habits and wishes of others. Naturally, he taught those whom the Lord had placed under his spiritual care to be similarly disposed.

As to the parenthesis, how could it make any difference to Paul, who had been divinely appointed and had received his gospel directly from Christ, exalted in heavenly glory, whether "those of repute" had been closely associated with Jesus during the latter's earthly ministry? Why were the Judaizers always emphasizing that earthly fellowship, as if, because of it, men like James, Cephas, John, etc., were intrinsically better than he and more to be trusted? "What (that is, *of what kind*) they once[56] were" makes no difference to Paul. God takes no account of a man's "face" or "person." An individual's *outward circumstances*—whether, for example, he has been closely associated with Jesus as a *disciple* (Cephas and John) or as his *brother* (James); whether he occupies a certain *position,* or has a *reputation*—matter nothing to God; hence, not to Paul either. Things of that nature can never determine the intrinsic value of the gospel as proclaimed by Paul. Cf. I Sam. 16:7; Matt. 22:16; Mark 12:14; Luke 20:21; II Cor. 12:5.

**7-9.** But though Paul is not impressed with the propaganda of the Judaizers, who are constantly playing off "those of repute" against him, he

---

[56] L.N.T. (A. and G.), p. 579, ascribes no separate meaning to ποτέ here (cf. A.V., Williams, R.S.V.); as if it were not a temporal modifier but simply a generalizing suffix; cf. the Latin *qualescumque*. However, *this* enclitic use has no other example in the New Testament.

is very definitely impressed by the divine influence upon James, Cephas, and John, causing them to welcome the grace of God when they saw its manifestation in the apostle to the Gentiles. Having stated that the Jerusalem leaders had imparted nothing to him, the writer continues: **On the contrary, when they saw that I had been entrusted with the gospel to the uncircumcised just as Peter (with that) to the circumcised—for he who was at work through Peter in apostolic mission activity for the circumcised was also at work in me for the Gentiles—, and when they perceived the grace that was given to me, James and Cephas and John, "those who were reputed" to be pillars, gave to me and Barnabas the right hand of fellowship, that we should (go) to the Gentiles, and they to the circumcised.**

At Jerusalem "those of repute" (see on verse 2), having taken note of the soundness of the gospel as proclaimed by Paul, of the enthusiasm with which he spoke of it, of the manner in which the Lord had been placing his seal of approval upon its proclamation among the Gentiles, namely, by means of conversions, signs and wonders (cf. Acts 15:4, 12; I Cor. 9:2; II Cor. 12:12), heartily and enthusiastically endorsed both him and his co-laborer, Barnabas. Literally, Paul speaks about "the gospel *of the uncircumcision* just as Peter *of the circumcision*." This is one and the same gospel (cf. Gal. 1:6-9), and the terms "the uncircumcision" and "the circumcision" use the abstract for the concrete (cf. Rom. 3:30; 4:9; Eph. 2:11; Col. 3:11). The distinction made is that between the gospel "to the Gentile world" and that "to the Jewish world."[57]

It is clear that equal honor is accorded to Paul and Peter. Since in this combination nothing is said about John, whereas we know, nevertheless, that Paul's designation "those of repute," a term borrowed from the Judaizers, included John, it would appear to be a fair conclusion that Peter represents The Twelve (cf. Matt. 16:15, 16; Acts 2:37), including John. Peter and John, in fact, were often found together (John 1:35-41; 13:23, 24; 18:15, 16; 20:1-10; 21:2, 7, 20-22; Acts 3:1-4, 11 ff.; 4:13 ff.; 8:14 ff.). That among the Twelve Peter was the recognized leader is shown by the fact that in every list of apostles his name is mentioned first of all (Matt. 10:2-4; Mark 3:16-19; Luke 6:14-16; Acts 1:13).

That the Lord had been *at work*—energetically operative—in connection with Peter, and this *especially* (though by no means exclusively) in connection with the latter's "apostolic mission activity"[58] for *the Jews,* is

---

[57] The genitives, accordingly, are objective.

[58] The word ἀποστολήν refers here not to the apostolic office as such (Acts 1:25; Rom. 1:5), but to its execution; hence, here: *apostolic mission activity.* Note absence of article, perhaps to prevent the idea from taking root that Peter had a monopoly on carrying out the apostolic mandate. The expression εἰς τὰ ἔθνη is probably an abbreviation of εἰς ἀποστολὴν τῶν ἐθνῶν, which is parallel to εἰς ἀποστολὴν τῆς περιτομῆς.

clear from many other passages besides Gal. 2:7, 8; namely, from Gal. 1:18 (by implication); Acts 1:15 ff.; 2:14 ff.; 2:37 ff.; 3:1 ff.; 4:8 ff.; 5:3 ff. (*notably* 5:15); 11:2 ff.; 12:1 ff.; 15:7 ff. That the same Lord who empowered Peter was also energizing Paul, but in his case *especially* (though by no means exclusively) in apostolic mission activity for the benefit of *the Gentiles,* was now being made clear at Jerusalem, where, both in the private interview and at the public gathering, Paul and Barnabas gave a run-down of the astonishing results that had been accomplished.

The result was that James and Cephas and John, the reputed "pillars," clearly recognized that a ministry carried on by Paul and Barnabas with such conscientious regard for the will and revelation of God, such unswerving and pious purpose, such boundless energy, such tender love for souls, and, last but not least, such marvelous results, must be the product of "the grace that was given" to the agents used by the Lord. They saw the amazing manifestation of God's undeserved, but energetically operating, favor.

Of the three Jerusalem leaders *James* is mentioned first. See on 1:19. As has been shown, he is definitely linked with Jerusalem, more so even than Peter and John. It is not surprising, therefore, that he is mentioned first. Though not properly an apostle (in the plenary sense), his position as "the Lord's brother," his moderation, wisdom, and sympathetic nature, assured him a place of special prominence in this stronghold of Jewry, in which many people had already accepted Christ, and many more were to follow (Acts 2:41; 4:4; 21:20). Peter, the leader of The Twelve, has just been described. See also on Gal. 2:11 ff. Probably because his influence and activity in Jerusalem are here emphasized, he is now called by his Aramaic name, *Cephas.* There follows *John,* Peter's frequent companion, as has been shown. Though for a while similarly linked with Judea, he probably left Jerusalem at the beginning of the Jewish War, and chose Ephesus as his headquarters. Banished to the island of Patmos, he was subsequently permitted to return to Ephesus. According to tradition he, "the disciple whom Jesus loved," survived all the other apostles.

By the Judaizers these three men were regarded as "pillars" (cf. I Tim. 3:15; Rev. 3:12), that is, those who gave stability to the church, its genuine leaders, whom they loved to contrast with Paul at the latter's expense. Paul does not begrudge the three the honor that is bestowed upon them. The real thrust of his argument is to show that these "pillars," far from disagreeing with him, enthusiastically approve of him, and acknowledge the fact that his gospel and their gospel are one and the same, to which nothing can be added, and from which nothing must be subtracted.

The singularly striking manner in which they confirmed their enthusiastic endorsement of the two foreign missionaries, herein following the example, years earlier, of "the common people" of Judea who were believers (1:22-24), is expressed in the words: "When they saw that I had been entrusted with the gospel to the uncircumcised . . . and when they perceived the grace that was given to me, they . . . gave to me and Barnabas the right hand of fellowship." Note that they themselves—James, Cephas, and John—took the initiative. This handshake, to be sure, was a sign of *mutual agreement and acknowledgment;* more than that, of *fellowship* (*koinonia*), one of the richest terms in the entire New Testament. See the detailed treatment of this concept in N.T.C. on Philippians, pp. 51–54; 93–95. But it also served as *the confirmation of a solemn covenant*[59] into which these five men now entered, as they divided the work-load: "that we [Paul and Barnabas] should (go) to the Gentiles, and they [James, Cephas, and John] to the circumcised." This division of labor must be interpreted in general terms. It amounted to a ratification of what had already begun; for, as has been indicated, Paul and Barnabas were bestowing their special attention upon the Gentiles; James, Cephas, and John, upon the Jews. This did not prevent the two from *first of all* addressing the Jews, wherever there was a synagogue, nor the three from reaching out also to the non-Jews. Thus, Peter did not have to apologize for having worked among the Samaritans (Acts 8:14 ff.) and having preached to the Roman centurion Cornelius and his friends and relatives (Acts 10:1 ff.; 11:1 ff., *especially* 15:7!). Nevertheless, from now on and as long as circumstances would permit it, the Jews and the country they inhabited would be the chief responsibility of the three and of those whom they represented, while Paul and Barnabas were to proclaim the gospel "far away to the Gentiles" (cf. Acts 22:21).

In verses 7-9 the following lessons stand out:

(1) Under God Paul's gospel is independent; that is, it is able to maintain itself in relation to friends and foes. It vanquishes the arguments of its foes, and is enthusiastically endorsed by its friends, who recognize it as the gospel which they themselves charish.

(2) *One* gospel suffices for every age and every clime. Methods of presentation may have to vary, but essentially the gospel for the first century A.D. is the gospel for today. Those who maintain that it is "not relevant" for this day and age are committing a tragic error. Only then when the message of the love of God in Christ has penetrated heart and mind, resulting in a life of unselfish dedication to God and grateful observance of the principles

---

[59] The handclasp as a pledge of friendship and allegiance has long existed among many nations; for example, Parthians, Persians, Hebrews, Greeks. Cf. II Kings 10:15; I Chron. 29:24; Ezra 10:19; Lam. 5:6; Ezek. 17:18. The right hand was given to signify the conclusion of an agreement: "Now then let us give the right hand to these men, and make peace with them" (I Macc. 6:58); "Vespasian . . . sent two tribunes . . . having ordered them to give right hands to Josephus" (*Jewish War* III.viii.1); "I received (from him) and extended (to him) the right hand" (Xenophon, *Anabasis* I.vi.6); "I know that both of us have taken oaths and given right hands [pledges]" (*Anabasis* II.v.3).

of conduct he has laid down in his Word, will solutions be found for the problems that now vex the individual, the family, society, the church, the nation, and the world.

(3) The New Testament is not a hodgepodge of conflicting theologies—the theology of John, the theology of Paul, etc.—but a harmonious, beautifully variegated, unit. It is a remarkable fact that the five men, whose handclasp of ringing harmony is here described, produced, between them, no less than twenty-one of the twenty-seven New Testament books![60]

**10.** To the major agreement touching the essence of the gospel and the division of the field of labor, one stipulation was added: **Only, we were to continue to remember the poor,[61] the very thing which I was also eager to do.** The difficult situation of the Judean poor required that special measures be taken to help them. It would seem that this situation, though more severe at one time than at another, was rather constant (Acts 11:27-30; 12:25; II Cor. 8:14). A few years earlier Barnabas and Paul had been sent on a relief mission. Paul and Barnabas now agree that such aid should be continued. Paul says that he was *eager*—was taking pains, making every effort—to do this. In fact, so eager was he to engage in this work of mercy that his third missionary journey, the one that was to follow immediately the present (second) trip during which Galatians was written, had as one of its chief objects, in the words of the apostle himself, "to bring alms to my nation" (Acts 24:17). The words, "We were *to continue to remember,*" probably do not only mean that the work already begun should be resumed and thus continued, but also that to help the poor should be and remain *the regular practice* of the church. I Cor. 16:1, 2 certainly points in that direction.

Work of this nature should be pushed with all vigor. This is demanded by the laws of God (Exod. 23:10, 11; 30:15; Lev. 19:10; Deut. 15:7-11), the exhortations of the prophets (Jer. 22:16; Dan. 4:27; Amos 2:6, 7), and the teaching of Jesus (Matt. 7:12; Luke 6:36, 38; cf. 21:1-4; John 13:29; Gal. 6:2). It also pertains to the expression of gratitude for benefits re-

---

[60] Paul, thirteen; John, five; Cephas (Peter), two; James, one. Tertullian's opinion that *Barnabas* was the author of Hebrews has recently been revived by the prominent Dutch New Testament scholar, Dr. H. Mulder, in his articles "De Eerste Lezers van de Brief aan de Hebreeën," *homiletica & biblica* (May, 1965), pp. 95–99, and in the same journal, "Barnabas en de Gemeente te Jeruzalem" (September, 1965), pp. 198–200. If that view should be correct, all five of the men who are joined in this handclasp would be represented in the list of authors of New Testament books. However, the statement of Origen is still a fact, namely, "But as to who actually wrote the epistle, God knows the truth of the matter."

[61] This ἵνα clause is probably co-ordinate with the one that immediately precedes it. Hence, the two ἵνα clauses could be rendered: ". . . *that* we should (go) to the Gentiles, and they to the circumcised" and "(adding only) *that* we should continue to remember the poor." The position of μόνον τῶν πτωχῶν before ἵνα emphasizes the idea that it was especially *the poor* who should be remembered.

ceived. Those to whom mercy has been shown should be merciful. Paul points to the fact that since the Gentiles have received so many *spiritual* blessings from the saints of Jerusalem, they should certainly be of service to them in matters *material* (Rom. 15:26, 27). *And the greatest text of all, in this connection, is surely II Cor. 8:9!* A rich reward awaits the generous (Matt. 25:31-40).

It is remarkable that Paul, the deep thinker, is at the same time the Christian benefactor, who believes wholeheartedly in "doing good to everybody, and especially to those who are of the household of the faith," as he says in this very letter (6:10). Such is Christianity. If it is genuine, it is concerned about the poor, their health and their housing, their spiritual but also their material welfare. It does all in its power to help the underprivileged, under-educated, undernourished, the migrants and those who belong to "minority" groups. Overwhelmed by the love of God in Christ, it is *eager* to do so! The five men who concluded this agreement must have been very happy, indeed, as they stood there, firmly clasping each other's right hand, brothers in a common cause. Accordingly, Paul and Barnabas entered into a solemn agreement with the others, promising that they would remind the Gentiles that they should help the poor; particularly, in the present instance, Jerusalem's saints. One of these five men was James, the Lord's brother, who, with respect to the rich and the poor, wrote the unforgettable words found in the second and fifth chapters of his epistle!

# Chapter 2

Verses 11-21

Theme: *The Gospel of Justification by Faith apart from Law-works Defended against Its Detractors*

I. *This Gospel's Origination: it is not of human but of divine origin: hence, is independent*

F. Far from receiving anything from Jerusalem's "pillars," at Antioch I even took Cephas to task for his reversion to legalism: separating himself from Gentile converts after first eating with them. A man is not justified by law-works but through faith in Jesus Christ. For I through law died to law, that I might live to God.

11 Now when Cephas came to Antioch I opposed him to his face because
he stood condemned. 12 For before certain individuals from James arrived he had
been in the habit of eating his meals with the Gentiles. But when they came he
began to draw back and to separate himself, being afraid of those who belonged
to the circumcision party. 13 And the rest of the Jews joined him in playing the
hypocrite, so that even Barnabas was carried along by their hypocrisy. 14 But when
I saw that they were not pursuing a straight course in accordance with the truth of
the gospel, I said to Cephas, in everybody's presence, "If you, though a Jew, can
live like a Gentile and not like a Jew, how can you (now) force the Gentiles to
live like Jews?"

15 "We ourselves, though by nature Jews and not 'Gentile sinners,' 16
yet, knowing that a man is not justified by law-works but only through faith in
Jesus Christ, even we believed in Christ Jesus in order that we might be justified
by faith in Christ, and not by law-works, because by law-works will no flesh be
justified. 17 But if, in seeking to be justified in Christ, we ourselves also turn out
to be sinners, is Christ then a sin-promotor? By no means! 18 For, if I start to
rebuild the very things which I have torn down, it is then that I prove myself
a transgressor. 19 For I through law died to law, that I might live to God. 20 I have
been crucified with Christ; and it is no longer I who lives, but Christ who lives in
me; and that (life) which I now live in flesh I live in faith, (the faith) which is
in the Son of God, who loved me and gave himself up for me. 21 I do not set
aside the grace of God; for if justification (were) through law, then Christ died in
vain."

### 2:11-21

### F. *The gospel as proclaimed by Paul maintained even over against Peter's deviation*

Paul continues to prove "the essential independence both of his gospel and of his position."[62] That gospel which had been so enthusiastically endorsed by the "pillars," etc. at Jerusalem was able to assert itself, when necessary, even *over against* one of those very "men of repute." The theory according to which the rebuke here administered was addressed to some other *"Cephas,"* not to the apostle, is without a shred of evidence. The *Cephas* or *Peter* indicated here in 2:11 ff. must have been the one to whom Paul referred previously in this same letter (1:18; 2:7-9). And that person was one of Jerusalem's "pillars," none other than Peter the apostle, the leader of The Twelve.

[62] R. A. Cole, *The Epistle of Paul to the Galatians* (*The Tyndale New Testament Commentaries*), p. 72. There is, accordingly, no sharp contrast between verses 1-10 and verses 11-21. Hence, (verse 11) can best be translated "now" or "and," not "but."

The episode in which Peter was involved may well have occurred during the interval between the Jerusalem Conference (Acts 15:1-29) and the beginning of the second missionary journey (15:40 ff.). We know from the book of Acts (15:22, 30-39) that it was then that Paul and Barnabas tarried for some time in Syrian Antioch. And here in Galatians the Paul-versus-Peter controversy immediately follows the conference (inclusive of private interview).

11. Paul writes: **Now when Cephas came to Antioch I opposed him to his face.** We are not told just why Cephas visited Antioch at this time. Various guesses have been made but none of them serves any useful purpose. The important fact is that Cephas committed an error of conduct so serious that Paul felt obliged to *oppose* or *resist*[63] him "to his face," that is, directly, openly, man to man. Peter's action was entirely inexcusable, to which Paul calls attention by adding: **because he stood condemned.** His own behavior condemned him. Why this was true will become clear from the discussion of verses 12-14.

These lines begin as follows: **12. For before certain individuals from James arrived he had been in the habit of eating his meals with the Gentiles. But when they came he began to draw back and to separate himself, being afraid of those who belonged to the circumcision party.**

The reference is, no doubt, to the fellowship meals or *agapae* ("love feasts") of the early Christians. The food which otherwise would have been consumed at home was brought to the meeting-place of the congregation. It would seem that originally the Lord's Supper took place at the conclusion of such a get-together. Whether such meetings were ordinary church services or congregational meetings is not always clear and, for the present purpose, does not matter. The abuses to which such social meals could lead are pointed out in I Cor. 11:17-34. In Corinth there was segregation according to wealth, the rich separating from the poor; in Antioch the segregation which threatened was of an ethnic character, the Jewish Christians separating from their Gentile brothers in the faith, as will become clear.

The question, "How can Jewish Christians eat with Gentile Christians?" was a very perplexing one in the apostolic age. It is true that, with a view especially to those who from the Gentiles turned to God (Acts 15:19), the Jerusalem Council had made an important decision, namely, "that y o u abstain from that which has been sacrificed to idols, and from blood, and

---

[63] The verb ἀνθίστημι occurs in Matt. 5:39; Luke 21:15; Acts 6:10; 13:8; Rom. 9:19; 13:2; Eph. 6:13; II Tim. 3:8; 4:15; James 4:7; and I Peter 5:9. It does not necessarily mean *to resist an attack,* though at times it should be so interpreted (Matt. 5:39; Eph. 6:13). Whether or not it does depends upon the context. The present context may well point in that direction. If so, then Paul regards Peter's conduct as an attack upon the freedom proclaimed by the gospel. See also W. Hendriksen, *The Meaning of the Preposition ἀντί in the New Testament* (doctoral dissertation), pp. 48, 58; also N.T.C. on Eph. 6:13, footnote 172.

from anything that has been strangled . . ." (15:29).[64] But even though this decision to a certain extent limits the area in which it was possible for Jews and Gentiles to enjoy meal-time fellowship, it did not by any means settle everything with reference to such eating and drinking.

First, there were the Old Testament rules concerning clean and unclean (Lev. 11). For centuries the Jews had observed such and similar divine ordinances. Josephus (*Antiquities* IV.vi.8) puts into the mouths of the Midianite women who came to entice the Israelites (cf. Num. 25 and 31) these words: "Y o u r kinds of food are peculiar to yourselves, and y o u r kinds of drinks are common to no others." Well-known is the Old Testament passage: "But Daniel resolved in his heart that he would not defile himself with the king's dainties, nor with the wine which he drank" (Dan. 1:8). From the apocryphal book Tobit (1:10-12) note the following: "And when I was carried away captive to Nineveh, all my brothers and those that were of my kindred ate the bread of the Gentiles, but I kept myself from eating because I remembered God with all my soul." There is also I Macc. 1:62: "And many in Israel were fully resolved and confirmed in themselves not to eat unclean things"; and the dramatic story of the mother and her seven sons who were martyred because they refused to eat "abominable swine's flesh" (II Macc. 7). In some of the cases listed above (for example, Dan. 1:8 ff.) the revulsion of the devout Jews aroused by the sight of heathen food may have been due to a combination of reasons; for example, some of the food set before them may have been *unclean* according to the regulations of Lev. 11, and most or all of it may have been previously consecrated to idols.

Secondly, there were the man-made restrictions and stipulations, handed down from generation to generation, by means of which the rabbis had sought to explain and expand the divinely imparted ordinances. These, in turn, were of various kinds. Some dealt with the purchase of meats from Gentile meat-markets; for example: "The Jews were permitted to get meat from a Gentile meat-market when the animal had not been slaughtered by a non-Israelite, when the meat had not been brought into contact with pagan religious ceremonies, and when the proprietor of the place where the meat was sold guaranteed that he did not handle inferior meat, the kind that had been prohibited for Jewish consumption."[65]

There was also the peculiar Pharisaic interpretation of the law of purity (Lev. 15). This may well furnish the true explanation of John 4:7-9 with reference to Christ's conversation with the Samaritan woman. Jesus said to her, "Give me a drink." Continued: "So the Samaritan woman said to him, 'How is it that you, a Jew, ask a drink of me, a Samaritan woman?'

---

[64] The question with respect to the value of the variant reading in the Western text belongs to commentaries on the book of Acts.

[65] Strack-Billerbeck, *op. cit.*, Vol. III, p. 420.

(For Jews do not use [vessels] together with Samaritans)." See N.T.C. on the Gospel according to John, Vol. I, pp. 160, 161.

Still another set of *halakoth* ("traditions of the elders") had to do with washing the hands before eating, a washing not for ordinary hygienic reasons but out of fear lest these hands had been contaminated by contact with a Gentile or with something that belonged to a Gentile (Matt. 15:1 ff.; Mark 7:1 ff.).

Finally, to mention only one more reason why it was so difficult for a devout Jew to eat with a Gentile, think of the many man-made rules which the rabbis had laid down regarding the consumption of food *on the sabbath!*

In view of all this, it is easy to see that for a Jew to eat in the company of a Gentile, whether on the sabbath or not, was considered by many to be positively wicked.

But had not Christ, by his death on the cross, fulfilled, and thereby abolished, the Old Testament "shadows"? And if even the divinely established rules had lost their validity, was not the same true—even more decisively—with respect to all the man-made regulations that had been embroidered upon these rules? True indeed, but this legitimate inference was not drawn by every believer in Christ. Many, especially in and around Jerusalem, held fast to their "traditions." Provided that no saving significance of any kind was ascribed to the continuation of such habits and that no offense was given, such persistence could be tolerated, particularly during what might be called the period of transition. However, in mixed communities problems immediately presented themselves. See I Cor. 8:1 ff.; 10:14 ff. Customs (Gentile versus Jewish) were bound to clash. The fact that the law of ordinances had been nailed to the cross was not always fully appreciated, and the further and closely related fact that "in Christ" the wall of separation between Jew and Gentile had been broken down, never to be rebuilt, was frequently ignored (as it is even today in certain circles!).

In *liberal* (I now use the word in its most favorable sense) Antioch the far-reaching *implication* of the Jerusalem Council had been fathomed. The logical deduction had been drawn, namely, that if the ceremonial ordinances regarding eating and drinking were not to be imposed upon the Gentiles, they should not be saddled upon the Jews either. Here it was understood that the unity of the church, consisting of Jew and Gentile, demanded, among other things, eating and drinking together in sweet fellowship, with restrictions reduced to the very minimum (those only that are described in Acts 15:20, 29). Were not *all* of the brothers "Christians," and was it not Antioch in which this beautiful new name had first been given to Christ's followers? (11:26). According to this principle of love and fellowship the members of the Antiochian church had now for some time been eating and drinking.

When Cephas arrived in Antioch he, too, had fallen in line with this new procedure and had continued in this manner for some time. But then something occurred which brought about an inexcusable and dangerous change in his behavior. Into the church-gathering walked "certain individuals from James."[66] In the light of such passages as Acts 15:1, 24 it is not necessary to conclude that these "investigators" actually represented the views of James or that they had been delegated by him. Far more natural would seem to be the explanation that they came from the church at Jerusalem, a church in which James occupied a position of special prominence. Although some cling to the theory that these "individuals from James" and "those who belonged to the circumcision party" are two different groups, the text does not demand this interpretation. In all probability the "individuals from James" belonged to the same group as the Judaizers to which reference is made in Acts 15:1. In the latter passage they demanded that the Gentiles, in order to be admitted to the church, be circumcised. Here we meet them once more in the same city of Antioch, and this time they insist (perhaps by their very presence and refusal to eat with Gentile believers) that Jews dine with Jews, Gentiles with Gentiles. And Cephas hesitates, then little by little begins to withdraw himself from the Gentiles, until at length he is completely separating himself and is no longer eating with the Gentiles.[67]

Peter, in so doing, was motivated by fear. Was he afraid that by means of continued eating with the Gentiles (believers in Christ, gathered from the Gentiles) he would antagonize the men from James to such an extent that the evil report which they would bring to their like-minded friends in Jerusalem would weaken his prestige in that city and might even cause him to be persecuted?

It is argued that the Peter who had spoken with such courage at the Council of Jerusalem would not have "turned around" so completely here at Antioch, certainly not so shortly afterward. This argument fails to give due consideration to two facts: *a.* Peter may not have been aware of the full implications of his action; for, after all, the decisions of that council *explicitly* dealt with Gentiles, not with Jews; *b.* inconsistency and momentary fear consituted the weak strain in Peter's character. Besides, though a believer's progress in sanctification is capable of being represented by a rising diagonal, so that the Peter of Acts 2:22-36; 4:19, 20; 5:12-16, 29 shows far more courage than the one of Matt. 27:69-75; Mark 14:66-72; Luke 22:54-62; and John 18:15-18, 25-27, nevertheless, this diagonal is not a straight line. It dips at times. And so it was here. Instability was again asserting itself,

---

[66] The word-order would seem to favor the construction of ἀπὸ Ἰακώβου with τινας rather than with ἐλθεῖν.

[67] The imperfects συνήσθιεν, ὑπέστελλεν, and ἀφώριζεν are very graphic.

as it had done so often before. Accordingly, far from saying that Cephas could not have changed so quickly from one kind of conduct to another, we should rather affirm that the description here given is exactly "in character" for that particular apostle. For proof see N.T.C. on the Gospel according to John, Vol. II, p. 232. The change from Peter's excellent emphasis on the unity of Jew and Gentile, when at the Council of Jerusalem he said, "And God made no distinction between us and them, cleansing their hearts by faith" (Acts 15:9) and his present encouragement of separation between these two groups, was certainly not any more drastic and sudden than that between his boast, "Even if I must die with thee, yet will I not deny thee" and his complete disavowal, "I do not even know the man."

13. Continued: **And the rest of the Jews joined him in playing the hypocrite.** Whether or not Peter had understood the full implications of the decisions of the Jerusalem Council, one thing at least is certain: he knew that in separating himself from the believing Gentiles he was acting contrary to his own inner convictions. He was hiding his real beliefs, just as an actor conceals his real face under a mask. He was playing the hypocrite. We know that this is true, for:

(1) During Christ's sojourn on earth Peter had been one of his closest disciples. He had heard the teaching of Jesus whereby he "made all meats clean" (Mark 7:19). He knew that this same Jesus had urged sinners, one and all, to come unto him and be saved by simple trust in him (Matt. 11:28-30). He knew, too, that the Master had welcomed non-Israelites (Matt. 8:11; 28:18-20; Mark 12:9; Luke 4:16-30; 17:11-19); and that in ever so many of his sayings he had emphasized the oneness in him of all believers throughout the whole wide earth (Matt. 13:31, 32; Luke 14:23; 19:10; John 3:16; 4:42; 10:16; 12:32; 17:19, 20).

(2) As if that were not sufficient, to Peter had been given—and this not once but three times!—the vision of the sheet. On the housetop at Joppa he had learned that it was wrong to regard as "unclean" that which God had cleansed (Acts 10:9-16).

(3) He had also understood the implication *of this vision* and had acted upon it. Boldly he had gone to Caesarea and had entered the house of the centurion Cornelius of the Italian band. It was to the group gathered at the home of this non-Jew that he had said, "You yourselves know how unlawful it is for a Jew to associate with or to visit a person of another nation; yet to me God has shown that I should not call any man common or unclean" (Acts 10:28).

(4) Not only had he visited the uncircumcised but *he had even eaten* with them. And when those of the circumcision party had criticized him for such conduct, Peter had come forth with a lengthy defense (Acts 11:1-18). And, in the full assurance of the fact that he was following the only divinely approved course, he had in the beginning repeated at Antioch

what he had already done at Caesarea. In both cases he had taken his meals with the Gentiles.

(5) In fact, if it was right for Peter to eat with Gentile *enquirers* at Caesarea, it certainly must have been right for him to eat with Gentile *believers* in Antioch!

Accordingly, when Paul accuses Peter of insincerity or hypocrisy he is not using too strong a word. Peter's conduct was all the more reprehensible because he was a recognized leader. His example was prone to be followed by others. So it was also in the present case. When the courage of Cephas was oozing out, faint-heartedness also took possession of "the rest of the Jews" (that is, all the other Jewish Christians who were present). Even Barnabas, whom we would never have accused of narrow-mindedness (see on Gal. 2:1), who had co-operated heartily with Paul in the establishment of several churches in Gentile regions, and who must have enjoyed many a meal with the young converts from the heathen world, now meekly went along with Peter in the latter's insincere behavior: **so that even Barnabas was carried along by their hypocrisy.**

The courage and firmness of Paul's reaction to this inexcusable hypocrisy merit profound admiration: **14. But when I saw that they were not pursuing a straight course in accordance with the truth of the gospel, I said to Cephas, in everybody's presence, "If you, though a Jew, can live like a Gentile and not like a Jew, how can you (now) force the Gentiles to live like Jews?"**

Paul saw that Peter and all those who followed his example "were not straight-footing *toward,* or in *accordance with,* the truth of the gospel," thus literally. In the New Testament the verb *they are straight-footing*[68] occurs only here. The meaning is probably either that, as Paul saw it, these people were not advancing *toward,* i.e., *in the direction of,* the gospel-truth, or that they were not pursuing a straight course *in accordance with*[69] that truth. According to the latter view, to which I would give a slight preference, the two lines—of which one is the guideline and represents the gospel-truth, and the other represents the conduct of these segregationists—were not running parallel. On the contrary, they were pulling farther and farther apart. The straight course in accordance with gospel-truth is the gospel message presented in all its purity.

When Paul, after due consideration, understood that Cephas and his imitators were deviating from the straight course, he addressed himself directly to his fellow-apostle. This is generally far better than "talking behind a person's back." It stands to reason that Paul could not very well have waited for an opportunity to speak to Peter *privately,* for even though

[68] ὀρθοποδοῦσιν: *present* active indicative retained because of indirect discourse, where we would use the *imperfect.*

[69] The reason for the slight difference in interpretation is that πρός with the accusative can here mean either *toward* or *in accordance with.*

Peter was the leader, he was not the only sinner. The rest of the Jews were also guilty, including even Barnabas. It would have been impractical to visit each one separately. Besides, on this matter of *publicly* rebuking those who have erred *publicly,* worthy of serious consideration is John Calvin's comment on this verse, "This example instructs us that those who have sinned publicly must be publicly chastised, as far as the church is concerned. The purpose is that their sin may not, by remaining unpunished, form a dangerous example; and elsewhere (I Tim. 5:20) Paul lays down this rule expressly, to be observed in the case of elders, 'Those who do wrong you must rebuke in the presence of all, so that also the others may have fear,' because the position which they occupy renders their example more pernicious. It was particularly advantageous that the good cause in which all had an interest, should be openly defended in the presence of the people, that Paul might have the better opportunity of showing that he did not shrink from the broad light of day."

In everybody's presence, then, Paul said to Cephas, "If you, though a Jew, can live like a Gentile and not like a Jew, how can you (now) force the Gentiles to live like Jews?" Meaning: "If even you, Cephas, *though you are a Jew,* can allow yourself the freedom of ignoring the Jewish traditions with respect to eating and drinking, as you certainly did when you were eating your meals with the Gentiles, then how can you now impose these very traditions upon *Gentiles,* forcing them to live like Jews? It is undeniable that by separating yourself from the Gentiles at dinner time, you are saying to them, 'If y o u Gentiles wish to have fellowship with us—and such, of course, is desirable—y o u will have to adopt our customs; y o u will have to live like Jews.' "

As to verses 15-21 the question arises, "To whom were they addressed?" To Peter? To the entire multiude present at the love-feast? To the Galatians? The best answer is probably this, that even though Peter is never absent from Paul's mind, for it was this very Cephas who had led the others into serious error, yet the attention is gradually shifted away from one individual to the entire group present, which includes even Paul himself. The very change in the employment of pronouns would seem to point in that direction, for having used the singular pronoun *you* (συ) in verses 14, Paul now shifts to the plural "we ourselves" (verse 15). It should be added immediately, however, that inasmuch as the error which *the Galatians* were committing was similar to that of Peter and his followers, for both groups allowed themselves to be influenced by the Judaizers, the entire address (verses 14-21) was intended to be taken to heart also by those *to* whom, or *by* whom, this letter would be read.

**15, 16.** Clear and forceful are the words: **We ourselves, though by nature Jews and not "Gentile sinners," yet, knowing that a man is not justified by law-works but only through faith in Jesus Christ, even we believed in Christ Jesus**

**in order that we might be justified by faith in Christ, and not by law-works, because by law-works will no flesh be justified.**

If a Jew who, having turned to Christ, has learned that strict obedience to legal requirements, divine and human, will not bring even *him* into the kingdom, tries, nevertheless, to impose such legalism upon *Gentiles,* his effort to place this yoke upon them is inexcusable. Such would seem to be the connection between verses 15, 16 and that which immediately precedes.

The content of the present verses may be briefly paraphrased as follows: "Though we ourselves are by birth (race, descent) Jews, highly privileged people, and not coarse sinners of Gentile descent, yet, when we learned that our works done in obedience to law could never suffice to make us righteous in God's sight, and that this standing could be attained only by trusting in Jesus Christ, *even we,* who in self-esteem were always looking down upon the Gentiles, began to see that before God we were not any better than they. Hence, *even we* embraced Christ by a living faith, in order that by means of the exercise of this faith we might receive, as a free gift, the standing of being 'not guilty but righteous' in God's sight. It was *by faith* in Christ and *his* merits, and definitely not by law-works, that we received this blessing, for by works done in obedience to law no weak, earthly, perishable human being,[70] whose works never reach the goal of perfection, will ever be able to attain to the standing of righteousness before God."

The verb *to justify*—here in the passive voice; hence, *to be justified*—occurs here for the first time in Paul's epistles, and no less than three times in this one passage (verses 15, 16).[71] Since we are dealing here with one of the most important concepts in the writings of Paul, a closer study is called for.

### *"To Be Justified"*

(1) *The Meaning Not Always the Same*

The exact connotation of the word will have to be determined in each case in accordance with the specific context. Thus it will become clear that its sense in I Tim. 3:16 differs from that in Rom. 3:24. Note also its difference in meaning in Rom. 2:13 as compared with Rom. 3:20. An appreciation of this fact is very important. It will greatly help in the solution of the problem *James versus Paul.* The latter again and again emphasizes the fact that a man is *not* justified by works, but the former states, "You see that by works a man is justified and not only by faith" (James 2:24). If

[70] The Greek word is σάρξ, "flesh." The various meanings of this word in Paul's epistles are summarized in N.T.C. on Philippians, p. 77, footnote 55.

[71] δικαιοῦται (third per. sing. pres. indic. passive); δικαιωθῶμεν (first per. plur. aor. subj. passive); and διακιωθήσεται (third per. sing. fut. indic. passive).

James means that by works the genuine character of man's faith *is demonstrated,* Paul is in perfect agreement with him (cf. Eph. 2:10).

(2) *Justification Defined*

When used, as here in Gal. 2:15, 16, in the dominant forensic sense, *justification* may be defined as *that gracious act of God whereby, on the basis solely of Christ's accomplished mediatorial work, he declares the sinner just, and the latter accepts this benefit with a believing heart.* In defense of this definition see, besides Gal. 2:15, 16, the following: Gal. 3:8, 11, 24; 5:4; Rom. 3:20, 24, 26, 28, 30; 4:3, 5; 5:1, 9; 8:30; Titus 3:7. *Justification* stands over against *condemnation* (Rom. 8:1, 33).

(3) *Justification Compared to Sanctification*

Justification is a matter of *imputation* (reckoning, charging): the sinner's guilt is imputed to Christ; the latter's righteousness is imputed to the sinner (Gen. 15:6; Ps. 32:1, 2; Isa. 53:4-6; Jer. 23:6; Rom. 5:18, 19). Sanctification is a matter of *transformation* (II Cor. 3:17, 18). In justification the Father takes the lead (Rom. 8:33); in sanctification the Holy Spirit does (II Thess. 2:13). The first is a "once for all" verdict, the second a life-long process. Nevertheless, although the two should never be identified, neither should they be separated. They are distinct but not separate. In justifying the sinner, God may be viewed as the Judge who presides over a law court. The prisoner is standing at the dock. The Judge acquits the prisoner, pronouncing him "not guilty but righteous." The former prisoner is now a free man. But the story does not end here. The Judge now turns to that free man and adopts him as his son, and even imparts his own Spirit to him (Rom. 8:15; Gal. 4:5, 6). Here justification and sanctification touch each other, as it were; for, out of gratitude, this justified person, through the enabling power of the Spirit, begins to fight against his sins and to abound in good works to the glory of his Judge-Father. Good works never justify anyone, but no truly justified person wants to be without them (Eph. 2:8-10).

(4) *The Basis of Justification*

As already implied in the definition (see point 2), justification, as a judicial act of God, rests not on human works (Rom. 3:20, 28; Gal. 3:11; 5:4), not even on faith as a work of man (Eph. 2:8), but solely on God's sovereign grace in Jesus Christ. It is *his* accomplished mediatorial work that furnishes the legal basis upon which man's justification becomes both possible and actual. Christ fully satisfied the demands of God's law: he both paid our debt and also rendered the obedience which we owed (Matt. 20:28; Rom. 3:24; II Cor. 5:21; Gal. 3:24; Eph. 1:7; Titus 3:7).

(5) *The Acquisition of Justification*

Man cannot earn it. He can only accept it as a gift. Faith is the hand that accepts this gift. Faith itself is also a gift. See N.T.C. on Eph. 2:8. This does not reduce man to sheer passivity. Is not a tree which *accepts* water and minerals from the soil, light from the sun, etc., very active? So it is also with faith. It is receptive but not passive. It is very active, indeed! (John 3:16; Phil. 2:12, 13).

(6) *Justification an Imperative Need*

Neither poverty nor disease nor pain nor imprisonment is man's most bitter woe. To remove any or all of these is not his most pressing need. His unbearable curse is the fact that by nature he is a child of wrath (Eph. 2:3). He has no peace (Isa. 48:22) but only a terrifying expectation of judgment (Heb. 10:27), so that he cannot even fully enjoy the natural blessings which God bestows upon him. What he needs more than anything else is to have his guilt removed. "How can man be just with God?" (Job 9:2; 25:4) is the question to which he must have an answer.

(7) *Justification and Man's Continuous Quest*

In his utterly lost condition, however, man fails to understand that by his own efforts he will never be able to dispel his guilt complex and to achieve peace. Over the years and the centuries man has employed various means and methods in order to "justify himself" (Luke 10:29); such as, a strenuous effort to live in accordance with law (human, natural, and/or divine), rigorous asceticism, physical torture, sacrifices to appease the deity, the invocation of angels and of saints, the purchase of letters of indulgence, masses, humanitarianism, becoming a zealous member of a political movement (Fascism, Nazism, Communism), submitting to psychoanalysis, etc.

(8) *Man's Failure to Obtain Justification by His Own Efforts*

None of these attempts succeed. *Man,* dead in sins and trespasses, is unable to atone for *man's* guilt or to bring an offering that will redeem either himself or his brother (Ps. 49:7). Moreover, he is also totally unable to perform even a single *perfect* deed. In God's sight no man living is righteous (Ps. 143:2; cf. 130:3; Job 9:3; 25:4; 40:4; 42:5, 6; Rom. 3:9-20).

(9) *Justification by Faith as God's Free Gift* (see point 5 above) *by the Gospel Offered to All, Regardless of Race, Social Position, Wealth, Degree of Education, Sex, etc.*

*All* have sinned and have fallen short of the glory of God. The invitation is that *all* should repent and accept the righteousness of Christ, including forgiveness of sins (Ps. 130:3, 4; Isa. 1:18) and life eternal (Isa. 45:22; 50:8; 53:11; Ezek. 18:23; 33:11; John 3:16; Rom. 3:23, 24; 5:19; II Cor. 5:20, 21).

**17a.** Paul has just said, "We believed in Christ Jesus in order that we might be justified by faith in Christ," etc. With a reflection, perhaps, on the Judaizers, who claim that such faith in Christ will not quite reach far enough and must be supplemented by law-works, the apostle continues: **But if, in seeking to be justified in Christ, we ourselves also turn out to be sinners, is Christ then a sin-promoter?** Of this difficult passage there are many interpretations. Three of the most important are:

(1) "If, in seeking to be justified in Christ, *our sins are laid bare,* so that it becomes evident that not only the Gentiles but also we, Jews, are great sinners before God, is Christ then a sin-promoter?"

*Objection.* The expression "turn out to be sinners" (literally "are found to be sinners") is not the same as "must submit to having our sins laid bare." Besides, in such a connection, the question, "Is Christ then a sin-promoter?" does not make good sense, for how would the laying bare of sin, so that it is seen in its true character, make Christ a sin-promoter, an encourager (literally "a servant") or abettor of sin? By itself it is true that Christ, by his Spirit, lays bare or reveals the seriousness of sin. However, he does this in order to bring the sinner to repentance, and so to the joyful assurance of having been forgiven, and to gradual victory over sin. Christ, in all this, proves himself a Deliverer from—and not an Encourager of—sin.

(2) "If, in seeking to be justified in Christ, we Jews, law-*respecters,* turn out to be sinners just like the Gentiles, law-*rejecters,* then why should we not all live as if there were no law? Moreover, if this doctrine of justification is of Christ, must we then conclude that he encourages sin (lawlessness)?" Cf. Rom. 6:1, 15.

*Objection.* The introduction, at this point, of a kind of antinomian distortion of the doctrine of grace seems rather unnatural. Nothing in the preceding context has prepared us for it, and nothing in the succeeding context links with it. Contrast Gal. 5:13, where the danger of turning liberty into license is clearly stated and condemned.

(3) *"If the Judaizers are correct* in maintaining that we, in seeking to be justified solely in Christ, and thus neglecting law, turn out to be gross sinners just like the Gentiles, then would y o u say that Christ, who taught us this doctrine, is a sin-promoter?"

In favor of this interpretation note the following:

(a) *It obviously suits the preceding context.* In substance Paul is saying, "Peter and all of y o u who have followed his example, consider what y o u are doing! By y o u r action y o u are really saying that Christ was wrong when he taught y o u: that it is not what enters a man from without that defiles him but rather what proceeds out of his heart (Matt. 15:1-20); that all meats are clean (Mark 7:19); and that men are saved by simply coming to him and trusting in him (Matt. 11:25-30; John 3:16). Is it really true, then, that Christ is a sin-promoter, that is, that he—by his teaching, example, death on the cross—makes y o u a greater sinner than y o u were already?"

(b) *It also establishes a smooth connection with the words which immediately follow,* for Paul continues:

**17b, 18. By no means!** A thousand times *NO* to the suggestion that Christ encourages sin, making y o u a greater transgressor than y o u were previously, *for* not by tearing down the ceremonial law and believing in salvation solely by grace, as y o u, Peter, etc., started out to do, do y o u show yourselves transgressors, but y o u very definitely prove yourselves transgressors by doing the very opposite, namely, rebuilding the very things which y o u have torn down. However, to spare their feelings, that is, to prevent those in his audience (*visible:* those actually present when the apostle was speaking—Peter, Barnabas, etc.—and *invisible:* the Galatians who would hear the letter as it was read to them) from thinking that they alone were capable of so great an error, Paul lovingly uses the first person instead of the third, as if to say, "The conclusion I am drawing holds for anyone who rebuilds what he had previously so wisely torn down. It holds in my own case, if I were to be guilty of it, as well as in y o u r s. Let each and every one of us then apply it to himself. Let him say, 'If *I* start to rebuild,'" etc. Accordingly, in close connection with the immediately preceding, as has now been shown, the apostle states: **For, if I start to rebuild the very things which I have torn down, it is then that I prove myself a transgressor.** I *prove* or *demonstrate* (cf. Rom. 3:5; II Cor. 7:11) myself a transgressor, because I know very well that what I am now doing—in rebuilding the doctrine of salvation by law-works—*a.* clashes with my deepest convictions based on past experience (see verse 19), and *b.* cancels the significance of Christ's death on the cross (see verses 20 and 21).[72]

**19.** Continued: **For I through law died to law.** If ever a man could have been saved by strict obedience to law, that man was Paul. He had tried O so hard! Elsewhere he reviews his life before his conversion in these words: "If anyone else imagines that he has reason for confidence in flesh, I (have) more: . . . *as to legal righteousness having become blameless*" (Phil. 3:4b-6). So strict had Paul been in his outward observance of the Old Testament law, as interpreted by the Jewish religious leaders, that in the pursuit of this legal rectitude he had become blameless, that is, in *human* judgment. His outward conduct, even during the days before he was converted to Christ, had been irreproachable. So it had seemed in the eyes of men, but not in the eyes of God! God's law, after all, demanded much more than the kind of behavior of which Paul's superiors approved. It demanded nothing less than *inward* (as well as outward) *perfection:* loving God with *all* the heart, soul, mind, and strength, and loving the neighbor as oneself. That standard Paul had been unable to meet. In fact, he had missed the target *by far.* In the meantime, moreover, the law had not relaxed its demands, nor its threats of punishment, nor its actual flagellations. It had not given Paul the peace with God which he so ardently desired. It had scourged him until, by the marvelous grace of God, he had found Christ (because Christ

---

[72] Others are of the opinion that Paul meant, ". . . then I prove that I *was* a transgressor previously" (e.g., Lenski, *op. cit.*, p. 113). But the more natural explanation would seem to be that Paul means: "*In the very act* of rebuilding the things which I have torn down, *I am, and show myself to be,* a transgressor." Besides, this explanation makes for a smoother connection with verse 19 ff.

had first sought and found him!) and peace in him. Thus, through the law he had died to the law. Through the law he had discovered what a great sinner he was, and how utterly incapable in himself of extricating himself from his position of despair and ruin (cf. Rom. 3:20; 7:7). Thus the law had been his custodian to conduct him to Christ (Gal. 3:24). And when by Christ he had been made alive, the law, viewed as being in and by itself a means unto salvation and as a cruel taskmaster who assigns tasks impossible of fulfillment and who lays down rules and regulations endless in their ramifications, had left him cold, dead like a corpse, without any response whatever. The response had been given *by Christ!* The satisfaction has been rendered *by him!*

Now in all this, God's wise purpose was being realized. What purpose? Answers Paul: **that I might live to God** (cf. Rom. 6:11; 14:7; II Cor. 5:15). And what is meant by living *to* or *for* God? Negatively, it means: no longer living for self. Positively it indicates: living as God wants me to live; hence, to his glory (I Cor. 10:31), according to his revealed will, his *law.*

It must never be overlooked that in the writings of the apostle the word *law*—as is true with respect to so many other great words—has more than one meaning. It is not my purpose at this point to present a detailed study of all the various meanings which this word has in Paul's epistles. That task would be more appropriate in a commentary on Romans. For the present the following must suffice. On the one hand Paul rejoices in the fact that he is not under law (Rom. 6:14, 15; cf. 7:6). He speaks of being delivered from the curse of the law (Gal. 3:13). He describes the law as "the hand-written document that was against us, which by means of its requirements testified against us" (Col. 2:14; cf. Eph. 2:15). And in the chapter now under study—see below—he even states, "If justification (were) through law, then Christ died in vain" (Gal. 2:21). Yet, on the other hand, he also tells us that he is "under law to Christ" (I Cor. 9:2), that he "delights in the law of God according to the inner man" (Rom. 7:22), that "the law is holy, and the commandment holy and righteous and good" (Rom. 7:12), and that love—the very love which is "the greatest of the three greatest" (I Cor. 13:13)—is the fulfilment of the law (Rom. 13:10; cf. Gal. 5:14; 6:2).

There is no warrant, therefore, to go to any extreme in denouncing the law. Whenever anything is said in disparagement of law, the concept *law* must be carefully described. The hue and cry of the present day, to the effect that as Christians "we have nothing whatever to do with the law" has no Scriptural justification at all. It is, in fact, a dangerous slogan, especially in an era of lawlessness!

Even in the passage now under consideration (Gal. 2:19) Paul does not think of *law* in an altogether negative sense or as something wholly useless. It was through a legal demand ("law")—the requirement that Paul be *perfect*—that Paul had died to the demand ("law"), and had been driven to Christ (cf. 3:24). That much good *law,* at least, had performed. Nevertheless, broadly speaking, it remains true that when Paul in Galatians places salvation *by law-works* over against salvation *by grace* (or "justification by faith"), he is using the term *law* in its definitely unfavorable sense. He is referring to the fact that man endeavors to save himself through his own efforts by means of strict adherence to the law of Moses, buried under a load of human regulations, many of them in direct conflict with the will of God (Matt. 5:43; Mark 7:9-13).

**20, 21.** Paul has shown that if he were to rebuild the very things—namely, salvation by law-works and everything connected with it—which he had torn down, he would prove himself a transgressor, because he would be doing something that would clash with his deepest convictions based on past experience (verses 18, 19). To this he now (in verses 20, 21) adds that such action would also destroy the meaning of Christ's death on the cross. In his own experience faith in Christ Crucified has thoroughly replaced confidence in whatever he might have been able to accomplish by means of law-works. That is the connection between verses 20, 21 and the immediately preceding context. Since the closing passage of the chapter has rightly endeared itself to believers of every age, I shall treat it in the manner in which similar most precious texts have been presented in this series of Commentaries, namely, in the form of a theme and a brief outline or summary:

*The Riddle of Having Been Crucified with Christ*

(1) *The Riddle Propounded*

Paul starts out by saying: **I have been crucified with Christ.** What a startling assertion! Here is the great apostle to the Gentiles at this love-feast of the Antiochian church. He is addressing an audience the bulk of which consisted of believers both of Gentile and Jewish origin. Peter and Barnabas are in this audience. Undoubtedly some of the men who had come from Jerusalem and who, though nominally confessing Jesus as their Savior, were always making trouble by stressing salvation by obedience to law far more than salvation by grace through faith, had also tarried in Antioch long enough to cause their presence at this particular meeting to be felt.

Now in this meeting-place that day there was a situation which at many a get-together would be considered improper, but which without any doubt is highly objectionable in a *church,* and most emphatically at a *love*-feast, a religious-social meeting characterized by all or most of the following elements: prayers, sacred songs, the reading and brief exposition of Scripture, eating and drinking together, and partaking of the Lord's Supper. That deplorable condition was this, that *the church-members were cliquing.* Segregation was being practiced, yes, right here in the church meeting:

Jews eating *exclusively* with Jews, leaving the Gentile believers no other choice than to eat with other Gentiles. This violation of the principle of the oneness of all believers "in Christ" occurred because undue respect was being accorded to the Judaizers. Peter, who previously had been freely eating with the Gentile believers, had allowed himself to be scared into withdrawing himself from them. He was now seen sitting or reclining in the company of Jews; Barnabas, ditto; and the same was true with respect to the rest of the Jews, as if *the cross of Christ* had been of no avail in taking down the barrier that had divided Jews and Gentiles!

It is under such circumstances that Paul arises and points to the significance which Christ Crucified had come to assume in his own life. Having first shown that "a man is not justified by law-works"—for example, by rigidly adhering to traditional regulations regarding eating and drinking—, but only through faith in Jesus Christ, the apostle closes his stirring address with the passage which starts out with these ringing words: "I have been crucified with Christ." Something marvelous had happened to Paul in the past, with abiding significance for the present and for all future time.[73]

But what can he mean by this? Must this saying be taken *literally?* Cases of survival after crucifixion have occurred, but certainly the present context, marked by use of words in an other-than-literal sense (for example, Paul also affirms that he is no longer alive!), cannot be interpreted literally. Are the words to be understood *emotionally,* perhaps (after the manner in which some explain Phil. 3:10)? Is it Paul's intention to convey the thought that with mind and heart he had been contemplating the story of Christ's great love for sinners, shown in his entire sojourn on earth but especially at Calvary, until he (Paul) had at last tearfully arrived at the point of identifying himself with the Great Sufferer, that is, of feeling, in some small degree, what *he* had felt and undergoing what *he* had experienced? But though such sharing in Christ's sufferings, when applied to the heart by the Holy Spirit, so that its boundaries are not overstepped, and its implications as to the sinner's guilt and his pardon are sanctified to the heart, can be very beneficial, this explanation would fail to do justice to the concrete situation that occasioned this famous testimony. Is it then to be explained *forensically,* that is, in terms of the law-court? Does Paul mean that he, too, along with all of God's children, had been declared *"Guilty* and exposed to the sentence of *eternal death,"* but that at Calvary, due to Christ's redemptive suffering as our Substitute and Representative, this sentence had been changed into its very opposite, namely, *"Righteous* and an heir of *eternal life"?* Certainly, in such a case the apostle would have had the perfect right to say that he had been crucified along with Christ and also that with Christ he had arisen from the dead. Moreover, this forensic

---

[73] Paul uses the perfect tense: *συνεσταύρωμαι.*

explanation would bring the passage into line with many others (for example, Isa. 53:4-6, 8, 12; Matt. 20:28; Mark 10:45; John 1:29; Gal. 1:4; 3:13; Eph. 2:1, 3, 5, 6; Col. 2:12-14, 20; 3:1; I Tim. 3:6). But even though this meaning may well have been included, does it exhaust the contents of Paul's remarkable affirmation? Does it solve the riddle, and does it do justice to the present historical, as well as literary, context?

No doubt the best procedure is to let Paul be his own interpreter. Accordingly, we proceed to:

(2) *The Riddle Partly Clarified but Also Partly Intensified*

Paul continues: **and it is no longer I who lives, but Christ who lives in me.** This at least shows that when the apostle said, "I have been crucified with Christ" (literally, according to word order: "With Christ I have been crucified"), he meant that the process of crucifixion had been carried to its conclusion: he had been crucified, abidingly experiences the effects of this crucifixion, and, therefore, he is now no longer alive! But in what sense has he been crucified and is he no longer alive? The answer that suits the present context is this, that Paul is saying: *"As a self-righteous Pharisee, who based his hope for eternity on strict obedience to law, I, as a direct result of Christ's crucifixion, have been crucified and am no longer alive."* That, after all, was exactly the issue here at Antioch! "In order to be saved, is it necessary that, in addition to believing in Christ, we observe the old traditions; particularly, that we adhere to the laws concerning eating and drinking, and that we accordingly separate ourselves from the Gentiles?" That was the question. It is as if the apostle were saying, "I used to be of that persuasion myself. I was 'as to law a Pharisee, as to legal righteousness blameless' (Phil. 3:5, 6). But when, by God's marvelous grace, I was rescued from my sinful folly, then, 'such things as once were gains to me, these I counted loss for Christ.' And now I rejoice in no longer having 'a righteousness of my own, legal righteousness, but that which is through faith in Christ' (Phil. 3:9). Therefore 'it is Christ who now lives in me': it is from him that I receive all my strength. In him I trust completely. On his righteousness, imputed to me, I base my hope for eternity. 'On Christ, the solid Rock, I stand; All other ground is sinking sand.' "

For those in the audience who were used to interpreting everything literally (and there are such people, now as well as then!), the riddle may not as yet have been cleared up, however. They may have said to themselves, "But how can Paul say that he is no longer alive? If he were no longer alive, how could he be addressing us?" For them, accordingly, the riddle propounded by the man who was addressing them may have been intensified instead of solved. The apostle does not ignore them. He clears up this point also, for in the next line we see:

(3) *The Riddle Fully Explained*

Paul had not been trying to say that in no sense whatever was he still alive. He had not fallen into the error of those mystics who, on the basis of the present passage and of other passages, proclaim the doctrine of the merging of the believers' personality with that of Christ, in such a way that in reality only one personality can be said to exist, namely, that of Christ. The apostle fully clears up this point by stating: **and that (life) which I now live in flesh**[74] **I live in faith, (the faith) which is in the Son of God.** Paul has not been deprived of his life "in flesh," that is, earthly existence. It is still Paul, the individual, who thinks, exhorts, bears witness, rejoices. Nevertheless, the bond between himself and his Lord is a very close one, for it is the bond of faith. Humble trust in Christ is the channel through which Paul receives the strength he needs to meet every challenge (Phil. 4:13). By means of this unshakable confidence in his Redeemer he surrenders all to him and expects all from him. This faith, moreover, is very personal, and this both as to *subject* and *object*. First, as to *subject*. Note the constant use of the pronoun *I*. In verses 19-21 it is *twice* spelled out fully as a separate pronoun (first at the beginning of verse 19: "For *I—ego*—through law died to law," and then in verse 20, at the end of the clause which A.V. renders literally, "nevertheless I live; yet not *I—ego*—"). In addition "I" occurs no less than *seven* times as part of a verbal form. Finally, there are the *three* occurrences of this same pronoun in a case other than nominative, translated *me* in each instance (verse 20). That makes no less than *twelve* "I's" in all in just three verses! It shows that salvation is, indeed, a very personal affair: each individual must make his own decision, and each believer experiences his own fellowship with Christ, relying upon him with all the confidence of his own heart. Then also this faith is personal as to its *object:* Christ, not something pertaining to Christ but Christ *himself*. When Paul, who had been a bitter persecutor, reflects on the manner in which his Lord and Savior had taken pity on him, unworthy one, he, perhaps in order to emphasize the greatness of Christ's condescending love, reminds us of the fact that the One who so loved him was no less than "the Son of God," hence, himself God! ("the faith which is in the Son of God"). He adds: **who loved me and gave himself up for me.** Note: not just *gave,* but *gave up*. In that act of giving himself up to shame, condemnation, scourging, the crown of thorns, mockery, crucifixion and abandonment by his Father, death, and burial, the love of the Son of God for his people—"for me"—had become most gloriously manifest. How, then, would it ever be possible for Paul to minimize in any way the significance of the cross? This leads to the conclusion:

(4) *The Riddle Applied to the Present Concrete Situation*

Paul writes: **I do not set aside the grace of God.** Of this simple line, too, there are several explanations, some of them without any reference to the

---

[74] The Greek phrase is ἐν σαρκί. See footnote 70.

present context. The simplest interpretation is surely this one: "I do not set aside—declare invalid, nullify—the grace of God, which I surely would be doing if I were attempting by means of law-works—for example, strict obedience to regulations concerning eating and drinking—to secure my acceptance with God, my state of righteousness before him." In complete harmony with this thought the apostle adds: **for if justification (were) through law,**[75] **then Christ died in vain.** Paul is saying, therefore, to Peter, to Barnabas, to all those present that day at this love-feast in Antioch, to the Galatians, who have allowed themselves to be influenced by the Judaizers, and certainly also *to the modern man who imagines that by doing good and giving everyone his due he can be saved,* that a definite choice must be made, namely, between salvation by grace and salvation by law-works, by Christ or by self.

We are firmly convinced that Peter knew in his heart—and was glad—that his "beloved brother Paul" (II Peter 3:15) had rendered an incalculably valuable service to the cause of the unity of *all believers* in Christ, to the demands of Christian love, and to the doctrine of the all-sufficiency of Christ unto salvation. Barnabas and many of the others must have been similarly persuaded.

## *Summary of Chapter 2*

This chapter consists of two paragraphs: verses 1-10; 11-21. The first describes what took place in Jerusalem fourteen years after the visit indicated in 1:18, 19. The apostle gives his version of The Jerusalem Conference (cf. Acts 15:1-29). The second paragraph concerns the Paul-versus-Peter affair in Syrian Antioch shortly afterward. In the first paragraph the foes are the Judaizers, Christians only in name, men who advocated faith plus law-obedience as the way to glory. One of their slogans was, "Unless y o u are circumcised according to the custom of Moses, y o u cannot be saved." Not being real Christians, they had no business at this synod. They were present as spies, bent on depriving true believers of their freedom in Christ. Now to this Conference the Antiochian church had delegated Paul and Barnabas, champions of Christian liberty. With them was Titus, a Christian of unmixed Gentile extraction, and thus uncircumcised, *a test case* therefore. Would the Judaizers succeed in persuading the assembly that Titus must be circumcised? If they do, then everywhere the position of Gentile Christians would be in jeopardy, Christianity would never become a worldwide religion, and the gospel of Christ's all-sufficiency for salvation

---

75 In the original the verb is not expressed. Hence, some translate this protasis as belonging to the *first class* or *simple condition* group; others as *second class* or *contrary to fact*. In the end it makes no difference, as in each case the interpreters agree that Paul meant to convey the thought: *a.* that justification is not actually through law, and *b.* that Christ did not die in vain.

would vanish from the earth. But by God's decree that cannot happen! In a private consultation the truly Christian leaders—Paul and Barnabas, on the one hand; James, Cephas, and John, on the other—plan their strategy. Concerning God's work among the Gentiles Paul and Barnabas bear witness with such conviction, both before the Jerusalem leaders and before the full convention, that the opponents fail completely. The paragraph closes by picturing James, Cephas, and John in the act of extending the hand of friendship and brotherhood to Paul and Barnabas. The work-load is divided and help for the poor is provided.

Hardly was this battle won when a second had to be fought, as shown in verses 11-21. And in this struggle the foe was no one less than Cephas, the leader of The Twelve. Not that Peter was at heart an enemy of the gospel of grace, but here at Antioch he suffered a temporary lapse (cf. Matt. 16:23). When, at a public church-gathering he withdraws himself from the Gentiles, refusing any longer to eat with them, he is saying, in effect, "To be saved, more is needed than trust in Christ. Adherence to the ceremonial law is also necessary." He knows better, having been taught by Jesus and by the vision of the sheet. He is playing the hypocrite, having become alarmed by the arrival of a party of Judaizers. For a while things looked bad, for Peter's example was followed by others, including even Barnabas. Paul, however, rises to meet the challenge. We see him at the height of his fortitude. By inserting the substance of his remarks in this letter to the Galatians, he shows that his words are now also meant for these similarly erring brothers. In substance he says, "If you, Cephas, though a Jew, can live like a Gentile, as you proved when you ate with Gentiles, how can you now, by withdrawing from them, force them to live like Jews, so that they may be able to eat and have fellowship with us?" Then, turning to the entire audience, he stresses that not by law-works is anyone justified, but only by faith in Christ, and that if the Judaizers were right, Christ would be a promoter of sin. The real sinner, however, is the man who rebuilds the very structure—salvation by law-works—which he had previously pulled down. As to law Paul states, "For I through law died to law, that I might live to God." For a thematic treatment of verses 20, 21 see the explanation.

In the room silence prevails. The gospel of grace has triumphed once more. And may we not assume that not only Cephas but all true but momentarily erring believers who had followed his example were grateful to the Lord that they had been corrected by "our beloved brother Paul"?

# Chapter 3

Verses 1-5

Theme: *The Gospel of Justification by Faith apart from Law-works Defended against Its Detractors*

II. *Its Vindication: both Scripture—i.e., the Old Testament—and life (experience, past history) bear testimony to its truth*

A. O foolish Galatians! Was it by doing what the law demands that you received the Spirit or was it by believing the gospel message?

# CHAPTER III

## GALATIANS

3 1 O foolish Galatians! Who has bewitched y o u, before whose very eyes Jesus was openly displayed as crucified? 2 This only would I learn from y o u: Was it by doing what (the) law demands that y o u received the Spirit, or was it by believing (the) gospel message?[76] 3 Are y o u so foolish? Having begun by the Spirit, now by fleshly means are y o u being made perfect? 4 Did y o u experience so many things in vain?—if (it be) really in vain. 5 He, accordingly, who supplies the Spirit to y o u and works miracles among y o u (does he bring this about) because y o u do what (the) law demands or because y o u believe (the) gospel message?[77]

---

3:1-5

A. *By what avenue did y o u receive the Spirit and its fruits?*

1. The apostle, having proved that the gospel as proclaimed by himself—that is, the good tidings of justification by faith apart from law-works—is of divine origin and is therefore able to maintain itself everywhere and at all times, now proceeds to show that both *Scripture* and *experience* bear testimony to its truth. He turns to *experience* first of all, that is, to that which the Galatians themselves had begun to experience when they, by sovereign grace, had accepted Jesus Christ as their Lord and Savior. He says: **O foolish Galatians! Who has bewitched y o u, before whose very eyes Jesus was openly displayed as crucified?** As is clear from a study of the word "foolish" or "senseless" in Luke 24:25; Rom. 1:14; I Tim. 6:9; and to a certain extent even in Titus 3:3, the original indicates an attitude of *heart* as well as a quality of *mind*. It refers not to bluntness but to a sinful neglect to use one's mental power to the best advantage. The Galatians, in lending a listening ear to the arguments of the legalists, must be considered not necessarily dull but thoughtless, not ignorant but senseless, not stupid but foolish. And is not everyone foolish who barters the truth of God for the lie of Satan, peace for unrest, assurance for doubt, joy for fear, and freedom for bondage?

---

[76] Alternate translation: "Was it as a result of law-works that y o u received the Spirit or was it as a result of faith-inspired listening?"
[77] Alternate translation: ". . . (does he bring this about) as a result of law-works or as a result of faith-inspired listening?"

Paul, deeply moved, asks, "Who has bewitched y o u?" Neither in Greek, however, nor in modern English does the word *bewitch* always have reference to literal witchcraft. In the interpretation of this passage much has been made of "the evil eye" (cf. Deut. 28:54, 56; Prov. 23:6; 28:22; Matt. 20:15; Mark 7:22). But Paul was probably not thinking about the sorcerer who had brought the Galatians under the baleful influence of his evil eye, but rather of the Judaizer who had cast a spell upon them *not* by means of his eyes but by means of his *words, his teaching;* specifically, by telling them that faith in Christ must be *supplemented* by Mosaic ritualism.[78] And the Galatians, by yielding to this influence, had failed to understand that a Christ *supplemented* is a Christ *supplanted.*

Moreover, such yielding was entirely inexcusable, since Jesus, as the source of salvation full and free to all who believe, had been *openly displayed, clearly and publicly proclaimed*[79] to the Galatians. With their very eyes, as it were, they had seen him. So clear and vivid had been the presentation of this Christ that they had formed a mental picture of him, dying for sinners and promising salvation to all who would accept him by true faith. When Paul says "before whose very eyes Jesus was openly displayed as crucified," he is thinking not so much of the historical details of the crucifixion as of the supreme value of Christ Crucified for a world lost in sin, and of the implication that obedience to law contributes nothing to this salvation.

2. Paul continues: **This only would I learn from y o u: Was it by doing what (the) law demands that y o u received the Spirit, or was it by believing (the) gospel message?** A somewhat different translation—not differing, however, in its basic idea—is also possible, namely, ". . . Was it as a result of law-works that y o u received the Spirit, or was it as a result of faith-inspired listening?"[80] The two renderings agree in this that according to

---

[78] See Delling, article *βασκαίνω*, Th.W.N.T., Vol. I, pp. 595, 596.

[79] The context makes clear that this rather than *written beforehand* (cf. Rom. 15:4; Eph. 3:3; Jude 4) is the sense of *προεγράφη*.

[80] The preference for either the one or the other translation hinges mainly on the answer which is given to the question, "What is the meaning of ἐξ ἀκοῆς πίστεως? The notion that πίστις is here used in the objective sense (body of doctrine, teaching) can be dismissed as being out of line with the context. It is also easy to agree on the meaning of ἐξ = *by, by way of, as a result of*. But the exact connotation, in the present instance, of ἀκοή-ῆς furnishes a real difficulty. Dismissing the meaning *ear, ears* (Mark 7:35; Luke 7:1; Acts 17:20; II Tim. 4:3), it is agreed that the word can refer to *a. hearing* or *listening* (*active* sense). It has this meaning in Rom. 10:17 and II Peter 2:8. The modifier πίστεως could then be interpreted as a qualitative genitive: "hearing characterized by faith, hearing with a believing heart," or as a subjective genitive: "hearing that comes of—or: is inspired by—faith." This interpretation of ἀκοῆς πίστεως as being, in either sense, the hearing or listening *of faith* yields a good sense in the passage now under discussion. There is then a contrast between *works performed in bondage to law* ("law-works"), on the one hand, and *listening inspired by (or: characterized by) faith,* on the other.

both *salvation by works* is placed over against *salvation by faith.* Paul's question is filled with significance and applies to every age. Let the tree be judged by the fruits it produces. It is as if Paul were asking, "My dear Galatians, does the course which you are now following make you more happy and contented than that which you previously selected? By what avenue were you first made conscious of having the Holy Spirit in your hearts? Was it by the avenue of rigorous bondage to ceremonial ordinances or was it by the exercise of faith in Christ, so that you listened and listened and eagerly took to heart the marvelous message of the gospel?" In verse 5 the apostle is going to come back to this question and is going to expand it. See on that verse.

3. Continued: **Are you so foolish?** What their folly consisted of has already been explained (see on verse 1). Nevertheless, there is a further explication of the concept *Galatian Folly* in these words: **Having begun by the Spirit, now by fleshly means are you being made perfect?** [81]

In the original there is a double contrast, namely, *a.* between "having begun" and "being made perfect," and *b.* between "by the Spirit" and "by flesh" (in the sense of "by fleshly means"). This double contrast is made all the more effective by the chiastic (or letter X) arrangement of the words in the sentence:

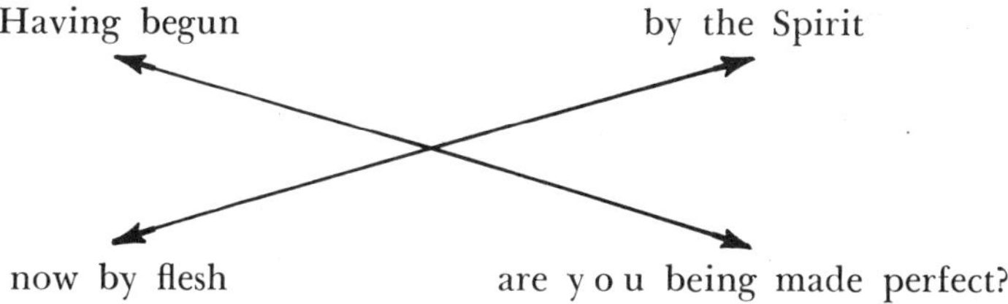


However, ἀκοή also has a *passive* meaning: *b. that which is heard, report, preaching, message;* particularly now *the gospel message.* It has this meaning in Isa. 53:1 (LXX) and at least also in the New Testament quotations of that passage (John 12:38; Rom. 10:16). So rendered ἐξ ἀκοῆς πίστεως could then be translated: *by* (or: *as a result of*) *the gospel message which demanded faith* or . . . *which was the object of faith,* or even more simply but still correctly: *by believing the gospel message.* Here, too, the contrast between *doing* what the law demands, on the one hand, and *believing* the gospel message, on the other, is very clear. What especially interested the present author, in making a study of this verse, was that noted interpreters, *in each group* (*a.* and *b.*) claim that *their* rendering of ἀκοή-ῆς does better justice to the contrast which Paul has in mind than does the opposite rendering. As I see it, both do equal justice to this contrast, and at bottom, both interpretations and translations of the passage amount to about the same thing, for what is this *faith-inspired* (or *faith-derived*) *listening* if it be not a "listening with a believing heart *to the gospel message*"?

[81] The verb ἐπιτελεῖσθε is probably passive, not middle. Nowhere else in the New Testament does this verb occur in the middle voice. It is always either active (Rom. 15:28; II Cor. 7:1; 8:6, 11; Phil. 1:6; Heb. 8:5; 9:6) or passive (I Peter 5:9).

By placing *Spirit* and *flesh* so near to each other (as is done in the original and in my translation) the difference between the two receives the proper emphasis. The active presence of *the Spirit* spells the indwelling of Christ; hence, rebirth, the implantation of the seed of true faith, the sense of forgiveness and sonship, and the further gifts of illumination, liberty, joy, assurance of salvation, power against Satan, answered prayers, effective witness-bearing, etc. It produces gifts both outward and inward, as will be indicated (see on verse 5). On the other hand, *the flesh*[82] is the absence of Christ's indwelling. It indicates anything apart from Christ on which one bases his hope for salvation. The Galatians were beginning to renounce Christ as the all-sufficient Savior. Having begun in the Spirit they were now tending to place their confidence in fleshly means—such as trusting in the advice of the Judaizers, hence also in legal works, strict observance of ceremonies, circumcision, etc.—in order that by means such as these they might become perfected. What stupendous and disastrous folly! They remind one of the prodigal son who leaves the home of his father, with the security, peace, love, and understanding which that home offered, in order that he might roam about in a strange and hostile environment, where he would suffer hunger and want. Flesh spells doubt, fear, darkness, weakness, bondage, gloom, defeat, etc.

It is as if Paul were saying, "How hopeful was your beginning, and how sad your continuation! And just think of it: those false guides whom you are now beginning to follow have a name for this process of going downhill. They call it *becoming perfected!* What tragic irony!"

What the apostle writes applies not only to the Galatians of his own day. It applies equally to those who today are trusting in such things as ritual, the moral life, scientific achievement, intellectual attainment, physical charm, financial resources, political power, doctrinal liberalism, or even doctrinal purity. If one bases his hope for this life or the next upon anything apart from Christ he is placing confidence in *flesh.*

**4.** In close connection with the words "Having begun by the Spirit" (verse 3 and cf. also verses 1 and 2) Paul continues: **Did you experience so many things in vain?** A.V. reads, "Have ye suffered so many things in vain?" This wording (with *suffered* instead of *experienced*) is found also in many other translations, both ancient and modern, and is recommended by many interpreters. If it be correct, Paul would be introducing an entirely new thought at this point, one about which he has said nothing whatever in the preceding, which he drops immediately, and to which he never again alludes in the remainder of the letter! Now, it can hardly be questioned that the Galatians, along with all others who turn to Christ, had suffered. Cf. John 16:33; II Tim. 3:12. Even the book of Acts which dwells in some detail

[82] On σάρξ see N.T.C. on Philippians, p. 77, footnote 55, meaning g.

on Paul's sufferings in South Galatia (13:50; 14:2, 5, 19) and says but little about the afflictions which the Galatians themselves endured, nevertheless implies that many tribulations awaited them (14:22). It is also true that the word used in the original and translated *suffered* in A.V., etc., generally has that meaning. And, *taken in and by itself,* the question, "Have ye suffered so much in vain?" yields an intelligible sense, for the Galatians might well be asked whether "the game had been worth the candle," if they now were at the point of deserting the very faith which they had once confessed and for which they had suffered a measure of persecution.

Notwithstanding these arguments in support of the rendering *suffered,* there remain a few considerations which have moved many to part company with the A.V. at this point. First, it should be borne in mind that the verb used in the original is neutral. It really means no more than *to experience.* Whether the things which have been experienced were good or bad, favorable or unfavorable, is not indicated in the verb as such.[83] Then also the argument based upon the prevalent meaning of the word (namely, to suffer) in Paul's epistles (and elsewhere) loses much of its force as soon as it is discovered, after detailed examination of all the other Pauline passages in which it is found (I Cor. 12:26; II Cor. 1:6; Phil. 1:29; I Thess. 2:14; II Thess. 1:5; and II Tim. 1:12) that *in all these other cases* the context clearly demands, as translation, a form of the verb *to suffer,* but that the present context, on the contrary, points in the opposite direction. Both preceding and succeeding verses speak of past *favors:* the public proclamation of the Christ to the Galatians, the reception of the Spirit, and the occurrence of miracles in their midst. See also Gal. 4:14, 15. It is in *this* general context that Paul asks, "Did y o u experience so many things *in vain* (that is, *to no effect*)?"

The implied lesson, always applicable, is surely this, that the Lord wants everyone to profit spiritually by the experiences through which he has passed. He wants his people to use those experiences—in the present case *blessings,* but the lesson applies to *all* experiences—to good advantage. In the old dispensation Laban, though he refers to what he has learned from experience, made a selfish application (Gen. 30:27). The Galatians likewise were showing by their erring ways that theirs was not the proper response. On the other hand, David, reflecting on God's mercies, proves that these tokens of divine love had not been lost on him. He said, "Who am I, O Lord Jehovah, and what is my house, that thou hast brought me thus far?" (II Sam. 7:18). Cf. also Ps. 103; 116; 119:67; Luke 17:11-19; Acts 3:23-31; I Tim. 1:12-17; and Rev. 15:2-4. Paul adds: **if (it be) really in vain.** Some interpret this to mean, "If (it be) only in vain and not worse than

---

83 Greek authors at times used an adverbial modifier—*εὖ, κακῶς*—to indicate whether the experience was good or bad.

in vain." I cannot agree with this—rather harsh (?) —interpretation. Gal. 5:10 definitely shows that Paul had not given up hope in connection with the Galatians. Even now he regarded them as being *his* "dear children" (Gal. 4:19), yes, as *God's* dear—but grievously erring—children. I agree with Calvin's remark on this verse: "But to mitigate the severity of this complaint, he [Paul] adds, 'if (it be) really in vain,' thus inspiring their minds with the expectation of something better, and rousing them to the exercise of repentance." Thus also Berkhof, Lightfoot, Luther, and most commentators. The opposite view is defended by Ridderbos (among others), *op. cit.,* pp. 115, 116.

**5.** As the word "accordingly" indicates, Paul now returns to the question which he had asked previously (see verse 2), changing the second person to the third, and the past tense to the present, for heightened effect: **He, accordingly, who supplies the Spirit to y o u and works miracles among y o u (does he bring this about) because y o u do what (the) law demands or because y o u believe (the) gospel message?**[84] Note the addition: "and works miracles among y o u." Instead of "among y o u" one can also translate "within y o u." This means that the *miracles, forces,* or *powers* of which the apostle makes mention can be viewed either as *outward charismata* (*special gifts*), such as healing, prophecy, tongues, interpretation of tongues (I Cor. 12:10; II Cor. 12:12), or as *inward moral and spiritual endowments,* such as faith, hope, and love. There would seem to be good reason to believe that Paul had both of these groups in mind, for when he himself enumerates the various blessings which the Holy Spirit had bestowed on another church, he proceeds, by a very easy transition, from the first group (in I Cor. 12) to the second (in I Cor. 13). Blessings of both kinds had been bestowed—yes, *liberally bestowed*[85]—upon the Galatians. But had they been imparted as a result of obedience to law or as a result of faith in the Lord Jesus Christ, as set forth in the gospel? And if the latter, as was most certainly true, then why are the Galatians turning away from *faith* to *works,* from *the Fountain* to *the broken cistern* that holds no water? "O foolish Galatians!" "O equally foolish modern man!"

---

[84] Or: "(does he bring this about) as a result of law-works or as a result of faith-inspired listening?" For a discussion of these different renderings see on verse 2.

[85] For the meaning of ἐπιχορηγέω see N.T.C. on Philippians, p. 74, footnote 50.

# Chapter 3

Verses 6-14

Theme: *The Gospel of Justification by Faith apart from Law-works Defended against Its Detractors*

II. *Its Vindication: both Scripture—i.e., the Old Testament—and life (experience, past history) bear testimony to its truth*

B. The law (Deut. 27:26) pronounces a curse upon the disobedient. Christ Crucified, by bearing this curse (Deut. 21:23), redeemed us from it, so that we are saved through *faith* in him. Abraham, too, was justified by faith (Gen. 15:6), and blessed with him are all those who are of faith, according to God's promise (Gen. 12:3; 18:18; 22:18; Hab. 2:4).

6 (It is) even as (recorded): "Abraham believed God, and it was
reckoned to him for righteousness." 7 Know then that those that are of faith,
it is they who are sons of Abraham. 8 Now Scripture, foreseeing that it was by
faith that God would justify the Gentiles, preached the gospel beforehand to
Abraham, (saying): "In you all the nations shall be blessed." 9 Therefore, those
that are of faith are blessed with Abraham, the man of faith.

10 For as many as rely on law-works are under a curse; for it is written,
"Cursed (is) everyone who does not continue in all the things that are written
in the book of the law, to do them." 11 Now it is evident that by law no one is
justified before God, for "The righteous shall live by faith." 12 But the law does
not belong to faith; on the contrary, "He who does them shall live by them."
13 Christ redeemed us from the curse of the law, having become a curse for us—for
it is written, "Cursed is everyone who is hanging on a tree"—14 in order that the
blessing of Abraham might come to the Gentiles in Jesus Christ, in order that we
might receive the promised Spirit through faith.

3:6-14

B. *Faith: blessing . . . works: curse. The promise to Abraham*

For the idea that justification—hence, salvation in all its fulness—is obtained by way of faith and not by reliance on law-works Paul now appeals to Scripture, and first of all to the story of Abraham. In fact, the present section begins and ends with a reference to Abraham (verses 6-8, 14). We may well believe that throughout this entire paragraph (3:6-14), and, in a sense, throughout the entire chapter (cf. verses 15-18, 29), Abraham is never absent from the apostle's mind. Paul probably selected the scriptural references to Abraham in order to show *a.* that already at the very beginning of Israel's history it is clearly evident that God had chosen this one nation in order that in and through its great "seed" it might not only receive a blessing but also become a blessing to *the world;* and *b.* that equally from the very beginning the divinely appointed means of receiving this blessing, so as to be able to impart it to the nations, was *faith,* not works.

**6.** Accordingly, Paul writes: **(It is) even as (recorded): "Abraham believed God, and it was reckoned to him for righteousness."** Probably an additional reason for devoting so much attention to Abraham was the fact that the opponents were constantly boasting about their descent from Abraham, as if this biological circumstance would give them a higher rating with God (Acts 15:5; Gal. 2:3; 5:2, 3; 6:12, 13, 15; cf. Matt. 3:9; Luke 3:8; John 8:33, 39, 40, 53), and as if the *righteousness* which Jehovah had "reckoned" to Abraham (Gen. 15:6) had been a *debt* which God owed him for his *work* (cf. Rom. 4:4).[86] So Paul refers to this very passage from Genesis and shows that it teaches the exact opposite, and places the emphasis on *faith, not* on *work.* "Abraham believed God," that is, believed what God had spoken. Moreover, this faith, says Paul, in complete harmony with Gal. 3:1-5, was not a matter of merit on Abraham's part, but was by God graciously "reckoned" or "imputed" to him for righteousness. Also, if the opponents imagine that for their emphasis on the necessity of *circumcision* as a means unto salvation they can appeal to the story of Abraham (Gen. 17:23-27), let it then be emphasized that *the patriarch's justification preceded his circumcision* by many years (Gen. 15:6; 16:16; 17:24). Righteousness was reckoned to him not after but long before he had been circumcised (Rom. 4:9-12); so that, as a result of this prior justification, he became the father of *all* believers, the uncircumcised as well as the circumcised. That, in brief, is Paul's argumentation, according to Gal. 3:6-10 as illumined by Rom. 4:1-12.

Abraham's life is, in fact, an illustration of the manner in which men, in all ages, are saved. *Confidence* in God, come what may, and *resulting obedience* to God's revealed will, characterize Abraham's life. Of these two—confidence and obedience—the former is basic throughout. Abraham obeyed because he believed. He heeded God's command because, *first of all,* he trusted God. The *work* of obedience proved that the confidence was genuine.[87]

Abraham's faith is being constantly put to the test. By God's grace he triumphs again and again. When God appears to him in Ur of the Chaldeans (Acts 7:3; cf. Gen. 11:28-32) he is told to leave country and kindred. Fully trusting that God will make all things well, he obeys. When Jehovah appears the second time, in Haran of Mesopotamia (Gen. 12:1), the test is even more severe: Abraham[88] must leave his father's house. Again he trusts and obeys (Heb. 11:8). It is at this time that he receives the wonderful promise, "In you shall all the families of the earth be blessed." Here we notice that God's particularism—in selecting Abraham from among all of mankind—had a universalistic purpose: the salvation of men of every nation. At Shechem in the land of Canaan Jehovah appears again, this time with the promise, "To your *seed* I will give this *land*" (Gen. 12:6, 7). This promise constitutes another test of faith, for Sarai is barren (Gen. 11:30), and the Canaanite, who was not at all eager to yield his soil to a stranger, was then in the land. Again Abraham believes, and builds an

---

[86] For λογίζομαι, here ἐλογίσθη ("it was reckoned") see Heidland, Th.W.N.T., Vol. IV, especially pp. 293, 294.

[87] It is for this reason that James (2:20-24), with his stress on *works,* is able to make use of this same passage (Gen. 15:6) and to apply it to prove his point, doing so without coming into any real conflict with Paul.

[88] Until his name is changed he is called "Abram" (Gen. 17:5).

altar to Jehovah. After an unhappy incident in Egypt (Gen. 12:10-20), in which the weaker side of the man's character becomes manifest, Jehovah appears to him at Bethel. This occurred when Abraham had separated himself from Lot (Gen. 13:1-13). "God's friend" (James 2:23) is promised *a.* all the land which he sees, extending in every direction, and *b.* a seed as the dust of the earth (Gen. 13:14-18). But Abraham himself during his lifetime did not see the fulfilment of these promises. He lived *by faith* (Heb. 11:18-13). After his return from the slaughter of Chedorlaomer and his associates the word of Jehovah comes to Abraham in a vision, saying, "Fear not . . . I am your shield and your exceeding great reward." Offspring is promised to him as the stars in multitude. There follows the passage which Paul quotes here in Gal. 3:6 (cf. Rom. 4:3, 20, 22; James 2:23): "Abraham believed God, and it was reckoned to him for righteousness." Subsequently, to Abraham, aged ninety-nine, the promise is repeated (Gen. 17). With him, as prospective father of a numerous race, the covenant of grace is established (17:7). Even before the promised child's birth it is already given a name (17:19). A little later the very time of the birth is revealed to Abraham and his wife (18:10). Abraham, though overcome with wonder, continues to cling to God's promise. Isaac is born, Abraham being now a centenarian (21:1, 2, 5).

The most excruciating test of Abraham's faith occurs when God says to him, "Now take your son, your only son, whom you love, even Isaac, and go to the land of Moriah, and offer him there as a burnt offering upon one of the summits which I will indicate to you" (Gen. 22:2). Yet Abraham knows that Isaac is the very son who, in the line of descent, must some day produce "the seed" (as to his human nature), the very One in whom all the nations of the earth were to be blessed! How then can God command Abraham to offer up Isaac? By divine grace the father of all believers sustains even this fearfully bitter trial. He triumphs through faith in God, being deeply convinced that God was able even to raise up Isaac from the dead (Heb. 11:19). His faith is gloriously rewarded.

It is with this climax of Abraham's faith (Gen. 22) that James in his epistle links Gen. 15:6. He had every right to make this application, for whether Abraham professes his faith at the terebinths of Mamre, at the tamarisk of Beer-sheba, or on a high hill in Moriah, that marvelous confidence is still the same subtle chain that binds him to the Infinite, the same resting on the promises, the same looking forward to the city with the solid foundations, whose Architect and Builder is God. Paul, on the other hand, leaves Gen. 15:6 in its own historical context, as is clear from Rom. 4:3, 10. For Paul's reasoning, both in Galatians and in Romans, this actual historical context was very meaningful, since, as has been indicated, it showed that *even before his circumcision* Abraham's faith was already reckoned to him for righteousness. Hence, it also proved that circumcision was not nearly as important as the Judaizers were trying to make it appear!

Two questions demand an answer, however. The first one is this: "Is not forensic righteousness or justification a matter of the imputation of Christ's righteousness to the sinner? But if this be true, then how is it that here in Gal. 3:6 (cf. Rom. 4:3, 20, 22), as in Gen. 15:6, Abraham's *faith* is said to have been reckoned for righteousness, and this without any reference to Christ? Does not Christ figure in this account of imputation? Or must a reference to him be artificially superimposed upon the story or dragged into it?" The answer is: Scripture itself shows us the Christ in the story. He is there, for all to see who are willing to see. Even better: it is Christ himself who reveals himself with respect to this story. It was he who said to the hostile Jews of his day, "Abraham, y o u r father, was extremely happy that he was to see my day, *and he saw it and rejoiced*" (John 8:56). When the promise concerning a son was made to Abraham, the latter believed, therefore, that in the line of Isaac "the blessed seed" would at length arrive through whom God would bless all the nations. Thus, as is stated clearly in Heb. 11:13, Abraham (and others before and after him) "died in faith, not having received (the fulfilment of) the promises, but *having greeted them from afar.*" See N.T.C. on John 8:56, Vol. II, pp. 64–66.

It is not necessary, however, to establish to what extent Abraham had received clarity with respect to the coming Redeemer and the task assigned to him by the Father. It is far more important to take note of the fact that Paul himself, here in Gal. 3, links the promise that was given to Abraham with Christ and his redemptive work (verses 13, 14, 16, 22, 29). For Abraham also, therefore, the real basis of justification—pardon for sin, right standing before God, adoption as a son—was Christ's voluntary and vicarious sacrifice. For him, too, faith was the hand that laid hold on God's promise, however dimly apprehended. It is in that sense that Gen. 15:6 and Gal. 3:6 must be understood.

The second question, which also is being asked again and again is this: "Does Paul have any right, in his defense of faith over against law-works, to appeal to the faith of Abraham, which, after all, is mentioned in an entirely different setting?" A quick, true, and also at times the only possible, answer would be that it was the Holy Spirit who inspired both Moses and Paul, both Genesis and Galatians, and who therefore had the right to apply his own previous utterances to new situations. Having granted this, however, must it not be added that *basically* the two situations were very similar? When, step by step, we followed the life of Abraham up to Moriah, did it not become clear that (with few exceptions) he was constantly rejecting the flesh for the Spirit, the earthly in favor of the heavenly, the visible in the interest of the invisible? Did he not do exactly this when, purely at God's bidding, he left his home and kindred for regions unknown; again when he rejected the well-watered Plain of the Jordan, giving Lot first choice;

and once more when, in obedience to God, the God in whom he trusted, he even suppressed his strong and natural desire to keep alive his own dear and long-awaited son, in order that he might do God's bidding with respect to him? Is it not clear then that Abraham's chief desire was to lean for his salvation entirely on God and his will, and not on the arm of "flesh"? And was not the latter, namely, leaning on the arm of flesh, exactly what the Judaizers of Paul's day were doing when, prompted by fleshly considerations (Gal. 6:12), they continued to demand that the Gentiles supplement their faith in Jesus with fleshly trust in fleshly ordinances? Over against all those who placed their confidence in *flesh*—anything apart from Christ on which one relies—both Abraham and Paul manifested their *faith,* and were able to say, "We look not at the things that are seen but at the things that are not seen; for the things that are seen are temporal, but the things that are not seen are eternal" (II Cor. 4:18). Therefore the appeal to Gen. 15:6 is not only fully justified but even natural.

7. Paul continues: **Know[89] then that those that are of faith, it is they who are sons of Abraham.** To be "of faith" means to be characterized or controlled by faith, to have *trust in God* as one's guiding principle. When this can be truly affirmed of persons, then they are sons of Abraham; and if sons then also heirs, true partakers of the spiritual promise that was made to Abraham. Note the emphasis on the fact that they, *they alone* but also *all of them,* are the true sons of Abraham.

What Paul is writing was nothing new. Christ in his teaching had emphasized the same truth, namely, that not physical descent but spiritual likeness makes a person a true son of Abraham. Those are sons of Abraham who do the works of Abraham (Luke 19:9; John 8:39, 40; cf. Matt. 8:11, 12). And John the Baptist had taught similarly (Matt. 3:9; Luke 3:8). Just as it is true that to be a child of God one must be like God (Eph. 5:1; I John 2:29; 3:1, 8, 9), so also it cannot be denied that to be a son of Abraham one must be like Abraham, imitate his conduct, and thus become a partaker of his blessedness. Therefore, even though a man should be a Hebrew of Hebrews, he is not, in the spiritual sense, a son of Abraham unless he be a true believer. Conversely, if he be a true believer in the Lord Jesus Christ, he is a son of Abraham, whether he be a Gentile or a Jew by race.

8. Continued: **Now Scripture, foreseeing that it was by faith that God would justify the Gentiles, preached the gospel beforehand to Abraham, (saying): "In you all the nations shall be blessed."** In the words "Scripture foreseeing . . . preached the gospel beforehand" we have a very emphatic identification of

---

[89] Though construing γινώσκετε as a present indicative yields a good sense (for example, "You are able, therefore, to draw the conclusion"), the imperative is more immediately understandable: the Galatians were forgetting that in the sight of God racial distinctions had no value, that faith was all that really mattered. Hence, they are called back to their duty of realizing this truth.

God and his Word: what Scripture promises God promises, for he is the Speaker. Since the Holy Spirit is Scripture's Primary Author the conclusion is inevitable that God and his Word are most closely connected. The thing *foreseen,* because it had been thus ordained before the foundation of the world (Eph. 1:4, 11), was that it was "by faith"[90] and not "by works" that God would justify the Gentiles. If the Galatians would only understand this, they would not allow themselves to be misled by the Judaizers. "By faith" means "by trustfully receiving" God's gift out of his hand. It is thus, thus *only,* that the nations of the world were to receive pardon, right standing in the sight of God and his holy law, and adoption as sons; in a word: justification. This precious doctrine had been previously "gospeled" to Abraham. It had been proclaimed to him as good tidings of great joy for the entire world. This promise, though always valid, was to be realized *on an international scale* with the coming of Christ and of the dispensation which that coming would usher in. The content of the promise proclaimed to Abraham, recorded in words varying slightly but always essentially the same, was this: "In you all the nations shall be blessed" (Gen. 12:3; 18:18; 22:18). The blessing of which Paul is thinking is that of "justification by faith," as the context indicates; and this, in turn, was basic to all the blessings of salvation full and free. But inasmuch as the fulfilment of this promise, on a world-wide scale, was a matter of the future, it is readily understood that the phrase "in you" must be understood as Abraham himself also certainly understood it, namely, "in the Messiah," "the seed of the woman" (Gen. 3:15), Abraham's seed (see on verse 16).

**9.** A significant and logical conclusion is drawn. The assurances were: *a.* Those that are *of faith, they alone* but also *all of them* without exception, are sons of Abraham (verse 7); and *b.* "in Abraham," that is, "in his seed," shall *all the nations* be blessed, for it was foretold that it would be *by faith* that God would justify *the Gentiles* (verse 8). Conclusion: **Therefore, those that are of faith are blessed with Abraham, the man of faith.**[91] This conclusion

---

[90] The forward position of ἐκ πίστεως, indicating strong emphasis, is inexcusably lost in most translations.

[91] The English translation of such a simple phrase as τῷ πιστῷ 'Αβραάμ, with retention of the sound similarity which in the original characterizes the words οἱ ἐκ πίστεως, πιστῷ, is not easy. This is due to the fact that English has no suitable adjective that is built on the stem *faith.* To a modern reader A.V.'s "faithful Abraham" is somewhat confusing, since the word "faithful" in the sense of "full of faith" is today obsolete. Today a "faithful person" is simply one who is true to his word and shows loyalty, fidelity. It is only fair to state that several other languages, besides English, present the same difficulty. In German, however, the sentence runs very smoothly: *"Also werden nun, die des Glaubens sind, gesegnet mit dem gläubigen Abraham."* Dutch similarly: *"Zij, die uit het geloof zijn, worden dus gezegend tezamen met den gelovigen Abraham."* In English the best that can be done with τῷ πιστῷ 'Αβραάμ is to render it "Abraham, the man of faith" or, with R.S.V., "Abraham who had faith."

is warranted, for those who are "of faith" are the ones who exercise faith. As such they are the sons of Abraham; hence, they are blessed with him, the man of faith, who "in hope believed against hope, in order that he might become a father of many nations" (Rom. 4:18).

The passage (Gal. 3:6-9; cf. verses 14, 26-29) clearly teaches the important truth—by many so deplorably rejected—that the church of both dispensations, the old and the new, is *one*. All believers dwell in the same tent (Isa. 54:1-3). When the old dispensation ended it was not necessary to pitch a new tent; the old one was simply enlarged. All of God's children are represented by the same olive tree. The old tree did not have to be uprooted; new branches were grafted in among the old (Rom. 11:17). To each of the saints the same promise is given: "I will be your God." Note how this promise runs through both Testaments (Gen. 15:1, 2; 17:7, 8; Exod. 20:2; Deut. 5:6; Josh. 1:5; II Chron. 20:17; Jer. 15:20; 24:7; 30:22; 31:33; Ezek. 11:20; Zech. 8:8; 13:9; II Cor. 6:16; Heb. 8:10; Rev. 21:3, 7). All are saved by the same faith in the same Savior (Gen. 15:6; Isa. 53; Jer. 23:5, 6; Matt. 1:21; John 3:16; Acts 4:12; 10:43; 15:11; Rom. 3:24; 4:11). Apart from us those of the old dispensation do not reach perfection (Heb. 11:40). The names of all God's people are written in the same book of life. There are not two of those books: one for the old and one for the new dispensation; there is only one (Exod. 32:32, 33; Ps. 69:28; Dan. 12:1; Mal. 3:16, 17; Luke 10:20; Phil. 4:3; Rev. 3:5; 13:8; 17:8, 20:12, 15; 21:27; 22:19). All are foreknown, foreordained, called, justified (by faith), and glorified (Rom. 8:29, 30). All partake and will partake of the glories of Jerusalem the Golden, the city on whose gates are written the names of the twelve tribes of the children of Israel, and on whose foundation stones are engraved the twelve names of the twelve apostles of the Lamb (Rev. 12:12, 14). Cf. John 10:16; 17:11.

Once this is understood the Bible becomes a living book, for we begin to realize that when God says to Abraham, "Fear not . . . I am your shield and your exceeding great reward . . . your God," he is speaking also to us. This *central*[92] promise concerns all believers of both dispensations, for all those that are of faith are Abraham's children and heirs (Gal. 3:29). No clearer language could have been used than that which is found in Rom. 4:22-24. There Paul, having again made mention of the fact that Abraham's

[92] It is true, of course, that blessings of a more temporal character were also promised to Abraham—for example, "To thy seed will I give this land" (Gen. 12:7)—but it is the *central* promise, "I will be your God," with all that it implies as to salvation full and free in and through the promised Messiah, that is repeated throughout both the Old and the New Testament, as has been shown. To say that God's covenant with Abraham has no significance for us because in addition to its central promise it also comprised elements of a temporal and national character amounts to affirming that a river loses its identity when it decreases or increases in width or depth. Besides, the promised *land* typifies Canaan above. See on 3:16.

faith "was reckoned to him for righteousness," adds, "But not for his sake alone was it written that it was reckoned to him, but for our sake also."

**10.** Having shown that righteousness comes by way of faith, Paul now expresses this same truth negatively. What he states in verse 10 ff. may therefore be considered a corollary of the thought expressed in verses 6-9. Moreover, his attack against the false doctrine of the Judaizers, by which the Galatians were being influenced, thus increases in intensity and directness. It develops into a head-on collision: **For as many as rely on law-works are under a curse; for it is written: "Cursed (is) everyone who does not continue in all the things that are written in the book of the law, to do them."** This is a modified quotation from Deut. 27:26, which, according to the Hebrew reads: "Cursed (is) he who does not confirm the words of this law, to do them." In the Old Testament these words form the conclusion of the chapter that contains the curses that were to be pronounced from Mt. Ebal after the children of Israel would have passed over the Jordan. Now the curse which the law here pronounces is very real. Unless this be granted Gal. 3:13 will be meaningless. Nevertheless, it is a fact, often ignored, that in Deuteronomy not only the blessing which was to be shouted from Mt. Gerizim but also the curse occurs in a setting of love, the idea being that by means of proclamation of this blessing and curse Israel, tenderly addressed as "the people of Jehovah thy God," shall live a consecrated life to the glory of their merciful Deliverer. Paul's intentional departure from the Hebrew text when he writes, "the book of the law" may have been occasioned by his desire to emphasize the thought that the entire law, with all its precepts, considered as a unity, is meant. His reference to "everyone" and to "all the things" reminds one of the LXX rendering: "Cursed (is) every man who does not continue in all the words of this law, to do them." But these changes are not of an essential nature.

Now what was really the purpose of God's law? God gave his law in order that man, by nature a child of wrath, and thus lying under the curse (Gal. 3:13), as definitely declared in Deut. 27:26; John 3:36; Eph. 3:2, might be reminded not only of his unchanged obligation to live in perfect harmony with this law (Lev. 19:2), but also of his total inability to fulfil this obligation (Rom. 7:24).[93] Thus this law would serve as a custodian to conduct the sinner to Christ (Gal. 3:24; cf. Rom. 7:25), in order that, having been saved by grace, he might, in principle, live the life of gratitude. That life is one of freedom in harmony with God's law (Gal. 5:13, 14). However, the Judaizers were perverting this true purpose of the law. They were relying on law-works *as a means of salvation*. On that basis they would fail

[93] That total inability is brought to light even more sharply when the law is interpreted in its true, inner meaning. Thus Jesus showed that, in order to qualify as a murderer, being angry with one's brother would suffice, while similarly the lustful glance would suffice to make one an adulterer (Matt. 5:21-48).

forever, and Deut. 27:26, when interpreted in that framework, pronounced God's heavy and unmitigated curse upon them; yes, *curse,*[94] not blessing. The law condemns, works wrath (Rom. 4:15; 5:16, 18).

**11.** The fact that the opponents were diverting the law from its true purpose and that this attempt was bound to result in tragic failure is brought out clearly, as Paul continues: **Now it is evident that by law no one is justified before God, for "The righteous shall live by faith."**[95] The law has no power to subdue man's sinful tendencies. It cannot destroy the power of sin within man (Rom. 8:3). How then can a sinner ever attain to the ultimate blessing of being righteous in the sight of God? How can that true, rich, full life in which man is at peace with his Maker, and abides in sweet communion with him, ever be reached? The answer, which holds for both dispensations, the old and the new, and for people of every race or nationality, whether Gentile or Jew, is this: "The righteous shall live by faith." It is the man who has placed his entire confidence in God, trusting him implicitly, and accepting with gladness of heart the gracious provision which that merciful Father has made for his salvation, it is he, he alone, who shall live. This *living* consists in such things as: *a.* enjoying the peace of God which passes all understanding (Phil. 4:7), in the knowledge that in the sight of God's holy majesty the believer is *righteous* (Rom. 5:1; 8:15); *b.* having fellowship with God "in Christ" (John 17:3); *c.* "rejoicing greatly with joy unspeakable and full of glory" (I Peter 1:8); *d.* "being transformed into the image of the Lord from glory to glory" (II Cor. 3:18); and *e.,* last but not least, striving to be a spiritual blessing to others to the glory of God (I Thess. 3:8).

Now if the Judaizers had only paid more attention to the Word of God and had accepted it, they would have known that not by trusting in his own reasoning or in his own accomplishments but "by faith" the righteous man attains to this bliss of "living." This had been clearly stated by Habakkuk the prophet (Hab. 2:4). That man of God appeared upon the scene of history during the reign of wicked Jehoiakim (608–597 B.C.). The words "The righteous shall live by his faith" may even be considered the theme of Habakkuk's prophecy. The divisions then would be: I. *Faith tested:* the prophet's questions and Jehovah's answers (chapters 1 and 2), and II. *Faith strengthened* by a vision shown in answer to the prophet's prayer. What bothered Habakkuk was that it seemed as if wicked men were getting away with their wickedness. Jehovah apparently tolerated such

---

[94] In verse 10 (contrast beginning of verse 13) the word κατάραν is used without preceding article, no doubt to emphasize the quality of this curse, as if to say "curse as opposed to blessing" (for the latter see verses 8, 9, 14).

[95] The correct rendering is not "the righteous by faith" but "shall live by faith." This is clear both from the preceding and the immediately following context; for "live by faith" is contrasted with "justified by law" and with "live by (doing) them."

evils as the exploitation of the needy, strife, contention, violence, etc. So the prophet begins to ask questions. He addresses these questions to Jehovah. He complains, objects, and waits for an answer. Habakkuk's first question amounted to this, "Why does Jehovah allow the wicked in Judah to oppress the righteous?" Jehovah answers, "Evil-doers will be punished. The Chaldeans (Babylonians) are coming." But this answer does not quite satisfy the prophet. So he asks another one, which was tantamount to this: "Why does Jehovah allow the Chaldeans to punish the Jews, who, at least are more righteous than these foreigners?" The prophet stations himself upon his watch-tower and awaits an answer. The answer arrives: "The Chaldeans, too, will be punished. In fact *all sinners* will be punished . . . but the righteous shall live by his *faith.*" It is his duty and privilege to trust, and to do this even then when he is not able to "figure out" the justice of Jehovah's doings. In this humble trust and quiet confidence he shall truly *live.*

But Jehovah does more than merely tell the prophet that he must exercise faith. He also strengthens that faith by means of a marvelous, progressive vision. Habakkuk sees the symbol of Jehovah's presence, descending from Mt. Paran. Having descended he stands firm and shakes the earth. The tent-hangings of Cushan and Midian are trembling and are being torn to shreds. One question worries the prophet: "Upon whom is Jehovah's wrath going to fall? Merely upon the realm of nature? Upon Judah perhaps?" Finally, the answer arrives: Jehovah destroys the Chaldeans and delivers his people.

So fearful and terrifying had been the appearance of Jehovah, so alarming the sound of the tempest, of crumbling mountains, etc., that the prophet is trembling in every part of his body. Nevertheless, having witnessed that Jehovah had descended for the defense of his own people, Habakkuk no longer questions the ways of God's providence. From now on he "waits quietly." He expresses his feelings in a beautiful Psalm of Trust: "For though the fig-tree shall not flourish. . . . Yet I will rejoice in Jehovah, I will joy in the God of my salvation."

In this case, too, as with the quotation from the story of Abraham (Gen. 15:6; cf. Gal. 3:6), I beg to differ from those who think that Paul's appeal to an Old Testament passage in his battle with the Judaizers is far-fetched. These interpreters seem to see little if any connection between "the faith versus law-works controversy" of Paul's day and the "faith versus Chaldean self-confidence contrast" described in Habakkuk's prophecy. It is an error, however, to restrict the latter contrast so narrowly. A rapid review of the contents of the Old Testament book has certainly shown that the quiet confidence which Jehovah so patiently teaches his servant is contrasted also—perhaps *especially*—with the prophet's own tendency to question the ways of God's providence. Fact is that the sinner is beset with enemies: the accusing voice of conscience, the doubting mind, etc. He must have peace. How will he obtain it? The Judaizers answer: "by trusting in his own works (circumcision, etc.)." Habakkuk, before he had fully learned the lesson which God was teaching him, gives evidence of answering: "by trusting in his own reason." That is why it was so difficult for him to harmonize the events that were happening in Judah with the existence of a holy God. That is why he had asked so many questions. But Habakkuk learned his lesson. When he sat down to write his prophecy he had learned it thoroughly, and gave an account of the experience through which he had passed. But whether a person trusts in his own *works* or in his own *reason*, in either case is he not trusting in "flesh"? As I see it, therefore, to clinch his argument Paul could not have chosen a better prophecy from which to quote than that of Habakkuk. The passage fits the situation exactly! In every age it remains true that "The righteous shall live by faith." "In quietness and confidence shall be y o u r strength" (Isa. 30:15).

12. Continued: **But the law does not belong to faith; on the contrary, "He who does them shall live by them."** In its own setting the included quotation from the book of Leviticus (18:5) is beautiful and comforting. It is introduced as follows: "Speak to the children of Israel and say to them, I am Jehovah y o u r God" (verse 2). This encouraging assurance is repeated in verse 4, and is followed by "Y o u must therefore keep my statutes and my ordinances; which, if a man do, he shall live by them: I am Jehovah" (verse 5). In summary this means: "As y o u r *sovereign* God I have a right to order y o u to keep my statutes, and as y o u r *faithful and loving God* I will help and strengthen y o u to observe these statutes out of gratitude." So interpreted, observing God's law is the believer's joy. Did not the Psalmist exclaim: "O how I love thy law! It is my meditation all the day"?

However, when one begins to *"rely* on law-works" (Gal. 3:10), as if such obedience to law amounts to a ticket of admission into the kingdom of heaven—and *that,* after all, is the context here in Galatians—he should bear in mind that, *so conceived, law* is the very opposite of *faith.* The two cannot be combined. Leaning on law means leaning on self. Exercising faith means leaning on Christ. As avenues by which men attempt to obtain salvation the two simply do not mix. They are thoroughly antagonistic. Paul himself supplies the best commentary: "But when the kindness of God our Savior and his love toward man appeared, he saved us, not by virtue of works which we ourselves had performed in a (state of) righteousness, but according to his mercy through the washing of regeneration and renewing by the Holy Spirit" (Titus 3:4, 5). Cf. John 1:17. Those who expect to be justified by observing all the statutes and ordinances of the law should remember that "He who does them shall live by them." They are even more foolish than those who imagine that they can quench their thirst by drinking salt water. Lev. 18:5 now becomes their accuser, but that is *their* fault!

**13.** The penitent sinner does not need to despair, however. To be sure, he is by nature under the curse of the law, as has been indicated. From this pitiable situation he is unable to deliver himself. But God has provided the remedy: **Christ redeemed us**—Gentiles as well as Jews (see verse 14) —**from the curse of the law, having become a curse for us.** Christ purchased us free from the curse of the law. He bought us back[96] from the sentence of condemnation which the law pronounced on us and from the punishment of eternal death which it exacted (Gen. 2:17; Deut. 30:15, 19; John 3:36; Rom. 5:12; 8:1; Eph. 2:3). He rescued us by the payment of a ransom (Exod. 21:30), the ransom price being his own precious blood (I Cor. 6:20; 7:23; Rev. 5:9; cf. I Peter 1:18, 19). He became a curse—that is, "an accursed one" —for us.

It is, indeed, difficult to conceive of the majestic Christ as being *accursed*. What! Jesus anathema? In the face of I Cor. 12:3 how would one dare to say that? This becomes all the more a problem when we consider that we generally—and rightly—associate the curse with *sin*, and Christ had no sin (Isa. 53:9; John 8:46; II Cor. 5:21; I Peter 2:22). The only solution is the one supplied by the beautiful words of Isa. 53:6: "Jehovah laid on him the iniquity of us all"; cf. also verses 10-12. Christ's curse-bearing, then, was vicarious: "Him who knew no sin he made to be sin for our sake, in order that in him we might become the righteousness of God" (II Cor. 5:21). This eminently scriptural truth of Christ's substitutionary atonement is being denied by ever so many people. It has been called "butchershop theology." Nevertheless, not only is it taught here in Gal. 3:13 in unmistakable language[97] but it is the doctrine of Scripture throughout (Exod. 12:13; Lev. 1:4; 16:20-22; 17:11; Ps. 40:6, 7; 49:7, 8; Isa. 53; Zech. 13:1; Matt. 20:28; 26:27, 28; Mark 10:45; Luke 22:14-23; John 1:29; 10:11, 14; Acts 20:28; Rom. 3:24, 25; 8:3, 4; I Cor. 6:20; 7:23; II Cor. 5:18-21; Gal. 1:4; 2:20; Eph. 1:7; 2:16; Col. 1:19-23; Heb. 9:22, 28; I Peter 1:18, 19; 2:24; 3:18; I John 1:7; 2:2; 4:10; Rev. 5:9; 7:14).

In support of the idea that Christ became a curse for us Paul appeals to Deut. 21:23: **for it is written, "Cursed is everyone who is hanging on a tree."** In its Old Testament context, however, that passage does not refer to death by crucifixion, which was not known among the Israelites as a mode of

---

96 The verb is ἐξηγόρασεν. In the New Testament, besides its occurrence here and in 4:5, it is found only in Eph. 5:16 and Col. 4:5. But other verbs express the same or a very similar idea. See N.T.C. on Eph. 1:7 and on Col. 1:14.

97 The idea of substitution, however, can hardly be derived solely from the preposition ὑπέρ. To say that in this passage ὑπέρ = ἀντί is precarious and wholly unnecessary. Entirely aside from the meaning of ὑπέρ the passage itself clearly teaches *a.* that we were under the law's curse; *b.* that we are now no longer under the curse; and *c.* that the reason for this changed situation is this: Christ took our curse upon himself. The logical conclusion, surely, is that Christ's curse-bearing was substitutionary.

capital punishment. It refers, instead, to the custom according to which after a wrong-doer had been executed, his dead body was nailed to a post or tree. But if, in the sight of God, the hanging of a *dead* body was a curse, how much more would not the slow, painful, and shameful death by crucifixion of a *living* person be a curse, especially when that dying one was experiencing anguish beyond the power of description! See Matt. 27:46.

**14.** The curse having thus been borne and lifted off our shoulders, the blessing can now flow forth: **in order that the blessing of Abraham might come to the Gentiles in Jesus Christ, in order that we might receive the promised Spirit through faith.** The two purpose clauses are co-ordinate. They cover the same ground, the second explaining the first. Among all the priceless gems sparkling in the crown of Abraham's blessing (the blessing he received) this surely was one of the most precious, namely, that through him—more precisely through his seed, the Messiah—a countless multitude of people was to be blessed. Through Christ and his Spirit (literally "the Spirit of promise," but this means "the promised Spirit," cf. Acts 1:4, 5; Eph. 1:13) the river of grace (cf. Ezek. 47:3-5; Ps. 46:4; Rev. 22:1, 2), full, flowing, freshening, fructifying, and free, would continue on and on, blessing first the Jews but subsequently men of every race, Gentiles as well as Jews. And to receive this blessing, namely, the realization of the promise, "I will be your God," all that is necessary is *faith,* confidence in Christ Crucified, for it is at Calvary that the fires of God's wrath have spent all their fury, and believers of every tribe and tongue and people and nation are therefore perfectly safe!

# Chapter 3

Verses 15-29

Theme: *The Gospel of Justification by Faith apart from Law-works Defended against Its Detractors*

II. *Its Vindication: both Scripture—i.e., the Old Testament—and life (experience, past history) bear testimony to its truth*

C. This promise or convenant is superior to the law, for the latter reached us through mediation, the former came directly from God, and is still in force. The law, which came later, far from annulling the promise, serves it, by revealing our sinfulness and leading us to Christ. All who belong to Christ are Abraham's seed, heirs according to promise.

15 Brothers, I speak from a human standpoint: even a human testament,
once ratified, no one sets aside or amplifies. 16 Now to Abraham were the promises
spoken, and to his seed. He does not say, "And to the seeds," as (referring) to
many, but as (referring) to one, "And to your seed," which is Christ. 17 Now
this is what I mean: a covenant that has been ratified by God, the law, which came
into existence four hundred thirty years afterward, does not annul so as to make
the promise ineffective. 18 For if the inheritance (is) due to law, it (is) no longer
due to promise; but to Abraham it was through a promise that God graciously
granted it.

19 Why then the law? By reason of the transgressions it was added, until
the seed should come to whom the promise had been made, having been ordained
through angels by the agency of an intermediary. 20 Now the intermediary does
not represent (just) one party, but God is one.

21 (Is) the law then contrary to the promises of God? By no means. For
if a law had been given that was able to impart life, then indeed righteousness
would have come by law. 22 But Scripture has locked up the whole world under (the
power of) sin, in order that as a result of faith in Jesus Christ the promise might be
given to those who believe.

23 Now before this faith came, we were kept in custody under law, being
locked up with a view to the faith that was to be revealed. 24 So the law became
our custodian (to conduct us) to Christ, that by faith we might be justified. 25 But
now that this faith has come we are no longer under a custodian.

26 For y o u are all sons of God, through faith, in Christ Jesus. 27 For
as many of y o u as were baptized into (union with) Christ have put on Christ.
28 There can be neither Jew nor Greek; there can be neither slave nor freeman;
there can be no male and female; for y o u are all one in Christ Jesus. 29 And if
y o u belong to Christ, then y o u are Abraham's seed, heirs according to promise.

3:15-29

## C. *The superiority of the promise over the law*

The promise is superior to the law because it was *earlier.* Moreover, being in the nature of a testament, already ratified and in force, this promise or covenant could not be set aside by the law which came so much later (verses 15-18). Besides, the promise came to Abraham *directly;* the law was given to Israel *indirectly,* by mediation (verses 19, 20). For both of these reasons the promise is superior to the law. The Galatians should remember this and repent of their error of listening to the Judaizers who exalt the law above the promise.

**15.** Paul writes: **Brothers, I speak from a human standpoint.** He is taking his illustration from human life so that the Galatians may understand all the better that those to whom they have been lending a listening ear are false guides. Jesus also often made use of earthly stories (parables) to illustrate heavenly realities. Note that Paul calls the Galatians "brothers." This shows that when he exclaimed "O foolish Galatians" he was scolding them as a father or mother rebukes an erring son who is the object of tender love (cf. 4:19, 20). Continued: **even a human testament, once ratified, no one sets aside or amplifies.** It is a matter of common knowledge that among men a last will or testament, legally ratified, cannot be nullified. Nor can it be amplified: not a single codicil can be added to it. Then would not this be true all the more with respect to the covenant-promise which the immutable Jehovah made to Abraham and his seed? Was not this covenant in the nature of a testament?[98] Was it not re-affirmed to Isaac, Jacob, etc.? Did it not begin to go into effect immediately, namely, when "Abraham believed God, and it was reckoned to him for righteousness"? Surely, when God's will or testament has been thus decreed and ratified it cannot be set aside or changed. This logical deduction, already implied here in verse 15, is going to be clearly expressed in verse 17. However, the inviolability and immutability of God's promise will become all the more evident when it is understood first of all that, in the final analysis, it is a promise that concerns not physical Israel but Christ together with those who are "in him," for all the promises of God find their Yes in him (II Cor. 1:20; cf. Eph. 1:3). If this be understood it will be seen that the words which now follow are not really a parenthesis but part of the argument: **16. Now to Abraham were the promises spoken, and to his seed. He does not say, "And to the seeds," as (referring) to many, but as (referring) to one, "And to your seed," which is Christ.** Is this argument a bit of rabbinical casuistry, ingenious perhaps but unconvincing? Does not Paul know that even in Hebrew the word *seed* is a collective noun, so that no plural is needed to indicate more than one? See Gen. 15:5; 16:10; 22:17; 46:6; II Kings 11:1; II Chron. 20:7; Mal. 2:15; etc.[99] And as to the Greek word for *seed,* namely, *sperma,* does the apostle not realize that this word also is a collective noun (Matt. 22:24; Rom. 4:18; Acts 7:6; II Cor. 11:22), so that *spermata* (seeds) would have been unnecessary in any case? Shall we say then that in arguing against rabbinical adversaries Paul was using rabbinical methods that belonged to the exegesis of that happily bygone day and age? How can Paul say that the singular *seed* indicates one person, namely, Christ, when in Gal.

[98] The LXX translators used the word διαθήκη to render the Hebrew *bᵉrīth*. It appears thus nearly three hundred times. The New Testament also uses διαθήκη rather than συνθήκη, probably because the former stresses the one-sided character of God's disposition with respect to salvation for man and all that this implies. In Heb. 9:16, 17 and also here in Gal. 3:15 the context favors the rendering *testament.* Elsewhere the translation *covenant* is probably the best.

[99] Biblical Hebrew does not use the plural of *zera'* (see I Sam. 8:15) in referring to one's *descendants;* and even the Greek σπέρματα though occurring in classical literature, is elsewhere not plentiful (LXX Dan. 11:31; IV Macc. 18:1).

3:29 he himself uses that very word *in the singular* as a collective noun which refers to all believers? Besides, did he not realize that the seed promised to Abraham would be "as the stars in multitude" (Gen. 15:5; 22:17)?

As I see it, the answer is as follows:

(1) It is not true that the Hebrew word for *seed* always refers to more than one person. In Gen. 4:25 it refers to Seth, to him *alone;* in 21:13 to Ishmael; in I Sam. 1:11 to Samuel; in II Sam. 7:12 to Solomon as a type of Christ; so also in I Chron. 17:11. And obviously—see the context in each case—the Greek equivalent *sperma* has a singular reference not only here in Gal. 3:16 but also in 3:19; Acts 3:25; Rom. 9:7, 8; and Heb. 11:18.

(2) It should be readily admitted that Paul knew that both the Hebrew and the Greek word for *seed* (singular) often refer to more than one person. He knew that Abraham's seed would be as the stars in multitude. However, in keeping with the point which he is driving home, namely, that God promised salvation not to Abraham's physical descendants but to true believers, to them *all* (whether Jew or Gentile) and to them *alone,* he is saying that this great blessing is concentrated in *one* person, namely, Christ. It is in him, in him *alone,* that all these multitudes of believing Jews and Gentiles are blessed. It is in this sense that *seed* is singular, definitely not plural. It is true that the physical descendants of Abraham inherited the physical land of Canaan, according to God's promise (Gen. 12:7; 13:15; 15:18; 17:8; 24:7), but even Abraham already knew that there was more to this promise than appeared on the surface. The promised country on earth was the type of "the better country," the heavenly, reserved for believers in the Lord Jesus Christ, for them *all* and for them *alone,* as is beautifully stated in Heb. 11:8-16. Now the one and only heir of that "country" is Christ, for he is the Son by nature. It is by his grace that believers, as children by adoption, are joint-heirs with him (Rom. 8:17). And as for the basic promise, expressed from the beginning in spiritual terms, the promise according to which God assures Abraham that he will be his God and that in Abraham's seed all the nations of the earth will be blessed (17:7; 22:18), is it not very obvious that this promise also, in its fulfilment, was centered exclusively in *one* person, namely, Christ? The many are blessed in the One!

(3) In promising these rich spiritual blessings God had from the very beginning turned Abraham's attention away from the plural to the singular, from *seeds to seed:* "As for Ishmael, I have heard you . . . but I will establish my covenant with Isaac. . . . In Isaac shall your seed be called" (Gen. 17:20, 21; 21:12; cf. Rom. 9:7). Similarly, at a later time God made it very clear to Isaac and Rebekah that not in the line of Esau but in that of Jacob the promise would be continued (Gen. 25:23; cf. 27:27-29). Accordingly, Paul's distinction here in Gal. 3:16 between *seeds* and *seed* is based on the words which God himself addressed to the patriarchs.

(4) It appears to be clearly implied in such passages as John 8:56; Heb. 11:13, 17-19 that Abraham understood that Isaac would not himself be the Hope of mankind. He knew that Isaac's birth would pave the way for the coming of the real Messiah, the genuine *seed,* the *One* through whom God would bless all the nations. He was aware of the fact that the promised blessings would be concentrated in this one great person. At the time of Christ's birth even the highest court in Israel, the Sanhedrin, interpreted the prophecy of Micah 5:2 *personally,* that is, as referring to the birth of one definite person, Christ (Matt. 2:4-6). Is not the personal interpretation of Isa. 53—"Surely he has borne our griefs and carried our sorrows. . . . He was wounded for our transgressions, he was bruised for our iniquities," etc.—better by far than the exclusively *nationalistic*? Were not Isaiah and Micah contemporaries? And can we not go back beyond these two prophets, and their Messianic utterances, to II Sam. 7:12, 13? Does a reference to Solomon *exhaust* the meaning of the words, "I will establish the throne of his kingdom forever"? Does not also that promise refer to one exalted person, one greater by far than Solomon? Does not the same thing apply to Gen. 49:10? And does not this series of promises, everyone of which refers ultimately to one definite person, a person who had not yet arrived but was eagerly awaited, finally point back to Gen. 3:15, which concerns *the seed of the woman,* the very culmination of God's promise not only to Adam but also to Abraham?

The words which, according to Gen. 3:15, God addressed to the serpent —that is, to Satan—were as follows: "And I will put enmity between you and the woman, and between your seed and her seed; he shall bruise your head, and you shall bruise his heel." Is it not probable that Abraham knew this prophecy? It refers to the woman's *seed,* and here, too, the primary reference would appear to be to *one* person, though a further collective reference is not thereby ruled out. Dr. G. Ch. Aalders makes the following comment (my translation from the Dutch): "There is more here than merely this, that man will gain the victory over the serpent. . . . In that serpent a definite personality is being addressed. . . . And if the enemy whose discomfiture is here announced must be a definite personality, then would it even be possible that the One who conquers him could be other than also a definite personality? Even the contrast *head* and *heel* suggests that the struggle will finally be fought between two contestants. Also the Hebrew demonstrative pronoun [*that one* or *he*] strongly suggests that the conqueror is to be regarded as one person." Having pointed out that this protevangelium does not exclude the reference to a collective interpretation of the concepts "your seed" and "her seed," Aalders continues: "But in the end the figure of the Mediator stands in the foreground, and this so much so that in the words in which the final struggle is described there is definite mention of only one person, who is indicated by this seed of the woman.

The real struggle is won by no one else than by our Lord Jesus Christ" (*Korte Verklaring, Genesis,* Vol. I, pp. 136–138).

As mentioned earlier, Abraham probably knew this prophecy. But more important is the fact that the Holy Spirit, who inspired Galatians as well as Genesis, knew what content he was pouring into Gen. 3:15; 13:15; 17:7, 8; 22:18; 24:7, as well as into Gal. 3:16. And is it not significant that in the echo of Gen. 3:15 which we have in Rev. 12:1-6 the struggle is again *primarily* between the two personal antagonists: Christ and Satan? To be sure, from this struggle "the woman" is not excluded (verses 6, 13); yet the central figure, the One who really conquers, is *Christ.*

Accordingly, Paul's intention in writing, "He does not say, 'And to the seeds,' as (referring) to many, but as (referring) to one, 'And to your seed,' which is Christ," is to show *a.* that God's promise to Abraham, in its richest, spiritual meaning, was to be fulfilled in connection with one—and not more than one—definite person, Christ, the true seed; *b.* that all those—and only those—who are "in him" are saved; *c.* that had the case been otherwise, that is, had the promised blessings been dispersed indiscriminately among an indefinite aggregate of individuals, such plurality would have been definitely indicated; and *d.* that being thus concentrated unchangeably in the one seed, Christ, nothing, not even the law, is able to nullify this promise, a truth to which the apostle gives further expression by continuing: **17. Now this is what I mean: a covenant that has been ratified by God, the law, which came into existence four hundred thirty years afterward, does not annul so as to make the promise ineffective.** "Even a human testament, once ratified, no one sets aside or amplifies" (verse 15); hence, this holds all the more with respect to a *testament* or *covenant* (same word in the original) ordained and ratified by God. Between the giving of the promise and the promulgation of the law at Sinai there had been an interval of "four hundred thirty" (Exod. 12:40) or, in round figures, "four hundred" years (Gen. 15:13; Acts 7:6). Surely a covenant that had been in effect for so long a time, that partook of the nature of a testament, and had been established by the unchangeable Jehovah, whose word never fails, could not be annulled by the law!

With reference to these "four hundred thirty years" there is much difference of opinion. The question has been asked: Was there not an interval of two hundred fifteen years between Abraham's call and Jacob's "descent" into Egypt (Gen. 12:4; 21:5; 25:26; 47:9)? These two hundred fifteen years plus the four hundred thirty years in Egypt (Exod. 12:40) add up to six hundred forty-five years from Abraham's call to the exodus, and the same number of years (plus a few months, Exod. 19:1) to the giving of the law (Exod. 20). If the *repetition* of the promise of Gen. 12:1-3 in Abraham's later years, with specific mention of *the seed* (Gen. 13:15; 15:5, 18; 21:12; 22:15 ff.; 24:7), be taken as the beginning of the interval between the promise and the law, some years could be subtracted from the two hundred fifteen and from the total of six hundred forty-five, but even then the question would remain: How can Paul say that the law came into existence four hundred thirty years after the covenant-promise? Was not the intervening period considerably longer? Among the answers that have been suggested are the following:

(1) Paul errs, having been misled by the Greek Bible (LXX) which in Exod. 12:40 gives a total of four hundred thirty (or, according to another text, 435) years as the duration of the sojourn of the Israelites in Canaan *and* in Egypt (literally, "in Egypt-land and in Canaan-land").

(2) The period from the giving of the promise to Abraham, as recorded in Gen. 12, to the giving of the law at Sinai, actually covered only four hundred thirty years, as is clear from such passages as Gen. 15:16; Exod. 6:15-19 [Hebrew text: verses 16-20]; and Num. 26:57-59. Of this entire period two hundred fifteen years belong to the stay in Canaan, two hundred fifteen to the sojourn in Egypt.

I cannot accept either of these theories. The round figure "four hundred years," and the more exact figure "four hundred thirty years," for the sojourn *in Egypt* are too definitely established in Scripture as an indication of the time that the Israelites spent there to be so easily dismissed (Gen. 15:13; Acts 7:6; and Exod. 12:40 Hebrew text). Paul, thoroughly at home in the Old Testament, knew this. Besides, would not two hundred fifteen years have been too short a period for "three score and ten" people at the outset (Gen. 46:27) to grow into a nation so great that at the time of the exodus it had produced "about six hundred thousand men on foot (Exod. 12:37) besides the women and children? [100]

(3) We have here a case of "intentional understatement" made by Paul so that the Galatians may say: "Paul is certainly not exaggerating, for when the law finally came into existence the covenant had been in force much longer than four hundred thirty years, hence could certainly not be annulled."

As I see it, the best answer is the following:

(4) The covenant which God made with Abraham was repeated and confirmed in identical language in the promise addressed to Isaac and to Jacob. Compare, for example, Gen. 22:18 (to Abraham), 26:4 (to Isaac), and 28:14 (to Jacob), in each of which are found the words: "And in your

---

[100] As to the small number of "generations" mentioned or implied in Gen. 15:16; Exod. 6:15-19; and Num. 26:57-59, it is a well-known fact that the ancients counted generations differently than we do today: for one reason or another they would often skip certain ancestors in their count. In 15:16 one generation may represent one century. As to skipping generations, compare Matt. 1:8 with II Kings 8:25; 12:1, 2; 15:1. Therefore no solid argument as to the length of Israel's stay in Egypt can be based on such passages.

seed shall all the nations (in 28:14: "families") of the earth be blessed." "It may not be unreasonable to suppose that it was from such a time, at which the promise was confirmed (to Jacob) that Paul is measuring the interval which extends to the giving of the law at Sinai" (C. R. Erdman, *op. cit.,* p. 69). This, as I see it, best accounts for the figure "four hundred thirty years afterward."

The reasonable character of this explanation is evident from the fact that Scripture itself definitely points in this direction, for again and again it mentions Abraham, Isaac, and Jacob in one breath. Not only this, but in nearly every case when this occurs *it is in connection with the divine promise that the three patriarchs are grouped together as if they were one* (Gen. 28:13; 32:9; 48:16; 50:24; Exod. 3:16; 6:3; 32:13; Deut. 1:8; 9:5, 27; 29:13; 30:20; I Chron. 29:18; Matt. 22:32; Mark 12:26; Acts 3:13; 7:32).

**18.** It has been established, therefore, that justification, hence salvation in all its fulness, the entire "inheritance," is the result of God's promise, a covenant-promise that could not have been abrogated by Sinai's law, which did not enter into the picture until much later. Salvation, then, is not the result of law or law-observance. Neither is it possible to combine the two, as if *law* and *promise,* merit and grace, were twin sources of eternal bliss for God's children. Says Paul: **For if the inheritance (is) due to law, it (is) no longer due to promise; but to Abraham it was through a promise that God graciously granted it.** The Galatians will have to make up their minds once for all. They will have to choose between God's way and man's way of being saved. They must fully return to the position of faith in God and in his promise. In this connection there are especially four words that deserve emphasis, all of them underscoring the same idea, namely, that salvation is God's gift, not man's achievement:

(1) It is the result of God's *covenant,* and, as shown earlier, this covenant is of the nature of a *testament,* a sovereign *grant* (verses 15, 17). It is not a *contract* or *compact* reached after lengthy bargaining, bickering, and wrangling. It was God who established this covenant. It was he who stipulated the manner in which it would attain its purpose for man, namely, through faith. It is even God who grants this faith. He grants what he demands (Eph. 2:8).

(2) The main feature of this covenant is therefore God's *promise,* his solemn *assurance:* "I am (will be) your God," "In your seed I will bless you," "I will give you the land" (ultimately "the better land, Canaan above," as has been indicated).

(3) God's covenant with Abraham was therefore a "covenant *of grace.*" "To Abraham it was through a promise that God *graciously* granted it." Human merit has nothing to do with it. In fact, God's gift would be deprived of its gracious character if it were afterward made to depend on strict compliance with law.

(4) The promised salvation is an *inheritance*. Paul says, "If *the inheritance* (is) due to law, it (is) no longer due to promise." An inheritance is freely bestowed. It is a gift; hence, is not bought with money, nor earned by the sweat of human toil, nor won by conquest. Moreover, it is duly acquired (by right rooted in grace), and inalienable (cf. I Kings 21:3). As an inheritance it is future glory of which, however, the first instalment has even now become our possession (Eph. 1:13, 14).

Now it is certainly true that in the historical realization of the divine arrangement for man's salvation action proceeds from two parties: God and man. *God* makes the promise and points out the way in which it is to be fulfilled, namely, through faith (Gen. 15:1, 4, 5; 17:7; etc.). *Abraham* believes (Gen. 15:6; 17:1b, 9; etc.). God does not believe for him. When the Philippian jailer asked Paul and Silas, "Men, what must I do to be saved?" Paul did not answer, "Nothing at all, just wait until it pleases God to come and save you." What he did say was this, "Believe in the Lord Jesus, and you will be saved, you and your household" (Acts 16:30, 31). Nevertheless, this two-sidedness is completely subsidiary to the one-sided character of the covenant, as has already been indicated. If strict compliance with the demands of the law could have saved anyone, Paul certainly would have entered heaven by that gateway (Phil. 3:1-6). But the Lord had revealed to him the utter impossibility of success in this direction. No wandering sheep ever returns to the fold unless the Master finds him and brings him home.

**19.** This, however, raises a question: **Why then the law?** If the law given at Sinai was unable to impart righteousness, then what possible good could it do? Of what use was it? Perhaps the opponents had already asked that question. If not, they could be expected to ask it. Paul answers: **By reason of**[101] **the transgressions it was added**; that is, it was given to man in addition to the promise in order to bring about within his heart and mind an awakened sense of guilt. A vague awareness of the fact that all is not right with him will not drive him to the Savior. Only when he realizes that his sins are transgressions of the law of that God who is also his Judge and whose holiness cannot brook such *digressions,* such constant *stepping aside* from the appointed path, will he, when this knowledge is applied to his heart by the Holy Spirit, cry out for deliverance. "Where there is no law, there is no transgression," no stepping aside from the law (Rom. 4:15). "The law came in besides, that *the trespass*—the act of *falling away from* the proper course, as indicated by the law—might abound" (Rom. 5:20).

[101] Here χάριν probably means "by reason of," cf. Eph. 3:1; I John 3:12. The statement must be explained, as always, in the light of the context; see especially verse 24. This refutes the interpretation, favored by some, that Paul here views the law as a means of *checking* or *restraining* transgressions.

This—"that the trespass might abound"—has been interpreted to mean that the law actually makes a person a more determined wrong-doer than he ever was before. The more he is forbidden to steal, the more he will steal. Illustration: Boys pass an apple orchard a hundred times without attempting to pick one from the tree's overhanging branches. But let a sign be put up: "Those who steal apples will be prosecuted," and see if the pockets of these boys do not begin to bulge with apples!—Nevertheless, that is probably not the meaning here, but rather this: "Through the commandment sin becomes exceedingly sinful." It is *knowledge* of sin that comes through law (Rom. 3:20; 7:7, 13). The law acts as a magnifying glass. That device does not actually increase the number of dirty spots that defile a garment, but makes them stand out more clearly and reveals many more of them than one is able to see with the naked eye. "By reason of the transgressions," therefore, the law was added, so that when that law demands nothing less than perfect love for God and the neighbor, and the man sees clearly that there is very little of this love in his heart, he may by means of this realization be led to the Savior. This interpretation brings the present passage into harmony with another one taken from this very chapter (see on 3:24). It also blends with the words which immediately follow, namely, **until the seed should come to whom the promise had been made.** When by God's grace the sinner has learned to see himself in the light of the law as being damnable in himself, he yearns for Christ, the true seed, and for redemption in and through him. To this *seed* the blessing and the right and power to impart it had been promised. Therefore, while the law was given through Moses, grace and truth came through Jesus Christ (John 1:17), the One who entered the world in order to minister, and to give himself a ransom for many (Matt. 20:28; Mark 10:45). There was nothing wrong with the law. It had been given by God through Moses. But there was one thing which the law was unable to do: it was unable to pardon transgressors. It could point out but could not remove their sins. That mighty work in which God's justice and his love embrace each other was reserved for the Mediator.

With respect to the law Paul adds: **having been ordained through angels.** The law of Sinai was *ordained* or authoritatively decreed. By whom was it thus ordained? Though this is not stated here, it is clear from such passages as Rom. 7:22, 25; 8:7, that the law's Author was God himself. It was he who decreed it. "And God spoke all these words saying, I am Jehovah your God," etc. (Exod. 20:1 ff.).

Now a king's decree is issued, published, or promulgated *through* his servants. Moreover, these messengers do not always convey the king's order directly to the public at large. At times the sequence of communication is as follows: king, messenger, provincial governor, citizenry. Something of this nature must have happened also in connection with the giving of the law. We cannot be more precise. Where Scripture is silent, it is not proper for us to try to break this reserve. Did the holy angels communicate God's commands to Moses? Is that the meaning of Heb. 2:2: "the word spoken through angels"? Stephen also held that the angels were active in the giving of the law at Sinai (Acts 7:53). This belief may perhaps be traced back to Deut. 33:2, but the meaning of that passage, whether read according to the Hebrew text or according to the Septuagint, is not entirely clear. Farther than this we cannot go.[102] All kinds of speculations have been built up around the theme of angelic activity in connection with the giving of the law. It has been said, for example, that the angels had made the law their hobby, which they intended to defend against every encroachment. With the coming of Christ, so continues this theory, these angels became as it were, competitors of Christ, and tried to maintain the law over against the doctrine of salvation by grace. In the present passage, then, and in Gal. 4:3, 9, Paul is supposedly warning the Galatians against putting themselves in bondage again to these angels. However, the idea that Paul regarded the keeping of the law to be a bondage to angels is devoid of every shred of evidence. Paul never makes the angels responsible in any way for the idea of salvation through law-works. Here in Gal. 3:19 he clearly represents the angels as adding luster to the law. The point which the apostle is trying to drive home is of an entirely different nature, as will become clear in a moment. See also on 4:3, 9.

Whatever function the angels may have performed in connection with the giving of the law, the real intermediary between God and the people was Moses. The law was ordained through angels **by the agency**—literally, "in (the) hand"—**of an intermediary.** This would seem to be a clear echo of Deut. 5:5, where Moses says, "I stood between Jehovah and y o u at that time." The lesson, then, which Paul is teaching the Galatians is clearly this: the law given at Sinai, though ordained by God through his holy angels by the agency of Moses, and though, accordingly, holy, righteous, and good (Rom. 7:12; cf. 2:18; 8:7; 9:4), is inferior to the promise, for while *the law came indirectly from God to his people, the promise was made to Abraham (and thus to all believers) directly by God himself.* When a ruler—whether president, king, or queen—wishes to communicate a message to his people, there are all kinds of indirect avenues by means of which he is able to do this, but when the message is of supreme importance, he will unburden his very heart by addressing his people directly, today by means of radio or television. Thus also, the gospel of salvation by grace alone is so precious

[102] For example, to identify these angels with "the Angel" mentioned in Acts 7:38 or with "the Angel of Jehovah" of the Old Testament (Gen. 22:11; 48:16; etc.) is unwarranted. That God's holy angels are, in a sense, "ambassadors" is true, though also the passage in Josephus (*Antiquities* XV.v.iii) where this comparison is drawn, fails to shed light on the exact nature of the function of the angels at Sinai.

to the heart of the God to whom the impartation of this salvation meant nothing less than the agonizing death of his only Son, that he appeals to each of us directly and personally, saying, "My son—my daughter—give me your heart" (Prov. 23:26).

**20.** Moses, to be sure, was a great man. But God is greater by far. The Galatians must not permit the Judaizers to exalt Moses above God. Says Paul: **Now the intermediary does not represent (just) one party**—literally, "Now the intermediary is not of one"—**but God is one.** Instead of vexing the reader with the four hundred thirty different interpretations to which this passage has given rise, I shall immediately state the one which appears to me to be the most consistent with the context. It is this: Though a human intermediary may be ever so important, he is, after all, only a third party acting between two other parties. Moses served as a human link between God and the people. Such an intermediary lacks independent authority. God, however, is *One*. When he made his promise to Abraham—and through him to *all* believers, whether Jew or Gentile (Rom. 3:30!)—he did this on his own sovereign account, directly, personally. He was speaking from the heart to the heart.

**21.** Continued: **(Is) the law then contrary to the promises of God?** Paul has indicated that the inheritance was due to promise, not to law, and that law is, accordingly, inferior to promise. Must the conclusion then be drawn that the law is an enemy of the promis*es,* that is, of the oft-repeated, rich and varied promise of God? See on verse 16. Paul answers: **By no means** (literally, "Let it not be") or "That never," "Certainly not," "Perish the very thought." Continued: **For if a law had been given that was able to impart life, then indeed righteousness would have come by law.**[103] Only then when law and promise (works and grace) are both regarded as means whereby the sinner obtains salvation, can they be viewed as opponents. But as soon as it is understood that the two differ in their objectives—*the law* aiming to lead the sinner to Christ and his gracious promise; *the promise* "in Christ" aiming to save him—it becomes clear that they cannot be viewed as being in conflict with each other. By reason of human perversity the law is unable to deliver a man from the sentence of condemnation and to impart to him the blessing of justification (Rom. 8:2, 3). The law can never make a man spiritually alive, cannot regenerate him, or impart faith to him whereby he would be enabled to accept the righteousness of God in Christ. If a law had been given that could have done that, then, of course, righteousness would have come by law, but the law is not a vivifying power. It takes God's grace to function in that capacity. Phrasing it differently, it

[103] This is a *contrary to fact* or *second class conditional sentence,* relating to past time: εἰ with aor. indic. passive in the protasis, and ἄν with a past indicative in the apodosis. In such sentences ἦν may be regarded as aorist *in meaning.*

takes the promise of God, savingly applied to the heart by the Holy Spirit, to raise the dead to life (II Cor. 3:6, 17). As to the law, it is useful indeed. It accomplishes its very design by showing what it cannot accomplish! It causes the sinner to say, "Wretched man that I am! Who shall deliver me out of the body of this death?" Grace, already operative *in principle* when the question was asked, makes possible the answer, "I thank God through Jesus Christ our Lord" (Rom. 7:24, 25). Another way of expressing this truth is found in verse **22. But Scripture has locked up the whole world under (the power of) sin.** Did the law ever justify anyone? Did it ever set anyone free? "On the contrary," says Paul, "Scripture, in which the law plays such a prominent role, has locked up," that is, has shut in from every side without possibility of escape, "the whole world[104] under (the power of) sin." The words, "Scripture has locked up, etc." probably indicate that Scripture, that is, the Old Testament, has authoritatively declared that the whole world is under the power of sin; in other words, that sin is the jail-keeper who holds all men under the sentence of condemnation. These men are as truly chained as are prisoners with iron bands around their legs, bands that are fastened to chains that are cemented into the walls of their cells. Such spiritual convicts are unable to break their fetters. On the contrary, every sin which they commit draws tighter their bonds, until at last they are completely crushed (John 8:34; Rom. 6:23a; I John 5:19).

That this is indeed the picture that is drawn in the Old Testament is clear from such passages as the following: Deut. 27:26, already discussed (see on Gal. 3:10); Ps. 130:3, "If thou, Jehovah, shouldest mark iniquities, O Lord, who could stand?"; Ps. 143:2, "In thy sight no man living is righteous"; Isa. 1:5, 6, "The whole head is sick, and the whole heart is faint. From the sole of the foot even to the head there is no soundness in it, but bruises and sores and raw wounds"; and Jer. 17:9, "The heart is deceitful above all things, and it is exceedingly corrupt; who can know it?" Add to this Gen. 6:11, 12; 8:21; Job 40:4; Dan. 9:4 ff.; Zech. 3:3; as well as all those Old Testament passages that are quoted or alluded to by Paul in Rom. 3:9-18. And these are but a few. Many more could easily be added.

But, with the help of the Holy Spirit, the prisoners' very consciousness of their galling bondage and of their total inability to burst their chains, causes them to yearn for a divine Deliverer and to shout for joy when they hear his approaching footsteps. All this was in God's plan. Therefore Paul continues: **in order that as a result of faith in Jesus Christ the promise might be given to those who believe.** Who will want to be delivered unless he knows that there is something from which he needs to be delivered? But once men know this, and this knowledge has been sanctified to their hearts, they

---

[104] The neut. τὰ πάντα can refer to persons, and the present context favors the meaning "all mankind."

will hail the Rescuer, and place their trust in him, that is, in Jesus Christ, the Anointed Savior, the One whose very purpose *was* and *is* to save the lost (Matt. 1:21; 9:12, 13; Luke 19:10; I Tim. 1:15). This wonderful Redeemer does something for sinners that the law was not able to do. He sets the prisoners free, delivering them from the curse by taking it upon himself, and speaks peace to their hearts. In a word, he gives *the promise* to those who were perishing. The term "promise," as used here, must be interpreted in its fullest, richest sense, for the wretched ones not only receive a verbal promise, cheering tidings—"Be not afraid," "Only believe and all will be well"—but also the *fulfilment* of this promise; hence, justification by faith, salvation full and free, as a gift to all those who embrace Jesus Christ by means of simple trust apart from the works of the law.

**23.** Looking back from the vantage ground of faith in Jesus Christ, both Jew and Gentile had to admit that bondage to law had served the purpose of preparing them for this wonderful gospel of justification by faith alone, a thought which Paul expresses as follows: **Now before this[105] faith came, we were kept in custody under law, being locked up with a view to the faith that was to be revealed.** Note the slight transition from "locked up the whole world *under sin*" (verse 22) to "kept in custody *under law,* being locked up" (verse 23). The difference is not essential. If *sin* is the jail-keeper, then so is *the law,* for sin derives its power from the law (I Cor. 15:56). It is through the commandment that sin becomes exceedingly sinful (Rom. 7:13; see also 7:9 and 4:15).

When Paul says, "Before this faith came," he is not denying what he had before so emphatically affirmed, namely, that even during the old dispensation people were saved *by faith* (Gal. 3:6, 11, 17, 18). He is speaking now of faith in the incarnate Christ, the Deliverer already arrived.[106] Essentially there is no difference: the Object is still the same and the nature of the activity remains unchanged. The difference is this, that Abraham and all the other saints of the old dispensation looked *forward* to the coming Redeemer; Paul and his fellow-believers were able to look *back* to a Redeemer

---

[105] In connection with abstract nouns—faith, hope, love, etc.—the Greek (as also German, Dutch, and French) often uses the definite article where English would omit it. Thus the correct English rendering of the phrase "through the faith" of the original (verse 26) is "through faith." However, if the abstract quality has been mentioned in the immediately preceding context *and* the article's omission would lead to confusion, it is better to insert it—or the demonstrative "this" or "that"—in English. Hence, at the beginning of verse 23 I favor the rendering "this faith" (with Williams and N.E.B.), and toward the close of that verse "the faith" (with Williams), and again "this faith" in verse 25 (with Williams). On the use of the article in the original in such cases see Gram.N.T., especially pages 758 and 762.

[106] Some hold that "faith" must here be interpreted in the objective sense (religion, doctrine) as in 1:23. See also 6:10. However, the word obviously refers to the "faith in Jesus Christ" of the preceding verse, the subjective activity of believing in him.

who had already come into the flesh, had carried out his redemptive program on earth, and had returned to heaven, so that believers could now look *up* to him as the One who had been exalted to the Father's right hand, from which he was ruling the entire universe in the interest of the church.

Now *before* this faith in the Christ of history arrived, hence during the old dispensation, "we," says Paul, "were kept in custody" under law. God's *moral* law filled the hearts of the Jews with a sense of guilt and inadequacy. They were obliged to fulfil it, yet were unable to do so. Of course, even then there was a way of escape provided by the Lord himself, namely, trust in God's promise concerning the "seed," and thus salvation "without money and without price" (Gen. 3:15; 22:18; 49:10; II Sam. 7:13; Job 19:23-27; Ps. 40:6, 7; Isa. 1:18; 9:1, 2, 6; 40:1-5, 11; 53; 55:1, 6, 7; Jer. 23:6; Mic. 5:2; Zech. 13:1), but most of the Jews had failed to avail themselves of this glorious opportunity. They refused to grasp the hand that was extended to them, and instead began to look upon strict obedience to law as a means whereby they must try to obtain salvation *for* and *by* themselves. Not only the moral law must be kept, however, but also the *ceremonial.* The latter was interpreted and re-interpreted. It was "embellished" by the rabbis, augmented almost beyond recognition, until its observance had become an oppressive burden, a galling yoke, from which no mere man offered any way of escape. Because of their own stubbornness the law, in its most comprehensive sense, thus *held* the Jews *in strictest custody;* just as, for example, the governor under king Aretas *rigidly guarded* (same word in the original) the city of Damascus, in order, as he thought, to prevent any possibility that Paul might escape. The Jews, then, were *locked up,* shut in from every side (as in verse 22). But God's grand design was to be openly revealed, so that the stubbornness of men, for which they, they alone, were responsible, would lead to the open display of *his* mercy: "being locked up *with a view to* the faith that was to be revealed" in connection with the coming and work of the Redeemer and the outpouring of his Spirit.

As to the manner in which the strict custody of the law could be a means of leading a formerly self-righteous Pharisee to humble faith in Christ, note this autobiographical fragment, in which some years later Paul was going to describe himself as having been in his pre-conversion years "as to law a Pharisee, as to zeal persecuting the church, as to legal righteousness having become blameless." He was going to continue: "Nevertheless, such things as once were gains to me these have I counted loss for Christ. Yes, what is more, I certainly do count all things to be sheer loss because of the all-surpassing excellence of knowing Christ Jesus my Lord, for whom I suffered the loss of all things, and I am still counting them refuse, in order that I may gain Christ, and be found in him, not having a righteousness of my own, legal righteousness, but that (which is) through faith in Christ, the righteousness (which is) from God (and rests) on faith" (Phil. 3:5-9).

The question might be asked, "But in view of the fact that the Galatians, for the greater part, had been won for Christ from the *Gentile* world (Gal. 4:8-11), how can the given explanation, which depicts a change from legal righteousness to all-out surrender to Christ, suit the concrete situation with which the addressed confronted Paul? Are we not forgetting that the apostle was writing not to Jews but to those who were Gentiles by race and formerly also by religion?" The answer would be:

(1) It is clear that these Gentiles had of late been in very close contact with the Judaizers (1:6-9; 3:1, 2; 4:10, 17, 21-31; 6:13-15).

(2) Even before this, by means of the synagogue-service, which a considerable number of them had attended (Acts 13:16, 44, 45; 14:1), and also by means of daily contact with Jews, the Galatians had become acquainted with a somewhat adulterated version of the Jewish religion, a religion which, in its modified presentation, insisted on strict compliance with law *as the way to salvation.*

(3) Even apart from any contact with the Jews or with Judaizers, was not the attempt to reach life's fulfilment by purely human means (such as sacrifices to appease the gods, the infliction of self-torture) characteristic of paganism? In their "Do it yourself" philosophy of obtaining salvation, *all* Galatians, of whatever racial or religious origin, were basically equal. Therefore all needed this letter. And since this same sinful tendency, one that leads but to bankruptcy and despair, is a true description of every human heart as it is by nature, this epistle is ever up-to-date in the lesson which it teaches.

God's holy law daily confronts every man with a "must" which he is unable to fulfil and with the threat of punishment if he does not fulfil it. The clear revelation of God's love revealed in the birth, teaching, suffering, death, burial, resurrection, ascension, and coronation of Christ and in the outpouring of the Holy Spirit was necessary to bring about a mighty change on earth. Not that even then the bulk of the people accepted the proffered grace (John 1:5, 10, 11). But compared to the rivulet of grace during the old dispensation there was a mighty stream now. "The church in the wilderness" (Acts 7:38) was, without loss of identity as to essence, being replaced by the world-conquering church (Rev. 17:14; cf. 20:1-3; Luke 10:17, 18; John 12:31, 32). And the tension which had been generated by the discipline of the law had contributed its very significant share to the bringing about of this change. It had prepared the hearts of multitudes for the reception of Christ and his promise. Paul expresses this thought by means of a striking figure: **24. So the law became our custodian (to conduct us) to Christ, that by faith we might be justified.** In view of the explanation of verse 23 little need be added. The rendering "schoolmaster" (A.V.) is not a happy one. It is true that the original calls the law "our pedagogue," but that word did not then have the meaning which it has now in our language.[107] It cannot be denied that in the execution of his duties the ancient "pedagogue" might also impart some elementary and useful instruction on various matters, but that was not his primary function. In the figure here used the "pedagogue" is the man—generally a slave—in whose custody the slave-owner's boys were placed, in order that this trusted servant might conduct them to and from school, and might, in fact, watch over their conduct throughout the day. He was, accordingly, an *escort* or *attendant,* and also at the same time a *disciplinarian.* The discipline which he exercised was often of a severe character, so that those placed under his guardianship would yearn for the day of freedom. And, as has been shown (see the explanation of verses 19, 22, and 23), that was exactly the function which the law had performed. It had been of a preparatory and disciplinary nature, readying the hearts of those under its tutelage[108] for the eager acceptance of the gospel of justification (for which concept see on 2:15, 16) by faith in Christ. Continued: **25. But now that this faith has come we are no longer under a custodian.** The time arrives when the boy is no longer a mere child. The grim discipline of his earlier days is not necessary any more. The rod can be laid aside, the custodian given a different assignment. Some parents seem to forget that little children grow up, and that there comes a time when from the discipline of *outward precepts* they can advance to the free expression of *inner principles.* Similarly the Judaizers, who were upsetting the Galatians, were forgetting that the tutelage of the law could not continue forever. They were ignoring the fact that when Christ himself had arrived, and trust in him had been established, those who had embraced him by this true and living faith had attained to majority and freedom.

**26.** This new-found freedom in Christ has nothing to do with race or former religion. Hence, Paul's "we" (verse 25) easily changes into "y o u" (verse 26), as he continues: **For y o u are all sons of God, through faith, in Christ Jesus.**[109] In proof, therefore, of the fact that the Galatians, too, are no

[107] In German one might say that the law is not here described as our *Schulmeister* but rather as our *Zuchtmeister;* or in Dutch: not as our *schoolmeester* but rather as our *tuchtmeester.*

[108] The rendering "the law became our *tutor,*" favored by many, is entirely proper, provided the figure be understood in the sense of *the guardian of a boy or girl below the age of puberty or majority,* and not in the sense which today many immediately attach to it, namely, that of *private instructor.*

[109] Thus the order of the words as in the original is maintained (as in A.R.V.); and at the same time, by the use of commas, room is provided for the probability that the phrase "in Christ Jesus" must here be regarded as a modifier of the entire statement. Another way of arriving at the same result would be to shift the phrase "in Christ Jesus" from the end of the sentence to the beginning: "For in Christ Jesus y o u are all sons of God through faith" (cf. R.S.V.). Although it is certainly possible to regard the phrase in question as modifying only the concept *faith* (cf.

longer under a custodian (verse 25) Paul emphasizes that they are no longer immature children but "in Christ Jesus" mature sons, yes, "sons of God," with all the rights and privileges implied in that term, and that this new state and condition has come about "through faith."

**27.** Let no one deny that in vital union with Christ *all* believers, Gentiles as well as Jews, are immediately sons of God, true Christians. Let no one deceive the Galatians into thinking that in order to become Christians they must first become Jews. Says Paul: **For as many of y o u as were baptized into (union with) Christ have put on Christ.** The "in Christ" relationship, therefore, expressed in verse 26 and here repeated in slightly altered form, is all that matters. And that holds for anyone, for the words "as many as" here in verse 27 are as wide in scope as is "all" (that is, "all believers") in verse 26. It should not be any matter of controversy that "being baptized into (union with) Christ" means more than being baptized with water, for surely not all those who were the objects of the outward administration of this sacrament have actually "put on Christ." The apostle is speaking, therefore, not about the merely outward administration of baptism, as if some magical healing power adhered to it, but about *the sign and seal in conjunction with that which is signified and sealed.* All those, then, who by means of their baptism have truly laid aside, in principle, their garment of sin, and have truly been decked with the robe of Christ's righteousness, having thus been buried with him and raised with him, have put on Christ (cf. Rom. 6:3 ff.; 13:14; Col. 2:12, 13). In Christ they have risen to newness of life. They have become united with him in the sense that he is the Life of their life, the Light of their light, the Strength of their strength. And this, let it be stressed once again, is true of *them all,* regardless of outward differences, for the apostle continues: **28. There can be[110] neither Jew nor Greek; there can be neither slave nor freeman; there can be no male and female; for y o u are all one in Christ Jesus.** In Paul's day fraticidal class-distinctions were the order of the day, just as they are still in many quarters. See N.T.C. on Colossians and Philemon, pp. 151–154, where this same

---

A.V.: "For we are all children of God by faith in Christ Jesus," note absence of commas), the alternative manner of construing the sentence (with ἐν Χριστῷ Ἰησοῦ regarded as a modifier of the whole) receives support from verse 27, in which not Christ as the object of faith but as the One with whom believers have become united is indicated. The *oneness* of Christ and his own is, moreover, not only a repeatedly recurring Pauline theme but also a central thought in the immediate context (verse 27).

[110] Though οὐκ ἔνι = οὐκ ἔνεστιν is rendered variously, the translators agree that Christianity cannot tolerate any actions or decisions which because of race, social standing, or sex, would degrade certain individuals to the status of second-rate citizenship in the kingdom of heaven, or would even exclude them entirely from such citizenship. Thus, Moffatt and also Goodspeed translate: "There is no room for"; A.V. and R.S.V.: "There is neither"; N.E.B.: "There is no such thing as"; and Weymouth: "There cannot be."

subject is discussed in some detail in connection with Col. 3:11. For the present purpose it is necessary only to note that the Jews drew a sharp line of separation between themselves and the "swarms" or "hordes" (*"goyim"*) of outsiders, heathen nations in contrast with Israel. Often such heathen were simply called "dogs." Even proselytes to the Jewish religion were never fully "accepted." After all, they were not "children of Abraham." It seems that the Judaizers of Paul's day had not broken away from this feeling of disdain for non-Jews. Gentiles, too, were often guilty of similar snobbery. They looked down upon the Jews as much as the latter looked down upon them. And as to their attitude toward slaves, it cannot have been far removed from that of Aristotle, who called a slave "an animated implement," a mere breathing tool. And as to the distinction between male and female, even such a man of culture as Josephus, if the passage in his work *Against Apion* (II.xxiv) be genuine, declared, "The woman, so says the law, is inferior in all things to man." What Paul is saying, then, is that all such distinctions—be they racial-religious ("neither Jew nor Greek"), social ("neither slave nor freeman"), or sexual ("no male and female")—must be thoroughly and forever abandoned, since in Christ all are equal.

This does not mean that common sense must now be cast overboard. Because of different historical backgrounds, different vocational interests, different skills, different degrees of educational advancement, and different geographic locations, it may be in the interest of all concerned that at times "birds of a feather flock together." The Bible recognizes this right. It was not wrong for Bezalel and Oholiab to work in conjunction with other artisans of similar ability in the construction of the tabernacle (Exod. 36:1, 2, 8). Neither was it wrong, as such, for Demetrius, "the silversmith," to meet with other men of his trade (Acts 19:25). Scripture clearly justifies distinctions of this nature. It teaches not only the unity but also the diversity of all believers and, in a sense, of all men (Acts 17:26; I Cor. 7:20; 12; 16:2; Eph. 4:7). Are there not some people today who, in their mania for unity and equality, have left common sense and genuinely scriptural teaching far behind? Is it not absurd, for example, in the interest of "integration" to force into the fourth grade children, of whatever race, who cannot do fourth grade work? Would it not be foolish for ministers, with little knowledge of electricity, to try to crash a Convention of Electrical Engineers? Or for *men* to barge into a meeting of the Sewing Circle?

On the other hand, it certainly remains true that in God's holy sight all men are, indeed, equal, for "all have sinned, and fall short of the glory of God" (Rom. 3:23; cf. 2:11; 3:9-18; 5:12, 18). Also, "the same Lord is Lord of all, and is rich to all that call on him" (Rom. 10:12). For a Jew to confess himself to be a Christian, and then to refuse to eat with Christians from the Gentiles, or to regard himself as being in any way superior to them in moral worth, is an abomination to the Lord. Similarly today the church cannot tolerate hurtful distinctions. All believers are in a sense one person, one body "in Christ" (I Cor. 10:17; 12:12; Col. 3:15), for he who is the Son of David is also the Son of man; he who is "the seed of Abraham" is also "the seed of the woman." From God's side the Holy Spirit, and from man's side Spirit-imparted faith, link believers with Christ, and thereby also with one another.

**29.** Paul concludes this beautiful chapter as follows: **And if**[111] **y o u belong to Christ, then y o u are Abraham's seed, heirs according to promise.** The close connection with verses 27, 28, as well as with verses 6-9 and 16-18, is immediately apparent. It is unnecessary, therefore, to repeat what has already been said in the discussion of these passages. Clearly, the apostle once again stresses the fact that "belonging to the seed of Abraham is not determined by physical descent but by faith" (Ribberbos, *op. cit.,* p. 150). "In Christ" the wall of separation between Jew and Gentile no longer exists. Therefore, the Judaizers have no right to demand of the Gentiles anything else than that which they demand of the Jews, namely, true and living faith in the Lord Jesus Christ. Throughout the whole vast earth the Lord recognizes *one,* and *only one,* nation as his own, namely, the nation of believers (I Peter 2:9). These are Abraham's seed. These, too, are the *heirs* (for this concept see on 3:18) according to the promise which centers in Christ.

*Summary of Chapter 3*

Having shown that the gospel which he, Paul, proclaims is of divine origin and therefore victoriously independent, the apostle now indicates that both Scripture and experience bear testimony to its truth. He begins (verses 1-5) with a lesson from *experience.* Now experience is very important. The way in which God has led men in the past must be constantly recalled and applied to new situations (cf. Ps. 78:1 ff.). This the Galatians had neglected to do. So in verse 1 Paul asks them, "O foolish Galatians! Who has bewitched y o u, before whose very eyes Jesus was openly displayed as crucified?" And in verse 2 he continues, "This only would I learn from y o u: Was it by doing what (the) law demands that y o u received the Spirit, or was it by believing (the) gospel message?" In verse 5 he repeats the question of verse 2 in somewhat expanded form. In verse 3 he asks, "Are y o u so foolish? Having begun by the Spirit, now by fleshly means are y o u being made perfect?" They had begun by yielding to the direction of the Spirit, but they were now continuing by placing their trust in fleshly means: observance of days, months, seasons, and years (4:10), believing in the necessity of circumcision (5:2, 3; 6:12-15); in short: adherence to

---

[111] The εἰ δέ in this *simple* or *first class conditional sentence* does not suggest doubt, however. The meaning is that whoever is "of Christ" certainly also belongs to Abraham's seed. Throughout this epistle Paul regards the Galatians as Christians (3:15; 4:12, 19; 5:10), though grossly erring (3:1).

law as a means of obtaining salvation. And *this* was progress? Has all their past experience—the manner in which at their conversion they had been enriched with both special gifts and spiritual endowments—been in vain? Paul refuses to believe it, and by saying, "if (it be) really in vain," he "rouses them to the exercise of repentance" (John Calvin).

For the idea that justification—hence, salvation in all its fulness—is obtained by way of faith and not by reliance on law-works Paul now (verses 6-14) appeals to *Scripture.* He shows that from the very beginning of Israel's history—that is, already in the promise God gave to Abraham—the divinely appointed means of obtaining the blessing was faith, not works (Gen. 15:6). Hence, all those, and only those, who have faith as their guiding principle are the true sons of Abraham. Those, on the contrary, who rely on law-works are under a curse from which they cannot deliver themselves, for they cannot "continue in all the things that are written in the book of the law to do them" (Deut. 27:26). Therefore "by law no one is justified before God, for 'The righteous shall live by faith' " (Hab. 2:4). Leaning on law means depending on self. Exercising faith means resting on Christ. Considered as means of obtaining salvation these two do not mix. But penitent sinners do not need to despair, for Christ has redeemed them from the curse by taking it upon himself (Deut. 21:23), in order that thus "the blessing of Abraham might come to the Gentiles in Jesus Christ, in order that we might receive the promised Spirit through faith."

In the final paragraph (verses 15-29) Paul shows that this promise made to Abraham-Isaac-Jacob is superior to law, for two reasons: (1) Because the latter came much later, and was therefore unable to annul the earlier promise, just as even among men a last will or testament that has been legally confirmed and has gone into effect cannot be abrogated. Surely a promise that centered in Christ, the one and only seed, could not be withdrawn. Nevertheless, the law performed a useful function, namely, by serving as custodian to bring sinners to Christ, having aroused within them the sense of guilt and the yearning for salvation through him. (2) Because the law reached us through mediation (Moses), but the promise came *directly* from God, who, in establishing his covenant with Abraham, and thus with *all believers,* regardless of racial-religious, social, or sexual distinctions, did this on his own sovereign account, being filled with love. Nothing can ever remove God's love for all who belong to Christ. Nothing can deprive them of their inheritance, for "If you belong to Christ, then you are Abraham's seed, heirs according to promise."

# Chapter 4

Verses 1-11

Theme: *The Gospel of Justification by Faith apart from Law-works Defended against its Detractors*

II. *Its Vindication: both Scripture—i.e., the Old Testament—and life (experience, past history) bear testimony to its truth*

D. We used to be in bondage to ordinances, regulations. God sent forth his Son to redeem those who were in bondage, that we might receive the adoption as sons. And because you are sons God sent forth the Spirit of his Son into our hearts, crying, "Abba! Father!" Do you then wish to exchange your former bondage to heathenism for bondage to Judaism? I am afraid about you, lest somehow I have labored among you in vain.

# CHAPTER IV

## GALATIANS

4 1 What I mean is this, that as long as the heir is a child he differs in no
respect from a slave though he is owner of all, 2 but is under guardians and
stewards until the time fixed by the father. 3 So also we, when we were children, were
enslaved by the rudiments of the world. 4 But when the fulness of the time came,
God sent forth his Son, born of a woman, born under law, 5 in order that he
might redeem them (who were) under law, that we might receive the adoption as
sons. 6 And because y o u are sons, God sent forth the Spirit of his Son into our
hearts, crying, "Abba! Father!" 7 So, no longer are you a slave but a son; and if a
son then also an heir through God.

8 However, at that time, since y o u did not know God, y o u were slaves
to those who by nature are no gods; 9 but now that y o u have come to know God,
or rather to be known by God, how (is it) that y o u turn back again to the weak
and beggarly rudiments by which all over again y o u wish to be enslaved? 10 Y o u
observe days and months and seasons and years. 11 I am afraid about y o u, lest
somehow I have labored among y o u in vain.

---

4:1-11

D. *Why exchange one bondage for another?*

Paul has shown that as many as rely on law-works are under a curse, that by law no one is justified before God, that no law was ever given that could impart life, and that the law served only in a preparatory way, namely, as a custodian to bring sinners to Christ. Here, so it might seem, the argument could have ended. Why is it that one entire chapter (ch. 4) is added to drive home the same central point: the sinners' inferiority "under law"? The answer is probably this, that the apostle loved his Galatians so very much (see verses 19 and 20) that he wished to leave no stone unturned in order to deliver them from their grievous error. Besides, what he now presents is by no means mere repetition. Though here, too, as in chapter 3, there is an appeal to past history and experience (verses 1-20), as well as to Scripture (verses 21-31), there is material difference. In chapter 3 the argument from experience centered about *the gifts* which at their conversion the Galatians had received, and the question was asked, "By what avenue did y o u receive them?" In chapter 4 it is rather *the joy or blessedness* that had accompanied the reception of these gifts that is recounted. Again, in chapter 3 the argument from Scripture centered about Abraham,

Habakkuk, and Moses. In chapter 4 the reference is to Abraham's wife Sarah and her son *versus* Abraham's concubine Hagar and her son.

In driving home his point Paul (in the present paragraph, verses 1-11, and the next, verses 12-20) appeals to both heart and mind: to feelings, desires, and considerations which could be counted on to affect profoundly the members of the Galatian churches. Accordingly he appeals to their desire for freedom, a yearning that dwells in every human breast (verses 1-11), their sense of honor, by reminding them of their past nobility in attitude and action (verses 12-14), their presupposed nostalgia for former bliss (verse 15), their presumed sense of fairness (verse 16), and their dread of being duped (verses 17, 18). Last but not least he mentions the birth-pangs endured at this very moment by his own tenderly loving heart (verses 19, 20).

The immediate connection with the preceding paragraph is found in the word *heir(s)*, which is found both in 3:29 and 4:1. Chapter 3 ended with the significant statement, filled with comfort for both Gentile and Jew, "And if y o u belong to Christ, then y o u are Abraham's seed, *heirs* according to promise." Hence, Paul continues: **1, 2. What I mean is this, that as long as the heir is a child he differs in no respect from a slave though he is owner of all, but is under guardians and stewards until the time fixed by the father.** When a young father dies[112] his minor child will have to wait for the inheritance until he is of age. Though this child is, accordingly, the legal heir and as such "lord," "master" or, as here, "owner" of everything, yet with respect to taking possession of, and exercising control over, the estate that has been left to him he is no better off than a slave. Until he attains to the age previously stipulated by the father, he is heir *de jure* (by right) but not as yet *de facto* (in fact). For the time being this child is under *guardians,* to whose care he has been personally entrusted, and under *stewards* (often slaves) to whom the oversight of his estate has been committed (cf. Luke 12:42; 16:1 ff.; Rom. 16:23). Continued: **3. So also we, when we were children, were enlsaved by the rudiments of the world.** Just as an immature child is governed by rules and regulations, so also before the dawning of the light of the gospel, *we* were in bondage to "the rudiments of the world." For a rather detailed study of this concept I refer the reader to N.T.C. on Colossians and Philemon, pp. 108–110, 130–137; especially to footnote 83 on pp. 135–137. The context in Gal. 3:3, 9 (see verse 10) and

[112] Several commentators point out that in the illustration here used it is not necessary to assume that the father has died, since sons would at times take active possession of their inheritance or allotment before the death of the father had occurred (Luke 15:12; cf. Gen. 25:6). Nevertheless, normally a will or disposition to divide an inheritance does not go into effect until the testator has died (Heb. 9:17). We are safe, therefore, in making that assumption also in the present case. Besides, it is not the condition of the father but that of the son that is in the foreground in the present illustration.

in Col. 2:8, 20 (see verses 16, 18, 21-23), demands, as I see it, that we interpret these "worldly rudiments" as *elementary teachings regarding rules and regulations, by means of which, before Christ's coming, people, both Jews and Gentiles, each in their own way, attempted by their own efforts, and in accordance with the promptings of their own fleshly (unregenerate) nature, to achieve salvation.*[113]

There was nothing wrong with the law given at Sinai, but when the Jews and the proselytes to the Jewish religion began to look upon law-observance as the way whereby salvation could be achieved, and when, with this in mind, the Jewish religious leaders began to add their own multitudinous rules and regulations to those previously received, that law became their tyrant, to which they became enslaved. The same was true with respect to the prescriptions and ordinances by which the worshipers of pagan deities sought to achieve redemption. By all such means, whether Jewish or pagan, men were putting themselves in bondage. This interpretation is also in harmony with Paul's previous statement in 3:23 (see on that verse). With the coming of Christ and the full light of special revelation which he brought (John 1:17, 18) there was even less excuse than there had ever been for this servitude, this catering to false philosophy and empty deceit. To the Colossians Paul was going to say, "If with Christ y o u died to the rudiments of the world, why, as though y o u were (still) living in the world, do y o u submit to regulations, 'Do not handle, Do not taste, Do not touch'—referring to things that are meant for destruction by their consumption—according to the precepts and doctrines of men? Regulations of this kind, though to be sure having a reputation for wisdom because of their self-imposed ritual, humility, and unsparing treatment of the body, are of no value whatever, (serving only) to indulge the flesh" (Col. 2:20-23). Continued: **4. But when the fulness of the time came, God sent forth his Son. . . .** Christ's coming supplied the basis of freedom for man. He came, moreover, "in the fulness of the time"; that is, he arrived upon the scene of human history at the time previously fixed by the Father (cf. the illustration, verse 2).

This is about all we can say with certainty about the phrase "the fulness of the time." Other ideas, however, may have been included in the concept; for example, to mention but one, that of *ripeness of opportunity* for the scattering, far and wide, of the seeds of the gospel. In this connection think

113 In my definition of these rudiments to which men were in bondage the two most important items are: *a.* "rules and regulations" (the law) and *b.* "fleshly nature." Essentially the same conclusion was reached independently by Dr. Andrew J. Bandstra, who on p. 71 (and elsewhere) of his doctoral dissertation states that the term *stoicheia* most probably refers to law and the flesh (for title of Bandstra's work see General Bibliography). Luther agrees, calling these "the two feeble beggars."

of: *a.* the spread of the *Greek* language throughout the civilized world, *b.* the presence of *Jewish* synagogues in many places, enabling Christian missionaries to reach both Jews and Gentiles (proselytes) simultaneously, and *c.* the help which these evangelists derived from the network of *Roman* roads and, to some extent, from the enforcement of *Roman* peace. But it is God alone who fully knows why, in his inscrutable decree, he had decided that *the long period of time* (*chronos*) in which all the preparatory events were to occur would run out at that specific moment. It was then that he "sent out from himself" his Son. We say that Jesus *was born* in Bethlehem, and that is correct. But in some respects his birth was not like that of any other child. Other children do not exist in any real sense before they are conceived in the womb. It is by means of conception and birth that they come into existence. But God's Son existed already from eternity with the Father (John 1:1; 8:58; 17:5; Rom. 8:3; II Cor. 8:9; Phil. 2:6; Col. 1:15; Heb. 1:3). He existed—and exists forevermore—*as to his deity.* Accordingly, the fact that he was now sent forth must mean that he now assumed the human nature (John 1:14), which was wondrously prepared in the womb of Mary by the Holy Spirit (Luke 1:35). Thus he now became, and would forever remain, the possessor of two natures, the divine and the human, united indissolubly in the one divine person. From the very beginning Christ's human (as well as his divine) nature was without sin and filled with positive holiness (Mark 1:24; Luke 1:35; John 4:34; 6:38; 8:29, 46; Acts 3:14; 22:14; II Cor. 5:21; Heb. 4:15; 7:26; I Peter 1:19; 2:21; 3:18; I John 2:1; 3:5). And so it will remain forever. Nevertheless, during the days of his humiliation it was oppressed by the effects of sin, for Paul continues: **born of a woman.**

Some have used this expression as a proof-text for the doctrine of the virgin birth, as if "born of a woman" meant "born without human paternity." Now it is certainly true that the Holy Spirit has seen to it that Paul expressed himself in a way which causes Gal. 4:4 to be in full harmony with the teaching elsewhere of the doctrine of the virgin birth. Nevertheless, direct evidence for the virgin birth—a most important truth, to be sure—is found not here in Gal. 4:4 but rather in Matt. 1:18-25 (cf. Isa. 7:14) and Luke 1:34, 35. The fact that Jesus was "born of a woman" does not *in and by itself* mean that he was virgin born. John the Baptist, too, was born of a woman, and so is everybody else, with the exception of Adam and Eve (Matt. 11:11).[114] J. G. Machen correctly observes: "This passage [Gal. 4:14] has

[114] In the defense of the theory that Gal. 4:4 is a proof-text for the virgin birth, some (Lenski, Orr, etc.) argue that the text should really be translated: ". . . his Son, *come to be* from a woman" (Lenski) or ". . . His Son, *become* of a woman" (James Orr, *The Virgin Birth of Christ,* New York, 1924, p. 119), instead of "*born* of a woman," since the aor. participle of the verb γίνομαι is used here, and not the aor. passive participle of the verb γεννάω, as in Gal. 4:29 (cf. forms of that same

sometimes been held to show that Paul did not believe in the virgin birth and sometimes also has been held to show that he did so. As a matter of fact both opinions are probably wrong; the passage does not enable us to draw any conclusion with respect to Paul's belief in the matter one way or the other" (*The Virgin Birth of Christ,* New York and London, 1930, p. 259).

Fact is that in order to save us Jesus Christ had to be in one person both divine and human, *divine* in order to give his sacrifice infinite value, to deliver us out of the realm of darkness, and to transplant us into the realm of everlasting light (Isa. 9:1, 2, 6; John 1:1-4; Col. 1:13, 14); and *human* because since it was man who sinned it is also man who must bear the penalty for sin and render his life to God in perfect obedience (Rom. 5:18; I Cor. 15:21; Heb. 2:14-17). It stands to reason that the Redeemer must be a *sinless* man, for one who is himself a sinner cannot satisfy either for himself or for others (Ps. 49:7, 8; Heb. 7:26, 27; I Peter 3:18). There is, accordingly, something special and something common about Christ's birth. That which is *special* is stressed in the words: "God sent forth his Son." That which is *common* is brought out in the phrase: "born of a woman," meaning: like any other human being, born to affliction, pain, trouble, etc. "Man that is born of a woman is of few days and full of trouble" (Job 14:1). Truly, Christ "was in every respect tempted as we are, yet without sin" (Heb. 4:15).

Continued: **born under law,** and this in the sense not only of being under *personal* obligation to keep that law, but also of being duty-bound (with a duty to which he voluntarily bound himself!) *vicariously* to bear the law's penalty and to satisfy its demand of perfect obedience.

The altruistic nature of Christ's coming is stressed in the purpose clause: **5. in order that he might redeem them (who were) under law.** Essentially we have here the same thought that was expressed previously in 3:13: "Christ redeemed us from the curse of the law, having become a curse for us." Even

---

verb in 4:23, 24). But, in speaking of Christ's conception and birth the sacred writers do not hesitate to use forms of the latter verb (Matt. 1:16; 2:1), not even in reproducing the message of Gabriel to Mary (Luke 1:35). In fact, Jesus himself, in speaking of his own birth, made use of this verb when he said to Pilate, "For this purpose *was I born,* and for this purpose I am come into the world, that I should bear witness to the truth" (John 18:37). Note, however, also a form of the verb γίνομαι—ultimately the two verbs can be traced to the same root—in the sense of *being born.* It is used in connection with the birth of Abraham (John 8:58, according to the best text), when Christ's Aramaic is rendered: "Before Abraham *was born* I am." As to *Paul's* usage in connection with Christ see also Rom. 1:3. In the Apocrypha this verb has reference to *being born* in such passages as Esd. 4:16; Tob. 8:6; Wisd. 7:3; etc. "To be born" or "to be begotten" is, accordingly, a recognized meaning of the verb γίνομαι. Hence, no argument in favor of the doctrine of the virgin birth can properly be derived from its use here in Gal. 4:4. See also L.N.T. (A. and G.), p. 157.

the verb—*redeem*—is the same. Hence, see the explanation of 3:13, and for the thought compare II Cor. 5:21. Yet, there is a difference, for here in Gal. 4:5 emphasis is placed on the fact that *we* (Gentiles, Jews; the addressed, the addressor, everybody destined to be redeemed) were "under law," and this not only in the sense of being subject to the moral law, which by nature we were unable to fulfil and whose curse we were unable to carry so as to get out from under it; but also (in the present context; see verses 3, 8-10; cf. Col. 2:8, 14, 20-23) in the sense that "we" regarded strict obedience to the ceremonial law and all its man-made additions to be necessary for salvation. Accordingly, the Father's object in commissioning his Son was that, in the most comprehensive sense, the latter might purchase those free that were under law; and not only that but also: **that we might receive the adoption as sons.** Cf. Rom. 8:15, 23; 9:4; Eph. 1:5. Plainly, then, the purpose of the Father in sending his Son, and of the Son in condescending to be born "of a woman, under law," was that we might not only be delivered from the greatest evil but might also be crowned with the choicest blessing. The best interpreter of Paul's statement in Gal. 4:4, 5 is Paul himself: "For you know the grace of our Lord Jesus Christ, that though he was rich, yet for your sake he became poor, that you through his poverty might become rich" (II Cor. 8:9).

Rich, indeed, we become, for we are made members of "the Father's Family" (see N.T.C. on Eph. 3:14, 15). With respect to this *adoption* it is rather useless to look for human analogies, for it surpasses anything that takes place on earth. It bestows upon its recipients not only a new name, a new legal standing, and a new family-relationship, but also a new image, the image of Christ (Rom. 8:29). Earthly parents may love an adopted child ever so much. Nevertheless, they are, to a certain extent, unable to impart their *spirit* to that child; but when *God* adopts, he imparts to us the *Spirit* of his Son, as Paul indicates by continuing: **6. And because you are sons, God sent forth the Spirit of his Son into our hearts, crying, "Abba! Father!"** The redeemed are now sons, not minors but majors. They have reached maturity and with it freedom. It is remarkable that the apostle is saying this to *the Galatians!* He says, as it were, "You, Galatians, weak, foolish, erring, must consider that you, yes even you, are sons of the heavenly Father, the Father of your Lord Jesus Christ." In other words, he is not giving up hope with respect to them, even though he is baffled about their present behavior (4:11).

Now because they are sons, God, the Father, having adopted them as sons, has sent forth the Spirit into their hearts. They are sons; hence they receive the Holy Spirit. They receive the Spirit; hence they become conscious of their sonship (Rom. 8:15). All three persons of the Holy Trinity are indicated in this passage, and their harmonious co-operation as the one true God is beautifully set forth. Moreover, the third person is called "the

Spirit of his (God the Father's) Son." He is the Spirit of the Son because he proceeds from the Son (John 15:26), as well as from the Father, and because he glorifies the Son, causing men to ponder the Son's teaching, love unto death, heavenly intercession, and constant care (John 16:14).

"God *sent forth* his Son" (verse 4); "God *sent forth* the Spirit of his Son" (verse 6). The same word is used with reference to the sending of the Spirit as was previously used in connection with the sending of the Son. The two are equally real, and also equally important. In fact, the salvation that was *bought* for God's people by the Son will not avail except it be also *wrought* in their *hearts* by that Son's Spirit. The heart, moreover, controls the entire personality. It is the core and center of man's being, man's inmost self. It is the hub whence radiate all the spokes of his existence, the fulcrum of feeling and faith as well as the mainspring of words and actions (Rom. 10:10; cf. Matt. 12:34; 15:19; 22:37; John 14:1). "Out of it are the issues of life" (Prov. 4:23).

In dwelling on the great mysteries of salvation, matters in which he himself has become intensely and lastingly involved, Paul frequently changes from the second to the first person plural (Gal. 1:3, 4; 2:14, 15; Eph. 1:17, 19; 2:1, 5; 2:8, 10; 2:13, 14; 5:1, 2; 6:11, 12; Phil. 3:2, 3; 3:15, 16; Col. 1:11-13; 2:13; etc.). So also here: "And because *y o u* are sons, God sent forth the Spirit of his Son into *our* hearts." About such marvelous realities he is unable to write in an abstract, detached manner; hence not *y o u . . . y o u r,* but *y o u . . . our.* And why is his soul thus lost in wonder, love, and praise? The very contents of verses 4-6 clearly shows why. First, the Father had sent the Son, sent him from his very heart, as it were: "he *spared not* his *own* Son!" (Rom. 8:32), his *only Son* (John 3:16). He sent him into a world of sin and ruin, where for our sake and in our stead he was to suffer innumerable reproaches. And what did *we* (all those who were to be redeemed) do? *We* (that is, *our* sins) nailed him to the cross! This we did to him who came to dwell *with* us. Yet, instead of casting us away forever from his presence of love, the Father then sent the *Spirit* of his Son, in order that this Spirit (and in him also the Father and the Son) might draw even closer to us, dwelling not just *with* but *within* us, in our very hearts, and transforming these hearts from being hateful to being loving, from being rebellious to being obedient, from being distrustful to being faith-filled, and from being despondent to being exuberant with praise and adoration. Within these hearts the Spirit speaks peace, assurance. He bears witness with our spirit that we are God's very children, his adopted sons and heirs. Is it any wonder that such hearts begin to respond to the Father's love, so that love answers love, and a blessed interchange takes place? Is it not natural that the Spirit, dwelling within these hearts, impels them to address their Benefactor jubilantly, calling him "Father"? The text reads: crying, "Abba! Father!" In reality the outcry of joyful recognition, sweet response, appropriating love, overwhelming gratitude, and last but not least, filial trust, is ascribed to the Spirit. Nevertheless, this must be understood mediately, meaning that it is the Spirit "whereby we cry Abba! Father!" (Rom. 8:15). Similarly, in connection with the church's yearning for Christ's return we read, "And the Spirit and the bride say, Come" (Rev. 22:17). Here, too, the bride is moved by the Spirit. Spirit and bride always work together (Rom. 8:16).

It is a well-known fact that those who have acquired proficiency in more than one language will at times give preference to their native tongue as a vehicle for the expression of their deepest emotions. Being "a Hebrew of Hebrews" (Phil. 3:5), a Hebrew son of Hebrew parents, Paul must have been fond of the language spoken by the Jews as they returned from the lands of the captivity, namely Aramaic, akin to Hebrew (Acts 21:40). Aramaic, in fact, was a very important language in those days, being spoken not only by the Jews but by many others besides, even far outside the borders of Palestine. Jesus, too, spoke Aramaic, and it is altogether probable that in his frequent teaching about the Father, he had often used the term *Abba*. His disciples, therefore, relished the use of this word. Thus it passed into the vocabulary of the primitive church. Naturally, in writing to churches consisting for the greater part of people who were non-Jews, the word *Abba* had to be translated into the Greek *páter,* as Paul does here. Paul, then, is giving expression to his own inner devotion as well as to the deepest feelings of the early church when he tells us that now that freedom has arrived, through the redemption accomplished by Christ, and the way of access to the throne of God has been opened wider than ever, redeemed humanity, both Jew and Gentile, takes hold on God by crying, "Abba! Father!" By means of this expression of filial trust and *closeness* to the Father believers echoed the words of their Lord, spoken at a time when, in order to obtain this closeness of fellowship for us, he himself was being driven into isolation, was losing this very sense of nearness to his Father. It was in Gethsemane that Jesus, in deep anguish, said, "Abba," which by the evangelist Mark is similarly rendered into the Greek equivalent for "Father" (Mark 14:36).

7. At this point there is a change in the form of address which Paul uses. He has been addressing the Galatians as a group. He now turns to each one individually, saying: **So, no longer are you a slave but a son. . . .** Once a man has accepted Christ's sacrifice as the only ground of his salvation, and has drawn near with confidence to the throne of grace, addressing God as *"Abba! Father!,"* the shackles of bondage to law have been thrown off. No longer is man a slave. He not only *is* a son now (4:1, 2), but *knows* that he is. For him the way to the Father's heart is no longer blocked. Every valley has been raised, every mountain and hill made low, the crooked turns have been straightened, and all rough places have been made smooth. There

are no longer any obstructions. Grace has removed them all. Continued: **and if a son then also an heir . . . ,** as was stated previously (3:29). For the comforting implications of heirship see on 3:18. The very word *heir* already implies that the son's salvation is not his own achievement but the gift of God's marvelous grace. But since this is hard for man's proud heart to admit, and since salvation by self-effort and not by grace was the very error against which Paul is here directing his attack, he adds: (according to the best reading) **through God.** Soli Deo Gloria! The sovereign, divine, nature of the work which made a man a son and an heir is stressed throughout Scripture (Deut. 7:7, 8; Isa. 48:11; Dan. 9:19; Hos. 14:4; John 15:16; Rom. 5:8; Eph. 1:4; I John 4:10, 19). This doctrine gives a person a sturdy foundation to stand on. It spells eternal security, without in any way violating personal responsibility.

"The glory, Lord, from first to last,
Is due to thee alone;
Aught to ourselves we dare not take,
Or rob thee of thy crown."
—Augustus M. Toplady

**8, 9.** Assurance of full redemption through Christ, sonship, the blessed indwelling of the Spirit, freedom of access to the Father, heirship—are the Galatians now ready to sacrifice all these? Are they really going back to their former state of slavery, with this difference that they will be exchanging one type of bondage (to heathenism) for another (to Judaism)? It is evident that the apostle is here returning to the very occasion that had led him to write this letter. There is thunder in the sky, and the lightning flashes again, as it had done in 1:6-10 and 3:1 ff. Paul writes: **However, at that time, since you did not know[115] God, you were slaves to those who by nature are no gods.** Formerly the Galatians, then mostly pagans, had been without saving knowledge of God. It is not denied that by virtue of the manner in which God created man there is a certain kind of knowledge of God and of his law inherent in man's mind. Even the heathen show the work of the law written in their hearts (Rom. 2:14, 15). Nor is it denied that all men—including, therefore, non-Christians—derive from general revelation a certain amount of knowledge of God's attributes (Rom. 1:19, 20). That all of this knowledge is indeed important is plainly taught in the passages referred to. But *saving* knowledge is not found outside of Christ. Though the heathen have knowledge of God, they fail to render to God

115 There is a cause and effect relationship between ignorance of God and slavery; hence, οὐκ εἰδότες is probably causal as well as temporal, with emphasis on the former.

the glory and the thanksgiving that is his due (Rom. 1:21). They do not *acknowledge* him but instead, in their perversity, serve the creature rather than the Creator, and for the glory of God they substitute "the likeness of an image of corruptible man and of birds and of four-footed beasts, and of creeping things," and make these the objects of their worship.[116] This foolish and wicked failure to acknowledge God results in slavery for those who are guilty of it, slavery to the products of their own wicked invention: gods which in reality are no gods at all, as is clear from their very nature, for they are but objects of wood, stone, etc. They have no breath, no power, no wisdom, and no concern for man. Instead of carrying man through his difficulties, they themselves must be carried (Isa. 46:1; contrast Isa. 63:9). Idolatry always spells slavery, not only the slavery of fear but also that of moral and spiritual degradation of every variety. Such, then, had been the former condition of most of those whom Paul here addresses.

A great change had occurred however, as Paul indicates by continuing: **but now that y o u have come to know God. . . .** In his marvelous grace it had pleased God to send Paul, Barnabas, etc. to preach the gospel to these wretched ones. And through the work of the Holy Spirit the Galatians had come to acknowledge the true God as he stands revealed in Christ. With respect to the dramatic and basic experience which these Galatians had undergone Paul is going to say more in verses 12-15. Here in verse 9 he adds one important point, however: **or rather to be known by God. . . .** This is an expression full of glorious significance. It means far more than that God would have a bare, factual knowledge with reference to them, or would simply be *acquainted* with them. In the case of the Galatians it indicates at least this, "that God had visited them in his mercy" (thus John Calvin). In view of what the apostle says in verse 6 ("Y o u are sons") is it not possible that also in the present passage the words are rich with such meaning as this: that they had been acknowledged as God's own; that, accordingly, God had set his love upon them and had chosen them to eternal life? This would certainly not have to apply to each and every one of them, but it could well apply to most of them, if we may assume that God blessed this letter to their hearts. We are reminded of such passages as: "I am the good shepherd, and I know my own" (John 10:14); "The Lord knows those who are his" (II Tim. 2:19). See also Gen. 18:19; Exod. 33:12, 17; Nah. 1:7; John 10:28; and Rom. 8:28, in all of which the statement that *God knows* or *has known* (or *foreknown*) a person is rich in meaning toward salvation. When Paul says, ". . . but now that y o u have come to know God *or rather* to be known by God" he is clearly stressing the fact

---

116 John Murray gives an excellent explanation of the pertinent passages in Paul's Epistle to the Romans. See his book *The Epistle to the Romans,* Grand Rapids, Mich., 1959, Vol. I, especially pp. 34–42; 72–76.

that "We love him because he first loved us." Here, as at the close of verse 7 (see on that passage), there is, accordingly, a renewed emphasis on God's sovereignty in the effectuation of man's salvation. And that was exactly the lesson which the Galatians needed, and which, in a sense, we all need.

Right at this moment these Galatians were guilty of backsliding, so that Paul continues: (in view of these facts) **how (is it) that y o u turn back again to the weak and beggarly rudiments by which all over again y o u wish to be enslaved?** The apostle was shocked to learn that men who had been so enriched with the gospel of God's free and bounteous grace in Jesus Christ would now, under the influence of false teachers, be turning back again to those "rudiments of the world" (verse 3), which here, in verse 9, are described as being "weak and beggarly." What makes matters worse is that they are doing this by choice. Formerly they had been enslaved by the childish teachings of pagan priests and ritualists. They had been taught to obey all kinds of prescriptions regarding the discovery of the will of the gods by means of omens, the benefit of afflicting the body and of submission to fate. See on 5:1. There had been moral stipulations derived from nature, custom, and arbitrary will. Having been delivered from all this folly, do they now wish to become enslaved all over again, this time by Judaistic regulations? Paul calls these "rudiments" *weak and beggarly* because they have no power to help man in any way. Luther, commenting on this verse and applying the lesson to his own day, tells us that he had known monks who zealously labored to please God for salvation, but the more they labored the more impatient, miserable, uncertain, and fearful they became. And he adds, "People who prefer the law to the gospel are like Aesop's dog who let go of the meat to snatch at the shadow in the water. . . . The law is weak and poor, the sinner is weak and poor: two feeble beggars trying to help each other. They cannot do it. They only wear each other out. But through Christ a weak and poor sinner is revived and enriched unto eternal life."

The apostle then gives an illustration which sheds much light on what he meant when he spoke about turning back to the weak and beggarly rudiments: **10. Y o u observe days and months and seasons and years.** Since Paul in the entire preceding argument has made it abundantly clear that he is mainly attacking the false doctrine that law-works are the road to salvation (2:16, 19; 3:2, 5, 10-13, 17, 21; 4:5), and since by "law" he is referring specifically to that of Sinai, which came into existence four hundred and thirty years after the promise had been given to Abraham, Isaac, and Jacob, it follows that here in 4:10 he is not referring to days, months, etc., that pertained to this or that pagan system of religious worship, or even to some mixed ("syncretistic") cultus, but definitely to *the sabbath-days, days of the new moon, festival seasons* belonging to the Jewish cycle, and *either a. the sabbath and jubilee years, or b. the New Year* (Rosh

Hashana) on the first day of the month Tishri (September or October).[117] Paul is saying that strict observance of such days and festivals has nothing whatever to do with securing the divine favor. As a foundation upon which to build one's hope of being justified in the sight of God such a superstition is utterly futile, nothing but sinking sand! In fact, though deep down in his heart Paul certainly has not given up hope regarding the eternal welfare of the Galatians, as he indicates again and again (1:11; 3:4, 15; 4:6, 7, 9, 15, 16, 19; 5:10), he, as it were, shakes his head in utter disgust when he reflects on the fact that rigid, painstaking, adherence to the Mosaic law regarding sacred days, and to all kinds of man-made rules and regulations with respect to such celebrations, was actually beginning to be substituted for the simplicity of faith in Jesus Christ unto salvation full and free. Such folly staggers him. Have these Galatians learned nothing then? That seems to be the meaning of the words: **11. I am afraid about you, lest somehow I have labored among you in vain.** Note the word *somehow* or *perhaps,* strangely ignored in several translations,[118] yet of some importance, as it shows that the apostle has *not* definitely decided that all his efforts in the interest of the Galatians have been a waste of time. In fact, though admittedly this verse is one of Paul's gloomiest utterances in the entire epistle, so that, as some see it, the pendulum of his emotions, which is swinging between hope and fear, has here swung all the way to the latter, even here the door of hope has not been shut. Gal. 4:11 is not really in conflict with the somewhat similar 3:4. And the noble purpose of 4:11 as well as of 3:4 is "to rouse the minds of the Galatians to the exercise of repentance."

---

[117] The fact that the reference to *years* is not entirely clear is one of several reasons why the attempt that has been made to found upon it a theory with respect to the date when the epistle was written must be considered a failure.

[118] Greek πώς. Among those who do justice to this word in their translations are Beck, Berkeley Version, Goodspeed, Moffatt, N.A.S.B. (N.T.), Norlie, and Weymouth.

# Chapter 4

Verses 12-20

Theme: *The Gospel of Justification by Faith apart from Law-works Defended against Its Detractors*

II. *Its Vindication: both Scripture—i.e., the Old Testament—and life (experience, past history) bear testimony to its truth*

E. Become as I am as I also became as y o u are. Where is now that blessedness which y o u experienced on that former occasion when y o u welcomed me so warmly? Those (perverters of the true gospel) who pay court to y o u do so selfishly. I could wish to be present with y o u now and to change my tone of voice, for I am perplexed about y o u.

12 Become as I (am), because I also became as y o u (are), brothers; (this) I beg of y o u. No wrong did y o u do me. 13 Y o u know, moreover, that it was because of an infirmity of the flesh that I preached to y o u the gospel on that former occasion; 14 and though my physical condition was a temptation to y o u, yet y o u did not despise or loathe me, but as an angel of God y o u welcomed me, as Christ Jesus. 15 Where, then, (is) y o u r (former) blessedness? For I testify to y o u that, had it been possible, y o u r very eyes y o u would have plucked out and given to me. 16 Have I then become y o u r enemy by telling y o u the truth? 17 These people are zealously courting y o u for no commendable purpose: on the contrary, they want to isolate y o u, in order that y o u may zealously court them. 18 Now (it is) commendable to be zealously courted in connection with a commendable cause (and this) always, and not only when I am present with y o u. 19 My dear children, for whom I am again suffering birth-pangs until Christ be formed in y o u, 20 I could wish to be present with y o u now and to change my tone of voice, for I am perplexed about y o u.

4:12-20

E. *Where is now y o u r blessedness?*

**12.** It is characteristic of Paul, the tactful shepherd of souls, the warm-hearted master-psychologist, that his rather sharp reproof (verses 8-11) is followed immediately by tender, urgent, intensely personal appeal. This paragraph is one of the most gripping in all of Paul's epistles. The apostle implores and agonizes, because he cannot endure the thought that those whom he addresses and who at one time had treated him with such sympathetic consideration and had accepted his gospel with such enthusiasm would now continue to wander farther and farther away from home. Hence, lovingly, as a parent speaking to children, for such in a sense they are (see verse 19), he writes: **Become as I (am), because I also became as y o u (are), brothers; (this) I beg of y o u.** In the light of such stirring passages as Gal. 2:16, 19, 20; Phil. 3:7 (cf. Titus 3:5) this must mean: "Cast aside all thought of being able, by means of law-works, to become righteous in the sight of God, for that is exactly what I by grace was taught to do. At one time, I, a proud Jew, imagined that I would be able to achieve my own righteousness before God. But I became as y o u Gentiles are, by nature condemnable in his sight, with nothing of self to appeal to."

Because Paul, by God's marvelous grace, has learned that this shedding of all self-righteousness is the only way to please and glorify God, he beseeches the Galatians to follow this course. They should return to the point from which they started out when they had accepted the gospel of salvation, full and free, on the basis solely of Christ's redemptive sacrifice. They should spurn once and for all the sinister teachings of the Judaizers. Let them, as his children, reveal their likeness to him. Let them return to that simple, childlike, faith which, in addressing the Savior, says, "Nothing in my hand I bring, Simply to thy cross I cling." Cf. 2:20; 6:14. That the plea is very earnest and touching appears from the affectionate word of address, "brothers" (1:11; 3:15; 4:28, 31; 5:11, 13; 6:1, 18), and from the emphatic appeal with which the sentence *ends:* " (This) I beg of y o u."[119] Continued: **No wrong did y o u do me.** At first glance this statement may surprise us because of its suddenness. Some have explained it as a response to an assertion made by the Galatians: "We have not wronged you in any way." But there is no basis for this theory. Nor is there any need for it. Paul's soul was in a state of intense agitation, brought about by grave concern about the present disloyalty of the Galatians, especially as contrasted with their past enthusiasm. Therefore, his abruptness is, after all, understandable. When he now says, "No wrong did y o u do me," he is reflecting on the manner in which he had been received by the Galatians when he had met them for the first time and worked among them, as is clear from verses 13-15. Continued: **13. Y o u know, moreover, that it was because of an infirmity of the flesh that I preached to y o u the gospel on that former occasion. . . .**[120] Paul had visited the Galatians twice, that is, on two separate missionary journeys: the first (see Acts 13 and 14) and the second (see Acts 15:40-16:5). He refers now to what had happened on the first of these two trips.

The apostle states that it was *because* of an infirmity of the flesh—an illness so severe that on the part of the Galatians it might have given rise to contempt and disgust (verse 14)—that he had preached the gospel to them on that former occasion. Some interpreters, however, do not look with favor on the rendering "because of." They prefer—or at least regard as worthy of very serious consideration—a translation such as "amid," or "while suffering from" or simply "in" bodily weakness.[121] Reference to this difference of opinion was made earlier. See p. 11. In favor of the idea that the infirmity of which Paul speaks was not *the cause* of the apostle's preaching but rather *the accompanying circumstance* it might be stated that not only Luke (see Acts 13:50; 14:5, 6, 19) makes some remarks about the physical

---

[119] This special emphasis is lost in most translations. It is retained, however, in N.E.B., and, in a way, also by Phillips.

[120] It is true that the Greek τὸ πρότερον at times simply means *formerly, before, previously* (John 6:62; 9:8; I Tim. 1:13). However, in the present instance Paul, by his very emphasis and rather lengthy expatiation on what had happened *on a definite earlier occasion,* shows that he is here using this expression in the sense of "on the former of two occasions."

[121] Thus respectively Cole (*op. cit.*, pp. 121, 122); Ridderbos (*op. cit.*, pp. 13, 30, 166); and Bruce (*The Letters of Paul, An Expanded Paraphrase,* p. 31).

afflictions which Paul, and to some extent also Barnabas, had to endure while working in Galatia, but so does also Paul himself, many years later. These experiences were never erased from the latter's memory. Even in his very last epistle that has been preserved the afflictions suffered on that journey march in rapid procession before his mind's eye, as he writes to Timothy: "You, however, followed my . . . persecutions, my sufferings, what kind of things happened to me at Antioch, at Iconium, (and) at Lystra, what kind of persecutions I underwent; yet from them all the Lord rescued me!" (II Tim. 3:10, 11). For this and other, more technical, reasons,[122] the *possibility* that this was actually what the apostle had in mind, and that what he wrote should be rendered, ". . . it was *amid bodily weakness* that I preached to you the gospel on that former occasion" must be granted. Nevertheless, it must also be admitted that the far more usual sense of the phrase found here is *because of an infirmity*. It is so understood by the vast majority of exegetes.[123] And on the basis of this interpretation of the phrase Ramsay's conclusion, that because of malaria with accompanying severe headaches Paul had been forced to leave the lowlands of Perga and vicinity for the considerably higher elevation of Antioch and the other cities of Galatia, has been accepted by many. It could be right. Yet, in reality we know nothing about the nature of the illness which, if the preferred rendering "because of an infirmity of the flesh" is accepted, caused the apostle to preach the gospel in Galatia and/or to continue his ministry there for a longer period than he had at first contemplated. The idea that verse 15 (cf. 6:11) points to an affliction of the eyes is not well grounded, since in that passage the apostle is no longer speaking about his physical infirmity. And so it is with the other guesses that have been made. Those who immerse themselves in such matters sometimes miss the real intention of the passage, as when a Bible study group, spending several evenings on the first few chapters of the book of Genesis, instead of taking to heart the marvelous spiritual lessons taught there, how God is there revealed in all his power, wisdom, and love, wholly concentrates its attention on the question: "How long were the days of the creation week?"

---

122 The question may well be asked whether Koine Greek is so inflexible as never to allow διά to be used even with the accusative to indicate attendant circumstance, as it certainly does at times when it is used with the genitive. At any rate prominent Greek fathers (Chrysostom, Theodoret, and Theodore of Mopsuestia), well-versed in Greek, seem to interpret Gal. 4:13 with this sense of διά in mind.

123 For example, by Burton (*op. cit.*, pp. 238, 239); Duncan (*op. cit.*, p. 139); Goodspeed (*Paul*, p. 42); Lenski (*op. cit.*, pp. 217, 218); Lightfoot (*op. cit.*, p. 174); and last but not least Ramsay (*St. Paul the Traveller and the Roman Citizen*, pp. 92ff.; Historical *Commentary on Galatians*, p. 424). Lightfoot states: "No instance has been produced, until a much later date, which would at all justify one explaining δι' ἀσθένειαν, as if it were δι' ἀσθενείας or ἐν ἀσθενείᾳ, as is frequently done."

By writing, "Y o u know that it was because of an infirmity," etc., the apostle causes the scenes and experiences of the not very distance past to flash vividly across the memory of the errant Galatians. Their thoughts are carried back to the events that had taken place at the time of the first meeting with the missionaries, and shortly afterward. The sentence continues: **14. and though my physical condition was a temptation to y o u, yet y o u did not despise or loathe me. . . .** This is a very compressed statement. Literally, according to what is probably the best reading, this clause reads: "And y o u r temptation in my flesh y o u neither despised nor loathed." Two ideas are here combined: *a.* "Y o u did not despise or loathe me because of my physical condition"; *b.* "Y o u did not yield to the temptation to do so." The resultant meaning is clear enough, just so also at this point we avoid wild conjectures. The first verb causes no difficulty: "Y o u did not regard (me) of no account, as good for nothing"; hence, "Y o u did not despise (me)." There follows, *if* the verb is to be taken literally: "or spit out (at me.)."[124] On the basis of that literal rendering some have said that Paul was surprised because the Galatians had not expectorated when they first met him, for that was their custom when they saw a person who was having an epileptic fit. The conclusion drawn from the use of this verb is, accordingly, that Paul was an epileptic. But since from very early times this verb was also used in a metaphorical sense—to loathe—, and since after "Y o u did not despise," this secondary meaning "or loathe" completes the pair of synonyms, the latter translation is certainly to be preferred. Besides, nowhere in Paul's epistles or in the book of Acts is there the slightest evidence to support the notion that Paul was an epileptic. Therefore, all we can really affirm is that when, during this first missionary journey, the Galatians saw Paul, they saw a man who was afflicted with a grievous physical illness. But even though such bodily infirmity was regarded by the Jews, and even more so by the Gentiles, as a token of God's displeasure (Job 4:7; John 9:2; Acts 28:4), so that the Galatians had been tempted to treat Paul with contemptuous scorn, they had done nothing of the kind. Continued: **but as an angel of God y o u welcomed me, as Christ Jesus.** So great had been their respect for Paul, so generous the welcome extended to him, as if his voice had been that of an angel of God, yes even that of Christ Jesus himself (cf. Acts 13:42, 44, 48; 14:1, 11-13, 21).

The Galatians had experienced a season of thrilling discovery, of joy unspeakable and full of glory. What had become of it? How completely different was their present condition. Says Paul: **15. Where,[125] then, (is) y o u r (former) blessedness,** the disposition of mind and heart in which,

---

[124] "At last, however, he [Odysseus] came up, and *spat forth* from his mouth the bitter brine that flowed in streams from his head" (Homer, *Odyssey* V. 322, 323).
[125] The textual evidence is decidedly in favor of the reading as here assumed.

because of our presence, you blessed or congratulated yourselves? Continued: **For I testify to you that, had it been possible, your very eyes you would have plucked out and given to me.**[126] In the original the words "your eyes" are, for the sake of emphasis, given a forward position: "your eyes, having plucked (or: dug) out, you would have given to me." My translation preserves this special stress. What the apostle evidently means is this: "You thought so highly of me at that time, and felt so happy in our presence, that, had it been possible, you would have given me the most precious member of your body." Continued: **16. Have I then become your enemy by telling you the truth?**[127] To what does Paul refer when he asks this question? In which way does he assume that he might have become their enemy? The opinions given may be classified as follows: *a.* by means of a previous letter which he had written to them but which was not preserved; *b.* by means of warnings against the Judaizers which he had issued on his *second* journey through Galatia (see Acts 15:40 ff.); *c.* by means of the strong language which he had used earlier in the very letter which he is now writing (1:6; 3:1 ff.; 4:11). For the first of these suggestions I see no need whatever, nor probability. The second is very well possible. The Galatians may not have taken kindly to these warnings. The third impresses me as being the most natural, though *b* and *c* may well be combined. What Paul is telling the Galatians by means of this question is that he has proved himself their real friend, for the mark of such a friend is that he tells those whom he loves the truth even though it may hurt. Nathan, for example, proved that he was David's genuine supporter when, in the name of his Sender, he rebuked the king, saying, "You are the man!" (II Sam. 12:7). Paul, then, is saying, "You have heard what I have said. Now what is your reaction? Have I become your enemy by rendering this service to you, namely, telling you the truth?" Are the Galatians unable to tolerate the truth? Are they like a foolish woman who breaks her mirror because it reveals the wrinkles on her face? Do they not realize that were the apostle, in this important matter, concealing the truth, he would be committing a crime? Do they resemble those fickle church-members who are always demanding that their minister says nothing but "nice things" to them? Paul's own stand on this matter is that one should always practice integrity in all his dealings, and that he should do so in the spirit of love (Eph. 4:15). Said Lincoln: "If it is decreed that I should go down because of this speech, then let me go down linked to the truth." This attitude gave him peace of

---

[126] I agree with Robertson (*Word Pictures,* Vol. IV, p. 305) that there is nothing unusual in the omission of ἄν in this *second class* or *contrary to fact* conditional sentence, but I disagree with his suggestion: "Did Paul not have at this time serious eye trouble?"

[127] For ἀληθεύω see N.T.C. on Eph. 4:15, footnote 118.

mind. And as to his influence? Though defeated in his bid for the Senate, he became President two years later.

It is but natural that Paul, who has just asked whether he had possibly become the enemy of the Galatians by telling them the truth, now states who are their *real* enemies. In what he is about to say he probes into and exposes the motives of the Judaizers, without mentioning them by name: **17. These people are zealously courting y o u for no commendable purpose: on the contrary, they want to isolate y o u, in order that y o u may zealously court them.** The Judaizers are trying to curry favor with the Galatians, ostensibly being deeply concerned about them. However, their purpose is not commendable, their motivation is not honorable. Literally Paul says "not properly," "not in the right way." Their real object is *to exclude* the Galatians, that is, to shut them out from all influences except their own; particularly, of course, *to isolate* them from any effect Paul and his associates might have upon them. But man cannot live in a vacuum. He is a social being. Once these opponents have succeeded in deluding the minds of the Galatians with an untrue image of Paul and of his message, the sadly deluded ones will then become wholly dependent upon these detractors of the only true gospel. Accordingly, the apostle states, "They want to isolate y o u, in order that y o u may zealously court them." *To zealously court someone* (active voice), to be deeply concerned about that person, and to bestow much attention upon him, need not be a bad thing. Good parents are deeply concerned about their children. The very idea that those so dear to them might succumb to the temptation of being led astray by evil companions, so that in that sense these parents might "lose" their children, fills them with dismay and incites them to earnest prayer and strenuous effort on their behalf. They are jealous for their children with God's own jealousy, as was, for example, Paul himself, with respect to the Corinthians (II Cor. 11:2: same verb in the original as here in Gal. 4:18). So also, says Paul, *to be zealously courted* (passive voice), diligently sought after, is not a bad thing in and by itself, no matter whom it concerns, provided, however, that it be "in something good," that is, "in connection with a commendable cause": **18. Now (it is) commendable to be zealously courted in connection with a commendable cause.** Then suddenly the apostle rivets the mind of the Galatians upon the fact that this rule applies also to himself. On that unforgettable "former occasion" had *he* not been the object of their whole-souled attention, intense interest, unmistakable favor, and genuine respect, and this in connection with the noblest of all causes, namely, the proclamation of the one and only true gospel? Would that this had endured and were true even today! Continued: **(and this) always, and not only when I am present with y o u.** That was the trouble. Their attachment to Paul had lost its warmth, to say the least. Their zeal for the truth had subsided. Their loyalty was in the process of being transferred from Paul to the proponents of dangerous error. Everything was fine, as long as Paul had been present with them. But once he was gone and the distorters of the true gospel had arrived, the alienation of affection had begun, to their own hurt!

This situation almost breaks Paul's heart. No wonder, for he knows so much better than they do what would be the result of such apostasy were it to run its full course. But this must not, this cannot be. So, in spite of the fact that their feelings toward him had cooled, he, still filled with the most tender love toward them, now addresses them in the language of warm, pastoral—and we may well add: parental—affection, as follows: **19, 20. My dear children,**[128] **for whom I am again suffering birth-pangs. . . .**

Paul compares himself to a mother who is giving birth to a child. Thus also in I Thess. 2:7[129] he says, employing a figure only slightly different: "But we were gentle in the midst of y o u, as when a nurse cherishes her own children," meaning: as when a mother-nurse warms, fondles, cherishes the children that are her very own because she gave them birth. Here in Gal. 4:19 note the word *again:* "for whom I am again suffering birth-pangs." Once before he had endured these labor pains for them, as Luke so vividly portrays in Acts 13 and 14. At that time he, as God's instrument, had brought these children to the point where they loved him and trusted him; even better: where they loved and trusted *Christ,* placing their hope for salvation in him alone. And now, having been displaced in their affections by others, Paul's birth-pangs have returned. He hopes with all the ardor of his soul that, for the sake of their own salvation, the Galatians will renew their former attachment to him. O that they might be his children once more, as children imitating him! O that they might become as he is (verse 12), trusting solely in Christ for their salvation! O that they would cast aside all reliance on self, on law-works, as he, by the grace of God, had learned to do!

The apostle is yearning for his children. He is afflicted. In his heartache also this element is included, "that the Galatians are making the maternal heart of Paul suffer all the birth-pains a second time, something which no offspring ever does in nature. . . . Unnaturally they are causing Paul to suffer all these pains over again, even in a more severe way" (Lenski, *op. cit.,* p. 227).

Though, according to the entire preceding context, it was especially the acceptance of legalism by the Galatians that made Paul suffer and yearn as he did, nevertheless the danger of libertinism (immorality) can hardly

---

128 Whether with Grk.N.T. (A-B-M-W) on reads τεκνία μου (literally: "my little children," cf. John 13:33; I John 2:1, 12, 28; 3:7, 18; 4:4; 5:21) or with N.N. τέκνα μου ("O my children!"), cannot the rendering "My dear children" be considered proper in either case?

129 This resemblance between Galatians and I Thessalonians can be added to those mentioned earlier. See p. 16.

have been absent from his mind, for in the very next chapter he earnestly warns the Galatians that they must not turn their freedom into an opportunity for the flesh (5:13, 16-24; cf. 6:7, 8). Hence, it is in that broad connection, reflecting on the situation in Galatia in its entirety, that he says: **until Christ be formed in y o u,** that is, until y o u r whole inner being[130] proclaims Christ's being and his ways, so that y o u will trust fully in y o u r Savior, will be like him in y o u r thoughts, wishes, and aspirations, and will reflect him in the common words y o u speak, in life's common looks and tones, in intercourse at hearth or board with y o u r beloved ones, in brief: in the entire gamut of y o u r existence and manifestation among men.[131] Continued: **I could wish to be present with y o u now and to change my tone of voice, for I am perplexed about y o u.** Though Paul was writing as a holy man of God who was being moved by the Holy Spirit (cf. II Peter 1:21; 3:15, 16), he, nevertheless, was conscious of the manner in which he was restricted by the limitations of time and space. Right now he wishes that he could be with those whom he addresses. However, with his hands full of work in Corinth (if that supposition be correct), he finds it impossible right now to rush off to distant Galatia. Ah, if he could only be with them, then, perhaps by hearing and seeing them and conversing with them, the change in them for which he so yearns might be brought about more speedily. Then possibly he might no longer have to rebuke them as he has done in this epistle, might not have to call them "foolish Galatians" any longer, but might be able to change his tone of voice. As of now, however, he is perplexed about them, at a loss to know why they have yielded to temptation. O that his dear children would return to the home from which they have wandered away! Yes, indeed, Paul is suffering birth-pangs . . . again!

The passage is one of the finest practical applications of I Cor. 13, written by Paul himself. Though the Galatians have failed Paul, his love toward them never fails, for love is longsuffering and kind, and even now hopes all things.

---

130 The verb μορφωθῇ points to a desired change in inner essence. See N.T.C. on Philippians, pp. 102–105.

131 The hymn "Fill Thou My Life" by Horatius Bonar provides an excellent commentary.

# Chapter 4

Verses 21-31

Theme: *The Gospel of Justification by Faith apart from Law-works Defended against Its Detractors*

II. *Its Vindication: both Scripture—i.e., the Old Testament—and life (experience, past history) bear testimony to its truth*

F. History of the slave-woman (Hagar) and her son versus the free-woman (Sarah) and her son (Gen. 16:1-4; 21:8-12). Application: Cast out the slave-woman and her son. Not of a slave-woman are we children, but of the free-woman.

21 Tell me, y o u who desire to be under law, do y o u not hear the law?
22 For it is written that Abraham had two sons, one by the slave-woman and one
by the free-woman. 23 But the son of the slave-woman was flesh-born; the son of
the free-woman (was born) through promise. 24 Now things of this nature were
spoken with another meaning in mind, for these two women represent two
covenants: one from Mount Sinai, bearing children destined for slavery. She is
Hagar. 25 Now Hagar represents Mount Sinai in Arabia, and corresponds to the
Jerusalem of today, for she is in bondage with her children. 26 But the Jerusalem (that is) above is free, and she is our mother; 27 for it is written:

"Rejoice O barren one, you who do not bear;
Break forth and shout, you who have no birth-pangs;
For more are the children of the desolate than of her who has a husband."

28 Now y o u, brothers, like Isaac, are children of promise. 29 But as at that time
he (who was) flesh-born persecuted the one (who was) Spirit-born, so (it is) also
now. 30 But what does Scripture say? "Cast out the slave-woman and her son; for
in no way shall the son of the slave-woman share in the inheritance with the son
of the free-woman." 31 Wherefore, brothers, not of a slave-woman are we children,
but of the free-woman.

4:21-31

### F. *Instructive "Allegory"*

The proposition that those—those *alone, all* those—who by a true and living faith accept God's promise are the children of God, is defended once more, and now for the last time, with an appeal to Scripture. Rigid adherence to law, as if this were the way to be saved, is exposed as being in reality nothing but bondage, spiritual slavery. Faith, on the contrary, spells freedom. Accordingly, this section, too, is true to the theme of the entire epistle, namely, "The gospel of justification by faith apart from law-works defended against its detractors."

This time, however, the apostle makes use of a type of argumentation which he has not employed before. He avails himself of an allegory. It is not wrong to call it that, provided that the term *allegory* be interpreted in the most favorable sense (see on verse 24). Paul sets forth the spiritual meaning of a familiar story, that of two women that dwelt in Abraham's tents: *a.* his wife Sarah, and *b.* Sarah's personal slave Hagar, whom she gave to Abraham in order that she, Sarah, might obtain children by her. Hagar bore Ishmael. Several years later Sarah bore Isaac. Sarah and her son are now described as representing all those freedom-loving people who live by faith, as contrasted with Hagar and her son who are designated as representing those spiritually enslaved individuals who live by law. Cf. Gen. 16:1-4; 21:1-12.

Those who suppose that by using this kind of an argument Paul arrives at an interpretation that is fallacious, far-fetched, and fantastic, betraying the influence of his own early training in worthless rabbinical methods of exegesis, do him an injustice, and are themselves guilty of misinterpretation, for they misinterpret the apostle. What his allegory really amounts to is *an obvious lesson* plus a *self-invited comparison,* both of them derived from the ancient narrative in a manner so natural that in a mood of surprise Paul says: **21. Tell me, y o u who desire to be under law, do y o u not hear the law?** Those people—the Judaizers and also the Galatians themselves to the extent in which they allow themselves to be influenced by these legalists—are always talking about the indispensable necessity of keeping the Mosaic law (see on verse 10) ; nevertheless, they seem to forget that the law itself clearly contradicts their belief. In this second reference to *law* ("the law") Paul uses the term in a wider sense: Torah or Pentateuch. With a lively "Tell me," he calls his opponents to account. Continued: **22. For it is written that Abraham had two sons, one by the slave-woman and one by the free-woman.** As has been shown earlier (see on 3:6), Paul's adversaries and their Jewish followers prided themselves in the fact that they were the descendants of Abraham, as if that biological relationship were of paramount significance for salvation, of such superior value that even the non-Jewish converts to Christianity should, by being circumcised, strive to resemble their Jewish co-religionists as closely as possible. Paul's argument, then, is this: Those who are always boasting about their descent from Abraham are forgetting that Abraham had not *one* son but *two* sons[132]: Ishmael by Hagar as well as Isaac by Sarah. Accordingly, if physical descent from Abraham is so all-important, then they who are Jews by birth are not any better off than are the Ishmaelites.

Nevertheless, so runs Paul's argument, there is, indeed, a marked difference between the son of Hagar, the slave-woman, and the son of Sarah, the free-woman, but that difference is not of a physical but of a spiritual nature. It represents the contrast between those who live by law and those who live by faith; in other words, between those who depend on that which they themselves are able to bring about and those who rely on the effectuation of God's gracious promise. The basic difference between Ishmael and Isaac, and between the two groups which they respectively represent, reveals itself in their contrasted birth (verses 23-28), their relation to each other (verse 29), and their lack of right, or right, to the inheritance (verse 30).

---

[132] The sons of Abraham's concubine Keturah are not within the range of vision here (Gen. 25:1 ff.; I Chron. 1:32, 33).

First, then, there is the contrast in birth: **23. But the son of the slave-woman was flesh-born; the son of the free-woman (was born) through promise.** Meaning: Ishmael was the product of his parents' natural power of procreation. He was born in accordance with that which Abraham and Hagar were able to accomplish in the ordinary course of nature (cf. John 1:13; Rom. 9:7-9). Accordingly, he represents all those who base their hope for eternity on what they themselves are able to effectuate, that is, on their own works.

There are those who think that this conclusion, already obvious, gains added strength when the full story, as related in Gen. 16:1-4, is taken into account. According to that passage Ishmael's birth was the result not only of a physical act but also of sinful deliberation. Abraham and Sarah, unwilling to bide God's time for the fulfilment of the promise, took matters into their own hands, so that, on the advice of Sarah, Abraham went in to Hagar, Sarah's Egyptian maid, with the result that she conceived and bore Abraham a son, Ishmael. However, the purpose of this scheme was not thereby realized, for Ishmael was not the child of promise. As these interpreters see it, therefore, when Paul here in Gal. 4:23 describes Ishmael as *flesh-born,* he attaches a double sense to this term, namely, "born according to carnal deliberation (Gen. 16:2), and by virtue of the physical capacity of both Abraham and Hagar, which had not yet died (Gen. 16:4)."[133] Thus, in the opinion of these exegetes, it becomes even more strikingly evident how the son of the slave-woman could represent all those who, instead of trusting in Christ for their salvation, labor slavishly to attain it by their own cunning, and are doomed to bitter disappointment. This double sense theory is attractive, but whether or not it be correct cannot be proved. Moreover, the theory is not necessary. Ishmael, as a son born in the usual, natural, way, is even so a true representative of all those who have experienced only the natural birth, not the birth from above. And on either theory he remains a slave, a fit symbol of all those who labor slavishly to enter into the kingdom.

Isaac, on the other hand, was born as a result of Abraham's faith in God's promise. It was as a reward for the exercise of this faith that God intervened miraculously, enabling Abraham, though he had become "as good as dead," to deposit seed, and making it possible for Sarah, heretofore barren, to conceive (Rom. 4:19; Heb. 11:11, 12). Isaac, then, was Spirit-born (verse 29), for it was the Holy Spirit who caused the promise to be realized. The conclusion, therefore, that Isaac is a symbol of all Spirit-born (now in the sense of *regenerated*) men is not far-fetched. It is all the more natural in view of the fact that he, in spite of his weaknesses, was going to manifest himself as a true believer, one who by faith rested in God's promise (Gen. 24:63; 26:18, 22-25; 28:1-4).

---

[133] Greijdanus, *Galaten* (Korte Verklaring), p. 126.

On the basis of the preceding it is not strange that Paul continues: **24. Now things of this nature were spoken with another meaning in mind, for these two women represent two covenants. . . .** Such historical events were designed to convey a meaning *other than*—in addition to—the strictly literal. God has given us such narratives not only to teach us what happened in the past, but also to enable us to apply the lessons of the past to our present situation (cf. Rom. 4:23, 24). Such things, then, are true as *history* and valuable as *graphic pedagogy*. It is in that sense that Paul is saying that things of this nature "are an allegory" (A.V.). The lesson here taught is derived as naturally from the narrative as an almond-kernel is picked out of an almond-shell. With this interpretation in mind we can understand that Paul was justified in saying, "Tell me, y o u who desire to be under law, do y o u not hear the law?" He meant, of course, that the lesson implied in the incident was so obvious that anyone who listened attentively to the narrative, when it was read, should have understood the deeper meaning immediately.

This shows that Gal. 4:24 provides no comfort whatever to "allegorizers" of the wild type; such, for example, as Rabbi Akiba, who was able to distil a mystical sense from the hooks and crooks of the Hebrew letters; Philo, who imagined that the cherubim placed at Eden's gates represented God's lovingkindness and his sovereignty; Origen, who on occasion "tortured Scripture in every possible manner, turning it away from the true sense" (Calvin); and the author of a certain very popular present day Bible which, though valuable in some respects, can hardly be considered a trustworthy guide when it pictures Asenath, the Egyptian wife of Joseph, as the type of the Christian church, called out from among the Gentiles to be the bride of Christ!

These two women, says Paul, *are* (that is, *represent*) two covenants, two distinct affirmations of God's one and only covenant of grace. See N.T.C. on Eph. 2:12. These two were: the covenant with Abraham (verse 18; cf. 3:8, 16-18) and the covenant of Sinai (Gal. 3:19, 24). Paul begins with the latter: **one from Mount Sinai, bearing children destined for slavery.** Though, as was shown earlier (see on 3:10, 25), God gave his law to Israel in a context of grace, that law was unable to save anyone. Besides, when it is, nevertheless, viewed as a force by means of which a person achieves deliverance and salvation, as the Jews and Judaizers actually viewed it, then it enslaves. It then not only leaves men in their bondage but more and more adds to their heavy burden. See on 2:4; 3:22, 23; 4:3, 7; 5:1; cf. Matt. 11:28, 29; Rom. 8:15. Paul adds: **She is Hagar,** for just as Hagar, being herself a slave, was able to bear only a slave-child, so also the law, as the Jews and Judaizers erroneously interpreted it, was able to bring forth none but drudges, whom it kept under its harsh dominion. Continued: **25. Now Hagar represents Mount Sinai in Arabia, and corresponds to the Jerusalem of today, for she is**

**in bondage with her children.**[134] In the preceding verse Hagar and Mount Sinai have been linked. It was shown that, in the sense explained, both can produce nothing but slaves. Now the comparison is brought a step farther. What was implied right along is now clearly stated, namely, that *in line with* Hagar and Mount Sinai is also the Jerusalem of Paul's own day, earthly Jerusalem with her children (cf. Matt. 23:37): all of carnal Israel that had rejected Christ and his glorious gospel. It is hardly necessary to add that here Paul is thinking not only of the Jews who had openly repudiated Christ, but definitely also of those Jews who were Christians only in name, the Judaizers. Now here in verse 25 the emphasis is entirely on the third element in the comparison: Jerusalem and her children. These, too, as well as Hagar and Ishmael, are now said to be in bondage. They have enslaved themselves to Sinai's law, for they imagine that by strict obedience to this legal code—with emphasis on its ceremonial regulations, expanded by man-made additions—they can work their way into the kingdom of heaven. But they are wrong. Mount Sinai is in Arabia, and Arabia is a desert. It is not the land of promise; it is not "Zion" (Heb. 12:22; Rev. 14:1). When a person bases his hope for eternity on his own endeavors he is engaged in a sterile business!

The clause: ". . . and corresponds to the Jerusalem of today," calls attention to the fact that Hagar, Mount Sinai, and Jerusalem of today all stand in the same *row* or *line,* the same *"stich"* (line of poetry); hence, the same *category,* for they all spell *slavery,* the bondage that results from trusting in works of the flesh. Their opposites spell *freedom,* the blessing which those enjoy who trust fully in Christ, their Lord, who will never put them to shame:

Hagar, Horeb, earthly Salem,
Works of flesh will not avail them.
Sarah, Zion, heavenly Salem,
Christ, their Lord, will never fail them.

Continued: **26. But the Jerusalem (that is) above is free, and she is our mother.** Over against "the Jerusalem of today" we might have expected Paul to mention "the Jerusalem of the future." But he cannot very well do this, for the church, as the sum-total of all believers, here contrasted with carnal Israel, is being gathered even now, though her glorious consumma-

[134] The text here is somewhat obscure. There are many variants. Some of these are not very important. So, for example, whether one reads *Now* or *For* at the beginning of verse 25, the basic sense of the entire passage remains the same. The most debated question is whether or not the proper name *Hagar* belongs to the text. Though lengthy arguments have been presented for its omission, that rejection does not rest on solid textual evidence but is an unsubstantiated conjecture. On the basis of the information supplied by N.N.'s textual apparatus there would seem to be no good reason to accept any changes in the reading that is given in the text of both N.N. and Grk.N.T. (A.B.M.W.).

tion belongs, indeed, to the future. Not until Christ's return will she have been brought to completion, to shine forth in all her beauty, to the glory of God Triune.

Now when Paul speaks about "the Jerusalem (that is) above," he is thinking not only of the Church Triumphant but also of the many blessings which the exalted Christ lavishes upon this object of his love. And since from heaven these blessings also descend to the earth (cf. Eph. 1:3), creating and strongly influencing the church here below, producing conditions on earth which in some measure reflect those in heaven, it is clear that "the Jerusalem (that is) above" becomes in a sense the mother of all God's true children on earth, be they Gentiles or Jews. Essentially the same idea is found in the book of Revelation (3:12; 21:2, 10). In a vision John sees the holy city, new Jerusalem coming down out of heaven from God. That is happening now: whenever sinners are reborn—born "from above" (John 3:3, 6, 7)—; whenever, in principle, God's will is done on earth as in heaven (Matt. 6:10); and whenever, as a result of Christ's coming and work (Isa. 7:14; cf. 9:6), heaven's peace is reflected in the hearts and lives of God's children here below (Isa. 11:6-9; cf. Jer. 23:6; 31:31-34). But this is only an anticipatory fulfilment of the prophecies. Perfection belongs to the day of the great consummation.[135]

Heaven, then, is the church's mother, for it was heaven that gave birth to her children. Though many of them are still on earth, is not heaven their homeland (Phil. 3:20)? Are not their lives governed from heaven in accordance with heavenly standards? Are not their names inscribed in heaven's register? Is it not there that their rights are secured, and their interests promoted? Is it not to heaven that their thoughts and prayers ascend and their hopes aspire? Their Savior dwells there, living evermore to make intercession for them. Some of their friends are there even now, and they themselves, if they place their trust in the heavenly Highpriest, will be there shortly, to receive the inheritance of which they have an earnest even now. See John 14:1-4; Rom. 8:17; Col. 3:1-3; Heb. 4:14-16; 6:19, 20; 7:25; 12:22-24; I Peter 1:4, 5; Rev. 7:9-17.

"The Jerusalem (that is) above is free," says Paul. See John 8:36. She has been delivered from every form of bondage and enjoys perfect peace in the presence of her Lord. She is, moreover, "*our* mother," the mother not only of the Jews who have gone to the deeps of God's promise but also of the Gentiles who have done the same thing; **27. for it is written:**

**"Rejoice O barren one, you who do not bear;**
**Break forth and shout, you who have no birth-pangs;**
**For more are the children of the desolate than of her who has a husband."**

---

[135] See my book *More Than Conquerors, An Interpretation of the Book of Revelation* (Grand Rapids, fifteenth edition, 1967), p. 237.

Isaiah, by prophetic vision, sees Zion bereft of her children, who have gone into Babylonian captivity. Jehovah, through his prophet, brings her a message of cheer. She, though now barren, will be fruitful; more so, in fact, than ever before (Isa. 54:1). The promise given to Sarah, who also was barren, will be fulfilled (Gen. 17:16). God's church will be extended among the Gentiles. Large multitudes will thus be added to the company of the saved. Zion, the Jerusalem (that is) above, will have an abundant posterity on earth. Hence, she will have to make her tent more spacious by lengthening its cords. At the same time she will have to see to it that the stakes are strengthened, that is, that the tent-pins are fixed into the ground more firmly, because the dwelling-place of the church as God sees it will never be broken up (Isa. 54:2, 3; Rev. 3:12; 7:9; cf. John 6:37, 39; 10:28).

Now all this is represented here as the work of the Lord, the result of the manifestation of his enduring lovingkindness (cf. Isa. 54:7, 8); not the product of human exertion but the realization of God's promise, the very promise that gave Isaac to Abraham and Sarah. This promise applies also to the Galatians if they accept it by means of a living faith: **28. Now y o u, brothers, like Isaac, are children of promise.** Here again we are pleased to take note of the affectionate manner in which Paul addresses those for whom the letter was intended. Again he calls them "brothers" (cf. 1:11; 3:15; 4:12, 28, 31; 5:11, 13; 6:1, 18). Are not all believers members of the same family, the Father's Family? See N.T.C. on Eph. 3:14, 15. They are brothers by grace, through the Spirit. Surely, if the Jerusalem (that is) above is their common mother (verse 26), then it follows that her children are brothers. Like Isaac, and by virtue of the promise realized in him but not in Ishmael, these Galatians who truly believe—whether they be Gentiles or Jews by birth makes no difference—are "children of promise." They are Abraham's legitimate sons, the true heirs. Let them understand, then, that what the Judaizers and their followers are doing is this: they are opposing the very work of God which he is gloriously effectuating whenever Gentiles, on equal terms with the Jews, are gathered into the church. See on 3:16-18, 29; 4:22.

The basic difference between Ishmael and Isaac, and between the two groups which they respectively represent, reveals itself not only in their birth (slave or free), but also in their relation to each other: **29. But as at that time he (who was) flesh-born persecuted the one (who was) Spirit-born, so (it is) also now.** The reference here is to Gen. 21:8, 9, which informs us that on the day when Isaac was weaned—which usually took place when the child was about three years of age—Abraham celebrated this event by means of a great feast. It was then that "Sarah saw the son of Hagar the Egyptian, whom she had borne to Abraham, mocking" (translation of the Hebrew text). Though the original lacks the words: (mocking) "her son Isaac," this object, added by the Septuagint and thus also by the Vulgate, etc., undoubtedly expresses what the writer had in mind, as the context clearly indicates. Since Ishmael was fourteen years older than Isaac (cf. Gen. 16:16 with 21:5), he must have been a lad of about seventeen at the time when this incident occurred.

There are those, however, who interpret the Hebrew verb which describes Ishmael's conduct toward his brother as indicating nothing more serious than innocent play. Thus R.S.V. renders the Genesis passage: "playing with her son Isaac."[136] On the basis of this rendering it is at times further assumed that the guilty one was Sarah, not Ishmael. When Isaac's mother sees the older boy and her own little child having a good time together, she is stricken with jealousy, as she considers the future. She begins to worry about the possibility that the two might some day become joint-heirs of Abraham's wealth. That must not be. Hence, she demands Ishmael's ejection, so that her own son Isaac may be the sole heir. On the basis of this interpretation Paul's statement that Ishmael *persecuted* Isaac would, of course, be wrong. But the facts do not sustain this view of that which actually took place. Note the following:

(1) The Old Testament does not support this meaning for the verb that is here used to describe what Ishmael was doing. That verb does not generally refer to innocent fun. There was, for example, nothing innocent in the "jesting" with which Lot's prospective sons-in-law greeted the announcement of Sodom's imminent doom (Gen. 19:14). That jesting was coarse ridicule, mockery. Again, Potiphar's wife was not at all in the mood to accuse Joseph of having been "guilty" of a little innocent play. On the contrary, by implication she charged him with *insult,* to put it mildly (Gen. 39:14). The unrestrained hilarity of the Israelites around the golden calf was by no means innocent merrymaking (Exod. 32:6), neither was the "amusement" of the Philistines in connection with their prisoner Samson (Judg. 16:25). It is evident that in all these cases the word has an unfavorable sense, an acrid taste.[137]

(2) A look at the historical and psychological background also favors the rendering *mocking* rather than *playing with.* It should be borne in mind that the birth of Isaac and, even more, the fact that the little one had survived the earliest and most critical stage of his life, had brought about an important change in Ishmael's prospects as an heir of Abraham's vast estate. *Before* Isaac's arrival Ishmael must have regarded himself as the sole heir of unassailable assets. He must have felt all the more secure because of his father's ripe old age. And now suddenly the ground gives way from under his feet. Someone else has replaced him. Not only that, but

---

[136] See also Strack-Billerbeck, *op. cit.,* Vol. III, pp. 575, 576.

[137] In Gen. 26:8 the verb is used in a different sense: of a man *fondling* his wife. In all these cases in which the word occurs in the Old Testament the Hebrew uses a strengthened (Piël) form of the verb *çāhaq* (Gen. 19:14; 21:9; 26:8; 39:14; Exod. 32:6; and Judg. 16:25: the only instances of the Piël form).

at this particular *feast* everyone's interest is focused on this little brother, not on Ishmael. Seen in this light, it is not so strange that Ishmael, out of envy, *mocked* Isaac.

(3) Children often imitate their parents. Is it not possible, indeed rather natural, that the contempt with which Hagar had looked down upon Sarah was copied by Ishmael in his attitude toward Sarah's son? Cf. Gen. 16:4 and 21:9.

Paul, accordingly, was entirely correct in interpreting the Old Testament passage as he did. The one who was born in the natural way *had persecuted* the one who was born in a supernatural way, that is, born through special intervention of the Holy Spirit, who had enabled Abraham, though the latter had become "as good as dead," to deposit seed, and had quickened Sarah's womb. Cf. verse 23. So also today, says Paul, himself formerly a legalist and persecutor, the flesh-born Judaizers are persecuting those who are Spirit-born (now in the sense of *regenerated*). The wicked world, whether represented by legalists or by libertines, begrudges believers their joy in the Lord. To be persecuted is therefore the lot of the Christian (Matt. 5:11; John 15:20; 16:33; II Tim. 3:12; Rev. 12:13).

If there be any implied idea of relative "innocence" in this passage, it would be on the part of Isaac. If he complained at all, it is not mentioned. It was his mother who noticed that Ishmael was mocking. It is true that a child of three can do very little in the way of opposing a young man of seventeen. But it is characteristic of Isaac that also later on in life he bears persecution with admirable patience (Gen. 26:13-22), a virtue for which the Lord rewarded him (Gen. 26:23-25). He was not a vengeful person.

But though vengeance is wrong, evil must be resisted. Moreover, it was the duty of both Abraham and Sarah to protect the son of promise. Ishmael and Isaac cannot live side by side. Hence, Paul continues: **30. But what does Scripture say? "Cast out the slave-woman and her son; for in no way shall the son of the slave-woman share in the inheritance**[138] **with the son of the free-woman."** The inheritance (see on 3:9, 18, 29) is not for mockers or persecutors. It is for believers, for them alone. This is the third item with respect to which the basic difference between Ishmael and Isaac reveals itself. For the others see on verses 23 and 29. *Law* (as interpreted by the Judaizers) *and grace cannot dwell in one camp.* Ishmael must be summarily ejected! Sarah demanded it (Gen. 21:10). What is more, God himself supported this demand (Gen. 21:12), giving Paul the right to imply that the order for Ishmael's expulsion was based on divine authority: "But what does *Scripture* say?"

**31.** With another, very affectionate, "brothers" (see on verse 28) the

---

[138] What we have here is a very strong negative, expressed by οὐ μή and the future indicative κληρονομήσει (the best reading).

apostle closes and summarizes the argument. He says: **Wherefore, brothers, not of a slave-woman are we children, but of the free-woman.** We—that is, Paul, the Galatians (as viewed by the judgment of love; cf. 4:6, 19; 5:10), all believers everywhere and throughout all time—are children not of *a* slave-woman—the definite article being omitted to emphasize her *slavish* quality—but of *the* free-woman, Sarah, as the true representative of "the Jerusalem (that is) above." We are the offspring of sovereign grace. Nevertheless, this in no way relieves us of responsibility, the very responsibility implied in the passage, namely, to guard the precious endowment which the Lord has bequeathed to us, and therefore to live by faith, in the joyful exercise of our freedom of access to the throne of grace. This freedom is at the same time a deliverance from the curse of the law. Let us then, so argues Paul, cling to this freedom, for Jerusalem (that is) above is a city of free men (Gal. 3:19-29; 4:26; 5:1).

## *Summary of Chapter 4*

This chapter can be divided into three sections under the headings: Recapitulation (verses 1-11), Reminiscence (verses 12-20), and Reasoning by means of an Allegory (verses 21-31). In the first section Paul, in close connection with the preceding argument,[139] points out the folly of exchanging one type of slavery for another. Judaistic bondage is not any better than paganistic. God sent his Son to redeem men from every type of spiritual slavery. He changed slaves into sons. Moreover, he sent the Spirit into their hearts in order that those who were sons *in position* might also be sons in *disposition,* for *adoption* implies *transformation.* Deliverance means freedom of access, so that the ransomed one cries out, "Abba!" ("Father!").

In the next paragraph the apostle asks, "Where is now your former blessedness?" His affectionate concern for the Galatians reveals itself as he recalls the warm welcome with which they had received him at the occasion of their first meeting. How blessed had been the experiences then enjoyed, how unforgettable the fellowship! What a contrast between then and now. One is reminded of the lines:

"Where is the blessedness I knew
  When first I sought the Lord?
Where is the soul-refreshing view
  Of Jesus and his Word?

[139] Cf. 4:1, 2 with 3:22, 25; 4:3, 8-10 with 3:23; 4:4 with 3:19; 4:5 with 3:13; 4:6 with 3:2, 3, 5, 14; 4:7 with 3:18, 29; and 4:11 with 3:4.

## GALATIANS

"What peaceful hours I once enjoyed!
How sweet their memory still!
But they have left an aching void
The world can never fill."
William Cowper

In the case of the Galatians the former blessedness had been lost because Paul's earnest warnings had been left unheeded. The apostle exposes the motives of the enemies of the faith. They make much of the Galatians in order that the latter may make much of them. Now making much of someone is not wrong if it be in connection with a good cause. Thus, the fact that the Galatians had previously paid special attention to Paul, and, far from treating him with contemptuous scorn because of his bodily infirmity, had been willing, if necessary, to give him their most precious possession, was not wrong, because he proclaimed to them the gospel of salvation. Would that this interest in Paul and his gospel had continued! With sadness of heart Paul asks, "Have I then become y o u r enemy by telling y o u the truth?" Do the Galatians not realize that his warnings and criticisms were for their own good? The apostle concludes this section by saying, "My dear children, for whom I am again suffering birth-pangs until Christ be formed in y o u, I could wish to be present with y o u now and to change my tone of voice, for I am perplexed about y o u."

The chapter closes with a reminder—in the form of an allegory—that those who hear the law should take it to heart. When the Judaizers pride themselves in the fact that they are "sons of Abraham," and the Galatians are influenced by this boast, let it be remembered that Abraham had two sons: one by the slave-woman, the other by the free-woman. Slavish law-observance, as if this were the pathway to salvation, makes one similar to Ishmael, slave-son of a slave-woman (Hagar). On the contrary, the exercise of one's freedom in Christ, basing one's trust in him alone, makes one a true son of Abraham, similar to the free-born son Isaac, born to the free-woman, Sarah.

# Chapter 5

Verse 1

Theme: *The Gospel of Justification by Faith apart from Law-works Defended against Its Detractors*

III. *Its Application: it produces true liberty. Let the Galatians stand firm, therefore, as does Paul, who glories in the cross of Christ*

A. For freedom Christ has set us free; continue to stand firm, therefore.

# CHAPTER V

## GALATIANS

5 1 For freedom Christ has set us free; continue to stand firm, therefore, and do not be loaded down again with a yoke of slavery.

---

5:1

A. *Maintain y o u r freedom!*

**1. For freedom Christ has set us free.**[140] There is every reason to agree with modern versions when they print Gal. 5:1 as a little paragraph all by itself, the first paragraph of a new chapter. That something new begins here is clearly evident from the contrast between the *argumentative* style of the earlier chapters, including the immediately preceding context, and the *hortatory* language that begins here in 5:1. Having been taught that in Christ we *are* free, we (here specifically the Galatians) are now encouraged to maintain that freedom (verse 1) and to interpret and apply it properly (verse 13 ff.). But this very statement also indicates the close connection between chapters 4 and 5. The truth stated and vigorously defended in the preceding chapters is applied to life in chapters 5 and 6.

That the idea of freedom is very much in the foreground is clear not only from verse 1 but also from verse 13 ff. The question arises: Just what does Paul mean when he speaks of freedom? It implies first of all *deliverance.* This deliverance is sometimes conceived of as rescue from the guilt and power of sin (Rom. 6:18); hence, from an accusing conscience (Heb. 10:22), from the wrath of God (Rom. 5:1; cf. Heb. 10:27), and the tyranny of

---

[140] Other translations of verse 1, such as, "Stand fast therefore in the liberty wherewith Christ hath made us free" (A.V.), though conveying the same meaning essentially, are not based upon the best text. Besides, in connection with the great central doctrines of salvation asyndetic expression is not uncharacteristic of Paul. Cf. Eph. 2:5b, "By grace y o u have been saved." Such omission of conjunctions produces emphasis. With respect to the question whether, with some, we should adopt the rendering, "For *this* freedom," or should favor the simple, "For freedom," my answer would be that it is probably best to allow either translation, since although the abstract quality *freedom* has not been mentioned in the immediately preceding context, it has nevertheless been implied in the words, "We are children of the free-woman." Translated either way, moreover, the close connection with the immediately preceding verses is clear. For the point of grammar see p. 145, footnote 105.

Satan (II Tim. 2:26; cf. Heb. 2:14). Nevertheless, although all of this is probably implied in Paul's use of the term here in Gal. 5:1, 13, the context indicates that he is thinking particularly of freedom from "the law," that is, deliverance from the curse which the law pronounces upon the sinner who had been striving—unsuccessfully, of course—to achieve his own righteousness (Gal. 3:13, 22-26; 4:1-7), but has now, by grace, turned to Christ and salvation in him. Cf. Phil. 3:4-9. For God's chosen one this freedom includes rescue from the results of the law's inability to make alive what is dead (Gal. 3:21). Implied is also freedom from fear, the fear that arises from *a.* the erroneous idea that both the moral and the ceremonial law must be strictly obeyed if one is to be saved, and *b.* the oppressing awareness of inability to meet this demand (Gal. 3:23; 4:21-31; Rom. 7:24-8:2).

*Deliverance* is, however, a negative concept, though the positive is clearly implied. *Freedom is more than deliverance. It is a positive endowment.* What the law could not do God has accomplished through Christ and the Spirit (Rom. 8:3, 4). Positively, then, freedom, as Paul sees it, is the state in which a person is walking and living in the Spirit (Gal. 5:25), so that he produces the fruit of the Spirit (5:22, 23), and with joy and gratitude does the will of God (5:14; Rom. 8:4), in principle fulfilling the law of Christ (Gal. 6:2), even "the law of liberty" (James 1:25). This liberty amounts to delighting in the law of God in one's inmost self (Rom. 7:22). The person who is truly free no longer acts from constraint but serves his God willingly, with cheerfulness of heart. Freedom of access to the Father is implied, of course, for the blessing of which Paul speaks is enjoyed by *sons* (Gal. 4:6; Rom. 8:15).

Such true freedom is therefore always a freedom *plus.* It is with freedom as with justification. See p. 98. When an accused man is declared not guilty, he is free. Likewise when a slave has been emancipated, he is free. But the judge or the emancipator does not, as a rule, adopt the acquitted individual as his son. But when the Son makes one free, he is free indeed (John 8:36). He then rejoices in the glorious liberty of sonship, with all that this implies as to "access," right to the inheritance, etc.

Paul emphasizes that it was Christ himself—not our own merits or our own deeds—that set us free. He did it by becoming a curse for us (Gal. 3:13); hence, by his blood (Heb. 10, 19, 22); and he did it and is constantly doing it through his Spirit (Gal. 3:2, 3, 14; 4:6, 29; cf. Rom. 8:4). Where the Spirit of the Lord is, there is liberty (II Cor. 3:17).

The thoroughly human Paul expresses himself in a manner which could almost be described as containing a bit of humor when he says, "For freedom Christ has set us free," as if to say, "Is it not ridiculous to imagine that Christ would have opened for us the gate of our prison—at such a cost!—merely to transfer us to another prison? Surely, he set us free in order that we might indeed be and remain free!" Continued: **continue to stand firm, therefore** (cf. II Thess. 2:15). Perseverance in the fight against re-enslavement is here prescribed. The Galatians had been running beautifully (5:7), but they had failed to carry on. They had, in fact, reversed their course. What Paul is saying, then, is that over against the opponents they should stand firm *and should so continue.* This standing firm is not that of a well-nigh unassailable fenced-in statue, but rather that of a tree firmly rooted in the midst of the raging storm. Even better, it is that of the soldier on the field of battle, not fleeing but offering stout resistance to the enemy and defeating him (Eph. 6:10-20). The very fact that it was no one less than Christ himself who had set the Galatians free, so that by standing firm, they are voluntarily continuing in the sphere of *his* activity, should encourage them; hence, "Continue to stand firm, *therefore.*" The crown of valor is victory (Matt. 10:22; Rev. 2:10).

Paul adds: **and do not be loaded down**[141] **again with a yoke of slavery.** Peter had spoken about an unbearable yoke (Acts 15:10). He was referring to the yoke of the law, including its many regulations, augmented subsequently by man-made "traditions." Under that yoke Israel had groaned. The Galatians, mostly of pagan origin (4:8), had been similarly subjected to rules and regulations pertaining to their former pagan religion. Ramsay speaks of "a highly elaborate system" of such burdensome stipulations, prevalent in Galatia. Hence, what the apostle is saying is that those who were delivered from this unbearable yoke of paganism should certainly not try to shoulder another similar yoke, that of Judaism. See also on 4:9. Having escaped from one ritualism are they now going to bow before another? Rather, let them flee for refuge to him whose yoke is easy and whose burden is light (Matt. 11:29, 30).

---

[141] The original uses a form of the verb ἐνέχω; literally, to *have or hold in.* Thus it is used in connection with Herodias who "had it in" for John the Baptist (had a grudge against him; Mark 6:19), and in connection with the scribes and Pharisees who were (violently) enraged against Jesus (Luke 11:53). In connection with a yoke, the best translation is probably "to be loaded down with" or "to be oppressed by."

# Chapter 5

Verses 2-6

Theme: *The Gospel of Justification by Faith apart from Law-works Defended against Its Detractors*

III. *Its Application: it produces true liberty. Let the Galatians stand firm, therefore, as does Paul, who glories in the cross of Christ*

B. Do not try to combine both principles: *a*. justification by way of law and *b*. justification by grace through faith. If y o u let yourselves be circumcised, Christ will be of no advantage to y o u. If y o u cling to law, y o u have lost y o u r hold on grace. Practice faith working through love.

2 Now I, Paul, say to you that if you let yourselves be circumcised Christ will be of no advantage to you. 3 And I testify again to every man who lets himself be circumcised, that he is under obligation to keep the whole law. 4 You are estranged from Christ, whoever (you are who) seek to be justified by way of law; you have fallen away from grace. 5 For, as to ourselves, it is through the Spirit, by faith, that we eagerly await the hoped-for righteousness. 6 For in Christ Jesus neither circumcision nor uncircumcision is of any avail, but faith working through love.

5:2-6

B. *Faith in Christ plus circumcision will not do*

It was a *gain* of incalculable value that Christ obtained for his people, namely, freedom. Over against this stands the frightful *loss* that is incurred by those who refuse to recognize him as their all-sufficient Savior. Therefore the text continues: **2. Now I, Paul, say to you that if you let yourselves be circumcised**[142] **Christ will be of no advantage to you.** From the stately style it is evident that the writer is conscious of his authority as an apostle of Jesus Christ. He has every right to speak thus, not only because he is, in fact, a true apostle, invested with this office by Christ himself (1:1, 12), but also because the matter at hand concerns the eternal weal or woe of those addressed. For "I, Paul" see also II Cor. 10:1; Eph. 3:1; Col. 1:23; and I Thess. 2:18. The substance of Paul's words is this, that a man's faith rests on Christ either entirely or not at all. God's Anointed One must be recognized and worshiped as the one and only Savior. Since the Galatians were already yielding to the Judaizers in the matter of observing "days and months and seasons and years" (4:10), the danger was great that they would yield also in the matter of circumcision, and that, as a result, their whole religion would be reduced to ritualism with a slightly Christian tinge. It is for this reason that the apostle uses such incisive language. If they accept circumcision, thinking that this is necessary for salvation, or at least for a full measure of salvation, Christ will be of no advantage to them whatever. A Christ supplemented is a Christ supplanted. Continued: **3. And I testify**

[142] It is important to note that this is a third class or future more vivid conditional sentence, implying that, considered from the viewpoint of human responsibility, the thing which Paul fears is possible, not that it necessarily has already occurred. On circumcision see N.T.C. on Colossians and Philemon, pp. 114-116, including footnote 85.

**again to every man who lets himself be circumcised, that he is under obligation to keep the whole law.** Continuing in the same solemn vein Paul *testifies,* so that the Galatians may act reverently, with a proper sense of respect for the will of God as revealed to them by his ambassador Paul. For *testify* see also Eph. 4:17 and I Thess. 2:12. The gravity of the expression is shown especially in the manner in which it is used in the speeches of Paul as reported by Luke in Acts 20:26 and 26:22. Paul testifies *to every man.* He is not only addressing the churches "en masse," or even the Galatian congregations one by one, but each *member* individually and personally. Let his warning be taken to heart by each and by all. Note the significant word *again* ("I testify again"). The sense, in connection with the preceding verse, is in all probability this, "Y o u must accept *the whole Christ* (Christ in all the fulness of his saving power and grace); *again,* if y o u refuse, then y o u will have to keep *the whole law.*" The one is implied in the other. If salvation is by law, why should one be obliged to keep just *one* ceremonial commandment, or even two or three, and not the rest? If the pathway to salvation is thought to lie in that direction one should travel it to the very end. He will discover, however, that the base from which he started was located in enemy territory—that his presupposition was a tragic error—and that the destination for which he is actually headed is "the curse" (3:10).

4. In this verse the same truth is reiterated: **Y o u are estranged[143] from Christ, whoever (y o u are who) seek to be justified[144] by way of law; y o u have fallen away from grace.** If the Galatians, whether all or some, should seek to be justified by way of law, and should persist to the end in this error, the cord that binds them to Christ would not be able to bear that strain. It would snap! They would then have fallen away from the domain of grace, would have lost their hold on grace. It would be with them like it is with withered flowers that fall to the ground and perish.

We should not try to diminish the force of these words, in the interest, perhaps, of this or that theological presupposition. It might seem as if what Paul is here saying is inconsistent with the doctrine of the preservation of the saints, a doctrine not only scriptural in general but also particularly dear to Paul. For evidence see N.T.C. on Philippians, pp. 54, 55. In reality, however, there is no conflict at all, as has been shown in connection with the explanation of Gal. 1:6, 7. Let it be borne in mind that Paul is speaking here from the standpoint of human responsibility.

5. In contrast with those who presumably might fall into the error against which the apostle issues his warning, Paul's own position, the

---

[143] Greek κατηργήθητε 2nd. person pl., aor. indic. passive of καταργέω. Cf. Rom. 7:2, 6.

[144] Greek δικαιοῦσθε 2nd. person pl. pres. indic. passive with conative force. See Gram. N.T., p. 880.

conviction of the Galatians who have remained loyal, and, in general, the firm persuasion of believers everywhere, is set forth in the following passage, in which the emphasis falls on the word which in the original heads the sentence, namely, "we" or, as we can also render it, "as to ourselves." Says Paul: **For, as to ourselves, it is through the Spirit, by faith, that we eagerly await the hoped for righteousness.** The conjunction γάρ can best be interpreted in its more usual sense as indicating the cause or reason for the thought that was expressed in the preceding verse. What Paul is saying then amounts to something along this line, "Those who yield to the Judaizers have fallen away from grace *because* they refuse to give due credit to the work of the Holy Spirit. On the contrary, as to ourselves, we recognize that Spirit as the source of all our striving and of our ultimate victory." That the word *pneuma,* which by itself can be rendered either *spirit* (6:1, 18) or *Spirit* (the Holy), must here be interpreted in the latter sense, as nearly always in Galatians, follows from all that Paul has been saying previously in this epistle and from all that he says elsewhere concerning the activity of the third person of the Trinity. Thus, the idea that it is through the Spirit that by faith we eagerly await the hoped-for righteousness is in line with the teaching that the law produces death (Rom. 7:10; 8:2), but the Spirit makes alive (Gal. 4:29; Rom. 8:3, 4, 10; cf. John 3:5); that the law creates fear and wretchedness (Rom. 8:15), but the Spirit brings about hope and assurance (Rom. 8:16; Eph. 1:13); that the law enslaves (Gal. 3:23; 4:24, 25), but the Spirit brings about freedom (Gal. 4:29-5:1). Considered from God's side, therefore, salvation is the gift of the Spirit (II Thess. 2:13; cf. Eph. 2:5, 8). Viewed from man's side it is received by faith, but even this faith, both in its initiation and at every step of the way, is Spirit-given. And if faith is God-given, why should not hope be also? And why should not the thing hoped for, in this case: the hoped-for righteousness,[145] be also assigned to the Holy Spirit, this all the more because the very presence of the Spirit in the hearts of believers is considered a pledge and first instalment of greater glories to come (Eph. 1:13, 14)?[146]

These greater glories to come are definitely in the mind of the writer, for he says that "through the Spirit, by faith we *eagerly await* (cf. Rom. 8:19, 23, 25; I Cor. 1:7) the hoped-for righteousness." To be sure, the verdict of acquittal has already been pronounced, so that even now the peace of God has smiled its way into our hearts (Rom. 5:1). But one day, namely, at Christ's glorious return, our righteousness will be declared *publicly*. Cf. Matt. 25:31-40; Luke 18:1-8; I Thess. 3:13; II Thess. 1:10. To

[145] Thus also in Col. 1:5 and Titus 2:13 "hope" refers to "the thing hoped for."

[146] For the reasons given I cannot accept the conclusion of Lenski (*op. cit.*, pp. 256, 257) who refuses to interpret Gal. 5:5 as containing a reference to the Holy Spirit. To be sure the Spirit may not be "a means that *we* use," but he may, nevertheless, very well be the Source of the exercise of our faith, hope, and love.

this day and to this blessing *we,* through the Spirit, by faith, eagerly look forward, not doubting that God will fulfil his promise.

**6.** This declaration concerning the eager forward look of Spirit-imparted faith is true, **For in Christ Jesus[147] neither circumcision nor uncircumcision is of any avail, but faith working through love.** As far as Christ Jesus is concerned —or, as one might say, in the sphere of Christian religion—*being circumcised* will be of no benefit toward salvation. But here as always Paul shows excellent balance by immediately adding, *nor being uncircumcised.* The circumcised person must not boast about the fact that his foreskin was removed, nor should the uncircumcised put on airs because he still has his. Cf. the similar statement in I Cor. 8:8 regarding food. What *is* important, however, is "faith working through love." Compare Rom. 14:17, "For the rule of God does not consist in eating and drinking but in righteousness and peace and joy in the Holy Spirit."

A controversy has long raged between Roman Catholic and Protestant interpreters with respect to the question whether Paul meant to say "faith wrought through love" or "faith working through love." According to the first view, generally favored by Rome, love precedes faith. Our works of love or "charity" give substance to faith. In this way the danger of ascribing too great a value to works and of making works basic in the effectuation of our salvation, is great indeed. This theory, therefore, contradicts the very thesis which the apostle is trying to establish in this epistle, namely, that justification is by faith, apart from works.[148] And as to which is first in order, whether *a.* love and the work it produces or *b.* faith, basically the priority should be given to faith. The works are fruits, not roots. Cf. Eph. 2:8-10; I Thess. 1:3; and see N.T.C. on I Tim. 1:5.

This having been said, it is well, nevertheless, to point out that just as in the natural sphere the young married woman who becomes the happy mother of a child, not only lavishes her love upon that child but is also herself reciprocally enriched, so also mother *faith,* having produced her child *love,* receives grace and glory from this child. Action begets reaction in this blessed circle of interrelationships.[149] The endowments with which

---

147 On the title "Christ Jesus" in distinction from "Jesus Christ" see N.T.C. on I and II Timothy and Titus, p. 51, footnote 19.

148 Moreover, also from the point of view of grammar this position is indefensible, for, in spite of articles that have been written in defense of the belief that ἐνεργουμένη, here used, is in the passive voice, the theory which regards it as a middle is far more natural and in keeping with Paul's usage elsewhere: "sinful passions are at work" (Rom. 7:5); "comfort—or patience—is at work" (II Cor. 1:6); so is also God's power (Eph. 3:20) and his word (I Thess. 2:13); and also "the mystery of lawlessness" (II Thess. 2:7). In each of these cases the verbal form is a middle, not a passive.

149 I consider Lenski's discussion of this subject (*op. cit.*, pp. 259, 260) to be, on the whole, excellent. I have difficulty, however, with his statement, "Faith is ever complete in itself."

the Holy Spirit graces the believer overlap. None stands by itself. And is not this implied in Paul's very statement that faith works through love? It works, becomes effective, proves its genuine character, by means of love and loving deeds. Indeed, by works faith is made perfect (James 2:22). Paul and James are in complete agreement!

Whether or not those are right who say that the Judaizers must have accused Paul of minimizing love, and that in this passage the apostle is answering this charge, we do not know. One fact, however, stands out clearly: the faith which Paul proclaims is always far richer than mere understanding. It is fruitful (5:22, 23; cf. John 16:2, 5, 8), not barren. It is warm, not cold. The man who wrote Gal. 5:6 also wrote I Cor. 13:2.

# Chapter 5

Verses 7-12

Theme: *The Gospel of Justification by Faith apart from Law-works Defended against Its Detractors*

III. *Its Application: it produces true liberty. Let the Galatians stand firm, therefore, as does Paul, who glories in the cross of Christ*

C. You were running well; who was it that threw you off your course? I am convinced that you will see the matter my way. If I am still preaching circumcision, why am I still being persecuted? Would that the disturbers might make eunuchs of themselves!

7 Y o u were running well; who cut in on y o u so that y o u did not continue to obey the truth? 8 This persuasion (is) not (derived) from him who is calling y o u. 9 A little leaven leavens the whole lump. 10 I on my part am persuaded in the Lord with respect to y o u, that y o u will not adopt a different view (than mine). And the one who is throwing y o u into confusion will have to pay the penalty, whoever he may be. 11 Now as for myself, brothers, if I am still preaching circumcision, why am I still being persecuted? In that case the stumbling-block of the cross has been removed. 12 Would that those who upset y o u might make eunuchs of themselves!

5:7-12

C. *Y o u were running well. I am persuaded that y o u will repent*

7. Turning back once more (cf. 1:8, 9; 3:2, 3; 4:9, 12-15) to the time when the Galatians had heard the gospel from the lips of Paul and had accepted Christ as their Savior and Lord, the apostle says: **Y o u were running well.** They had started out beautifully. Proof for this statement is found in 4:13, 14; cf. the account in Acts 13 and 14. The metaphor is taken from the foot-race in the stadium. A similar figure underlies Gal. 2:2; Phil. 2:16; I Tim. 4:7, 8; Heb. 12:1, 2. If Paul was in Corinth when he wrote this letter, as seems probable, he must have been hearing about such and other athletic contests, and may even have been a spectator at one time or another. But rivalry in games and sports was not confined to the city famous for its Isthmian contests, but was prevalent in greater or lesser extent throughout the world, then as well as now. The Galatians understood the metaphor. Continued: **who cut in on y o u so that y o u did not continue to obey the truth?** Paul is not asking for information. He is not necessarily referring to any ringleader. In all probability he is simply saying to the Galatians, "Before y o u continue to yield to the wishes of *any* person who belongs to this group, would it not be wise to consider carefully what kind of a person it was that threw y o u off y o u r course?" It is not the *identity* but the *character* of the Judaizers which the apostle is bringing into the foreground. This is in harmony with 6:12, 13. The Galatians, having been diverted from their proper course, were now proceeding on a path that would lead them to ruin, unless they returned to the base from which they had started out. They had discontinued to obey the truth. By this "truth" is meant God's special revelation as embodied in the gospel proclaimed by Paul and the other apostles and fellow-workers. Cf. 2:5, 14. That *truth* is full of practical implications. It concerns both doctrine and life. It not only tells men what to believe but also how they should conduct themselves. It reveals to them

that God gave his Son as a complete and perfect Savior, and that, out of gratitude for the salvation that is freely given to all who embrace him by a living faith, the redeemed should spend their days showing forth God's praise in thought, word, and deed. Continued: **8. This persuasion**[150] **(is) not (derived) from him who is calling y o u.** For "calling" see on 1:6. The Galatians are being told that the persuasion that draws them away from the truth does not have its source in him who not only *called* them in the beginning but *is calling* them even now: "Day by day his sweet voice soundeth, Saying, 'Christian, follow me'" (Mrs. Cecil F. Alexander). They must realize that their present course of action means that they are saying "No" to no one less than God himself (cf. 1:15). And this is a mild way of declaring that they have begun to say "Yes" to Satan, who is using the Judaizers in the distortion of the only true gospel (cf. Matt. 13:25, 28).

**9.** The warning continues, this time in the form of a proverbial saying, found also in I Cor. 5:6: **A little leaven leavens the whole lump.** Seemingly insignificant causes can lead to momentous consequences, whether for good (as in Matt. 13:33) or for evil, as in the present case. Principles penetrate! When a person has forsaken the sound principle of salvation *by grace alone through faith* (the latter considered as God's gift; see N.T.C. on Eph. 2:8), and has taken his stand on a new "persuasion," namely, salvation *by grace plus works,* the attention is gradually shifted to works, until grace has disappeared completely, and so has Christ, on whom grace rests. Illustrations of the penetrating power of evil: *a.* In ancient Israel the deceptively *innocent* worship of Jehovah under the symbolism (and by means) of an image soon led to gross idolatry; *b.* it took only a "worm" to destroy Jonah's "gourd" (Jonah 4:7); *c.* cancer spreads (metastasizes), so that a malignant tumor, ever so small in its beginning, may in the end destroy the entire body (cf. II Tim. 2:17); *d.* a "little" (?) carelessness starts a forest-fire, with destruction of thousands of valuable lumber-producing trees, or sets fire to a hotel, killing several people; *e.* someone tosses a few roots of a "beautiful" flower into a stream; result: many of the rivers, canals, lakes, and bayous of beautiful Florida, etc., are choked with the water hyacinth, which menaces wildlife, causes floods, strangles navigation, costs a fortune in attempts at eradication, so far with no completely satisfactory remedy in sight; and *f.:*

"For want of a nail the shoe was lost; for want of a shoe the horse was lost; for want of a horse the rider was lost; for want of a rider the battle

---

[150] As is clear from the textual evidence presented in N.N., this is the best text. The words πείθεσθαι (verse 7), πεισμονή (verse 8), and πέποιθα (verse 10), present a sound-similarity that is difficult to reproduce in English. An attempt would be: "Who cut in on y o u so that y o u did not continue *to be persuaded by* (hence, to obey) the truth? This (new) *persuasion* of y o u r s is not derived from him who is calling y o u. . . . I on my part *am persuaded* in the Lord, . . ."

was lost; and for want of a battle the kingdom was lost. All this for want of a horseshoe nail" (Benjamin Franklin, according to one version).

**10.** But though again and again the apostle has expressed his deep concern with reference to the Galatians (1:6, 7; 3:1-5; 4:11-20; 5:1-4, 7), he now reiterates his conviction that the letter which he is writing will have the desired effect. For other traces of this confidence see 3:4b; 4:6, 7, and the frequent use of the endearing form of address: "brothers" (1:11; 3:15; 4:12, 28, 31; 5:11, 13; 6:1, 18). He writes: **I on my part am persuaded in the Lord with respect to y o u, that y o u will not adopt a different view (than mine).** His conviction or persuasion regarding the Galatians rests not on any innate goodness of theirs, but solely on *their* and *his* relation to Christ, *their* and also *his* Lord. It is that Lord who, having begun a good work in the Galatians, will carry it on toward completion. See N.T.C. on Phil. 1:6. Continued: **And the one who is throwing y o u into confusion will have to pay the penalty, whoever he may be.** For the meaning of the verb *to throw into confusion* see on 1:7. Here in 5:10, as in verse 7 above, some see a reference to a ringleader. Some venture even farther away from shore, embarking boldly upon the sea of speculation when they suggest that either the apostle Peter, or else James the brother of the Lord, was that ringleader. But as to Peter see II Peter 3:15; and as to James see Acts 15:19, 24-26. Fact is that in referring to the disturbers Paul again and again uses the plural (1:7; 4:17; 5:12; 6:12, 13). But he also does not hesitate to use the plural and the singular in one breath (1:7; cf. 1:9: "certain individuals . . . anyone"). Does that mean that from the *many* disturbers he suddenly turns to the *one* ringleader? That would be rather strange. So also here the very wording would seem to point in the opposite direction: "the one who is throwing y o u into confusion . . . whoever he may be." The probable meaning is: "There are several disturbers. Be on y o u r guard, therefore, so that if *one*—anyone at all—of these creators of confusion approaches, y o u resist him, bearing in mind that, whoever he may be, he will have to pay the penalty." Implication: "and y o u also will have to pay the penalty (literally: bear the judgment) if y o u become involved in his guilt."

That the apostle is referring to *God's* judgment upon the distorters of the truth is not open to doubt. Whether Paul was thinking of punishment *here and now,* or rather of retribution *in the hereafter,* is not indicated. He may well have been thinking of both.

**11.** It is but natural that in connection with the strong condemnation of the teachers of error Paul would be reminded of an accusation which, in all probability, these men had hurled against him; namely, that he himself was inconsistent in his presentation of the gospel; specifically, that in regard to circumcision, the very matter with respect to which he censured his opponents so unmercifully, he himself was not to be trusted. They charged him with duplicity. At one time, so they said, Paul would have nothing whatever to do with this rite, and would denounce those who honored it. At another time he himself would preach it. Had he not circumcised Timothy? Viewed in the light of this accusation we understand what the apostle means when he continues: **Now as for myself, brothers, if I am still preaching circumcision, why am I still being persecuted?**[151] If there had *not* been a radical change in Paul's philosophy of life, so that he who at one time had been a self-righteous Pharisee and an ardent advocate of the Jewish traditions had even now *not* been truly converted, but was still clinging to his earlier beliefs, then why would he nevertheless be persecuted? In that case the Judaizers would have welcomed him as one of their own circle!

As to the circumcision of Timothy (Acts 16:3), it certainly was *one thing* to circumcise a person of mixed parentage, as was Timothy, in order to make him a more effective missionary among the Jews, and to do this without the least suggestion that in some way this circumcision would contribute toward his salvation; it was *an entirely different matter* to force circumcision upon the Gentiles, with the implication that unless they were circumcised they could not be saved! See Acts 15:1. In matters in which no principle was involved Paul was very accommodating, flexible, and conciliatory (cf. Acts 21:17-26), but when a deep principle was at stake—for example, Christ's all-sufficiency for salvation—he was unbending, and rightly so. Moreover, far from being inconsistent when, on the one hand, he circumcised Timothy, yet on the other hand strongly condemned the circumcision of the Galatians, he was most gloriously consistent, for in both instances he was promoting the spread of the one true gospel, subordinating everything else to this marvelous cause. If, therefore, the opponents, in charging Paul with inconsistency, were thinking of what he had done to Timothy, and were implying that by that very act he had been "preaching circumcision," they really had no case at all.—For a different interpretation of the passage see footnote.[152] See also on 2:5.

---

[151] This is a first class conditional sentence, with εἰ and the first per. pres. indic. active in the protasis; first per. pres. indic. passive in the apodosis. The sentence assumes the thought expressed in the protasis to be true, but in the present instance (as in Matt. 12:27) only *for the sake of the argument*, to show how absurd the conclusion would be if the assumption in the protasis were true.

[152] There are those who think that Paul's hypothetical clause bears no relation to his controversy with the Judaizers. In support of their theory they state that the Judaizers could hardly have called such an alleged inconsistency as the circumcision of Timothy "a *preaching* of circumcision." See Ridderbos, *op. cit.*, p. 266. I believe Lenski answers this objection when he points out that, as the Judaizers saw it, "Did Paul not thus preach circumcision by his own acts?" He refers to such acts as circumcising Timothy and refusing to object when Jewish Christians chose to circumcise their male children, as long as no legalistic and Judaistic ideas were connected with such circumcisions.

*Certainly one also preaches by means of his actions and refusals to act!* Besides, the explanation which I, along with many others—Berkhof, Burton, Lenski, Robert-

Paul continues: **In that case the stumbling-block of the cross has been removed.** For the Jews the death of the Messiah—even more so, the *accursed* death of the cross!—was a stumbling-block, a definite obstacle or hindrance to their acceptance of the Christian religion (I Cor. 1:23). They would say, "What, the Messiah crucified? Perish the thought!" What added to the offensiveness of this doctrine, as they saw it, was the claim that by means of this cross the old shadows had been fulfilled, the old ceremonial ordinances abrogated. Moreover, the burden of obedience to the law as a precondition of salvation had been lifted. And, to make things even worse *in their eyes,* by this cross the wall of separation between Jew and Gentile had been removed once for all, never to be rebuilt. Therefore, the all-sufficiency of Christ Crucified for salvation, completely obliterating the need of any additional props such as circumcision, was the stumbling-block for the Jews. But if the apostle were still preaching circumcision as a means of salvation, that offense would have been removed. Also, in that case Paul would no longer be persecuted by his kinsmen. Hence, the very fact that this persecution had not been discontinued was adequate proof that the charge of the opponents was false.

**12.** Paul closes this brief paragraph with a rather startling expression: **Would that those who upset y o u might make eunuchs of themselves!**[153]

In view of the fact that the basic meaning of the verb which Paul uses in expressing his wish is *to cut off,* there are those who think that the apostle voices his desire that the opponents may be "cut off" from the church ("I would that they were even cut off which trouble you," A.V.), or, better still, that they would *cut themselves off* (". . . would cut themselves off from you altogether," Phillips; cf. Ramsay, *Historical Commentary,* pp. 437–440). A more reasonable interpretation, however, one which (because it agrees with the use of the verb in such contexts in contemporary sources)[154] is supported by most commentators both ancient and modern, interprets the meaning to be this, that the apostle is saying, "As for these agitators, they had better go the whole way and make eunuchs of themselves!" (N.E.B). Paul reasons, as it were, as follows: Since circumcision has lost its religious value, it is nothing more than a concision (cf. Phil. 3:2), which differs only in degree but not essentially from the practices of pagan priests, practices well-known to the Galatians. But since the Judaizers who are upsetting the Galatians believe *a little* physical mutilation is of

---

son, etc.—accept, is also in harmony with the charge of *duplicity* which the Judaizers preferred against Paul (1:10).

[153] The text accepted by both N.N. and Grk.N.T. (A-B-M-W) has the third person pl. fut. indic. middle ἀποκόψονται. Some texts, including p[46], favor the subjunctive -ψωνται, with very little difference in resultant meaning. The verb is used elsewhere in connection with the cutting off of a member of the body (Mark 9:43, 45; John 18:10, 26) or of the ropes by which a boat is held (Acts 27:32).

[154] See the entry ἀποκόπτω in L.N.T. (A. and G.), p. 92.

spiritual value, let them be consistent and cut away *more radically*. Let them go all the way, and castrate themselves, thus making eunuchs of themselves like the priests of Cybele in their wild "devotions."

The question arises whether Paul was justified in uttering this wish. A few points should be borne in mind in this connection:

(1) In the final analysis Paul, in expressing this wish, was responsible to God, not to us. It is God alone who is able to judge the ethical value of such an utterance.

(2) Did not even the sinless Jesus say, "Whoever causes one of these little ones who believe in me to stumble, it is better for him that a heavy millstone be hung around his neck, and that he be drowned in the depth of the sea"? (Matt. 18:6; cf. Mark 9:42; Luke 17:2).

(3) The situation in which Paul found himself was similar: the Galatians, who were very dear to him (4:19) were being led astray. Also, the purity of the gospel was being undermined. Paul loved the Galatians and the true gospel deeply enough to be disturbed!

(4) Accordingly, instead of saying, "Shame on you, Paul, for wishing such a thing!" should we not rather say, "Shame *on ourselves,* that when in our own day and age the soundness of the gospel is being sacrificed upon the altar of ecumenism, and when ever so many people are being led astray by a so-called gospel that recognizes no contrast between saved and unsaved, but only "the brotherhood of all men" (as if, *in a redemptive sense,* all men were brothers), our own cheeks have lost the ability to glow with righteous indignation!

(5) Nevertheless, in all our thoughts, wishes, and expressions, may the prayer of the Psalmist, uttered in connection with a somewhat similar revelation of indignation, be ours also:

> "Search me, O God, and know my heart;
> Try me, and know my thoughts;
> And see if there be any wicked way in me,
> And lead me in the way everlasting"
> (Psalm 139:23, 24).

Such language reminds us of Paul's own sentiments (Eph. 4:31, 32; Col. 4:4, 6; Titus 3:2).

# Chapter 5

Verses 13-26

Theme: *The Gospel of Justification by Faith apart from Law-works Defended against Its Detractors*

III. *Its Application: it produces true liberty. Let the Galatians stand firm, therefore, as does Paul, who glories in the cross of Christ*

D. Remember that true liberty does not mean license. It means love. It does not welcome the works of the flesh but the fruit of the Spirit. It produces unity, not strife.

13 For you were called to freedom, brothers; only (do) not (turn) this
freedom into an opportunity for the flesh, but through love be serving one another.
14 For the whole law is fulfilled in one word, namely, in this: "You must love your
neighbor as yourself." 15 But if you bite and devour one another, watch out lest
you be consumed by one another.

16 But I say, walk by the Spirit, and you will definitely not fulfil the
desire of the flesh; 17 for the flesh sets its desire against the Spirit, and the Spirit
against the flesh: for these are opposed to each other, so that these very things
which you may wish to be doing, these you are not doing. 18 But if you are
being led by the Spirit you are not under law. 19 Now obvious are the works of
the flesh, which are: immorality, impurity, indecency, 20 idolatry, sorcery, quarrels,
wrangling, jealousy, outbursts of anger, selfish ambitions, dissensions, party intrigues, 21 envyings, drinking bouts, revelries, and the like, of which I forewarn
you, as I previously forewarned you, that those who indulge in such practices
will not inherit the kingdom of God. 22 But the fruit of the Spirit is love, joy,
peace, longsuffering, kindness, goodness, faithfulness, 23 meekness, self-control;
against such there is no law. 24 And those who believe in Christ Jesus have crucified
the flesh with its passions and desires.

25 If we live by the Spirit, by the Spirit let us also walk. 26 Let us not
become boasters, challenging one another, envying one another.

5:13-26

## D. *Freedom means love, not license*

Having previously dealt with the subject of freedom (2:4; 4:21-30; 5:1), Paul feels that further treatment is necessary, and this, it may well be surmised, particularly for two reasons: *a.* the charge of the Judaizers, that Paul's rejection of the law as a precondition of salvation would lead to lawlessness, and *b.* the presence of leftovers of pagan vices in the hearts and lives of the formerly chiefly pagan Galatians.

The Christian religion resembles a narrow bridge over a place where two polluted streams meet: one is called legalism, the other libertinism. The believer must not lose his balance, lest he tumble into the refined (?) faults of Judaism on the one side, or into the gross vices of paganism on the other. He must tread the safe and narrow path. Whether fashionable or coarse, both kinds of evils are products of "the flesh," that is, of sinful human nature. Since the apostle had devoted a large part of his epistle to the task of combating Judaistic self-righteousness, arrogance, exclusivism, etc., he now turns the attention of the Galatians, and of all who then or now read these warnings, to those sins which, though to a certain extent also present among the Jews (Rom. 2:1, 21-24), were *especially* conspicuous among the Gentiles. He fully realizes that even though the Galatians were now "brothers" in Christ, they were still plagued and beset by the sinster influences of contaminated heredity, long-existing habit, and dissolute environment. Generally speaking, sanctification does not complete its task in one day. So, this new section begins as follows: **13. For y o u were called to freedom, brothers; only (do) not (turn) this freedom into an opportunity for the flesh. . . .** For the meaning of *freedom* see on 5:1. The present passage is linked in thought especially with verse 8. When these two verses (8 and 13) are combined the meaning of *for* and of both passages becomes clearer: "This persuasion (is) not (derived) from him who is calling y o u. . . . For y o u were called to freedom, brothers; only (do) not (turn) this freedom into an opportunity for the flesh." When God applies the *outward* call, the gospel message, to the heart, thereby producing the *effectual* call, the person who experiences this basic change is introduced into the realm of freedom, the sphere of grateful and spontaneous living to the glory of his marvelous Benefactor, and is invited to roam about freely in this new country, delighting in its treasures and making full use of its opportunities. The Galatians must beware, nevertheless, that they do not accept a distorted interpretation of the concept *freedom,* as if it were an *opportunity,* that is, bridgehead, springboard, pretext, or incentive (cf. II Cor. 5:12; 11:12; I Tim. 5:14) for sinful human nature to assert itself.

Paul is not tilting at windmills when he issues this warning. Cf. Rom. 3:8; 6:1; Rasputin (cf. R. K. Massie, *Nicholas and Alexandra,* New York, 1967, p. 196). Turning liberty into license is an evil ingrained in sinful human nature. It is so easy to interpret *liberty* as "the right to sin," and to construe *freedom* as "the privilege to do whatever one's evil heart *wants to* do," instead of looking upon it as *the Spirit-imparted ability and desire to do what one should do.* Even today how often does it not happen that such baneful practices as attending places of *worldly* amusement, chain-smoking, "boozing," desecrating the sabbath, and reading smutty novels are defended with an appeal to "Christian liberty!" The apostle's own inspired interpretation of the meaning of true liberty is set forth both here in Galatians and in equally touching passages of his first epistle to the Corinthians: see especially 6:12; 8:9, 13; 9:12, 19, 22; 10:23, 24, 31; 11:1.

Surely no loftier description of the essence of true freedom has ever been offered than the one given in the words: **but through love be serving one another.** For the concept *love* see the explanation of verse 6, where Paul speaks about "faith working through love." Here in verse 13 note the paradox: "freedom . . . serving." A paradox, indeed, but not a self-contradiction, for such service is voluntary, from the heart. It is a service rendered in imitation of him who "took the form of a servant" (Phil. 2:7), and who, during the solemn night when he stepped upon the threshold of his most profound and indescribable agony, "rose from the supper, laid aside his garments, and having taken a towel, tied it around his waist, poured water into a basin, and began to wash the disciples' feet and to dry them with the towel" (John 13:4, 5). He was the thoroughly consecrated, wise and willing servant pictured by Isaiah (42:1-9; 49:1-9a; 50:4-11; and 52:13-53:12), the spontaneously acting servant who resolutely fulfilled his mission, so that with reference to him Jehovah said: "Behold, my servant, whom I uphold; my chosen, in whom my soul delights." It is such service that Paul has in mind when he says: ". . . through love be serving one another."[155] And what is meant by this *love* by means of which one brother voluntarily *serves* the other? Such ingredients as deep affection, self-sacrificing tenderness, genuine sympathy, readiness to render assistance, yearning to promote the brother's (and in a wider sense the neighbor's) welfare, spontaneous giving and forgiving: all these enter into it. But would it not be easier to count the glistening beads in the descending chains of rain than to catalogue all the elements that enter into that mysterious force which causes many hearts to beat as one?[156]

When Paul warns the Galatians not to turn freedom into an opportunity for the flesh but through love to be serving one another, he is placing *service* over against *selfishness,* the *positive* over against the *negative.* Paul does this frequently: see Rom. 12:21; 13:14; I Cor. 6:18-20; Eph. 4:28, 31, 32; 5:28, 29; 6:4; Col. 3:5-17; I Thess. 4:7, etc. Vice can only be conquered by virtue, which is the Spirit's *gift,* man's *responsibility.* Continued: **14. For the whole law is fulfilled in one word, namely, in this: "You must love your neighbor as yourself."** Paul quotes Lev. 19:18. One can also say that he is quoting the words of Jesus (Matt. 22:39, 40; Mark 12:31; Luke 10:27; cf. Matt. 7:12; 19:19; Rom. 13:8-10; and I Cor. 13). Love, then, is both the *summary* (interpretive epitome or condensation) and the *realization in practice* of the entire God-given moral law, viewed as a unit. True, in harmony with the immediately preceding context ("through love be serving *one another*"), the apostle here refers specifically to the second, not to the first, table of the law, but that first table is in the background, for the two are inseparable (I John 4:20, 21). Paul's teaching throughout is that though it would be a gross error to say that the sinner must love God and his neighbor *in order to be saved,* it is entirely true that the "saint," saved by grace, out of gratitude for (and by dint of) this salvation loves God and his neighbor.

155 Accordingly, the rendering here given is to be preferred to that of Lenski: "by means of love slave for each other." On this point see also N.T.C. on Philippians, pp. 44, 109.

156 The significance which Paul ascribes to *love* is evident from the fact that in his writings forms of the verb ἀγαπάω occur more than thirty times, and of the noun ἀγαπή more than seventy times. For the difference between ἀγαπάω and φιλέω see N.T.C. on the Gospel according to John, Vol. II, pp. 494–501.

Though love and the deeds which it produces must not be considered preconditions of salvation, they are, nevertheless, very important, namely, as fruits of the work of the Holy Spirit in man's heart. Once this is understood it becomes clear that Paul is entirely consistent when, on the one hand, he maintains that believers are not under law, yet, on the other hand, emphasizes that they are "under law to Christ" (I Cor. 9:21; and see on Gal. 6:2).

It has been maintained that the rule here quoted differs in no respect from that of the non-Christian moralist. The resemblance, however, is only superficial. The believer's *incentive* to obey this summarizing command is gratitude for the redemption accomplished by Christ; the *strength* to observe it is furnished by the Spirit of Christ (Gal. 5:1, 13, 25; cf. Eph. 3:16, 17; 4:20 ff.; 5:1 ff.); and it was also Christ who himself supplied the *example* of obedience (John 13:34).

When the question is asked, "But who is my neighbor?" (Luke 10:29), the answer is: anyone with whom, in God's providence, we come into contact; anyone whom we can assist in any way, even though he hates us and in that sense is our "enemy" (Matt. 5:43-48). Here, too, Christ himself has given us the supreme example (Luke 23:34; cf. I Peter 2:21-24). The parable of The Good Samaritan (Luke 10:25-37) proves, moreover, that, instead of asking, "But who is my neighbor?" each person should "prove himself a neighbor" to the one whom he is able to benefit in any way. Continued:

**15. But if y o u bite and devour one another, watch out lest y o u be consumed by one another.** The attitude toward "one another" that is described and condemned in this passage is the very opposite of the one that was urged upon the addressed in verses 13 and 14. Here, in verse 15, people—church-members at that!—are pictured in the act of rushing at each other like wild beasts. By means of an ascending series of gruesome acts their violence and its threatening woeful result is pictured: they bite each other, "gulp each other down," and, if they persist, will in the end be totally consumed by one another. They obey the dictates of their old self, and resemble nature "raw in tooth and claw." Robertson reminds us of the story of "two snakes that grabbed each other by the tail and each swallowed the other." (*Word Pictures,* Vol. IV, p. 311). And Cole refers to "the two Kilkenny cats of Cromwellian times who fought so furiously that not a scrap of fur remained of either" (*The Epistle of Paul to the Galatians,* in *The Tyndale New Testament Commentaries,* p. 158). One might expect such acts of terror and violence from the enemies of God's people in their onslaught upon the righteous (Ps. 35:25; 79:2, 7; 80:13; 124:3), but surely those who style themselves "believers in the Lord Jesus Christ" and "members of the one holy universal church" cannot be accused of such behavior?

The question arises, therefore, "Just what does Paul have in mind? Is he merely warning the Galatians against certain sins which they might be considering, without in any way implying that such evils as 'biting' and 'devouring' already existed in their midst? Or, on the other hand, has he received information regarding actual conditions of dissension and strife, and is he now warning the churches as to what will be the inevitable result of the continuation of such discord and contention?" Some commentators favor the first,[157] some the second[158] alternative. I side with the latter. My reason is as follows. It is clear from the entire epistle—especially from 1:1-5:12—that a considerable segment of the membership here addressed was in the process of yielding to the wishes of the Judaizers. Also, it is equally obvious (see 5:19, 21) that there were others who leaned in the exactly opposite direction, and were abusing the doctrine of grace, as if it implied a license to sin. Paul surely must have had a reason to dwell in such detail on the vices enumerated in the verses that follow. And finally, does not the fact that he knew so much about the conditions that prevailed in these churches indicate that he must have had close friends there, who shared his views, were infected neither with legalism nor with libertinism, and were his informers? Does it not seem reasonable, therefore, to believe that, at least to some extent, there were "parties" or "factions" in these churches? Besides, as Ramsay points out, older rivalries, as between person and person, town and town, race and race, etc., may not have been *completely* and *immediately* eliminated with the coming of Christianity to these parts. Of course, it is not necessary or even reasonable to suppose that *all* the Galatians were engaged in internecine strife. If we accept the theory that at least *some* of the addressed were thus engaged, and that Paul writes as he does not only to prevent these quarrels from becoming more extensive and/or intensive, but also to put an end to them completely by urging the contending parties to adopt "the more excellent way" of love, have we not done justice to the meaning of his words? At any rate, the apostle shows "how distressing, how mad it is that we, who are members of the same body, should be leagued together, of our own accord, for mutual destruction" (Calvin).

---

[157] Thus Lenski, who states, "We thus decline to accept the conclusion that biting and devouring were actually in progress among the Galatians at this time" (*op. cit.*, p. 278). Rendall, *op. cit.*, p. 186; and Ridderbos, *op. cit.*, p. 202, express themselves more cautiously.

[158] This is the more general view. See, for example, the commentaries of Burton, Calvin, Duncan, Findlay, Greijdanus, and Ramsay. Duncan states, "Paul tactfully puts the case hypothetically, but we may be sure that he believes that these conditions actually exist."

Grammar does not help us to solve the puzzle. The condition here expressed is first class, assumed as true. The protasis has εἰ with two pres. indic. verbs. The apodosis has ἀναλωθῆτε, first aor. passive subjunctive of ἀναλίσκω in a negative final clause. Whether, in such a conditional sentence the condition *actually* corresponds with reality or whether it is a *mere* assumption, to show what would happen granted that the condition were real, must be established from the general context.

What, then, is the remedy for this evil? Paul mentions it in these words: **16. But I say, walk by the Spirit,**[159] **and y o u will definitely not fulfil the desire of the flesh.**[160] Let y o u r conduct be governed by the Spirit, that is, by God's gift imparted to y o u (3:2, 5). If y o u follow his directions and promptings y o u will not be dominated by y o u r human nature regarded as the seat and vehicle of sinful desire (as in 5:13), but instead will conquer it. It takes the tender leaves of early springtime to rid the oak tree of the remnants of last autumn's withered foliage. It is only the living that can expel the dead. It is only the good that can push out the bad. See also on verse 13 above.

Verse 16 clearly implies that there is a conflict between the Spirit and the flesh, therefore also between the believer's new, Spirit-indwelt, nature and his old, sinful, self. Hence, Paul continues: **17. for the flesh sets its desire against the Spirit, and the Spirit against the flesh: for these are opposed to each other. . . .** True, as long as one allows himself to be led by the Spirit he will definitely not fulfil the desire of the flesh, but how often does it not happen that the person in question does not allow the Spirit to be his Leader? And so, because the Spirit persists, a fierce conflict takes place inside the believer's heart. The antagonists are: the Spirit—hence also the Spirit-indwelt new nature—, on the one side; and on the other side: the flesh, that is, "the old man" of sin and corruption (same meaning as in verses 13 and 19 of this chapter, and as in 6:8; cf. Rom. 7:25; 8:4-9, 12, 13).

In connection with this contest, note the following:

(1) The *libertine* experiences no such struggle at all, for he follows his natural inclinations.

(2) The *legalist,* who is destined for grace and glory, having been reminded of his sinfulness by the law but for a while unwilling to accept grace, struggles and struggles but without achieving victory or experiencing the sense of certain, ultimate triumph. This condition lasts until grace finally breaks down all the barriers of opposition (Phil. 3:7 ff.).

(3) The *believer,* while still on earth, experiences an agonizing conflict in his own heart, but *in principle,* has already gained the victory, as the very

---

[159] Also here πνεῦμα refers to the Holy Spirit. Says Duncan, "Throughout this passage it is important to remember that Paul is writing to Christians, i.e., to men who have received the Spirit of God" (*op. cit.,* p. 166). I believe this to be the correct position, and over against Lenski's rendering and exegesis (*op. cit.,* pp. 278, 279) I would also refer to my interpretation of 5:5 above, including footnote 146 on p. 197. It seems to me that the only instances in Galatians of πνεῦμα in a sense other than Holy Spirit are 6:1: "a *spirit* of gentleness," and 6:18: "The grace of our Lord Jesus Christ (be) with y o u r *spirit,* brothers."

[160] For a word-study of ἐπιθυμία see N.T.C. on I and II Timothy and Titus, pp. 271, 272, footnote 147; and for σάρξ see N.T.C. on Philippians, p. 77, footnote 55; also pp. 152, 153 on Phil. 3:3.

presence of the Holy Spirit in his heart testifies. In full measure this victory will be his portion in the hereafter; hence,

(4) For *the redeemed-soul in glory* the battle is over. He wears the victor's wreath.

As to (3), therefore, the very wording of the text—note: "sets its desire against" and "are opposed to each other"—indicates the intensity of the life-long tug of war. This shows that the Christian life means far more than stepping forward to register one's decision at a great revival meeting, after listening to a powerful, evangelical, and heart-warming message, and while one is under the influence of the singing of old familiar hymns by a massive choir. When, under such circumstances, the sudden change is genuine, it is wonderful, but it must be borne in mind that as a rule a sinner is not *wholly* saved all at once ("Presto!"). He does not leap into heaven in one prodigious bound. On the contrary, he has to *work out* his own salvation (Phil. 2:12). This takes time, struggle, intense effort and exertion. He is his own most powerful enemy, as Paul proves by continuing: **so that these very things which y o u may wish to be doing, these y o u are not doing.** What a battle between the will and the deed! Paul, writing as a converted man (Rom. 7:14-25) and recording his *present, "state of grace"* experiences (for proof see Rom. 7:22, 25), complains bitterly about the fact that he practices that in which his soul no longer takes delight; in fact, practices that which his regenerated self *hates* (Rom. 7:15). He cries out, "Wretched man that I am! Who will deliver me out of the body of this death?" (Rom. 7:24). Nevertheless, he is also fully aware of the fact that in the struggle between his own flesh and God's Spirit, the latter's victory—hence also Paul's—is certain; in fact, *in principle* is a fact even now. Would there have been this genuine, *God-centered* sorrow for sin, had not Paul been a truly converted man? Of course not! This very conflict, therefore, is a charter of the apostle's salvation. We are not surprised, therefore, that the exclamation "Wretched man! . . . Who will deliver me?" is followed by "I thank God through Jesus Christ our Lord. . . . There is therefore now no condemnation to them that are in Christ Jesus" (Rom. 7:25; 8:1; cf. I Cor. 15:57). Similarly here in Galatians the thought of victory through the Spirit is basic to the understanding of verse **18. But if y o u are being led by the Spirit y o u are not under law.**[161] Being "under law" spells defeat, bondage, the curse, spiritual impotence, for the law cannot save (Gal. 3:11-13, 21-23, 25; 4:3, 24, 25; 5:1). It takes the Spirit to set one free (4:29; 5:1, 5; II Cor. 3:17).

---

[161] This is a first class conditional sentence. Accordingly, the thought expressed in the protasis is assumed to be a fact. Upon the presupposition that it is a fact the thought expressed in the apodosis is the truth. Whether the protasis states an *actual* fact, let each Galatian—and let each hearer or reader down the centuries—decide for himself, after thorough examination in the light of the Word. Note present tense: "are being led."

### *Being Led by the Spirit*

(1) *Whom It Concerns*

According to a rather popular view "spiritual leading" is the Spirit's gift to the select few, "the holiest men," the flower of the flock. It is imparted to them to protect them from physical harm, especially while traveling, to deliver them from dangerous situations, and sometimes even to insure them success in their business enterprises.

However, when, with Gal. 5:18 as our starting-point, we trace *back* the line of Paul's thinking, it becomes evident that this limitation of "spiritual leading" to a group of super-saints is completely foreign to his mind. Those who are being led by the Spirit (5:18) are the same as those who walk by the Spirit (5:16), and vice versa. Going back a little farther, we notice that these, in turn, are the ones who have been set free (5:1; 4:31, 26), who belong to Christ (3:29), and are "of faith" (3:9). All true believers, therefore, are being led by the Spirit.

Moreover, the powerful influence that is being exercised upon and within them by the Spirit is not of a sporadic character, being, as it were, injected into their lives now and then in moments of great need or danger. On the contrary, it is steady, constant, as even the tense here in Gal. 5:18 implies: they *are being led* by the Spirit. Even when they disobey the Spirit—and they certainly do, as has just been set forth (verses 13-17)—the Spirit does not leave them alone but works repentance within their hearts.

This representation is in keeping with the only other truly parallel passage in Paul's epistles, namely, Rom. 8:14: "For as many as are being led by the Spirit of God, these are sons of God." Here, too, being led by the Spirit is set forth as the indispensable characteristic of God's children. If a person is a child of God he is being led by the Spirit. If he is being led by the Spirit he is a child of God.

(2) *What It Is*

Before giving a positive answer to this question it may be well to point out what is *not* meant by being led by the Spirit. Naturally, it cannot refer to being governed by one's own sinful impulses and inclinations, nor to "being easily led" into waywardness by evil companions. Also definitely excluded here is the idea of those moral philosophers, ancient and modern, who hold that in every man there is a higher and a lower nature, and that each human being has within himself the power of causing the former to triumph over the latter. This idea is excluded even if for no other reason than this, that throughout, in Paul's teaching, the Holy Spirit is a distinct person, of one substance with the Father and the Son. He is not "our other or better self." See Rom. 8:26, 27; I Cor. 2:10; II Cor. 13:14. This also shows that, strictly speaking, being led by the Spirit cannot even be identified with the triumph of "the new man" (the regenerated nature) within us over "the old man" (our corrupt nature, not yet fully destroyed). That victory and that implied struggle are certainly very real; yet they are not *in and by themselves* what is meant by being led by the Spirit, but are rather *the result* of the Spirit's active indwelling. They are certainly *implied,* but are not basic.

What then does *the leading of the Spirit*—to change from the passive to the active voice, for the sake of the definition—actually mean? It means sanctification. *It is that constant, effective, and beneficent influence which the Holy Spirit exercises within the hearts of God's children whereby they are being directed and enabled more and more to crush the power of indwelling sin and to walk in the way of God's commandments, freely and cheerfully.*

By so defining it extremes are avoided. Thus, on the one hand, to be *led* by the Spirit means more than to be *guided* by him, though, to be sure, the Spirit is also our Guide (John 16:13; cf. Matt. 15:14; Luke 6:39; Acts 8:31; Rev. 7:17). But the very fact that, according to the passage now under consideration (Gal. 5:18), the enslaving power of the law has been broken for all those who are being *led* by the Spirit, indicates that this *leadership* which the Spirit provides implies more than "pointing out the right way." It reminds us not so much of the Indian guide who pointed out to the pioneer white explorers the pass through the Rockies, as of the blind man of Jericho who *was led* to Jesus (Luke 18:40; cf. Matt. 21:2; Luke 10:34; John 18:28; Acts 6:12; 9:2). Merely pointing out the way to him would not have helped him. When the Holy Spirit *leads* believers he becomes *the controlling influence* in their lives, bringing them at last to glory.

On the other hand, however, this representation also steers clear of the opposite extreme, that of denying human responsibility and activity. The blind man of Jericho was not *carried* or *borne* (II Peter 1:21) to Jesus, but did his own walking. Warfield has said very aptly: "It is his [the Holy Spirit's] part to keep us in the path and to bring us at length to the goal. But it is we who tread every step of the way; our limbs that grow weary with the labor; our hearts that faint, our courage that fails—our faith that revives our sinking strength, our hope that instills new courage into our souls—as we toil over the steep ascent" (*The Power of God unto Salvation,* p. 172). Being led by the Holy Spirit, to be fully effective, implies that one allows himself to be led. As to the interrelation of these two factors—the believers' self-activity and God's (the Holy Spirit's) leading—, Paul's own Spirit-inspired statement cannot be improved upon: "With fear and trembling continue to work out y o u r own salvation; for it is God who is working in y o u both to will and to work for his good pleasure" (Phil. 2:12, 13; and see N.T.C. on that passage).

(3) *Its Blessed Results*

*a.* Those who are being led by the Spirit breathe the exhilarating and invigorating air of moral and spiritual freedom. Being no longer under law's bondage, they obey God's precepts with gladness of heart (Gal. 5:1, 18).

*b.* They detest and vigorously oppose "the works of the flesh" (5:17, 19-21, 24).

*c.* They love the Word (whose very Author is the Spirit) and the Triune God revealed therein in all his marvelous attributes (Rom. 7:22; cf. Ps. 119; John 16:14).

*d.* "The fruit of the Spirit" abounds in their lives (Gal. 5:22, 23; 6:2, 8-10).

*e.* This enhances their freedom of access in approaching the throne of grace (Eph. 2:18; cf. Rom. 5:1, 2; Heb. 4:14-16).

*f.* It also goes hand in hand with the testimony of the Spirit in their hearts, assuring them that they are children of God (II Peter 1:5-11; cf. Rom. 8:16).

*g.* Finally, it (the fruit of the Spirit abounding in their lives) greatly strengthens their testimony to the world, all this to the glory of God Triune (Acts 1:8; cf. John 15:26, 27).

**19-21.** The various ways in which the desire of the flesh (verse 17) manifests itself are now set forth. With the majority of commentators I hold that the apostle mentions the particular vices in the list that follows because they needed to be mentioned. In other words, the Galatians had not as yet gained a complete victory over these evils, though here as always the degree of success must have varied with the individual.

The list which follows may be compared with similar ones in Paul's other epistles (Rom. 1:18-32; 13:13; I Cor. 5:9-11; 6:9, 10; II Cor. 12:20, 21; Eph. 4:19; 5:3-5; Col. 3:5-9; I Thess. 2:3; 4:3-7; I Tim. 1:9, 10; 6:4, 5; II Tim. 3:2-5; and Titus 3:3, 9, 10). Striking, for example, is the similarity (note, however, also the differences) between Gal. 5:19, 20 and II Cor. 12:20, 21. Whether there were factors other than identity of authorship (for example, already existing lists) that account for this and similar resemblances is difficult to ascertain. Paul writes: **Now obvious**—hence undeniable, self-evident as vices—**are the works of the flesh, which are: immorality, impurity, indecency, idolatry, sorcery,**[162] **quarrels, wrangling, jealousy, outbursts of anger, selfish ambitions, dissensions, party intrigues, envyings, drinking bouts, revelries, and the like. . . .**

There are fifteen items in the list. In content there is, of course, consider-

[162] Thus rendered, the first five, in addition to being true to the meaning of the Greek words, all end in "-y," and the originals of these five all end in -ια.

able overlapping. Thus, while each of the three vices *immorality, impurity,* and *indecency,* has a distinct meaning, yet the three have something in common, namely, departure from the will of God in the matter of sex. And so it is also with the other items in the list.

The first three vices, accordingly, are in the realm of *sex*. The next two pertain to *false gods*. There follow eight that have to do with *strife*. The last two indicate abuses in the sphere of *drink*. Or, dropping these monosyllables, the fifteen items can be grouped as follows:

*Immorality* and kindred evils; hence, immorality, impurity, indecency

*Idolatry* and the sin associated with it; hence, idolatry, sorcery

*Rivalry:* quarrels, wrangling, jealousy, outbursts of anger, selfish ambitions, party intrigues, envyings

*Inebriety:* drinking bouts, revelries.

First on the list, then, is *immorality,* a term which in Paul's writings is used also in I Cor. 5:1; 6:13, 18; 7:2; II Cor. 12:21; Eph. 5:3; Col. 3:5; and I Thess. 4:3. It refers basically to unlawful sexual intercourse. It probably includes illicit, clandestine relationships of every description. Evil in the sexual realm was, and is today, a characteristic feature of life apart from Christ. In paganism it is often closely associated with idolatry. That even among those who had turned to Christ it was not unheard of is clear from I Cor. 5:1 ff. Closely associated with immorality, *impurity* (II Cor. 12:21; Eph. 4:19; 5:3; Col. 3:5; I Thess. 2:3; 4:7) is mentioned next. It is a very comprehensive concept, and includes not only uncleanness in deeds but also in words, thoughts, and desires of the heart. *Indecency* or *licentiousness* ("lasciviousness," Rom. 13:13; II Cor. 12:21; Eph. 4:19) emphasizes the lack of self-control that characterizes the person who gives free play to the impulses of his sinful nature.

The next group begins with the mention of *idolatry*. As the other passages in which Paul uses the word indicate (I Cor. 10:14; Col. 3:5), it refers not only to the worship of images as such but also to any evil practice in connection with such worship; for example, to eating meats that had been offered to idols, when conscience forbids this, and, in fact, to the substitution of anything at all for the adoration of the true God who has revealed himself in Jesus Christ. Thus, greed, too, is idolatry, for by means of it a person has substituted self for God. Closely associated with idolatry is *sorcery*. The Greek word is *pharmakeia;* cf. our "pharmacy." Though basically *pharmakeia* is a term without moral implications, it is not difficult to understand how—particularly in an unscientific age—a "mixer of drugs" could be—or could be viewed as being—a "magician." "Pharmakeia," accordingly, is used here in the sense of *sorcery,* by means of which mysterious powers were erroneously ascribed to certain articles, formulas, or incantations (cf. Acts 8:9; 13:8; 19:13, 19). The sorcerer generally claimed to have access to this or that super-human power by means of which he plied his trade. The apostle uses the word "sorcery" or "magic" only in this one instance. See, however, also Rev. 9:21; 18:23; cf. Exod. 7:11, 22; 8:14; Isa. 47:9, 12; Rev. 21:8; 22:15. When faith in magic replaces trust in God it is exposed as a form of idolatry.

The third is the largest group and refers to *rivalry* of the baser sort. The reason why so much prominence is given to this category of sinful practices has been stated above (see on verse 15). The list begins with *quarrels*. Cf. Eph. 2:16 where the singular occurs in the sense of "hostility." Next is *wrangling*[163] (also rendered "variance," "strife," "contention," cf. Rom. 1:29; 13:13; II Cor. 12:20; Phil. 1:15; I Tim. 6:4; Titus 3:9), which, for example, occurs when people begin to choose sides, and each of the wranglers fairly worships his hero (I Cor. 1:11, 12; 3:3). Something of this nature may have occurred also in Galatia, as was suggested previously. *Jealousy*[164] is mentioned in connection with "strife" also in Rom. 13:13; I Cor. 3:3; II Cor. 12:20.[165] Psychologically the two—wrangling and jealousy—go together, for what started out as intense devotion to a leader, so that every other name is immediately dismissed amid much wrangling, degenerates into a jealous craving to retain the feeling of closeness to that leader, to "possess" him, as it were, and to enhance his prestige come what may. In such a context *outbursts of anger* or fiery flashes of rage, when a "rival's" name is mentioned, are natural. The men who are guilty of this vice pant with fury (Rom. 2:8; II Cor. 12:20; Eph. 4:31; Col. 3:8). Though the people who engage in such practices may never be willing to admit it, yet it is a fact that such and similar sins are often rooted in *selfish ambitions* (Rom. 2:8; II Cor. 12:20). That such ambitions at times invade even "the Christian ministry" is shown in Phil. 1:17; 2:3 (see N.T.C. on these passages). *Dissensions* (Rom. 16:17) result when men are actuated by selfish motives, each craving honor for himself. *Groups* working and scheming against each other (cf. I Cor. 11:19: "factions"), hence *party intrigues,* come into existence when one member *chooses* the side of this, and another the side of that leader.[166] The group of eight vices that can be summarized

---

[163] The textual evidence favors the singular.

[164] Here, too, the textual evidence supports the singular rather than the plural.

[165] The resultant meaning of ζῆλος in other Pauline passages is somewhat different. Thus, in Rom. 10:2; II Cor. 7:7, 11; 9:2; Phil. 3:6 *zeal* is the preferred translation. II Cor. 11:2 refers to a "godly" (or "divine") *jealousy.*

[166] The party that becomes guilty of error in doctrine or ethics advocates "heresy," which is the English form of the very word that is used in the original. But this was a later development of the meaning of the Greek word. Hence the rendering of "heresies" here in Gal. 5:20 (A.V.) is an error. Though at first the term simply indicated a "sect," as of the Pharisees (Acts 15:5; 26:5) or of the Sadducees (Acts 5:17), with no odium attached, passages such as Acts 24:5 ("a ringleader of the *sect* of the Nazarenes"); 24:14 ("according to the Way which they call a *sect*"); and 28:22 ("as to this *sect,* we know that everywhere it is being spoken against") show its gradual tendency toward the meaning "heretical sect."

under the caption *rivalry* closes with *envyings*[167] (Rom. 1:29; Phil. 1:15; I Tim. 6:4; Titus 3:3). Paul has already mentioned "jealousy." Whenever these two—jealousy and envy—are distinguishable, as here, the former can be defined as the fear of losing what one has, while the latter is the displeasure aroused by seeing someone else have something. One of the most soul-destroying vices is envy, an evil which, as the probable etymology of the Greek word implies, causes one *to waste away*. Has not envy been called that vice whose rage nothing can allay, "the eldest born of hell"? Is it not "the rottenness of the bones" (Prov. 14:30)? Our English word *envy* is from the Latin *in-video,* meaning "to look against," that is, to look with ill-will at another person because of what he is or has. It was envy that caused the murder of Abel, threw Joseph into a pit, caused Korah, Dathan, and Abiram to rebel against Moses and Aaron, made Saul pursue David, gave rise to the bitter words which "the elder brother" (in the Parable of the Prodigal Son) addressed to his father, and crucified Christ. *Love* never envies (I Cor. 13:4).

The fourth group denounces and warns against *inebriety,* that is drunkenness and the evils associated with it. The first member of this group is *drinking bouts* (Rom. 13:13; cf. Luke 21:34). No doubt it refers to repeated manifestations of intemperance. The entire list of vices closes with *revelries* (Rom. 13:13; cf. I Peter 4:3). It should be distinctly noted that Scripture considers alcoholism to be a *sin,* not *merely* a *disease.* It states in words clear and simple that drunkards will not inherit the kingdom of heaven (I Cor. 6:10). The last part of the verse which we are now considering speaks likewise. Though the *disease* aspect of this evil should, to be sure, be given its due, the *responsibility* aspect must not be ignored. Minimizing personal accountability has been the destroyer of several civilizations. Is not our own civilization in danger of being destroyed by it? As to the pagan revelries to which the apostle makes reference here, we see, as it were, the disorderly night-time procession of fellows parading through the streets, with their torches and songs honoring Bacchus. The boisterous parade of half-drunks stops in front of the houses of friends, and the merrymaking is protracted until the small hours of the morning. To practices such as these the Galatians, too, had been accustomed. When they turned to the Lord it must have seemed difficult for some of them to break off, once and for all, every association with this kind of a past.

The given list of vices is not meant to be exhaustive. It is representative, as is indicated by the words, "and the like" or "and things like these."

Continued: **of which I forewarn y o u, as I previously forewarned y o u,**

---

[167] As the textual apparatus of N.N. clearly indicates, the addition (A.V.) of "murders" (φόνοι) after "envyings" (φθόνοι) rests on an inferior text. Perhaps it is due to Rom. 1:29.

**that those who indulge in such practices will not inherit the kingdom of God.** It is clear from these words that to the Galatians Paul, during his visits, must have imparted a considerable amount of instruction, and this not only theological but also moral, the two being very closely related. This gives the lie to the charge of his opponents that he taught, "Let us do evil, that good may come" (Rom. 3:8; cf. 6:1). It should also be observed that although according to Paul's argumentation it is not possible to gain entrance to the kingdom of God by means of what were deemed to be *good* practices (law-works), it is definitely possible to shut oneself out by *evil* practices. A person must bid farewell to *all* the works of darkness. Otherwise he proves that he is not as yet walking in the light (I Cor. 6:11; Eph. 4:20; 5:7-11). He must realize that even though he is *in* the world and has a mission to fulfil, he is not *of* the world, but is a sojourner or pilgrim on the earth (cf. Ps. 119:19).

Here, too, Paul has a message for every age, including the present, in which the complaint is often heard that the tenor of certain so-called *Christian* organizations is that of "paganism on the basis of the creed." The constitution of the organization demands loyalty to the creed on the part of every member, and declares that all the activities must be carried on in harmony with Scripture as interpreted by this confession, but the facts of life tell an altogether different story, if published reports by those "on the scene" are reliable. Those who confess Jesus Christ as their Savior and Lord must bear in mind that far more worldly people "read" *them* than read the Bible (II Cor. 3:2).

With a pastor's loving heart, therefore, Paul issues his warning that those who continue to indulge in their former evil habits will not *inherit* (see on 3:18) the kingdom of God: the new heaven and earth with all their glory.[168]

---

[168] In its broadest connotation "the kingdom of God" indicates *God's kingship, rule, or sovereignty recognized in the hearts and operative in the lives of his people, and effecting their complete salvation, their constitution as a church, and ultimately a redeemed universe.* However, in various passages now this, then that, aspect of the βασιλεία (τοῦ) θεοῦ is stressed. Thus, at times it is obedience *to the rule of God* upon which the emphasis falls: "Thy kingdom come, thy will be done" (Matt. 6:10; cf. Luke 17:21). Then again the main idea is *complete salvation,* i.e., all the spiritual blessings that result when God is recognized as King in heart and life: "It is easier . . . than for a rich man to enter the kingdom of God. And they said, 'Then who can be saved?'" (Mark 10:25, 26). A third meaning is *the community of men in whose hearts God is recognized as King.* Here the terms "kingdom of God" and "church" begin to approach each other in meaning: "And upon this rock will I build my church. . . . I will give to you the keys of the kingdom of heaven" (Matt. 16:18, 19). Finally, the term has reference to the final realization of God's saving power: *the new heaven and earth with all their glory:* "Inherit the kingdom prepared for y o u" (Matt. 25:34). These four meanings are not separate or unrelated. They all proceed from the central idea of the rule of God, his supremacy in the sphere of saving power.—For the theory according to which there is a sharp distinction between the kingdom of *God* and that of *Christ* see N.T.C. on Colossians and Philemon, p. 64, footnote 47.

The *works* of the flesh have been reviewed. Over against these is now placed the *fruit,* that is, the organic, spontaneous product, of the Spirit, for it is only by means of the Spirit that the flesh can be conquered. It is the good that expels the evil. By no means does this representation cancel human responsibility. On the contrary, it is by means of the operation of the Spirit in the hearts of God's children that the latter become very active. But such activity is no longer slavery. It is the free, voluntary, and grateful response of hearts and lives to God for favors received (Luke 6:44, 45). It is the natural expression of the new life, the life "in the Spirit." It should also be noted that the apostle is not now speaking about *extraordinary* and *temporary* manifestations of the Spirit's power in the lives of certain individuals, *special gifts* (*charismata*), such as speaking in tongues (see I Cor. 12), but rather about endowments bestowed upon all those who love the Lord. These endowments are here considered as a unit: "the fruit," that is, the harvest.

Paul writes: **22, 23. But the fruit of the Spirit is love, joy, peace, longsuffering, kindness, goodness, faithfulness, meekness, self-control. . . .** Perhaps the nine pleasing endowments can be divided into three groups, each group comprising three gifts. *If* this should be correct—it is by no means certain!—, the first group would refer to the most basic spiritual qualities: love, joy, peace. The next group would describe those virtues that reveal themselves in social relationships. We assume that it views believers in their various contacts with each other and with those who do not belong to their company: longsuffering, kindness, goodness. In the last group, though here especially there is room for a difference of opinion, the first item listed may well refer to the relation of believers to God and to his will as revealed in his Word: faithfulness or loyalty. The second probably pertains to their contact with men: meekness. The last, to each believer's relation to himself, that is, to his own desires and passions: self-control.

Mentioned at the very beginning of the first group is "the greatest of the three greatest," namely, *love* (I Cor. 13; Eph. 5:2; Col. 3:14). For this virtue see on 5:6 and 5:13 above. Not only Paul but also John assigns priority to this grace of self-giving (I John 3:14; 4:8, 19). And so does Peter (I Peter 4:8). In this they clearly followed the example that was given by Christ (John 13:1, 34; 17:26). Although, as these passages indicate, it is hardly legitimate *strictly to limit* this basic virtue to "love *for the brethren,*" yet, on the other hand, in the present context (over against quarrels, wrangling, jealousy, etc.," and see also verse 14) the reference may well be *especially* to this mutual affection. When love is present, *joy* cannot be far behind, for has not the author told us that love is the law's fulfilment, and does not the doing of God's law bring *delight* (Ps. 119:16, 24, 35, 47, 70, 174)? Moreover, the truth of this statement becomes even clearer when it is borne in mind that the ability to observe this divine ordinance of love is God's gift, being an element in that wonderful salvation which in *his* great love he has freely bestowed upon his children. Moreover, since all things work together for good to those that love God (Rom. 8:28), it is evident that believers can rejoice even amid the most distressing circumstances, as Paul himself proved again and again (Acts 27:35; II Cor. 6:10: "as sorrowful, yet always rejoicing"; 12:9; Phil. 1:12, 13; 4:11; II Tim. 4:6-8). Their gladness, moreover, is not that of the world, a mirth which is superficial and fails to satisfy the deepest needs of the soul, but is a "joy unspeakable and full of glory" (I Peter 1:8), and a foretaste of the radiant raptures that are still in store for Christ's followers. *Peace,* too, is a natural result of the exercise of love, for "Great *peace* have they that *love* thy law" (Ps. 119:165; cf. 29:11; 37:11; 85:8). This peace is the serenity of heart that is the portion of all those who, having been justified by faith (Rom. 5:1), yearn to be instruments in the hand of God in causing others to share in their tranquility. Hence, the peace-*possessor* becomes, in turn, a peace-*maker* (Matt. 5:9). Moreover, the one who is truly conscious of this great gift of peace which he has received from God as a result of Christ's bitter death on the cross, will, within the Christian fellowship, "make every effort to preserve the unity imparted by the Spirit by means of the bond (consisting in) peace" (Eph. 4:3).

The mention of peace is, as it were, a natural link between the first and the second group, for this virtue is often contrasted with strife among men, and this second group describes those virtues which believers reveal in their contacts with each other and with other men. The first of the Spirit's gifts mentioned in this second group is *longsuffering.* It characterizes the person who, in relation to those who annoy, oppose, or molest him, exercises patience. He refuses to yield to passion or to outbursts of anger. Longsuffering is not only a human but also a divine attribute, being ascribed to God (Rom. 2:4; 9:22) and to Christ (I Tim. 1:16) as well as to man (II Cor. 6:6; Eph. 4:2; Col. 3:12, 13; II Tim. 4:2). As a human attribute it is inspired by trust in the fulfilment of God's promises (II Tim. 4:2, 8; Heb. 6:12). Emphasis on this virtue was greatly needed by the Galatians, who, as has been shown, were probably being torn by strife and the party spirit. Besides, longsuffering is a mighty weapon over against the hostility of the world in its attitude toward the church. Hand in hand with this virtue goes *kindness.* It is mildness, benignity. The early Christians by means of it commended themselves to others (II Cor. 6:6). This endowment, as exercised by believers, is a faint reflection of the primordial kindness manifested by God (Rom. 2:4; cf. 11:22). We are, moreover, admonished to become like him in this respect (Matt. 5:43-48; Luke 6:27-38). The Gospels contain numerous illustrations of Christ's kindness shown to sinners. To mention but a few, see Mark 10:13-16; Luke 7:11-17; 36-50; 8:40-56; 13:10-17; 18:15-17; 23:34; John 8:1-11; 19:25-27. *Goodness,* which completes this group, is Spirit-created moral and spiritual excellence of every description.

Perhaps in the present connection, being mentioned after kindness, it could refer especially to generosity of heart and action.

Finally, the apostle mentions the three graces that conclude the entire summary. First is *faithfulness.* The word that is used in the original is often properly rendered *faith.* However, here occurring after "kindness" and "goodness," the rendering "faithfulness" would seem to strike a more consonant harmony. It means *loyalty, fidelity.* Since in this very letter Paul complains about the lack of loyalty toward himself which had become evident in the conduct of many of the Galatians (4:16), we can see that mentioning this virtue was definitely in order. However, in the final analysis it was not so much disloyalty to himself as to the gospel—hence, to God and his Word—that, to a considerable extent, had been lacking, as is evident from 1:6-9; 3:1; 5:7. Faithfulness *to God and to his will* is, accordingly, the virtue which, in all probability, Paul is here commending as a gift of the Spirit. This, however, does not exclude but includes loyalty toward men. In connection with the preceding context, which speaks of strife in its various manifestations (see verses 20, 21), it would seem to be proper *here* to interpret the next item, namely, *meekness,* as gentleness *toward one another and toward all men.* Cf. I Cor. 4:21. Also *this* virtue reminds one of Christ (Matt. 11:29; II Cor. 10:1). Meekness is the very opposite of vehemence, violence, and outbursts of anger. The final virtue which Paul mentions, and by implication commends, is *self-control,* a relation of the self *to the self.* The person who is blessed with this quality possesses "the power to keep himself in check," which is the meaning of the word that is used in the original. The previous mention of immorality, impurity, and indecency, among the *vices* (verse 19), shows that it was very appropriate to list self-control as an opposing *virtue.* Of course, the reference is to other things besides sex. Those who truly exercise this virtue compel *every* thought to surrender itself in obedience to Christ (II Cor. 10:5).

Continued: **against such there is no law.** Since Paul has just completed a list of virtues, which are *things,* not *people,* it is natural to interpret his words as meaning: "against such *things*—such *virtues*—there is no law." Grammar does not forbid this construction. It is also evident that, as was true with respect to the vices, so also this list of virtues is representative. By no means every item of Christian excellence is included in the list. Hence, Paul says, "against *such.*" By saying that there is no law against such things he is encouraging every believer to manifest these qualities, in order that, by so doing, the vices may be annihilated.

The *incentive* to exhibit these fine traits of character was furnished by Christ, for it is out of gratitude to him that believers adorn their conduct with them. The *example,* too, in connection with all of them, was given by him. And *the virtues themselves,* as well as the *strength* to exercise them, are imparted by his Spirit.

Though Paul has called the enumerated virtues "the fruit of the Spirit," he now shifts the emphasis from the Spirit to Christ. That he is able to do this so readily is due to the fact that when the Spirit occupies the heart, so does Christ (Eph. 3:16, 17). Christ and the Spirit cannot be separated. "In the Spirit" Christ himself inhabits the inner selves of believers (Rom. 8:9, 10). Was not the Spirit given by Christ (John 15:26; II Cor. 3:17)? The reason for the shift in emphasis is that the apostle is going to remind the Galatians of the fact that they *have crucified* the flesh. This, of course, immediately rivets the attention upon Christ and his cross. So Paul continues: **24. And those who believe in Christ Jesus have crucified the flesh with its passions and desires.** Christ Jesus had been openly displayed to them as the One who had been crucified for their sins (3:1). They had seen his amazing love, and along with it they had learned to recognize the horrible nature of their sins which had required such a death. And they themselves had accepted this crucified Savior as their own, had reposed their trust in him, and through union with him had made a definite break with "the flesh," their old, evil nature. By God's grace they had administered the death-blow to it. They, like Paul, had been crucified with Christ (see on 2:20). Let them therefore *be* what they *are*. Let them be *in practice* what they are *in principle,* for in principle they had crucified their old human nature, together with its sinful yearnings, whether these be viewed more passively as *passions* (probably the evil promptings working within their subconsciousness) or actively as *desires* (the wicked cravings which they consciously support and enliven).[169]

Because of the supreme importance of living a consistent Christian life, that is, of being in practice what one is already in principle, this thought is now rephrased as follows: **25. If we live by the Spirit, by the Spirit let us also walk.** This translation, favored also by A.R.V., is better than the one that is found in A.V., R.S.V., N.E.B., and others. It preserves the chiastic structure of the original. The phrases "by the Spirit," "by the Spirit" are in the center, and thus receive the strongest emphasis. Nevertheless, by means of placing the words "if we live" at the very beginning of the sentence, and the words "let us also walk" at the very close, the contrast between *living* and *walking,* as these terms are here employed, is brought out with full force. Meaning: "If the source of our life is *the Spirit, the Spirit* must also be allowed to direct our steps, so that we make progress, advancing step by step toward the goal of perfect consecration to the Lord." This walking by the Spirit is the only way to administer the finishing touch to that which has already been dealt a mortal blow. It is the only way to deal with "the flesh along with its passions and desires." We should destroy the power of the negative by means of The Invincible Positive, the Holy Spirit.

[169] See N.T.C. on I and II Timothy and Titus, pp. 271, 272, especially footnote 147.

Continued: **26. Let us not become boasters, challenging one another, envying one another.** In other words, "Let us neither brag about that which we have (or think we have), thereby calling forth equally pretentious swagger on the part of the person to whom we are speaking, nor grudge that other person what he has." Haughtiness and conceit, the "know-it-all" attitude, brutal aggressiveness, these ill become those who claim to be followers of him who was always showing the very opposite spirit (Isa. 42:2; Zech. 9:9; Matt. 11:29; 20:28; John 13:5; II Cor. 10:1; Phil. 2:8). God does not approve of windbags. If there had not been a special need for this warning Paul undoubtedly would not have issued it. Paul's main idea, accordingly, is this: Allow the fruit of the Spirit to expel the works of the flesh!

*Galatians 5: Seed Thoughts*
(one thought for each verse)

See Verse

1. Freedom is a precious gift. It is also an immense responsibility.
2. Christ is either our complete Savior or is not our Savior at all.
3. Whoever would be saved by works must render perfect obedience to the whole law. Nothing less will do!
4. Those who would be saved by their good works have lost their hold on grace. Nevertheless, it is grace alone that saves.
5. For the Christian it is true that "the best is yet to be."
6. Faith without love is not true faith.
7. "Excelsior" is the Christian's motto. He should allow no one to throw him off this course.
8. "Consider the source!" whenever anyone urges you to do that which is morally or spiritually questionable.
9. An evil intention, if unchecked, leads to a shameful deed. A shameful deed, if unrepented of, becomes a bad habit. A bad habit, if not discarded, will grow into a depraved character, which, in turn, leads to perdition.
10. Showing that you have confidence in a person, if you are at all able to do this with candor, is excellent psychology.
11. The devil does not persecute those whom he already has captured.
12. Are we becoming so selfish that our cheeks no longer glow with indignation when harm is being done to those whom, supposedly, we love?
13. *True liberty* is not the privilege to do whatever one's evil heart desires to do, but is the Spirit-imparted ability and desire to do what one should do.
14. The Christian's law is love.
15. Bitter (= biting) words harm the biter as well as the one bitten. They tend to destroy the fellowship.

16. "Overcome evil with good."
17. Satan has a "fifth column" in our hearts. But the Holy Spirit also resides there. Hence, the conflict!
18. A person enjoys true freedom when the Holy Spirit has taken the helm of the ship which bears him over the troubled sea of life.
19. What today is often called "sickness" is by Scripture called "obvious work of the flesh."
20. We should practice self-denial, not self-indulgence.
21. "Private" sins, such as jealousy and envy, are not any better than "public" sins, such as drinking bouts and revelries.
22. *Love* heads the list of virtues.
23. The true Christian is loyal to his God, gentle to his neighbor, and has himself under control, all this as the result of God's grace.
24. Be in practice what you are (have confessed to be) in principle!
25. You derive all your strength from the Spirit. Then let the Spirit lead you in every phase of your life and conduct.
26. Rude self-assertion is displeasing to the Lord.

# Chapter 6

Verses 1-10

Theme: *The Gospel of Justification by Faith apart from Law-works Defended against Its Detractors*

III. *Its Application: it produces true liberty. Let the Galatians stand firm, therefore, as does Paul, who glories in the cross of Christ*

E. Restore the fallen in a spirit of gentleness. Bear one another's burdens. Share all good things with y o u r instructor. Bear in mind that a man will reap what he sows. Let us do good to everybody, and especially to those who are of the household of the faith.

# CHAPTER VI

## GALATIANS

6 1 Brothers, even if a man be overtaken in any trespass, y o u who are
spiritual should restore such a person in a spirit of gentleness, constantly looking to yourself, lest also you be tempted. 2 Bear one another's burdens, and so fulfil
the law of Christ. 3 For if anyone imagines that he amounts to something, while he
amounts to nothing, he is deluding himself. 4 But let each one test his own work;
then his reason to boast will be in himself alone, and not in (comparing himself
with) someone else; 5 for each person will have to bear his own load.

6 Let him who receives instruction in the Word share all good things
with his instructor. 7 Do not be deceived; God is not mocked; for whatever a man
sows, that also will he reap; 8 for he who sows to his own flesh will from the flesh
reap corruption, and he who sows to the Spirit will from the Spirit reap life everlasting. 9 And let us not grow weary in well-doing, for in due season we shall reap
if we do not give up. 10 So then, as we have opportunity, let us do good to everybody, and especially to those who are of the household of the faith.

---

### 6:1-10

### E. *Show this love to all*

Over against rudeness (5:26) the apostle places gentleness. He says: **1. Brothers, even if a man be overtaken in any trespass, y o u who are spiritual should restore such a person in a spirit of gentleness. . . .** Here, let us say, is a person who, without deliberately planning to perform a wicked deed or to embark upon a devious course, "is overtaken in a trespass."[170] Before he even realizes to the full extent the ethically reprehensible or injurious nature of the act he has already committed it. He "was overtaken." The

---

[170] For the verb προλαμβάνω see M.M., p. 542. Perhaps the various meanings of the word can be subsumed under the general heading: to take or undertake—or in the passive, to be taken—before (hand). Thus in Corinth each person grabbed his food *before* sharing it with the less-privileged (I Cor. 11:21). The woman whose deed is described in Mark 14:8 undertook to anoint Christ's body *before* the usual time. So here in Gal. 6:1 also, the person in question is ensnared by the tempter *before* he fully realizes what he is doing.

This also sheds some light on the meaning *here* of the word *trespass.* In general it indicates a deviation from the path of truth and righteousness. Such deviations may be of a gross or of a less serious nature. The milder sense—fault, error, mistake—would seem to attach to the word in the present instance (as perhaps also in Rom. 5:15, 17, 18). At least the serious nature of the offense is not here stressed. See R. C. Trench, *op. cit.,* par. lxvi.

question then arises, "How must such a case be handled?" The answer is that those members of the churches who are more consistent in following the promptings of the Spirit (5:16, 18, 25) should, *in the spirit of gentleness or meekness* (cf. 5:23), restore the one who committed the trespass. This word *restore* means *to mend,* to bring something or someone back to its or his former position of wholeness or soundness. Thus, it is used with respect to mending nets (Matt. 4:21; Mark 1:19), and perfecting human character (II Cor. 13:11: "Be perfected"). Cf. Luke 6:40; I Thess. 3:10. The main idea certainly is this: "Follow a positive, not a negative course with respect to the trespasser. Do not hurt him but help him. Treat him as you yourselves would wish to be treated if you were in his place." Continued: **constantly looking to yourself**—note change from plural ("You who are spiritual, etc.") to singular—**lest also you be tempted.** Rudeness or boastfulness ill befits the person who at any moment may himself also be tempted. Instead of being self-righteous and arrogant let each one offer the prayers suggested in such passages as Matt. 6:14; 26:41; Mark 14:38; Luke 22:40. The man who thinks that he is standing erect should all the more take heed to himself lest he fall (I Cor. 10:12, 13).

Note how Paul himself practices what he preaches. Was it not true that many Galatians had erred, not mildly but grievously? Nevertheless, though he did not spare them (1:6; 3:1 ff.; 4:11; 5:7), did he not treat them gently, tenderly (4:12 ff., 19, 20)? For the endearing word of address "Brothers," with which this chapter opens, see on 6:18.

Entirely in line with the preceding verse is verse **2. Bear one another's burdens, and so fulfil the law of Christ.** This does not merely mean "Tolerate each other," or "Put up with each other." It means: "Jointly shoulder each member's burdens." Everybody should put his shoulder under the burdens under which this or that individual member is groaning, whatever these burdens may be. They must be carried[171] jointly. Though the term "one another's burdens" is very general, and applies to every type of oppressing affliction that is capable of being shared by the brotherhood, it should be borne in mind, nevertheless, that the point of departure for this exhortation (see on 6:1) is the duty to extend help to the brother so that he may

---

171 The verb βαστάζω occurs more than twenty-five times in the New Testament. It is especially common in the Gospels and in Acts. It is used in connection with *carrying* a water-jar (Mark 14:13; Luke 22:6), a coffin (Luke 7:14), stones (John 10:31), money (carrying it away, stealing it: John 12:6), a corpse (transferring it from one place to another: John 20:15), a yoke (Acts 15:10), a man: Paul (Acts 21:35), and a woman (Rev. 17:7). Hence, here in Gal. 6:2 (and cf. Rom. 15:1) it can best be taken in the figurative sense of "carrying" each other's burdens, lightening each other's loads *of difficulty and grief.* For a slightly different metaphorical sense see Gal. 5:10 (bear one's judgment, pay the penalty). We should not allow the exceptional sense which the word has in Rev. 2:2 (tolerate, put up with) to determine the meaning here in Gal. 6:2, but should interpret it in accordance with its usual sense.

overcome his spiritual weaknesses.[172] Continued: **and so fulfil the law of Christ.** This law of Christ is the principle of love for one another laid down by Christ (John 13:34; see also on Gal. 5:14; cf. James 2:8). However, Christ not only promulgated this law; he also exemplified it. Note how tenderly he dealt with: the sinful woman (Luke 7:36-50), the pentitent thief (Luke 23:43), Simon Peter (Luke 22:61; cf. John 21:15-17), an invalid (John 5:14), and the woman taken in adultery (John 8:11). And note also the marvelously generous reception which, according to Christ's *Parable of the Prodigal Son* (commonly so described), is accorded to the returning penitent. Paul constantly holds before us the *example* of Christ (Rom. 15:3-8; II Cor. 8:9; Phil. 2:5-8), as well as Christ's *precept.*

What follows stands in very close connection with the thought of verses 1 and 2. The connection with verse 1 might be stated as follows: "Constantly look to yourself, lest you also be tempted . . . for if anyone imagines that he amounts to something. . . ." And with verse 2, thus: "Bear one another's burdens, for no one can stand by himself alone . . . for if anyone imagines that he amounts to something, . . ." Accordingly, the apostle writes: **3. For if anyone imagines that he amounts to something, while he amounts to nothing, he is deluding himself.** What makes us tender and generous, meek and humble, sympathetic and helpful, toward others is the realization that we ourselves amount to so little. This does not mean that anyone should lose courage, thinking, "I amount to nothing, and am completely unfit to perform any kingdom work." On the contrary, Paul says, "I can do all things through him that infuses strength into me" (4:13). Morbid self-contempt is unfair to the Giver of all good gifts. Paul would have none of this. He recognizes that when the Holy Spirit distributed his gifts he (Paul) had not been passed by. Accordingly, he calls himself a wise master-builder (I Cor. 3:10), and a steward of the mysteries of God (I Cor. 4:1; cf. 9:17). He ranks himself higher than ten thousand tutors (I Cor. 4:15). He knows that he is able to speak with tongues "more than y o u all" (I Cor. 14:18). He is convinced that as an apostle he has "labored more abundantly" than anyone else (I Cor. 15: 10). See also II Cor. 11:22-33; Gal. 1:1, 14; and Phil. 3:4-6. But he ascribes all of these gifts to the Giver (Rom. 12:3; Gal. 6:14), and never claims personal credit for any virtue or talent (Rom. 7:24, 25; I Cor. 4:7). Besides, it should be borne in mind that Paul does not say, "For if anyone imagines that he amounts to something he is deluding himself." He says, "For if anyone imagines that he amounts to something, *while he amounts to nothing,* he is deluding himself." Paul is attacking the spirit of overconfidence in oneself. It was this error that caused Peter to deny his Lord (Matt. 26:33, 35; Mark 14:29, 31; Luke 22:33; John 13:37), and that

---

[172] Excellent is the article written by H. P. Berlage, "De juiste verklaring van Gal. 6:2," *TT,* 25 (1891), pp. 47–61.

denied the blessing to the Pharisee (Luke 18:9-14), just as much earlier it had brought about the discomfiture of Goliath (I Sam. 17:42-44), of Benhadad (I Kings 20:1 ff.), of Edom (Obad. 1-4), and of Nebuchadnezzar (Dan. 4:30; cf. Isa. 14:12 ff.). See also Rev. 3:17; 18:7.

Instead, therefore, of looking down upon the rest of the members, each member should examine himself. Says Paul: **4. But let each one test**[173] **his own work; then his reason to boast will be in himself alone, and not in (comparing himself with) someone else.** "He who mirrors himself in the mirror of another person's conduct mirrors himself gently."[174] He should mirror himself in the mirror of God's law and of Christ's example. If, after doing this, there is still room for making any claims—as there may be, indeed![175]—then the possibilities of glorying will have arisen from himself, that is, from that which God has accomplished in his heart, not from comparing himself with someone else. The man who is constantly comparing himself with others is senseless (II Cor. 10:12). He that boasts, let him boast in the Lord (cf. 6:14; II Cor. 10:17; cf. I Cor. 9:16; 10:31).

The folly of trying to derive comfort for oneself by comparing oneself with someone else is obvious, **5. for each person will have to bear his own load.**[176] Responsibility cannot be transferred. Each man will be judged in accordance with his own deeds (Jer. 17:10; 32:19; Ezek. 18:20; Matt. 16:27; Rom. 2:6; Rev. 2:23; 20:13). Works do not save anyone. That truth has been emphasized over and over again in this epistle. Nevertheless, the "reward" will be measured out in harmony with each man's works. These works will show the degree in which each man has been true to his trust, the extent to which grace has been operative in his life. *Burdens* should be carried jointly, but

---

[173] The verb δοκιμάζω has various meanings: *a. to put to the test, examine* (I Cor. 11:28; II Cor. 13:5); *b. to prove or verify by means of testing* (I Cor. 3:13; Eph. 5:10; I Peter 1:7); and *c. to approve* (I Cor. 16:3). Here the first meaning best suits the context.

[174] Dutch: Die zich aan een ander spiegelt, spiegelt zich zacht.

[175] For example, he can claim to be a sinner, saved by grace!

[176] In such cases in which βάρος (verse 2) and φορτίον (verse 5) have reference to that which oppresses, is there a difference in meaning between the two words? As to βάρος, Matt. 20:12 refers to "the burden of the day and the scorching heat." There is also Acts 15:28: "to lay upon y o u no greater burden" (cf. 15:10; and see Rev. 2:24). As to φορτίον Matt. 23:4 mentions "heavy burdens," and Luke 11:46 says that these burdens are "grievous to be borne." Contrast Matt. 11:30. It would seem, therefore, that when these two words are used in the aforementioned sense (they also have other meanings which are not relevant to our present purpose) they are quite indistinguishable. This, however, does not mean that here in Gal. 6:5 the word φορτίον must be interpreted in a manner identical with that of βάρος in 6:2. It is the context in each case that must decide. And that context clearly shows that the resultant meaning in these two cases is not identical. And since this is true, and besides, the words used in the original are different, the decision to use two different terms in the translation, a decision reached by most of the more recent translators, was, I believe, a wise one. Contrast A.V. and A.R.V. (text), which have the word "burden" in both passages.

the *load of responsibility* differs for each individual, and in the Judgment Day the manner in which brother *A* has assumed his responsibility will not make things easier or harder for brother *B*. The latter, too, will have to carry his own load.

At first glance it might well seem as if there is no connection between verses 1-5, on the one hand, and what now follows in verse 6. This may, in fact, be the case. It is entirely possible that Paul, realizing that what he mainly wanted to say has been said, asks himself, "Are there any other matters on which I must briefly comment before dispatching the letter?" And it is possible that it then occurred to him—under the direction of the Spirit—that there was, indeed, one rather important matter, namely, that pertaining to providing materially for those in need, including those who had been entrusted with the oversight of the various flocks. Nevertheless, there may, after all, have been a closer connection between verses 1-5, on the one hand, and verse 6 ff., on the other. Ministers who are serving large congregations or have done so at one time or another, will probably sense the possibility of this connection at once. Paul has been speaking about restoring the erring brother. One should not immediately draw the conclusion that this weakling has deliberately cast aside the truth. He may have been caught in a trap. Before he knew it, he had allowed himself to be deceived. Or, theoretically he may have stood for the truth, but in defending it he completely lost his temper. In any event, as was pointed out previously, the party-spirit had left its mark upon these churches. Much work had to be done, and it had to be done firmly, yet lovingly, tactfully. And in this connection a disproportionate burden would rest on the leaders, particularly on those who gave instruction in the Word. We can well imagine that in these early days of the establishment of the church and of its growth in the midst of much opposition both from within and from without, it must have seemed almost impossible, at times, for a church-leader to earn his living and, in addition, to perform all of his spiritual functions. Could this possibly be the reason why the apostle now adds: **6. Let him who receives instruction**—literally, *the catechumen,* a word that is still being used in religious circles—**in the Word share all good things with his instructor,** that is, with *the catechist?* It is worthy of note that even at this very early date there was in existence something similar to today's official Christian ministry. Cf. I Cor. 12:28; Eph. 4:11. In a letter that was probably written very shortly afterward the apostle says, "Now we request y o u, brothers, to appreciate those who labor among y o u and are over y o u in the Lord and admonish y o u, and to esteem them very highly in love for their work" (I Thess. 5:12, 13). Paul was a great organizer (Acts 20:17; Phil. 1:1; Titus 1:5). Even during his first missionary journey he was already appointing "elders in every church" (Acts 14:23). That among the several duties of these elders there was also that of imparting instruction is understandable.

Just how long it took the church to divide the work of the elders between those who governed but did not specialize in imparting instruction, on the one hand, and those, on the other hand, who in addition to governing also specialized in catechizing, we do not know. It may not have taken very long. In any event the Galatians must bear in mind that there is such a thing as the principle of reciprocity (Rom. 15:27; I Cor. 9:4-14; II Cor. 8:7-9, 14; I Tim. 5:8). Hence, those who receive instruction in the Word should *share* (see also Rom. 15:26; II Cor. 9:13; and Heb. 13:16) all good things—including material things—with their instructor. Paul had laid the foundation. He asks nothing for himself. He does, however, definitely urge the Galatians to provide adequately for those who are building on the foundation that had been laid.[177]

With respect not only to what he has just said with reference to attending to the needs of the ministers but also to all the admonitions contained in this letter, the apostle summarizes as follows: **7. Do not be deceived; God is not mocked; for whatever a man sows, that also will he reap. . . .** This rule holds not only for church-members; it holds for everybody. God is not mocked. He does not permit anyone to make light of his gospel or of the exhortations that are implied in it. To sneer at him, thinking, "God is dead," will not go unnoticed. On the contrary, every person will be rewarded according to his works (see on verse 5). This also means, of course, that the manner in which anyone reacts toward the present letter, in which the doctrine of justification by faith apart from law-works is defended against its detractors (be they legalists or libertines), does not escape God's notice, and will definitely be taken into account. Continued: **8. for he who sows to his own flesh will from the flesh reap corruption, and he who sows to the Spirit will from the Spirit reap life everlasting.** *Sowing to the flesh* means to allow the old nature to have its way. So also, *sowing to the Spirit* means to allow the Holy Spirit to have his way. The one who does the latter is walking by the

---

[177] I have carefully read the completely different interpretation of this verse in Lenski's *op. cit.*, p. 299ff. Lenski regards the idea that the Galatians should be "generous with their money," and that "congregations should pay their pastors" to be "a cheap thought," one that would have been especially out of place "so close to the end of the entire epistle." But the apostle was a very practical man. He who wrote I Cor. 9:14 could certainly also urge the Galatians to support their pastors. And as to the place which this admonition occupies in the entire letter, namely, a place toward the close, also in Romans it is toward the close of the epistle that the obligation to reciprocate by means of giving of one's physical substance in return for spiritual goods, is tactfully imposed upon those addressed.

Moreover, in I Corinthians the marvelous chapter with reference to Christ's resurrection and ours (I Cor. 15), ending with the words of triumph: "Thanks be to God who gives us the victory through our Lord Jesus Christ, . . ." is followed, at the beginning of the very last chapter, by "Now concerning the collection"! All this is really not surprising, for Paul considers the putting into practice of Christian stewardship *a sacred ministry* (II Cor. 8:4; 9:1).

Spirit (5:16), and is being led by the Spirit (5:18). What happens to these contrasted representative individuals? Already in this life, but especially in and after the resurrection at the last day, he who has been sowing to please his flesh will from the harvest-field of the flesh reap destruction, decay. On the other hand, he who has been sowing to please the Spirit will from the harvest-field of the Spirit reap life everlasting.

The two terms "corruption" and "life everlasting" must be understood in a double sense: quantitative and qualitative. With respect to the former, the two are alike: both last on and on and on. "Corruption," for example, far from amounting to annihilation, indicates "everlasting destruction" (II Thess. 1:9). "Life everlasting" (occurring frequently in the Gospels, especially in the Gospel according to John—3:16, etc.—; further also in Acts 13:46, 48; Rom. 2:7; 5:21; 6:22, 23; I Tim. 1:16; 6:12; Titus 1:2; 3:7; frequently also in I John—3:15, etc.—; Jude 21) is equal in duration (Matt. 25:46). Qualitatively, and this with reference to both body and soul, the two—"corruption" and "life everlasting"—form a striking contrast. Those who have sown to the flesh will awaken unto shame and everlasting contempt (Dan. 12:2). Their worm will not die, neither will their fire be quenched (Mark 9:48). Their dwelling-place will be outside the banquet-hall (Matt. 8:11, 12; 22:13; 25:10-13). On the other hand, those who have sown to the Spirit will then shine as the brightness of the firmament and as the stars forever and ever (Dan. 12:3). They will bear the image of the heavenly (I Cor. 15:49), and physically will be conformed to the body of Christ's glory (Phil. 3:21). They will be like Christ, for they will see him even as he is (I John 3:2). For the qualitative content of the term "life everlasting" see also on Gal. 3:11; cf. N.T.C. on John 3:16.

9. The idea of *reaping* (verses 7 and 8) is continued in this verse, now with emphasis on the perseverance in well-doing that is required of believers if they are going to reap the blessings of life everlasting. There would also seem to be a connection between verse 9 and the matter mentioned in verse 6. Moreover, with respect to "well-doing" the connection between verses 9 and 10 is obvious. Says Paul: **And let us not grow weary in well-doing, for in due season we shall reap if we do not give up.** "Well-doing"—literally, doing that which is *beautiful*—is a very broad concept, as comprehensive as is "walking by the Spirit" and "being led by the Spirit." See also Rom. 7:21; II Cor. 13:7; and II Thess. 3:13. In each of these passages the meaning is general; that is, the term "well-doing" is not limited to "giving to the poor." This having been admitted, it should now also be affirmed that the idea of providing for *the needy* (in any sense) is certainly not excluded. Is not this work of charity and of giving spiritual guidance an essential ingredient of well-doing? In fact, it is entirely possible that in the present context Paul was thinking especially of "helping anyone who is in need," whether it be of things physical: food, clothing, shelter (see Gal. 2:10; II

Cor. 16:1); things spiritual: instruction, encouragement, advice, etc.; or both. The admonition contained in this verse may well be viewed as a commentary on verse 2: "Bear one another's burdens, and so fulfil the law of Christ."

When the apostle says, "Let us not *grow weary* (see especially Luke 18:1; II Thess. 3:13) in well-doing," he is pointing his finger at a well-known weakness of human nature (see 5:7). Well-doing requires *continued* effort, *constant* toil; but human nature, being fond of ease, lacks staying-power, is easily discouraged. This is especially true when results are not always apparent at once, when those who should help refuse to co-operate, and when no reward seems ever to be coming our way. It is entirely possible that it was especially this last thought—namely, the apparent delay with respect to the fulfilment of the promise regarding Christ's return to reward his servants—that troubled the Galatians. So the apostle reminds them of the fact that we shall reap "in due season," that is, "at the moment of time that is exactly right," not, however, as determined by us but as fixed in God's eternal plan. It is then that the reward of grace—not of merit!—will be conferred. We shall receive it *if we do not lose heart and give up* (cf. Heb. 12:3, 5). Continued: **10. So then, as we have[178] opportunity, let us do good to everybody. . . .** Here again the negative—"Do not grow weary," "Do not give up"—is followed by the positive, "Let us do good." Perseverance in good works as a product of grace is what Paul is constantly urging (3:3; 5:7, 18, 25; 6:2). God preserves his people by means of their perseverance. The power to persevere is from him; the responsibility is theirs. Accordingly, as long as—and since—we have opportunity, let us at each and every occasion that presents itself do good to everybody. The believer has been placed on this earth for a purpose. The best way to prepare for Christ's second coming is to use to the full every opportunity of rendering service. Moreover, this service should be rendered to everybody regardless of race, nationality, class, religion, sex, or anything else. As our Lord's active love overleaped boundaries (Luke 9:54, 55; 10:25-37; 17:11-19; John 4:42; I Tim. 4:10), so should ours. This, however, does not mean that there is no sphere of special concern. This is altogether to be expected. Parents, for example, have a duty toward their neighbors. Nevertheless, their first obligation is toward their own children. So also here. Paul says: **and especially to those who are of the household of the faith.** In this respect, too, we should imitate our heavenly Father, "who is the Savior of all men, especially of those who believe." For explanation see N.T.C. on I Tim. 4:10. Note the term, full of comfort, "the

[178] There is considerable textual support for both ἔχομεν and ἔχωμεν, as the textual apparatus in N.N. indicates. However, when ὡς is used with the subjunctive we also expect ἄν, which is absent here. Hence, with N.N. and Grk.N.T. (A-B-M-W) I accept ἔχομεν. In ὡς ("as") "while" and "since" are probably combined.

household of the faith." All believers constitute one family, "the Father's Family" (see N.T.C. on Eph. 3:14, 15). See also I Cor. 3:9; Eph. 2:19; I Tim. 3:15; and let us not forget Ps. 133. By the term "the household of the faith" is meant those who share the gospel. With respect to material aid, is it not altogether probable that it was exactly this "household of the faith" that was most direly in need of such assistance?

# Chapter 6

Verses 11-18

Theme: *The Gospel of Justification by Faith apart from Law-works Defended against Its Detractors*

III. *Its Application: it produces true liberty. Let the Galatians stand firm, therefore, as does Paul, who glories in the cross of Christ*

F. The Letter's End: Paul's "huge letters." Final warning against the disturbers and exposure of their motives: ease, honor. Concluding testimony: Far be it from me to glory except in the cross of our Lord Jesus Christ. Last plea: From now on let no one cause trouble for me, etc. Closing benediction.

11 Look with what huge letters I am writing to y o u with my own hand.
12 It is those who desire to make a fine outward impression that are trying to
compel y o u to be circumcised, their sole purpose being that they may not be persecuted for the cross of Christ. 13 For even those who favor circumcision are not
law-observers themselves, but want y o u to be circumcised that they may glory in
y o u r flesh. 14 As for myself, however, far be it for me to glory except in the
cross of our Lord Jesus Christ, by which the world has been crucified to me, and
I to the world. 15 For neither is circumcision anything, nor uncircumcision, but a
new creation. 16 And as many as shall walk by this rule, peace (be) upon them and
mercy, even upon the Israel of God.
17 From now on let no one cause trouble for me, for I, on my part, bear
on my body the marks of Jesus.
18 The grace of our Lord Jesus Christ (be) with y o u r spirit, brothers.
Amen.

6:11-18

### F. *Conclusion*

Paul has arrived at the conclusion. This he introduces as follows: **11. Look with what huge letters I am writing[179] to y o u with my own hand.** Another translation is: "Ye see how large a letter I have written unto you with mine own hand" (A.V.). The Greek allows either rendering. Galatians is, indeed, larger than any of eight other epistles that tradition ascribes to Paul. Only Romans, I Corinthians, II Corinthians, and Ephesians[180] are larger (the last one only slightly). So, especially if, of all Paul's letters that have been preserved, Galatians was the very first one he wrote, as we have assumed, he could perhaps have written, "See (or "y o u see") what a big letter I wrote y o u." Nevertheless, today very few interpreters would adopt the translation found in A.V. The most valid reason for this rejection is probably this: whenever the apostle refers to a *letter,* in the sense of "a communication in writing," as distinguished from "a character of the alphabet," he always uses the word *epistle* (Rom. 16:22; I Cor. 5:9; II Cor. 7:8; Col. 4:16; I Thess. 5:27; etc.). That word is not found here in Gal. 6:11.[181]

---

179 Robertson (Gram.N.T., p. 846) calls ἔγραψα "a true epistolary aorist." He states that "it probably refers to the concluding verses 11-18." The reasons given by others who contend that this is not an epistolary aorist have not convinced me. If in essentially similar cases this would be an epistolary aorist, showing that the writer looks at what he writes as the recipient will look at it, why would it be different in this case?

180 Hebrews, of anonymous authorship, is, of course, excluded from this list.

181 Besides, if Paul had an epistle in mind the accusative of the word "letter" (6:11) would have been more natural.

Having then adopted the rendering, "Look with what huge letters I am writing to y o u with my own hand," the next question would be, "Does Paul say this with respect to the entire epistle or only in connection with the closing paragraph (verses 11-18)?" Although there are those who have expressed very positively that the apostle wrote the entire Galatians with his own hand, I cannot go along with this conclusion. It would mean a departure, at the very outset, from what was going to be Paul's usual course, namely, to write *the closing greeting* (and perhaps a few words in connection with it) with his own hand. Thus we read, *"The greeting* by the hand of me, Paul, which is a token of genuineness in every epistle; so I write" (II Thess. 3:17). Cf. I Cor. 16:21; Col. 4:18.[182] This also indicates *why* the closing words were written by the author himself. Besides, it may well be that—especially in the case of Galatians—there was still another reason, namely, to add emphasis to the concluding words. In reading verses 11-18 one seems to sense the author's special emphasis, as if he were saying, "Let me summarize the entire argument, and let me give y o u one final, emphatic fatherly warning."

This, therefore, may also account for the fact that these letters were huge, namely, for the sake of special emphasis. But there may have been other reasons for this. Here, however, we have already entered the realm of speculation; for example: *a.* Paul's eyesight was impaired; *b.* his writing hand was sore; *c.* he had never learned to write very well; etc.

The next five verses contain a final warning against the Judaizers. Paul once again exposes their motives and in no uncertain terms blasts their compromising doctrine. In the course of doing this he comes up with one of his marvelous sayings, a profession of his personal faith. The warning begins as follows: **12. It is those who desire to make a fine outward impression that are trying to compel y o u to be circumcised, their sole purpose being that they may not be persecuted for the cross of Christ.** Whatever the apostle has said earlier about these opponents (see especially 1:7-9; 2:4, 5, 12; 3:1, 10; 4:17; 5:2-5, 7, 11, 12) is here brought to a head. In a few crisp phrases he makes clear that these Judaizers are not at all interested in the welfare of the Galatians. On the contrary, they are concerned only about themselves: their own honor, their own ease (freedom from persecution). They desire to make a good outward impression; literally: "to present a pleasing front *in flesh*," that is, *outwardly*. They are eager to cut a respectable figure when they come face to face with other Jews, those who have not even nominally accepted Christ. By making so much of circumcision—as if that were far more important than the cross of Christ—they are trying to work their way back into the good graces of their relatives and former friends. They know

[182] It was not unusual in those days for a writer to employ a secretary, and then to write the conclusion with his own hand. See A. Deissmann, *op. cit.*, pp. 171, 172.

very well that a Jew who departs from the Jewish traditions and accepts Christ wholeheartedly can expect nothing but bitter presecution: ostracism, threats, calumny, physical and mental torture, etc. (Matt. 10:17; John 11:57; Acts 4:27, 28; 5:33; 13:45, 50; 14:2, 19; 21:27-36; II Cor. 11:24; Col. 1:24; I Thess. 2:14-16; II Tim. 3:10-12; Rev. 2:9). They are trying to escape all this, therefore, by means of effecting a compromise; something like: "Salvation is achieved by means of faith in Jesus plus law-works, especially circumcision." Their hypocrisy and selfishness is evident: **13: For even those who favor circumcision[183] are not law-observers themselves, but want y o u to be circumcised that they may glory in y o u r flesh.** By all kinds of devious means and subterfuges these legalists tried to circumvent the law's real intention. The relation between the Judaizers and the Pharisees is clear from Acts 15:5. Jesus again and again characterized the Pharisees as being "hypocrites" (Matt. 23:13, 14, 15, 23, 25, 27, 29). He also called them "serpents and offspring of vipers" (Matt. 23:33), and declared that they made void the word of God by their tradition (Matt. 15:6). Relevant to the present context is also this saying of the Lord: "They tie together heavy loads, and lay them on men's shoulders; but they themselves are unwilling to raise a finger to lift them" (Matt. 23:4).

Paul therefore tells the Galatians: These hypocrites "want y o u to be circumcised that they may glory in y o u r[184] flesh," that is, that y o u r circumcised organ may provide them with a reason to boast. They would then be able to step up to their fellow-countrymen with an air of confidence, bragging, "Just think of it, we persuaded so many Galatians to become circumcised!"

Over against this type of "glorying" Paul now sets his own: **14. As for myself, however, far be it for me to glory except in the cross of our Lord Jesus Christ, by which the world has been crucified to me, and I to the world.**

### *The Cross: Paul's Only Reason for Glorying*

(1) *Why Paul Glories Only in the Cross*

The cross is about the last thing which natural man would ever have selected as a reason for boasting. It was "to the Jews a stumbling-block, and to the Greeks foolishness" (I Cor. 1:23). The cross exposes man's desperate state, his utter bankruptcy that made such suffering necessary. Accordingly,

---

183 The perfect: "those who have been circumcised," may have seemed more correct to a copyist than the present, which could be interpreted to mean, "those who have themselves circumcised." But the present can also be interpreted as indicating, "those who favor and advocate circumcision." The context points in the direction of the latter interpretation for it is clear that Paul is referring to the Judaizers.

184 The original may imply a degree of emphasis, especially in the light of *a.* the emphatic "as for myself" at the beginning of verse 14, and *b.* verse 17 (see on that verse).

it reveals the folly of all human pride. It teaches man to say: "I never knew myself as a sinner, nor recognized Christ as my Savior,

> Until upon the cross I saw
> My God, who died to meet the law
> That I had broken; then I saw
> My sin, and then my Savior."

No one is ever able to see on that cross "the wonder of God's glorious love" unless he also sees "his own unworthiness," and "pours contempt on all his pride."

By God's marvelous grace Paul had come to view that cross as:

*a. The M irror,* and this not only of his own unworthiness but also of God's resplendent attributes, that is, of such "excellencies" as God's righteousness which must receive its due (Rom. 8:3, 4) ; God's power and wisdom (I Cor. 1:24) ; and his love, mercy, and grace (II Cor. 5:19-21; Gal. 2:20) ; all of these in sublime harmony with each other (Ps. 85:10) .

*b. The M eans of Redemption* in its most comprehensive sense (Justification, Sanctification, Glorification) . See such passages as Rom. 3:25, 26; 6:6; Gal. 3:13; Eph. 1:7; 2:16; Col. 1:20; 2:14. Cf. Heb. 9:22; Rev. 7:14.

*c. The M agnet* by means of which men of every tribe and nation, being drawn to Christ Crucified, are also drawn together as one body (Gal. 3:23-29; Eph. 2:16, 18; Col. 3:11. Cf. John 3:13, 14; 12:32) .

*d. The M odel* for men to imitate. The redemptive acts can never be imitated, but the spirit of self-sacrifice and love that is revealed in these acts should be reflected in the hearts and lives of God's children (Rom. 15:1, 2; II Cor. 8:9; Eph. 5:1, 2; Phil. 2:5-8) . Cf. John 13:14, 34; I Peter 2:21-24.

Is it any wonder, then, that Paul glories only in the cross?

(2) *How Paul Glories in the Cross*

*a.* By surrendering himself to Christ Crucified as his own Lord and Savior (Gal. 2:20) ;

*b.* By praying that the power of the crucified and risen Savior may more and more assert itself in his own life (Phil. 3:7-16) ;

*c.* By proclaiming the crucified and risen Lord—notice full title "our Lord Jesus Christ"—wherever he is sent (Gal. 1:16) , the love of Christ constraining him to do so (I Cor. 9:16; II Cor. 5:14) ; and

*d.* By courageously defending the gospel of Christ Crucified over against every attack upon it (as is shown by this very epistle to the Galatians, in its entirety) .

(3) *What Effect Paul's Glorying in the Cross Has upon the Relation between Paul and the World*

*a.* By this cross, says Paul, "the world has been crucified to me." He does not say, "I crucified the world," but "the world has been crucified to me."

In other words, he bears testimony to the fact that the Holy Spirit, by means of the pure doctrine of the cross, had wrought a mighty work in his soul. The "world," that is, all those earthly pleasures and treasures, honors and values, that tend to draw the soul away from Christ, had lost their charm for Paul. *The world had become dead to Paul.* I am in complete agreement with Calvin when, in commenting on this expression, he states: "This exactly agrees with the language which Paul employs on another occasion," and then refers to Phil. 3:7, 8: "Nevertheless, such things as once were gains to me these have I counted loss for Christ. Yes, what is more, I certainly do count all things to be sheer loss because of the all-surpassing excellence of knowing Christ Jesus my Lord, for whom I suffered the loss of all these things, and I am still counting them refuse, in order that I may gain Christ" (my translation, not Calvin's).

*b.* Paul adds, "and I (have been crucified) to the world." Logic would seem to demand that, as far as possible, the two statements (*a.* and *b.*) be interpreted, in such a manner that the words "has—or: have—been crucified" have the same meaning in both cases. Hence, this second clause must mean that *Paul had become dead to the world,* an object of contempt to all those who place their confidence in earthly pleasures and treasures, honors and values, that tend to draw the soul away from Christ. Duncan expresses it very aptly: "Paul's ideals and outlook have now become so spiritual and unworldly that the world can ignore him, just as if he had ceased to be."

Paul continues: **15. For neither is circumcision anything, nor uncircumcision, but a new creation.** The conjunction *for* indicates the relation between this and the preceding verse. It shows that what Paul means is this: salvation by means of the cross of Christ is everything to me; worldly inventions, on the contrary, such as salvation through circumcision, mean nothing, "For (or: the reason being that) neither is circumcision anything. . . ." The present passage (6:15) comes very close to saying what Paul had said before, namely, "For in Christ Jesus neither circumcision nor uncircumcision is of any avail, but faith working through love" (5:6). See the explanation of that passage. Cf. I Cor. 7:19; II Cor. 5:17; Gal. 3:28; and Col. 3:10, 11. Being circumcised contributes nothing toward being saved, nor does *not* being circumcised; neither is it possible for either of these two states to assure us of salvation—or to make us effective witnesses for God. The one and only thing that really matters is "a new creation," that is, the new life, the life of regeneration, which the Holy Spirit brings about in a person's heart (John 3:3, 5; Rom. 2:29). That "creation" is "new," as contrasted with man's old, outworn nature. It is infinitely *better* than the old. It is *God's* work, and is therefore what really counts. It is the product of him who says, "Behold, I make all things new" (Rev. 21:5). It has come *fresh* from the heart of God Almighty, and is a firm pledge of even greater glories to follow, as a result of *his* transforming power, "For his handiwork are we, created in Christ Jesus for good works, which God prepared beforehand that we should walk in them" (Eph. 2:10).

Paul continues: **16. And as many as shall walk by this rule, peace (be) upon them and mercy, even upon the Israel of God.** According to the preceding context, this rule[185] is the one by which before God only this is of consequence, that a person places his complete trust in Christ Crucified, and that, therefore, he regulates his life by this principle. This will mean that his life will be one of gratitude and Christian service out of love for his wonderful Savior. Upon those—*all* those and *only* those—who are governed by this rule *peace and mercy* are pronounced. *Peace* is the serenity of heart that is the portion of all those who have been justified by faith (Rom. 5:1). In the midst of the storms of life they are safe because they have found shelter in the cleft of the rock. In the day of wrath, wasteness, and desolation God "hides" all those who take refuge in him (Zeph. 1:2 ff.; 2:3; 3:12). See on 1:3. Hence, peace is spiritual wholeness and prosperity. *Peace* and *mercy* are inseparable. Had not the *mercy* of God been shown to his people they would not have enjoyed *peace*. God's mercy is his love directed toward sinners viewed in their wretchedness and need. See N.T.C. on Philippians, p. 142, for a list of over one hundred Old and New Testament passages in which this divine attribute is described.

So far the interpretation runs smoothly. A difficulty arises because of the last phrase of this verse. That last phrase is: "*kai* upon the Israel of God." Now, varying with the specific context in which this conjunction *kai* occurs, it can be rendered: *and, and so, also, likewise, even, nevertheless, and yet, but,* etc. Sometimes it is best left untranslated. Now when this conjunction is rendered *and* (as in A.V., A.R.V., N.E.B.), it yields this result, that after having pronounced God's blessing upon all those who place their trust exclusively in Christ Crucified, the apostle pronounces an additional blessing upon "the Israel of God," which is then interpreted to mean "the Jews," or "all such Jews as would in the future be converted to Christ," etc.

Now this interpretation tends to make Paul contradict his whole line of reasoning in this epistle. Over against the Judaizers' perversion of the gospel

---

[185] Greek κανών was probably borrowed from the Hebrew word *qāneh*. According to etymologists our English word "cane" may be related to this. At any rate the Greek word has the basic meaning: *reed* or *measuring rod*. Thus, figuratively, it developed into the meaning *norm, standard*. Something similar has happened in connection with our English word "rule." The sense *norm, standard of measurement in ethical and spiritual matters,* clearly pertains to the word here in Gal. 6:16. In II Cor. 10:13-16 the meaning is slightly different: "sphere of action or influence," "boundary." The meaning "collection of divinely inspired, normative writings" was a later development. The word does not have that meaning in the New Testament.

he has emphasized the fact that "the blessing of Abraham" now rests upon all those, and only upon those, "who are of faith" (3:9); that all those, and only those, "who belong to Christ" are "heirs according to promise" (3:29). These are the very people who "walk by the Spirit" (5:16), and "are led by the Spirit" (5:18). Moreover, to make his meaning very clear, the apostle has even called special attention to the fact that God bestows his blessings on all true believers, regardless of nationality, race, social position, or sex: "There can be neither Jew nor Greek; there can be neither slave nor freeman; there can be no male and female; for y o u are all one in Christ Jesus" (3:28). By means of an allegory (4:21-31) he has re-emphasized this truth. And would he now, at the very close of the letter, undo all this by first of all pronouncing a blessing on "as many as" (or: "all") who walk by the rule of glorying in the cross, be they Jew or Gentile by birth, and then pronouncing a blessing upon those who do not (or: do not yet) walk by that rule? I refuse to accept that explanation. Appeals to the well-known "Eighteen petition prayer of the Jews," to the meaning of the word *Israel* in other New Testament passages, etc., cannot rescue this interpretation. As to the former, Gal. 6:16 must be interpreted in accordance with *its own specific context* and *in the light of the entire argument of this particular epistle*. And as to the latter, it is very clear that in his epistles the apostle employs the term *Israel* in more than one sense. In fact, in the small compass of a single verse (Rom. 9:6) he uses it in two different senses. Each passage in which that term occurs must therefore be explained in the light of its context.[186] Besides, Paul uses the term "the Israel of God" only in the present passage, nowhere else.

What, then, is the solution? In harmony with all of Paul's teaching in this epistle (and see also Eph. 2:14-22), and also in harmony with the broad, all-inclusive statement at the beginning of the present passage, where the apostle pronounces God's blessing of peace and mercy upon "as many as" shall walk by this rule, an object from which nothing can be subtracted and to which nothing can be added, it is my firm belief that those many translators and interpreters are right who have decided that *kai,* as here used, must be rendered *even,* or (with equal effect) must be left untranslated. Hence, what the apostle says is this: "And as many as shall walk by this rule, peace (be) upon them and mercy, even upon the Israel of God." Cf. Ps. 125:5. Upon all of God's true Israel, Jew or Gentile, all who truly glory in the cross, the blessing is pronounced.[187]

---

[186] See also my little book *And So All Israel Shall Be Saved,* an interpretation of Rom. 11:26a. It was published in 1945 by Baker Book House, Grand Rapids, Mich., but is out of print at this writing.

[187] The rendering according to which *kai* is translated *even,* or is left untranslated, is also favored by the following: The Amplified New Testament, Berkeley Version, Calvin, Erdman, Lenski, Lightfoot, Phillips, Rendall, R.S.V., and Williams.

**17.** Paul presents a final request: **From now on[188] let no one cause trouble for me, for I, on my part, bear on my body the marks of Jesus.** The apostle, loaded down with many responsibilities, asks that in the future he may not again be troubled by departures from the truth in the Galatian churches. He asks, in other words, that these churches may take his message to heart. Troublesome churches, and also troublesome individuals, at times forget that, while their own misbehavior is bad enough in itself, they also deprive others of the attention that could have been bestowed upon them. Cf. Luke 13:7. Besides, on the part of the person who must set them straight they often require energy that is exhausting. It is especially the latter thought which Paul has in mind when he reminds the Galatians that he bears on his body the marks of Jesus.

Evidently the apostle was referring to the scars (literally: *stigmata*)[189] that had been left on his body by the persecutions which he had endured while traveling through Galatia on his first missionary journey (Acts 13:50; 14:19; II Cor. 11:25; II Tim. 3:10, 11). At Lystra, for example, he had been almost stoned to death! Up to this point there is very little disagreement among commentators. However, when the question is asked, "In what sense were these scars the marks of Jesus?" the opinions vary widely. Some of them are as follows: They characterized Paul as *a.* a slave of Jesus, *b.* a prisoner of Jesus, *c.* a soldier of Jesus, *d.* in possession of an amulet or "Jesus-charm," as if the apostle were warning the Galatians: "Do be sensible, y o u cannot make any trouble for me, for I am protected by a charm" (a most unlikely explanation!). The best explanation, as far as I can see, is the one offered by Lenski (among others): "The scars on Paul's body belonged to Jesus, like the wounds he himself suffered, for Paul's scars were truly suffered because of Christ. Cf. II Cor. 1:5; 4:10; Col. 1:24" (*op. cit.*, p. 321). The wounds inflicted on Paul's body were evidence of the closeness of the fellowship between Jesus and Paul (Gal. 1:8-12, 15, 16; 2:19 ff.; 4:12-20).

It is just possible that Paul's emphatic "I, on my part"[190] forms a contrast with 6:13, where Paul tells the Galatians that the purpose of the Judaizers is "that they may glory in *y o u r* flesh." If that be so, then the apostle is, as it were, saying, "I, too, have *marks* or *scars,* namely those that link me with my Savior. Remember that, Galatians! And be reminded that when,

---

188 Here τοῦ λοιποῦ probably means *in the future* (= τοῦ λοιποῦ χρόνου), in distinction from τὸ λοιπόν, as for the rest. At times the two are equivalent in meaning. and may both be rendered "finally." See N.T.C. on Eph. 6:10.

189 These *stigmata* must not be identified in nature with the wounds in the hands, feet, and side of Francis of Assisi and many others after him. See the interesting account in E. M. Wilmot-Buxton, *St. Francis of Assisi,* New York, 1926, pp. 154-157. As some see it, such marks are connected with nervous or cataleptic hysteria. In any case, this subject has nothing to do with the explanation of Gal. 5:17.

190 Note emphatic ἐγώ at the beginning of the last clause; also: "on *my body.*"

because of departure from the faith, y o u trouble me, y o u are grieving my Savior, whose ambassador I am" (cf. Acts 9:4, 5; 22:7, 8; 26:14, 15).

Verse **18.** contains the closing benediction: **The grace of our Lord Jesus Christ (be) with y o u r spirit, brothers. Amen.** It has been remarked that the brevity which characterizes this benediction reflects the tension under which the apostle wrote this letter. Accordingly, these few words have been compared with the rich and bountiful parting salutations found in Rom. 16:25-27; II Cor. 13:14; Eph. 6:23, 24; and Jude 24, 25. Nevertheless, further reflection indicates that Paul's final word, here in Gal. 6:18, is by no means wanting in beauty and meaning. Note the following:

*a.* It concentrates the attention of those to whom it is addressed on "the marvelous grace of our loving Lord." This is the grace (love to the undeserving) that had atoned for their sin, had brought about the operation of the Holy Spirit in their hearts, and their adoption as children and heirs. It is the grace that sustains them, equips them to be living witnesses, fills their hearts with peace that passes understanding and with joy unspeakable and full of glory, and brings them at last to their inheritance, incorruptible, undefiled, and never-fading. Is it not true that throughout the letter the emphasis is on the marvel of *God's grace* as contrasted with *human work?*

*b.* It mentions Jesus in all the fulness of his saving power, giving him his full title "our Lord Jesus Christ." The solemnity with which the apostle utters this full name deserves attention. As *Lord* he owns us, governs and protects us, and we belong to him and should do his bidding. As *Jesus* he, he *alone,* is our Savior (Matt. 1:21; Acts 4:12). And as *Christ* he was appointed and (as to his human nature) gloriously qualified to be, in his capacity as our Mediator, "our chief Prophet, only Highpriest, and eternal King." See Acts 2:36.

*c.* It focuses the attention of the Galatians on the necessity of having this grace of the Lord Jesus Christ in their *inner personality,* viewed as contact-point between God and his children: " (be) with y o u r spirit." The Judaizers were fond of making a good *outward* impression. The Galatians are reminded of the fact that what they need is "grace that will strengthen and cleanse *within.*"

*d.* Finally, it does not take leave of these Galatians, many of whom were erring grievously, before it has once more, as so often before (1:11; 3:15; 4:12, 28, 31; 5:11, 13; 6:1), addressed them with that term of endearment and close Christian fellowship: "brothers," members—by grace!—of the same family, "the Father's Family" (see N.T.C. on Eph. 3:14, 15).

A church that was dear—in fact, very dear—to the heart of Paul was that at Philippi. Note how he was going to describe it in Phil. 4:1: "my brothers, beloved and longed for, my joy and crown . . . beloved." Surely Paul would put just as much love into the closing benediction addressed to that church as he now puts into the final blessing which he pronounces on the Galatians. Now compare the two:

| Phil. 4:23 | Gal. 6:18 |
|---|---|
| "The grace of the Lord Jesus Christ (be) with y o u r spirit." | "The grace of our Lord Jesus Christ (be) with y o u r spirit, brothers. Amen. |

Note: "brothers" in Gal. 6:18. The Philippians did not need to be reassured of this. They knew it (Phil. 1:12; 3:1, 13, 17; 4:1, 8). The Galatians must hear it once more; for the heart of Paul, that warm, throbbing heart, feels the need of once again embracing these erring "children" of his with his love!

The solemn word of affirmation and confirmation, "Amen," closes this epistle.

### *Galatians 6: Seed Thoughts*
(one thought for each verse)

See Verse

1. Restore lovingly those who were caught in temptation's net.
2. Burdens must be shouldered jointly.
3. Be conceited and be cheated!
4. He who mirrors himself in the mirror of another person's conduct mirrors himself gently.
5. Responsibility's load cannot be transferred.
6. Provide well for God's servant, the minister.
7. Those who sow weeds must not expect to reap wheat.
8. "The wages of sin is death, but the free gift of God is life everlasting in Christ Jesus our Lord."
9. "Blessed are the merciful, for they will receive mercy."
10. Love overleaps—yet also recognizes—boundaries.
11. Do not soft-pedal the gospel.
12. Beware of compromising when principles are at stake.
13. Practice what y o u preach.
14. The cross of Christ: our only glory.
15. "On Christ, the solid Rock, I stand; All other ground is sinking sand."
16. This (No. 15) is the Rule of Gratitude for every Christian.
17. Do not trouble those who bear the marks of Jesus, but help them in every way.
18. The man who preaches "Salvation through Imitation" forgets that it even takes grace to imitate.

# Paul's Epistle to the Galatians

## Chapter 1

1 Paul, an apostle—not from men nor through man but through Jesus Christ and God the Father, who raised him from the dead—2 and all the brothers who are with me, to the churches of Galatia; 3 grace to y o u and peace from God our Father and the Lord Jesus Christ; 4 who gave himself for our sins, that he might rescue us out of this present world dominated by evil; (having thus given himself) according to the will of our God and Father, 5 to whom (be) the glory forever and ever. Amen.

6 I am amazed that y o u are so quickly moving away from him who called y o u (and turning) to a different gospel, 7 which (in reality) is not (even) another; but (the fact is that) certain individuals are throwing y o u into confusion and are trying to pervert the gospel of Christ. 8 But even though we ourselves or an angel from heaven were to preach to y o u any gospel other than the one which we preached to y o u, let him be accursed! 9 As we have said before, so now I say again, If anyone is preaching to y o u any gospel other than that which y o u have received, let him be accursed! 10 There! Is it the favor of men that I am now seeking to win or of God? Or is it men whom I am seeking to please? If I were still trying to please men, I would not be a servant of Christ.

11 For I make known to y o u, brothers, with respect to the gospel that was preached by me, that it is not a human invention; 12 for as concerns myself, I did not receive it from men nor was I taught it; on the contrary (I received it) through the revelation of Jesus Christ. 13 For y o u have heard of my former manner of life when I practiced the Jewish religion, how beyond all bounds I was persecuting the church of God and was trying to destroy it; 14 and I advanced in the Jewish religion more than many of my contemporaries among my people, and was a more ardent enthusiast for the traditions of my fathers. 15 But when it pleased him, who separated me from my mother's womb and called me through his grace, 16 to reveal his Son in me, in order that I might preach his gospel among the Gentiles, I did not at once confer with flesh and blood, 17 nor did I go up to Jerusalem to those who were apostles before me, but I went away to Arabia; and again I returned to Damascus.

18 Then after three years I went up to Jerusalem to become acquainted with Cephas, and I remained with him fifteen days; 19 but none of the other apostles did I see, only James the Lord's brother. 20 Now take note: with respect to the things which I am writing to y o u, in the presence of God (I affirm) that I am not lying. 21 Then I came to the districts of Syria and Cilicia. 22 But I was still unknown by sight to the Christian churches of Judea. 23 They simply kept hearing, "He who formerly persecuted us is now preaching the gospel of the faith which he formerly was trying to destroy." 24 And they were glorifying God on my account.

## Chapter 2

1 Then, after an interval of fourteen years, I went up again to Jerusalem with Barnabas, also taking Titus with me. 2 I went up, moreover, as a result of a

revelation, and I set before them the gospel which I am accustomed to preach among the Gentiles; but (I did this) privately to "those of repute," to make sure that I was not running or had not run in vain. 3 Yet even Titus who was with me, Greek though he is, was not compelled to be circumcised; 4 (in fact, the suggestion would never have arisen) but for the uninvited sham brothers, who had infiltrated our ranks to spy on our liberty which we have in Christ Jesus, and thus to reduce us to slavery; 5 to whom not even for a moment did we yield submission, in order that the truth of the gospel might continue with y o u. 6 Well, from those "who were reputed" to be something—whatever they once were makes no difference to me; God accepts no man's person—to me "those of repute" imparted nothing; 7 on the contrary, when they saw that I had been entrusted with the gospel to the uncircumcised just as Peter (with that) to the circumcised 8—for he who was at work through Peter in apostolic mission activity for the circumcised was also at work in me for the Gentiles—, 9 and when they perceived the grace that was given to me, James and Cephas and John, "those who were reputed" to be pillars, gave to me and Barnabas the right hand of fellowship, that we should (go) to the Gentiles, and they to the circumcised. 10 Only, we were to continue to remember the poor, the very thing which I was also eager to do.

11 Now when Cephas came to Antioch I opposed him to his face because he stood condemned. 12 For before certain individuals from James arrived he had been in the habit of eating his meals with the Gentiles. But when they came he began to draw back and to separate himself, being afraid of those who belonged to the circumcision party. 13 And the rest of the Jews joined him in playing the hypocrite, so that even Barnabas was carried along by their hypocrisy. 14 But when I saw that they were not pursuing a straight course in accordance with the truth of the gospel, I said to Cephas, in everybody's presence, "If you, though a Jew, can live like a Gentile and not like a Jew, how can you (now) force the Gentiles to live like Jews?"

15 "We ourselves, though by nature Jews and not 'Gentile sinners,' 16 yet, knowing that a man is not justified by law-works but only through faith in Jesus Christ, even we believed in Christ Jesus in order that we might be justified by faith in Christ, and not by law-works, because by law-works will no flesh be justified. 17 But if, in seeking to be justified in Christ, we ourselves also turn out to be sinners, is Christ then a sin-promoter? By no means! 18 For, if I start to rebuild the very things which I have torn down, it is then that I prove myself a transgressor. 19 For I through law died to law, that I might live to God. 20 I have been crucified with Christ; and it is no longer I who lives, but Christ who lives in me; and that (life) which I now live in flesh I live in faith, (the faith) which is in the Son of God, who loved me and gave himself up for me. 21 I do not set aside the grace of God; for if justification (were) through law, then Christ died in vain."

## Chapter 3

1 O foolish Galatians! Who has bewitched y o u, before whose very eyes Jesus was openly displayed as crucified? 2 This only would I learn from y o u: Was it by doing what (the) law demands that y o u received the Spirit, or was it by believing (the) gospel message? 3 Are y o u so foolish? Having begun by the Spirit, now by fleshly means are y o u being made perfect? 4 Did y o u experience so many things in vain?—if (it be) really in vain. 5 He, accordingly, who supplies the Spirit to y o u and works miracles among y o u (does he bring this about) because y o u do what (the) law demands or because y o u believe (the) gospel message?

6 (It is) even as (recorded): "Abraham believed God, and it was reckoned to him for righteousness." 7 Know then that those that are of faith, it is they who are sons of Abraham. 8 Now Scripture, foreseeing that it was by faith that God would justify the Gentiles, preached the gospel beforehand to Abraham, (saying): "In you all the nations shall be blessed." 9 Therefore, those that are of faith are blessed with Abraham, the man of faith.

10 For as many as rely on law-works are under a curse; for it is written, "Cursed (is) everyone who does not continue in all the things that are written in the book of the law, to do them." 11 Now it is evident that by law no one is justified before God, for "The righteous shall live by faith." 12 But the law does not belong to faith; on the contrary, "He who does them shall live by them." 13 Christ redeemed us from the curse of the law, having become a curse for us—for it is written, "Cursed is everyone who is hanging on a tree"— 14 in order that the blessing of Abraham might come to the Gentiles in Jesus Christ, in order that we might receive the promised Spirit through faith.

15 Brothers, I speak from a human standpoint: even a human testament, once ratified, no one sets aside or amplifies. 16 Now to Abraham were the promises spoken, and to his seed. He does not say, "And to the seeds," as (referring) to many, but as (referring) to one, "And to your seed," which is Christ. 17 Now this is what I mean: a covenant that has been ratified by God, the law, which came into existence four hundred thirty years afterward, does not annul so as to make the promise ineffective. 18 For if the inheritance (is) due to law, it (is) no longer due to promise; but to Abraham it was through a promise that God graciously granted it.

19 Why then the law? By reason of the transgressions it was added, until the seed should come to whom the promise had been made, having been ordained through angels by the agency of an intermediary. 20 Now the intermediary does not represent (just) one party, but God is one.

21 (Is) the law then contrary to the promises of God? By no means. For if a law had been given that was able to impart life, then indeed righteousness would have come by law. 22 But Scripture has locked up the whole world under (the power of) sin, in order that as a result of faith in Jesus Christ the promise might be given to those who believe.

23 Now before this faith came, we were kept in custody under law, being locked up with a view to the faith that was to be revealed. 24 So the law became our custodian (to conduct us) to Christ, that by faith we might be justified. 25 But now that this faith has come we are no longer under a custodian.

26 For y o u are all sons of God, through faith, in Christ Jesus. 27 For as many of y o u as were baptized into (union with) Christ have put on Christ. 28 There can be neither Jew nor Greek; there can be neither slave nor freeman; there can be no male and female; for y o u are all one in Christ Jesus. 29 And if y o u belong to Christ, then y o u are Abraham's seed, heirs according to promise.

## Chapter 4

1 What I mean is this, that as long as the heir is a child he differs in no respect from a slave though he is owner of all, 2 but is under guardians and stewards until the time fixed by the father. 3 So also we, when we were children, were enslaved by the rudiments of the world. 4 But when the fulness of the time came, God sent forth his Son, born of a woman, born under law, 5 in order that he might redeem them (who were) under law, that we might receive the adoption as sons. 6 And because y o u are sons, God sent forth the Spirit of his Son into our

hearts, crying, "Abba! Father!" 7 So, no longer are you a slave but a son; and if a son then also an heir through God.

8 However, at that time, since you did not know God, you were slaves to those who by nature are no gods; 9 but now that you have come to know God, or rather to be known by God, how (is it) that you turn back again to the weak and beggarly rudiments by which all over again you wish to be enslaved? 10 You observe days and months and seasons and years. 11 I am afraid about you, lest somehow I have labored among you in vain.

12 Become as I (am), because I also became as you (are), brothers; (this) I beg of you. No wrong did you do me. 13 You know, moreover, that it was because of an infirmity of the flesh that I preached to you the gospel on that former occasion; 14 and though my physical condition was a temptation to you, yet you did not despise or loathe me, but as an angel of God you welcomed me, as Christ Jesus. 15 Where, then, (is) your (former) blessedness? For I testify to you that, had it been possible, your very eyes you would have plucked out and given to me. 16 Have I then become your enemy by telling you the truth? 17 These people are zealously courting you for no commendable purpose: on the contrary, they want to isolate you, in order that you may zealously court them. 18 Now (it is) commendable to be zealously courted in connection with a commendable cause (and this) always, and not only when I am present with you. 19 My dear children, for whom I am again suffering birth-pangs until Christ be formed in you, 20 I could wish to be present with you now and to change my tone of voice, for I am perplexed about you.

21 Tell me, you who desire to be under law, do you not hear the law? 22 For it is written that Abraham had two sons, one by the slave-woman and one by the free-woman. 23 But the son of the slave-woman was flesh-born; the son of the free-woman (was born) through promise. 24 Now things of this nature were spoken with another meaning in mind, for these two women represent two covenants: one from Mount Sinai, bearing children destined for slavery. She is Hagar. 25 Now Hagar represents Mount Sinai in Arabia, and corresponds to the Jerusalem of today, for she is in bondage with her children. 26 But the Jerusalem (that is) above is free, and she is our mother; 27 for it is written:

"Rejoice O barren one, you who do not bear;
Break forth and shout, you who have no birth-pangs;
For more are the children of the desolate than of her who has a husband."

28 Now you, brothers, like Isaac, are children of promise. 29 But as at that time he (who was) flesh-born persecuted the one (who was) Spirit-born, so (it is) also now. 30 But what does Scripture say? "Cast out the slave-woman and her son; for in no way shall the son of the slave-woman share in the inheritance with the son of the free-woman." 31 Wherefore, brothers, not of a slave-woman are we children, but of the free-woman.

## Chapter 5

1 For freedom Christ has set us free; continue to stand firm, therefore, and do not be loaded down again with a yoke of slavery.

2 Now I, Paul, say to you that if you let yourselves be circumcised Christ will be of no advantage to you. 3 And I testify again to every man who lets himself be circumcised, that he is under obligation to keep the whole law. 4 You are estranged from Christ, whoever (you are who) seek to be justified by way of law; you have fallen away from grace. 5 For, as to ourselves, it is through the Spirit, by faith, that we eagerly await the hoped-for righteousness. 6 For in Christ

Jesus neither circumcision nor uncircumcision is of any avail, but faith working through love.

7 You were running well; who cut in on you that you did not continue to obey the truth? 8 This persuasion (is) not (derived) from him who is calling you. 9 A little leaven leavens the whole lump. 10 I on my part am persuaded in the Lord with respect to you, that you will not adopt a different view (than mine). And the one who is throwing you into confusion will have to pay the penalty, whoever he may be. 11 Now as for myself, brothers, if I am still preaching circumcision, why am I still being persecuted? In that case the stumbling-block of the cross has been removed. 12 Would that those who upset you might make eunuchs of themselves!

13 For you were called to freedom, brothers; only (do) not (turn) this freedom into an opportunity for the flesh, but through love be serving one another. 14 For the whole law is fulfilled in one word, namely, in this: "You must love your neighbor as yourself." 15 But if you bite and devour one another, watch out lest you be consumed by one another.

16 But I say, walk by the Spirit, and you will definitely not fulfil the desire of the flesh; 17 for the flesh sets its desire against the Spirit, and the Spirit against the flesh: for these are opposed to each other, so that these very things which you may wish to be doing, these you are not doing. 18 But if you are being led by the Spirit you are not under law. 19 Now obvious are the works of the flesh, which are: immorality, impurity, indecency, 20 idolatry, sorcery, quarrels, wrangling, jealousy, outbursts of anger, selfish ambitions, dissensions, party intrigues, 21 envyings, drinking bouts, revelries, and the like, of which I forewarn you, as I previously forewarned you, that those who indulge in such practices will not inherit the kingdom of God. 22 But the fruit of the Spirit is love, joy, peace, longsuffering, kindness, goodness, faithfulness, 23 meekness, self-control; against such there is no law. 24 And those who believe in Christ Jesus have crucified the flesh with its passions and desires.

25 If we live by the Spirit, by the Spirit let us also walk. 26 Let us not become boasters, challenging one another, envying one another.

## Chapter 6

1 Brothers, even if a man be overtaken in any trespass, you who are spiritual should restore such a person in a spirit of gentleness; constantly looking to yourself, lest also you be tempted. 2 Bear one another's burdens, and so fulfil the law of Christ. 3 For if anyone imagines that he amounts to something, while he amounts to nothing, he is deluding himself. 4 But let each one test his own work; then his reason to boast will be in himself alone, and not in (comparing himself with) someone else; 5 for each person will have to bear his own load.

6 Let him who receives instruction in the Word share all good things with his instructor. 7 Do not be deceived; God is not mocked; for whatever a man sows, that also will he reap; 8 for he who sows to his own flesh will from the flesh reap corruption, and he who sows to the Spirit will from the Spirit reap life everlasting. 9 And let us not grow weary in well-doing, for in due season we shall reap if we do not give up. 10 So then, as we have opportunity, let us do good to everybody, and especially to those who are of the household of the faith.

11 Look with what huge letters I am writing to you with my own hand. 12 It is those who desire to make a fine outward impression that are trying to compel you to be circumcised, their sole purpose being that they may not be persecuted for the cross of Christ. 13 For even those who favor circumcision are

not law-observers themselves, but want y o u to be circumcised that they may glory
in y o u r flesh. 14 As for myself, however, far be it for me to glory except in the
cross of our Lord Jesus Christ, by which the world has been crucified to me, and I
to the world. 15 For neither is circumcision anything, nor uncircumcision, but a
new creation. 16 And as many as shall walk by this rule, peace (be) upon them and
mercy, even upon the Israel of God.

17 From now on let no one cause trouble for me, for I, on my part, bear on my body the marks of Jesus.

18 The grace of our Lord Jesus Christ (be) with y o u r spirit, brothers. Amen.

# Bibliography

For other titles see List of Abbreviations at the beginning of this volume.

Aalders, G. Ch., *Het Boek Genesis* (*Korte Verklaring der Heilige Schrift met Nieuwe Vertaling*), 3 volumes, Kampen, 1949.

Ante-Nicene Fathers, ten volumes, reprint, Grand Rapids, Mich., 1950, for references to Clement of Alexandria, Irenaeus, Justin Martyr, Origen, Tertullian, etc.

Bacon, B. W., "The Reading οἷς οὐδέ in Gal. 2:5," *JBL*, 42 (1923), pp. 69–80.

Bandstra, Andrew J., *The Law and the Elements of the World, An Exegetical Study in Aspects of Paul's Teaching*, doctoral dissertation submitted to the Free University at Amsterdam, Kampen, 1964.

Barclay, W., *The Letters to the Galatians and Ephesians* (*The Daily Study Bible*), Philadelphia, 1958.

Barton, G. A., "The Exegesis of ἐνιαυτούς in Galatians 4:10 and Its Bearing on the Date of the Epistle," *JBL*, 33 (1914), pp. 118–126.

Bavinck, H., *Gereformeerde Dogmatiek*, Vol. 11, *Over God;* English translation by W. Hendriksen, *The Doctrine of God*, Grand Rapids, 1955.

Berkhof, L., *New Testament Introduction*, Grand Rapids, 1916.

Berkhof, L., *Brief aan de Galatiërs, Hoofdstuk 3.* Student notes on class-lectures on Gal. 3, given at Calvin Seminary, Grand Rapids, during the school year 1925-1926. Redactor: W. Hendriksen. Contents: a broad introduction to the epistle and detailed exegesis of the entire third chapter.

Berkhof, L., *Systematic Theology*, Grand Rapids, 1949.

Berkouwer, G. C., *Dogmatisch Studiën* (the series), Kampen, 1949, etc.

Berlage, H. P., "De juiste verklaring van Gal. 6:2," *TT*, 25 (1891), pp. 47–61.

Bible, Holy, In addition to references to Bible-versions other than English, there are references to the following English translations: A.V., A.R.V., R.S.V., N.E.B., N.A.S.B.(N.T.), Amplified New Testament, Beck, Berkeley, Goodspeed, Moffatt, Phillips, Weymouth, Williams. These are *references*. The *translation* which is found in N.T.C. and followed in the exegesis is the author's own.

Bruce, F. F., "The Date of the Epistle to the Galatians," *ET*, 51 (1939–1940), pp. 396–397.

Bruce, F. F., *Commentary on the Book of Acts* (*New International Commentary on the New Testament*), Grand Rapids, 1964.

Bruce, F. F., *The Letters of Paul, An Expanded Paraphrase*, Grand Rapids, 1965.

Bultmann, Rudolf, ΔΙΚΑΙΟΣΥΝΗ ΘΕΟΥ, *JBL* (March 1964), pp. 12–16.

Burton, Ernest DeWitt, "Those Trouble-Makers in Galatia," *BW*, 53 (1919), pp. 555–560.

Burton, Ernest DeWitt, *A Critical and Exegetical Commentary on the Epistle to the Galatians* (*The International Critical Commentary*), New York, 1920.

Calvin, John, *Commentarius in Epistolam Pauli Ad Galatas* (*Corpus Reformatorum*, Vol. LXXX), Brunsvigae, 1895; English Translation (*Calvin's Commentaries*), Grand Rapids, 1948.

Cole, A., *The Epistle of Paul to the Galatians* (*Tyndale Bible Commentaries*, edited by R. V. G. Taker), Grand Rapids, 1965.

## GALATIANS


Conybeare, W. J. and Howson, J. S., *The Life and Epistles of St. Paul,* Grand Rapids, 1949.

Crownfield, F. R., "The Singular Problem of the Dual Galatians," *JBL,* 64 (1945), pp. 491–500.

De Boer, W. P., *The Imitation of Paul, An Exegetical Study,* doctoral dissertation, Kampen, 1962.

Deissmann, A., *Light from the Ancient East* (translated by L. R. M. Strachan), New York, 1927.

Duncan, George S., *The Epistle of Paul to the Galatians* (*Moffatt New Testament Commentary*).

Ellis, E. Earle, *Paul and his Recent Interpreters,* Grand Rapids, 1961.

Emmet, C. W., "Galatians, the Earliest of the Pauline Epistles," *Exp,* 7th series, 9 (1910), pp. 242–254.

Erdman, C. F., *The Epistle of Paul to the Galatians,* Philadelphia, 1930.

Findlay, G. G., *The Epistle to the Galatians* (*The Expositor's Bible,* Vol. V, pp. 811–925), Grand Rapids, 1943.

Goodspeed, E. J., *Paul,* Philadelphia and Toronto, 1947.

Greijdanus, S., *Is Hand. 9 (met 22 en 26) en 15 in tegenspraak met Gal. 1 en 2?,* Kampen, 1935.

Greijdanus, S., *Bizondere Canoniek,* two volumes, Kampen, 1949.

Greijdanus, S., *De Brief van den Apostel Paulus aan de Galaten* (*Korte Verklaring der Heilige Schrift met Nieuwe Vertaling*), Kampen, 1953.

Grosheide, F. W., *De Openbaring Gods in het Nieuwe Testament,* Kampen, 1953.

Grosheide, F. W., "De Synode der Apostelen," *GTT,* 11 (1910), pp. 1–16 [Gal. 2].

Hendriksen, W., *"And So All Israel Shall Be Saved," An Interpretation of Romans 11:26a,* Grand Rapids, 1945.

Hendriksen, W., *The Meaning of the Preposition ἀντί in the New Testament,* doctoral dissertation, Princeton, 1948.

Hendriksen, W., *Bible Survey,* Grand Rapids, 1961.

Hendriksen, W., *More Than Conquerors, An Interpretation of the Book of Revelation,* fifteenth printing, Grand Rapids, 1966.

Jackson, F. J. Foakes, and Lake, Kirsopp, eds., *The Beginnings of Christianity,* five volumes, especially Vol. IV and V, London, 1920–1933.

Johnson, Sherman E., "Early Christianity in Asia Minor," *JBL,* 77 (March 1958), pp. 1–17.

Johnson, Sherman E., "Laodicea and its Neighbors," *BA,* Vol. XIII (Feb. 1950), pp. 1–18.

Jones, Maurice, "The Date of the Epistle to the Galatians," *Exp,* 8th series, 6 (1913), pp. 193–208.

Kerr, John H., *An Introduction to the Study of the Books of the New Testament,* Chicago, New York, Toronto, 1892.

Knox, D. B., "The Date of the Epistle to the Galatians," *EQ,* 13 (1941), pp. 262–268.

Kouwenhoven, H. J., "Paulus' beroep op de litteekenen van den Heere Jezus in zijn lichaam," *GTT,* 13 (1912), pp. 105–115 [Gal. 6:17].

Lambert, J. C., "'Another Gospel that is not another'—Galatians 1:6, 7," *ET,* 12 (1900–1901), pp. 90–93.

Lenski, R. C. H., *Interpretation of St. Paul's Epistles to the Galatians, to the Ephesians, and to the Philippians,* Columbus, Ohio, 1937.

Lietzmann, Hans, *An die Galater* (*Handbuch zum Neuen Testament*), 2nd ed., Tübingen, 1923.

## GALATIANS


Lightfoot, J. B., *The Epistle of St. Paul to the Galatians,* reprint, Grand Rapids, no date.

*Loeb Classical Library,* New York (various dates), for The Apostolic Fathers, Eusebius, Josephus, Philco, Pliny, Plutarch, Strabo, etc.

Luther, Martin, *In Epistolam S.Pauli ad Galatas commentarius.* The edition that was used by the author of N.T.C. contains the lectures that were *delivered* in 1531. They are found in *D. Martin Luthers Werke,* kritische gesamtausgabe, 40.Band, two volumes, Weimar, 1911–1914. Among the translations there is also Th. Graebner's *New Abridged* [English] *Translation,* Grand Rapids, no date.

Machen, J. G., *The Origin of Paul's Religion,* Grand Rapids, 1947.

Mackintosh, Robert, "The Tone of Galatians 2:1-10," *ET,* 21 (1909–1910), pp. 327–328.

Menzies, Allan, "The Epistle to the Galatians," *Exp,* 8th series, 7 (1914), pp. 137–147.

Moffatt, J., *An Introduction to the Literature of the New Testament (The International Theological Library)*, 3rd ed., New York, 1918.

Moulton, J. H., "The Marks of Jesus," *ET,* 21 (1909–1910), pp. 283–284 [Gal. 6:17].

Mulder, H., "De Eerste Lezers van de Brief aan de Hebreeën," *homiletica & biblica* (May, 1965), pp. 95–99.

Mulder, H., "Barnabas en de Gemeente te Jeruzalem," *homiletica & biblica* (September, 1965), pp. 198–200.

Murray, J., *Christian Baptism,* Philadelphia, 1952.

Murray, J., *The Epistle to the Romans,* two volumes, Grand Rapids, respectively 1959 and 1965.

Parker, P., "Once More, Acts and Galatians," *JBL,* 86 (June 1967), pp. 175–182.

Parker, Thomas D., "A Comparison of Calvin and Luther on Galatians," *Int,* 17 (Jan. 1963), pp. 71–75.

Prins, J. J., "Nog iets over Gal. III:20 en, in verband daarmede, over vs. 13 en 16. Open brief aan Dr. A. H. Blom," *TT,* 12 (1878), pp. 410–420.

Ramsay, W. M., *Historical Geography of Asia Minor,* London, 1890.

Ramsay, W. M., *The Church in the Roman Empire,* London, 1893.

Ramsay, W. M., *Cities and Bishoprics of Phrygia,* two volumes, London, 1895–1897.

Ramsay, W. M., "A New Theory as to the Date of the Epistle to the Galatians," *ET,* 12 (1900–1901), pp. 157–160.

Ramsay, W. M., *The Letters to the Seven Churches of Asia,* London, 1904.

Ramsay, W. M., *The Cities of St. Paul,* reprint, Grand Rapids, 1949.

Ramsay, W. M., *The Bearing of Recent Discovery on the Trustworthiness of the New Testament,* reprint, Grand Rapids, 1953.

Ramsay, W. M., *St. Paul the Traveler and the Roman Citizen,* reprint, Grand Rapids, 1949.

Ramsay, W. M., *A Historical Commentary on St. Paul's Epistle to the Galatians,* reprint, Grand Rapids, 1965.

Rendall, F., *The Epistle to the Galatians (The Expositor's Greek Testament,* Vol. III, pp. 123–200), Grand Rapids, no date.

Ridderbos, H. N., *The Epistle of Paul to the Churches of Galatia (New International Commentary on the New Testament)*, Grand Rapids, 1953.

Robertson, A. T., *Word Pictures in the New Testament,* New York and London, 1931, Vol. IV, on Galatians, pp. 272–319.

Robinson, D. W. B., "The Circumcision of Titus and Paul's 'Liberty,'" *AusBibRev,* 12 (1–4, '64), pp. 24–42.

## GALATIANS


Ropes, J. H., *The Singular Problem of the Epistle to the Galatians,* Cambridge, 1929.

Schaff, P., *History of the Christian Church,* Vol. 1, New York, 1920.

Schlier, Heinrich, *Der Brief an die Galater* (*Meyer's Kommentar*), 10th ed., Göttingen, 1949.

Schmoller, Otto, *The Epistle of Paul to the Galatians* (*Lange's Commentary on the Holy Scriptures*), reprint, Grand Rapids, no date.

Scott, E. F., *The Literature of the New Testament,* New York, 1940.

Shedd, W. A., "The Date of the Epistle to the Galatians upon the South Galatian Theory," *ET,* 12 (1900–1901), p. 568.

Stamm, R. T., *The Epistle to the Galatians* (*Interpreter's Bible,* Vol. X), New York and Nashville, 1953.

Stewart, J. S., *A Man in Christ, the Vital Elements of St. Paul's Religion,* New York and London, no date.

Strack, H. L. and Billerbeck, P., *Kommentar zum Neuen Testament aus Talmud und Midrasch,* München, 1922–1928; especially volume III.

Tenney, M. C., *The New Testament, an Historical and Analytic Survey,* Grand Rapids, 1953.

Thiessen, H. C., *Introduction to the New Testament,* Grand Rapids, 1943.

Van Leeuwen, J. A. C., "Galaten (Brief aan de)," article in *Christelijke Encyclopaedie,* Kampen, 1925, Vol. II, pp. 218, 219.

Warfield, B. B., "The Date of the Epistle to the Galatians," *JBL* (June and December, 1884), pp. 50–64.

Warfield, B. B., *The Power of God Unto Salvation,* Grand Rapids, 1930.

Wood, H. G., "The Message of the Epistles; the Letter to the Galatians," *ET,* 44 (1932–1933), pp. 453–457.

Zahn, Th., *Einleitung in das neue Testament,* 1897–1900.

NEW TESTAMENT COMMENTARY

# NEW TESTAMENT COMMENTARY

*By*

WILLIAM HENDRIKSEN

*Exposition*
*of*
*Ephesians*

BAKER BOOK HOUSE

GRAND RAPIDS, MICHIGAN

PRINTED IN THE UNITED STATES OF AMERICA

Dedicated to

my faithful wife

RETA (DE BOER) HENDRIKSEN

who types all my manuscripts

# TABLE OF CONTENTS

# LIST OF ABBREVIATIONS

The letters in book-abbreviations are followed by periods. Those in periodical-abbreviations omit the periods and are in italics. Thus one can see at a glance whether the abbreviation refers to a book or to a periodical.

A. *Book Abbreviations*

| | |
|---|---|
| A.R.V. | American Standard Revised Version |
| A.V. | Authorized Version (King James) |
| Gram.N.T. | A. T. Robertson, *Grammar of the Greek New Testament in the Light of Historical Research* |
| Gram.N.T. (Bl.-Debr.) | F. Blass and A. Debrunner, *A Greek Grammar of the New Testament and Other Early Christian Literature* |
| Grk.N.T. (A–B–M–W) | *The Greek New Testament,* edited by Kurt Aland, Matthew Black, Bruce M. Metzger, and Allen Wikgren, 1966 Edition |
| I.S.B.E. | *International Standard Bible Encyclopedia* |
| L.N.T. (Th.) | Thayer's *Greek-English Lexicon of the New Testament* |
| L.N.T. (A. and G.) | W. F. Arndt and F. W. Gingrich, *A Greek-English Lexicon of the New Testament and Other Early Christian Literature* |
| M.M. | *The Vocabulary of the Greek New Testament Illustrated from the Papyri and Other Non-Literary Sources,* by James Hope Moulton and George Milligan (edition Grand Rapids, 1952) |
| N.A.S.B. (N.T.) | New American Standard Bible (New Testament) |
| N.N. | *Novum Testamentum Graece,* edited by D. Eberhard Nestle, revised by Erwin Nestle and Kurt Aland, 25th edition, 1963 |
| N.E.B. | New English Bible |
| N.T.C. | W. Hendriksen, *New Testament Commentary* |
| R.S.V. | Revised Standard Version |
| S.H.E.R.K. | *The New Schaff-Herzog Encyclopedia of Religious Knowledge* |
| Th.W.N.T. | *Theologisches Wörterbuch zum Neuen Testament* (edited by G. Kittel) |
| W.D.B. | *Westminster Dictionary of the Bible* |
| W.H.A.B. | *Westminster Historical Atlas to the Bible* |

B. *Periodical Abbrevations*

| | |
|---|---|
| *EQ* | *Evangelical Quarterly* |
| *ET* | *Expository Times* |
| *Exp* | *The Expositor* |
| *Int* | *Interpretation* |
| *JBL* | *Journal of Biblical Literature* |
| *NTSt* | *New Testament Studies* |
| *RE* | *Review and Expositor* |
| *TSK* | *Theologische Studien und Kritiken* |
| *TT* | *Theologisch Tijdschrift* |
| *TTod* | *Theology Today* |

*Please Note*

In order to differentiate between the second person singular (see Eph. 6:2, 3) and the second person plural (see Eph. 2:1; 6:1), we have indicated the former as follows: "you," "your"; and the latter as follows: "y o u," "y o u r."

# Introduction
# to
# The Epistle to the Ephesians

# I. Timeliness

Loathsome wickedness marked the world of Paul's day (Eph. 2:2; cf. Rom. 1:18-32). Efforts to improve this condition were largely unsuccessful. Mankind was "without hope" (2:12). The same perversity coupled with pessimism obtains today. At the present time, too, efforts are being put forth to banish crime and to improve man's environment. Among the means to this end are the following: slum clearance, better housing, development of parks and playgrounds, a higher minimum wage scale, job retraining, rehabilitation of educational drop-outs, and psychiatric aid for those who find it hard "to adjust themselves." Some call for better laws. Others emphasize the need of more rigid law-enforcement or the establishment of rules that will no longer favor the criminal at the expense of society. The merit in all this must not be *under*-estimated. But neither should it be *over*-estimated. Government totalitarianism, the tendency to look upon the state to provide for every need "from the cradle to the grave," with consequent loss of the sense of individual responsibility and initiative, is one danger. Another is the misapprehension of man's *basic* need. That need is nothing less than the removal of the load of guilt by which he, being by nature a child of wrath (2:3), is oppressed. What he needs is something more than *job rehabilitation.* He needs *reconciliation to God.* Ephesians proclaims that for all true believers this great blessing has been provided by means of the vicarious, atoning death of God's own Son (2:13). The motivation for this supreme sacrifice was "his great love" (2:4).

Another fallacy that is implied in today's approach to the problem of relieving man's misery is the notion that human happiness can be brought about by means that operate *from without inward.* "Improve the environment and man's inner condition will be improved" seems to be the slogan. But man's inner condition is one that does not offer much hope for the success of this method. He is "dead through trespasses and sins." Apart from Christ he is living "in the lusts of his flesh and its reasonings" (2:1, 3). An act of God is necessary to save him. The removal of the *guilt* of his sin is not sufficient. *Sin itself,* the urge to do that which is contrary to God's holy law, must be removed. A mighty work must be accomplished within man's heart, so that as a result, man, having been basically renewed and being gradually transformed by the Holy Spirit, can now, in consequence, begin to react *from within outward* upon his environment, calling upon all of it to function *Pro Rege* ("for the King"). This regenerating and transforming work of the Holy Spirit, procured by the death of Christ (John 16:7), is beautifully described in Eph. 3:14-19. Those who by nature are dead must be made alive (2:1).

Now all this does not in any way cancel human responsibility. On the contrary, it rather increases the sense of man's obligation to dedicate his life to his Benefactor. The believer, object of God's sovereign love, feels indebted to his Savior and Lord. He loves in return for love received (5:1, 2; cf. I John 4:19). Moreover, it stands to reason that, being drawn to God, the recipient of divine grace is in this very process also attracted to his brothers and sisters in the Lord. Thus Jew and Gentile, reconciled to God, are also reconciled to each other. The barrier between the two ethnic groups is removed by the same cross that made peace between the offended God and the offending sinner (2:11-22; cf. John 12:32; 15:12; I John 4:21); yes, by that very cross which to unconverted Jews was a stumblingblock and to unconverted Gentiles foolishness (I Cor. 1:23). Thus the divine mystery becomes disclosed to human view, and the church universal is born.

Since a new day has now dawned upon those who had surrendered themselves to Christ and to the influences of his Spirit, it follows that these children of light show in their new life the fruits of light: goodness and righteousness and truth (5:9). Spirit-born virtue drives out vice of every description, as is clearly indicated in the lengthy section, Eph. 4:17–5:21. Here then is the true solution to the "loathsome wickedness" which marked Paul's day as it does ours. It is God himself who "in Christ" has provided this way out of darkness and pessimism. It is the business of the church "to make all men see" that this is *the only solution.* The church must sing its mighty chorus of salvation by faith in Jesus Christ, in order thereby to drown out the thoroughly unrealistic paean of atheism. The latter also sings, to be sure, but its song has a hollow sound. It sings *the lie* in (the spirit of) *hatred.* The church sings "the truth in love" (4:15). Its daily life is, in fact, a walking in love, for it imitates the God of love (5:1). Thus, firmly united, it bids defiance to Satan and all his hosts, and for this purpose makes use of the weapons provided by God himself (6:10-20).

Never futile is the work of the church, for it is a product not of the mind of man but of the sovereign grace of God. The apostle, in exuberance of spirit, describes this church, dwelling in some detail on its eternal foundation, universal scope, lofty ideal, organic unity (amid diversity) and growth, glorious renewal, and effective armor. It is a church that exists for the purpose of serving as an agent for the salvation of men to the glory of God Triune, "principalities and authorities in the heavenly places" joining in the praise as they behold, in a kaleidoscope of changing colors, the wisdom of God reflected in his masterpiece, the church (3:10).

# II. Comparison with Colossians

## A. *Introduction*

With a view to answering those that deny the Pauline authorship of Ephesians and affirm that this epistle "is nothing but a verbose amplification of Colossians" it is necessary to compare the two. This comparison will also serve another purpose, for, once having established that Paul was indeed the author of both letters, we will have the right, in exegeting Ephesians, to allow parallel passages in Colossians to illumine the interpretation. By way of anticipation let it be affirmed even now that, as I see it, the traditional view which ascribes both epistles to the great apostle to the Gentiles is correct. Hence, the present chapter will become a handy tool for exegesis.

Observe, however, the following:

(1) Not all the parallels are equally striking, nor are they all of the same character. Though there are a goodly number of verbal resemblances, there are also many similarities in thought rather than in the actual words that are used.

(2) In a few instances the actual *word* resemblances are even closer in the original than in the translation. However, translations that have tried to eliminate this discrepancy (between Greek and English) in every instance by supplying a so-called "standard" (or "identical") English equivalent for each Greek word in whatever context the latter occurs, have not proved to be very satisfactory. Reasons: *a.* the same Greek word does not always have the same meaning, hence cannot always be faithfully rendered by the same English equivalent; *b.* idiomatic use in Greek does not always parallel idiomatic use in English.[1]

(3) As this is a Commentary on Ephesians – not on Colossians – it is proper that the basis for comparison be first of all the text of Ephesians, newly translated from the original. That text is accordingly to be found in the left main column, with comparable Colossian passages printed in the right column. It has not always been possible to place all the parallel passages *exactly* opposite each other. However, let the reader look not only directly opposite the Ephesian passage but also a little higher or lower in the column.

(4) It is impossible to present a list of parallels that will satisfy everyone. The question: "Is the resemblance in this or that passage in Colossians close enough to consider it a parallel to an Ephesian passage?" will not receive a unanimous answer. Some, for example, might wish to add, to the ones given below, such a "parallel" (?) as Eph. 4:10 = Col. 1:19; and even more remote parallels. I have chosen not to do so. But there is room here for difference of opinion.

[1] Moreover, for the Greek parallels one can use two Greek New Testaments, one for Ephesians, one for Colossians.

B. *Comparison*

| **In Ephesians Compare** | **Ephesians** | **Colossians** |
|---|---|---|
| | *Chapter 1* | |
| | 1 Paul, an apostle of Christ Jesus through the will of God, to the saints and believers who are in Ephesus in Christ Jesus; 2 grace to y o u and peace from God our Father and the Lord Jesus Christ. | 1:1 Paul, an apostle of Christ Jesus through the will of God, and Timothy our brother, 2 to the saints and believing brothers in Christ at Colosse; grace to y o u and peace from God our Father. |
| **2:6** | 3 Blessed (be) the God and Father of our Lord Jesus Christ, who has blessed us with every spiritual blessing in the | |
| **5:27** | heavenly places in Christ, 4 just as he elected us in him before the foundation of the world, that we should be holy and faultless before him, 5 having in love foreordained us to adoption as sons through Jesus Christ for himself, accord- | 3:12 **Put on,** therefore, as God's elect, holy and beloved. . . .<br>1:22 . . . in order to present y o u holy, fault-less, and blameless before himself. . . . |
| | ing to the good pleasure of his will, 6 to the praise of the glory of his grace, which he graciously bestowed on us in the | 1:13 **the kingdom of the Son of his love.** |
| **1:18; 2:7; 3:8, 16** | Beloved, 7 in whom we have our redemption through his blood, the forgiveness of our trespasses, according to the riches of his grace, 8 which he caused to over- | 1:14 **in whom we have our redemption, the** forgiveness of our sins.<br>1:20 . . . having made peace through the blood of his cross. . . . |

| | | |
|---|---|---|
| 3:9 | flow toward us in the form of all wisdom and insight, 9 in that he made known to us the mystery of his will, according to his good pleasure, the purpose which he cherished for himself in him, | 1:9 . . . in all spiritual wisdom and understanding. . . .<br>1:26 the mystery hidden for ages and generations but now made manifest to his saints . . . .<br>2:2 . . . with a view to the clear knowledge of the mystery of God, namely Christ. . . .<br>4:3 . . . to speak forth the mystery concerning Christ. . . . |
| | 10 to be put into effect in the fulness of the times, to bring all things together under one head in Christ, the things in the heavens and the things on the earth; in him | 1:16 for in him were created all things in the heavens and on the earth, the visible and the invisible, whether thrones or dominions or principalities or authorities, all things through him and with a view to him have been created. . . .<br>1:19 For in him he [God] was pleased to have all the fulness dwell, 20 and through him to reconcile all things to himself, . . . through him, whether the things on the earth or the things in the heavens. |
| 3:11 | 11 in whom we also have been made heirs, having been foreordained according to the purpose of him who accomplishes all things according to the counsel of his will, 12 to the end that we should be to the praise of his glory, we who beforehand had centered our hope in Christ; | 1:12 with joy giving thanks to the Father who qualified you for a share in the inheritance of the saints in the light. . . .<br>1:23 . . . and are not moved away from the hope that is derived from the gospel which you have heard. . . .<br>1:27 to whom God was pleased to make known what (is) the riches of the glory of this mystery among the Gentiles, which is Christ |

| In Ephesians Compare | Ephesians | Colossians |
| --- | --- | --- |
| 4:30 | 13 in whom you also (are included, hav-<br>ing listened to the message of the truth,<br>the gospel of your salvation; and hav-<br>ing also believed in him, you were sealed<br>with the promised Holy Spirit, 14 who is<br>the first instalment of our inheritance,<br>for the redemption of (God's) own posses-<br>sion, to the praise of his glory. | in you, the hope of glory. . . .<br>1:5 . . . of which you have previously heard<br>in the message of the truth, the gospel. |
| 4:4 | 15 For this reason, because I have<br>heard of the faith in the Lord Jesus that<br>(exists) among you and of your love<br>for all the saints, 16 I do not cease to<br>give thanks for you, while making men-<br>tion of you in my prayers, 17 (asking)<br>that the God of our Lord Jesus Christ, the<br>Father of glory, may give you the Spirit<br>of wisdom and revelation in the clear<br>knowledge of him, 18 (having) the eyes of<br>your hearts illumined, so that you may<br>know what is the hope for which he called | 1:3 While praying for you we are always<br>thanking God, the Father of our Lord Jesus<br>Christ, 4 because we have heard of your<br>faith in Christ Jesus and of the love which<br>you cherish for all the saints, 5 by rea-<br>son of the hope laid up for you in the<br>heavens, of which you have previously<br>heard in the message of the truth, namely,<br>the gospel. . . . 9 And for this reason, from the<br>day we heard it we never stopped praying for<br>you, asking that you may be filled with<br>clear knowledge of his will (such clear knowl- |

| | | |
|---|---|---|
| | you, what the riches of the glory of his inheritance among the saints, | edge consisting) in all spiritual wisdom and understanding, 10 so as to live lives worthy of the Lord, to (his) complete delight, in every good work bearing fruit, and growing in the clear knowledge of God. . . . |
| 3:20<br>3:10<br>6:12 | 19 and what the surpassing greatness of his power (displayed) with respect to us who believe, as seen in that manifestation of his infinite might 20 which he exerted in Christ when he raised him from the dead and made him to sit at his right hand in the heavenly places, | 1:11 being invigorated with all vigor, in accordance with his glorious might, so as to exercise every kind of endurance and long-suffering; 12 with joy giving thanks to the Father who qualified you for a share in the inheritance of the saints in the light. . . .<br>1:29 for which I am laboring, striving by his energy working powerfully within me.<br>2:12 having been buried with him in your baptism in which you were also raised with him through faith in the operative power of God who raised him from the dead.<br>3:1 If then you were raised with Christ, seek the things that are above, where Christ is seated at the right hand of God. . . . |
| | 21 far above every principality and authority and power and dominion and every name that is named, not only in this age but also in the coming one; 22 and he ranged everything in subjection under his feet, and him he gave as head over everything to the church, | 1:16 for in him were created all things . . . whether thrones or dominions or principalities or authorities. . . .<br>3:15 . . . for which you were called in one body.<br>1:18 And he is the head of the body, the church; who is the beginning, the firstborn from the dead, that in all things he might |

| In Ephesians Compare | Ephesians | Colossians |
|---|---|---|
| 4:12;<br>5:30 | 23 since it is his body, the fulness of<br>him who fills all in all. | have the pre-eminence, 19 for in him he<br>[God] was pleased to have all the fulness<br>dwell. . . .<br>1:24 I am now rejoicing amid my sufferings<br>for you and what is lacking in the afflic-<br>tions of Christ I in his stead am supplying<br>in my flesh, for his body, which is the<br>church. . . .<br>2:9 for in him all the fulness of the godhead<br>dwells bodily, 10 and in him you have at-<br>tained to fulness, namely, in him who is the<br>head of every principality and authority. . . . |
| | *Chapter 2* | |
| <br><br>1:21 | 1 And you, even though you were<br>dead through your trespasses and sins,<br>2 in which you formerly walked in line<br>with the course of this world, in line<br>with the prince of the domain of the air,<br>(the domain) of the spirit now at work in<br>the sons of disobedience, 3 among whom we<br>also once lived in the lusts of our flesh,<br>fulfilling the desires of the flesh and<br>its reasonings, and were by nature chil- | 2:13 And you, who were dead through<br>your trespasses and the uncircumcision<br>of your flesh, you he made alive to-<br>gether with him, having forgiven us all<br>our trespasses. . . .<br><br><br><br><br>3:6 on account of which things the wrath |

dren of wrath even as the rest, 4 God, being rich in mercy, because of his great
love with which he loved us, 5 even though
we were dead through our trespasses made
us alive together with Christ – by grace
1:3 y o u have been saved – 6 and raised us
up with him and made us sit with him in
the heavenly places in Christ Jesus, 7
1:7 in order that in the ages to come he
might show the surpassing riches of his
grace (expressed) in kindness toward us
in Christ Jesus. 8 For by grace y o u
have been saved through faith; and this
not of yourselves, (it is) the gift of
God; 9 not of works, lest anyone should
boast, 10 for his handiwork are we, created in Christ Jesus for good works,
which God prepared beforehand that we
should walk in them.
2:19 11 Therefore remember that formerly
4:17, 18 y o u, the Gentiles in flesh, who are
5:8 called "uncircumcision" by that which is
called "circumcision" – in flesh, handmade! – 12 that y o u were at that time
separate from Christ, alienated from the
commonwealth of Israel, and strangers to
the covenants of the promise, having no
hope and without God in the world. 13

of God is coming; 7 in which things y o u
also walked at one time, when y o u were
living in them.

3:1 If then y o u were raised with Christ,
seek the things that are above, where Christ
is, seated at the right hand of God. . . .

1:10 . . . in every good work bearing fruit. . . .

2:11 . . . in whom also y o u were circumcised
with a circumcision made without hands.
1:20 and through him to reconcile all things
to himself, having made peace through the
blood of his cross, through him, whether the
things on the earth or the things in the
heavens. 21 And y o u, who once were estranged and hostile in disposition, as shown
by y o u r wicked works, 22 he in his body

| In Ephesians Compare | Ephesians | Colossians |
|---|---|---|
| | But now in Christ Jesus you who formerly were far away have been brought nearby through the blood of Christ. 14 For he himself is our peace, who made both one and has broken down the barrier formed by the dividing wall, the hostility, 15 by abolishing in his flesh the law of commandments with its requirements, in order that in himself he might create of the two one new man, (so) making peace, | of flesh through his death has now reconciled, in order to present you holy, faultless, and blameless before himself. . . .<br>3:15 And let the peace of Christ . . . rule in your hearts.<br>2:14 having blotted out the handwritten document that was against us, which by means of its requirements testified against us, and he took it out of the way by nailing it to the cross. . . .<br>3:10 and have put on the new man, who is being renewed for full knowledge according to the image of him who created him. . . . |
| 6:15<br>3:12 | 16 and might reconcile both of them in one body to God through the cross, having slain the hostility by means of it; 17 and he came and proclaimed the good news: "Peace to you, those far away, and peace to those nearby"; 18 for through him we both have our access in one Spirit to the Father. | |
| 3:6 | 19 So then you are no longer strangers and aliens, but you are fellow-citizens with the saints and mem- | |

| | | |
|---|---|---|
| | bers of the household of God, 20 built upon the foundation of the apostles and prophets, Christ Jesus himself being the chief cornerstone, 21 in whom the entire building, harmoniously fitted together, is growing into a holy sanctuary in the Lord, 22 in which you also together with (all the others) are being built up for a dwelling-place of God in the Spirit. | 2:7 rooted and being built up in him and being established in the faith, just as you were taught, overflowing with thanksgiving.<br>2:19 and not keeping firm hold on the Head, from whom the entire body, supported and held together by joints and ligaments, grows with a growth (that is) from God. |
| | *Chapter 3* | |
| 6:19-20<br><br><br><br><br>1:7-11<br>2:13, 18, 19 | 1 For this reason I, Paul, the prisoner of Christ Jesus for the sake of you Gentiles — 2 for surely you have heard of the stewardship of God's grace that was given to me for your benefit, 3 how that by revelation there was made known to me the mystery, as I wrote before in few words, 4 whereby, as you read it you can perceive my insight into the mystery of Christ, 5 which in other generations was not made known to the sons of men as it has now been revealed by the Spirit to his holy apostles and prophets, 6 namely, that the Gentiles are fellow-sharers in the inheritance and fellow-members of the body and fellow-partakers | 1:23 . . . the gospel . . . of which I, Paul, became a minister.<br>1:24 I am now rejoicing amid my sufferings for you, and what is lacking in the afflictions of Christ I in his stead am supplying in my flesh, for his body, which is the church, 25 of which I became a minister, according to the stewardship of God given to me for your benefit, to give full scope to the word of God, 26 the mystery hidden for ages and generations but now made manifest to his saints; 27 to whom God was pleased to make known what (is) the riches of the glory of this mystery among the Gentiles, which is Christ in you, the hope of glory; 28 whom we proclaim, admonishing |

| In Ephesians Compare | Ephesians | Colossians |
| --- | --- | --- |
| | of the promise (realized) in Christ Jesus (as conveyed) through the gospel, 7 of which I was made a minister according to the gift of God's grace that was given to me according to the working of his power. | every man and teaching every man in all wisdom in order that we may present every man perfect in Christ; 29 for which I am laboring, striving by his energy working powerfully within me. |
| | 8 To me, the very least of all saints, was this grace given: to proclaim to the Gentiles the good tidings of the unfathomable riches of Christ, 9 and to enlighten all on what is the administration of the mystery which for ages has been hidden in God who created all things; 10 in order that now to the principalities and the authorities in the heavenly places might be made known through the church the iridescent wisdom of God, 11 according to the eternal purpose which he formed in Christ Jesus our Lord, 12 in whom we have the courage of confident access through faith in him. 13 Therefore I ask (y o u) not to lose heart over what I am suffering for y o u, which is y o u r glory— | 2:2 . . . in order that their hearts may be strengthened, they themselves being welded together in love, and this with a view to all the riches of assured understanding, with a view to the clear knowledge of the mystery of God, namely, Christ. . . .<br>4:3 . . . to speak forth the mystery concerning Christ, on account of which I am in prison. . . .<br>1:24 I am now rejoicing amid my sufferings for y o u. . . . |
| | 14 For this reason I bend my knees to the Father, 15 from whom the whole | 1:16 for in him were created all things in the heavens and on the earth, the visible and the invisible, whether thrones or dominions or principalities or authorities, all things through him and with a view to him have been created. |

family in heaven and on earth derives
its name: the Father's Family, 16 (praying) that according to the riches of his
glory he may grant you to be strengthened with power through his Spirit in
the inner man, 17 that Christ may dwell
in your hearts through faith; in order that you, being rooted and founded
in love, 18 may be strong, together with
all the saints, to grasp what is the
breadth and length and height and
depth, 19 and to know the love of
Christ that surpasses knowledge; in order
that you may be filled to all the fulness of God.

22 Now to him who is able to do infinitely more than all we ask or imagine,
according to the power that is at work
within us, 21 to him be the glory in the
church and in Christ Jesus to all
generations forever and ever; Amen.

*Chapter 4*

1 I, therefore, the prisoner in the
Lord, entreat you to live lives worthy
of the calling with which you were
4:32 called, 2 with all lowliness and meekness,
5:1 with longsuffering, enduring one another

1:27 the riches of the glory of this mystery
1:11 being invigorated with all vigor, in accordance with his glorious might. . . .

1:23 if, indeed, you continue in the faith, founded and firm. . . .
2:7 rooted and being built up in him and being established in the faith.

1:29 . . . striving by his energy working powerfully within me.
1:26 the mystery hidden for ages and generations.

1:10 so as to live lives worthy of the Lord. . . .
3:12 Put on, therefore, as God's elect, holy and beloved, a heart of compassion, kindness, lowliness, meekness, longsuffering, 13

**In Ephesians Compare**

**Ephesians**

in love, 3 making every effort to preserve
the unity imparted by the Spirit by means
of the bond (consisting in) peace. 4
(There is) one body and one Spirit, just
as also you were called in one hope
which your calling brought you;

5 one Lord, one faith, one baptism; 6 one
God and Father of all, who (is) over all
and through all and in all. 7 But to
each one of us this grace was given within
the limits which Christ apportioned. 8
Therefore he says: When he ascended on
high he led captive a host of captives,
and he gave gifts to men. 9 — Now this
expression, *he ascended,* what can it mean
but that he had (previously) descended
into the regions lower than the earth?
10 The one who descended is himself also
the one who ascended higher than all the
heavens in order that he might fill all
things — 11 And it was he who gave some

**Colossians**

enduring one another and forgiving each
other if anyone have a complaint against
anyone. Just as the Lord has forgiven you,
so do you also. 14 And above all these
things (put on) love, which is the bond of
perfection. 15 And let the peace of Christ,
for which you were called in one body,
rule in your hearts, and be thankful.

(to be) apostles; and some, prophets;
and some, evangelists; and some, pastors
1:23 and teachers; 12 in order fully to equip
the saints for the work of ministry, with
a view to the building up of the body of
Christ, 13 until we all attain to the
unity of the faith and of the clear knowledge of the Son of God, to a full-grown
man, to the measure of the stature of
the fulness of Christ, 14 so that we may
6:11 no longer be children tossed to and fro by
the waves and whirled around by every gust
of doctrine, by the trickery of men, by
(their) talent for deceitful scheming; 15
but adhering to the truth in love, may
grow up in all things into him who is the
head, even Christ, 16 from whom the entire
body, harmoniously fitted together and
held together by every supporting joint,
according to the energy that corresponds
to the capacity of each individual part,
brings about bodily growth with a view to
its own upbuilding in love.
17 This I say, therefore, and testify
in the Lord, that y o u should no longer
walk as the Gentiles also walk, in the
2:12 futility of their mind, 18 being darkened
in their understanding, alienated from

1:24 . . . for his body, which is the church.
2:2 . . . with the view to the clear knowledge of the mystery of God.
2:9 for in him all the fulness of the godhead dwells bodily.

2:22 . . . according to the precepts and doctrines of men.

1:18 And he is the head of the body, the church. . . .
2:19 and not keeping firm hold on the head, from whom the entire body, supported and held together by joints and ligaments, grows with a growth (that is) from God.

1:21 And y o u, who once were estranged

**In Ephesians Compare**

| **Ephesians** | **Colossians** |
| --- | --- |
| the life of God because of the ignorance that is in them due to the hardness of their hearts, 19 because they have become callous and have abandoned themselves to licentiousness for the greedy practice of every type of impurity. 20 You, however, did not so learn Christ, 21 for surely you heard of him and were taught in him, just as it is in Jesus that truth resides, 22 (having been taught) that with respect to your former manner of life you must put off the old man, which is being corrupted through deceitful lusts, 23 and must be renewed in the spirit of your minds, 24 and put on the new man, created after (the likeness of) God in true righteousness and holiness. | and hostile in disposition, as shown by your wicked works. . . . |
| | 3:5 Put to death therefore your members that (are upon the earth): immorality, impurity, passion, evil desire, and greed, which is idolatry. |
| 25 Therefore, laying aside falsehood, speak truth each (of you) with his neighbor, for we are members of one another. 26 Be angry but do not sin; let not the sun go down on that angry mood of yours, 27 and do not give the devil a | 3:8 But now you, too, lay them all aside: wrath, anger, malice, slander, shameful language from your mouth. 9 No longer lie to one another, seeing that you have put off the old man with his practices, 10 and have put on the new man, who is being renewed for full knowledge according to the image of him who created him. . . . |

foothold. 28 Let him who steals steal no
longer but rather let him labor, with his
own hands accomplishing what is good, so
that he may have something to share with
5:4 the needy one. 29 Let no corrupt speech
proceed from y o u r mouth, but (only)
such (speech) as is good for edification,
as fits the need, that it may impart
grace to the listeners. 30 And do not
1:13 grieve the Holy Spirit of God in whom
y o u were sealed for the day of redemption. 31 Let all bitterness and anger
and wrath and brawling and slander be put
away from y o u, along with all malice.
4:2, 3 32 And be kind to each other, tender-
hearted, forgiving one another, just as
God in Christ forgave y o u.

*Chapter 5*

1 Be therefore imitators of God, as
beloved children, 2 and walk in love, just
as Christ loved y o u and gave himself up
for us, an offering and a sacrifice to God,
for a fragrant odor.

4:6 Let y o u r speech always be gracious, seasoned with salt, so that y o u may know how to answer each individual.

3:12 Put on, therefore, as God's elect, holy and beloved, a heart of compassion, kindness, lowliness, meekness, longsuffering, 13 enduring one another, and forgiving each other if anyone have a complaint against anyone. Just as the Lord has forgiven y o u, so do y o u also.

3:14 And above all these things (put on) love which is the bond of perfection.

| In Ephesians Compare | Ephesians | Colossians |
|---|---|---|
| | 3 But immorality and impurity of any kind, or greed, let it not even be mentioned among y o u, as is fitting among saints, 4 also filthiness and silly talk or wittiness in telling coarse jokes, which things are improper, but rather the expression of thankfulness. 5 For of this y o u can be very sure, that no immoral or impure person or greedy individual — which is the same as an idolater — has any inheritance in the kingdom of | 3:5 Put to death therefore y o u r members that (are) upon the earth: immorality, impurity, passion, evil desire, and greed, which is idolatry. . . .<br>3:8 But now y o u, too, lay them all aside: wrath, anger, malice, slander, shameful language from y o u r mouth. |
| 2:2 | Christ and of God. 6 Let no one deceive y o u with empty words; for it is because of these things that the wrath of God comes upon the sons of disobedience. 7 Therefore do not be their partners, 8 | 2:4 I say this in order that no one may mislead y o u by persuasive argument.<br>3:6 on account of which things the wrath of God is coming. . . . |
| 2:11, 13 | for y o u were formerly darkness, but now (y o u are) light in the Lord; as children of light ever walk 9 — for the fruit of light (consists) in all goodness and righteousness and truth — 10 verifying what is pleasing to the Lord. 11 And do not take any part in the unfruitful works of darkness but instead even expose them, 12 | 3:20 . . . for this is well-pleasing in the Lord. |

5:10

for the things done by them in secret it
is a shame even to mention. 13 But when
all these (wicked practices) are exposed
by the light they are made visible; for
everything that is made visible is light.
14 Therefore he says,
"Awake, sleeper,
And arise from the dead,
And Christ will shine on you."
15 Be most careful therefore how
you walk, not as unwise but as wise, 16
making the most of the opportunity, because the days are evil. 17 Therefore do
not be foolish but understand what (is)
the will of the Lord. 18 And do not get
drunk on wine, which is associated with
unrestrained living, but be filled with
the Spirit, 19 speaking to one another in
psalms and hymns and spiritual songs,
singing and making melody from your
heart to the Lord; 20 giving thanks always for all things in the name of our
Lord Jesus Christ to (our) God and Father, 21 subjecting yourselves to each
other out of reverence for Christ.

4:5 Conduct yourselves wisely toward outsiders, making the most of the opportunity.

3:16 Let the word of Christ dwell among
you richly; in all wisdom teaching and
admonishing one another (and) by means of
psalms, hymns, and spiritual songs singing
to God in a thankful spirit, with all
your heart. 17 And whatever you do in
word or in deed (do) all in the name of
the Lord Jesus, giving thanks to God the
Father through him.

| In Ephesians Compare | Ephesians | Colossians |
|---|---|---|
| 5:33b | 22 Wives, (be subject) to your own husbands as to the Lord, 23 for the husband is head of the wife as also Christ is head of the church, he himself (being) the Savior of the body. 24 Then just as the church is subject to Christ so also wives (should be subject) to their husbands in everything. | 3:18 Wives, be submissive to your<br>**1:18 And he is the head of the body, the church. . . .**<br>husbands, as is fitting in the Lord. |
| 5:28, 33a | 25 Husbands, love your wives, just as also Christ loved the church and gave himself up for her; 26 that he might sanctify her, cleansing her by the washing of water in connection | 3:19 Husbands, love your wives, and do not be harsh toward them. |
| 1:4 | with the spoken word; 27 in order that he might present the church to himself brilliant in purity, having no spot or wrinkle or any such thing, but that she might be holy and faultless. 28 That is the way husbands also ought to love their own wives as their own bodies. He who loves his own wife loves himself; 29 for no one ever hated his own flesh; on the contrary, he nourishes it and cherishes it, just as | 1:22 . . . in order to present you holy, faultless, and blameless before himself. . . .<br>1:28 . . . in order that we may present every man perfect in Christ. . . .<br>3:19 Husbands, love your wives and do not be harsh toward them. |
| 1:23 | also Christ (does) the church, 30 because we are members of his body. 31 "There- | |

fore shall a man leave his father and
mother, and shall cleave to his wife; and
the two shall become one flesh." 32 This
mystery is great, but I am speaking with
reference to Christ and the church. 33
Nevertheless, let each one of you also
love his own wife as himself, and let the
wife see to it that she respects her husband.

*Chapter 6*

1 Children, obey your parents in
the Lord, for this is right. 2 "Honor
your father and your mother," which is a
commandment of foremost significance,
with a promise attached: 3 "that it may
be well with you" and that you may be on
earth a long time. 4 And fathers, do not
provoke your children to anger but
rear them tenderly in the discipline and
admonition of the Lord. 5 Slaves, be
obedient to those who according to the
flesh are your masters, with fear and
trembling, in the sincerity of your
heart, as to Christ, 6 not in the way of
eye-service as men-pleasers, but as slaves
of Christ, doing the will of God from the
heart, 7 with ready mind rendering service

3:19 Husbands, love your wives, and do
not be harsh toward them.
3:18 Wives, be submissive to your husbands, as is fitting in the Lord.

3:20 Children, obey your parents in all
things, for this is well-pleasing in the
Lord.

3:21 Fathers, do not exasperate your
children, in order that they may not lose
heart. 22 Slaves, obey in all things those
who according to the flesh are your
masters, not with eye-service as men-pleasers
but with singleness of heart, fearing the
Lord. 23 Whatever you do, put your
soul into the work, as for the Lord and not
for men, 24 knowing that from the Lord
you will receive the recompense, namely,
the inheritance. (It is) the Lord Christ

| In Ephesians Compare | Ephesians | Colossians |
| --- | --- | --- |
| | as to the Lord and not to men, 8 knowing that whatever good each one does this he will receive back from the Lord, whether (he be) slave or free. 9 And masters, do the same things for them, and stop threatening, knowing that (he who is) both their master and yours is in the heavens, and there is no partiality with him. | (whom) you are serving. 25 For, the wrong-doer will receive (the consequences of) what he has wrongly done. And there is no partiality. 4:1 Masters, render to your slaves that which is fair and square, knowing that you also have a Master in heaven. |
| 4:14 | 10 Finally, find your (source of) power in the Lord and in the strength of his might. 11 Put on the full armor of God in order that you may be able to stand firm against the crafty methods of the devil. | 1:11 being invigorated with all vigor, in accordance with his glorious might. |
| 1:21; 2:2 | 12 For not against flesh and blood is our wrestling but against the principalities, against the authorities, against the world-rulers of this darkness, against the spiritual forces of evil in the heavenly places. | 1:16 . . . whether . . . principalities or authorities. . . . |
| 6:11 | 13 Therefore take up the full armor of God, in order that you may be able to stand your ground in the day of evil, and having done everything, to stand firm. 14 Stand firm therefore, | |

having fastened the belt of truth around
y o u r waist and having put on the
breastplate of righteousness, 15 and having shod y o u r feet with readiness de-
2:17 rived from the gospel of peace, 16 and in
addition to everything else, having taken
up the shield of faith, by means of which
y o u will be able to extinguish all the
flaming missiles of the evil one; 17 and
take the helmet of salvation, and the sword
of the Spirit which is the spoken word of
God, 18 by means of all prayer and supplication, praying at all times in the
Spirit, and with a view to this, being on
the alert in all perseverance and supplication, for all the saints; 19 and
(praying) for me that when I open my
mouth I may be given a message, so that
I may make known courageously the mystery
of the gospel, 20 for which I am an ambassador in a chain, that when I proclaim
it I may speak with courage as I ought to
speak.

21 But in order that y o u also may
know my affairs how I am getting along,
Tychicus, the beloved brother and faithful minister in the Lord, will make them
all known to y o u, 22 whom I am sending

4:2 Persevere in prayer, keeping alert in
it with thanksgiving; 3 at the same time
praying also for us, that God may open to
us a door for the message, to speak forth
the mystery concerning Christ, on account
of which I am in prison, 4 (praying) that
I may make it clear, (and may speak) as I
ought to speak.

4:7 All my affairs will Tychicus make
known to y o u, the beloved brother and
faithful minister and fellow-servant in
the Lord, 8 whom I am sending to y o u for
this very purpose, that y o u may know our

| In Ephesians Compare | Ephesians | Colossians |
|---|---|---|
| | to you for this very purpose, that you may know our circumstances and that he may strengthen your hearts. 23 Peace (be) to the brothers, and love with faith, from God the Father and the Lord Jesus Christ. 24 Grace (be) with all those who love our Lord Jesus Christ with (a love) imperishable. | circumstances and that he may strengthen your hearts. |

## INTRODUCTION

In order to be able to arrive at an objective conclusion regarding the relation between Ephesians and Colossians it is now also necessary to refer to the *Colossian* text as a basis for comparison. (For the actual *text,* as newly translated, see N.T.C. on Colossians and Philemon, pp. 202–205.)

In the following presentation the numbers in roman type (1 2 3 4, etc.) indicate those verses in the Colossian chapter that have parallels in Ephesians. Those in italics (*6 7 8 15,* etc.) refer to the verses that are without significant duplicate in the longer epistle. Those printed in boldface (**1:1 1:16 1:15 1:13, 18,** etc.) immediately under the corresponding Colossian references, indicate the Ephesian parallels.[2]

### C. *Conclusions*

The above comparisons have made clear that there is, indeed, a substantial degree of resemblance between Colossians and Ephesians. To begin with *Colossians,* of its 95 verses about two-thirds are clearly or rather clearly paralleled in Ephesians, entirely or (more often) *in part,* either in thought conveyed or else both verbally and materially. This, however, by no means forces one to accept the conclusion that Ephesians is therefore the result of a skilful incorporation and amplification of phrases either remembered from Colossians or else copied from that shorter letter of Paul. Would a post-Pauline writer, whether he be thought of as writing from memory or from script, have rephrased the wording of Col. 1:12 into that of Eph. 1:11, that of Col. 1:13 into that of Eph. 1:6, that of Col. 2:11 into that of Eph. 2:11, that of Col. 2:4 into that of Eph. 5:6, and that of Col. 2:22 into that of Eph. 4:14, to list but a few parallels? Would not an imitator have adhered much more rigidly to the remembered or copied text? Surely, the remark of E. F. Scott is to the point: "When a writer borrows from himself he does what he likes with his own material. He cannot help revising and modifying in every sentence. It is only the unwarranted imitator who feels that he must stick

---

[2] If anyone compares the list here printed with that found in the work of C. L. Mitton, *The Epistle to the Ephesians,* pp. 316–318, he will discover that the two differ in some important details. Mitton, it must be remembered, denies the Pauline authorship of Ephesians. He sees a resemblance between Col. 1:8 and Eph. 3:5 and 6:18. However, the only item with respect to which all three passages are alike is the phrase "in the Spirit." This phrase, occurring both in those letters that are ascribed to Paul by almost everyone (Rom. 8:9; 9:1; 14:17; I Cor. 12:3), and in the Pastoral Epistles (I Tim. 3:16), is of little value in determining whether Paul himself or an imitator composed Ephesians. Further, it is hard to see any resemblance between Col. 1:17 and Eph. 5:1; between Col. 4:16 and Eph. 3:4, except for the fact that both refer to *reading.* And as to the closing benediction in Col. 4:18, though it is admitted that the words, "Grace (be) with y o u" resemble "Grace (be) with all those" of Eph. 6:24, yet when the two benedictions, in their entirety, are compared it is the contrast rather than the similarity that stands out. In certain other details also the list here given differs from that found in Mitton's work. It was made after careful examination of each individual passage.

## Colossians

### *Chapter 1*

| | | | | |
|---|---|---|---|---|
| 1<br>1:1 | 2<br>1:1 | 3<br>1:16 | 4<br>1:15 | 5<br>1:13, 18 |
| *6* | *7* | *8* | 9<br>1:8, 15–17 | 10<br>1:17; 2:10; 4:1 |
| 11<br>1:19; 3:16; 6:10 | 12<br>1:11, 16 | 13<br>1:6 | 14<br>1:7 | *15* |
| 16<br>1:10, 21; 3:9, 10, 15; 6:12 | *17* | 18<br>1:22; 5:23 | 19<br>1:23 | 20<br>1:10; 2:13, 14, 16 |
| 21<br>2:12, 13, 16; 4:18 | 22<br>1:4; 2:13, 16; 5:27 | 23<br>3:1, 2, 6, 7, 17 | 24<br>1:22, 23; 3:1, 13 | 25<br>3:2, 7 |
| 26<br>3:3–5, 9, 10, 21 | 27<br>1:9, 18; 3:6, 9, 10 | 28<br>3:10; 5:27 | 29<br>3:7, 10, 20 | |

### *Chapter 2*

| | | | | |
|---|---|---|---|---|
| *1* | 2<br>1:9; 3:9, 10 | *3* | 4<br>5:6 | *5* |
| *6* | 7<br>2:20; 3:17 | *8* | 9<br>1:23; 4:13 | 10<br>1:21 |
| 11<br>2:11 | 12<br>1:20 | 13<br>2:1 | 14<br>2:15 | *15* |
| *16* | *17* | *18* | 19<br>2:21; 4:15, 16 | *20* |
| *21* | 22<br>4:14 | *23* | | |

*Chapter 3*

| | | | | |
|---|---|---|---|---|
| 1<br>**1:20; 2:6** | *2* | *3* | *4* | 5<br>**5:3, 5; 4:19** |
| 6<br>**2:2, 3; 5:6** | 7<br>**2:3** | 8<br>**4:22, 29, 31; 5:4** | 9<br>**4:22, 25** | 10<br>**2:15; 4:24** |
| *11* | 12<br>**1:4; 4:2, 32** | 13<br>**4:2, 32** | 14<br>**4:2, 3; 5:2** | 15<br>**2:14; 4:1, 3, 4** |
| 16<br>**5:19, 20** | 17<br>**5:20** | 18<br>**5:22, 24, 33** | 19<br>**5:25, 28, 33** | 20<br>**5:10; 6:1** |
| 21<br>**6:4** | 22<br>**6:5–7** | 23<br>**6:5, 7** | 24<br>**6:6, 8** | 25<br>**6:8, 9** |

*Chapter 4*

| | | | | |
|---|---|---|---|---|
| 1<br>**6:9** | 2<br>**6:18** | 3<br>**1:9; 3:9; 6:19, 20** | 4<br>**6:20** | 5<br>**5:15, 16** |
| 6<br>**4:29** | 7<br>**6:21** | 8<br>**6:22** | *9* | *10* |
| *11* | *12* | *13* | *14* | *15* |
| *16* | *17* | *18* | | |

closely to his copy lest he may betray himself" (*The Epistles of Paul to the Colossians, to Philemon, and to the Ephesians,* p. 121).

It is true that even so the lists given above, in which the four chapters of Colossians form the basis for comparison, show remarkable resemblance. Yet, this resemblance is by no means uniform. Similarities abound especially in chapters 1 and 3. It is but fair, however, to take note also of the *differences.* In Colossians 2 and 4 (with exception of 4:7, 8; cf. the almost identical passage Eph. 6:21, 22) the *contrast* is as conspicuous as is the resemblance or even more so. We now clearly see that the theory according to which whoever wrote Ephesians simply copied Colossians but added a paragraph here and a phrase there, is not in accord with the facts. There is definite *material* difference between the two letters. No *contradiction,* to be sure, but *difference.* Alongside of everything that is similar there is a line of thought developed in Colossians which does not reappear *with similar emphasis* in Ephesians. As especially the second chapter of Colossians indicates, with confirmation in the other chapters, the smaller epistle places great stress on Christ, the Pre-eminent One, the Only and All-Sufficient Savior. Its style, moreover, is *polemical.* It is a defense of the truth over against heresy. The theme of Ephesians is a different one, for which see this Introduction, Chapter V. And its style is *doxological.* The longer epistle is an outburst of humble praise and adoration.

Turning now to *Ephesians,* passages paralleled in Colossians are clear from the parallel columns on pp. 6–26 in which the basis of comparison is the text of the longer epistle, printed consecutively in the first column. It is, accordingly, not necessary at this point to give a table of references for Ephesians as we did for Colossians. Ephesians contains 155 verses, well over half of which are paralleled, or *partly* paralleled, in Colossians. Sometimes more than one Ephesian passage is paralleled by the same Colossian passage. Thus both Eph. 4:2-4 and 4:32–5:2 resemble Col. 3:12-15. And for both Eph. 5:22 and 5:33b see Col. 3:18; for both Eph. 5:25a and 5:33a see Col. 3:19; etc. (The converse is also true: for both Col. 1:11 and 1:29 see Eph. 1:19; for both Col. 1:22 and 1:28 see Eph. 5:27; etc.)

Also with respect to *Ephesians,* however, it is necessary to point out not only the passages which correspond with those in Colossians but also those which do not. Though the two epistles have been called twins, these twins are by no means identical.

Thus, taking as our starting point for comparison *the first chapter of Ephesians,* we note that the paragraph concerning the church's *eternal foundation in Christ* and the ascription of praise for every spiritual blessing to Father, Son, and Holy Spirit (vss. 3-6, 7-12, 13, 14), has no parallel in Colossians. The references to the third person of the Holy Trinity (1:13, 17; and see also 2:18, 22; 3:16; 4:3, 4, 30; 5:9, 18; 6:17, 18) are not duplicated, as to frequency of occurrence, in the smaller epistle, which mentions the Holy

Spirit only once (Col. 1:8).[3] And the *many* references to "the church" in its most comprehensive sense, references beginning already in chapter 1 and continuing in later chapters (1:22; 3:10, 21; 5:23-25, 27, 29, 32), distinguish Ephesians from Colossians.

When we turn to *the second chapter of Ephesians* we are again reminded that this letter is by no means a copy of Colossians. Though, to be sure, Colossians, as well as Ephesians, magnifies God's grace (1:6), yet nowhere in that smaller epistle do we find anything that equals Eph. 2:7-10 in clearly stating and emphasizing the sovereign character of this grace and its relation to faith and to works. Moreover, the truth concerning *the universal scope* of the salvation which grace provides, so that through the blood of Christ men who were formerly bitter enemies are not only reconciled to *the Father* but also, because of that very fact, *to each other* (Eph. 2:11-18), though *implied* also in Colossians, *is brought into the foreground* only in Ephesians.

There is little in Colossians that parallels the closing paragraphs of *the third chapter of Ephesians,* the section containing the stirring prayer (3:14-19) and the doxology (3:20, 21). To be sure, the little there is suffices to show the reasonability of believing that he who wrote Col. 1:9b-14 (and Phil. 1:9-11) was also the author of Eph. 3:14-21 (cf. also Eph. 1:17-23). Yet, *the lofty goal* described in the words, "in order that y o u . . . may be enabled, together with all the saints, to grasp what is the breadth and length and height and depth, and to know the love of Christ that surpasses knowledge, that y o u may be filled to all the fulness of God" (Eph. 3:17-19) is unique.

As the parallel columns also clearly indicate, there is much in *Ephesians 4:1-16* to which there is no parallel in Colossians. *The organic unity (amid diversity) and growth* of the church is described in a paragraph which is unlike anything in the twin epistle, though, to be sure, *the idea* itself is not altogether absent from the latter (cf. Col. 3:15).

The *glorious renewal* on which *Eph. 4:17–6:9* dwells (note especially 4:23, 24; 5:14) and which becomes evident not only in the relation of believers to outsiders but also in the reciprocal attitudes of members of the same family (wives, husbands; children, fathers; slaves, masters), though paralleled to a considerable extent in Colossians, is in Ephesians described as a work of the Holy Spirit (4:30), by whom men are turned from "darkness" to "light" (5:6-14). The *darkness to light* metaphor occurs in a touching paragraph which, again, has no real parallel in Colossians, though *the germinal idea* occurs there also (Col. 1:13). And the striking thought that the relation between the believing husband and his wife is rooted in and patterned after that between Christ and his church (Eph. 5:23-32) stands by itself.

[3] This reference is, however, disputed, though, as I see it, without good reason. See N.T.C. on Colossians and Philemon, pp. 53, 54.

In *Eph. 6:10-24* it is especially the section that describes the believers' *effective armor* (Eph. 6:10-20) that distinguishes the two epistles. Except for verses 18-20 Colossians has little that corresponds to it.

It has become clear that those paragraphs – some of them lengthy – and those many individual passages in which Ephesians differs from Colossians are too numerous and too significant to be considered mere amplifications. On the contrary, they form a pattern and give to Ephesians a distinct character. This will become even clearer in Chapter V of this Introduction, where the theme of Ephesians is discussed and the distribution of the material under this theme is considered.

## III. Authorship

### A. *Arguments Against Pauline Authorship Answered*

The epistle to the Ephesians has been called "the divinest composition of man," "the distilled essence of the Christian religion," "the most authoritative and most consummate compendium of the Christian faith," "full to the brim with thoughts and doctrines sublime and momentous," etc. It has made that impression upon professional scholars and laymen, upon believers throughout the history of the church and of every nationality. Accordingly, to deny the universal testimony of the early church, namely, that it was the apostle Paul, richly endowed by his Lord with talents of heart and mind, who wrote it, would seem to require what some call "courage," others "temerity." This is true all the more when to this denial is added the suggestion that the writer was a person far more obscure than the apostle. Nevertheless, such denials have been lashed out and such suggestions have been propounded.[4]

[4] It should not be necessary at this point to dwell on the denial by F. C. Baur (b. 1792, d. 1860) and his school. For men of that type the question whether an epistle is characterized by the anti-Judaistic line of argumentation seemed to settle everything. Thus, all of Paul's thinking was forced into one groove. The historical Paul, as Baur and his disciples saw him, was ever ready for combat. Hence, when, as is the case with Ephesians, a letter is conciliatory in tone, picturing the church universal, Jew and Gentile having become reconciled not only with God but also with each other through the cross, no further mark of its un-Pauline and post-Pauline origin was required. But if any were needed it would be (according to Baur c.s.) the evidence, in both Colossians and Ephesians, of gnostic trends, and in Eph. 4:9, of the doctrine of the descent into Hades. However, the fact that already in Paul's days *incipient* gnosticism had raised its head is today undisputed, and as to Eph. 4:9, see on that passage.

After Baur a vigorous attack upon the authenticity of Ephesians, resembling in some of its arguments that of more recent criticism, was made by S. Hoekstra of The Netherlands in his article "Vergelijking van de Brieven aan de Efeziërs en de Colossers, vooral uit het Oogpunt van Beider Leerstelligen Inhoud," *TT* (1868), pp. 562–599. Hoekstra viewed Ephesians as an attempt to rephrase the contents of Colossians in such a manner that Ephesians would resemble more closely the doc-

The main arguments that have been urged against Pauline authorship are two which, at least to a certain extent, cancel each other out:

1. *The Resemblance Is Too Close*

a. *Ephesians resembles Colossians*

The statement is made that this similarity is so very close that if Paul wrote Colossians he cannot have written Ephesians.

Answer: This argument has been fully answered in the preceding chapter. The traditional theory, according to which the same author at about the same time wrote letters to people living in the same Roman province, but elaborated on themes which, though closely related, are yet essentially different, fits all the data. Moreover, several Colossians-Ephesians parallels are found also in Paul's other epistles. In such cases, therefore, assuming that Colossians was written prior to Ephesians,[5] can it be said that whoever wrote

---

trine of the real Paul. As Hoekstra saw it, the author, whoever he was, was averse to all those theosophic theories about Christ which were found in Colossians, theories which severed Christianity from its historic foundation and from its abiding connection with the old dispensation.

Among those who more recently have rejected the Pauline authorship of this epistle are the British scholars James Moffatt, *Introduction to the Literature of the New Testament,* New York, 1918, who does not even classify Ephesians with Pauline literature; B. H. Streeter, who discusses "The Pauline Corpus" in his work *The Primitive Church,* New York, 1929; W. L. Knox, *St. Paul and the Church of the Gentiles,* Cambridge, 1939; and especially C. L. Mitton, *The Epistle to the Ephesians, Its Authorship, Origin and Purpose,* Oxford, 1951; see also, by the same author, *The Formation of the Pauline Corpus of Letters,* London, 1955; "Unsolved New Testament Problems: E. J. Goodspeed's Theory Regarding the Origin of Ephesians," *ET,* 59 (1947–1948), pp. 323–327; "E. J. Goodspeed's Theory Regarding the Origin of Ephesians," *ET,* 60 (1948–1949), pp. 320–321; "Important Hypotheses Reconsidered; VII. The Authorship of the Epistle to the Ephesians," *ET,* 67 (1955–1956), pp. 195–198. In America it was especially E. J. Goodspeed who attacked the Pauline authorship and suggested that Onesimus (the fugitive slave for whom Paul interceded in his letter to Philemon), in his later capacity as Bishop of the church at Ephesus, not only made a collection of the Pauline epistles but also himself wrote Ephesians as a covering letter or introductory commentary, *The Meaning of Ephesians,* Chicago, 1933; cf. also by the same author *New Chapters in New Testament Study,* New York, 1937, p. 32; and *The Key to Ephesians,* Chicago, 1956, xvi. F. W. Beare (Toronto, Canada) states his reasons for rejecting Pauline authorship in his commentary, *The Epistle to the Ephesians* (*Interpreter's Bible,* Vol. X, pp. 597–601).

Among the defenders of Pauline authorship the scholarly work of E. Percy, *Die Probleme der Kolosser-und Epheserbriefe,* Lund, 1946, deserves to be mentioned first of all. It is deplorable that C. L. Mitton, in a Preface to his aforementioned work: *The Epistle to the Ephesians, Its Authorship, Origin and Purpose,* had to admit that his book was already in the printer's hands before he had been able to gain access to Percy's dissertation. The traditional view, that Paul wrote Ephesians, is also defended by the following, to mention only a few: Abbott, Barclay, Barry, Bartlett, Bowman, Brown, Bruce, Findlay, Greijdanus, Grosheide, Hodge, Hort, Moule, Robinson, Scott and Westcott. For titles see General Bibliography at end of this volume.

[5] Whether Colossians preceded Ephesians or vice versa cannot be established with certainty. The usual — and it would seem logical — view is that Paul, having written Colossians which deals with a particular situation (the denial of Christ's all-

the Ephesian passages was necessarily using *only Colossians* as a basis for composition? May he perhaps also have had in mind Romans, I or II Corinthians, Galatians or some other Pauline epistle(s)? This leads to the next proposition:

b. *Ephesians resembles too closely Paul's other epistles*

The claim is made that words and phrases from the other Pauline epistles, for the moment leaving out not only Colossians but also the Pastorals, reappear far more frequently in Ephesians than in any genuine letter written by the great apostle. The conclusion is drawn that a capable imitator, having been a disciple of the renowned master, and being well acquainted with his genuine epistles and thus able to reproduce their words and phrases from memory, must have composed Ephesians.

Answer:

(1) There is wide divergence of opinion among scholars as to the actual extent of this resemblance. E. J. Goodspeed claims that out of 618 short phrases into which Ephesians may be divided as many as 550 have unmistakable parallels in Paul, in words or substance. On the other hand, A. S. Peake and T. K. Abbott see in Ephesians no or very little evidence of borrowing from any of Paul's epistles other than Colossians. C. L. Mitton, though convinced that the percentage as given by Goodspeed is an exaggeration, agrees with him in his general conclusion that the similarities are so numerous and of such a character that someone other than Paul must have written Ephesians. Nevertheless, detailed examination of the borrowings which Mitton considers the most striking has left many unconvinced. Would a disciple, reproducing from memory or even from the written page, Romans 3:24, "justified freely by his grace through the redemption that is in Christ Jesus," have reformulated this into "even though we were dead

---

sufficiency for salvation), afterward passed from the particular to the more general, from conditions existing in one particular church or in the churches of the Lycus Valley to God's plan of redemption with reference to the church universal. The fact that Ephesians is the longer epistle, enlarging on certain subjects that are merely touched upon in Colossians, can also be interpreted as pointing to that conclusion. Colossians 4:16b ("see to it that y o u also read the letter from Laodicea") is not a refutation of this theory. It does not indicate that Ephesians must have preceded Colossians. Even if the letter "from Laodicea" should refer to Ephesians, a supposition that cannot be proved (see N.T. on Colossians and Philemon, pp. 196, 197), this would still leave room for at least two possibilities neither of which would preclude the priority of Colossians: *a.* the apostle wrote (i.e., dictated) Colossians in its entirety, including 4:16, *having already planned to write Ephesians very soon afterward,* the two letters (plus the letter to Philemon) to be carried to their respective destinations by the same carrier, Tychicus, on the same trip (cf. Col. 4:7-9; Eph. 6:21, 22); or *b.* having written Colossians, with the exception of 4:16 (at least) and having afterward also composed Ephesians, Paul then revised the former by adding 4:16. For the very complicated theory of H. J. Holtzmann regarding the composition of the two letters see N.T.C. on Colossians and Philemon, p. 29. For defense of Colossian priority cf. E. P. Sanders, "Literary Dependence in Colossians," *JBL* (March 1966), p. 29.

through our trespasses (he) made us alive together with Christ — by grace y o u have been saved — " (Eph. 2:5) ? To be sure, there is agreement in doctrine here and the phrase "by grace" is used in both passages. But is it not more reasonable to ascribe the significant alteration in general phraseology to an original author who has thoroughly digested this central fact of redemption and is recasting his own thought? And the same holds also with respect to other parallels such as Rom. 8:28, cf. Eph. 1:11; I Cor. 3:6, cf. Eph. 2:21; Gal. 1:15, cf. Eph. 3:8; Philem. 13, cf. Eph. 6:20; etc. In all these cases there is, to be sure, a degree of similarity, but resemblance close enough to disprove Pauline authorship, not at all! In each case, if *the same author* wrote both corresponding passages, neither their resemblance nor their divergence is strange or in need of further explanation.

(2) Since the author of Ephesians has as his theme *The Church Glorious,* a church enriched by all the blessings of salvation which God, *solely by grace,* bestows upon both Jew and Gentile, "to the praise of his glory," it is not at all strange that at least as to content many passages in this prison epistle resemble those in the other letters where the same or a very similar theme is expressed. The theme *Salvation* ("Justification") *by Grace Alone* is also central in Romans and Galatians and is the basis for the exhortations in all the other epistles.

(3) Ephesians offers very little material of a polemical character, and there are *few* — according to some there are *no* — local references. This leaves more room for resemblances in positive teaching.

(4) Ephesians was written later than most of the other epistles. It contains, as it were, *a summary of doctrine.* Also for this reason in reading it one would expect to hear more echoes of the other epistles than one could expect to detect elsewhere.

Now in comparing Ephesians with Paul's other epistles there is not any good reason to omit the Pastorals (I and II Timothy and Titus), as if it is an established fact that these were not written by Paul. On the contrary, the attempt to disprove their Pauline authorship must be considered a failure. See N.T.C. on I and II Timothy and Titus, pp. 4–33; 377–381. The most reasonable explanation for the extent of the resemblances, often in substance or thought-content but at times even in exact phraseology, between Ephesians and the Pastorals, is that these four letters sprang from the same mind and heart. Note the following:

| **Ephesians** | **I and II Timothy and Titus** |
|---|---|
| Doxologies break in suddenly | |
| "Now to him who is able to do infinitely more than all we ask or im- | "So to the King of the ages, the imperishable, invisible, only God (be) |

| Ephesians | I and II Timothy and Titus |
| --- | --- |
| agine . . . be the glory . . . forever and ever" (3:20). Cf. 1:3 ff. | honor and glory forever and ever!" (I Tim. 1:17). Cf. I Tim. 6:15, 16; II Tim. 4:18. |

Believers are God's *elect*

| | |
| --- | --- |
| ". . . just as he elected us in him before the foundation of the world" (1:4). | "On account of this I endure all things for the sake of the elect" (II Tim. 2:10). |

Man's chief purpose is God's glory

| | |
| --- | --- |
| ". . . to the praise of the glory of his grace" (1:6); ". . . to the praise of his glory" (1:12, 14). | "to him (*be* or *is*) the glory forever and ever. Amen" (II Tim. 4:18). |

The gospel is "the *word* or *message* [logos] of the truth"

| | |
| --- | --- |
| ". . . the message of the truth, the gospel of y o u r salvation" (1:13). | ". . . rightly handling the word of the truth" (II Tim. 2:15). |

It was because of God's *love* that sinners were saved

| | |
| --- | --- |
| ". . . among whom we also once lived in the lusts of our flesh . . . God, being rich in mercy, because of his great love with which he loved us, even though we were dead through our trespasses, made us alive together with Christ" (2:3-6). | "For at one time we also were . . . enslaved to various passions and pleasures. . . . But when the kindness of God our Savior and his love toward man appeared he saved us" (Tit. 3:3-5). |

It is grace — not works — that saved us

| | |
| --- | --- |
| "For by grace y o u have been saved through faith; and this not of yourselves, (it is) the gift of God; not of works, lest any one should boast" (2:8, 9). | "(God) who saved us and called us with a holy calling, not according to our works but according to his own purpose and grace" (II Tim. 1:9). Cf. Tit. 3:5. |

Nevertheless, good works are necessary,
as the fruit (never the root!) of grace

| | |
| --- | --- |
| "For his handiwork are we, created in Christ Jesus for good works, which God prepared beforehand that we should walk in them" (2:10). | ". . . (our great God and Savior Christ Jesus) who gave himself for us in order . . . to purify for himself a people, his very own, with a zest for noble deeds" (Tit. 2:14). Cf. I Tim. 2:10; 6:18; II Tim. 3:17; Tit. 3:8. |

| **Ephesians** | **I and II Timothy and Titus** |
|---|---|
| *Christ is the one and only Mediator* | |
| "... for through him we both have our access in one Spirit to the Father" (2:18). | "For (there is but) *one* God, and (there is but) *one* Mediator between God and men, the man Christ Jesus" (I Tim. 2:5). |
| *Paul considers himself unworthy* | |
| "To me, the very least of all saints, was this grace given" (3:8). | "Reliable (is) the saying, and worthy of full acceptance, that Christ Jesus came into the world sinners to save, foremost of whom am I" (I Tim. 1:15). |
| *The mystery of salvation, once hidden, has now been disclosed* | |
| "... the mystery which for ages has been hidden in God ... in order that now ... might be made known through the church the iridescent wisdom of God, according to the eternal purpose which he formed in Christ Jesus our Lord" (3:9-11). | "... his own purpose and grace which was given to us in Christ Jesus before times everlasting but now has been manifested through the appearing of our Savior Christ Jesus" (II Tim. 1:9, 10). |
| *The ascended Christ has instituted the offices for the perfecting of believers* | |
| "And it was he who gave some (to be) apostles ... fully to equip the saints for the work of ministry, with a view to the building up of the body of Christ" (4:12). | "... that the man of God may be equipped, for every good work thoroughly equipped" (II Tim. 3:17). |
| *Wives should be submissive to their own husbands* | |
| "Wives (be subject) to your own husbands as to the Lord" (5:22). | "... so that they may train the young women to be ... submissive to their own husbands" (Tit. 2:4, 5). |
| *We are saved through a spiritual washing, that of regeneration, symbolized by baptism* | |
| "... cleansing her by the washing of water ..." (5:26). | "... through a washing of regeneration" (Tit. 3:5). |

| Ephesians | I and II Timothy and Titus |
|---|---|
| The mystery which centers in Christ is great | |
| "This mystery is great . . ." (5:32). | "And confessedly great is the mystery of (our) devotion" (I Tim. 3:16). |
| The grace and power of the Lord is the believers' source of strength | |
| "Finally, find your (source of) power in the Lord and in the strength of his might" (6:10). | "You then, my child, be strengthened in the grace (that is) in Christ Jesus" (II Tim. 2:1). |
| When grace, love, and faith combine true peace results | |
| "Peace (be) to the brothers and love with faith, from God the Father and the Lord Jesus Christ. Grace (be) with all those who love our Lord Jesus Christ with (a love) imperishable" (6:23, 24). | "And it super-abounded (namely) the grace of our Lord, with faith and love in Christ Jesus" (I Tim. 1:14). |

Now in all this the complete *harmony* with the leading ideas found in those epistles that are by nearly everyone ascribed to Paul, coupled, however, with rich *variety* of expression, points to identity of authorship and not to either of two suggestions, namely, *a.* that a disciple of Paul refurbished passages from Ephesians, thus producing material now found in the Pastorals, or *b.* that he who composed Ephesians borrowed from the Pastorals.

c. *Ephesians resembles I Peter*

It must not be overlooked that some of the material found in Ephesians is similar to that contained in *non-Pauline New Testament literature.* There are, for example, significant resemblances between Ephesians and I Peter. Note the following:

| | Ephesians | I Peter |
|---|---|---|
| "Blessed (be) the God and Father of our Lord Jesus Christ" | 1:3 | 1:3 |
| "before the foundation of the world" | 1:4 | 1:20 |
| "so that you may know what is the *hope* . . . what the *inheritance* . . . and what the . . . *power* . . . which he exerted in Christ when he raised him from the dead" | 1:18-20 | cf. 1:3-5 |

| | Ephesians | I Peter |
|---|---|---|
| "he (God) raised him (Christ) from the dead, and made him to sit at his right hand . . . far above every principality and authority and power" | 1:20, 21 | cf. 3:21b, 22 |
| "the sons of disobedience" . . . "children of wrath" | 2:2, 3 | cf. 1:14; 2:2 |
| "Christ Jesus himself being the chief cornerstone" | 2:20 | cf. 2:4, 8 |
| "in other generations not made known . . . that now might be made known . . . ." | 3:5, 10 | cf. 1:10-12 |
| "lowliness . . . meekness . . . longsuffering . . . love," etc. | 4:2, 3 | cf. 3:8, 15; 5:5 |
| "laying aside falsehood . . . bitterness and anger and wrath and brawling and slander, along with all malice" | 4:25, 31 | cf. 2:1 |
| "tenderhearted" | 4:32 | 3:8 |
| table of household duties | 5:22–6:9 | cf. 2:18–3:7 |
| "Put on the full armor of God in order that you may be able to stand firm against the crafty methods of the devil" | 6:11 | cf. 5:8, 9a |

d. *Ephesians resembles Luke and Acts*

Similarly there are resemblances between Ephesians and the Lucan writings. In all three the divine love and grace, mercy and forgiveness are prominently displayed (Eph. 1:4, 6-8; 2:5-8; Luke 1:48; 4:18; 5:20; 7:47, 48; Acts 5:31; 11:23; 13:38, 43; 14:3, 26; 15:11, 40; 26:18). There is emphasis on prayer, often intercessory in content (Eph. 1:15, 16; 3:14; 6:18; Luke 1:9, 10, 13; 2:37; 3:21; 5:16; 6:12, 28; etc.; Acts 1:14; 2:42; 4:24-31; 10:4; 12:5; etc.). There is thanksgiving, praise, and song (Eph. 1:6, 12, 14, 16; 5:19, 20; Luke 1:46; 2:13, 14, 20, 29-32, 47; 3:8, 9; 5:67-79; 24:52, 53; Acts 2:47; 15:31; 16:25, 34). This is not surprising, for a world-embracing gospel is being proclaimed (Eph. 2:18; Luke 1:78, 79; 2:32; 13:29; Acts 2:17-21; 13:46, 47; 15:7-9; 22:21). It is the gospel of full and free salvation through the shedding of Christ's blood (Eph. 1:7; 2:13; Luke 22:20, 44; Acts 20:28). In the final analysis, therefore, every blessing proceeds from God, was included before the foundation of the world in his all-comprehensive decree, and flows forth from his sovereign "good pleasure" (Eph. 1:4, 5; Luke 2:14; 17:26-28).

Nothing either good or evil ever happens apart from his all-comprehensive, eternal decree (Eph. 1:11; Luke 22:22; Acts 2:23; 13:29). The blessings received on earth descend from heaven, from the ascended and exalted Mediator (Eph. 1:3, 20-22; 4:8-10; Luke 24:50, 51; Acts 1:6-11; 2:32-36; 7:55, 56). It is from that heavenly home that Jesus sent the Comforter, so that his own might be "filled with the Holy Spirit" (Eph. 5:18; Luke 1:15, 41, 53, 67; Acts 2:4, 33; 4:8, 31; etc.). In receiving these marvelous blessings men do not remain passive. On the contrary, by the power of the Holy Spirit, they, "with loins girded" (Eph. 6:14; Luke 12:35), and walking in the *light,* expose the works of *darkness* (Eph. 5:8-14; Luke 1:79; 11:33-36; 12:3; 16:8).

e. *Ephesians resembles the Johannine writings*

The last mentioned contrast — *light* versus *darkness* — is found, however, not only in Ephesians and Luke but also in other sacred literature, notably in the writings of *John* (John 1:4-9; 3:19-21; 8:12; I John 1:5, 7; 2:8-10, etc.; cf. also Rev. 21:22-26). The claim has often been made that Ephesians emits a Johannine fragrance. Note, accordingly, not only the light-darkness contrast but also the very similar opposition between *life* and *death* (Eph. 2:1, 5; 4:18; John 1:4; 5:24; I John 3:14; Rev. 3:1). Another contrast — in this case not hostile but complementary — with respect to which Ephesians reminds one of John's terminology, is that between Christ's *descent* and his *ascent* (Eph. 4:9, 10; John 3:13; 6:38, 41, 50, 51, 58, 62; 16:28). Many blessings descend upon the church from the ascended Christ. Now it was in Christ that even "before the foundation of the world" (Eph. 1:4; John 17:24; cf. 17:5; Rev. 13:8; 17:8) believers were chosen. They were fore-ordained to adoption as *sons* (Eph. 1:5; John 1:12; I John 3:1). Moreover, all of them having been elected from eternity "in Christ," (Eph. 1:3, 4, 6, 7, etc.; John 15:5) who dwells in them (Eph. 3:17; John 14:20; cf. Rev. 1:13), form a unity and must do their utmost to promote spiritual unity (Eph. 4:1-16; John 15:12; 17:21-23). The purpose of Christ's active and energetic indwelling is that he may present the church to himself brilliant in purity, having no spot or wrinkle, thoroughly sanctified (Eph. 5:27; cf. 3:14-19; 4:17-24; John 15:2; 17:17-19), cleansed by the spoken word (Eph. 5:26; John 15:3). This church is the object of his love. Of very frequent occurrence both in Ephesians and in the Johannine literature is this word *love,* both as noun and as verb (*noun:* Eph. 1:4, 15; 2:4; 3:14-19; *verb:* 2:4; 5:2; *noun:* John 5:42; 13:35; 15:9; I John 2:5, 15; II John 3, 6; III John 6; Rev. 2:14, 19; *verb:* John 3:16; I John 2:10; II John 1, 5; III John 1, to list only a few references). And is it not true that, according to both Ephesians and John, Christ is "the Beloved" of the Father? (Eph. 1:6; John 3:35; 10:17; 15:9; 17:23, 24, 26). Because of his infinite and tender love and in his Spirit believers are "sealed" (Eph. 1:13; 4:30; John 6:27; Rev. 5:1-9; 6:1; 7:3-8). They receive the reassuring testimony of the Holy Spirit. *Within the limit* ("according to the measure," Eph. 4:7) in which, in any situation of life, believers have need of pardoning and sustaining grace, their Savior apportions it to them, for it is he who has received the Spirit *in unlimited degree* ("without measure," John 3:34). He has "known" his sheep from all eternity, and they aim "to *know* the *love* of Christ that surpasses knowledge" (Eph. 3:19). Note this combination of these two entities that match perfectly: *a.* experiential *knowledge* and *b. love* that is experienced. As has already been indicated, John's writings, too, refer to this *love* again and again. They also enlarge on this *knowledge* (John 8:32; 10:15; 17:3, 25; I John 2:3-5, 13, 14; 4:7, 8, 16; 5:2, 20; II John 1; Rev. 3:9).

f. *Ephesians resembles Hebrews*

Both teach redemption through blood (Eph. 1:7; Heb. 9:12, 22); Christ's exaltation at God's right hand (Eph. 1:20; Heb. 1:3; 8:1; 10:12); and access to the Father through Christ (Eph. 2:18; 3:12; Heb. 4:16; 7:25). They also describe in similar terms those who are immature (Eph. 4:14; Heb. 5:13); warn against being whirled around or carried away by every gust of doctrine, that is, by strange and deviating teaching (Eph. 4:14; Heb. 13:9); recognize Christ's one and only offering of himself for the sin of his people (Eph. 5:2; Heb. 10:10); pronounce God's judgment upon every form of immorality (Eph. 5:5; Heb. 13:4); tell us that Christ offered himself for the church in order that he might sanctify it (Eph. 5:26; Heb. 10:10, 22; 13:12); and compare the word of God to a sword (Eph. 6:17; Heb. 4:12).

g. *Ephesians resembles the Epistle of James*

The same figure of speech is used to describe the unstable person. He is said to be "driven" or "tossed to and fro" by the wind (Eph. 4:14; cf. James 1:6). Ephesians 5:8 calls believers "children of light." James 1:17 describes God as "the Father of lights." "Be angry but do not sin" (Eph. 4:26) reminds one of "Let every man be . . . slow to anger" (James 1:19). For other resemblances compare Eph. 4:2, 3 with James 3:17; 5:8; Eph. 4:29 with James 3:10; Eph. 4:31 with James 3:14; Eph. 5:19 with James 5:13; Eph. 6:18, 19 with James 5:16. To represent James as Paul's opponent with respect to the doctrine of good works is unfair. On the contrary, James championed the cause of Paul (Acts 15:13-29). To the very end he remained Paul's friend (Acts 21:18-25). Paul and James were not in conflict, but faced different issues. James valued genuine faith highly (1:3, 6; 2:1, 5, 22-24; 5:15). The "faith" which he condemns is that of dead orthodoxy and of demons (2:19). Paul would condemn that just as vehemently. And, on the other hand, Paul was a firm believer in the necessity of good works as a fruit of faith (Eph. 2:10; cf. Rom. 2:6-10; II Cor. 9:8; I Thess. 1:3; II Thess. 2:17; Tit. 3:8, 14).

As to any conclusion with respect to authorship that can be drawn from these resemblances between Ephesians and other New Testament writings see below, under heading 3.

2. *The Difference Is Too Great*

a. *Different Words*

It is claimed that the letter contains too many exceptional or new words; that is, either words found nowhere else in the New Testament (forty-two of them), or else words which, though occurring elsewhere in the New Testament, are not found in any genuine epistle of Paul.

Answer:

(1) The same argument, if applied to Romans, Galatians, Philippians, or I and II Corinthians, would also exclude them from the list of Pauline letters. The number of new words in Ephesians is not disproportionately large.

(2) A different subject requires different words. In Ephesians, more than elsewhere, the apostle discusses "the unity of all believers in Christ." Hence, it is not surprising that here he uses such new words (those *in italics* which follow) as: *unity* (4:3, 13), which resulted because Christ "made *both* one and has broken down the *barrier* formed by the *dividing wall*" (2:14). In connection with this same stress on spiritual togetherness, this letter contains many sun-compounds, the prefix "sun-" meaning "together" or "fellow-." Paul uses the expressions: *harmoniously fitted together* (2:21), *built together* (2:22); *fellow-citizens* (2:19), *fellow-members of the body, fellow-partakers of the promise* (3:6). The last two are preceded by *fellow-sharers in the inheritance* (co-heirs), but this is not a new word, as it already occurs in Rom. 8:17.

Also, Paul stresses the fact that this entire united church should bid defiance to the forces of evil, and that in order to do so it should put on the spiritual armor which God provides (6:11 ff.). In that striking little paragraph this battle and this panoply of faith are described with a fulness of detail found nowhere else in Paul's epistles. We therefore expect to find new words. When they occur they certainly cannot be used as an argument against Pauline authorship. The apostle speaks about *crafty methods of "the devil"* (*ho diábolos,* a word found, however, also in the Pastorals; see No. [4] below). He reminds us of the fact that our *wrestling* is against . . . *world-rulers* of this darkness, against the spiritual forces of evil in *the heavenly places* (see No. [3] below). He urges us *to fasten* the belt of truth *around* the waist, *to put on* (lit., "to bind beneath") shoes that symbolize the *readiness* derived from the gospel of peace, and to take up *the shield* of faith by means of which we shall be able to extinguish all the flaming *missiles* of the evil one. In all this, for the reason given, there is nothing that argues against Pauline authorship for Ephesians.

(3) It is not very convincing to say that Paul could write "God," but not *without God* (Eph. 2:12); "shameful" (I Cor. 11:6; 14:35) but not shamefulness or, as here, *filthiness* (Eph. 5:4); that he could use the verb "to

open" (I Cor. 16:9; II Cor. 6:11), but not the noun *opening* (Eph. 6:19); could call a man "wise" (I Cor. 1:26) but not *unwise* (Eph. 5:15); could write "to equip," to make complete (I Cor. 1:10), but not *equipment* (Eph. 4:12); "to persevere" (Col. 4:2), but not *perseverance* (Eph. 6:18); "holily" (I Thess. 2:10), but not *holiness* (Eph. 4:24); and "heavenly" (I Cor. 15:40 – twice; 48, 49), also "the heavenly beings" (Phil. 2:10, "of those in heaven"), but not *the heavenlies,* at least not five times (Eph. 1:3, 20; 2:6; 3:10; 6:12).

(4) The statement, made so often, that many words are found in Ephesians "but not in any genuine Pauline writing," generally proceeds from the tacit assumption that the Pastorals (sometimes also Colossians) are not "genuine Pauline writings." But, as has been indicated (N.T.C. on I and II Timothy and Titus, pp. 4–33; also footnote 193 on pp. 377–381), for this assumption there are no real grounds. It was Paul who wrote the Pastorals. Hence, from the list of exceptional words that have any value as an argument against Pauline authorship for Ephesians must also be subtracted those which this letter has in common with the Pastorals though they do not occur in any other Pauline epistle: *chain* (Eph. 6:20; II Tim. 1:16); *deceive* (Eph. 5:6; I Tim. 2:14); *dissolute behavior* or *unrestrained living* (Eph. 5:18; Tit. 1:6); *devil* (Eph. 4:27; 6:11; I Tim. 3:6, 7, 11; II Tim. 2:26; 3:3; Tit. 2:3; also used by Matthew, Luke, John, James, Peter, and the author of Hebrews, often interchangeably with *Satan*); *evangelist* (Eph. 4:11; II Tim. 4:5); *discipline* or *training* (Eph. 6:4; II Tim. 3:16) and the verb *to honor* (Eph. 6:2; I Tim. 5:3).

(5) As to the "exceptional" words that still remain after all of these others have been subtracted because they can have no value in supporting the proposition that Paul could not have written Ephesians, we may well ask whether Paul, an able writer, with originality and a fertile mind, should not be credited with a sufficient command of language to enable him to use synonymous words and phrases. At the beginning of his writing-career was the apostle handed a list of words with the requirement that, no matter what the circumstances might be, either of himself or of the readers, and no matter what might be the purpose of any epistle or the subject on which he would write, he must invariably use *these* words, and *only* these, and, in addition, must distribute them in equal proportion over all his letters, like the spots on a polka-dot dress? Vocabulary proves nothing at all against Pauline authorship of Ephesians! [6]

---

[6] The manner in which this argument, however, is still being used even in a relatively recent commentary, with many excellent features, leaves something to be desired. I refer to F. W. Beare's work on Ephesians in *The Interpreter's Bible,* Vol. 10, p. 598. After informing the reader that the number of new words is extraordinarily large in Ephesians, he *mentions* five of them. However, no less than *three* of

b. *Different Meanings*

It is also maintained that in Ephesians Pauline words are used in a new sense. Thus the word *plērōma,* fulness, in Col. 1:19; 2:9 indicates the fulness of deity dwelling in Christ, but in Eph. 1:23 it is used in a different connection. In Col. 1:26, 27 the term *mystery* indicates eschatological glory, but in Ephesians it refers to the acceptance of the Gentiles (1:9; 3:3 ff.). So also in Col. 1:22 the word *sṓma, body,* refers to the physical body of Jesus Christ offered as a sacrifice for sin, and in Col. 2:19 its English equivalent is cosmos or universe, but in Ephesians the body is the church. Finally, the word *oikonomía* (whence our "economy"), which in Colossians and elsewhere has reference to the special task or assignment which by God was entrusted to Paul, has the abstract meaning "God's wise planning or generalship" in Ephesians.

Answer: The word *fulness,* in Greek as well as in English, can be used in many different connections. See N.T.C. on Colossians and Philemon, footnote 56, pp. 79, 80. Its exact reference in Eph. 1:23 is disputed. Certainly no argument of value can be based on such a controversial passage. See also the explanation of Eph. 1:10, 23; 3:19; 4:13. As to the word *mystery,* it is clear from the context that even in Col. 1:26, 27, though the setting is eschatological, the reference is to "the glory of the mystery *among the Gentiles* . . . Christ *in y o u,* the hope of glory." As to the word *sṓma, body,* is it fair to demand that it must have exactly the same reference in Ephesians as in Col. 1:22, when only in the latter case the author speaks of "his body *of flesh*"? It is not true that in Col. 2:19 the word *body* refers to the cosmos or universe. See N.T.C. on that passage. What is true is that (in Ephesians) the well-nigh consistent reference of this word to *the church,* with the human body in the background (1:22, 23; 2:16; 3:6; 4:4 ff.; 5:23, 30; exception 5:28) is also well represented in Colossians (1:18; 2:19; 3:15). Hence, there is no real problem here. And finally, as to *oikonomía,* this word, wherever it occurs in the New Testament, is based upon the idea of *stewardship.* It has this meaning not only in Luke 16:2-4; I Cor. 9:17; Col. 1:25; and I Tim. 1:4 but also in Eph. 3:2. However, by a slight semantic shift the meaning "administration of one's stewardship" arises, and so, in general, *administration,* execution, effectuation, the carrying into effect of a plan or purpose (Eph. 1:10; 3:9). One and the same author must certainly be allowed the privilege of using the same word both in its basic meaning and also, in a different context, in a somewhat modified sense. Is it not true that

---

these five are found in 6:11 ff., the paragraph on the Christian's spiritual armor, a new subject (at least as to detail), with respect to which we *expect* new words (see No. [2] above). The remaining *two* words are not "new" at all: one is found also in Romans; the other in II Corinthians. Negative criticism will have to do better than this!

even in the same short sentence a word, used twice, can have two different connotations (see Luke 9:60; Rom. 9:6) ? It is clear, therefore, that the argument based on "different meanings" lacks validity.

Sometimes *an entire phrase* is used in Ephesians in a connection in which it is not found in Colossians or elsewhere in Paul. This, too, has been used as an argument against Pauline authorship. The most remarkable instance of this exception to the rule is held to be Eph. 5:20 as compared with Col. 3:17. The latter passage reads, "And whatever y o u do in word or in deed, (do) all in the name of the Lord Jesus, giving thanks to God the Father *through him";* but the former reads, "giving thanks . . . *in the name of our Lord Jesus Christ* to (our) God and Father." Mitton tells us that in the Ephesian passage the phrase "in the name of Jesus" is artificially associated with giving thanks. As he sees it this phrase is added "rather pointlessly." To him this wrenching of a phrase from its proper Colossian context speaks, more than perhaps any other item, against Pauline authorship. But should we not rather say that this type of reasoning speaks more than perhaps anything else against the convincing nature of Mitton's argumentation? What could be wrong with the idea that in Paul's mind the giving of thanks was associated with the name of Jesus? Does not the very passage in Colossians clearly state that *everything* – hence, also the giving of thanks – must be done "in the name of the Lord Jesus"? Is not the clause, "giving thanks to God the Father *through him,*" synonymous with giving thanks to God the Father *in the name of* the Son? If it be true that in Christ's name knees will bend (Phil. 2:20), commands are issued (II Thess. 3:6), and, in fact, all things must be done (Col. 3:17), is it then pointless to say that in his name thanksgiving must also be offered? Is it not rather true that since the Father blesses us through the Son, thanksgiving should also be brought to the Father through the Son, that is, "in his name"?

c. *A Different Style*

The style employed by the author of Ephesians is said to be too diffuse, deferential, and dulcifying to belong to the real Paul. First, it is said to be *diffuse.* It is a wordy epistle, and the words are widely spread. By means of almost interminable sentences the letter moves along slowly and majestically like a glacier that worms its way down the valley inch by inch. See 1:3-14; 1:15-23; 2:1-10; 2:14-18; 2:19-22; 3:1-12; 3:14-19; 4:11-16; and 6:13-20. Within these lengthy sentences there is often a descriptive verbosity that is completely uncharacteristic of the real Paul. Titles are written out in full, followed by modifying clauses; example, "Blessed (be) the God and Father of our Lord Jesus Christ, who has . . ." etc. Frequently, a noun is followed by its synonym, the latter being in the genitive or being preceded by a preposition: "the dividing wall of the barrier," probably meaning "the barrier formed by the dividing wall," to which, as if this were not enough, is added another synonym "the hostility" (2:14); "the law of commandments in ordinances," indicating "the law of commandments with its requirements" (2:15); and "the measure of (the) stature of the fulness of Christ" (4:13). See also 1:5, 11, 19. Now all this is in sharp contrast with the concise, abrupt, lively, impetuous style that characterizes the real Paul.

Answer: Much of Ephesians is in the nature of a prayer offered by a deeply grateful apostle who is witnessing the realization of his life's dream, namely, the coming into existence of a new and glorious spiritual entity, the *one* church of Jew and Gentile, the product of the marvelous grace of God. Now elevated language with its many synonyms is characteristic of adoration. See N.T.C. on Colossians and Philemon, p. 30. Also, by far the most of these lengthy sentences occur in the first of the two major divisions of the letter, that is, in the part that can be described as *Adoration* in contrast with Part II: *Exhortation.* It is not fair to contrast the style of this Adoration section of Ephesians with that of the Exhortation section of the other epistles, and then to say that, therefore, Paul cannot have written Ephesians. It is true that Ephesians contains more long and lofty sentences than is usual with Paul. There is, however, a reason for this. Nowhere else is there such an outpouring of the heart, such unrestrained praise, as there is in this letter. The author is moved to the very depths of his being by *a.* the contemplation of God's sovereign, eternal, redemptive love for sinners, *both Jew and Gentile, b.* the inner conviction that he, the author himself, is a recipient of this grace, and *c.* the reflection that he, Paul, yes even he himself, formerly a vehement persecutor of the church, had been predestined by God to play a very important role in the proclamation and realization of God's marvelous plan of the ages.

Yet, as already indicated, the described stylistic difference in this respect between Ephesians and the other epistles is one *in degree* only. Hence, it cannot be properly used as an argument against Pauline authorship. Lengthy sentences are also found in other epistles traditionally ascribed to Paul. Rom. 1:1-7 has 93 words in the original; 2:5-10 has 87; Phil. 3:8-11 has 78; and Col. 1:9-20 has no less than 218. And as to piling up closely connected synonyms, this feature, too, is by no means confined to Ephesians. On the contrary, such and similar pleonasms are found also in Rom. 11:33; Phil. 3:8; Col. 1:5, 11, 27; I Thess. 1:3, to mention only a few.

Secondly, the style of Ephesians has been described as *deferential.* It is maintained that an admirer of the great master is here speaking. Paul himself, according to this manner of argumentation, could never have written such a boastful clause as the following: "whereby, as y o u read it, y o u can perceive my insight into the mystery of Christ" (3:4). Surely, the man who wrote, "I am the least of the apostles, unfit to be called an apostle" (I Cor. 15:9), was far too humble to write Eph. 3:4 (or 3:4-9).

Answer: It is exactly characteristic of Paul to make enormous claims. He claims to have fully preached the gospel amid signs and wonders (Rom.

15:19); calls himself "a wise master-builder" (I Cor. 3:10), and a "steward of the mysteries of God" (I Cor. 4:1; cf. 9:17). He even dares to make comparisons between himself and others. He ranks himself higher than ten thousand tutors (I Cor. 4:15). He is able to speak with tongues "more than y o u all" (I Cor. 14:18). As an apostle he has "labored more abundantly" than any of the others (I Cor. 15:10). See also II Cor. 11:22-33; Gal. 1:1, 14; Phil. 3:4-6. Hence, the claim made by the author of Eph. 3:4 is in line with those made elsewhere in Paul's epistles and cannot be used as a valid argument against the traditional ascription of Ephesians to the great apostle to the Gentiles.

It should be noted, however, that Paul's claims are entirely valid, are made in order that, through confidence in his message, men may be benefited spiritually and may be won for Christ (I Cor. 9:19-21), and that the glory may be given not to the recipient of the enumerated distinctions but to God alone (I Cor. 9:16; 10:31; Gal. 6:14). The apostle never claims personal credit for any virtue or talent (Rom. 7:24, 25; I Cor. 4:7; Gal. 6:3). Here in Ephesians he is just as humble as he was in I Corinthians, perhaps even more so (cf. Eph. 3:8 with I Cor. 15:9). But that he, nevertheless, makes these great claims cannot be denied. In the light of all the evidence it is clear that also on this score there is no essential difference between Ephesians and the other Pauline epistles.

Finally, a *dulcifying* character has also been ascribed to the style of Ephesians. It has been said by those who deny the Pauline authorship of both Colossians and Ephesians that in addition to the desire to soften the extreme doctrinal utterances of the former, the author of the latter, whoever he may have been, tried to tone down the *exhortations* found in the shorter epistle. Hence, the demand that children obey their parents and that slaves obey their masters "in all things" (Col. 3:20, 22) is in Ephesians reproduced in the weakened form which omits the offensive modifier (6:1, 5).

Answer: It is not difficult to suggest possible reasons for the change, reasons that will in no way imply a rejection of Pauline authorship for both epistles. In the case of the exhortation addressed to the children, the author here in this longer epistle wishes to stress another aspect of the matter, namely, that such submission is proper and will be rewarded. And in connection with the admonition to the slaves we may well ask whether the command (6:5) does not already have a sufficient number of predicate modifiers (verses 5b, 6, 7, 8) to be able to dispense with an additional "in all things." Besides, was not the flight of Onesimus from his Colossian master a sufficient reason why exactly in *Colossians* the demand that slaves obey their masters had to be emphasized by the addition of the modifier? But there may have been other reasons. What, however, especially shuts the door against this type of argumentation against Pauline authorship for Ephesians is the fact that in connection with the requirement that wives obey their husbands it is exactly *Ephesians,* not Colossians, that adds, "in everything" (cf. Eph. 5:24 with Col. 3:18).

It has become clear, therefore, that there is nothing in the style of Ephesians that prevents it from being a genuine letter written by Paul.

d. *Different Doctrines*

(1) *The Doctrine of God*

Objection: According to Ephesians *God's eternal decree* is the source of salvation for his people (Eph. 1:4, 5, 11). Paul, however, glories in the cross (Gal. 6:14; cf. Rom. 3:24).

Answer: Ephesians, too, glories in the cross (2:16; cf. 1:7), and the other Pauline epistles also trace salvation to its source in God's sovereign, eternal plan (Rom. 8:29, 30; 11:2, 28, 36; Col. 3:12).

(2) *The Doctrine of Man*

Objection: Ephesians describes man's condition apart from grace in milder terms than does Paul in Colossians and elsewhere. Contrast the strong language of Col. 3:5-9 with the mere negatives of Eph. 2:12.

Answer: No language used to describe the sinner in his natural state could be stronger than that used in Eph. 2:1-3. Moreover, there is dynamite in those negatives of Eph. 2:12! See on that passage.

(3) *The Doctrine of Christ*

(a) Objection: Ephesians calls Christ "the head" of the church (1:21, 22; 4:15, 16; 5:23). According to Paul the head is merely one of the members of the body (I Cor. 12:21).

Answer: Different themes require different metaphors. The passage from I Corinthians describes the mutual obligations of church-members. Ephesians deals with the unity of all believers in Christ, their head. There is no contradiction here. Even in I Corinthians the fact that "the head of every man is Christ" is clearly taught (I Cor. 11:3). Colossians, too, recognizes Christ's headship in relation to his church (Col. 1:18; 2:19).

(b) Objection: According to Eph. 2:16 it is *Christ* who achieves reconciliation; according to Col. 1:20; 2:13, 14 it is *God* who does this. Similarly, Eph. 4:11 teaches that it is *Christ* who appoints apostles, prophets, evangelists, etc. This is contradicted by I Cor. 12:28 which indicates that it is *God* who exercises that function.

Answer: As is clear from II Cor. 5:18 and Eph. 4:32, it is ever *God in Christ* who is at work. Hence, deeds of this kind can be ascribed to either person. It is as the late Professor L. Berkhof remarks in his *Systematic Theology,* Grand Rapids, Mich., 1949, p. 89, *"Opera ad extra,* or those activities and effects by which the Trinity is manifested outwardly . . . are never works of one person exclusively, but always works of the Divine Being as a whole." Thus also according to John 14:16, 26 the "giving" or "sending" of the Holy Spirit is ascribed to *the Father,* but in 15:26 this "sending" is ascribed to *the Son.* There is no contradiction: it is "in the Son's name" that the Father sends the Spirit; it is "from the Father" that the Son sends him.

(c) Objection: In Ephesians *Christ's death* is no longer basic. All the attention is concentrated on *his exaltation* (1:20 ff.; 2:6; 4:8).

Answer: Although, due to the central theme of Ephesians, the emphasis has changed somewhat, Christ's death is basic, even for the author of Ephesians (1:7; 2:13; 2:16).

(d) Objection: According to Paul sinners are reconciled *to God* through the cross (II Cor. 5:20, 21; Col. 1:21, 22), but according to Ephesians the cross effects a reconciliation *between Jew and Gentile* (2:14-18; cf. 2:19-22; 3:5 ff.; 4:7-16).

Answer: There is no contradiction. By means of the cross Jew and Gentile are reconciled to God; *therefore also to each other.* That basically the reconciliation is "to God" is clearly taught in Eph. 2:16; cf. also verse 18. But, in harmony with the central theme of Ephesians — the unity of all believers in Christ; hence, the church universal — it is on the reconciliation between Jew and Gentile that the emphasis falls here.

(e) Objection: Ephesians emphasizes *Christ's ascension* (4:8 ff.). Paul has no ascension doctrine.

Answer: Christ's ascension is clearly implied in such passages as Rom. 8:34; Phil. 2:6-11; 3:20; I Thess. 1:10; 4:16; and I Tim. 3:16.

(f) Objection: Ephesians teaches Christ's descent into Hades (4:19), and is therefore clearly post-Pauline. The real Paul nowhere teaches this doctrine.

Answer: See the explanation of Eph. 4:8-10.

(4) *The Doctrine of Salvation*

(a) Objection: Ephesians teaches the doctrine of *salvation* — "for by grace you have been saved through faith"; Paul that of *justification* (Rom. 3:24; 5:1).

Answer: It is true that over against Jewish and Judaistic legalism the forensic aspect of the sinner's deliverance is stressed in some Pauline epistles, notably in Romans and Galatians, leading to the use of the terms "justification" and "no condemnation," while, in harmony with the theme of Ephesians — the *oneness* of all believers "in Christ" — here the mystical experience and fellowship with Christ receives somewhat more extensive treatment. However, this does not imply any contradiction. The essence of the doctrine of justification, the "not of works, but solely by grace" doctrine, is clearly expressed in Eph. 2:8, 9. See also on 4:24; 6:14. Paul never departed from this, and even subsequent to the writing of Ephesians gave eloquent expression to it (Titus 3:4-7). As to Paul's emphasis on being *saved,* and being used as God's agent in *saving* others, see Rom. 10:9, 13; 11:14; I Cor. 9:22; 15:2.

(b) Objection: The manner in which Ephesians treats *the law* is un-

Pauline. In Ephesians the law is viewed not as something of benefit to man but as an instrument of division between man and man (2:15). Paul, however, establishes a definite relation between the law and the process of salvation: he pictures the law as our guide ("tutor") who brings us to Christ (Gal. 3:24). According to him "the law is holy, and the commandment holy and righteous and good" (Rom. 7:12).

Answer: In Romans and Galatians Paul views the law from several different aspects. Viewed from one aspect it is good, as just indicated; from another it is inadequate (Rom. 8:3); and from still another it even pronounces a curse upon a person (Gal. 3:10, 13). Hence, here, too, there is no contradiction. It certainly was not necessary for the author of Ephesians to discuss *all* the various phases of the law. What he does say about it here is in harmony with what he says elsewhere.

(5) *The Doctrine of the Church*

(a) Objection: In Ephesians the term *church* always refers to the church universal (1:22; 3:10, 21; 5:23, 24, 25, 27, 29, 32). In the genuine Pauline epistles it does not (or: does not always) have this meaning.

Answer: Examples of the use of the word *church* without local reference are I Cor. 12:28; 15:9; Gal. 1:13; Phil. 3:6 (cf. Acts 20:28). In Col. 1:18, 24 the reference is to the church universal; in Col. 4:15, 16 a local congregation is indicated. Accordingly, the use of this term in Ephesians cannot be a good reason for denying Pauline authorship. Since in writing Ephesians it was not Paul's purpose to enlarge on any local conditions but rather to glorify God for the work of his grace in the church at large, the apostle naturally used the word here in this broad sense.

(b) Objection: The author's emphasis on the unity of the church shows that this epistle must have been written after Paul's death, at a time when various sects had arisen, and when it had become necessary to stress the need of a centralized ecclesiastical government.

Answer: The unity that is described and urged in Ephesians is of a spiritual character. Cf. John 17:21. It is not the organizational unity for which, in a later day, Ignatius pleaded.

(c) Objection: The extreme importance attached to "apostles and prophets" (2:20-22; 3:5), as if they were "holy" and "the foundation" of the church, befits a generation later than Paul. The apostle himself would never have written this. To him Jesus Christ is the only true foundation (I Cor. 3:11).

Answer: It is exactly because these men gave a true and enthusiastic testimony about Christ that, in a secondary sense, they could be called the foundation of the church. Not at all in themselves or because of any intrinsic merit were they entitled to this distinction, but as divinely appointed witnesses and ambassadors who were constantly pointing *away from themselves, to Christ.* This manner of speaking about Christ's plenipotentiaries originated with Christ himself (Matt. 16:18). John, the disciple whom Jesus loved, made use of the same symbolism in describing Jerusalem the Golden. He says, "And the wall of the city had twelve foundations, and on them twelve names of the twelve apostles of the Lamb" (Rev. 21:14). The fact that the author of Ephesians calls these men "holy" is no objection. They were, indeed, holy, that is, set apart and qualified by God for a unique office. All this does not plead *against* Paul as the author of Ephesians but rather *for* him. It is in strict harmony with all that he has to say about himself and about the other apostles and prophets. See the following passages: Rom. 1:1; I Cor. 3:10; 5:3, 4; 9:1; 12:28; II Cor. 10:13, 14; 12:12; Gal. 1:1, 11-17; 2:6-9.

(d) Objection: Paul could not have written Eph. 2:11. No true Jew could have viewed the sacrament of circumcision with such utter contempt.

Answer: Read what Paul says about this in Gal. 5:1-12; Phil. 3:2, 3.

(6) *The Doctrine of the Last Things*

Objection: Paul could not have written Ephesians, for in this epistle there is no suggestion of any second coming or of any event in connection with it.

Answer: The following Ephesian passages cannot be understood apart from an implied doctrine of the consummation: 1:14; 2:7; 4:13, 30; 5:5, 6, 27.

3. *Conclusion*

a. *as to the resemblance being too close*

(1) The striking *similarity* between Colossians and Ephesians is due *chiefly* to identity of authorship, time and place of writing, and general situation of those addressed. Identity of authorship also explains numerous *variations* in expressions and emphases. An imitator or forger would have adhered more closely to the original. Another reason for the *divergence* of the two letters is their different purpose, as has been explained.

(2) Since *the other letters* (that is, other than Colossians) that are traditionally ascribed to Paul were written under different circumstances with respect to both addressor and addressees (exception: Philemon), the resemblances between them and Ephesians are not quite as striking. Nevertheless, here too there are many clear parallels. And here also the same thought is frequently given a new turn. In addition to identity of authorship, hence also of doctrine, a second factor must be taken into consideration, namely, the rise, throughout the early Christian church, of common forms of expression, such forms as generally come into being whenever people become united by ties of deep convictions to which they feel impelled to bear unanimous testimony in the midst of a generally hostile environment. The increasing prevalence of such *forms* is also a factor in explaining the parallels existing between Ephesians, etc., and *the non-Pauline New Testament literature.* Among the forms there are *doxologies* of two types:

*a.* "Blessed be . . ." (Eph. 1:3; cf. Rom. 1:25; 9:5; II Cor. 1:3; 11:31; I Peter 1:3) and *b.* "Now to him be . . ." (Eph. 3:20, 21; cf. Rom. 11:36; Jude 24, 25); *hymns* or *hymn-fragments* (Eph. 5:14; cf. the nativity account in Luke; Col. 1:15-19; I Tim. 3:16; Book of Revelation); *tables of duties for the respective members of the family* (Eph. 5:22–6:9; cf. Col. 3:18–4:1; I Tim. 2:8-15; 6:1, 2; Titus 2:1-10; I Peter 2:12–3:7); *lists of virtues* (Eph. 4:1-3, 32; Col. 3:12-15; James 3:17; 5:8); and various others.[7] Some of these forms have an Old Testament origin. Hence, see also No. 5 below.

(3) The need of imparting uniform catechetical instruction to enquirers and recent converts would also promote unanimity in thought-expression.

(4) Similarity in form and content, whenever it occurs among New Testament writers, must also be traced further back, namely, to Christ, that is, to the Spirit-guided reflection on his person, work, and teaching. Thus, one can hardly fail to see the words recorded in Matthew 6:12 and the similar words *and action* in Luke 23:34 (forgiveness) reflected in Ephesians 4:32; I Peter 2:21-23; 3:8, 9; etc.; Christ's title, God's "beloved Son" (Matt. 3:17) echoed in Eph. 1:6; II Peter 1:17; the reference to this son's stoneship (Matt. 21:42) recurring in Eph. 2:20 and I Peter 2:4, 8; and the mention of his glorious exaltation to the Father's right hand (implied in Matt. 26:64) reaffirmed in Eph. 1:20; Acts 7:55; Heb. 1:3; 10:12; 12:2; I Peter 3:22; Rev. 12:5. Paul and the other New Testament authors were drawing water from the same Well, namely, Christ.

(5) The apostle and the other sacred writers were versed in the same Old Testament background. Thus, to take but two examples mentioned under No. (4) above, the idea of Christ's stoneship can be traced to Psalm 118:22; that of his exaltation to the Father's right hand, to Psalm 110:1.

(6) The combination of all these factors constitutes a far more satisfying explanation of the listed similarities than does the assumption that the traditional ascription of the authorship of Ephesians to Paul must be regarded as an error and that an imitator must have been at work.

b. *as to the difference being too great*

When this argument is applied to such matters as vocabulary and style, it has been shown in detail that whatever remains of it, after due allowance has been made for exaggeration, is accounted for by the overpowering emotion of gratitude which prompted Paul to write the letter and by the purpose he had in mind. As to alleged differences in doctrine, the following conclusion has been established: though it is certainly true that in Ephesians various doctrines receive not only greater emphasis but also broader amplification than elsewhere and new facets of well-known gems of truth are displayed, no doctrines found in other Pauline epistles find any contradiction here.

[7] See A. C. King, "Ephesians in the Light of Form Criticism," *ET* 63 (1951–1952), pp. 273–276.

### B. *Arguments in Favor of Pauline Authorship Stated*

1. The writer calls himself "Paul, an apostle of Christ Jesus" (1:1); and "I, Paul, the prisoner of Christ Jesus for the sake of y o u Gentiles" (3:1; cf. 4:1). Just before he pronounces the final benediction he states, "But in order that y o u also may know my affairs, how I am getting along, Tychicus, the beloved brother and faithful minister in the Lord, will make them all known to y o u, whom I am sending to y o u for this very purpose, that y o u may know our circumstances and that he may strengthen y o u r hearts" (6:21, 22). Would a disciple of Paul, a collector of his letters whose mind was saturated with Pauline teaching, have dared to identify himself with Paul so brazenly? The burden of proof surely rests on those who say that the writer, though calling himself Paul and delegating someone to tell those for whom the letter was intended how he, Paul, was getting along, was not actually Paul but Onesimus, Tychicus, or someone else.

2. Ephesians has all the characteristics of such almost universally recognized Pauline epistles as Romans, I and II Corinthians, Galatians, and Philippians. It resembles Colossians in many ways, as has been shown. To prove this remarkable similarity between Ephesians and the other Pauline epistles one need only compare the list given below with that found in N.T.C. on Colossians and Philemon, pp. 33, 34. Limiting ourselves now to Ephesians note the following:

| | *Ephesians* |
|---|---|
| a. The author is deeply interested in those whom he addresses | 1:16; 3:14-19; 5:15-21 |
| b. He loves to encourage and praise them | 1:15; 2:1 |
| c. He traces every virtue of those whom he addresses to God, ascribing all the glory to him alone | 1:3-5; 2:1 |
| d. He writes touchingly about the supremacy of love | 5:1, 2, 25, 28, 33 |
| e. He is filled with gratitude to God who laid hold on him and made him, though unworthy, a minister of the gospel | 3:6-9 |
| f. He lists virtues and vices | 4:17–5:21 |
| g. He is never afraid to assert his authority | 3:4; 4:17–6:22 |
| h. When conditions are at all favorable he thanks God for those addressed and at times assures them of his constant prayer for them | 1:15 ff.; 3:14-19 |
| i. He warns earnestly against those who are seeking to lead others astray | 4:14, 17-19; 5:3-7; 6:10 ff. |
| j. He loves "the gospel" | 1:13; 3:6; 6:15, 19 |

3. It is hard to believe that somewhere in the early church there existed a genius of a forger who blended the genuine writings of Paul into a com-

posite so excellent in style, logical in arrangement, and lofty in content that he must have been at least the apostle's peer in intellectual ability and spiritual insight, able even to provide the church with a further development of Pauline thoughts, and then leave no trace behind as to his identity.

4. The testimony of the early church is in harmony with the conclusion that has been established. Thus, Eusebius, having made a thorough study of the sources within his reach, states: "But clearly evident and plain are the fourteen (letters) of Paul; yet it is not right to ignore that some dispute the (letter) to the Hebrews" (*Ecclesiastical History* III.iii.4, 5). It is clear, therefore, that this great church-historian, writing at the beginning of the fourth century, was well aware of the fact that the entire orthodox church of his day and age recognized Ephesians as an authentic epistle of Paul.

From Eusebius we go back to Origen (fl. 210–250), who in his work *On Principles* (*De Principiis*) quotes several passages from Ephesians, assigning them to "the apostle" or to "Paul himself" (II.iii.5; II.xi.5; III.v.4). In his chief apology *Against Celsus* (*Contra Celsum*) he says (chapter 72), "The apostle Paul declares," and then quotes Eph. 2:3.

From Origen we go back still further, to his teacher, Clement of Alexandria (fl. 190–200). In his work *The Instructor* (*Paedagogus* I.5) he quotes Eph. 4:13-15, ascribing it to "the apostle" (according to the preceding context).

About the same time Tertullian (fl. 193–216) in his work *Against Marcion* (*Adv. Marcionem* V.17) declares, "We have it on the true tradition of the church that this epistle was sent to the Ephesians, not to the Laodiceans. Marcion, however, was very desirous of giving it the new title, as if he were extremely accurate in investigating such a point. But of what consequence are the titles, since in writing to a certain church the apostle did in fact write to all." Again (V.11), "I here skip the discussion concerning another epistle, which we hold to have been written to the Ephesians, but the heretics to the Laodiceans."

Earlier by a few years, but still for a long time a contemporary of Clement of Alexandria and of Tertullian, was Irenaeus, who in his work *Against Heresies* (*Adversus Haereses,* I.viii.5) states, "This also Paul declares in these words," and then quotes Eph. 5:13. Similarly (V.ii.3), ". . . even as the blessed Paul declares in his epistle to the Ephesians, 'We are members of his body and of his flesh and of his bones.' " Cf. Eph. 5:30. This testimony of Irenaeus, in which he clearly names Paul as the author of Ephesians, is very significant, for Irenaeus had traveled widely and was rather thoroughly acquainted with the entire church of his day and age, a period of early history in which the traditions of the apostles were still very much alive.

*The Muratorian Fragment* (about 180–200), a survey of New Testament books, definitely names Paul as the author of Ephesians.

But we can go back even further than the latter part of the second century A.D. Skipping disputed allusions to Ephesians in *The Shepherd of Hermas, The Teaching of the Apostles* (*Didache*), the so-called *Epistle of Barnabas,* etc., because such controversial passages have but little if any decisive value, we come now to such authors who not only flourished at one time or another during the period 100–170, but also furnished clear evidence for the existence and recognition of this epistle in their day. At a time so close to that of the apostles it was not necessary to mention the very names of the latter. Quoting their *writings,* with implied assumption that these were well known and were considered authoritative by the church, is all that we can expect from these early witnesses. I do not deny that those who reject the Pauline authorship of Ephesians will, of course, even deny the relevancy of the passages about to be quoted. But in doing so they labor under difficulties that are but too evident. Note, then, the following:

Polycarp states, ". . . knowing that 'by grace y o u have been saved, not by works' " (*Letter to the Philippians* I.3, quoting from Eph. 2:8, 9). Again, "Only as it is said in these Scriptures, 'Be angry but do not sin,' and 'Let not the sun go down on that angry mood of y o u r s' " (XII.1, Latin, quoting Eph. 4:26). Anent this letter of Polycarp see also N.T.C. on Philippians, p. 16.

We come now to Ignatius and his letter *To the Ephesians.*[8] The clearest reference to Paul's Ephesians is found in the opening paragraph (I.1), ". . . being imitators of God." These words immediately remind one of Paul's exhortation, "Be therefore imitators of God" (Eph. 5:1). And when Ignatius compares believers to "stones of the sanctuary of the Father, made ready for the building of God our Father" (IX.1), is not the reference to Paul's statement in Eph. 2:20-22 rather obvious?

Clement of Rome (as representing the church of Rome) writes, "Through him the eyes of our hearts were opened" (*The First Epistle of Clement to the Corinthians* XXXVI.2). Is not this a near-quotation of Eph. 1:18: ". . . that the eyes of y o u r hearts may be illumined"? Compare also: "Or have we not one God and one Christ and one Spirit of grace poured out upon us, and one calling in Christ?" (XLVI.6) with this sentence from Paul, "There is . . . one Spirit, just as also y o u were called in one hope which y o u r calling brought y o u [lit. 'of y o u r calling'], one Lord . . . one God and Father of all" (Eph. 4:4-6).

According to Hippolytus, the Basilides, Ophites, and Valentinians used Paul's Ephesian letter. Now these three were among the earliest of the Gnostic sects. The Epistle to the Ephesians was, moreover, also included in Marcion's Canon (though, as has already been indicated, under a different

[8] However, I purposely skip the debate with reference to XII.2. It is not needed to prove the point.

title), in the Old Latin, and in the Old Syriac. Finally, there is the possibility that Col. 4:16 refers to this letter. See N.T.C. on that passage.

It has been shown, therefore, that as soon as the church began to assign the New Testament writings to definite authors it "with one accord" named Paul as the author of Ephesians. There was no doubt or dissent. This definite ascription began about the latter part of the second century. But even earlier than this the existence of the letter and the high value which the church attached to it as inspired Scripture was everywhere recognized. There is no reason to depart from these traditional convictions.

## IV. Destination and Purpose

### A. *Destination*

#### 1. *The Facts and the Problem Arising from Them*

A real difficulty confronts us because Eph. 1:1, which in A.V., etc., mentions those to whom the letter was addressed, does not read the same in all the Greek manuscripts. The opening words, "Paul, an apostle of Christ Jesus through the will of God, to the saints and believers in Christ Jesus who are," furnish no serious textual problem. The difficulty arises with the additional phrase "in Ephesus" (ἐν Ἐφέσῳ). This phrase is not found in the oldest extant manuscripts: it is absent from p[46], dating from the second century, and from the unrevised *Sinaiticus* and *Vaticanus,* dating from the fourth.[9] As most scholars see it, a comment by Origen (early third century) implies that it was not in the text he used. A remark by Basil (about A.D. 370) has led to a similar conclusion with respect to the text on which he commented.

On the other hand, with one exception, from the middle of the second century *the title* above the letter has always been "To the Ephesians." The one exception was Marcion's copy in which the epistle bore the title "To the Laodiceans." It is commonly held, with good reason, that this departure from the rule was due to a misinterpretation of Col. 4:16. The manner in which Tertullian criticized Marcion for accepting (or originating?) this error has been noted (see III B 5 above). Also, with near-unanimity later manuscripts have "in Ephesus" in *the text* of 1:1. The versions also with one accord support this reading.

The problem, accordingly, is this: How can we explain the absence of the phrase "in Ephesus" from the earliest extant manuscripts in the light of the otherwise well-nigh unanimous testimony in favor of its inclusion? And what light do these facts shed on the real destination of Ephesians?

[9] It was also left out by the corrector of 424, whose corrections were based on a very ancient manuscript, and by 1739.

2. *Various Proposed Solutions*

a. *The letter was not intended for any specific locality whether large or small but rather for believers everywhere and at any time.*

According to this view, whatever *the title* may say, the words "in Ephesus" were never meant by Paul to be inserted. There are two main forms of this theory. According to the first, Paul addressed his message to the saints "who *are*," that is, who alone have true *being*, since Christ, in whom they live, is the one who truly IS. Is not he the great I AM? (cf. Ex. 3:14; John 6:35, 48; 8:12; 10:7, 9, 11, 14; etc.; Rev. 1:8; 22:13). This interpretation was suggested by Origen. Basil also adopts it. According to the second, Paul is simply writing "to the saints who are also faithful in Christ Jesus." This, with omission of the words "in Ephesus," is found not only in the text of R.S.V. but favored also, with some variation in wording, by many others, both translators and expositors: Beare, Findlay, Goodspeed, Mackay, Williams, etc.

Evaluation: Elsewhere in Paul's epistles the words "who are" or (the church) "which is," when present in the original, are consistently followed by a place-designation (Rom. 1:7; I Cor. 1:2; II Cor. 1:1; Phil. 1:1). Accordingly, there is no valid reason to assume that the occurrence of the words "who are" in Ephesians was to be an exception to this rule. There is nothing in Paul's other epistles that lends support to the metaphysical explanation presented by Origen and Basil. And as to the similarly non-local rendering "the saints who are also faithful," this rendering, besides being likewise exposed to the objection just mentioned, can be given a reasonable sense only if it be not interpreted to mean that there were some saints who were faithful and other saints who were not.

Though for the reason stated (Pauline usage elsewhere) I cannot accept the theory endorsed by R.S.V., etc., I am, nevertheless, of the opinion that it contains a point of value that should not be passed by. What Tertullian already pointed out is true, namely, that "in writing to a certain church the apostle did in fact write to all" (see above III B 5). In Ephesians, as well as in all the other epistles, etc., the Spirit is addressing *all* the churches both then and now. In fact the ecumenical theme of Ephesians adds emphasis to this point! It is possible to stress too strongly the local reference. However, this does not mean that the question whether or not the words "in Ephesus" should be retained can be dismissed as of no value whatever.

b. *The letter, though sent to believers living in a definite and limited region, was not in any sense meant for Ephesus.*

This theory is defended, among others, by T. K. Abbott in his work *The Epistles to the Ephesians and to the Colossians* (*International Critical Commentary*), New York, 1916, p. viii; and by E. F. Scott in his brief exposition, *The Epistles of Paul to the Colossians, to Philemon and to the Ephesians* (*Moffatt New Testament Commentary*), New York, 1930, pp. 121, 122.

According to Abbott Ephesians was meant for the Gentile converts in Laodicea, Hierapolis, Colosse, etc. Scott writes, ". . . nothing is certain except that the letter was not written to the Ephesians." Grounds: "in Ephesus" is lacking in the best manuscripts; there are no intimate touches; the implication of 1:15; 3:2; 4:21, 22 altogether rules out Ephesus.

Answer: It is hardly conceivable that Paul, who had spent so much time and energy in Ephesus, would write a letter to the churches of Proconsular Asia, excluding Ephesus!

The next two theories should be considered together. They agree basically, for both proceed from the assumption that in one sense or another the letter was sent to Ephesus. They differ in that c. interprets "in Ephesus" regionally; d. locally.

c. *The letter was addressed to the believers who resided in the province of which Ephesus was the chief city. It was a circular letter intended not only for the local church but also for the surrounding congregations in Proconsular Asia.*

Today this is a widely accepted view.

d. *The letter was sent to one specific, local church, namely, the one at Ephesus, just as Philippians was sent to the church at Philippi, and I and II Corinthians to the church at Corinth.*

For the defense of this view and the refutation of the circular-letter or encyclical idea in any form see especially R. C. H. Lenski, *op. cit.*, pp. 329–341.

Those who favor the circular letter theory, c., advance the following reasons for their view (these being the same as those under b. but with less rigid application):

(1) The words "in Ephesus" are omitted in the best and most ancient manuscripts. Hence, there is really no good reason to retain this place-designation unless we interpret it as referring to the region of which Ephesus was the metropolis.

(2) The words ". . . because *I have heard* of the faith in the Lord Jesus that (exists) among y o u" (1:15) and ". . . *if so be that y o u have heard* of the stewardship of God's grace that was given to me" (3:2; cf. 4:21, 22) clearly imply that among the addressed there were those with whom Paul was not acquainted and who had never stood in close personal relationship to him. Had the letter been intended solely for believers living in the city of Ephesus, with whom the apostle had established such very close ties (read especially Acts 20:36-38), he could never have expressed himself in this manner.

(3) In every epistle addressed by Paul to a congregation which he had founded or with which he had become personally acquainted there is a reference to the fact that he was the spiritual father of the church and had

labored in its midst (I Cor. 1:14; 2:1; 3:5-10; 11:23; 15:1-11; II Cor. 3:3; Gal. 1:8; 4:13-20; Phil. 1:27-30; I Thess. 1:5; 2:1-5). No such reference occurs in Ephesians. On the contrary, the epistle is completely lacking in intimate touches, items of personal information, or allusions to the work which the apostle had performed in the city and church of Ephesus, as recorded in Acts 18:18-21; 19; 20:17-38. If Ephesians was never intended as a letter to one specific congregation but rather as a circular letter sent to *several* churches, including Ephesus, this is understandable.

(4) Sometimes – *but now seldom* – a fourth reason is added: The epistle contains no personal greetings; yet, if it had been intended exclusively for the congregation at Ephesus these would not have been lacking.

Those who believe that the epistle was addressed solely to the church at Ephesus and was not a circular letter answer as follows:

(1) In all ancient manuscripts (except Marcion's) the letter bears *the title: To the Ephesians.* All the ancient *versions* have "in Ephesus" in verse 1. How shall we explain that title and those versions if the letter was not originally intended for the congregation at Ephesus? As to the absence of "in Ephesus" from 1:1 of the most ancient manuscripts, is it not possible that someone tampered with the text? Nearly all the later Greek *manuscripts* contain the disputed phrase. How do those who reject its genuine character explain that?

(2) As to 1:15, 3:2, and 4:21, 22, this is a matter of interpretation. See Commentary on these passages.

(3) It is not certain that there is no connection between the record of Paul's work found in Acts and the contents of this epistle. On the contrary, of which letter can it be said more truly that it proclaims "the whole counsel of God" (cf. Eph. 1:3-14)? Now according to Acts 20:27 that is exactly the characterization of Paul's preaching at Ephesus. See also on Eph. 2:20-22. Absence of major local problems that troubled the congregation may explain why Paul does not in this letter refer to the manner in which he had been received when he founded the church. Moreover, as to intimate touches and news with respect to himself, this is explained in 6:21, 22: Tychicus was able to supply full information.

(4) II Corinthians, Galatians, I and II Thessalonians also lack greetings though written to churches founded by Paul. On the other hand, Romans, addressed to a church not founded by the apostle, contains a great many greetings.

Evaluation: It is clear that *not all the reasons advanced in favor of the circular letter theory are valid.* No. (4) particularly is weak, and has been dropped by many proponents of the encyclical idea. It is doubtful, though, whether the rebuttal to No. (3) is fully satisfying. The lack or rather inconsiderable amount of local color and of personal touches as well as the broad and exalted theme (the church universal) would seem to harmonize better with the encyclical theory than with the purely local. There is, moreover, another fact that would seem to lend even greater support to this circular letter view. It would have been almost impossible for Paul to address a letter to the believers in Ephesus and not also to include those in the surrounding churches. Ephesus was the heart and center of the Christian community, as is very clear from Acts 19:10, which implies that when Paul was laboring in this city people from all around came streaming to hear him. As a result, "all those who were living in Asia heard the word of the Lord, both Jews and Greeks." In the Book of Revelation, too, the very first of the circle of seven letters is addressed to the church at Ephesus (Rev. 2:1-7). Accordingly, I favor theory c. But on the basis of either view (c. or d.) the words "in Ephesus" can be safely retained in our translation of Eph. 1:1.

Now in elaborating on the circular letter theory a popular view (proposed by Beza and endorsed by Archbishop Ussher) is that originally a blank had been left after the words "who are," and that Tychicus or someone else had been asked to make several copies, one for this church, one for that, in order, in each separate case, to fill in this blank by *writing* into it the name of the church for which the particular copy was intended. Furthermore, according to this theory, in the end the phrase "in Ephesus" became standardized because the church in that city was the most important one.

Possible objections to this theory are the following: First, are we not thus assuming for Ephesians a method of letter-distribution which "savors more of modern than of ancient manner" (Abbott)? Secondly, how do we explain the fact that a totally different method of letter-circulation is clearly indicated in Col. 4:16? Thirdly, if this seriatim labeling of blank spaces is what actually took place, how is it that there is no trace of copies in which 1:1 has any other name than that of Ephesus?

We shall have to admit that we do not know how and why the change from omission of "in Ephesus" to its insertion (or vice versa) occurred. Lenski, proceeding from the idea that the words "in Ephesus" were in the text from the very beginning, conjectures that Marcion may have tampered with the text of his day. However, this is not the only and perhaps not even the most charitable manner of solving the problem. Another suggestion — *again, a mere possibility!* — would be that *in full harmony with the expressed wishes of the apostle* and with thorough candor toward all concerned, the following took place:

The original letter, the autograph, left a blank, let us assume, after the words "who are." When this letter was read to any congregation assembled for worship, this blank was filled in *orally*, in each case in a manner suitable to the place where it was read. After the letter had been thus read to the church at Ephesus, it began its circular journey, arriving next at Laodicea. Here, before it was sent forward on its way to the next church,

Colosse (Col. 4:16?), a copy was made, enabling the members of the Laodicean church and also the brothers and sisters across the river (in Hierapolis) to be reminded again and again of the beauty of the inspired contents. This copy was true in every way to the *written* original, even to the point of retaining the blank space. This state of the letter is reflected in *the oldest extant manuscripts.* Finally, each church having made a copy, the autograph, having completed its circuit of the various congregations for which it was originally intended, was returned to Ephesus to rest in the archives of that church. However, by previous direction from Paul, the words "in Ephesus" were now inserted, for by now believers everywhere would understand that this place-designation had reference to *Greater* Ephesus, that is, to *Ephesus proper and the surrounding churches.* Just how far out this circle extended we do not know. Moreover, though the letter was now resting in the Ephesian archives, it was not unproductive. From this great center copies went out whenever they were needed. These copies contained the phrase "in Ephesus," exactly as reflected in nearly all *the later manuscripts.*

I repeat: all this is merely one of many possibilities. What actually happened may have been something entirely different. Nevertheless, the suggested possibility is not burdened with the three objections, mentioned earlier, to which the theory of the immediate seriatim labeling of blank spaces is exposed. Neither does it heap even more odium on the name of Marcion. As to doing this, did not Tertullian take care of it in an astoundingly thorough manner? (*Against Marcion* I.1).

3. *Conclusion*

The destination of the letter was "Ephesus," in the sense explained: the churches of Ephesus and surroundings. Place and time of writing: Rome, somewhere near the middle of the period A.D. 61–63. See N.T.C. on Colossians and Philemon, p. 28; on Philippians, pp. 21–30.

### B. *Purpose*

1. Paul wrote this letter in order to express his inner satisfaction with the Christ-centered faith of the addressed and their love for all the saints (1:15). The departure of Tychicus and Onesimus for Colosse (6:21, 22; cf. Col. 4:7-9) enabled the apostle to convey his warm greetings, etc., to the believers in Ephesus, through which city these emissaries would be passing. The same message must be communicated to the surrounding churches.

2. A closely related purpose was to picture God's glorious redemptive grace toward the church, bestowed upon it in order that it might be a blessing to the world and might stand united over against all the forces of evil and thus glorify its Redeemer.

In what Paul says about this glorious church he pushes every line of thought to its very limit. Thus he makes clear that neither good works nor even faith but the gracious plan of God "in Christ" from eternity, hence

*Christ himself,* is the church's true *foundation* (1:3 ff.). Christ controls nothing less than *the entire universe* in the interest of the church (1:20-22). *Both* Jew and Gentile are included in the *scope* of redemption (2:14, 18), in connection with which *all things* are brought under the headship of Christ, the things in the heavens and the things on the earth (1:10). The saving process does not stop when men are "converted." On the contrary, the believers' *goal* must be to attain to "the measure of the stature of the fulness of Christ" (4:13). In order to reach this goal *all* must manifest their *oneness* in Christ and must *grow up in all things* into him (4:1-16). Paul prays that believers may be enabled to know the love of Christ that surpasses knowledge, that they may be filled *to all the fulness* of God (3:19). The wisdom of God *in all its infinite variety* must be proclaimed by the church. Moreover, not only to the world must it be made known but also "to the principalities and the authorities in the heavenly places" (3:10). *Every* member of the household must make his *renewal* manifest (5:22–6:9). In the struggle against evil the church, acting as one body, must make effective use of *the entire panoply* provided by God (6:11 ff.).

It is not impossible that Paul's exuberant doxology at the beginning of this letter was due *in part* to the fact that he saw in the hearts and lives of the addressed, as reported to him, a partial but significant degree of progress in the realization of God's plan for his church. But this was not the only reason for joy and praise. See on 1:3.

3. It is possible that in writing this letter the apostle also intended to draw a contrast between the Roman empire, by which he was being held a prisoner, and the church. That this possibility cannot be entirely dismissed appears from another letter composed during this same imprisonment (Phil. 3:20). If so, then Rome's *glamor* may have suggested to him the church's *glory;* Rome's stern dictator who ruled over a vast yet limited domain, the church's gracious Lord, sovereign over all; its political consolidation by physical force, the church's organic unity in the bond of peace; its military might, the church's spiritual armor; and its foundation in time and "change and decay," the church's eternal foundation and endless duration.

## V. Theme and Outline

If it be true that in Colossians Paul dwells on "Christ, the Pre-eminent One, the Only and All-Sufficient Savior," then in Ephesians he discusses its corollary, namely, "The Unity of All Believers *in Christ.*" For "All Believers" one can substitute "The Church Glorious." The ideas of "unity" and of the "in Christ" relationship can be given their proper place in the Outline. Careful study of Ephesians has led an ever-increasing number of exegetes to arrive at the conclusion that the concept of *the church* receives such emphasis in this epistle that the entire contents can be grouped around it without superimposing one's own subjective opinions upon the apostle's thinking.[10]

The term *church,* as here used, indicates the *body* (Eph. 1:22, 23; 4:4, 16; 5:23, 30), *building* (2:19-22), and *bride* (5:25-27, 32) of Christ; the totality of those, whether Jew or Gentile, who were saved through the blood of Christ and through him have their access in one Spirit to the Father (2:13, 18).

As in Romans and Colossians so also here in Ephesians there is a rather clear-cut division between *Exposition* and *Exhortation,* between the truth *stated* and the truth *applied;* chapters 1–3 belonging to the first, chapters 4–6 to the second part. The style, especially of the first division, is, however, so exalted that *Adoration* more precisely expresses what is offered here than *Exposition.* The soul of the apostle is filled with humble gratitude to God, the Author of the Church Glorious. He pours out his heart in sincere, spontaneous, lavish praise. *With Paul doctrine is doxology!* It is a matter not only of the mind but also of the heart, of Christian experience under the guidance of inspiration.

After the opening salutation (1:1, 2) the body of the letter begins, in the original, with the word *E u l o g ē t ó s* (Blessed!). The apostle *eulogizes* (bestows high praise upon) God for his marvelous blessings to the church. To aid the memory an *acronym* can be made of the first six letters of this opening word, read downward: E This yields the following

U<br>L<br>O<br>G<br>E

Brief Summary of Ephesians

Theme: *The Church Glorious*

I. *Adoration*
*for its*

ch. 1 *E* ternal Foundation "in Christ"

After the salutation (verses 1, 2) the doxology begins as follows:

"Blessed (be) the God and Father of our Lord Jesus

[10] See W. E. Ward, "One Body — the Church," *RE,* Vol. 60, No. 4 (Fall, 1963), pp. 398–413; F. W. Beare, *The Epistle to the Ephesians* (*Interpreter's Bible,* Vol. X), New York and Nashville, 1953, pp. 606, 607; and L. Berkhof, *New Testament Introduction,* Grand Rapids, 1916, p. 189. The latter points out that while Colossians discusses Christ, the head of the church, Ephesians is concerned more emphatically with the church, the body of Christ.

Christ, who has blessed us with every spiritual blessing in the heavenly places in Christ, just as he elected us in him before the foundation of the world, that we should be holy and faultless before him" (1:4, 5).

ch. 2 *U* niversal Scope (embracing both Jew and Gentile)
"For through him we both have our access in one Spirit to the Father" (2:18).

ch. 3 *L* ofty Goal
"in order that now to the principalities and the authorities in the heavenly places might be made known through the church the iridescent wisdom of God . . . (and) to know the love of Christ that surpasses knowledge; in order that y o u may be filled to all the fulness of God" (3:10, 19).

II. *Exhortation*
*describing and urging:*

ch. 4:1-16 *O* rganic Unity (amid Diversity) and Growth into Christ
"I, therefore, the prisoner in the Lord, entreat y o u to . . . make every effort to preserve the unity imparted by the Spirit by means of the bond (consisting in) peace . . . so that we . . . adhering to the truth in love may grow up in all things into him who is the head, even Christ" (4:1, 3, 14, 15).

ch. 4:17–6:9 *G* lorious Renewal
". . . with respect to y o u r former manner of life y o u must put off the old man . . . and must be renewed in the spirit of y o u r minds, and put on the new man" (4:22-24).

ch. 6:10-24 *E* ffective Armor
"Put on the full armor of God in order that y o u may be able to stand firm against the crafty methods of the devil" (6:11). Conclusion (verses 21-24).

Below is a more extended

Outline of Ephesians

Theme: *The Church Glorious*

I. *Adoration*
*for its*

ch. 1 *E* ternal Foundation "in Christ"
After the opening salutation (verses 1 and 2) Paul "blesses" God for the fact that this is a foundation:

1. resulting in "every spiritual blessing" for believers, unto the praise of the glory of God the Father and the Son and the Holy Spirit (1:3-14); and
2. leading to thanksgiving and prayer, that the eyes of those addressed may be illumined in order to see God's saving power, exhibited in the resurrection and coronation of Christ (1:15-23).

ch. 2 *U* niversal Scope (embracing both Jew and Gentile),

1. secured by the great redemptive blessings *for both* which center "in Christ" and parallel his resurrection and triumphant life (2:1-10);
2. shown by the reconciliation of Jew and Gentile through the cross (2:11-18);
3. and by the fact that the church of Jew and Gentile is growing into *one* building, a holy sanctuary in the Lord, of which Christ Jesus is himself the chief cornerstone (2:19-22).

ch. 3 *L* ofty Goal

1. *To make known* to the principalities and the powers in the heavenly places *God's iridescent wisdom,* reflected in the mystery revealed especially, though not exclusively, to Paul, namely, that the Gentiles are . . . fellow-members of the body of Christ (3:1-13); and
2. *To know the love of Christ that surpasses knowledge* so as to be filled to all the fulness of God (3:14-19).
Doxology (3:20-21).

II. *Exhortation*
*describing and*
*urging upon all:*

ch. 4:1-16 *O* rganic Unity (amid Diversity) and Growth into Christ

*urging*

ch. 4:17–6:9 *G* lorious Renewal

1. *upon all* (4:17–5:21)
   a. "Put off the old man. Be renewed. Put on the new man."
   b. "Do not give the devil a foothold. Be imitators of God."
   c. "Y o u were formerly darkness, but now y o u are light in the Lord; as children of light ever walk."
   d. "Do not get drunk on wine, but be filled with the Spirit."

2. *upon special groups* (5:22–6:9)
   a. "Wives, be subject to y o u r own husbands. Husbands, love y o u r wives."
   b. "Children, obey y o u r parents. Fathers, rear them tenderly."
   c. "Slaves, obey y o u r masters. Masters, stop threatening."

*urging all to put on*
*the Church's God-given*

ch. 6:10-24 *E* ffective Armor. Conclusion
1. "Put on the full armor of God" (6:10-20);
2. Conclusion (6:21-24).

# Commentary
# on
# The Epistle to the Ephesians

# Chapter 1

Verses 1-14

Theme: *The Church Glorious*

I. *Adoration*
*for its*

*E* ternal Foundation "in Christ"

After the opening salutation (verses 1 and 2) Paul "blesses" God for the fact that this is a foundation:

1. resulting in "every spiritual blessing" for believers, unto the praise of the glory of God the Father and the Son and the Holy Spirit (verses 3-14)

# CHAPTER I

## EPHESIANS

1 1 Paul, an apostle of Christ Jesus through the will of God, to the saints
and believers who are in Ephesus in Christ Jesus; 2 grace to y o u and
peace from God our Father and the Lord Jesus Christ.
3 Blessed (be) the God and Father of our Lord Jesus Christ, who has
blessed us with every spiritual blessing in the heavenly places in Christ, 4 just as
he elected us in him before the foundation of the world, that we should be holy
and faultless before him, 5 having in love foreordained us to adoption as sons
through Jesus Christ for himself, according to the good pleasure of his will, 6 to
the praise of the glory of his grace, which he graciously bestowed on us in the Beloved, 7 in whom we have our redemption through his blood, the forgiveness of
our trespasses, according to the riches of his grace, 8 which he caused to overflow
toward us in the form of all wisdom and insight, 9 in that he made known to us
the mystery of his will, according to his good pleasure, the purpose which he cherished for himself in him, 10 to be put into effect in the fulness of the times, to
bring all things together under one head in Christ, the things in the heavens and
the things on the earth; in him 11 in whom we also have been made heirs, having been foreordained according to the purpose of him who accomplishes all things
according to the counsel of his will, 12 to the end that we should be to the praise
of his glory, we who beforehand had centered our hope in Christ; 13 in whom
y o u also (are included), having listened to the message of the truth, the gospel
of y o u r salvation; and having also believed in him, y o u were sealed with the
promised Holy Spirit, 14 who is the first instalment of our inheritance, for the redemption of (God's) own possession, to the praise of his glory.

---

### 1:1, 2

*Opening Salutation*

1. As is not unusual with Paul, the letter opens with a salutation and closes with a benediction. At the beginning God, as it were, walks into the church assembled for worship and breathes his blessing upon it. He remains throughout and at the close of the worship-service walks out again, not out *of* the church but out *with* the church. Yet, it is **Paul** himself who is speaking in this letter. And he is not playing back electrically recorded dictation. Ephesians is not a belt from a transcriber or a reel from a recorder. On the contrary, here is Paul in person, pouring out his heart in praise and thanksgiving. What he writes is in very fact the product of his own meditation and reflection. It is both a spontaneous utterance of *his* heart and a careful composition of *his* mind. The gold that pours forth from his heart has been

molded into definite and (one may even say) artistic shape by his mind. But this heart and this mind are so thoroughly Spirit-controlled that the *ideas* expressed and the very *words* by means of which they are conveyed are also (in a sense, were first of all) the ideas and the words of the Holy Spirit. Hence, the word of Paul is the Word of God. Ephesians, as well as the rest of Scripture, is God-breathed. Cf. II Peter 1:21; II Tim. 3:16; and on the latter passage see N.T.C. on I and II Timothy and Titus, pp. 301–304.

The author of this epistle was a man whose Hebrew name was Saul, and whose Latin name was Paul*us* (here, in the original, grecized to Paul*os*). He is not just any private individual who happens to have something on his mind to which he wants to give expression. No, he is, and wants the Ephesians to know that he is, **an apostle of Christ Jesus,** and this not in the broader sense merely but in the fullest meaning that can properly be given to the word *apostle*. Has he not received his call to office directly from Christ? Were not the marks of plenary apostleship abundantly evident in his life and work? He belongs to Christ, and represents him, so that *Paul's* message is *Christ's* own message. When Paul salutes the Ephesians, "God the Father and the Lord Jesus Christ" are bestowing *their* blessing upon them.

Paul continues, **through the will of God.** The apostle has attained his high office neither through *aspiration* nor through *usurpation* nor yet through *nomination* by other men but by divine *preparation,* having been set apart and qualified by the activity of God's sovereign will.

Having thus in some detail set forth the name of the addressor, Paul now turns to the addressees. He is writing **to the saints and believers who are in Ephesus in Christ Jesus.** The saints are those who by the Lord have been *set apart* to glorify him, *the consecrated ones,* whose task it is to proclaim God's excellencies (I Peter 2:9). The phrase "the saints and believers" forms a unit. The same people who are called *saints* are also called *believers,* for saints who are true to their calling do, indeed, repose their trust in the one true God who has revealed himself in Christ.[11]

The phrase "in Ephesus" has been fully discussed in the *Introduction,* IV A. Destination. Paul writes to God's people in Ephesus and surroundings. Those addressed are "in Christ Jesus," that is, they are what they are by virtue of union with him.[12] This phrase may without exaggeration be

---

[11] That the expression is a unit is shown also by the fact that in the original the definite article is not repeated before the second word. This non-repetition also indicates that it is correct to translate the second as well as the first of the two words as a noun, not an adjective; hence, *believers,* not *faithful.* The *believers* here in Eph. 1:1 are comparable to the *believing brothers* in Col. 1:2.

[12] The rendering "to the saints and believers in Christ Jesus" (instead of "to the saints and believers who are in Ephesus in Christ Jesus") makes it appear as if Christ Jesus were here conceived as the object of the implied verb *believe.* But this would be contrary to the usual meaning of the phrase "in Christ Jesus," and would

called the most important one in all the Pauline epistles. In Ephesians it or its equivalent ("in him," "in whom," "in the Beloved") or near-equivalent ("in the Lord") occurs in 1:1, 3, 4, 6, 7, 9-13, 15, 20; 2:5-7, 10, 13, 21, 22; 3:6, 11, 12, 21; 4:1, 21, 32; 5:8; and 6:10, 21. It also occurs with greater or lesser frequency in Paul's other epistles (exception Titus). It was *by virtue of union with Christ* that the addressees were saints and believers, for in connection with him they receive "every spiritual blessing" (1:3); here particularly and basically *election* before the foundation of the world (1:4-6), *redemption* through blood (1:7-12), and *certification* ("sealing") as sons and therefore heirs (1:13, 14). It will be clear that this interpretation of the phrase fits the present context. Had it not been for their connection with Christ, a connection infinitely close, these people would not now be saints and believers. Moreover, their present life of faith has its center in him. For them "to live is Christ" (Phil. 1:21). They now love him because he has first loved them.

2. The salutation proper is as follows: **grace to y o u and peace from God our Father and the Lord Jesus Christ.** Thus, there is pronounced upon the Ephesian saints and believers *grace.* This word may at times indicate *kindness, as a quality or attribute of God or of the Lord Jesus Christ.* It may also describe *the state of salvation,* and thirdly, the *believer's gratitude* for the salvation received or for any gift of God. But in the present instance it refers undoubtedly to *God's spontaneous, unmerited favor in action, his freely bestowed lovingkindness in operation, bestowing salvation upon guilt-laden sinners. Grace* is the fountain. *Peace* belongs to the stream of spiritual blessings which issues from this fountain. This peace is the smile of God as it reflects itself in the hearts of the redeemed, the assurance of reconciliation through the blood of the cross, true spiritual wholeness and prosperity. It is the great blessing which Christ by his atoning sacrifice bestowed upon the church (John 14:27), and it surpasses all understanding (Phil. 4:7).

Now this grace and this peace have their origin in God the Father (James 1:17), and have been merited for the believer by him who is the great Master-Owner-Conqueror ("Lord"), Savior ("Jesus"), and Office-Bearer ("Christ") and who, because of his threefold anointing – namely, as Prophet, Priest, and King – "is able to save to the uttermost them that draw near to God through him" (Heb. 7:25).[13]

For further details about certain aspects of Paul's opening salutations see N.T.C. on I and II Thessalonians, pp. 37–45; on Philippians, pp. 43–49; and on I and II Timothy and Titus, pp. 49–56; 339–344.

---

also destroy the unity of the pair "saints and believers," as if the words "in Christ Jesus" modified the second word only.

[13] The *one* preposition *from* introduces the entire expression "God our Father and the Lord Jesus Christ," showing that these two Persons are placed on the level of complete equality.

1:3-14

Proceeding now to the body of the letter, Paul "blesses" God for the church's *Eternal Foundation* "in Christ," a foundation:

1. *resulting "in every spiritual blessing" for believers, to the praise of the glory of God the Father and the Son and the Holy Spirit.*

3. **Blessed (be) the God and Father of our Lord Jesus Christ.** Goodness, truth, and beauty are combined in this initial doxology, in which the apostle, in words that are *beautiful* both in the thoughts they convey and in their artistic arrangement, pours out his soul in *true* adoration for God's *goodness* in action. He ascribes to God the honor due him for spiritual blessings *past* (election), *present* (redemption), and *future* (certification as sons with a view to complete possession of the inheritance reserved for them). The apostle realizes that divine blessings bestowed upon God's people should be humbly, gratefully, and enthusiastically acknowledged in thought, word, and deed. That response is the only proper way in which these spiritual bounties can be "returned" to the Giver. The circle must be completed: what comes from God must go back to him! That is the meaning of saying, "Blessed (be) . . . ."[14]

The sentence begun by "Blessed (be)" rolls on like a snowball tumbling down a hill, picking up volume as it descends. Its 202 words, and the many modifiers which they form, arranged like shingles on a roof or like steps on a stairway, are like prancing steeds pouring forward with impetuous speed. Says John Calvin, "The lofty terms in which he [Paul] extols the grace of God toward the Ephesians, are intended to rouse their hearts to gratitude, to set them all on flame, to fill them even to overflowing with this disposition." Paul's "heart aflame" is bent on setting other hearts aflame also, with sincere, humble, overflowing praise to "the God and Father of our Lord Jesus Christ." Cf. Rom. 15:6; II Cor. 1:3; 11:31. Since Jesus was and is not only God but also man, and since he himself addressed the first Person of the Trinity as "my God" (Matt. 27:46), it is evident that the full title "the *God* and Father of our Lord Jesus Christ" is justified. As to the term "Father," it is evident that if the title *"God* of our Lord Jesus Christ" places emphasis on Christ's *human* nature, that of *"Father* of our Lord Jesus Christ"

[14] On *blessedness* as applied to God see N.T.C. on I and II Timothy and Titus, pp. 71, 72 (including footnote 34). Although according to its form εὐλογητός is a verbal adjective properly meaning "worthy of praise," yet, according to later usage, there is nothing that prevents it from having the sense of a perfect participle. As to the copula, Lenski would leave it out entirely. He says, "Supply nothing, read the word as an exclamation." But even an exclamation of this type has an *implied* verb. Some favor the indicative ἐστίν (cf. Rom. 1:25 and LXX Ps. 118:12) and the rendering "Worthy of blessing is"; more usual is the translation "Blessed be" or "Praise be to," on the basis of the optative εἴη. Ultimately the difference is minimal, as even the expression "Worthy of blessing is" would imply, "Therefore, let him be blessed (or praised)."

calls attention to the Son's *divine* nature, for not *nativistic* but *trinitarian* sonship is referred to in this thoroughly trinitarian epistle, in which the Beloved, by whatever name he is called, is constantly placed on a par with, and mentioned in one breath with, the Father and the Spirit (2:18; 3:14-17; 4:4-6; 5:18-20). Christ is the Son of God by eternal generation. See also N.T.C. on the Gospel according to John, Vol. I, pp. 86–88. Now, calling the first person of the Holy Trinity "the Father of our Lord Jesus Christ" has a very practical purpose, as the apostle shows plainly in II Cor. 1:3. In his capacity as Father of our Lord Jesus Christ he is "the Father of mercies and God of all comfort." Via Christ every spiritual blessing flows down to us from the Father. And if Christ is "the Son of God's love" (Col. 1:13), then God must be the Father of love, the loving Father. Note also that beautiful word of appropriating faith, namely, *our:* "the Father of *our* Lord Jesus Christ." How close this draws Christ to the believers' hearts, and not only Christ but the Father also. Truly, Christ and the Father are *one!* On the title "Lord Jesus Christ" see verse 2 above.

Paul continues, **who has blessed us with every spiritual blessing in the heavenly places in Christ.** The Father blesses his children when he lavishes gifts upon them in his favor so that these bounties or these experiences, of whatever nature, work together for their good (Rom. 8:28). Together with the gift he imparts himself (Ps. 63:1; cf. Rom. 8:32). While it is *not* true that the Old Testament regards material goods as being of higher value than spiritual, for the contrary is clearly taught in such passages as Gen. 15:1; 17:7; Ps. 37:16; 73:25; Prov. 3:13, 14; 8:11, 17-19; 17:1; 19:1, 22; 28:6; Isa. 30:15; cf. Heb. 11:9, 10, it is true, nevertheless, that between the two Testaments there is a difference of degree in the fulness of detail with which earthly or physical blessings are described (Exod. 20:12; Deut. 28:1-8; Neh. 9:21-25). God is ever the wise Pedagogue who takes his children by the hand and knows that in the old dispensation, "when Israel is a child" it needs this circumstantial description of earthly values in order that by means of these as symbols (e.g., earthly Canaan is the symbol of the heavenly), it may rise to the appreciation of the spiritual (cf. I Cor. 15:46). The New Testament, while by no means deprecating earthly blessings (Matt. 6:11; I Tim. 4:3, 4), places all the emphasis on the spiritual (II Cor. 4:18), and it may well have been that in order to emphasize this difference between the old and the new dispensation it is here stated that the God and Father of our Lord Jesus Christ blessed us with every *spiritual* blessing. It is best to allow the context to indicate the nature and content of these blessings. Though, to be sure, the very word *every* clearly proves that it would be wrong to subtract even a single invisible bounty from the list of those "vast benefits divine which we in Christ possess," yet the context indicates that the apostle is thinking particularly of – or subsuming all these benefits under – those that are mentioned in the present paragraph, namely, *election* (and its accompaniment, foreordination to adoption), *redemption* (implying forgiveness and grace overflowing in the form of all wisdom and insight), and *certification* ("sealing") as sons and heirs.

The phrase "in the heavenly places" or simply "in the heavenlies" (used in a local sense also in 1:20; 2:6; 3:10, and probably also locally in 6:12) indicates that these spiritual blessings are heavenly in their origin, and that from heaven they descend to the saints and believers on earth (cf. 4:8; and see N.T.C. on Phil. 3:20 and on Col. 3:1).

For the meaning of "in Christ" see on verse 1 above. It or its equivalent occurs more than ten times in this short paragraph (1:3-14), clear evidence of the fact that the apostle regarded *Christ* as *the very foundation of the church,* that is, of all its benefits, of its complete salvation. It is in connection with Christ that the saints and believers at Ephesus (and everywhere else) have been blessed with every spiritual blessing: election, redemption, certification as children and heirs, and all the other benefits subsumed under these headings. Apart from him they not only *can do nothing* but *are nothing,* that is, amount to nothing spiritually.

4. Paul continues, **just as he elected us in him before the foundation of the world.**

### *Election*

#### (1) *Its Author*

The Author is "the God and Father of our Lord Jesus Christ," as has been indicated (see on verse 3). This, of course, by no means cancels the fact that all the activities which affect extra-trinitarian relationships can be ascribed to Father, Son, and Holy Spirit. Nevertheless, it is the Father who, as here shown, takes the lead in the divine work of election.

#### (2) *Its Nature*

*To elect* means *to pick* or *choose out of* (for oneself). Although the passage itself does not indicate *in so many words* the mass of objects or individuals out of which the Father chose some, this larger group is, nevertheless, clearly indicated by the purpose clause, "in order that we should be holy and faultless before him." Accordingly, the larger mass of individuals out of which the Father chose some are here viewed as *unholy and vile.* This interpretation suits the context. It supplies one of the reasons (see Synthesis at end of chapter for more reasons) why the soul of the apostle is filled with such rapture that he says, "Blessed (be) the God and Father of our Lord Jesus Christ, who . . . elected *us.*" He means: us, thoroughly unworthy in his sight! He does not try to explain how it was possible for God to do this. He fully realizes that when men are confronted with this manifestation of amazing grace their only proper response is *adoration,* not *explanation.*

### (3) *Its Object*

The object is "us," not everybody. This pronoun "us" must be explained in the light of its context. Paul is writing to "saints and believers" (verse 1). He says that the Father has blessed "us," that is, "all saints and believers" (here with special reference to those at Ephesus) including Paul (verse 3). Therefore, when the apostle now continues, "just as he elected *us,*" this "us" cannot suddenly have reference to *all men whatever,* but must necessarily refer to all those who are (or who at one time or another in the history of the world are destined to become) "saints and believers"; that is, to all those who, having been set apart by the Lord for the purpose of glorifying him, embrace him by means of a living faith.

It is for this contextual reason (and for others also) that I cannot agree with the contention of Karl Barth that in connection with Christ *all men whatever* are elect, and that the basic distinction is not between elect and non-elect but rather between those who are aware of their election and those who are not.[15]

### (4) *Its Foundation*

The foundation of the church, of its entire salvation from start to finish, hence surely also of its election, is Christ. Paul says, "He ("the God and Father of our Lord Jesus Christ") elected us *in him.*" The connection between verses 3 and 4 hinges on this phrase. One could bring this out in the translation as follows, "God the Father blessed us with every spiritual blessing in the heavenly places *in Christ, just as in him* he elected us. . . ." In other words, *in time* the Father *blessed* us in Christ, just as *from all eternity* he *elected* us in him. Though some maintain that this "just as" denotes no more than *correspondence,* in the sense that there is perfect agreement between the blessings and the election, for both are "in Christ," it may well be asked whether this interpretation exhausts the meaning of the word used in the original.[16] Aside from a point of grammar (for which see the footnote), it is the teaching of Paul that election from eternity and the further steps

---

[15] For the teaching of Karl Barth on this subject see his "Gottes Gnadenwahl," *Die Lehre Von Gott, Die Kirchliche Dogmatik,* II/2 (3e.Auflage, 1948). See also G. C. Berkouwer, *De Triomf der Genade in de Theologie van Karl Barth* (Kampen, 1954); C. Van Til, *The New Modernism: an appraisal of the theology of Barth and Brunner* (Philadelphia, 1946), and by the same author, *Has Karl Barth Become Orthodox?* (Philadelphia, 1954); F. H. Klooster, *The Significance of Barth's Theology: An Appraisal, With Special Reference to Election and Reconciliation* (Grand Rapids, 1961); and Edwin D. Roels, *God's Mission, The Epistle to the Ephesians in Mission Perspective,* doctoral dissertation presented to the Free University at Amsterdam (Franeker, 1962).

[16] In similar case καθώς, at the beginning of a clause, is used as a conjunction and in a sense not merely of comparison or correspondence but of cause (4:32; also Rom. 1:28; I Cor. 1:6; 5:7; Phil. 1:7).

in the order of salvation are not to be considered as so many separate items but rather as links in a golden chain, as Rom. 8:29, 30 makes abundantly clear. Election, then, is the root of all subsequent blessings. It is as Jesus said in his highpriestly prayer, ". . . that to all whom thou hast given him he might give everlasting life" (John 17:2). See also John 6:37, 39, 44; 10:29. Hence, since election is from eternity, and since it is the foundation of all further blessings, and since it is "in him," Christ is not only the *Foundation* of the church but its *Eternal Foundation.*

The question must now be answered, "How is it to be understood that it was *in Christ* that saints and believers were chosen?" The answer that is often given is this, that it was determined in the counsel of God that *in time* these people would come to believe in Christ. Though, to be sure, that, too, is implied, it is not a sufficient answer and fails to do justice to all that is taught by Paul and other inspired writers with respect to this important point. The basic answer must be that from before the foundation of the world Christ was the Representative and Surety of all those who in time would be gathered into the fold. This was necessary, for election is not an abrogation of divine attributes. It has already been established that in the background of God's decree is the dismal fact that those chosen are viewed as being, at the very outset, totally unworthy, having involved themselves in ruin and perdition. Now sin must be punished. The demands of God's holy law must be satisfied. The God and Father of our Lord Jesus Christ does not, by means of election, cancel his righteousness or abolish the demands of his law. How then is it ever possible for God to bestow such a great, glorious, and basic blessing as election upon "children of wrath," and to do so without detriment to his very essence and the inviolability of his holy law? The answer is that this is possible because of the promise of the Son (in full co-operation with the Father and the Spirit), "Lo, I come; in the roll of the book it is written of me; I delight to do thy will, O my God; thy law is within my heart" (Ps. 40:7, 8. Cf. Heb. 10:5-7; Gal. 4:4, 5; Phil. 2:6-8). "In Christ," then, saints and believers, though initially and by nature thoroughly unworthy, are righteous in the very sight of God, for Christ had promised that *in their stead* he would satisfy all the requirements of the law, a promise which was also completely fulfilled (Gal. 3:13). This forensic righteousness is basic to all the other spiritual blessings. Therefore,

"To thee, O Lord, alone is due
All glory and renown;
Aught to ourselves we dare not take,
Or rob thee of thy crown.
Thou wast thyself our Surety
In God's redemption plan;

In thee his grace was given us,
Long ere the world began."
(Augustus M. Toplady,
1774; revised by Dewey Westra, 1931)

(5) *Its Time*

This election is said to have occurred "before the foundation of the world," that is, "from eternity." Moreover, since it occurred "in him," this is altogether reasonable, for he is the One who and whose "precious blood as of a lamb without blemish and without spot" were *foreknown even before the foundation of the world* (I Peter 1:19, 20).[17] The fixity of God's eternal plan with respect to his chosen ones was not a Pauline invention. It was the teaching of Jesus himself. It was he who referred to those whom he loved as *the given ones* (see John 6:39; 17:2, 9, 11, 24; cf. 6:44). The fact that from all eternity he had promised to make atonement for them may well have been an element that entered into the Father's love for him; cf. the words of the highpriestly prayer, "Father, I desire that they also, whom thou hast given me be with me where I am, in order that they may gaze on my glory, which thou hast given me, for thou lovedst me before the foundation of the world" (John 17:24). In such and similar passages (see also Matt. 13:35; Heb. 4:3) the universe is viewed as a building, and its creation as the laying of the foundation of this building.

The point that should be emphasized in this connection is the fact that if already before the foundation of the world those destined for everlasting life were elected, then all the glory for their salvation belongs to God, and to him alone. Hence, "Blessed (be) the God and Father of our Lord Jesus Christ!" See 2:5, 8-10.

(6) *Its Purpose*

The purpose of election is found in the words, **that we should be holy and faultless before him.** It is worthy of special note that Paul does not say, "The Father elected us *because* he foresaw that we were going to be holy," etc. He says, *"that* [or: *in order that*] we should be holy," etc. Election is not conditioned on man's foreseen merits or even on his foreseen faith. It is salvation's root, not its fruit! Nevertheless, it remains true that man's responsibility and self-activity are not diminished even in the least. When the divine decree unto salvation is historically realized in the life of

---

[17] If, with A.V. (and very similarly Berkeley Version and Lenski) Rev. 13:8 be rendered "the Lamb slain from the foundation of the world," the doctrine of election from eternity "in him" would receive additional support. And is it so certain that A.R.V., R.S.V., N.A.S.B. (N.T.), N.E.B., etc., are correct in linking the modifier ("from the foundation of the world") to the words "written in the book of life" (after the analogy of Rev. 17:8)? The word-order of Rev. 13:8, in the original, would seem to support A.V., etc., here.

any individual it does not operate by means of external compulsion. It motivates, enables, actuates. It *im*pels but does not *com*pel. The best description is probably that which is found in *Canons of Dort* III and IV. 11, 12:

"Moreover, when God accomplishes this, his good pleasure, in the elect, or works in them true conversion, he not only provides that the gospel should be outwardly preached to them, and powerfully illuminates their minds by the Holy Spirit, that they may rightly understand and discern what are the things of the Spirit of God, but he also, by the efficacy of the same regenerating Spirit, pervades the innermost recess of man, opens the closed, softens the hardened, and circumcises the uncircumcised heart, infuses new qualities into the will, and makes that will which had been dead alive, which was evil good, which had been unwilling willing, which had been refractory pliable, and actuates and strengthens it, that, as a good tree, it may be able to bring forth the fruit of good works. . . . Whereupon the will, being now renewed, is not only actuated and moved by God, but being actuated by God, itself also becomes active. Wherefore man himself, by virtue of that grace received, is rightly said to believe and repent." See Phil. 2:12, 13 and II Thess. 2:13.

From the stated purpose it is evident that election does not carry man half-way only; it carries him all the way. It does not merely bring him to conversion; it brings him to perfection. It purposes to make him *holy* – that is, cleansed from all sin and separated entirely to God and to his service – and faultless – that is, without any blemish whatever (Phil. 2:15), like a perfect sacrifice. Nothing less than this becomes the conscious goal of those in whose hearts God has begun to work out his plan of eternal election. It is their goal in this present life (Lev. 19:2), and it attains ultimate realization in the hereafter (Matt. 6:10; Rev. 21:27).

The absolute and undiminished perfection of the ethical goal is given added emphasis by the phrase "before him," that is, before God in Christ. Not what we are in the estimation of men but what we are in the sight of God is what counts most.

(7) *Its Further Description*

**5.** A further definition of election, showing the form it takes, is found in the words, **having in love** [18] **foreordained us to adoption as sons.** This fore-

---

[18] With N.N., F. W. Grosheide, *De Brief Van Paulus Aan De Efeziërs* (*Commentaar op het Nieuwe Testament*), Kampen, 1960, p. 18, R.S.V. (text), Berkeley Version, and many others, I construe ἐν ἀγάπῃ with verse 5, not with verse 4. In favor of linking it with verse 4 – with Grk. N.T. (A-B-M-W) – it is claimed:

(1) that it is Paul's habit to place this phrase after the clause which it modifies (S. D. F. Salmond, *The Epistle to the Ephesians, The Expositor's Greek Testament,* Vol. 3, Grand Rapids, Mich., no date, p. 251); and

(2) that the rhythm of the sentence requires this (R. C. H. Lenski, *op. cit.,* p. 359).

ordination is not to be regarded as a divine activity prior to election. It is the latter's synonym, a further elucidation of its purpose. The Father is described as having *pre-horizoned* or *pre-encircled* his chosen ones. In his boundless *love,* motivated by nothing outside of himself, he set them apart to be his own sons. "As the hills are round about Jerusalem, so Jehovah is round about his people" (Ps. 125:2). He destined them to be members of his own family (cf. Rom. 8:15; Gal. 4:5). It is rather useless to look for human analogies, for the adoption of which Paul speaks surpasses anything that takes place on earth. It bestows upon its recipients not only a new name, a new legal standing, and a new family-relationship, but also a new image, the image of Christ (Rom. 8:29). Earthly parents may love an adopted child ever so much. Nevertheless, they are, to a large extent, unable to impart their spirit to the child. They have no control over hereditary factors. When God adopts, he imparts his Spirit! This adoption is **through Jesus Christ for himself.** It is through the work of Christ that this adoption becomes a reality. By his atonement the new standing and also the transformation into the spirit of sonship were merited for the chosen ones. Thus, they become God's children who glorify him.

The modifier **according to the good pleasure of his will** not only fits the immediate context ("for himself"), but also harmonizes excellently with the words "having *in love* foreordained us." When the Father chose a people for himself, deciding to adopt them as his own children, he was motivated by love alone. Hence, what he did was a result not of sheer determination but of supreme delight. A person may be fully determined to submit to a very serious operation. Again, he may be just as fully determined to plant a beautiful rose garden. Both are matters of the *will.* However, the latter alone is a matter of *delight,* that is, of his will's *good pleasure.* Thus, God, who does not afflict from the heart (Lam. 3:33), delights in the salvation of sinners (Is. 5:4; Ezek. 18:23; 33:11; Hos. 11:8; Matt. 23:37; cf. Luke 2:14; Rom. 10:1).

---

However, as to (1) it may be replied that the passages referred to (Eph. 4:2, 15, 16; 5:2; Col. 2:2; I Thess. 5:13) prove that it is Paul's habit to place this phrase *close to the clause which it modifies;* and as to (2), why rhythm would require the linking of this phrase with the preceding clause is not made clear.

In favor of viewing the phrase as a modifier of προορίσας the following may be mentioned:

(1) There would seem to be no good reason to link the phrase with the far removed ἐξελέξατο instead of with the nearby προορίσας. With ἁγίους καὶ ἀμώμους it is unnatural.

(2) The idea that God *in his love* would foreordain his people to *sonship* – a son being the object of the love of his Father – makes excellent sense.

(3) The fact that in man's redemption God (or Christ) was motivated by love is in harmony with other passages in this very epistle (2:4; 3:19; 5:2, 25).

(4) It is Pauline doctrine throughout (Rom. 5:8; 8:28, 35, 37; II Cor. 5:14; 13:11; Gal. 2:20; II Thess. 2:16; Titus 3:4).

**6.** This election, which was further described as a foreordination to adoption as sons, is **to the praise of the glory of his [the Father's] grace.** That is its *ultimate* purpose. The *immediate* (or intermediate) design has already been designated, namely, "that we should be holy and faultless before him," and along the same line, that we should receive "adoption as sons." The final goal, to which everything else is contributory, is the adoring recognition ("praise") of the manifested excellence ("glory") of the favor to the undeserving ("grace") of him who was called "the God and Father of our Lord Jesus Christ." (The concept *glory* has been treated rather fully in N.T.C. on Philippians, p. 62 footnote 43. For the meaning of *grace* see also on 1:2; 2:5, 8.)

It is clear that it is especially that marvelous *grace* to which the emphasis now shifts. It was the rapturous contemplation of that freely bestowed love to those viewed as lost in sin and ruin which moved the soul of the apostle to cry out, "Blessed (be) the God and Father of our Lord Jesus Christ." That exclamation, moreover, was genuine. Heathen also at times ascribe praise and honor to their gods, but in their case the motivation is entirely different. They do it to appease them or to extract some favor from them. Actually, therefore, such praise ends in man, not in the god to whom honor is ascribed. It resembles Cain's offering, which the Lord could not accept. Here in Ephesians, however, at the close of each paragraph (see verses 6, 12, 14) there is genuine adoration, such adoration as was not only God's intention in saving man, but also the thanksgiving offering presented to God by his servant Paul, whose heart is in harmony with the purpose of his Maker-Redeemer.

It is but natural that the grace of "the God and Father of *our Lord Jesus Christ*" should center in the Beloved. Hence, Paul continues, **which** [19] **he graciously bestowed on us in the Beloved.** One might translate as follows: "with which he has generously blessed us." But the rendering, as given in bold type above, to some extent preserves the wordplay of the original.[20] When the Father imparts a favor he does so with gladness of heart, without stint. Moreover, his gift reaches the very heart of the recipient and transforms it. It is, of course, as explained earlier, in connection with the Son that the Father so generously bestows his grace on us (see on verses 3 and 4 above). That Son is here called "the Beloved." Cf. Col. 1:13, "the Son of his love." Since Christ by means of his death earned every spiritual blessing for us, and therefore wants us to have these goods, and since the Father loves the Son, it stands to reason that, for the sake of this Beloved One, the Father would gladly grant us whatever we need. To this must be added the

---

[19] ἧς is attracted to the case of its antecedent *χάριτος*.

[20] Even more literal, but not as euphonious in English, would be, "grace by which he graced us." Cf. Luke 1:21. Both the sense and the wordplay are beautifully preserved in the Dutch translation: "genade, waarmede hij ons begenadigd heeft."

fact that the Father himself gave his Son for this very purpose. Hence, "He that spared not his own Son, but delivered him up for us all, how shall he not also together with him *graciously give* us all things?" (Rom. 8:32).

It is said at times that Christ is the Father's Beloved because he always obeyed the Father. This is true and scriptural (John 8:29). However, it is necessary in this connection to point out that it was especially the *quality* of this obedience that evoked the Father's love. The Son, knowing what is pleasing to the Father and in harmony with his will, does not wait until the Father orders him to do this or that, but willingly *offers himself.* He *volunteers* to do the Father's will. He is not passive even in his death, but *lays down* his life. "For this reason the Father loves me because I lay down my life in order that I may take it again. No one has taken it away from me; on the contrary, I lay it down of my own accord" (John 10:17, 18; cf. Is. 53:10). It is this marvelous *delight,* on the part of the Son, in doing the Father's will and thereby saving his people even at the cost of his own death, yes, death by means of a cross (Phil. 2:8), that causes the Father, again and again, to exclaim, "This is my beloved Son." In substance the Father already made this exclamation "before the world began." Even then he bestowed his infinite love upon his Son (John 17:24), moved, no doubt, among other things, by the latter's glorious resolution, "Lo, I come" (Ps. 40:7; cf. Heb. 10:7). To be sure, this is a very human way of speaking about these realities, but how else can we speak about them? The Father's exclamation was repeated in connection with the Son's baptism (Matt. 3:17), when in a visible manner the Son took upon himself the sin of the world (John 1:29, 33); and once more in connection with the transfiguration (Matt. 17:5; II Peter 1:17, 18), when again, and most strikingly, the Son voluntarily chose the way of the cross.[21]

**7.** In the second paragraph the attention is shifted from heaven to earth, from the past to the present, and, in a sense, from the Father to the Son. I say "in a sense," for the change is by no means abrupt. The infinitely close connection between the Father and the Son in the work of redemption is fully maintained. It is *the Father* who caused *his* grace to overflow toward us (verse 8), made known to us the mystery of *his* will according to *his* good pleasure (verse 9), etc. Nevertheless, the emphasis has changed from the work of the Father to that of the Son. It is *the Beloved,* that is, *the Son,* in whom we have our redemption. It is *he* who shed *his* blood for us (verse 7). It is *he* also in whom the Father's purpose of grace was concentrated (verse 9), under whose headship all things are brought together (verse 10), in connection with whom we have been made heirs (verse 11), and in whom we centered our hope (verse 12). Accordingly, Paul continues: (the Beloved) **in whom we have our redemption.** *Redemption* here, as in Col. 1:14 (cf. also

[21] The subject of *election* has also been treated in N.T.C. on I and II Thessalonians, pp. 48–50.

Exod. 21:30; Matt. 20:28; Mark 10:45; Rom. 3:24; Heb. 9:12, 15), indicates *deliverance as a result of the payment of a ransom.*[22] There was no other way for sinners to be saved. God's justice must be satisfied. Anyone who doubts the necessary, objective, voluntary, expiatory, substitutionary, and efficacious character of the act of the Father's Beloved whereby he offered himself for his people should make a diligent study of the passages mentioned in N.T.C. on I and II Timothy and Titus, p. 376.

This redemption implies: *a. emancipation* from the curse, that is, from the guilt, punishment, and power of sin (John 8:34; Rom. 7:14; I Cor. 7:23; Gal. 3:13), and *b. restoration* to true liberty (John 8:36; Gal. 5:1). It was, moreover, a redemption **through his blood,** a redemption, therefore, which implied *substitution* of the life of One for the life of others. Thus, thus *only,* atonement could be made (Lev. 17:11; Heb. 9:22). Moreover, the blood through which alone redemption could be accomplished was *his* blood, that of the perfect Redeemer. The blood of animals was merely symbolical and typical (Ps. 40:6-8; Heb. 9:11-14; 10:1-14). Yet, when mention is made of redemption through his *blood,* this blood must never be dissociated from the voluntary sacrifice of the entire *life,* the *self* (Lev. 17:11; Isa. 53:10-12; Matt. 26:28; cf. 20:28; I Tim. 2:6). Expressions such as, "He gave his blood," "He gave his soul," and "He gave himself," are synonymous. They all indicate that the Redeemer was made (and made himself) an offering for sin (Isa. 53:10; II Cor. 5:21); that he suffered the eternal punishment due to sin; that he did this vicariously, and that he did all this for those who by nature were "children of wrath" (Eph. 2:3). What enhances the glory of this sacrifice even more is the fact that although the Beloved came into the world to do many things, for example, to still the boisterous waves, cast out demons, cleanse lepers, open the eyes of the blind, unstop the ears of the deaf, feed the hungry, heal the sick, and even raise the dead, yet the overarching purpose of his coming was to seek and to save the lost, to give himself a ransom for many (Isa. 53:12; Matt. 20:28; Mark 10:45; Luke 19:10; I Tim. 1:15). Truly, "Jesus from his throne on high came into this world *to die.*" No wonder that Paul cries out, "Blessed (be)," that Peter urges upon those committed to his charge the thankful response of a holy life, adding "knowing that y o u were redeemed not with corruptible things, with silver or gold . . . but with precious blood, as of a lamb without blemish and without spot, (even the blood) of Christ" (I Peter 1:15-19), that "angels desire to look into the sufferings of Christ and the glories that were to follow them" (I Peter 1:10-12), that, with their minds and hearts fixed on the infinite greatness of this sacrifice, the four living creatures and

[22] The more general connotation that adheres to the word in Luke 21:28; Rom. 8:23; I Cor. 1:30; Eph. 1:14; 4:30; Heb. 11:35, passages in which the idea of the payment of a ransom is dropped, and only that of deliverance, release, etc., is retained, does not change this fact.

the twenty-four elders in their new song are forever exclaiming, "Worthy art thou . . . for thou wast slain, and didst purchase with thy blood men of every tribe and tongue and people and nation" (Rev. 5:9), and that the ten thousand times ten thousand and thousands of thousands of angels join in with this grand jubilation by lifting up their voices in exuberant adoration, shouting, "Worthy is the Lamb who has been slain!" (Rev. 5:12).

Now the purpose of this redemption was "that we might from sin be free." It was with that objective in mind and heart that he "bled and died upon the tree." Hence, Paul says, "the Beloved, in whom we have our redemption through his blood," **the forgiveness of our trespasses.** These two – *a.* redemption by blood and *b.* forgiveness of trespasses – go together. Redemption would not be complete without procuring pardon. Even Israel in the old dispensation understood this. On the day of atonement the *blood* of one goat *was sprinkled* on the mercy-seat. The other goat, over whose head the people's *sins* had been confessed, *was sent away,* never to return. Now here in Eph. 1:7 this idea of *complete removal of sin* constitutes the very meaning of the word, used in the original, rendered *forgiveness* (or *remission*). Other passages that shed light on the meaning are Ps. 103:12 ("As far as the east is from the west, so far has he removed our transgressions from us"), Isa. 44:22 ("I have blotted out, as a thick cloud, your transgressions, and as a cloud your sins: return to me, for I have redeemed you"), Jer. 31:34 (". . . and their sin I will remember no more"), Mic. 7:19 ("Thou wilt cast all their sins into the depths of the sea"), and I John 1:9 ("If we confess our sins, he is faithful and righteous to forgive us our sins, and to cleanse us from all unrighteousness").

As to its derivation, the word rendered *trespass* means *a falling to the side of.* A trespass, then, is *a deviation from the path of truth and righteousness.*[23] Such deviations may be either of a gross or of a less serious nature. That in Ephesians no deviation is excluded, and that the totality of these deviations is regarded as a serious matter, one that is rooted in the very nature of man as corrupted by the fall, is clear from 2:1, "And y o u (he made alive) when y o u were *dead* through y o u r trespasses and sins" (cf. 2:3, 5). With reference to *forgiveness* see also N.T.C. on Colossians, pp. 118–120.

Now forgiveness takes place **according to the riches of his [the Father's] grace.** Forgiveness and grace are in complete harmony. The standard established by God's grace determines the measure of his forgiveness. For the meaning of *grace* see on 1:2 above; cf. also 1:6; 2:5, 7, 8. Note that the Father forgives not merely *of,* but *according to,* his riches, riches of grace. Illustration: Here are two very rich persons. When asked to contribute toward a good cause, both give *of* their riches. The first one, however, donates a

[23] See R. C. Trench, *Synonyms of the New Testament,* par. lxvi. He points out that although the milder meaning (fault, error, mistake) attaches to the word at times (see Rom. 5:15, 17, 18; Gal. 6:1), this is by no means always the case.

very paltry sum, far less than had been expected of him. He merely gives *of* his riches, not *according to*. The second is lavish in his support of every noble cause. He gives *according to* the amount of his wealth. God ever gives and forgives *according to* his riches. And *he* is rich, indeed! His favor toward the undeserving is infinite in character. 8. The apostle continues, **which**[24] **he caused to overflow**[25] **toward us in the form of all wisdom and insight.** In a similar passage (I Tim. 1:14) the apostle states, "And it *superabounded,* namely, the grace of our Lord, with faith and love in Christ Jesus." Just as in that passage grace is said to have kindled *faith* and *love,* so here grace floods the souls of believers with *wisdom* and *insight. Wisdom* is *knowledge plus.* It is the ability to apply knowledge to the best advantage, enabling a person to use the most effective means for the attainment of the highest goal. *Insight* (cf. Col. 1:9, *understanding*) is the result of *setting one's mind on* God's redemptive revelation in Christ, the mystery of his will, for Paul continues: **9. . . . in that he made known to us the mystery of his will.** God had made it known to Paul (3:3), who, in turn, rejoices in being able to proclaim it to others. In addition, grace sanctifies this knowledge to the hearts of those destined to be saved. Paul says, "He made it known to *us*" (cf. "toward us" in verse 8), that is, to myself and to those whom I am addressing (see verse 1).

He caused his grace to overflow . . . in that *he made known* to us the mystery of his will! He did not keep it to himself. The Father did not desire that the saints and believers in Ephesus (and everywhere else) should be like the people in the city of Samaria, described in II Kings 7:3-15, who were unaware of their riches. The greatest story ever told, that of God's grace in Christ, *must be made known.* In that respect, too, the true gospel of salvation differs from "other gospels" invented by men. In the days of Paul certain cults imposed on their devotees "tremendous oaths" *not* to reveal their secrets to the uninitiated. Even today there are societies which demand that their members make similar solemn promises on pain of dire punishment if they fail to keep them. It was the Father's will that the most sublime secret be broadcast far and wide, and that it penetrate deeply into the hearts of those who were his own. God's plan of salvation, moreover, must be made known in order that it may be accepted by faith, for it is by faith that men are saved.

Exactly what did Paul mean when he mentioned "the mystery"? Here in Ephesians the answer is not given until we reach verse 10, and even then it is merely *introduced.* Even so, however, we are told that the mystery of

---

[24] ἧς attracted to the case of its antecedent, as in verse 6 above.

[25] The verb περισσεύω is used in various senses: such as, to be left over (John 6:12), surpass (Matt. 5:20; II Cor. 8:2), grow or abound (Phil. 1:9), have more than enough (Phil. 4:18), excel (I Cor. 15:58). For the meaning *to cause to overflow,* as here in Eph. 1:8, see also I Thess. 3:12.

which the apostle is thinking is that of God's *will,* that is, of the Father's *desire.* The mystery and the Father's *desire, good pleasure, cherished purpose,* go together. They cannot be separated, for the mystery is that *of* his eternal purpose. Its disclosure, too, was **according to his good pleasure.** Cf. verse 5 above, where *foreordination* is also ascribed to the Father's good pleasure. We learn from this that the Father, far from being less loving than the Son, *takes special delight* in planning whatever must be planned in order to bring about the salvation, full and free, of men who had plunged themselves into misery and ruin, and takes equal pleasure in telling them about this marvelous plan! Is it any wonder that Paul's heart was filled with adoration so that he exclaimed, "Blessed (be) the God and Father of our Lord Jesus Christ"?

The apostle further defines this *good pleasure* by adding: **the purpose which he cherished for himself in him.**[26] This "in him" must mean "in the Beloved," as the preceding context indicates. The Father "has blessed us with every spiritual blessing . . . *in Christ*" (1:3), "elected us *in him*" (verse 4), and "graciously bestowed his grace upon us *in the Beloved*" (verse 6). It is natural, therefore, that we should now be referred to the purpose which he cherished for himself "in him." In what sense this purpose of the Father was cherished *in* the Beloved has been explained above (see on verse 4).

**10.** The Father's good pleasure, his cherished purpose, the plan in which his soul delighted, a plan drawn up *in eternity,* was to be realized *in time.* Hence, Paul continues: **to be put into effect in the fulness of the times.** Literally, "for administration [or: for effectuation]," etc.[27] The expression "fulness of the times" (or: seasons) and the similar (though not exactly identical) one in Gal. 4:4 indicate *the moment* (Gal. 4:4) or *the period* (Eph. 1:10) when, as it were, the lower compartment of the hourglass of God's eternal decree had become filled, that is, when all the preceding times and seasons which the Father had set within his own authority had been completed (Acts 1:7; cf. 17:26). It is, in other words, "the appropriate time." As is evident from 1:20-23, in the present case the reference is to the entire New Testament era, particularly to the period which began with Christ's resurrection and coronation. It will not end until the Lord, upon his glori-

---

[26] Literally, the original reads: "(his good pleasure) which he purposed for himself in him." But since such a rendering is hardly idiomatic and fluent English, for we do not generally speak about "purposing a good pleasure," and since the shade of meaning in the word *good pleasure,* when its underlying idea is continued in the relative clause "which, etc.," shifts somewhat, so that it no longer refers exclusively to a divine disposition but also to the plan in which this disposition is expressed, I translated as I did. My rendering is somewhat similar to that proposed by R. F. Weymouth, *The New Testament in Modern Speech,* though I do not agree with his translation of this clause in its entirety. He offers: "the purpose which he has cherished in his own mind."

[27] The word οἰκονομία has been explained in Introduction, III A 2 b, p. 44.

ous return, will have pronounced and executed judgment (I Cor. 15:24, 25). It is well, in this connection, to stress what was said before, namely, that *mystery* and *purpose* go together: *the effectuation of the purpose is the revelation of the mystery,* for it was exactly the Father's purpose of love to reveal that which to men was a mystery. This effectuation and revelation was destined to take place, therefore, in the present Messianic age.

The purpose actualized in the fulness of the times, the mystery *then* revealed, is expressed in these words: **to bring all things together under one head in Christ,**[28] **the things in the heavens and the things on the earth.** What Paul is saying here receives amplification in verses 20-22. Therefore it is not necessary to enlarge upon it here. It is the identical doctrine expounded also in other letters that belong to this same imprisonment; see especially Col. 1:20 and Phil. 2:9-11, and the N.T.C. on these passages. As to the *mystery* which the apostle here introduces, but on which he later on expatiates in far greater detail (2:11-22, though in that paragraph the word *mystery* is not used; 3:1-13, note especially verse 4; 6:19), suffice it at this point to say that this mystery centers in Christ, and that one element in it is that which is expressed here, namely, that literally *everything,* things in heaven, things on earth, everything above us, around us, within us, below us, everything spiritual and everything material, has even now been brought under Christ's rule. This is, indeed, *a mystery,* for no one would ever have

[28] There is a great variety of opinion in connection with the rendering of *ἀνακεφαλαιώσασθαι*. On the one hand there are those who insist that since the cognate *noun* *κεφάλαιον* never means *head* but *sum* ("For a large sum of money I acquired this citizenship," Acts 22:28) or *summary, main point* ("Now the main point in what we are saying is this," Heb. 8:1); and since similarly, in its only other New Testament occurrence, the *verb* means *to sum up* ("For this, You must not commit adultery . . . and any other commandment, is summed up in this word, You must love your neighbor as yourself," Rom. 13:9), hence the only proper translation of the words of Paul here in Eph. 1:10 is *"to sum up* all things in Christ." Others, however, are of the opinion — I believe correctly — that this A.R.V. rendering is somewhat obscure, for just what does "summing up in Christ" really mean? Accordingly, they suggest various alternative renderings. A rather popular one centers about the concept of *bringing about unity* (cf. Col. 1:20). Hence, already A.V. translated, "that he might gather together in one all things in Christ." Similarly, R.S.V. offers, "to unite all things in him"; N.E.B., "that the universe might be brought into a unity in Christ"; and L.N.T. (A. and G.), "to bring everything together in Christ." This type of translation, provided that it be not interpreted to mean that in the end everybody will be saved, is undoubtedly on the right track. Is it possible, however, to be still more definite? Does the word used in 1:10 at all indicate what kind of bringing together Paul has in mind? A. T. Robertson (*Word Pictures in the New Testament,* Vol. IV, pp. 518, 519) points out that *κεφάλαιον* is derived from *κεφαλή*. Accordingly, he translates "to head up all things in Christ." F. F. Bruce (*The Letters of Paul, An Expanded Paraphrase,* pp. 267, 268) gives the sense of the passage in these words, "that all things in heaven and earth alike should find their one true head in Christ." As this is exactly what the apostle teaches in this very chapter (1:10-22; cf. also 4:10), it is difficult to believe that he can have meant anything else here in 1:10. This explains my rendering, "to bring all things together under one head in Christ."

guessed it, had it not been revealed. "Now we do not yet see all things subjected to him" (Heb. 2:8). It takes nothing less than *faith* – and not a very weak faith either – to "see Jesus crowned with glory and honor" (Heb. 2:9), actually ruling the entire universe from his heavenly abode. It is as Dr. Herman Bavinck has so aptly expressed it, "Round about us we observe so many facts which seem to be unreasonable, so much undeserved suffering, so many unaccountable calamities, such an uneven and inexplicable distribution of destiny, and such an enormous contrast between the extremes of joy and sorrow, that anyone reflecting on these things is forced to choose between viewing this universe as if it were governed by the blind will of an unbenign deity, as is done by pessimism, or, upon the basis of Scripture and by faith, to rest in the absolute and sovereign, yet – however incomprehensible – wise and holy will of him who will one day cause the full light of heaven to dawn upon these mysteries of life" (*The Doctrine of God,* my translation from the Dutch; Grand Rapids, Mich., second printing, 1955).

This bringing together of all things under one head in Christ, so that things are not allowed to drift by themselves but our Lord is fully in charge, is taught by many passages in Scripture. In heaven the exalted Mediator lives and reigns (Rev. 20:4), receiving the adoration of all the redeemed and of all the angelic hosts (Rev. 5). But the thoughts of this great Uniter are turned earthward also, so much so, in fact, that he not only *intercedes* for his people who are still engaged in struggle and turmoil (Rom. 8:34), but even *lives to make intercession* for them (Heb. 7:25), and is already preparing places for them (John 14:2). He imparts gifts to men (Eph. 4:8), performs acts of healing (Acts 3:6, 16), and through his Spirit dwells in the midst of "the seven light-bearers" (Rev. 1:13). This indwelling is very active and produces fruits of sanctification in the lives of believers (Eph. 3:17-19). At the same time Christ wages war victoriously against the dragon (Satan) and his allies (Rev. 17:14), and, in general, governs the entire universe in the interest of his church (Eph. 1:22).

That Christ's interest in this church is deep, indeed, is shown also in the statement which follows, namely, **in him 11. in whom we** – **I,** Paul, and y o u, the addressed – **also have been made heirs.** Note the word "also," meaning: *not only* did we, in vital union with Christ, receive such blessings as redemption, forgiveness of sin, and spiritual illumination (wisdom, insight), favors which have already been mentioned (verses 7-10 above), but, in addition to these initial favors, which, though they have *abiding* significance, focus the attention upon *the past* (deliverance from that terrible power by which we *were* bound, pardon of *past* sins, banishment of *former* darkness), the right to *future* glory was bestowed upon us. "We were made heirs,"[29] says Paul. Heirs are those who, apart from any merit of theirs,

---

[29] The verb used in the original should be interpreted as a true passive, in harmony with such passives as "having been foreordained" (verse 11) and "were sealed"

were given the right to all the blessings of salvation in Jesus Christ, nevermore to lose them. The inheritance is given to them in two stages: certain blessings are bestowed upon them in the here and now, others in the hereafter (see on verses 13 and 14 below).

The objection might occur, "But will all the blessings of salvation – *future* as well as present – really be ours? Does God's plan for our lives also *secure* the future?" The apostle answers this by continuing: **having been foreordained according to the purpose of him who accomplishes all things according to the counsel of his will.**[30] Neither fate nor human merit determines our destiny. The benevolent purpose – that we should be holy and faultless (verse 4), sons of God (verse 5), destined to glorify him forever (verse 6, cf. verses 12 and 14) – is fixed, being part of a larger, universe-embracing plan. Not only did God *make* this plan that includes absolutely all things that ever take place in heaven, on earth, and in hell; past, present, *and even the future,* pertaining to both believers and unbelievers, to angels and devils, to physical as well as spiritual energies and units of existence both large and small; he also *wholly carries it out.* His providence in time is as comprehensive as is his decree from eternity. Literally Paul states that God *works* (*operates with his divine energy in*) all things. The same word occurs also in verses 19 and 20, which refer to the *working* (*energetic operation*) of the infinite might of the Father of glory, which he *wrought* (*energetically exerted*) in Christ when he raised him from the dead. Hence, nothing can upset the elect's future glory.

Moreover, although everything is included in God's universe-embracing

---

(verse 13). Moreover, the rendering "we were made a heritage" (A.R.V., and similarly, Barry, Berkeley Version, Greijdanus, Salmond, Van Leeuwen), though also passive, loses sight of the following facts:

*a.* the immediate context speaks of "*our* inheritance" (verse 14a). Though it is true that believers are regarded as God's own *possession* (verse 14b) yet *heirship* is not ascribed to God but to them.

*b.* In the New Testament *the inheritance* is ever said to be *ours* or *intended for us* (Acts 20:32; Gal. 3:18; Col. 3:24; Heb. 9:15; I Peter 1:4). Even Eph. 1:18 is no exception to this rule. See on that passage.

*c.* Eph. 1:5 informs us that the Father "in love foreordained us to adoption as sons." Now this very idea of being sons by adoption is elsewhere by Paul brought into immediate connection with the thought that *we* are therefore heirs (Rom. 8:15-16).

*d.* The parallel, Col. 1:12, also supports the idea that believers are the heirs: "with joy giving thanks to the Father who qualified y o u for a share in the inheritance of the saints in the light."

N.E.B. offers a translation which is essentially correct: "In Christ indeed we have been given our share in the heritage."

[30] It is not easy to distinguish between *will, counsel,* and *purpose.* Yet, Paul seems to have had a distinction in mind. Probably it is the best to regard God's *will* (θέλημα) as basic here. It is his sovereign volition. The βουλή would then be the *plan* or *counsel* that is viewed here as belonging to, springing forth from, his θέλημα. It would seem to indicate that God never acts arbitrarily, but with deliberation. Finally, God's πρόθεσις indicates the *purpose* of this plan, or, perhaps, *the plan itself* from the point of view of what it *aims* to accomplish; God's *design.*

plan and in its effectuation in the course of history, there is nothing in this thought that should scare any of the children of God. Quite the contrary, for the words clearly imply that the only true God, who in Christ loves his own with a love that passes all understanding, acts with divine deliberation and wisdom. All his designs are holy, and he delights to reward those who trust in him. Human responsibility and the self-activity of faith are never violated in any way. There is plenty of room for them in the decree and in its effectuation. Scripture is very clear on this (Luke 22:22; Acts 2:23; Phil. 2:12, 13; II Thess. 2:13).

Besides, God is not like the heathen deities who are moved by changing circumstances, by whim and caprice, so that one never knows how long their favor is going to last. He who in his love has foreordained his people to adoption as sons will never forsake them, but will finish that which he began in them (Phil. 1:6). He will carry out his plan to the very finish. Nothing will ever be able to frustrate his design. "Nor sin, nor death, nor hell can move his firm predestinating love."

**12.** If, then, God's decree from eternity is thus all-embracing, and if it is fully carried out in history, and if the destiny of his children was included in this plan, then Paul and the readers have no reason whatever for boasting in themselves. Whatever they *are* or *have* or *do* is from God. Hence, in language similar to that employed in verse 6 above, Paul concludes this section by saying: **to the end that we should be to the praise of his glory, we who beforehand had centered our hope in Christ.** *Before* the inheritance has been *fully* received – for only the first instalment has been received here and now (see verses 13, 14) – Paul and those addressed (see verse 1) have already centered their hope in Christ. That hope will not be crushed. "And the ransomed of Jehovah will return, and come with singing to Zion; and everlasting joy will be on their heads: they will obtain gladness and joy, and sorrow and sighing will flee away." (For contrasting interpretations of "we" in verse 12 and "y o u" in verse 13, see on verse 13.)

**13.** As the center of interest shifts once more, this time from the Son ("Christ," mentioned at the close of verse 12) to the Holy Spirit, here again instead of an abrupt change there is a gradual transition (cf. the beginning of verse 7, with its stair-step transition from the Father to the Son). Paul writes, **in whom y o u [31] also (are included), having listened to the message**

---

[31] On the basis of the words *"we,* those having previously hoped in Christ" (verse 12) as contrasted with *"y o u . . .* having also believed in him" (verse 13), many have endorsed the position that two ethnic groups are indicated here; namely, in verse 12 Jewish Christians; in verse 13 believers from the Gentiles.

Objections:

(1) This is a very unnatural interpretation, for in the preceding verses "we" and "us" always refer to Paul and all those addressed (see verses 11, 9, 8, 7, 6, 5, 4, 3). By far the most of those addressed were believers from the Gentiles, not from the Jews. Why, then, the sudden change of meaning in verse 12?

**of the truth, the gospel of y o u r salvation.**[32] The Ephesians must not doubt their inclusion in Christ and all his benefits. They have heard, have listened attentively to, the message of the truth. Did not Luke report, "All those who lived in Asia heard the word of the Lord, both Jews and Greeks"? (Acts 19:10). Such *hearing* was necessary in order that by faith they might be saved. The answer to be given to those who say that men who can properly be considered objects (or potential objects) of missionary activity are able to be saved without hearing the gospel is, "And how will they believe in him whom they did not hear?" (Rom. 10:14; cf. Matt. 1:21; John 14:6; Acts 4:12). Of course, it makes a difference *how* men hear. Some hear and become gospel-hardened. As men may become deaf because of a constant pounding noise, so also hearers of the gospel may become completely immune to the preaching of the truth. ("And I heard him a bumming away like a buzzard clock over my head.") Moreover, to some the proclamation of the gospel is like a love-song sung beautifully and played well (Ezek. 33:32). They hear but do not take to heart (Mark 4:24; Luke 8:18). Christ told his audiences to take care *how* they heard. By means of unforgettable parables he emphasized this lesson (Matt. 7:24-27; 13:1-9, 18-23).

Christ, however, also stressed that men should give heed *what* they heard. The Ephesians had listened attentively to "the message of the truth." There were many errors abroad in those days, many false gospels (Col. 1:23; 2:4, 8; cf. Gal. 1:6-9). The Ephesians, by and large, had ignored or rejected them. They wanted to hear only the very best. It is called the message of *the truth* because it reveals man's true condition, proclaims and advocates the only true way of escape, and admonishes saved sinners to show true gratitude in

---

(2) The perfect participle προηλπικότας from προελπίζω, in the New Testament occurring only here, does not necessarily mean *having hoped before others did* or *having hoped before Christ arrived.* It may equally well mean *having hoped before having fully attained.* With "we had previously hoped" compare "y o u have previously heard" (Col. 1:5). In the latter passage, too, no contrast is implied between two groups of believers of different national origin.

(3) Finally, if such a contrast in origin must be maintained here in 1:12, 13, it would almost seem as if the apostle were writing, "We Jewish Christians, we alone, are destined for the praise of his glory," and "Y o u believers from the Gentiles, y o u alone, were sealed with the promised Spirit." The apostle obviously would never have taught this.

The only element of value I can see in the theory which I reject is this, that when Paul, who in verses 3-12 has been referring constantly to himself and the addressed as one group ("we," "us"), now in verse 13 (and see also 1:15-18; 2:1, 2, 8) begins to substitute the second person plural for the first person plural — meaning, however, *y o u as well as all believers* —, he is gradually preparing the hearers for the clear-cut distinction between Gentile Christians and Jewish Christians which begins at 2:11.

[32] This clear and positive statement, showing that the addressed had indeed heard the true gospel, sheds light on the proper explanation of 3:2; 4:21, passages which have often been enlisted in defense of the theory that this letter could not have been addressed to the Ephesians and/or that Paul could not have written it. See on these passages.

their whole lives. It is, accordingly, "the gospel of y o u r salvation," not in the sense that in and by itself it saves anyone, but thus that, when accepted by true faith in Christ, its good tidings of great joy become "the power of God for salvation" (Rom. 1:16). This true faith the Ephesians had shown, for Paul continues: **and having also believed in him. . . .** They had surrendered their lives to their Lord, had reposed their trust in him. The better they knew him, the more they had trusted him. The more they had trusted him, the better they had learned to know him. Hence, Paul says: **y o u were sealed with the promised Holy Spirit.** A seal – not stamped on but attached to an object in ancient times – was used *a. to guarantee* the *genuine character* of a document, etc. (Esther 3:12), or, figuratively, of a person (I Cor. 9:2); *b. to mark ownership* (Song of Sol. 8:6); and/or *c. to protect against tampering or harm* (Matt. 27:66; Rev. 5:1). The context (see verse 14) would seem to indicate that the first of these three ideas, that of authentication or certification, is basic in the present passage. The Spirit had testified within their hearts that they were children of God (Rom. 8:16; I John 3:24), and "if children, then heirs, heirs of God, and joint-heirs with Christ" (Rom. 8:17), people whom nothing can harm, and to whom "all things work together for good" (Rom. 8:28). It is immediately apparent that in such matters the three aforementioned purposes for which a seal is used combine: *authentication* implies *ownership* and *protection.* In this connection see also N.T.C. on I and II Timothy and Titus, pp. 266–270.

When the very practical question is asked, "How did the Ephesians – or how does anyone – get that seal, that inner assurance?" the answer is: not merely or mainly as the result of agonizing self-searching to see whether all the "marks" of having been elected are present, but rather by a *living* faith in the triune God, as revealed in Christ, a faith "working through love" (Gal. 5:6). That those addressed had indeed received it in no other way is a fact to which the apostle immediately calls attention (Eph. 1:15).

The Spirit who had given them this seal is here called by his full name, "the Holy Spirit," to indicate not only that he is holy in himself but also that he is the source of holiness for believers, a holiness which in the case of the addressed was expressed not only by their inner disposition but also by their loving words and deeds. Moreover, this third person of the Trinity is here called "the Holy Spirit *of promise,*" that is, *the promised Holy Spirit,* the One given in fulfilment of divine promises (John 14:16, 17; 15:26; 16:13; Acts 1:4). Does not the very fact that in his coming and work divine promises were gloriously fulfilled indicate that promises of future blessings for believers will also attain fruition? In that vein the apostle continues by writing, **14. who is the first instalment of our inheritance.** For "first instalment" Paul uses the word *arrabōn* (also spelled *arabōn*). In the papyri it often refers to earnest money in the purchase of an animal or even of a wife. In the LXX rendering of Gen. 38:17-20 the word occurs three times. It is of Semitic, probably Phoenician, origin. The Phoenicians were sea-faring traders who had not copyrighted their business-terminology. In the New Testament the word occurs also in II Cor. 1:22; 5:5, passages from which we learn that when God deposited the Spirit in the hearts of his children he obligated himself to bestow upon them subsequently the full remainder of all the blessings of salvation merited for them by the atoning sacrifice of Christ. The *first instalment* is, accordingly, a *pledge* or *guarantee* of glory to come, a glory arriving not only when soul and body part but also and especially in the great consummation of all things at Christ's return. The fruits which this indwelling and sanctifying Spirit bestows (Gal. 5:22, 23) – such as love, joy, peace, longsuffering, kindness, faithfulness, meekness, self-control, and their marvelous product: assurance of salvation (II Peter 1:5-11) – are "first-fruits" (Rom. 8:23). They are a foretaste of future, ineffable bliss.[33] The full *inheritance* – salvation viewed as God's gracious and abiding gift, not bought with money, nor earned by the sweat of human toil, nor won by conquest – will one day be the believers' portion, for them to possess and to enjoy, *to God's glory*.

Now the end or purpose of all things lies never in man but always in God: **for the redemption of (God's) own possession.**[34] At the moment when

---

[33] On ἀρραβών see also L.N.T. (A. and G.), p. 109; and Th.W.N.T., Vol. I, p. 474.

[34] Rather popular is the idea that the apostle has in mind not *God's* possession but *ours*. This is the view of T. K. Abbott, *op. cit.*, pp. 23, 24, who contends, "It is our inheritance that is in question; it is of it that the earnest is received. . . . Instead of this, the interpretation quoted supposes the figure entirely changed, so that, instead of receiving an inheritance, it is we that are the possession; a figure . . . involving a confusion of thought which we can hardly attribute to St. Paul." E. F. Scott, *op. cit.*, pp. 149, 150 reaches the same result. This type of reasoning is probably also basic to the rendering found in such translations as Berkeley, Moffatt, Goodspeed, and R.S.V. My objections are as follows:

(1) Is not the fact that it will become abundantly clear that we are *his* possession the very climax of *our* inheritance? A Christian young lady who is engaged to a young man of similar deeply rooted conviction, one who loves her with a love patterned after that of Christ for his church, looks forward with joyful anticipation to the moment when she will *belong to* her beloved.

(2) He who gives the engagement ring, in *pledge*, expects to receive the bride. It is God who gave the *arrabōn*. The word *arrabōn* and its cognates are used in modern Greek to indicate matters pertaining to a wedding engagement.

(3) The idea that God's people (in the Old Testament *Israel;* in the New Testament, *the church*) constitutes "his own possession," "a people, his very own," is repeated so often in Scripture that it may almost be said to belong to technical phraseology. For the linguistic aspect of the term see N.T.C. on I and II Timothy and Titus, p. 379, footnote 193. It occurs in one form or another in such passages as Exod. 19:5; 23:22; Deut. 7:6; 14:2; 26:18. Paul himself in Titus 2:14 states, "(our great God and Savior Jesus Christ) who gave himself for us in order to . . . purify for himself *a people, his very own,* with a zest for noble deeds." Peter states, "But y o u are . . . *a people for (God's) own possession,* in order that y o u may proclaim the excellencies of him who called y o u out of darkness into his marvelous light." Add also Isa. 43:20, 21; Ezek. 37:23; and Mal. 3:17. Surely Paul knew his Old Testament!

believers receive *their* full inheritance, which includes a glorious resurrection body (4:30), the redemption[35] of God's own possession takes place, that is, the full release to him of that which is his by virtue of the fact that he both made it and bought it. Fully released from all the effects of sin, his people will then be made manifest as being in very deed "his peculiar treasure." When the apostle also at the close of this third paragraph, which centers in the work of the Holy Spirit, adds **to the praise of his glory,** he is echoing what he had said in an earlier epistle: "You are not your own, for you were bought with a price; glorify God therefore in your body" (I Cor. 6:19, 20). The fact that believers do not belong to themselves but to God (or: to Christ) is familiar Pauline doctrine: "You belong to Christ" (I Cor. 3:23); "Whether we live, we live to the Lord, and whether we die, we die to the Lord; therefore, whether we live or whether we die, we are the Lord's" (Rom. 14:8). This, too, is the believers' only comfort both in life and in death. It is exactly as the Heidelberg Catechism expresses it:

*"Question 1:* What is your only comfort in life and death?

*"Answer:* That I, with body and soul, both in life and death, am not my own, but belong to my faithful Savior Jesus Christ; who with his precious blood has fully satisfied for all my sins, and delivered me from all the power of the devil; and so preserves me that without the will of my heavenly Father not a hair can fall from my head; yea, that all things must be subservient to my salvation, wherefore by his Holy Spirit he also assures me of eternal life, and makes me heartily willing and ready, to live unto him."

Moreover, the combination which we have here in Eph. 1:14, namely, "(God's) own possession . . . to the praise of his glory" reminds one immediately of Isa. 43:20, 21, "my people, my chosen, the people which I formed for myself, in order that they might proclaim my praise." Is it any wonder that when the apostle ponders the fact that he himself and also those addressed had been emancipated from the most dreadful evil and had been restored to the most unimaginable good, and this by the very God against whom they had rebelled, and at such a cost, and that God had even given to them the Holy Spirit as a pledge and foretaste of future climactic bliss when they would receive their full inheritance and would stand forth in dazzling splendor as God's very own, — in view of all this is it any wonder that he begins his magnificent doxology by saying, "Blessed (be)" and that he ends it with "to the praise of his glory"?

---

[35] For the two meanings of the word "redemption" see above, on verse 7, footnote 22; also N.T.C. on Colossians and Philemon, p. 64, footnote 48.

# Chapter 1

Verses 15-23

Theme: *The Church Glorious*

I. *Adoration*
*for its*

*E* ternal Foundation "in Christ"

2. leading to thanksgiving and prayer, that the eyes of those addressed may be illumined in order to see God's saving power, exhibited in the resurrection and coronation of Christ (verses 15-23)

15 For this reason, because I have heard of the faith in the Lord Jesus that (exists) among y o u and of y o u r love for all the saints, 16 I do not cease to give thanks for y o u, while making mention of y o u in my prayers, 17 (asking) that the God of our Lord Jesus Christ, the Father of glory, may give y o u the Spirit of wisdom and revelation in the clear knowledge of him, 18 (having) the eyes of y o u r hearts illumined, so that y o u may know what is the hope for which he called y o u, what the riches of the glory of his inheritance among the saints, 19 and what the surpassing greatness of his power (displayed) with respect to us who believe, as seen in that manifestation of his infinite might 20 which he exerted in Christ when he raised him from the dead and made him to sit at his right hand in the heavenly places 21 far above every principality and authority and power and dominion and every name that is named, not only in this age but also in the coming one; 22 and he ranged everything in subjection under his feet, and him he gave as head over everything to the church, 23 since it is his body, the fulness of him who fills all in all.

1:15-23

## 2. *Thanksgiving and Prayer*

*Christ as the eternal foundation of the church* (cf. I Cor. 3:11), of its complete salvation, so that it was "in Christ" that believers received every spiritual blessing, is the theme not only of verses 3-14, as has been shown, but also of the rest of the chapter. This is evident from the fact that the apostle *begins* this single sentence of 169 words (in the original) by expressing gratitude because he has heard of the faith of those addressed "in the Lord Jesus." He *ends* it by describing the Christ as the One who *in the interest of the church* "fills all in all."

15. Paul's gratitude of heart was called forth by the blessings enumerated and described in verses 3-14 as well as by the report that had reached him, as he now relates: **For this reason, because I have heard of the faith in the Lord Jesus that (exists) among y o u. . . .** Traffic by sea was brisk in those days; visitors were allowed to see the famous prisoner in Rome; the bond of Christian fellowship was very strong. For all these reasons it is not surprising that although about four years had now elapsed since the apostle carried on his labors in Ephesus — labors from which the people of the surrounding territories also benefited (Acts 19:10, 26) — he had been kept well informed. Now not all of the information that had reached Paul was favorable. He knew that there were grave faults against which the Ephesians had to be warned, and he is going to do just that, but not immediately. Very tactfully he keeps these admonitions in reserve until the close of the letter is in sight (4:17–6:9). Paul was the kind of man who took pleasure in be-

stowing sincere praise upon those whom he loved, and in doing so at once. At the particular place in the letter where, had the apostle been a heathen, he would have thanked this or that deity for having kept the writer and/or the readers in good health, Paul expresses his humble gratitude to the only true God for having imparted to the addressed the quietness and confidence that is the portion of all those who lean on the everlasting arms of their Savior, *Jesus,* and revere him as their *Lord* who bought them and to whom they render joyful obedience. The rosebud of *faith,* moreover, had burst forth into the flower of *love,* for of this, too, Paul had received cheerful tidings: **and of your love** [36] **for all the saints.** *Faith,* if it be genuine, and *love* go together, for the Magnet that draws sinners to himself draws them together also. Or, to change the figure, as the spokes of a wheel approach the hub they at the same time approach each other (see Gal. 5:6; I John 4:21). And because of this feeling of warm personal attachment to, and concern for, one another, present among the addressed, a disposition from which *all* of the saints benefited, Paul continues: **16. I do not cease to give thanks for you, while making mention of you in my prayers.** Honor to whom honor is due! It was God to whom gratitude was due for the marvelous changes which, by his grace, had been wrought in Ephesus and the region round about. Paul is shown here as a man who believed with all his heart in the necessity of thanksgiving, the latter being an essential element in every prayer that proceeded from his heart. As to prayer for others see also Rom. 1:9; Phil. 1:4; Col. 1:9; I Thess. 1:2; II Thess. 1:11; Philem. 4. All the more striking and beautiful is this expression of thanksgiving and prayer when it is seen in the light of the fact that it was uttered a. with great regularity ("I do not cease") and b. by a prisoner. The latter reminds one of Jonah's prayer "out of the fish's belly," a prayer which similarly included the note of thanksgiving (Jonah 2:1, 9). The content of the prayer is found in the words: **17. (asking) that the God of our Lord Jesus Christ, the Father of glory, may give you the Spirit of wisdom and revelation in the clear knowledge of him.** See verse 3 above for a similar manner in which the Object of prayer is indicated, and the explanation there given. Here in verse 17, however, we read "the Father of glory." Paul has just shown how magnificently the attributes of God shone forth in the works of election, foreordination, redemption, spiritual illumination, certification. It is understandable, therefore, that he speaks of "the Father *of glory,*" that is, "the glorious Father." See also Acts 7:2; I Cor. 2:8; and James 2:1. The apostle asks that the Spirit of wisdom and revelation be given to the Ephesians.

---

[36] Though p[46] Sinaiticus A B lack the word *love,* the alternative reading which includes *love* must be accepted. Otherwise the statement does not make sense. Though it is true that πίστις can mean both *faith* and *faithfulness,* it cannot have both meanings in any *single* occurrence. Hence, the rendering "faith in the Lord Jesus and faithfulness toward all the saints" must be rejected.

Most of the translations have "spirit" instead of "Spirit" (= the Holy Spirit). In favor of *Spirit,* however, are the following arguments:

(1) Paul writes ". . . of *revelation.*" We do not generally associate revelation with the purely human spirit or state of mind.

(2) As to ". . . of *wisdom,*" in Isa. 11:2 this is mentioned as the first of several gifts imparted by the Spirit of Jehovah.

(3) Such expressions as "Spirit of truth" (John 15:26) and "Spirit of adoption" (Rom. 8:15) also refer to the Holy Spirit.

(4) Ephesians abounds with references to the third Person of the Holy Trinity. Since the Comforter figured so prominently in this epistle, we may well believe that also in the present instance Paul has him in mind.

(5) It is rather characteristic of Paul that, having made mention of God the Father and of Christ the Son – and both have already been mentioned here in 1:16 – he then also refers to the Spirit. Cf. Rom. 8:15-17; II Cor. 13:14; Eph. 1:3-14; 3:14-17; 4:4-6; 5:18-21.[87]

(6) When the Father gives *enlightened eyes,* does he not do so through the Holy Spirit? See John 3:3, 5. Men cannot *see* the Kingdom of God, *to enter* it, except through the Spirit. Cf. Eph. 5:8; I John 1:7.

A question may occur, however, in this connection. It may be asked, "But how is it possible that Paul prayed that the Spirit of wisdom and revelation *be given* to those who already possessed that Spirit; in fact, according to verse 13, had been sealed by him?" One cannot escape this difficulty by reading "spirit" (state of mind) instead of Spirit (Holy Spirit). For even then the question would occur: "How can the apostle ask that a spirit of wisdom *in the clear knowledge of him* [that is, of God] *be given* to those who already knew him so well that they had reposed their trust in him?" (verse 13). However, this difficulty confronts us not only here in Ephesians, but throughout Paul's epistles. To give but two examples: contrast Col. 1:4 with 3:12; I Thess. 1:3; 2:13 with 5:15. If Paul could say the one how could he say the other also?

The answer is provided by Paul himself. It amounts to this: what is already present *must be strengthened.* The Holy Spirit is present, to be sure, but the apostle prays that the Ephesians "may be strengthened with power through his Spirit in the inner man" (3:16). The work begun in the heart must "be carried on toward completion" (Phil. 1:6). Love and all the other graces must "abound more and more" (Phil. 1:9; cf. I Thess. 3:12; 4:10). It is clear, therefore, that Paul's prayer here in Eph. 1:15-23, includ-

---

[87] Having recently made a contextual study and tabulation of every New Testament occurrence of πνεῦμα I have arrived at the conclusion that one should not rely too heavily on the rule, "When the article is used, the reference is to the Holy Spirit; when omitted, the reference is to an operation, influence, or gift of the Spirit." Each occurrence should be studied in the light of its own immediate context.

ing therefore also verse 17, is entirely consistent with what he had solemnly declared in verses 3-14. In fact, the connection between verses 15 and 16, on the one hand, and 17 ff., on the other, shows that it was exactly because so many spiritual gifts had been received that the apostle takes courage to ask for even more.

Paul, then, asks that the addressed may receive a continually growing supply of *wisdom* and *clear knowledge*. Combine the two, and note that he is asking that the Ephesians be given deeper penetration into the meaning of the gospel and a clearer insight into the will of God for their lives, enabling them at all times to use the best means for the attainment of the highest goal, namely, the glory of God Triune.

Now it was the Spirit who imparted wisdom, the Spirit also who revealed the truth. For these early Christians, who so recently had emerged from pagan fear, superstition, and immorality, who were able to communicate with Paul only by letter or through a messenger, and who were living in the midst of a heathen environment, wisdom and revelation were doubly needed, and this not only in order to gain a clearer insight into the way of salvation but also to know just what was the right course to follow in any given situation. What they needed above all was *clear knowledge* of God, including joyful *recognition* of God's way for their lives and a willingness to follow his direction. Now this was not merely a matter of the intellect. Far more than this was at stake. Hence the apostle continues his prayer as follows: **18. (having) the eyes of y o u r hearts illumined.**[38] In Scripture the heart is the fulcrum of feeling and faith as well as the mainspring of words and actions (Rom. 10:10; cf. Matt. 12:34; 15:19; 22:37; John 14:1). It is the core and center of man's being, man's inmost self. "Out of it are the issues of life" (Prov. 4:23). "Man looks on the outward appearance, but Jehovah looks on the heart" (I Sam. 16:7). Now apart from the work of the Holy Spirit the eye of the heart is blind (Isa. 9:2; John 9:39-41; I Cor. 2:14-16). Men thus blinded need two things: the gospel and spiritual apperception. The latter is what is meant by *eyes illumined* or *enlightened*. See also on 5:8 for the meaning of *light* versus *darkness*. In order to bring about this illumination the Spirit causes men to be reborn. He removes their mists of ignorance, clouds of lust, selfish and jealous dispositions, etc., and imparts to them sorrow for sin and faith working through love. The spiritual eye is enlightened when the heart is purified. "Blessed are the

[38] The construction of *πεφωτισμένους τοὺς ὀφθαλμούς* is not easy. One solution would be to infer that, because of the following infinitive, the dative (*πεφωτισμένοις*) is here replaced by the accusative (*πεφωτισμένους*). Another would be to regard the words in question as an accusative absolute. The simplest, and perhaps the best, would be the construction which looks upon these words as being governed by *δώῃ*, and accordingly as in apposition with the preceding *πνεῦμα*. This would yield the sense, ". . . that he may give y o u the Spirit of wisdom and revelation . . . (hence) eyes illumined."

pure in heart, for they shall see God" (Matt. 5:8). Paul continues: **so that y o u may know what is the hope**[39] **for which he called y o u.** Paul knows that the best way to drive away old sinful tendencies is no longer to concentrate on *them* but rather on the blessings of salvation. The Ephesians had received *the effectual call.* The urgent invitation of the gospel (the *external* call) had been applied to their hearts by the Holy Spirit, producing the *internal* call. In the latter sense *calling* is referred to everywhere in the New Testament; cf. Rom. 11:29; I Cor. 1:26; 7:20; Eph. 4:1, 4 (in addition to the present 1:18); Phil. 3:14; II Tim. 1:9; Heb. 3:1; I Peter 2:9; II Peter 1:10. Let those addressed then ponder how rich they are because of *the hope* for which God had called them (literally, "the hope of his calling"). This hope is firmly grounded in God's infallible promises. It is the soul's anchor, moored to the very throne of God; hence, to the very heart of Christ (Heb. 6:18-20). It is therefore a fervent yearning, confident expectation, and patient waiting for the fulfilment of God's promises, a full *Christ-centered* (cf. Col. 1:27) assurance that these promises will indeed be realized. It is a living and sanctifying force (I Peter 1:3; I John 3:3). Paul continues: (so that y o u may know) **what (is) the riches of the glory of his inheritance among the saints.** "His" inheritance means the one given by him, just like "his" calling was the call issued and made effective by him. Paul is speaking about the glorious riches, the marvelous magnitude, of all the blessings of salvation, particularly those still to be bestowed in the great consummation of all things. See N.T.C. on Col. 1:12 ("the inheritance of the saints in the light"). These blessings are called an *inheritance* because they are the gift of God's grace, and once received will never be taken away again ("I will not give you the inheritance of my fathers," I Kings 21:4). See also above, on verse 14. The phrase "among the saints" (cf. Acts 20:32; 26:18) deserves special attention. When a believer's hope is what it should be, he never looks forward to an inheritance *just for himself.* What will make the inheritance so glorious is exactly the fact that he will enjoy it *together with* "all who love his appearing" (II Tim. 4:8).

**19.** Paul continues by adding one more item to *the hope* and *the inheritance.* He says, "I pray that the eyes of y o u r hearts may be illumined, so that y o u may know what is the hope . . . what the riches of the glory of his inheritance among the saints," **and what the surpassing greatness of his power (displayed) with respect to us who believe, as seen in that manifestation of his infinite might. . . .** This "surpassing greatness of his [God the Father's] power" is needed as a link between the two other items which were mentioned in the preceding verse, namely, the *hope* and the *inheritance.* The *power* (Greek *dúnamis,* cf. "dynamite") of God is necessary in order that the *hope* may be realized, the *inheritance* obtained. The words

[39] Note the triad faith, love (verse 15) and hope (verse 18). See N.T.C. on Colossians and Philemon, pp. 47–50.

"with respect to us who believe" show that this power is exerted in the interest of believers, of no one else. They alone receive the inheritance. Paul is asking God to give the addressed enlightened eyes in order that they may know what is the surpassing greatness of God's power ". . . according to that working of the strength of his might," etc., thus literally. The three words which he employs to show how this *power* is used are: *enérgeia* (whence our "energy"), that is, *activity, working, manifestation; krátos: exercised strength;* and *ischús: might, great inherent strength.* Nevertheless, when such synonyms are piled up, as happens in this part of the sentence, it is a question whether we should distinguish them so sharply. F. W. Grosheide is probably correct when he says, "It is difficult to indicate an accurate distinction between the various words used for power. It is permissible to conclude that the apostle uses more than one term to indicate the fulness and the certainty of this power" (*op. cit.*, p. 30). In harmony with this view I suggest the translation "power . . . as seen in that manifestation of his infinite might," (continued) **20. which he exerted in Christ when he raised him from the dead and made him to sit at his right hand in the heavenly places.** The main thought expressed by these words when they are viewed in the light of what immediately precedes is this: the apostle prays that the Ephesians be given enlightened eyes so that they may see and discern that, in order to translate their steadfast hope into glorious realization so that they will receive their full inheritance, God has at his disposal *as great a power* as he exhibited when he raised his Son from the dead and set him at his own right hand. It is as if the apostle were saying, "Do not despair. Y o u can rely on God's infinite power. One day the inheritance held in store for y o u will be fully y o u r s."

But is it necessary to limit the meaning of Paul's words to *a comparison* between *a.* the power displayed in Christ's resurrection and coronation, and *b.* the power exercised in bringing believers to their ultimate victory? In the light of Rom. 6:8-11; I Cor. 15:20; Col. 3:1, may he not also have had in mind the fact that Christ's resurrection and session at the Father's right hand are *typical* of what happens to believers? They, too, will conquer death when they arise gloriously from their graves to live and reign with Christ forevermore. And even now Christ's resurrection is a type of their spiritual resurrection, their gradual victory over sin. There is, in fact, even a *causal* connection. Christ's resurrection, being proof-positive of the believers' justification, is a *pledge* of their eternal glory. His sitting at the Father's right hand, whence he has poured out his Spirit into their hearts, *guarantees* and *brings about* their ultimate bliss.

The tremendously important place which Christ's resurrection occupied in the thinking of the apostolic age is apparent not only from the present passage but also from the following: Matt. 28; Mark 16; Luke 24; John 20, 21; Acts 1:22; 2:32; 3:26; 10:40; 13:34; 17:31; 23:6; 26:8, 23; Rom. 4:25;

8:34; I Cor. 15; I Peter 1:3; etc. Similarly, the significance attached to Christ's coronation, so that as a reward for his mediatorial work he rules the entire universe in the interest of his church, is clear in the present epistle from 1:20-23; 4:8 ff., and elsewhere from Acts 2:33, 36; 5:31; 7:56; Rom. 8:34; Phil. 2:9; Col. 3:1; Heb. 2:8, 9; etc. See also Ps. 110:1. Two chapters of the Book of Revelation are devoted mainly to this theme (chapter 5, see verse 7; chapter 12, see verses 5 and 10). The living and ruling Christ was a living reality to the consciousness of the early church. For the phrase "in the heavenly places" see above, on verse 3.

**21.** The fact that the apostle was not thinking first of all of a particular point in space when he spoke of Christ's exaltation to the Father's right hand but rather of the extent or degree of this high position is clear from the words: **far above every principality and authority and power and dominion and every name that is named.** The enumeration of the mighty ones "far above" whom Christ was assigned his place of pre-eminence is almost the same as that in Col. 1:16. From that passage, in the light of Col. 2:18, as well as from the present Ephesian passage when compared with 3:10, it is clear that the reference is, or is primarily, to angels. Teachers of error, who at this very time were disturbing the churches of provincial Asia, particularly those of the Lycus Valley, grossly overestimated the position of the angels in relation to Christ and the work of salvation. The names of angels, the various categories into which they were to be classified, and the worship due to them, seem to have been some of the topics on which the heretics concentrated their attention. What Paul is saying, then, is this: the angels (whether good or bad) have no power apart from Christ. Call them by whatever name you wish, far above them all reigns Christ. (See on 4:10.) Moreover, his position of majesty will last forever, for he has been exalted above all these eminent ones and above every title that can be conferred **not only in this age,**[40] the present dispensation, **but also in the coming one,** the one that will be ushered in at the consummation of all things (cf. 2:7).[41]

---

[40] αἰών has been defined as "the world in motion," as contrasted with κόσμος, "the world at rest." However, the latter term is used in a great variety of senses; see N.T.C. on John, Vol. I, p. 79, footnote 26. The term αἰών may be said to indicate the world viewed from the standpoint of time and change; hence, the *age,* whether present or future ("coming"), and its prevalent mood.

[41] At this point Lenski gets into a difficulty. Having interpreted "the coming" age as the one that Christ will usher in at his Parousia – a correct interpretation of the term as here used, I believe – and proceeding from the tacit assumption that at that moment time will cease to be, he must explain how the text can, nevertheless, speak about *a coming age.* His solution is as follows: "it is called 'the eon to come' only because we now wait for it in hope. Also we may note that human language is compelled to use terms indicating time when speaking of eternity [a fact which I do not call in question], although eternity is timelessness, the opposite of time, succession, progress, etc." On this point I differ. Nowhere does Scripture teach that the soul, either when it enters heaven or when it is reunited with the body at

22, 23. Accordingly, the God of our Lord Jesus Christ, the Father of glory manifested his infinite might when he raised Christ from the dead and made him to sit at his right hand **and he ranged everything in subjection under his feet.** In him, as *the Ideal Man* ("Son of Man" as well as "Son of God") Psalm 8 (of which verse 6 is here quoted; cf. LXX Ps. 8:7) attains its absolute fulfilment. See also I Cor. 15:27 and Heb. 2:8. The expression "everything" or "all things" must not be narrowed down to "all things in the church." Nor does it merely include such things as "sheep and oxen, the beasts of the field, the birds of the heavens, the fish of the sea, whatever passes through the paths of the seas" (Ps. 8:7, 8). Though, in a very limited manner, mankind, even after the fall, exercises a degree of dominion over these "lower" creatures, the sway that he thus wields is nothing compared to Christ's universal sovereignty, a dominion from which absolutely nothing that exists is excluded. Therefore *nothing* can prevent the realization of the believers' "hope." *Nothing* will be allowed to stand in the way of their acquisition and enjoyment, to the full, of that glorious "inheritance" of which they have a foretaste even here and now. Moreover, God's power does not lie dormant. In a manner that was clearly exhibited in Christ's exaltation it is being used for the government of the universe in the interest of the church. Hence, Paul continues: **and him [42] he gave as head over everything to the church, since [43] it is his body** . . . ; that is, since he is so intimately and indissolubly united with it and loves it with such profound, boundless, and steadfast love. It is the closeness of the bond, the unfathomable character of the love between Christ and his church that is stressed by this head-body symbolism, as is clearly indicated in 5:25-33. In this connection an important fact must not be ignored, namely, that throughout the letter Paul emphasizes God's (or Christ's) great love for his people, and the love they owe him and one another in return (1:5; 2:4; 3:19; 4:1, 2; 5:1, 2 ff.; 6:23, 24). There is not a single chapter in which this theme is not stressed. One who has not grasped this point does not understand Ephesians!

In the twin epistles, Colossians and Ephesians, the figure head-body appears for the first time in Paul's epistles, to indicate the relation between Christ and his church. It is true, of course, that here in Eph. 1:22, 23 Christ is not actually said to be the head of the church but rather "head over everything to the church . . . his body." But this manner of expressing it merely enhances the beauty of the symbolism. The meaning, then, is this:

---

Christ's return, acquires the divine attribute of timelessness. Also, "perfection" for believers does not necessarily rule out "progress." For my own views on this subject and also the views of others see my book *The Bible on the Life Hereafter*, pp. 70–78.

[42] Note forward position of αὐτόν for emphasis.

[43] The relative pronoun ἥτις has causal force. See Gram. N.T., p. 728.

since the church is Christ's body, with which he is organically united, he loves it so much that *in its interest* he exercises his infinite power in causing the entire universe with all that is in it to co-operate, whether willingly or unwillingly. Accordingly, the idea *Christ the Ruling Head over everything* (cf. Col. 2:10) does not cancel but rather strengthens and adorns the clearly implied doctrine *Christ the Ruling (and Organic) Head of the Church* (cf. Eph. 4:15; 5:23; Col. 1:18; 2:19). When, therefore, many commentators, dogmaticians, as well as the Heidelberg Catechism (Lord's Day XIX, edition with textual references, Q. and A. 50) appeal to Eph. 1:20-23, among other passages, in support of the position that Christ is head of the church, they are not committing an error. For further remarks on Christ's headship see above, on verse 10; also N.T.C. on Colossians, pp. 76–78, the latter particularly for the distinction between *ruling* and *organic* headship.

As a further description of the church as body of Christ, Paul adds: **the fulness**[44] **of him who fills all in all.**

The argument with respect to the exact meaning of *fulness* in this particular case covers many pages in scores of commentaries. With due respect for the reasoning of those who defend other theories, and whose pleas in corroboration of their views have been examined in detail,[45] I have, after

---

[44] The idea of G. G. Findlay and others that πλήρωμα modifies αὐτόν, and refers, therefore, to Christ rather than to the church, has found but little approval, the reason being that words used in apposition or as a modifier must be construed with a near, not with a remote, antecedent, unless a very good reason can be given for construing them differently.

[45] Some interpret πλήρωμα as "the full number of aeons as well as the uncreated monad from which they have proceeded" or, in general, as a term belonging to second century gnostic speculation. Nothing in the context favors this theory. Others, many of whom depend heavily on J. B. Lightfoot's contention (defended in his work, *Saint Paul's Epistle to the Colossians and to Philemon,* pp. 255–271) that "Substantives in *ma,* formed from the perfect passive, appear always to have a passive sense," favor the interpretation: (the church as body of Christ is) "that which is filled – or is being filled – by Christ." With variations as to detail this view is defended, among others, by Greijdanus, Percy ("die Gemeinde als von Christus erfüllt), Robertson, Salmond, Scott. It is also favored by L.N.T. (A. and G.), p. 678, and by *The Amplified New Testament.* In support of this theory it can be said that the apostle stresses the fact that the church finds its fulness in Christ, in him alone (Col. 2:10), in whom God was pleased to have all the fulness dwell (Col. 1:19; cf. Eph. 4:10). Also, the combination of the noun πλήρωμα and the participle πληρουμένου then runs smoothly: the church is filled by him who fills all things. The theory is very attractive. It is weakened somewhat, however, by the contention of other interpreters that "In every other case in which πλήρωμα occurs it is used actively – *that which does fill*" (thus Hodge, *op. cit.,* pp. 89, 90; and for the titles of other sources showing that Lightfoot's position is indefensible see M.M., on πλήρωμα, p. 520). At any rate, contextual study of all the New Testament instances in which πλήρωμα is used shows that in interpreting Eph. 1:23 it is rather precarious to make use of Lightfoot's contention. See also N.T.C. on Colossians and Philemon, pp. 79, 80, footnote 56, for complete tabulation of the meaning of πλήρωμα in the New Testament. What is, perhaps, an even more cogent argument against the passive sense of the noun as here used is the fact that in that case the head-body metaphor which the apostle employs would seem to be hardly fitting. One can say that

lengthy study reached the conclusion that the following is the correct interpretation: *the church is Christ's complement.* In other words:

"This is the highest honor of the church, that, until he is united to us, the Son of God reckons himself in some measure imperfect. What consolation it is for us to learn that, not until we are in his presence, does he possess all his parts, or does he wish to be regarded as complete." (John Calvin in his comments on this passage. See Bibliography for title of work.) With variations as to detail, this view, namely, that the church is, indeed, represented here as *filling* or *completing* him who fills all in all, is also defended by Abbott, Barry, Bruce, Grosheide, Hodge, Lenski, Simpson, and many others.

This interpretation to which I, along with all of those just mentioned, cling does not in any degree or manner detract from the absolute majesty or self-sufficiency of Christ. As to his divine essence Christ is in no sense whatever dependent on or capable of being completed by the church. But as *bridegroom* he is incomplete without the *bride;* as *vine* he cannot be thought of without *the branches;* as *shepherd* he is not seen without *his sheep;* and so also as *head* he finds his full expression in *his body,* the church.

There are also the following additional reasons that have induced me to regard this interpretation as being the correct one:

(1) The fact that the One who fills all in all does, nevertheless, have that which fills or completes him, is clearly taught by Christ himself and also by his disciple John (John 6:56; 15:4, 5; 17–21; I John 3:24). "Abide in me, and I in y o u" shows that not only are the branches incomplete apart from the vine – which is the point that is stressed in John 15 – but, in a sense, the vine also finds fulfilment in the branches.

(2) In Col. 1:24 Paul speaks about himself as "supplying what is lacking

---

the church is filled by Christ, and conversely that, accordingly, Christ fills the church. But can one also say that the body is filled by the head, hence, that the head fills the body? Beare answers, "The head cannot be said 'to fill' the body." Is it not rather the body that fills, completes, expresses, carries out the directives of, the head?

Finally, there is an interpretation which would avoid placing any emphasis either on the active or on the passive sense of πλήρωμα. It interprets this noun as indicating simply "the full number or totality of those individual believers who are represented in the redemptive activity of the incarnate Christ." As I see it, this, too, is a plausible interpretation. The word πλήρωμα does at times seem to have the meaning *full number.* Rom. 11:12 and 11:25 ("total number of elect Jews," "total number of elect Gentiles") merit consideration here. And it is also true that, numerically speaking, the reference in Eph. 1:23 is, indeed, to none other than the full number of the elect. Why is it, then, that by far the most commentators insist that πλήρωμα, as used here in Eph. 1:23, must be interpreted either *passively,* "that which is – or is being – filled," or *actively,* "that which fills or completes," but not *quiescently,* "totality." Is it, perhaps, because it is felt by both classes of interpreters that the noun and the participle form a unit, and that if the latter implies *action,* whether received or exerted, the former must do the same?

in the afflictions of Christ." There is a sense in which the church, as it were, completes Christ's suffering. See N.T.C. on Col. 1:24. Those, therefore, who reject the idea that the church is the complement of the Christ, will experience great difficulty in interpreting Col. 1:24. Similarly, the church recapitulates Christ's death and resurrection (Rom. 6:4, 5; Col. 2:20; 3:1; II Tim. 2:11, 12).

(3) The head-body metaphor, when interpreted as meaning that the body fills or completes the head, resulting in an organic unity, so that the body carries out the will and purpose of the head, makes good sense. Christ uses the church in the realization of his plan in the government of the world and for the salvation of sinners.

(4) The idea stressed by Calvin, namely, that Christ refuses to regard himself as complete until he possesses all his parts, also harmonizes beautifully with the love-motif which, as I have shown, dominates this entire epistle.

(5) The description of the church as "the fulness of him who fills all in all" is, indeed, a "tremendous paradox" (to use Lenski's expression, *op. cit.*, p. 403). This, too, is exactly what we expect to find in Paul. Oxymora or seeming contradictions abound in his writings: "They are not all Israel that are of Israel" (Rom. 9:6). "In everything we commend ourselves . . . as deceivers, yet true; as unknown, yet well-known; as dying but behold we live; . . . as sorrowful, yet always rejoicing; as poor, yet making many rich; as having nothing, and yet possessing all things" (II Cor. 6:4-10). "When I am weak, then I am strong" (II Cor. 12:10). It is Paul who wants the Thessalonians to be ambitious about living calmly (I Thess. 4:11). And in this very epistle of Ephesians he speaks about *knowing* the love of God *that passes knowledge* (3:19)! The paradox of Eph. 1:23 fits nicely into this style category.

Commenting on the words "of him who fills all in all" Calvin continues as follows, "This is added to guard against the supposition that any real defect would exist in Christ if he were separated from us. His desire to be filled and, in some respects, to be made perfect in us, arises from no want or necessity; for all that is good in ourselves, or in any of the creatures, is the gift of his hand."

The words "who fills [46] all in all" mean that Christ fills *all* the universe *in all* respects; that is, the entire universe is not only dependent on him for the fulfilment of its every need but is also governed by him in the interest

---

[46] The participle is to be interpreted as a middle, not as a passive, which would result in a harsh construction. Whether or not this middle has retained something of its reciprocal or reflexive force — hence, "who fills the whole universe *for himself*" (or, according to others, "from himself as the center") — or simply has the sense of the active, would be difficult to establish, though the former alternative seems probable.

of the church, which, in turn, must serve the universe, and is replenished by his bounteous gifts. Thus he is constantly pervading all things with his love and power (cf. Jer. 23:24; I Kings 8:27; Ps. 139:7). I agree with the statement of Roels, "Paul most probably refers to the fact that the Christ, exalted over all, is now involved in the historical realization of the already accomplished reconciliation of the universe by directing all things to their determined, divinely appointed, end" (*op. cit.*, p. 248).

With such a Christ as *the Eternal Foundation* of its salvation the church has nothing to fear. Its *hope* will be realized, its *inheritance* fully enjoyed.

### *Summary of Chapter 1*

The chapter consists of two main parts (after the opening salutation, verses 1-3). In the first of these (verses 4-14) Paul praises God Triune for the blessings of election by the Father, redemption through the Son, and certification in the Spirit. In the second (verses 15-23), having given utterance to his deep and humble thanksgiving, the apostle prays that the Ephesians may be enlightened so that they may behold: *a.* what is the *hope* for which they have been called; *b.* what the *inheritance* that awaits them; and *c.* what is the *power* of God to cause this hope to be realized and the inheritance to become their everlasting possession. Was not the proof of the operation of this power given when "the Father of glory" raised his Son from the dead and made him to sit at his right hand in the heavenly places?

In this chapter, more than in any other, the apostle underscores the fact that it is "in Christ" that every spiritual blessing descends upon God's people from "the heavenly places." Apart from him they are desperately poor. In intimate fellowship with him they are inexpressibly rich. Christ is, accordingly, in a very real sense the church's *Eternal Foundation.* Cf. I Cor. 3:11.

The question may be asked, "How is it that in this chapter and also in chapters 2 and 3 the apostle, a *prisoner,* gives expression to his profound gratitude in words of unrestrained adoration, beginning with 'Blessed (be) the God and Father of our Lord Jesus Christ!'?" The answer is that he had meditated on the following facts:

(1) The Father's *special delight* in planning the salvation of people who in themselves were entirely unworthy (1:5b; 2:3).

(2) The Father's *marvelous decision* to adopt these people as his very own, and to call them "the Father's Family" (1:5; 3:15).

(3) The Son's *solemn pledge,* made before the foundation of the world, whereby he became his people's Surety (1:4).

(4) The fact that "not until we are in his presence does he [the Son] wish to be regarded as complete" (Calvin's interpretation of the expression that the church is "the fulness of him who fills all in all" 1:23).

(5) The Spirit's willingness to dwell in the hearts of God's people, by his very presence assuring them of greater glory to come (1:13, 14).

(6) The Spirit's activity of enlightening the eyes, so that believers, thus illumined, may have a clear and definite knowledge of their *hope,* their *inheritance,* and of *the power of God* which transforms the hope into the actual possession of the inheritance (1:17-23).

(7) The revelation to Paul of the "mystery," namely, the establishment of the church gathered out of Jews and Gentiles and welded into *one* spiritual community with equality of membership for all regardless of race or nationality (1:15; 2:16; 3:6).

(8) The fact that this "united church" is being established before Paul's very eyes, the congregations of Ephesus and surroundings furnishing the proof (1:15).

(9) The fact that even he, Paul, once a bitter persecutor, had, in God's marvelous grace, been chosen to reveal the mystery to men and to see it go into effect (3:3-5).

(10) The reign of the resurrected and ascended Christ over the entire universe in the interest of the church, his body (1:22, 23).

# Chapter 2

Verses 1–10

Theme: *The Church Glorious*

I. *Adoration*
*for its*

*U* niversal Scope (embracing both Jew and Gentile),

1. secured by the great redemptive blessings *for both* which center "in Christ" and parallel his resurrection and triumphant life

# CHAPTER II

**EPHESIANS**

2 1 And y o u, even though y o u were dead through y o u r trespasses and
sins, 2 in which y o u formerly walked in line with the course of this world,
in line with the prince of the domain of the air, (the domain) of the spirit now
at work in the sons of disobedience, 3 among whom we also once lived in the lusts
of our flesh, fulfilling the desires of the flesh and its reasonings, and were by nature
children of wrath even as the rest, 4 God, being rich in mercy, because of his great
love with which he loved us, 5 even though we were dead through our trespasses
made us alive together with Christ — by grace y o u have been saved — 6 and raised
us up with him and made us sit with him in the heavenly places in Christ Jesus,
7 in order that in the ages to come he might show the surpassing riches of his
grace (expressed) in kindness toward us in Christ Jesus. 8 For by grace y o u have
been saved through faith; and this not of yourselves, (it is) the gift of God; 9 not
of works, lest anyone should boast, 10 for his handiwork are we, created in Christ
Jesus for good works, which God prepared beforehand that we should walk in them.

---

## 2:1-10

### 1. *Redemptive Blessings for Both Jew and Gentile*

The record of the prayer and thanksgiving has ended. But the deep feeling continues, as is evident from such expressions as "*rich* mercy . . . *great* love . . . *surpassing* riches of grace." This, too, as well as in chapter 1, is the language of gratitude and adoration. Nevertheless a new subdivision begins here. There is no sudden break. In chapter 2, as in chapter 1, Christ, in whom the Holy Trinity is revealed, is regarded as the basis of blessing (2:6, 7, 9, 13, 21, 22). But the emphasis has shifted, as is shown by the fact that in this second chapter the phrase "in Christ" or its equivalent occurs with far less frequency. It is the *universal scope* or *extent* of the church on which chapter 2 concentrates our attention. The apostle begins to show that "in Christ" the palace of salvation has opened its gates to all, that is, to Gentiles as well as to Jews. When Jesus died on the cross the wall between these two formerly hostile groups came tumbling down, never to be re-erected (2:14). In him all are now *one,* that is, all those who have embraced him by a living faith.

The easy manner in which Paul shifts from "y o u" to "we" and back again, in verses 1-10 — with "y o u" in verses 1, 2, and 8; "we" in verses 3, 4, 6, 7, and 10; and a "we" that clearly includes a "y o u" in verse 5 — indicates that though a distinction is being drawn at times, it is upon what all have in common that the emphasis falls. The blessings enumerated are shared by addressor and addressed, by Jew and Gentile alike, for all, being by nature dead through sins and trespasses, had to be made alive. Not until verse 11 is reached are we told how the two groups – Jew and Gentile – erstwhile bitter enemies, have become friends. The logic is simple and clear. The establishment of peace between God and man (verses 1-10), so that "children of wrath" stand revealed as objects of love, naturally precedes and brings about peace between man and man, in this case between Jew and Gentile (verse 11 ff.). The horizontal line is the proliferation of the vertical.

Not only does chapter 2 contain an echo of the main emphasis of chapter 1, namely, that Jesus Christ, as the revelation of God Triune, is the One "in whom" all blessings, past, present, and future, are bestowed upon believers, so that in that sense he is the church's *eternal foundation,* but it also foreshadows the ideas on which the apostle is going to dwell in greater detail in later chapters. Particularly, does it give a preview of 4:1-16: the church's *organic unity and growth.*

In the main, however, chapter 2, by implication, assails the spirit of sinful exclusivism, and stresses the fact that God's love is broader than the ocean, and embraces not only Jews but also Gentiles (cf. Rom. 1:14; Gal. 3:28; Col. 3:11; then also John 3:16; 10:16; Rev. 5:9; 7:9), welding them into an organic unity, and doing this by the strangest instrument imaginable, namely, a death upon a cross! The church's *universal scope* is the thought on which Paul's mind is centered here, and which he introduces as follows:

**1. And y o u, even though y o u were dead through y o u r trespasses and sins . . .** The word *y o u* is the object of the sentence, placed first for the sake of emphasis. It is as if the apostle were saying, "It was on *y o u,* so unworthy, that God took pity." Yet, in the original the subject of the sentence, namely, "God," and the predicate, "made alive," are not mentioned until verses 4 and 5. And even then Paul does not really say, "God made *y o u* alive," but "God made *us* alive." In dwelling on the great mysteries of salvation, matters with which the apostle is himself so vitally concerned, and the effects of which he has experienced so dramatically in his own life and is still experiencing, it was impossible for him to leave himself out of the picture. He is unable to write about such things in an abstract, detached manner. Hence, he is going to substitute "us" for "y o u." This "us" is, however, broad enough to include "y o u."

In many English translations, however, already in verse 1 subject and predicate are inserted, so that verse 1 reads, "And y o u did he make alive." Sometimes the words "did he make alive" (A.R.V.) or "hath he quickened" (A.V.) are printed in italics (A.R.V.; A.V.), to indicate their absence in the original; sometimes they are not (R.S.V.), which, as I see it, is worse.

Either way, their insertion in verse 1 beclouds Paul's purpose.[47] The apostle, I believe, was so completely overwhelmed by the sense of gratitude when he contrasted the former utter wretchedness of the addressed with their present riches in Christ that he purposely postponed the description of the latter until he had portrayed the former. No doubt he did this in order that the Ephesians, having been reminded at some length (verses 1-3) of the dreaded darkness of death in which they formerly walked, would rejoice all the more when at last (verse 4 ff.) they are told that all this is now past, since God, in his infinite mercy, love, and grace, had caused the light of life to dawn upon them (yes, upon "us"). The more men learn to see the dimensions of their utterly lost condition the more they will also, by God's grace, appreciate their marvelous deliverance.

Before their conversion, then, the addressed were "dead" in their trespasses (deviations from the straight and narrow path; see on 1:7) and sins (inclinations, thoughts, words, and deeds which "miss the mark" of glorifying God). Now the fact that these people are here described as having been *dead* does not mean that in their hearts and lives the process of moral and spiritual corruption had run its full course. Ursinus, in his explanation of the Heidelberg Catechism, John Calvin, and many, many others, have pointed out that even the unregenerate can perform *natural* good: eating, drinking, taking exercise, etc., and *civic* or *moral* good. Some worldly men have "uniformly conducted themselves in a most virtuous manner through the whole course of their lives." So wrote John Calvin, *Institutes of the Christian Religion* (translated by John Allen, Philadelphia, 1928), Vol. I, p. 263. To deny this would be to close our eyes to facts that confront us every day of our lives.[48] Also such a denial would amount to a rejection of the plain teaching of Scripture. King Joash "did what was right in the eyes of Jehovah all the days of Jehoiada the priest" (II Chron. 24:2). But note how his life ended (II Chron. 24:20-22). Jesus said, "If y o u do good to those who do good to y o u, what credit is that to y o u? For even sinners

---

[47] The Swedish Bible (Stockholm, 1946) inserts the words in verse 1. So do the Frisian (Amsterdam, 1946), the South African, though in italics (Kaapstad, 1938), etc. On the other hand, the Dutch (*Nieuwe Vertaling,* Amsterdam, 1951) and several others, including French and German versions, do not have this insertion. Some translators have taken Paul's one beautiful sentence (consisting at least of verses 1-7) and have chopped it up into so many brief statements, each followed by a period, that, whether in verse 1 they insert or omit these words, the resultant translation misses something of the flavor of the real Paul.

[48] The fact that *sinners* sometimes turn out better than expected, while *saints* often disappoint us, is discussed by A. Kuyper in his three-volume work *De Gemeene Gratie* (second edition, Kampen, no date); see especially Vol. II, p. 13 ff. Whatever one may think of Kuyper's solution, it is at least more scriptural and satisfying than that which is offered by Reinhold Niebuhr in his work *Man's Nature and His Communities: Essays on the Dynamics and Enigmas of Man's Personal and Social Existence* (New York, 1965). That author sees no real difference between saints and sinners!

do the same thing" (Luke 6:33). Truly at times "the barbarians" show us "no common kindness" (Acts 28:2; cf. Rom. 2:14). In an emergency the crowd that is willing to donate blood is frequently so numerous that at the proper time an announcement has to be issued, "No more blood needed." When a case of pitiable poverty makes the headlines, and is covered by an emotional write-up, accompanied by sensational pictures, men's feelings are stirred to such an extent that food, clothing, money, toys, etc., come pouring in to help those in distress. And by no means all the givers are believers!

However, though it would be foolish to deny that even apart from regenerating grace men "show some regard for virtue and for good outward behavior" (Canons of Dort, III and IV, article 4), such conduct does not even begin to compare with *spiritual* good. Only the Lord knows to what extent, in each man's life, the outwardly good deed springs from genuine sympathy because God's image in him was not completely lost, and in how far it resulted from the realization that absolute self-seeking is self-defeating, or from some other not exactly altruistic motive. In any event such a good deed does not spring from the root of gratitude for the salvation merited by Jesus Christ. It is not a work of faith, therefore. It is not done with a conscious purpose to please and glorify God and to obey his law. Now it is with respect to such *spiritual* good that men are by nature *dead*. It is a fact that even men with a reputation for virtue have been known to answer every gospel appeal with utter disdain. Their proud heart refuses to accept the urgent invitation to confess their sins and to accept Christ as their Savior and Lord. Natural man is not even able properly *to discern* God. The things of the Spirit are "foolishness" to him (I Cor. 2:14). He lacks the ability to bestir himself so as to give heed to that which God demands of him (Ezek. 37; John 3:3, 5). Only when God turns him is he able to turn from his wicked way (Jer. 31:18, 19). Besides all this, he is under the sentence of death, under the curse because of his sin in Adam (original sin) to which he has added his own trespasses and sins. 2. With respect to these trespasses and sins Paul continues: **in which**[49] **y o u formerly walked in line with the course of this world,** that is, in which environment y o u formerly moved about freely, feeling perfectly at home, conducting yourselves in complete harmony with "the spirit of the age that marks mankind alienated from the life of God,"[50] **in line with the prince of the domain**[51]

---

[49] In view of the last antecedent the relative is feminine (αἷς). The reference is, however, to both trespasses and sins.

[50] αἰών see on 1:21, footnote 40.

[51] Just as βασιλεία can mean both *kingship* (or *rule*) and the realm in which it is exercised: *kingdom,* so also ἐξουσία can mean *authority, one who wields authority* (or at least *supposedly* does so, an angel for instance), or the *domain* or *realm* over which this authority extends. I believe that much of the difficulty with respect to the proper interpretation of this passage has arisen from failure to recognize this

**of the air . . .** Must this word "air" be taken more or less literally as indicating the region above the earth but below the heaven of the redeemed, or must it be interpreted in an ethical or figurative sense: "the moral atmosphere" or "prevailing mood" of the period in which one happens to live? Lenski's candor must be admired. He confesses that he does not know what to do with this term (*op.cit.,* pp. 408–410). He does, however, reject both the literal and the figurative meaning. Simpson accepts the figurative sense. In rejecting the literal meaning, calling it "a queer fancy," he adds, "else we should earnestly dissuade all Godfearing souls from setting foot in an aeroplane" (*op.cit.,* p. 48). At this point I allow myself the following observations:

(1) Why only "Godfearing souls"? If air-travel is so dangerous because of all those minions of evil, should not the wicked be warned also? Moreover, should not *the earth* be avoided also, or, in spite of Rev. 16:14, is its terrain "off limits" to the evil spirits? But if that be true why did Jesus call Satan "the prince of this world" (John 12:31; 14:30)?

(2) Is there even one other instance in Scripture where the word "air" is used in this figurative sense?

(3) As to Satan — for it is he who, in line with the references just mentioned, is "the prince of the domain of the air" — is he omnipresent like God? Are his servants, the demons, omnipresent? Is it wrong to ascribe *whereness* to them because they are spirits? Obviously the distinguished and scholarly author of the work on Ephesians in *New International Commentary* would not endorse such a view, for it would be in conflict with the demonology of the New Testament. According to Mark 5:13 "the unclean spirits came out (of the man) and entered into the swine." If, then, a *place* must be assigned to Satan's servants, so that, by means of them he can influence men, can that domain be restricted to *hell,* even in this present dispensation before Christ's return? But that opinion would clash with such passages as Matt. 8:29; 16:18; I Peter 5:8. Surely, neither Satan nor his agents are in the heaven of the redeemed (Jude 6). If, therefore, according to the consistent doctrine of Scripture, the evil spirits must be *somewhere,* but not in the heaven of the redeemed, and if in this present age they cannot be restricted to hell, is it so strange that Eph. 2:2 speaks about "the prince of the domain of the air"? Is it not rather natural that the prince of evil is able, as far as God in his overruling providence permits, to carry on his sinister work by sending his legions to our globe and its surrounding atmosphere?

(4) Does not also 6:12 ("the spiritual forces of evil in the heavenly

---

last meaning. Illustrations of its use in this sense are the following: in the Septuagint IV Km. 20:13 ("or in all his realm"); Psalm 113:2 ("Judah became his sanctuary; Israel his domain"). See further Luke 4:6, in the light of Matt. 4:8 ("all this domain"). Cf. Luke 23:7. And note Col. 1:13 ("the domain of darkness").

places") point in this same general direction? Surely, if the cherubim in Ezekiel's vision were able to be on earth one moment but "lifted up from the earth" into the sky the next moment (Ezek. 1:19; cf. 10:19; 11:22), it is not impossible that the demons too would have that power. Accordingly, whatever figurative overtones the word "air" may have – due to the fact that the air is the region of fog, cloudiness, darkness – *the literal meaning here is basic.* This passage, in conjunction with others (3:10, 15; 6:12), clearly teaches that God has tenanted the supermundane realm with innumerable hosts, and that in its lower region the minions of Satan are engaged in their destructive missions. Grosheide is right when in his comments on this passage he states that according to the New Testament "the atmosphere is inhabited by spirits, including evil spirits, who exert an evil influence on people" (*op.cit.,* p. 36).[52] Note this word "including." The *evil* spirits do not have it all to themselves by any means! And as far as they and their leader are concerned, the Christian's real comfort is found in such passages as 1:20-23; Col. 2:15; Rom. 16:20; Rev. 20:3, 10. Cf. Gen. 3:15; John 12:31, 32.

The Ephesians, then, had formerly conducted themselves "in line with the course of this world, in line with the prince of the domain of the air," to which Paul now adds: **(the domain) of the spirit now at work in the sons of disobedience.** That *spirit,* again, is Satan, who, by means of his agents, the demons, and probably even directly and personally (Zech. 3; I Peter 5:8), is busily engaged in the hearts and lives of those wicked people who by the use of a Semitic expression are here designated as "the sons of disobedience," that is, those who, as it were, spring from disobedience as the mother that gave them birth. Cf. II Thess. 2:3. This is the disobedience *of unbelief* (Heb. 4:6), and hence of rebellion against God and his commandments. Note the fact that this "prince" or "spirit" is said to be "at work," that is *energetically* engaged to make what is bad even worse. Satan never rests. Now it was in line with this spirit that the Ephesians had previously conducted themselves. **3.** But not the Ephesians only. Paul is careful to add: **among whom we also once lived in the lusts of our flesh, fulfilling the desires of the flesh and its reasonings.** It is touching to read, "Among these sons of disobedience were also we," we Jews as well as y o u Gentiles.

[52] Salmond also adopts the literal meaning. Scott calls this idea "an out of date theory." Several commentators, however, are of the opinion that Paul is merely accommodating himself to current belief, and that the words he uses by no means necessarily imply that he himself held to this belief (thus Abbott, Robinson, and to a certain extent Van Leeuwen). Westcott emphasizes that the popular notion contained an element of truth, namely, "the unseen adversaries are within reach of us." Findlay interprets "air" figuratively. Hodge, having rejected the literal sense, wavers between the figurative sense "power of darkness" and the meaning "incorporeal power." No one today attaches any value to the grotesque and highly speculative notions of rabbinical literature regarding the abode, etc., of the demons.

Paul includes himself. Yet, this is the apostle who during this same imprisonment said concerning his own pre-Christian life, ". . . as to legal righteousness . . . blameless" (Phil. 3:6). The point is that both the Gentile, steeped in immorality, and the Jew, who imagines that he can save himself by obeying the law of Moses, are *living* (a synonym of *walking* in verse 2) "in the lusts of the flesh," for when the word *flesh* is used in such a context it refers to the corrupt human nature, or, more in general, to anything apart from Christ on which one bases his hope for happiness or salvation. "The moral man came to the judgment, But his self-righteous rags would not do." Cf. Rom. 7:18: ". . . in my flesh dwells no good thing." As to *desires,* in the present connection this can refer only to *unrighteous* cravings, such as belong to and are spawned by the flesh. For the Jew this undoubtedly included a yearning to enter the kingdom on the basis of his own supposedly meritorious law-works. For the Gentile the reference is to such matters as immorality, idolatry, drunkenness, and, in general, self-assertiveness in its several sinister manifestations.[53] The flesh or depraved human nature, accordingly, produces evil desires. These, in turn, in order to be realized, lead to reasonings, all kinds of hostile (cf. Col. 1:21), self-righteous, and/or immoral plans and cogitations, which finally result in wicked deeds. Cf. James 1:14, 15; 4:1. Illustrations of this process: the story of Cain and Abel (Gen. 4:1-8); of Amnon and Tamar (II Sam. 13:1-19); of Absalom in his rebellion against his father David (II Sam. 15 ff.); and of Ahab and Naboth (I Kings 21). However, though the indicated sequence of the elements in the progress of evil is as here summarized, life itself is too complex for such a simplification. There is constant interaction.[54] This is a matter that demands attention, for it shows how terrible is man's lost condition: the one sin breeds another which not only, in turn gives rise to still another but also "turns around," as it were, and reacts upon its begetter, adding to the latter's virility and effectiveness for evil! No wonder that Paul continues: **and were by nature children of wrath even as the rest.** This wrath is not to be compared to fire in straw, quickly blazing and quickly burnt out. On the contrary, it is *settled indignation,* the attitude of God toward men viewed as fallen in Adam (Rom. 5:12, 17-19) and refusing to accept the gospel of grace and salvation in Christ. It is with respect to them that it is written: "He who . . . disobeys the Son shall not see life, but the wrath of God remains on him" (John 3:36). "By nature" must mean "apart from regenerating grace." It refers to men as they are in their natural condition, as descendants of Adam; specifically, as included

[53] For a word-study of ἐπιθυμία see N.T.C. on I and II Timothy and Titus, pp. 271, 272, footnote 147; and for σάρξ see N.T.C. on Philippians, p. 77, footnote 55; also pp. 152, 153 on Phil. 3:3.

[54] Cf. the various sequences of the elements of Christian experience – such as knowledge, love, and obedience – in Scripture. See N.T.C. on the Gospel according to John, Vol. II, pp. 10, 11.

in him as their representative in the covenant of works. Such, then, says Paul, were we before the great change took place. It was true with respect to the addressed and true also with respect to the one who was addressing them. Moreover, in order that no one might conclude that among the children of men there were any at all to whom these words would not apply, Paul adds "even as the rest." Cf. Rom. 3:9-18. "Children of wrath" (another Semitism) means objects of God's settled indignation now and for all time to come (again John 3:36), unless God's marvelous grace intervenes to crush sinful pride and stubborn disobedience, the disobedience of unbelief.

"But is not God also merciful?" Yes, indeed, for though he hates the stubborn sinner because of his stubbornness, his inexcusable impenitence, yet he loves him as his creature. As such he loves all men. He loves *the world* (John 3:16). The amazing character of that love makes it understandable, at least to some extent, that God's wrath should rest on those who spurn it.

**4, 5.** And now the great change is vividly portrayed. Upon men so totally unworthy *such* mercy, love, and grace is bestowed: **God,[55] being rich in mercy, because of his great love with which he loved us, even though we were dead through our trespasses made us alive together with Christ — by grace y o u have been saved —.**

As far as the present paragraph is concerned the tragic account of man's forlorn condition is finished. But the main idea with which the apostle started out has not yet been expressed. The words "and y o u," as the *object* of the chapter's opening sentence, must not be left hanging in mid-air. *The Ephesians* cannot be left in their state of wrath and condition of misery. Both object and Ephesians must be "rescued." And it is high time that this be done. The great throbbing heart of this marvelous missionary, a heart so filled with compassion,[56] can wait no longer. Here then finally, after all these modifiers and in connection with the repetition in verse 5 of the words of verse 1 — "even though . . . dead through . . . trespasses" — comes the main clause: the subject and the main verb: "God (verse 4) . . . made alive" (verse 5). However, for the reason already given, the apostle chooses to take his stand alongside of the Ephesians. He is convinced that his own state (and, in fact, the state of all the Jews who in former days were

---

[55] Probably because spiritual darkness and light are here so strongly contrasted, and because of the particle δέ at the beginning of verse 4 (ὁ δὲ θεός), many feel that a new sentence begins here (A.V., R.S.V., N.E.B., etc.). However, the fact that in verse 5 the apostle (according to what appears to be the best reading) repeats the words of verse 1 in only slightly altered form, and now, in verses 4 and 5, adds the required subject and predicate, would seem to indicate that there was no serious "break" in the sentence structure. The anacoluthon which many see here is more apparent than real, and δέ in the present instance (as often) is best left untranslated. On this point I agree with Lenski (*op.cit.,* pp. 413, 414) over against many others.

[56] On this see N.T.C. on Philippians, p. 181.

trusting in their own righteousness for salvation) was basically no better than that of the Gentiles, and also that the new-found joy is the same for all. So instead of saying, "And *y o u* he made alive," he says, "And *us* he made alive." Now if this be a case of syntactical inconsistency it is one of the most glorious cases on record!

Paul ascribes the dramatic and marvelous change that has taken place, in his own life and in that of the others, to the *mercy, love,* and *grace* of God. *Love* is basic, that is, it is the most comprehensive of the three terms. Paul says, "God, being rich in mercy, because of his great love with which he loved us . . . made us alive," etc. This love of God is so great that it defies all definition. We can speak of it as his intense concern for, deep personal interest in, warm attachment to, and spontaneous tenderness toward his chosen ones, but all this is but to stammer. Those, and those only, who experience it are the ones who know what it is, though even they can never fully comprehend it (3:19). They know, however, that it is unique, spontaneous, strong, sovereign, everlasting, and infinite (Isa. 55:6, 7; 62:10-12; 63:9; Jer. 31:3, 31-34; Hos. 11:8; Mic. 7:18-20; John 3:16; I John 4:8, 16, 19). It is "the love that has been shed abroad in our hearts" (Rom. 5:5), "his own love toward us" (Rom. 5:8), the love from which no one and nothing "will be able to separate us" (Rom. 8:39).

Now when this love is directed toward sinners viewed in their wretchedness and need of commiseration and succor, it is called *mercy*. See N.T.C. on Philippians, p. 142 for a list of over 100 Old and New Testament passages in which this divine attribute is described, showing how "rich" this mercy is. It is as "rich" as God's love is "great." God's *grace* of which mention is made in the statement, "By grace y o u have been saved," is his love viewed as focused on the guilty and undeserving. Mercy *pities.* Grace *pardons.* But it does more than that. It *saves* all the way, delivering men from the greatest woe (everlasting damnation), and bestowing upon them the choicest blessing (everlasting life for soul and body). Being saved by grace is the opposite of being saved by merit, the merit that supposedly accrues from inherent goodness or from strenuous effort. Cf. 2:8, 9. The expression clearly indicates that the ground of our salvation lies not in us but in God. "We love him because he first loved us" (I John 4:19). This sovereign nature of divine love in its various aspects is illustrated in such beautiful passages as Deut. 7:7, 8; Isa. 48:11; Dan. 9:19; Hos. 14:4; John 15:16; Rom. 5:8; Eph. 1:4; I John 4:10.

It was because of the riches of his mercy, greatness of his love, and amazing character of his grace, that God "made us alive *together with Christ* even though we were dead through our trespasses." [57]

[57] With many expositors, but contrary to Lenski, *op.cit.,* p. 415, I adhere to N.N.'s punctuation which construes the words "even though we were dead through our trespasses" as a modifier of "God made us alive together with Christ." It seems to

"Together with Christ," for when the Father made his Son alive, by causing the latter's soul to return from Paradise in order to re-inhabit the body which it had left, he in this very act furnished proof that the substitutionary atonement had been accepted, and that, accordingly, the sentence of death which otherwise would have doomed believers had been lifted, their sins forgiven. And this justification, in turn, is basic to all the other blessings of salvation. **6.** This is true because vivification does not stand by itself, for the apostle continues: **and raised us up with him and made us sit with him in the heavenly places in Christ Jesus.** Christ's resurrection and exaltation to the Father's right hand in "the heavenly places" (here and in 1:3 the heaven of the redeemed is meant; contrast 6:12) not only foreshadows and guarantees our glorious bodily resurrection and all the consequent glory that will be our portion at the great consummation, but is also the basis of *present* blessings. Whatever happens to the Bridegroom has an immediate effect upon the Bride. This effect has reference not only to the church's *state* or legal standing before God's law, but also to its *condition,* the latter because from the place of his heavenly glory and majesty Christ sends forth the Spirit into the hearts of believers, so that they die to sin and are raised to newness of life. Therefore, both as to state and as to condition we can say that with Christ Jesus we ourselves were tried, condemned, crucified, buried (Rom. 6:4-8; 8:17; Col. 2:12; II Tim. 2:11), but also, made alive, raised, and set in heavenly places (Rom. 6:5; 8:17; Col. 2:13; 3:1-3; II Tim. 2:12; Rev. 20:4). To be sure, there is a time factor. Not at once do we receive this glory in full measure. But the right to receive it fully has been secured, and the new life has already begun. Even now our life "is hid with Christ in God." Our names are inscribed in heaven's register. Our interests are being promoted there. We are being governed by heavenly standards and motivated by heavenly impulses. The blessings of heaven constantly descend upon us. Heaven's grace fills our hearts. Its power enables us to be more than conquerors. And to heaven our thoughts aspire and our prayers ascend.

**7.** What now was the purpose which God had in mind when he bestowed on us this great salvation? Paul answers: **in order that in the ages to come he might show the surpassing riches of his grace (expressed) in kindness toward us in Christ Jesus.** Therefore, God's purpose in saving his people

---

me that this punctuation is justified by the consideration that Paul is here carrying toward completion the thought begun in verse 1. Lenski's objection, namely, that the apostle would certainly not mention the obvious fact that vivification concerns dead persons (*op.cit.,* p. 415) is not convincing. The point is: the addressed, as well as Paul, were dead *because of their own guilt.* This is clearly implied when they are called "children of wrath" and are pictured as in need of God's *grace.* Accordingly, when God makes them alive, in spite of the fact that they deserved nothing less than everlasting damnation, this is a marvelous deed, worthy to be mentioned.

reaches beyond man. His own glory is *his own* chief aim. It is for that reason that he displays his grace in all its matchless beauty and transforming power. To some this may seem somewhat cold or even "selfish." Yet, on rereading the passage one will soon discover that God's overshadowing majesty and his condescending tenderness combine here, for the glory of his attributes is placed on exhibition as it reflects itself "in kindness toward us!" *We* are his sparkling jewels. Illustration: A Roman matron when asked, "Where are your jewels?" calls her two sons, and, pointing to them, says, "These are my jewels." So also, throughout eternity the redeemed will be exhibited as the monuments of "the marvelous grace of our loving Lord," who drew us from destruction's pit and raised us to heights of heavenly bliss, and did all this at such a cost to himself that he spared not his own Son, and in such a manner that not a single one of his attributes, not even his justice, was eclipsed.

In Christ Jesus this divine kindness [58] was displayed in various ways, mostly, of course, in the death on the cross. It was displayed also in such sayings as are recorded in Matt. 5:7; 9:13; 11:28-30; 12:7; 23:37; Mark 10:14; Luke 10:25-37, to mention only a few; and in such attitudes and actions, among many others, as are commemorated in Matt. 9:36; 14:14; 15:21-28; 20:34; Luke 7:11-17, 36-50; 8:40-42, 49-56; 23:34; John 19:27; 21:15-17.

Paul does not say "God's grace," nor even "the riches of his grace," but "the sur- (super) passing riches of his grace." This is characteristic Pauline language. Earlier he had written to the Romans, "Where sin abounded, grace *super*-overflowed" (Rom. 5:20). During the present imprisonment he was going to tell the Philippians about the peace of God which "*sur*- (super) passes all understanding" (Phil. 4:7). And, during his brief period of freedom between the first and second Roman imprisonments he would write to Timothy, "And it *super*-abounded (namely) the grace of our Lord, with faith and love in Christ Jesus" (I Tim. 1:14). See also II Cor. 7:4; I Thess. 3:10; 5:13; II Thess. 1:3. As Paul sees it, there is nothing narrow about this grace of God, nothing stingy. Its loving arms embrace both Gentile and Jew. It reaches even to "the chief of sinners" (Paul himself), and so "rich" is it that it enriches every heart and life which it touches, filling it with marvelous love, joy, peace, etc.

God will display the surpassing riches of his grace "in the ages to come." But what is meant by these ages? In the main, there are three opinions:

(1) *The ages that will precede Christ's Parousia.* The expression *ages to come* "must not be understood to refer to 'the future' world. Paul is speaking about the earthly dispensation which has not yet run its course" (Grosheide; cf. Barry). A possible objection to this view would be that in that case Paul would probably have spoken about "the fulness of the times" (as

[58] In the New Testament the word χρηστότης is used only by Paul (Rom. 2:4; 3:12; 11:22; Col. 3:12; Titus 3:4, etc.).

in 1:10) or about "this age" (as in 1:21). Though not even in his early epistles did he proceed from the assumption that the second coming was the very next item on God's program for the history of the world (see II Thess. 2:1-12), nevertheless, it was not his custom to posit continuing lengths of time that would intervene between his own day and Christ's return.

(2) *The ages that will follow Christ's Parousia.* With variations as to detail this view is held by Abbott, Greijdanus, Lenski, Salmond, Van Leeuwen, and many others. In its defense an appeal is made to 1:21: "the coming age." However, it is debatable whether this argument is valid, for in 1:21 a contrast is drawn between "this age" and "the coming one." That is not the case in 2:7. Also 1:21 has the singular *aeon;* 2:7, the plural *aeons.* And when, with one commentator, these post-Parousia ages, as they affect us, turn out to be "the timeless [?] aeons of eternity," while another – perhaps forgetting that in that glorious life there will be no more sin and misery? – in his comments on the grace that will then be expressed "in kindness toward us," interprets this to mean personal pity shown to those in need, one begins to wonder whether, after all, the restriction of "the ages to come" to the post-Parousia era is legitimate.

(3) *All future time.* In commenting on this passage John Calvin says, "It was the design of God to hallow in all ages the remembrance of so great a goodness." Scott expresses the same idea in these words, "The new life now begun will endure forever, so that the manifestation of God's grace will be always renewing itself. To bring out more forcibly this idea of goodness that will extend through all eternity Paul speaks not of the 'age' but *the ages* yet to come." And Hodge states, "It is better therefore to take it [the phrase "in the ages to come"] without limitation, for all future time."

Since nothing in the context limits the application of the phrase to any one period either before or after Christ's return, and since the apostle himself when he dwells more fully on the church's *lofty goal* (chapter 3) speaks about both the gathering in of the Gentiles in the present pre-Parousia age, and of the ultimate perfection of the church in the coming age, I regard explanation (3) as the best. The purpose, then, which God had in mind when he bestowed on us this great salvation described in verses 4-6, was that "in Christ Jesus" (see on 1:1, 3, 4) throughout this entire new dispensation and forever afterward he might place *us, Jew and Gentile alike,* on exhibition as monuments of the surpassing riches of his grace expressed in kindness of which we are and forever will be the recipients.

**8.** Reflecting on what he has just now said about grace, and repeating the parenthetical clause of verse 5b, the apostle says, **For by grace**[59] **you**

---

[59] The original has τῇ γὰρ χάριτι. Note the anaphoric use of the article. This is very common in Greek. See Gram. N.T., p. 762. Some translate: "this grace."

**have been saved. . . .** For explanation see on verse 5. He continues: **through faith; and this not of yourselves, (it is) the gift of God . . .**

Three explanations deserve consideration:

(1) *That offered by A. T. Robertson.* Commenting on this passage in his *Word Pictures in the New Testament,* Vol. IV, p. 525, he states, "Grace is God's part, faith ours." He adds that since in the original the demonstrative "this" (and *this* not of yourselves) is neuter and does not correspond with the gender of the word "faith," which is feminine, it does not refer to the latter "but to the act of being saved by grace conditioned on faith on our part." Even more clearly in Gram. N.T., p. 704, he states categorically, "In Eph. 2:8 . . . there is no reference to *διὰ πίστεως* [*through faith*] in *τοῦτο* [this], but rather to the idea of salvation in the clause before."

Without any hesitancy I answer, Robertson, to whom the entire world of New Testament scholarship is heavily indebted, does not express himself felicitously in this instance. This is true first because in a context in which the apostle places such tremendous stress on the fact that from start to finish man owes his salvation to God, to him alone, it would have been very strange, indeed, for him to say, "Grace is God's part, faith ours." True though it be that both the responsibility of believing and also its activity are ours, for God does not believe for us, nevertheless, in the present context (verses 5-10) one rather expects emphasis on the fact that both in its initiation and in its continuation faith is entirely dependent on God, and so is our complete salvation. Also, Robertson, a grammarian famous in his field, knew that in the original the demonstrative (*this*), though neuter, by no means always corresponds in gender with its antecedent. That he knew this is shown by the fact that on the indicated page of his Grammar (p. 704) he points out that "in general" the demonstrative "agrees with its substantive in gender and number." When he says "in general," he must mean, *"not always* but most of the time." Hence, he should have considered more seriously the possibility that, in view of the context, the exception to the rule, an exception by no means rare, applies here. He should have made allowance for it.[60] Finally, he should have justified the departure from the rule that unless there is a compelling reason to do otherwise the antecedent should be looked for in the immediate vicinity of the pronoun or adjective that refers to it.

(2) *That presented, among others, by F. W. Grosheide.* As he sees it, the words "and this not of yourselves" mean *"and this being saved by grace through faith* is not of yourselves" but is the gift of God. Since, according to this theory – also endorsed, it would seem, by John Calvin in his Com-

---

[60] Though Lenski calls Robertson's statement ("Grace is God's part, faith ours") careless, his own explanation (*op.cit.,* p. 423), in which he likewise bases everything on the fact that *τοῦτο* is neuter but *πίστις* feminine, is *basically* the same as that of Robertson.

mentary — *faith is included in the gift,* none of the objections against theory (1) apply with respect to theory (2).

Does this mean then that (2) is entirely satisfactory? Not necessarily. This brings us to

(3) *That defended by A. Kuyper, Sr. in his book* Het Werk van den Heiligen Geest (Kampen, 1927), pp. 506–514.

Dr. Kuyper is, however, not this theory's sole defender, but his defence is, perhaps, the most detailed and vigorous. The theory amounts, in brief, to the following: Paul's words may be paraphrased thus, "I had the right to speak about 'the surpassing riches of his grace' *for* it is, indeed, by grace that y o u are saved, through faith; and lest y o u should now begin to say, 'But then we deserve credit, at least, for *believing,*' I will immediately add that *even this faith* (or: even this exercise of faith) is not of yourselves but is *God's gift.*"

With variations as to detail this explanation was the one favored by much of the patristic tradition. Supporting it were also Beza, Zanchius, Erasmus, Huigh de Groot (Hugo Grotius), Bengel, Michaelis, etc. It is shared, too, by Simpson (*op. cit.,* p. 55) and by Van Leeuwen and Greijdanus in their commentaries. H. C. G. Moule (*Ephesian Studies,* New York, 1900, pp. 77, 78) endorses it, with the qualification, "We must explain *τοῦτο* [*this*] to refer not to the feminine noun *πίστις* [*faith*] precisely, but to the fact of our exercising faith." Moreover, it is perhaps no exaggeration to say that the explanation offered is also shared by the average man who reads 2:8 in his A.V. or A.R.V. Salmond, after presenting several grounds in its favor, particularly also this that "the formula *καὶ τοῦτο* might rather favor it, as it often adds to the idea to which it is attached," finally shies away from it because "*salvation* is the main idea in the preceding statement," which fact, of course, the advocates of (3) would not deny but do, indeed, vigorously affirm, but which is not a valid argument against the idea that faith, as well as everything else in salvation, is God's gift. It is not a valid argument against (3), therefore.

I have become convinced that theory (3) is the most logical explanation of the passage in question. Probably the best argument in its favor is this one: If Paul meant to say, "For by grace y o u have been saved through faith, and this being saved is not of yourselves," he would have been guilty of needless repetition — for what else is *grace* but that which proceeds from God and not from ourselves? — a repetition rendered even more prolix when he now (supposedly) adds, "it, that is, salvation, is the gift of God," followed by a fourth and fifth repetition, namely, "not of works, for we are his handiwork." No wonder that Dr. A. Kuyper states, "If the text read, 'For by grace y o u have been saved, not of yourselves, it is the work of God,' it would make some sense. But first to say, 'By grace y o u have been saved,' and then, as if it were something new, to add, '*and* this having been saved is not of yourselves,' this does not run smoothly but jerks and jolts . . . . And while with that interpretation everything proceeds by fits and starts and becomes lame and redundant, all is excellent and meaningful when y o u follow the ancient interpreters of Jesus' church." [61] This, it would seem to me also, is the refutation of theory (1) and, to a certain extent, of theory (2).

Basically, however, theories (2) and (3) both stress the same truth, namely, that the credit for the entire process of salvation must be given to God, so that man is deprived of every reason for boasting, which is exactly what Paul says in the words which now follow, namely, **9, 10. not of works, lest anyone should boast.** This introduces us to the subject:

*Works in relation to our salvation*

(1) *Rejected*

As a basis for salvation, a ground upon which we can plead, works are rejected. "Not the labors of my hands can fulfil thy law's demands." In this connection it must be remembered that the apostle is not thinking exclusively or even mainly of works in fulfilment of the Mosaic law, by means of which the Jew, unconverted to Christ, sought to justify himself. Surely, also by such "works of the law" "no flesh will be justified in his sight" (Rom. 3:20; cf. Gal. 2:16). But in view of the fact that Paul was addressing an audience consisting mostly of Christians from the Gentile world it is clear that he wishes to emphasize that God rejects every work of man, be he Gentile, Jew, or believer in his moments of spiritual eclipse, *every work on which any man bases his hope for salvation.* If, then, salvation is completely from God, "who spared not his own Son but delivered him up for us all" (Rom. 8:32), *every* ground of boasting in self is excluded (Rom. 3:27; 4:5; I Cor. 1:31). When the Lord comes in his glory, those at his *left* hand will do all the boasting (Matt. 25:44; cf. 7:22); those at his *right* hand will be unable even to recall their good deeds (Matt. 25:37-39).

Now all boasting is excluded,
Unearned bliss is now my own.
I, in God thus safely rooted,
Boast in sovereign grace alone.
Long before my mother bore me,
E'en before God's mighty hand
Out of naught made sea and land,

[61] As to grammar, from the works of Plato, Xenophon, and Demosthenes several instances of the use of τοῦτο to indicate a masculine or feminine antecedent are cited by Kuyper. He also quotes the following from a Greek Grammar: "Very common is the use of a neuter demonstrative pronoun to indicate an antecedent substantive of masculine or of feminine gender when the idea conveyed by that substantive is referred to in a general sense." The quotation is from the work of Kühnhert, *Ausführliche Grammatik der Griech. sprache* (Hanover, 1870), Vol. II, p. 54.

His electing love watched o'er me.
God is love, O angel-voice,
Tongues of men, make him your choice.[62]

(2) *Confected*

Paul continues: **for his handiwork are we, created in Christ Jesus for good works, which God prepared beforehand . . .** Fact is that though good works are non-meritorious, yet they are so important that God created us in order that we should perform them. We are his *handiwork:* that which he made, his product (cf. Ps. 100:3). To him we owe our entire spiritual as well as physical existence. Our very birth as believers is from God (John 3:3, 5). We are created "in Christ Jesus" (see on 1:1, 3, 4), for apart from him we are nothing and can accomplish nothing (John 15:5; cf. I Cor. 4:7). As "men in Christ," believers constitute a new creation, as the apostle had said previously (II Cor. 5:17): "Wherefore if any man is in Christ, there is a new creation: the old things are passed away; behold they are become new" (II Cor. 5:17). Believers were "made alive together with Christ" (see above on verse 5; and below on 4:24; also Gal. 6:15).

Now along with *creating us* God also *prepared good works.* He did this *first* by giving us *his Son,* our great Enabler, in whom good works find their most glorious expression (Luke 24:19; Acts 2:22). Not only does Christ enable us to perform good works but he is also our Example in good works (John 13:14, 15; I Peter 2:21). God did this *secondly* by giving us *faith in his Son.* Faith is God's gift (verse 8). Now in planting the seed of faith in our hearts, and causing it to sprout and with great care tending it, making it grow, etc., God also in that sense prepared for us good works, for good works are the fruit of faith. Living faith, moreover, implies a renewed mind, a grateful heart, and a surrendered will. Out of such ingredients, all of them God-given, God *confects* or *compounds* good works. Thus, summarizing, we can say that by giving us his Son and by imparting to us faith in that Son God prepared beforehand our good works. When Christ through his Spirit dwells in the hearts of believers, his gifts and graces are bestowed upon them, so that they, too, bear fruits, such as "love, joy, peace, long-suffering, kindness, goodness, faithfulness, meekness, and self-control" (Gal. 5:22, 23).

(3) *Expected*

Paul concludes this paragraph by adding: **that we should walk in them.** Though good works are a divine preparation, they are at the same time a human responsibility. These two must never be separated. If salvation can be illustrated by the figure of a flourishing tree, then good works are symbolized not by its roots nor even by its trunk but by its fruit. Jesus requires

[62] This is the product of my attempt to translate into English, with retention of meter, the first stanza of the beautiful Dutch hymn "Alle roem is uitgesloten."

of us fruit, more fruit, much fruit (John 15:2, 5, 8). He said, "I am the vine, y o u are the branches. He who abides in me, with me abiding in him, he it is that bears much fruit, for apart from me y o u can do nothing." *To bear much fruit* and *to walk in good works* is the same thing. When a certain occupation has the love of a man's heart, he is "walking" in it. Note: walk *in them,* no longer in "trespasses and sins" (verses 1, 2).

(4) *Perfected*

Combining (2) and (3) we see that by walking in good works we have entered into the sphere of God's own activity. Hence, we know that though our own efforts may often disappoint us, so that we are ashamed even of our *good* works, victory will arrive at last; not fully, to be sure, in the present life but in the next. Moral and spiritual perfection is our *goal* even here, but will be our *portion* in the life hereafter, for we are confident of this very thing that he who began a good work in us will carry it to completion (Phil. 1:6). Cf. Eph. 1:4; 3:19; 4:12, 13.

This doctrine of good works, when accepted by faith, deprives man of every reason for boasting in self but also takes away from him every ground for despair. It glorifies God.

---

# Chapter 2

Verses 11–18

Theme: *The Church Glorious*

I. *Adoration*
*for its*

*U* niversal Scope (embracing both Jew and Gentile),
2. shown by the reconciliation of Jew and Gentile through the cross

11 Therefore remember that formerly y o u, the Gentiles in flesh, who
are called "uncircumcision" by that which is called "circumcision" – in flesh, handmade! – 12 that y o u were at that time separate from Christ, alienated from the
commonwealth of Israel, and strangers to the covenants of the promise, having
no hope and without God in the world. 13 But now in Christ Jesus y o u who
formerly were far away have been brought nearby through the blood of Christ.
14 For he himself is our peace, who made both one and has broken down the barrier formed by the dividing wall, the hostility, 15 by abolishing in his flesh the law
of commandments with its requirements, in order that in himself he might create
of the two one new man, (so) making peace, 16 and might reconcile both of them
in one body to God through the cross, having slain the hostility by means of it;
17 and he came and proclaimed the good news: "Peace to y o u, those far away,
and peace to those nearby"; 18 for through him we both have our access in one
Spirit to the Father.

2:11-18

## 2. *The Reconciliation of Jew and Gentile*

When Paul wrote the present paragraph he was in high spirits. This is very clear from the fact that the prayer and the doxology found in chapter 3 are the natural climax to 2:11-18 and 2:19-22. In order to understand the present paragraph it should be borne in mind that the apostle knew by personal experience how difficult it was to weld Jew and Gentile into an organic unity, a unity of perfect equality. Jewish Christians had often been loath to admit Gentiles into the church except via Judaism. Immediately after Paul's return to Syrian Antioch from his first missionary journey "certain men came down from Judea and were teaching the brothers, 'Unless y o u are circumcised according to the custom of Moses, y o u cannot be saved' " (Acts 15:1). Even Peter, who, because of the vision he had received, should have known better (Acts 10, 11), refused for a while to eat with the Gentiles, and by his conduct merited Paul's stinging rebuke (Gal. 2:11-21). When Paul wrote Galatians the controversy over the question "How can salvation be obtained?," implying the further question "On what terms can the Gentiles be accepted into the church?," was at its height. The apostle reminded these "foolish Galatians" that those who desired to be justified by the law were severed from Christ (Gal. 5:4). The epistles to the Romans and to the Corinthians clearly indicate that when these were written the battle had not yet been completely won. In fact, until the end of Paul's life the fire which at one time had been raging furiously was never *completely* put out but showed intermittent flashes. That was true during the present Roman imprisonment (see Col. 2:11-17; Phil. 3:2-11), during the brief period of freedom that followed it (I Tim. 1:6-11; Titus 3:5, 9), and even during the apostle's final incarceration (II Tim. 1:9, 10). But though this is true, yet *officially* the answer had been given long before the present letter was written. It had been furnished by the Synod of Jerusalem, before the apostle started on his second missionary journey. See Acts 15. The great principle that salvation in all its riches is freely given to all those – whether Jew or Gentile – who accept Christ through a living faith (this faith *also God-given*) had become the accepted doctrine of the church. Whatever remained of the struggle after the Jerusalem Synod had been held and Galatians had been written was "aftermath." The ferocious attack upon the truth had been repulsed. Yet all was not over. To the very end Paul defended the principle of freedom from the law in its saving and ceremonial aspects, the principle of salvation for "all men" without any distinction as to national or racial origin and without the requirement that anyone reach the church by means of a detour. (See I Tim. 2:3-7; Titus 2:11; II Tim. 4:1-8.)

Now it was especially in Ephesus and its surroundings that Jew and Gentile who had accepted Christ lived together in love and unity and constituted *one ecumenical church*. It was a flourishing church, from which, as from a center, many other congregations were founded (Acts 19:10; cf. Rev. 1:11; 2:1-7). This was one reason why Paul, though a prisoner, rejoiced greatly and glorified his God. Though even in Ephesus conditions were by no means perfect, yet, by and large, the apostle witnessed here the realization of his own ideal and, more important, of God's plan! Moreover, he bears testimony to the fact that Jew and Gentile, reconciled to God through faith in Christ, *are reconciled to each other also!* Hence, in the spirit of exultation he desires that the Ephesians, *mostly formerly Gentiles,* will rejoice with him in God's works. This goal can best be achieved by comparing their past wretchedness with their present reason for cheerfulness. **11, 12.** So Paul writes, **Therefore remember that formerly y o u, the Gentiles in flesh, who are called "uncircumcision" by that which is called "circumcision" – in flesh, handmade! – that y o u were at that time separate from Christ,**[63] **alienated from the commonwealth of Israel, and strangers to the covenants of the promise, having no hope and without God in the world.** "Therefore," that is, because y o u Ephesians, once dead, were made alive by grace through faith and for good works (verses 1-10), consider y o u r

---

63 I do not agree with those expositors (including Lenski, *op.cit.,* p. 432, but see his translation, p. 429) who deny the predicative position of the phrase "separate from Christ." A harsh construction results, as was pointed out by Abbott (*op.cit.,* p. 57). Both the periphrastic nature of the predicate in verse 12 and the re-emphasis in verse 13 on the formerly "separate from Christ" idea, cause me to agree with most translators and exegetes in accepting *five* (not only four) predicate terms in verse 12: *separate from Christ, alienated, strangers, hopeless,* and *without God.*

present high estate in the light of y o u r former low position, that y o u may glorify God, y o u r Benefactor. As to y o u r past, y o u r case was in a sense even more hopeless than that of *the highly privileged* Jews, for y o u were Gentiles. Y o u carried the evidence of y o u r Gentile state in y o u r very flesh, for y o u were uncircumcised. Hence the Jews, unconverted to Christ, call y o u "uncircumcision" (that is, "the uncircumcised"). They do this even though they themselves, proud of being called "circumcision" (that is, "the circumcised"), possess only *the sign,* not *the thing signified.* They were circumcised only "in flesh," not in their hearts (Lev. 26:41; Deut. 10:16; 30:6; Jer. 4:4; Ezek. 44:7, ears (Jer. 6:10), and lips (Exod. 6:12, 30). It was all merely a matter of minor surgery, a manual operation, the cutting away of foreskin. It was outward, not inward. The real meaning or value of circumcision has been erased with Christ's death on the cross. Yet in this outward mark the Jews continue to glory, while they despise all others, including y o u Ephesians. Now at that time when y o u, as also now, were being held in such low esteem, y o u r misery was great, for y o u were *Christless, stateless, friendless, hopeless, and Godless.*

(1) *Christless: "separate from Christ"*

Paul cannot have meant that before their conversion Christ had paid no attention to them, for the apostle has clearly indicated that those whom he addresses had been included in the number of the elect from all eternity (1:3 ff.). He must mean that before their conversion this oneness "in Christ" had not been *experienced* by them in any sense whatever. They had been groping in the darkness, filth, and despair of sin. The light, holiness, and hopefulness of those who come to know Christ had not as yet become their portion. Hence, in that former state they had been unspeakably wretched. The Christians' greatest joy is the solemn assurance that no one and nothing can ever *separate* them from the love of Christ (Rom. 8:35). From this great joy the Ephesians had been *far removed.*

(2) *stateless: "alienated from the commonwealth of Israel"*

To be sure, they had not been stateless in every conceivable sense. But though included in the Roman province of Asia, they were excluded from the many blessings that pertained to the Jewish theocracy. They lacked citizenship among the chosen people. This was, indeed, a deplorable lack, for it was to Israel (for the meaning of the name see Gen. 32:28) that God of old had revealed himself in a special manner. To that people he had given his law, his special protection, his prophecies and promises. Read the following stirring passages: Deut. 32:10-14; 33:27-29; Ps. 147:20; Isa. 63:9; Ezek. 16:6-14; Amos 3:2. From all this the Ephesians had been excluded.

(3) *friendless: "strangers to the covenants of the promise"*

The essence of the covenant of grace, to which the present passage refers, is the experience of "the friendship of Jehovah" (Ps. 25:14). Now in their unconverted state the Ephesians had been strangers to this friendship. They had been mere "foreigners" from whom the rights and privileges of citizens had been withheld. Ranking high among these withheld privileges were "the covenants of the promise." Paul speaks about *covenants,* plural. He has reference, no doubt, to *the many reaffirmations of the one and only covenant of grace.* He calls it the covenant "of promise," because its main element is, indeed, God's promise: "I will be your (or at times *y o u r*) God." That this promise was made to Abraham, reaffirmed to Isaac, to Jacob, and, in fact, to all God's people in both dispensations, so that, while in a sense there is only *one* covenant of grace, there were *many* reaffirmations (and in *that* sense many *covenants*), is clear from such passages as the following: Gen. 17:7, 8; 26:1-5; 28:10-17; Exod. 20:2; Deut. 5:2, 3, 6; Jer. 24:7; 30:22; 31:33; Ezek. 11:20; Zech. 13:9; II Cor. 6:16; Gal. 3:8, 9, 29; Rev. 21:3. On the basis of all the passages that refer to it, this covenant can be defined as *that divinely established arrangement between the triune God and his people whereby God carries out his eternal decree of redemption by promising his friendship, hence full and free salvation, to his people, upon the basis of the vicarious atonement of Christ, the Mediator of the covenant, and they accept this salvation by faith.* Because of the greatness of God and the lowliness of man it stands to reason that such a covenant cannot be a fifty-fifty agreement but must be a one-sided disposition, a divine *grant, settlement, ordinance,* or *institution.* It is never a mere contract between two parties — God and man — each with equal rights. Though *in a sense* it is two-sided, because man must exercise faith, as has been indicated, yet even that faith is God's gift (see on verse 8 and cf. Jer. 31:33). In that respect this covenant partakes of the nature of a *testament.* In fact, the word used in the original, namely, *diathēkē,* has both meanings: *testament* and *covenant.* It means *testament* in Heb. 9:16, 17. See also Gal. 3:15. Elsewhere both in Hebrews and in the rest of the new Testament (as in the LXX) the translation *covenant* is probably the best. Now to this covenant, too, the Ephesians, in their lost condition, had been strangers. At that time God had never revealed himself to them as their special Friend. And the Jews, having robbed God's covenant of its real, spiritual meaning, and having substituted for it the hope of earthly glory, had not even been able to convey to the Ephesians the glory of God's promise. See Matt. 23:15.

(4) *hopeless: "having no hope"*

This follows very naturally, for the Christian's *hope* is based on the divine *promise.* Accordingly, since in the earlier period the covenant-promise had not been revealed to the Ephesians, as has just been indicated, hence they also lacked hope: solid, firmly-anchored assurance of salvation. Such hope is one of God's most precious gifts, and is mentioned alongside of faith and love (1:15, 18; cf. I Cor. 13:13). It is knowledge of God's promise plus confidence with respect to its fulfilment (cf. II Cor. 1:7). It is the proliferation of faith. It amounts to the conviction that all things will be well, even when all things seem to be wrong (Rom. 4:18). It never disappoints, because it, too, like faith and love, is a divine gift (Rom. 5:5).

In their state of unbelief the Ephesians had lacked this hope. Instead, they had been filled with fear and despair. The Greek and Roman world of Paul's day was, indeed, a *hopeless* world. For details on this see N.T.C. on I and II Thessalonians, pp. 110, 111.

(5) *Godless: "and without God in the world"*

Surely they had gods, but these were vain. The Ephesians were without the one true God. This cannot mean that they were "utterly abandoned by God," for we know that this is not true, for from eternity they had been included in God's decree of election. Moreover, for them, too, Christ had died (see 1:4 ff.). Besides, on the Ephesians, as well as on the people of Lystra, God had bestowed many blessings which they shared with all earth's inhabitants, though not with all in the same degree, namely, "rains and fruitful seasons, filling their hearts with food and gladness" (Acts 14:17). But they had been in truth "without God in the world" in the sense that they had been without the true knowledge of God, and therefore without holiness, righteousness, peace, and the joy *of salvation*. They had resembled mariners who without compass and guide were adrift in a rudderless ship during a starless night on a tempestuous sea, far away from the harbor. Nothing less than that is meant by the gloomy, awe-inspiring phrase "without God in the world." That world is the mass of fallen mankind, lost, sin-laden, and exposed to the judgment.

**13.** Out of the darkness and despair of heathendom the Ephesians had emerged *directly* into the radiance and rapture of Christianity. The great change is described in the following words: **But now in Christ Jesus you who formerly were far away have been brought nearby through the blood of Christ.** The words "but now" indicate a sharp contrast with "formerly" (verse 11) and "at that time" (verse 12). Formerly "far away," now "nearby." These expressions have an Old Testament background. In the old dispensation Jehovah, in a sense, had his dwelling in the temple. That temple was in Jerusalem. Israel, therefore, was "nearby." On the other hand, the Gentiles were "far away." [64] Not only was this true literally, but even more so in a spiritual sense: they generally lacked the true knowledge of God. All this, however, was going to change. Isaiah records, in words reflected here in Eph. 2:17: "I create the fruit of the lips: Peace, peace to him that is far off and to him that is near . . . and I will heal him" (Isa. 57:19). The fact that this type of phraseology was carried over into the New Testament is clear from Acts 2:39, "The promise is to you and your children and to all that are *far away*." It should be evident that a person could be "nearby" and yet "far away." He could be "nearby" in a merely external

[64] In later days a *proselyte*, as the very name implies, was one who had come to be nearby.

sense, namely, because he was a sharer in the privileges of the Old Testament economy, or simply, a Jew. His heart, however, could still be "far away from God." Taken in the *external* sense, then, those who are "far away" are the Gentiles, those "nearby" are the Jews (as in verse 17). Through faith in Christ all those to whom the gospel is proclaimed have the opportunity *to draw near.* In the *spiritual* sense, however, those "nearby" are genuine *believers;* or as we today would say: Christians. The expression "nearby through the blood of Christ," here in 2:13, must mean *spiritually nearby.* Moreover, in order to do justice to the entire context, the idea "formerly far away but now nearby" must be explained in the light of verse 12 taken in its entirety. The meaning that results is this: formerly separate from Christ; now "in Christ Jesus" saved by grace through faith (verse 8); formerly alienated from the commonwealth of Israel, now "fellow-citizens with the saints and members of the household of God" (verse 19); formerly strangers to the covenants of the promise, now covenant members (Gal. 3:29); formerly without God, now at peace with him (verse 17) and in possession of the privilege of blessed access (verses 16-18).

With this explanation justice is done to the context, which shows that the terms "far away" and "nearby" must be construed both *perpendicularly* and *horizontally.* As to the first – the *God-man* relationship – the Ephesians in their former state had been so far removed from God that the intervening distance could be measured only by the greatness of the sacrifice required to bring them nearby. But by faith they had been brought close to God's heart. As to the second, the annihilation of the perpendicular distance had brought about the cessation of the horizontal also, for at the cross Jew and Gentile, both reconciled to God, had embraced each other. "Through the blood of Christ" (for explanation see on 1:7) *sin,* the great separator, had been vanquished. With reference to this horizontal reconciliation brought about by Christ crucified, the apostle continues: **14. For he himself is our peace, who made both one and has broken down the barrier formed by the dividing wall, the hostility.**[65] The forward position of the pronoun that

---

[65] With respect to the grammatical construction of verses 14 and 15 there is much difference of opinion among exegetes. Many connect τὴν ἔχθραν with the words that follow. This results in the rendering which is favored by A.V. and A.R.V., "having abolished in his flesh the enmity, *even* the law of commandments *contained in* ordinances." This makes good sense, for the law is, in a sense, an adversary, the accuser of transgressors (cf. Deut. 27:26; Gal. 3:10). Nevertheless, it is, perhaps, better to connect τὴν ἔχθραν with the immediately preceding λύσας, so that it would be in apposition with τὸ μεσότοχον. The participle καταργήσας has enough modifiers as it is. Hence, in harmony with N.N., I, too, would place a comma after τὴν ἔχθραν.

Essentially there is little difference between (a) the rendering favored by A.V. and A.R.V., and (b) that which R.S.V., I, and many others endorse. In both cases it remains true that when Jesus abolished in his flesh the law of commandments with its requirements, the barrier between Jew and Gentile ceased to be.

refers to Christ shows that the proper English translation is "he himself," or "he alone." He himself is our peace, that is, what everything else — whether the law with its ordinances, human merit, law-works of whatever kind, sacrifices, etc. — could not do, he, he alone in his own person, has done, for he is the very embodiment of peace. In his capacity as the Prince of Peace (Isa. 9:6) he, by means of his voluntary sacrifice, has brought about peace (cf. John 14:27; 16:33; 20:19, 20): reconciliation between God and man, hence also between Gentiles and Jews. As to the latter groups, he has made both [66] one, has welded them into one organic unit, namely, the church. That the reference is here to the reconciliation between Gentiles and Jews is clear from the fact that these are the two groups mentioned in the immediate context (verses 11 and 12).

Between the Gentiles and the Jews there had long been a formidable obstacle, a hatred-barrier.[67] It is called a barrier "of" or "formed by" "the dividing wall" or "fence," a figurative reference to the law considered as a cause of separation and enmity between Jews and Gentiles. See on verse 15. When Paul speaks about this *barrier* of hostility, there may be an allusion to the barricade which in Jerusalem separated the court of the Gentiles from the temple proper, and on which there was an inscription threatening death to any non-Jew who tried to pass it:

"No foreigner may enter within the barricade which surrounds the sanctuary and enclosure. Anyone who is caught doing so will have himself to blame for his ensuing death." [68]

But the allusion, if any, to that literal barricade is only by way of illustration. What the apostle was actually speaking of was something far more serious and dreadful, namely, *inveterate hostility* between the two groups. Humanly speaking, the wall of hatred and contempt that divided Jew and Gentile had been strengthened by centuries of mutual disparagement and mudslinging. A few more years and the pent-up hostility of generations would burst into an open flame, and one of the most cruel and bitter wars would be fought. It would result in the destruction of Jerusalem, A.D. 70. To the Jews the Gentiles were "dogs." Many other vituperative expressions

---

[66] Though some suggest that the neuter here (*τὰ ἀμφότερα*), contrasted with the masculine (*οἱ ἀμφότεροι*) in verses 16, 18, indicates an ellipsis, so that a word like *γένη* should be applied, this is doubtful. Abbott (*op.cit.*, p. 60) may well be right when he says, "It is simply an instance of the neuter being used of persons in a general sense." Another instance of this same usage of the neuter is found in Heb. 7:7. Cf. also the use of the neuter *τοῦτο* in 2:8. See on that passage.

[67] The word *μεσότοιχον* is of rare occurrence. In the New Testament it is found only here. Outside of the New Testament, too, it is found but seldom. See M.M., p. 400; also L.N.T. (A. and G.), p. 509. Josephus, *Jewish Antiquities* VIII. 71, speaks about a *middle wall*. Here in 2:14 the context favors the translation *barrier*.

[68] See J. H. Iliffe, "The ΘΑΝΑΤΟΣ Inscription from Herod's Temple: Fragments of a Second Copy," *Quarterly of Department of Antiquities in Palestine* VI (1938), pp. 1 ff.

were used. Non-Jews were considered "unclean," people with whom one must have almost none but unavoidable dealings. By many prominent Jews and rabbis even *proselytes* were despised. Close association with Gentiles meant "defilement" (John 18:28). To be sure, the temple had its "court of the Gentiles," but even this space was at times filled with Jewish merchants and money-changers, with oxen, sheep, and doves, instead of being reserved for holy purposes. The result was that it failed to contribute its share in making the temple "a house of prayer" (Luke 19:46) *"for all peoples"* (Isa. 56:7). And, of course, the Gentiles treated the Jews similarly. By them the Jews were considered "enemies of the human race," a people "filled with a hostile disposition toward everybody." We can well imagine with what gesture of disdain and in what tone of contempt Pilate must have said, "I, surely, am not *a Jew,* am I?" (John 18:35). Across the centuries we can still hear the owners of the Philippian slave-girl denounce the Jewish trouble-makers (Paul and Silas!) in these words of contempt, "These men, *being Jews,* do exceedingly trouble our city" (Acts 16:20). Cf. Acts 18:2.

Yet, wonder of wonders, Christ Jesus, the Peace-maker, had broken down this barrier of hostility. *Believers* from the Jews and *believers* from the Gentiles were dwelling together in unity in the midst of a world of bitterness and turmoil. How had this been accomplished? Christ had broken down the barrier formed by the dividing wall, the hostility, **15. by abolishing** [69] **in his flesh the law of commandments with its requirements.** That law, in the sense here meant, was the dividing wall which had to be abolished if peace was to be established between Jew and Gentile. Now "in his flesh," that is, in his body nailed to the cross where he shed his blood (see verses 13 and 16; cf. Col. 1:20; 2:14; cf. Heb. 10:20), Christ abolished the law. Of course, this cannot mean that he did away with the law as a moral principle embedded in man's very conscience (Rom. 1:21; 2:14, 15), formalized in the decalogue (Exod. 20:1-17; Deut. 5:6-21), summarized in the rule of love for God and for one's neighbor (Matt. 22:34-40; Mark 12:28-34; Luke 10:25-28; Rom. 13:8-10; Gal. 5:14), and climaxed in "the new commandment" (John 13:34, 35). By God's grace and through the indwelling Spirit the believer, in principle, obeys this law out of gratitude for salvation received. He delights in it (Rom. 7:22). Also, since his obedience *in this life* is only in principle, never perfect, the believer rejoices in the fact that Christ, by means of his active and passive obedience, has fully satisfied the demands of this law and borne

---

[69] The verb καταργέω of which the aorist active participle occurs here is a favorite with Paul. It occurs frequently in Romans and in I Corinthians; also four times in II Corinthians and thrice in Galatians. In II Thess. 2:8 it indicates that the Lord Jesus *will utterly defeat* the lawless one; in II Tim. 2:8, that he *has utterly defeated* or *abolished* death. Another, rather common, meaning is *nullify, render useless or ineffective* (Rom. 3:3; 4:14; Gal. 3:17). In I Cor. 13:11 it means *set aside.* In the New Testament, outside of Paul, it is found only in Luke 13:7 and Heb. 2:14.

its curse. But while, according to many, the apostle here in verse 15, also refers to this satisfaction rendered by Christ, which opinion I believe to be correct, I agree with Grosheide (*op. cit.,* p. 45) that Paul was thinking *especially* of the ceremonial law. The very wording "the law of commandments with its requirements" points in that direction. So, and very clearly, does the parallel passage, Col. 2:14 (in the light of Col. 2:11, 16, 17). The reference then is especially to the many rules and regulations of the Mosaic Code, stipulations with respect to such matters as fasts, feasts, foods, offerings, circumcision, etc. The great error committed by the Jews was that they had shifted the emphasis from the moral to the ceremonial law, and as to the latter, had "made void the law of God by their tradition," having added ever so many rules and regulations of their own (cf. Matt. 15:3, 6). Since the return from the exile the Jewish religion had become formalistic to a very great extent. Obedience to traditional ordinances was stressed. Now it was this very emphasis on ceremonial stipulations, even those stipulations contained in the law of Moses, that formed the dividing wall between Jews and Gentiles. For example, the latter could see no reason why a man had to be circumcised in order to be saved. The passage (verse 15) teaches that Christ, by his suffering and death, put an end to the law of ceremonies, and caused its binding power to cease. These ceremonial regulations had served their purpose. During his entire life on earth, especially on Calvary, Christ fulfilled all these shadows **in order that in himself** [70] **he might create of the two one new man, (so) making peace.** Since Christ is both "the seed of the woman" and "the seed of Abraham" it is not surprising that in him Jew and Gentile meet so as to become "one new man," a new humanity (cf. 4:24; Col. 3:10, 11). In him the two were "created" (cf. verse 10) one! When the Christian was able to say to the Gentile, as well as to the Jew, "Believe in the Lord Jesus, and you will be saved, you and your household" (Acts 16:31), meaning, "Nothing less than this is required of you, but also *nothing more,*" the dividing wall, which for so long a time had been a hostile barrier between Jew and Gentile, came crashing down. It was in that way that Christ by his atonement made peace, the very peace referred to in verse 14. In further explanation of the purpose of Christ's sacrifice whereby he abolished in himself the law of commandments in ordinances, the apostle adds, **16. and might reconcile both of them in one body to God through the cross, having slain the hostility by means of it.** What Paul describes in the present verse is not only the reconciliation between Jews and Gentiles but also that basic reconciliation, namely, between *a.* the two groups, *now viewed as one body, the church* (as in 1:22, 23; 3:6; 4:4 ff.; 5:23, 30), and *b.* God. In fact it is on that basic reconciliation that the emphasis falls in the first part of the verse. The meaning is that Christ's atoning death had

[70] Whether one reads αὐτῷ or ἑαυτῷ makes no essential difference, as, in either case, the sense is reflexive.

achieved its purpose: the proper relation between the Ephesians and their God had been established. By grace those estranged from God, having heard and accepted the gospel, had laid aside their wicked alienation from God and had entered into the fruits of Christ's perfect atonement. This miracle had been achieved "through the cross," that very cross which to the Jews was a stumblingblock and to the Gentiles folly (I Cor. 1:23). It was by means of Christ's death on the cross that the curse had been borne, and, having been borne, had been lifted off the hearts and lives of all believers (Gal. 3:13). The miracle of Calvary, however, was even more thrilling, for, *through the strange instrument of the cross,*[71] the Sufferer not only reconciled to God both Jews and Gentiles but also slew the deeply-rooted antipathy that had existed for so long a time between the two groups.

The basic lesson holds for all time. The reason why there is so much strife in this world, between individuals, families, social or political groups, whether small or large, is that the contending parties, through the fault of either or both, have not found each other at Calvary. Only then when sinners have been reconciled to God through the cross will they be truly reconciled to each other. This shows how very important it is to preach the gospel to all men, and *to beseech them* (!) on behalf of Christ to be reconciled with God (II Cor. 5:20). For a world torn by unrest and friction the gospel is the only answer.

**17.** The idea of *peace* between God and man, consequently also between man and man (Jew and Gentile), brought about by Christ's self-sacrifice (verses 14–16), is continued in the words: **and he came and proclaimed the good news: "Peace to y o u, those far away, and peace**[72] **to those nearby."** The *emphasis* here is on basic peace (between God and man), as verse 18 indicates. Not only did Christ by means of his substitutionary suffering merit this peace for his people, he also wanted them to know about it and to experience it in their hearts. This peace is the inner assurance that all is well because the curse of the law has been removed, the guilt transferred, the punishment borne, salvation procured. "He came" to proclaim this peace. This "coming" refers, in all probability, to all of Christ's work on earth, that which he himself in person performed during his earthly sojourn and that which he continued to accomplish by means of the apostles and others (John 14:12; Acts 1:1 ff.; 4:10, 30). That it was peace which he not only brought about but also proclaimed appears from the passages already referred to (see on verse 14). It is implied also in such beautiful texts as

[71] Contrary to Lenski, *op. cit.*, p. 444, but in agreement with most versions and commentators, I take αὐτῷ in verse 16 to refer to *its closest logical antecedent,* namely, τοῦ σταυροῦ. Col. 1:20, "having made peace through the blood of his cross" confirms this more common interpretation.

[72] The omission (see A.V.) of the second mention of *peace* is not supported by the best manuscripts.

Matt. 9:13; Luke 19:10; and I Tim. 1:15. Notice also the "wideness" of the mercy here revealed: he came to call *sinners, the lost.* Destined to be included in that category were not only Israelitish sheep but also "other sheep" (John 10:16). Christ, when lifted up from the earth, drew "all men," regardless of blood or race, to himself. Cf. Matt. 28:18-20; John 1:29; 3:16; 11:51. He, accordingly, *gospeled* [73] the gladsome message of that which the Triune God through him had done, urging *all* to receive it: both those *far away, the Gentiles* (see on verses 12, 13), and those *nearby, the Jews,* here called *nearby* because of the many privileges they had received, including the knowledge of the one true God.

**18.** Paul continues, as it were, We know that both Jew and Gentile have obtained this peace through Christ's suffering on the cross **for through him we both have our access in one Spirit to the Father.** It is through Christ, through him alone – that is, through the shedding of his *blood* (verse 13), the sacrifice of his *flesh* (verse 15), the curse borne by him on the *cross* (verse 16) – that access to the Father was made possible and real. There was and there is no other way. See 3:12; John 3:16-18; 10:9; 14:6; Acts 4:12; Rom. 5:1, 2 (note same sequence of *peace* and *access* there as here in Eph. 2:17, 18); 5:10; Heb. 4:14-16; Rev. 7:14. It was he who supplied the *objective* basis apart from which access would have been impossible. The word *access* occurs only here and in 3:12 and Rom. 5:12. It follows from 3:12 that it may be defined as *freedom of approach to the Father, in the confidence that we, Jew and Gentile, have found favor with him. Subjectively* speaking, it is "in" or "by means of" the Spirit that man has access to the Father. Though there are those who reject the common view that the reference is here to the Holy Spirit, the third person of the Holy Trinity, this departure from the usual interpretation is not well grounded. Here in 2:18, as well as so often in Ephesians (1:3-14; 1:17; 3:14-17; 4:4-6; 5:18-20), there is a clear confession of the doctrine of the Trinity. Besides, elsewhere, too, confident approach to the Father is associated with the indwelling and enabling power of the Holy Spirit (Luke 10:21, 22; Rom. 8:15, 16; Rev. 22:17).

However, to appreciate more fully how inestimably glorious is this privilege of *access* it should be seen in the light of concrete reality, that is, of actual cases in which it is superbly illustrated. In some of the instances about to be mentioned it is *one* quality that strikes us, in others it is *another.* Often it is a combination of two or more qualities. Among these pleasing attributes of access to the Father may be mentioned the following: reverence, earnestness, pertinacity ("importunity"), concern for the welfare of others and/or for the glory of God's name, ability to distinguish between what is needful and what is merely wishful, world-embracing sympathy, spontaneity or naturalness, pleasing simplicity of faith. Illustrations: Abra-

[73] For "proclaimed the good news" the original has *εὐηγγελίσατο* (cf. evangelize). See N.T.C. on Philippians, pp. 81–85.

ham's intercession for the cities of the plain (Gen. 18:23 ff.) ; Jacob's wrestling at the Jabbok (Gen. 32:26) ; Moses' entreaty for the people of Israel (Exod. 32:32) ; Hannah's prayer for a child (I Sam. 1:10, 11) ; Samuel's answer to Jehovah's call (I Sam. 3:10) ; his "cry" to God at Ebenezer (I Sam. 7:5-11) ; David's many confessions, pleas, expressions of thanksgiving and adoration (in the Psalms) ; Solomon's prayer at the dedication of the temple (II Chron. 6:12 ff.) ; the supplications of Jehoshaphat when beset by enemies (II Chron. 20:5 ff.) , of Elijah on Carmel (I Kings 18:36 ff.) , and of Hezekiah when he had received Sennacherib's defiant letter (II Kings 19:15 ff.) ; the prayerful "interjections" of Ezra (Ezra 9:5) and of Nehemiah (Neh. 5:19; 6:9, 14; 13:22, 29, 31) ; Daniel's confession (Dan. 9:3-19) ; the prayers of the publican (Luke 18:13) , of the early church (Acts 4:24-31) , of Stephen (Acts 7:59, 60) , and of Paul (Eph. 1:15 ff.; 3:14-21; etc.) ; and the yearning of the bride for the coming of the Bridegroom (Rev. 22:17) .

In a place all by itself, yet full of instruction for all his followers, is the manner in which Jesus, while on earth, approached his Father (Luke 10:21, 22; 23:34, 46; John 11:41, 42; 17) . From these prayers not a single virtue of *access* is excluded.

It must be borne in mind, however, that, as defined above, *access* is more than prayer. It is first of all the condition of the soul that rests in the Lord, surrendering itself fully to him, trusting that he will, in answer to prayer, fulfil every need. Prayer, being the natural result of this state of heart and mind, is an essential element in access. And since Jew and Gentile, on equal terms, through the Son, have access in one Spirit to the Father, the world-embracing extent of Christ's church is once more emphasized. See Col. 3:11; cf. Gal. 3:28.

# Chapter 2

Verses 19–22

**Theme:** *The Church Glorious*

I. *Adoration*
*for its*

*U* niversal Scope (embracing both Jew and Gentile).

3. shown by the fact that the church of Jew and Gentile is growing into *one* building, a holy sanctuary in the Lord, of which Christ Jesus is himself the chief cornerstone

19 So then y o u are no longer strangers and aliens, but y o u are fellow-citizens with the saints and members of the household of God, 20 built upon the foundation of the apostles and prophets, Christ Jesus himself being the chief cornerstone, 21 in whom the entire building, harmoniously fitted together, is growing into a holy sanctuary in the Lord, 22 in which y o u also together with (all the others) are being built up for a dwelling-place of God in the Spirit.

2:19-22

### 3. *A Sanctuary of Jew and Gentile*

Since, therefore, Christ has reconciled both Gentile and Jew to God through his suffering on the cross, and both have their access in one Spirit to the Father, hence all inequality between the two groups, as far as their *standing* in the sight of God is concerned, has ceased, a thought to which Paul gives expression in the words: **19. So then y o u are no longer strangers and aliens, but y o u are fellow-citizens with the saints and members of the household of God . . .** The Ephesians, believers from the Gentiles for the greater part, had been "strangers" (see verse 12), as it were citizens of another country, but no longer were they to be considered mere foreigners who happened to be visiting the people of another land. Nor were they even to be regarded as aliens or sojourners, mere Gibeonites who dwelt in the midst of Israel without having obtained full rights of citizens. Cf. Exod. 2:22; Acts 7:6. On the contrary, they are "fellow-citizens" (a word occurring only here in the New Testament) with the saints, that is, with all those who were separated from the world and consecrated to God as a people for his own possession. The church is not to be divided into first-class members (Jewish converts to Christianity) and second-class members (Gentile converts to Christianity). The *terms of admission* are the same for all: faith in the Lord Jesus Christ, a faith working through love. The *rank* or *standing* is also the same. Expressing this thought in language still more intimate, the apostle declares that these former Gentiles are now "members of the household" of God. The household or family is a more intimate unit than the state. "Brothers and sisters" (household-members) is a more endearing term than "fellow-citizens." **20.** The double sense of the Greek word *oikos* (household, house) makes it natural for the apostle, by an easy transition, to change his metaphor from family-life to architecture. Hence, he continues: **built upon the foundation of the apostles and prophets.**[74] The

[74] The fact that the article is not repeated before *prophets* does not mean that apostles and prophets indicate the same individuals. In fact, 3:5 and especially 4:11

sense in which the apostles and prophets were, indeed, though in a secondary sense, the foundation of the church,[75] has been indicated in the Introduction, p. 50. Not in the least does such a statement constitute any contradiction of I Cor. 3:11, where Paul teaches that *the real or primary foundation is, and can be none other than, Jesus Christ.* In fact, by calling Christ "the cornerstone," that is, that part of this foundation in which the latter achieves its super-excellence, luster is added to the metaphor. The joyful testimony made by the apostles and prophets *in confirmation of the very fact* that the *basic* or *primary* foundation is Christ makes it possible that, *in a secondary sense,* they, too, can be called the church's foundation. On the term *apostles* see 1:1; 4:11. The position that the term *prophets* as here used refers to the Old Testament bearers of that appellative, such as Moses, Elijah, Isaiah, Jeremiah, etc. (thus Lenski, *op. cit.,* pp. 450–453), is open to serious objections; such as the following: (1) Apostles are mentioned first, then prophets; (2) the designation "foundation" of the house, a dwelling shared *equally* by Jew and Gentile, suits the New Testament prophets better than those of the old dispensation; (3) according to 4:8-11 the prophets there mentioned immediately after the apostles, just as here in 2:20, are "gifts" bestowed on the church by the *ascended* Christ; hence, prophets of the New Testament era; and (4) 3:5, where the same expression "apostles and prophets" occurs in a context from which the reference to the prophets of the old dispensation is definitely excluded, would seem to clinch the argument in favor of New Testament prophets. As to the office or function which these New Testament prophets performed, in distinction from the apostles, see on 4:11.

Paul continues: **Christ Jesus himself being the chief cornerstone.**[76] Other references to this stone, clearly showing that it symbolizes Christ, are Isa. 28:16; Ps. 118:22; Matt. 21:42; Acts 4:11. The cornerstone of a building,

---

show that this is not the case. True explanation of the non-repetition of the article: the apostles and prophets belong to the same large category, namely, that of teachers of the church.

[75] Among other interpretations the main ones are: (1) "the foundation of the apostles and prophets" means "Christ, the foundation on which the apostles and prophets have built." Objection: this introduces a confusion of metaphors, for here in 2:20 Christ is represented as the cornerstone, not the foundation. (2) It means "the foundation laid by the apostles and prophets," namely, Christ's teaching. Although both Matt. 16:18 and Rev. 21:14 point in the direction of the genitive of apposition (the apostles and prophets are themselves the foundation), nevertheless, if it be understood that they are referred to as such not because of what they are in themselves but because of their office, representing Christ and his teachings to men, it will become evident that in the end meaning (2), though probably not technically correct, does not miss the truth by much.

[76] With reference to this cornerstone see G. H. Whitaker, "The Chief Cornerstone," *Exp,* Eighth Series (1921), pp. 470–472; also J. M. Moffatt, "Three Notes on Ephesians," *Exp,* Eighth Series (1918), pp. 306–317.

in addition to being part of the foundation and therefore *supporting* the superstructure, finalizes its shape, for, being placed at the corner formed by the junction of two primary walls, it determines the lay of the walls and crosswalls throughout. All the other stones must adjust themselves to this cornerstone. So also, in addition to resting in Christ, the spiritual house is determined as to its character by him. It is he who settles the question as to what this house is to be in the sight of God, and as to what is its function in God's universe. It is Christ who gives the house its needed *direction.* Believers, as "living stones" (I Peter 2:5), must regulate their lives in accordance with the will of the cornerstone, Christ. **21.** The apostle adds: **in whom the entire building,**[77] **harmoniously fitted together, is growing into a holy sanctuary in the Lord.**

Another thought is added now to the one just expressed. We now learn that Christ, in addition to being the principle of the church's *stability* and *direction* is also the principle of its *growth.* It is in vital union with *him* that the entire building is "growing" or "rising." There is nothing static about this edifice. It is a living building consisting of living stones: believers. And since each living stone makes his own contribution to the growth and beauty of the building, the latter is described as "harmoniously fitted together." Compare 4:16. Thus the building becomes, ever increasingly, "a holy sanctuary in the Lord." It is *holy,* that is, cleansed and consecrated, because of the blood and Spirit of Christ.

Turning now from the general thought to the special application, Paul states: **22. in which y o u also together with (all the others) are being built up for a dwelling-place of God in the Spirit.** Very comforting is this assurance. The apostle says, as it were, The business of being built up concerns y o u, Ephesians, as well as all other believers; it has reference to y o u, who are for the most part Gentiles, as well as to the Jews. God's love is as wide as

---

[77] Although the best text omits the article, and Gram. N.T., p. 772, states that πᾶσα οἰκοδομή in Eph. 2:21 = "most probably 'every building,' " I, along with many others, believe that only one building is here indicated. Reason: verse 20 describes a *house* with a *foundation* and *cornerstone,* not several buildings. The unity of the church has been stressed right along. Nowhere in the context has the reader been prepared for the idea of several separate buildings or congregations. Besides, abstract nouns do not need the article to be definite, and "the entire building" may perhaps be viewed as "whatever is being (or *has been*) built." Again, it has been suggested that it is possible to regard the word in question as being in the nature of a proper name. Also in that case no article would be necessary. Cf. Matt. 2:3; Rom. 11:26. The renderings offered by A.V., R.S.V., and N.E.B. are to be preferred, therefore, to A.R.V.'s confusing "each several building."

As to the meaning of the word οἰκοδομή itself, in Matt. 24:1 and Mark 13:1 the literal meaning *building, edifice* is clear. In Eph. 4:12, 16, 29 *edification, building up* is indicated. This seems also to be the meaning in Rom. 14:19; 15:2; II Cor. 10:8; 12:19; 13:10, and in the several occurrences of the word in I Cor. 14. Subject of much controversy is the exact reference of the word in II Cor. 5:1.

the ocean. It is all-embracing. Moreover, y o u are being built up *together,* in the closest possible association with each other, through active fellowship. Thus, the church universal gradually rises. It will not be finished until the day of the consummation of all things. Then it will be *in perfection* what it is even now *in principle,* namely, "a dwelling-place of God *in* (that is, by virtue of the cleansing and transforming operation of) *the Spirit.*"

That this house(hold) of God, rising building, holy sanctuary in the Lord, dwelling-place of God, is *a spiritual and not a physical entity* requires no proof. Paul is clearly speaking about the church glorious, gathered out of all the nations, until at last "the number of the elect is complete." The question arises, however, Is there any allusion here, however faint, to a physical temple, so that the image of the latter would serve as a kind of background? And if there be such an allusion is it possible that it might shed light on the meaning of the passage? In favor of the idea of an implied and indirect reference to a literal temple or to literal temples is the fact that when, during his second missionary journey, the apostle had made a tour of the city of Athens, observing closely its sacred places and objects, he had remarked, "The God who made the world and everything in it . . . does not live in sanctuaries made by (human) hands" (Acts 17:24). In the given context the meaning must have been: "he cannot be localized in (or restricted to) one of y o u r (heathen) temples." Yet the same words also applied to the temple at Jerusalem, as is shown by the use Stephen makes of them in Acts 7:46-50. It would seem to be established, therefore, that when the apostle concentrated his attention on God's dwelling-place, the contrast between the true and the false was not absent from his mind; and also that, being a Jew, the contrast between shadow and reality, type and antitype, was appreciated by him. He was "of the tribe of Benjamin, a Hebrew of Hebrews" (Phil. 3:5), and had received his early training in Jerusalem, at the feet of Gamaliel (Acts 22:3). After his conversion, the heavenly voice had spoken to him while he was praying in the temple (Acts 22:17, 18). Moreover, it was in this same temple at the close of his third missionary journey, that he had been mobbed and arrested (Acts 21). The result had been his incarceration, first at Caesarea, then at Rome for his first Roman imprisonment, during which Ephesians was written, as were also Colossians, Philemon, and Philippians. It would have been almost impossible, therefore, for Paul to have written Eph. 2:21, 22 without at least alluding to the Jerusalem temple. Most commentators who refer to this question at all – many skip it entirely – agree with this position. "He [Paul] thinks of the Sanctuary at Jerusalem, which was a type and symbol both of Christ (see John 2:18-22) and of his Church" (Lenski, *op. cit.,* p. 459). The same author definitely rejects the idea that in Paul's words there might also be an indirect reference to a pagan sanctuary. Others, however, stress the idea that "the famous image of the spiritual temple, in which perhaps we may trace some recollection of the magnificent temple of Artemis,[78] which all Asia and the world worshiped, belongs in Eph. 2:20-22, nowhere else." Though it is not possible to prove an allusion to the image which, according to popular belief, had fallen from heaven, there are, nevertheless, certain facts that would seem to favor it. Note the following: (1) It has already been pointed out that the words of Paul quoted in Acts 17:24 are applicable to *any* man-made temple, whether at Jerusalem or elsewhere. (2) The apostle was writing this letter to the people who lived in and around the very city which housed the temple of Artemis (by the Romans identified with Diana), one of the seven wonders of the ancient world. (3) During Paul's ministry at Ephesus his preaching had collided head-on with the cult of the goddess, a fact that had been thoroughly grasped by Demetrius and his fellow-craftsmen. Demetrius, in addressing his colleagues, had pointed out that because of Paul's preaching there was "danger that the temple of the great goddess Artemis would cease to command respect." This address had stirred up a riot so filled with excitement that for two hours the mob had shouted, "Great is Artemis of the Ephesians" (Acts 19:23-41). After the uproar ceased Paul had taken his departure, to continue on his missionary journey (the third), which, as was indicated, led to his arrest and imprisonment.

Now if we accept as probable the theory that in 2:20-22 the apostle is, by implication, contrasting the spiritual sanctuary with any and all others, whether the one at Jerusalem or the one at Ephesus,[79] exactly in what respect is there a contrast? What was the most important function of any earthly temple which the apostle may have had in mind when he wrote as he did? The answer must be that the literal temple — more definitely, the inner enclosure or *sanctuary* — "was not built for the comfort of the worshipers, but as a shrine to house the deity" (Moffatt). Thus, even though Solomon was well aware of the fact that "heaven and the heaven of heavens cannot contain God," nevertheless, he believed that Jehovah would reveal his glorious Presence in a special manner in the temple which had just been completed (II Chron. 6:1, 2, 41; 7:1; cf. Exod. 40:34 ff.). *The sanc-*

---

[78] Helpful is the full-color picture (No. 5) of "The Temple of Diana, Ephesus" in the View-Master reel "The Seven Ancient Wonders of the World." Also, the accompanying *Story Guide* with its description of this temple (Sawyer's, Inc., Portland, Oregon, 1962). On Ephesus and its famous temple see also Merrill M. Parvis, "Ephesus in the Early Christian Era," *The Biblical Archaeologist Reader*, 2 (edited by D. N. Freedman and E. F. Campbell, Jr.), New York, 1964, pp. 331–343. In the same volume also Floyd V. Filson, "Ephesus and the New Testament," pp. 343–352. See also: J. T. Wood, *Discoveries at Ephesus* (1877); D. J. Hogarth, *The Archaic Artemisia* (1908); and *Forschungen in Ephesos* (1906–37), published by the Österreiches Archaeologisches Institut of Vienna.

[79] "In order that he may dwell among men God requires the community of his people, which is henceforth to replace all the old temples made with hands" (Scott, *op. cit.*, p. 179).

*tuary on Zion is God's dwelling-place* (Ps. 132:1-5, 8, 13, 14; 135:21; etc.). Similarly, the "cella" (inner shrine, sanctuary) of the temple at Ephesus was by far the most important part of that marvelous building. It excelled the rest of the temple in the value that was attached to it, the reason being that *it contained the statue of the goddess. She dwelt there.* It is true, of course, that between the dwelling-place of Jehovah at Jerusalem and that of Artemis at Ephesus there was this vast contrast, namely, that it was, indeed, *the living God* who had made Zion his special abode, whereas, on the contrary, it was a *mere statue,* perhaps a large meteorite, shaped into the form of a human figure by a skillful artist, that was adored at Ephesus. But, in contrast with both, what Paul is bringing out is this beautiful and comforting thought: *"Y o u yourselves, Ephesians, are now God's earthly sanctuary* (Isa. 57:15; 66:1, 2; I Cor. 3:16, 17; II Cor. 6:16; Rev. 21:3). *Y o u are his dewlling-place, his home."* [80] "Dwelling-place, home" indicates permanence, beauty, close fellowship, protection, love. That dwelling-place is very large. It is a home "where there cannot be Greek and Jew, circumcision and uncircumcision, barbarian, Scythian, slave, freeman" (Col. 3:11), and where the "one new humanity" (Eph. 2:15) is at peace with its Maker-Redeemer.

*Summary of Chapter 2*

The church's *Universal Scope,* its extent broader than any ocean, is described in this chapter. It embraces *both Jew and Gentile,* that is, *everybody* who appropriates Christ by true faith. In verses 1–10 we are told that this universality was secured by the great redemptive blessings *for both* which center "in Christ," and which parallel his resurrection and triumphant life.

Paul shows that by nature *all* men are dead through trespasses and sins. They are "children of wrath," and servants of "the prince of the domain of the air." The great change, when it occurs, is due exclusively to the *rich mercy* and *great love* of God, the *surpassing riches of his grace.* Salvation in its entirety is from God, *even faith itself being "God's gift."* As to *good works,* considered as a ground upon which to plead they are *rejected.* Yet by God good works were "prepared" or *confected,* for he gave his Son and imparted to his chosen ones faith in that Son, and good works are the fruit of faith. Moreover, God prepared them in order that his people should walk in them. In other words, these works are *expected* of them, as works of gratitude. These good works, having been prepared by God, will by him be *perfected,* for God always finishes what he has begun. Besides, Christ's resurrection from the dead implies our resurrection from sin, for it is the Spirit of the raised and ascended Christ who "raised us up with him." In

[80] Similarly, the church is "the Israel of God" (Gal. 6:16), the true "seed of Abraham" (Gal. 3:7, 16; cf. Rom. 4:16), "an elect race, a royal priesthood," etc. (I Peter 2:9).

glory we shall be sinless. All this applies to all of God's children, both Jews and Gentiles.

The cross whereby Jew and Gentile were reconciled to God also brought about their mutual reconciliation (verses 11-18). This is an amazing fact, namely, that the very cross which to the Jews had been a stumblingblock and to the Gentiles foolishness was the means whereby the double reconciliation was secured. Paul shows how thankful *all* should be for this divine arrangement. The Jews should praise God because through the cross "the law of commandments with its requirements" had been abolished. But the Gentiles, too, had a reason for special thanksgiving. They should consider what great benefits Christ through his death on the cross had bestowed upon them. Formerly they had been separate from Christ; now they are "in him"; formerly alienated from the commonwealth of Israel, now, "fellow-citizens with the saints and members of the household of God"; formerly, strangers to the covenants of the promise, now covenant-members; formerly, hopeless, now filled with buoyant hope; formerly, without God, now at peace with him. To both Jews and Gentiles Jesus by his coming and work had proclaimed and was still proclaiming the good news: "Peace to y o u, those far away and peace to those nearby." Through him both have access in one Spirit to the Father.

Thus the church of Jew and Gentile is growing into one building, a holy sanctuary in the Lord, of which Christ Jesus is himself the chief cornerstone (verses 19-22). Of course, the real and primary foundation is, and can be none other than, Jesus Christ (I Cor. 3:11). But *in a secondary sense* the apostles and New Testament prophets can truly be called the church's foundation, namely, because they direct everyone's attention to Christ as the only true Savior. A parallel would be the fact that Jesus called himself "the light of the world" (John 8:12), but he also called his disciples "the light of the world" (Matt. 5:14). They derive their light from him. When the apostles are called the church's foundation, Christ is called that foundation's *cornerstone,* that is, the principle of the church's stability, direction, and growth. Day by day living stones are added to this building, the church. No earthly temple, whether Jewish or pagan, but the church alone is God's dwelling-place. Here he homes. That home is very large. It is peaceful, for Jew and Gentile being at peace with their Maker-Redeemer, are also at peace with each other.

# Chapter 3

Verses 1–13

Theme: *The Church Glorious*

I. *Adoration*
*for its*

*L* ofty Goal

1. *To declare* to the principalities and the powers in the heavenly places *God's iridescent wisdom,* reflected in the mystery revealed especially, though not exclusively, to Paul, namely, that the Gentiles are fellow-members of the body of Christ

# CHAPTER III

**EPHESIANS**

3 1 For this reason I, Paul, the prisoner of Christ Jesus for the sake of
you Gentiles – 2 for surely you have heard of the stewardship of God's
grace that was given to me for your benefit, 3 how that by revelation there was
made known to me the mystery, as I wrote before in few words, 4 whereby, as you
read it, you can perceive my insight into the mystery of Christ, 5 which in other
generations was not made known to the sons of men as it has now been revealed
by the Spirit to his holy apostles and prophets, 6 namely, that the Gentiles are
fellow-sharers in the inheritance and fellow-members of the body and fellow-
partakers of the promise (realized) in Christ Jesus (as conveyed) through the gospel, 7 of which I was made a minister according to the gift of God's grace that
was given to me according to the working of his power. 8 To me, the very least of
all saints, was this grace given: to proclaim to the Gentiles the good tidings of the
unfathomable riches of Christ, 9 and to enlighten all on what is the administration
of the mystery which for ages has been hidden in God who created all things;
10 in order that now to the principalities and the authorities in the heavenly places
might be made known through the church the iridescent wisdom of God, 11 according to the eternal purpose which he formed in Christ Jesus our Lord, 12 in
whom we have the courage of confident access through faith in him. 13 Therefore
I ask (you) not to lose heart over what I am suffering for you, which is your
glory –

---

3:1-13

1. *The Church Should Strive to Declare God's Marvelous Wisdom to the Principalities and the Powers in the Heavenly Places*

1. The very beginning of the present chapter, namely, the words **For this reason,** already indicate its close *material connection* with the preceding one. The meaning, accordingly, must be, Because blessings so great have been bestowed upon both Gentile and Jew – reconciliation with God and with one another, and the erection of *one* sanctuary consisting of Jew and Gentile – therefore, etc. In fact, in view of the equally close relation between chapters 1 and 2, and the recurrence in 3:4, 9 of the concept *mystery,* first mentioned in 1:9, it is very probable that the connection goes back even further and includes *all* that has gone before in this epistle.

The *mode* of humble gratitude and adoration also continues; see especially verses 8, 14-21. "Paul is about to resume his prayer on behalf of his readers. . . . This prayer forms the framework of the whole first half of the epistle. . . . His thought is pitched in a solemn key" (Scott, *op. cit.,*

p. 181). The first part of the epistle (chapters 1–3), which after the salutation began with one main type of doxology, namely, "Blessed (be)" (1:3 ff.), is going to end with the other main type, "Now to him . . . be the glory" (3:20, 21). That closing doxology is immediately preceded by one of the most glorious prayers to be found anywhere (3:14-19), a prayer which, in a sense, is already introduced in 3:1.

Nevertheless, there is *progress* in thought. Chapter 2 has shown what God has done. Chapter 3, therefore, is going to indicate what the church, mentioned distinctly in verse 10, now must do. It indicates the church's *Lofty Goal.* In the realization of this purpose Paul himself has played a prominent role, for to him, to him *especially* though not exclusively, the great mystery, to be published far and wide, has been disclosed.

So Paul continues, **I, Paul** (cf. II Cor. 10:1; Gal. 5:2; Col. 1:23; I Thess. 2:18; Philem. 19), **the prisoner of Christ Jesus** (cf. 4:1; Philem. 1, 9; II Tim. 1:8). In every reference to himself as a prisoner Paul stresses the fact that as such *he belongs to his Lord,* for it was while engaged in *his* service and thus for *his* sake that he was imprisoned. Moreover, all the details of the imprisonment as well as the outcome, whether it be the death-sentence or acquittal, are in the hands that were pierced for this prisoner, those very hands that now control the entire universe in the interest of the church (1:22). Paul's imprisonment is therefore a very honorable one. In fact, it strengthened his claim as an apostle of Jesus Christ. And since he is going to remind the church of its exalted task, its *Lofty Goal,* namely, to declare God's marvelous wisdom, it is entirely proper for him to make mention of his chains in authentication of his apostleship (cf. II Cor. 11:16-33). This is true all the more since enemies were constantly questioning his claims, as is clear from I and II Corinthians, Galatians, I and II Thessalonians, and from passages scattered here and there throughout his epistles. It is not improbable that these opponents viewed his very *imprisonment* as a sign of the falsity of his pretensions. So, instead of carefully avoiding this subject he starts right out by boldly calling attention to it. He emphasizes, however, that he is a prisoner in a righteous cause, so that his very confinement is a reason why they should listen all the more attentively to what he has to say. He regards it, in fact, as an honor, and this not only for himself but even *for them* (verse 13), for he is the prisoner of Christ Jesus **for the sake of y o u Gentiles** — It was because of the fact that he had been proclaiming the love of God for Gentile and Jew alike, without any racial or national distinction whatever, that he had been imprisoned (Acts 21:17 ff.; 22:21-24). The *Ephesians* especially knew about this, for surely they must have heard that at the close of his third missionary journey his association with Trophimus *the Ephesian* had led to the false charge which resulted in his capture and incarceration. Moreover, not only had his work *for the Gentiles* brought about his imprisonment but he had been specifically charged by his Lord to be an apostle *to Gentiles* as well as to Jews (Acts 9:15). In fact, to him, in distinction from the other apostles (Gal. 2:9), had been entrusted the glorious assignment of being above all else the apostle *to the Gentiles* (see verse 8; also: Acts 13:47; 22:21; 26:12 ff.; Rom. 11:13; 15:16; Gal. 2:8, 9; I Tim. 2:7; Titus 1:7).

It must be borne in mind, in this very connection, that big-hearted Paul wanted everybody to share his joy in the Lord. It was he who had said in a letter written previously, "I have become all things to all men, that in one way or another I may save some" (I Cor. 9:22). But in order to be saved men must accept the gospel-message which Paul had been commissioned to bring. And confidence in his credentials was necessary if his message was going to be accepted, his exhortations obeyed, his prayers appreciated. This also explains the digression (verses 2-13), in which he dwells at some length on the charge given to him by the Lord. Hence, having said, "For this reason I, Paul, the prisoner of Christ Jesus for the sake of y o u Gentiles," he does not at once add "bend my knees to the Father," but postpones this until verse 14 is reached. He never loses sight of this petition, however. It is definitely on his mind throughout the paragraph. But by inserting the words of verses 2-13 he adds strength to the prayer that he was about to utter and to the doxology which follows that prayer. **2.** Paul continues, accordingly: **for surely y o u have heard of the stewardship of God's grace that was given to me for y o u r benefit.** A strictly literal translation of what Paul actually writes is perhaps impossible in English. The nearest to it would be something like this: "If, indeed, y o u have heard." Cf. A.V., "If ye have heard"; A.R.V., "If so be that ye have heard." However, that type of rendering will hardly do, since it might suggest that Paul is questioning whether or not the Ephesians, by and large, have ever heard about the task committed to him by his Lord. There are those who, upon the basis of this kind of rendering, have argued that *Paul* could not have written Ephesians, and/or that this letter was never meant for *them*. They base their argument upon the fact that the book of Acts assigns a lengthy ministry to Paul at Ephesus, making it impossible for *him* to write to *the Ephesians, "If* y o u have heard of my stewardship," for Paul knew that *they* must have heard of his stewardship. However, such reasoning is not convincing. It proceeds from the assumption that the little word "if" – whether in Greek or in English – must indicate *uncertainty*. But that is incorrect. Two contrasted examples in the English language will make this clear: (1) *"If* our team wins, there will be a celebration." Here "if" expresses uncertainty, mere possibility. (2) *"If* you do not know the day of your death, you should be prepared now." Here "if" indicates an assumption that is taken for granted. This "if" could be translated "since." [81] But what ground have we for believing that in the

[81] Many commentators mention the fact that the expression εἰ γε, used here in Eph. 3:2, has the sense of "since" or "inasmuch as." They refer to II Cor. 5:3 as a paral-

present instance "if" means *"since* y o u heard" rather than *"maybe* y o u heard, *and maybe* y o u did *not* hear"? The answer is that this epistle, which from the beginning has been almost universally viewed as a writing of Paul "to the Ephesians" (in some sense), elsewhere clearly *states* (1:13; 2:17; 4:20) and throughout *implies* that the readers have heard the gospel. Would they then not have heard about *Paul's* part in it? Anent *Paul's* work in Ephesus Luke writes: "All those who lived in Asia *heard* the word of the Lord, both Jews and Greeks." With this cf. Eph. 3:2: ". . . y o u *have heard* of the stewardship of God's grace that was given to me for y o u r benefit." Therefore, such renderings as the following must be considered excellent: "Y o u have heard – have y o u not? – of the stewardship of God's grace" (Bruce's paraphrase); "If y o u have heard, as I presume y o u have" (Grosheide); ". . . assuming that y o u have heard" (R.S.V.); "Y o u must have heard" (Phillips); "Surely y o u have heard" (Moffat; N.E.B.). Of course, even on the basis of this translation and interpretation it must be granted that the "if" of the original may, perhaps, leave room for the possibility that a relatively small number of people living in the province of Asia, and addressed here, might never have heard about Paul and his commission, or that they might *claim* not to have heard. After all, the people to whom the epistle was addressed did not all live inside the city of Ephesus. The circle addressed was very wide! And some time had elapsed since Paul had labored in this region.

The apostle says that the addressed, by and large, must have heard about the *stewardship* of God's grace that had been granted to him. For a discussion of the word *stewardship* see Introduction, p. 44. The gospel of the *grace* (see on 1:2; 2:5, 8) of God in Christ had been assigned to Paul as a sacred trust (I Cor. 4:1, 2; 9:17; I Tim. 1:4; Titus 1:7). It had been given to him for the benefit of the Ephesians. Cf. Col. 1:25. In their case that was true in a special sense, for most of them had been won over from the Gentiles (3:1, 8), and, as has already been indicated, it was especially to the Gentiles that Paul had been sent. Paul continues, **3. how that by revelation there was made known to me the mystery.** Here begins a brief description of the stewardship of grace that had been entrusted to Paul. It had reference to "the mystery," that is, to something that would have remained unknown had it not been *revealed,* as Paul also indicates by writing "how that *by revelation* there was made known to me the mystery." Such revelation is generally in the form of a divine communication by means of voice or vi-

lel case. The probability of the correctness of this rendering does not depend exclusively on the particle γε, however. Even in the absence of this particle doubt is often excluded. Thus, the words, *"If* therefore there is any encouragement in Christ" (Phil. 2:1), do not mean that the apostle wonders whether there be such encouragement. On the contrary, the sense is, "If then there is any encouragement in Christ, *as there surely is."* For similar illustrations of this second sense of "if" see I Cor. 11:6; 15:12, 32; II Cor. 3:7; Philem. 17; Heb. 2:2.

sion. Paul's stewardship with respect to the Gentiles had been made known to him by both of these forms of thought-transmission, as is clear *directly* from such passages as Acts 16:9; 22:21; 26:17, 18; and *indirectly* from Acts 9:15; Gal. 1:11-17; 2:8. Paul always insisted, over against the allegations of his critics, that the stewardship which he had received was not of human origin. As he had been one of the strictest of Pharisees it could not have occurred to him that God's grace would be extended to Gentiles as well as to Jews and on equal terms. And as far as Peter and other leaders of the church were concerned, Paul could not *originally* have received his commission as the apostle *to the Gentiles* from them, for the Book of Acts shows how difficult it had been for them to divest themselves of their Judaistic exclusivism. They only agreed *after* they had perceived the grace that had been given to Paul (Gal. 2:9). Peter, in fact, needed the vision of the sheet (Acts 10:9-16) and Paul's rebuke (Gal. 2:11 ff.) to get over his error.

In connection with the fact that the mystery had been made known to him *by revelation* Paul adds, **as I wrote before in few words.** Calvin prefers the translation "as I wrote a little before," that is, somewhat earlier. He inclines to the view, rather popular in his day, that the reference is to an earlier letter to the Ephesians, one that has not been preserved. But of such earlier epistles to the Ephesians there is no hint anywhere, and it would seem far more reasonable to interpret Paul's word as having reference to the brief account he had already given *in this same letter,* with respect to God's plan of salvation for both Gentiles and Jews, with special emphasis on the changed position of the former (2:11-22; cf. 1:9 ff.). Accordingly, the clause, "as I wrote before in few words" is tantamout to "as I briefly indicated above."

Continued, **4. whereby, as y o u read it, y o u can perceive my insight into the mystery of Christ.** When, in the various churches for which this epistle was intended, those of Ephesus and surroundings, this letter was read, particularly also 2:11-22, lectors and listeners would be able *to perceive* (cf. 3:20; I Tim. 1:7) Paul's insight into this Christ-mystery, that is, the mystery of which Christ is both the source and the substance. One can say that the mystery is, in a sense, Christ himself, that is *Christ in all his glorious riches actually dwelling through his Spirit in the hearts and lives of both Jews and Gentiles, united in one body, the church.* Cf. Col. 1:26, 27.[82] However,

[82] I prefer this interpretation to that which tries to distinguish sharply between "the mystery" in verse 3 and "the mystery of Christ" in verse 4, so that ὁ at the beginning of verse 5 would have to refer to the former, and 3b, 4 would have to be construed as a parenthesis (as in A.V.). More natural, it would seem to me, is the construction according to which ὁ refers to its nearest possible antecedent. Moreover, if the expression "this mystery . . . Christ" (Col. 1:27) can refer to the calling of the Gentiles (as it actually does according to the context), why should not the phrase "the mystery of Christ" (here in Eph. 1:4) describe the same theme?

here in Ephesians the actual *content* of the mystery is not given until verse 6 is reached.

We find no fault with Handel who said that when he began to compose the "Hallelujah Chorus" it seemed as if all heaven and earth were lying open to his gaze. Why then should we criticize Paul for saying, "You can perceive my insight into the mystery of Christ"? The reason which prompted him to write this was altogether honorable, as was pointed out previously. See Introduction, p. 46, and also on verse 1 above. Besides, as did Handel in later days, Paul, too, gives the credit for his insight to God, not to himself (verses 3, 7, 8).

**5, 6.** In verse 5 Paul continues to speak about the mystery mentioned in verses 3 and 4, but still no description of its content is given. In verse 6, however, this description is finally supplied. Unless we know the content of the mystery it is impossible to interpret it, and to show in what sense it is true that it was concealed "in other generations." Therefore verses 5 and 6 should be considered together. The apostle writes: **which in other generations was not made known to the sons of men as it has now been revealed by the Spirit to his holy apostles and prophets, namely, that the Gentiles are fellow-sharers in the inheritance and fellow-members of the body and fellow-partakers of the promise (realized) in Christ Jesus** (as conveyed) **through the gospel.** It is a mystery which "in other generations," that is, at other times (cf. Acts 14:16: "in past times or ages"), was not made known to the sons of men (not even to *anybody*) *as* – meaning "as clearly as" – it has now *been revealed* or *unveiled* by the Spirit (the Holy Spirit, who imparts different gifts to different men, I Cor. 12:4-11) to his holy apostles and prophets (see on 1:1; 2:20; 4:11).[83] Cf. Rom. 16:25, 26; Col. 1:26, 27. This does not mean that before Pentecost no one, not even prophets, like Moses, Isaiah, etc., knew anything about the future blessing in which the Gentiles, too, would share. The Old Testament writers, in fact, did know about it and referred to it again and again (Gen. 12:3; 22:18; 26:4; 28:14; Ps. 72; 87; Isa. 11:10; 49:6; 54:1-3; 60:1-3; Hos. 1:10; Amos 9:11 ff.; Mal. 1:11, to mention only a few references). *But what these prophets did not make clear was that in connection with the coming of the Messiah and the outpouring of the Spirit the old theocracy would be completely abolished and in its place would arise a new organism in which the Gentiles and the Jews would be placed on a footing of perfect equality.* As has already been shown, even some of the leaders in the early church were slow to grant this point. Moreover, there is nothing which sheds so much light on the full meaning of a prophecy – a meaning not always *fully* grasped even by the Old Testament prophets (I Peter 1:10) – as does its fulfilment! The holy

[83] The connection of αὐτοῦ with *apostles,* and not with *prophets,* probably indicates "in the first place *to the apostles,* then also *to prophets* who followed them" (Grosheide, *op. cit.*, p. 52, footnote 8).

apostles and prophets of the *new* dispensation lived in the era of fulfilment. Illumined by the Spirit given to the church on the day of Pentecost, they were able to set forth with greater clarity than ever before the meaning of the prophecies and their application to the new order of events. Hence, for Gen. 12:3; 22:18 see Gal. 3:8; for Isa. 49:6 see Acts 13:47; for Isa. 54:1-3 see Gal. 4:27; for Amos 9:11 ff. see Acts 15:16-18; etc.

Paul makes it very clear that God's unveiled secret ("mystery") has to do not merely with an *alliance* of Jew and Gentile, or perhaps a friendly *agreement* to live together in peace, or even an outward *combination* or *partnership,* but, on the contrary, with a complete and permanent *fusion,* a perfect spiritual union of formerly clashing elements into *one* new organism, even a "new humanity" (2:15). In God's house there are no boarders; all are children. Note the climactic arrangement: the Gentiles are, in the first place, *fellow-sharers in the inheritance* (implied already in 1:14; cf. Gal. 3:29; 4:7). In the abstract it might, however, be possible for someone outside the inner family-circle (for example, a slave) to receive a share of an inheritance. So the next term makes the picture even clearer, namely, *fellow-members of the body;* [84] that is, the Gentiles are actually members of God's church (see 1:23; 2:16; 4:4, 16). As such they are equal in standing with all the other members. The blessed result and climax is that they are *fellow-partakers of the promise* (see on 2:11-13; cf. II Tim. 1:1). Full salvation is their portion, all this "in Christ Jesus," who merited it for them and apart from whom there can be no share in the inheritance or in the body or in the realization of the promise. And this marvelous union of the two who were formerly enemies but now in Christ have become *one* "elect race, royal priesthood, holy nation, people for God's own possession" (I Peter 2:9), was effected "through the gospel" preached, heard, and accepted by faith (Rom. 10:14, 15; I Cor. 4:15). On *the gospel,* its essence, power, author, emphasis, etc. see N.T.C. on Philippians, pp. 81–85.

**7.** Paul returns now to the very personal manner of speaking begun in verses 1-4. Perhaps the reason for this is that he has just made mention of *the gospel.* Paul and the gospel are friends. In Rom. 2:16 he speaks of "my gospel." It is a gospel in which he glories (Rom. 1:16, 17). In fact, he tells us that he was set apart in a special way to preach the gospel (Rom. 1:1). He just "cannot get over it" that God chose *him,* even himself, Paul, the great persecutor of the church, to proclaim the gospel of the grace of God in Christ. So, speaking about this glorious gospel and about his share in it, he writes: **of which I was made a minister.** That was the task that had been assigned to him, the cause which he had been called to serve **according to the gift of God's grace that was given to me.** Paul had not arrogated to himself the distinction of being a gospel-minister. He was no self-constituted

---

[84] Greek σύσσωμα, a word used only by Paul and Christian writers.

ambassador. The office with which he had been invested was a gift of God's grace, a fact which is stressed over and over in Paul's letters (Rom. 1:1; I Cor. 1:1, 17; 15:10; II Cor. 1:1; Gal. 1:1; etc.). The bountiful nature of this grace becomes all the more clear in the light of verse 8. But before coming to that the apostle adds: (God's grace that was given to me) **according to the working of his power.** How mightily that power of God had operated, and continued to operate, in the life and ministry of the apostle is clear from II Cor. 11:16-33; 12:9; cf. Phil. 4:13; and I Tim. 1:15, 16. For "the working of his power" see on 1:10. However, the thought which Paul emphasizes is rather this, that not he but his Lord deserves all the credit for whatever he, as gospel-minister, in proportion to the talents and opportunities given to him, may have accomplished. He continues: **8. To me, the very least of all saints,**[85] **was this grace given: to proclaim to the Gentiles the good tidings of the unfathomable riches of Christ.** That the man who wrote verse 4 – "whereby, as y o u read it, y o u can perceive my insight into the mystery of Christ" – was not a proud individual, appears very clearly here in verse 8. A similar note is struck in I Cor. 15:9, "For I am the least of the apostles, not fit to be called an apostle, because I persecuted the church of God"; and in I Tim. 1:15, "Reliable (is) the saying, and worthy of full acceptance, that Christ Jesus came into the world sinners to save, foremost of whom am I." Since in the present passage Paul does not give the reason for calling himself "the very least of all saints," it is impossible for any interpreter to supply this reason. The nearest we can come to a sensible conjecture would be to quote the apostle's own reference to his former life as a persecutor of the church. Note forward position of "to me," for emphasis. On "to the Gentiles" see 3:1, 2, 6. "Unfathomable riches" are riches that cannot be *tracked* or *traced,* the illimitable resources of the grace of God in Christ, ocean-depths that can never be plummeted, treasure-stores that are inexhaustible. See on 1:7 and on 3:17-19. Any one who wishes to learn how magnificently Paul fulfilled his God-given task, what excellent use he made of the "grace" (here "blessed but undeserved privilege") given to him should read such chapters and passages as the following: Rom. 5; 8; 12; 13:11-14; I Cor. 13; 15; II Cor. 4; 5; II Cor. 8 (see especially 8:9); 11; Gal. 5; 6; Phil. 2; 3; Col. 3:1-17; I Thess. 4; 5; etc.; also, of course, the account of Paul's life and preaching in the book of Acts.

**9.** To proclaim to the Gentiles the unfathomable riches of Christ was, however, only part of Paul's task. In two respects his mission was broader: *a.* it concerned not only the Gentiles but *all* men. Had not God described him as "a chosen vessel, to bear my name before the Gentiles and kings and the children of Israel"? (Acts 9:15); *b.* it had to do not only with the *proclamation* of the gospel but also with the *illumination* of men's eyes so that

---

[85] The word ἐλαχιστοτέρῳ is a comparative formed on a superlative.

they might see how this gospel, accepted by faith, was operating in the hearts and lives of men. Not only must the mystery of the unfathomable riches of Christ be set forth. To be sure, that mystery is great and marvelous, and reveals salvation for both Jew and Gentile by grace through faith. But the attention must also be focused upon the manner in which in Paul's own day that mystery *was actually working out,* replacing fear by trust, gloom by gladness, hatred by love, and separation by fellowship. Speaking, then, about the *administration* or *effectuation* of the mystery, the apostle continues: **and to enlighten all on what is the administration of the mystery which for ages has been hidden in God who created all things.** In connection with the expression "to enlighten" see on 1:18 and 5:7-9. The original light is Christ himself. It is with reference to him that it was said, "The true light, which illumines every man, was coming into the world" (John 1:9). Jesus called himself "the light of the world" (John 8:12). In a secondary sense, Christ's followers, too, are "the light of the world" (Matt. 5:14). They are *light-bearers* (Rev. 1:20). The great missionary, Paul, was functioning in this capacity in a pre-eminent manner by bearing testimony, *even while in prison,* to "the light of the gospel of the glory of Christ" (II Cor. 4:4). As such he had become all things to *all men* that in one way or another he might save some. Hence, here in 1:9 he says, "to enlighten *all,*[86] (Jews and Gentiles alike) on what is the administration of the mystery." He describes the mystery as the one "which for ages has been hidden in God." Cf. Col. 1:26. From the beginning of time the mystery had been concealed. *Now,* however, it is being revealed both by the worldwide preaching of the gospel and by the crystallization of its precious truths in the life and conduct of the church universal. It is not clear why Paul adds: (God) "who created all things." If I may be permitted to add just one more guess to all those that have been made by others, I would say that the expression may, per-

[86] It is my conviction that πάντας should be retained. In the text of N.N. it is omitted. Grk. N.T. (A–B–M–W) retains it, though between brackets and with a D ("very high degree of doubt") rating. The external evidence is inconclusive. In such cases one must not slavishly follow the old rule "The more difficult reading must be adopted." That rule has long been in need of serious modification. Ernest C. Colwell in his article, "Biblical Criticism: Lower and Higher," *JBL* (March, 1948), p. 4, is correct when he states, "Today textual criticism turns for its final validation to the appraisal of individual readings, in a way that involves subjective judgment. The trend has been to emphasize fewer and fewer canons of criticism." One of the two canons which he mentions would apply especially in the present instance, I believe. It is this, "That reading is to be preferred which best suits the context." Surely, the words in the preceding context, namely, "to proclaim *to the Gentiles* the good tidings," etc., are followed very naturally by "and to enlighten *all* (*men*)." Note that the verb φωτίζω is followed by an object also in I Cor. 4:5 and in II Tim. 1:10. Cf. Rev. 21:23. However, in the present instance it really makes very little difference which reading one follows. It is as Abbott says (*op. cit.*, p. 87), "The general meaning is, indeed, pretty much the same with either reading, since the result of bringing οἰκ to light is that all men are enabled to see it."

haps, rivet the attention on God's sovereignty. He is the God who, by virtue of the very fact that he *created* all things, also proves himself to be the sovereign Disposer of their destinies. In other words, he does not owe it to any one to explain why for a long time the mystery was concealed from the Gentiles, and why it is now revealed to all, regardless of race or nationality.

The purpose which Paul has in mind in *proclaiming to the Gentiles the good tidings* of the unfathomable riches of Christ, *and in enlightening all men* on what is the administration of the mystery, is that by means of these two (to some extent overlapping) activities, the church, being formed and strengthened, might display God's marvelous wisdom even to the angelic world. He writes, **10. in order that**[87] **now to the principalities and the authorities in the heavenly places might be made known through the church the iridescent wisdom of God.** The church, therefore, does not exist for itself. It exists for God, for his glory. When the angels in heaven behold the works and the wisdom of God displayed in the church, their knowledge of the God whom they adore is increased and they rejoice and glorify him. That the designation "principalities and authorities" refers to angels has been established. See on 1:21 and N.T.C. on Col 1:16 and 2:18. By no means all commentators who adopt this position are in agreement, however, with respect to the kind of angels indicated here (3:10). Some defend the position that the reference is to evil powers exclusively.[88] Robertson, in his *Word Pictures,* Vol. IV, p. 531, equates them with "gnostic aeons or what not." Greijdanus states that although the reference is, first of all, to the good angels, the fallen angels need not be excluded (*op. cit.,* p. 72). Now it is true, indeed, that the expression "principalities and authorities" is neutral just like "angels." Gabriel is an angel, but so is Satan. In each case it is the context that determines whether the designation refers to angels in general, as in 1:21, to evil angels, as in 6:12, or to good angels. Even the addition here in 3:10 of the words "in the heavenly places" is not decisive in determining whether good angels or demons are meant, as 6:12 proves. Nevertheless, I still see no reason for disagreeing with Calvin, Bavinck, Grosheide, Hodge, Lenski, and a host of other leading theologians and commentators, in believing that 3:10 refers to the good and not to the evil angels. My reasons are as follows:

---

[87] The purpose clause thus introduced must not be linked with the immediately preceding subordinate clause. According to that construction the sense would be, "God created all things in order that the principalities and the authorities might learn more about God's marvelous wisdom in the sphere of redemption." I agree with Hodge, *op. cit.,* when he states, "This connection of the clauses is unnatural, because the words 'who created all things' are entirely subordinate . . . and therefore not the proper point of connection for the main idea in the whole context."

[88] Thus, for example, Franz Mussner, in *Christus, Das All und die Kirche,* Trierer Theologische Studien, V, Trier, 1955, p. 21; E. F. Scott, *op. cit.,* p. 189.

(1) Here (3:10) there is no reference to any *conflict* between believers and spiritual hosts of wickedness. In 6:12 the matter is entirely different.

(2) Both language and thought-content are elevated. Calvin's comments may well be taken to heart. Says he, "Some prefer to refer these words to devils, but without due reflection . . . There can be no doubt about the fact that the apostle labors to place in the strongest light the mercy of God toward the Gentiles, and the high value of the gospel . . . Paul's meaning is, The church, composed of both Jews and Gentiles, is a mirror, in which the angels behold the astonishing wisdom of God displayed in a manner unknown to them before. They see a work which is new to them, and the reason whereof was hid in God."

(3) The fact that the church, as God's masterpiece in which his excellencies are mirrored forth, is an object of interest and scrutiny to the good angels is clear also from other passages (Luke 15:10; I Cor. 11:10; I Peter 1:12; Rev. 5:11 ff.). Eph. 3:10 harmonizes beautifully with all this.

Now what the principalities and powers see reflected in the church is "the iridescent wisdom" of God. The adjective that modifies *wisdom* means literally *multi-colored* or *much-variegated.* Unless the word used in the original has lost its full etymological significance, and should therefore simply be rendered *manifold* (as in A.V., A.R.V., R.S.V.) or *many-sided* (L.N.T. – A. and G.), which in the present highly elevated context is improbable, it calls attention to the *infinite diversity* and *sparkling beauty of* God's wisdom. For both of these characteristics one is reminded of the rainbow. Hence, *iridescent* or something on that order (like *"many-splendoured"* suggested by Bruce) would seem to be a reasonable English equivalent, unless one wishes to retain the literal rendering *multi-colored.* In every phase of redemption (as well as of creation) the brilliance of God's wisdom reveals itself. Since in chapters 2 and 3 of Ephesians (see especially 2:16; 3:6) the matter of the reconciliation of Jew and Gentile to God and to each other through the cross – which to the Jew was a stumblingblock and to the Gentiles foolishness (I Cor. 1:22-25) – is never absent from Paul's mind, it would seem that this is one of the manifestations of the divine "wisdom" which he mentions. Cf. Rom. 16:25-27, where *the revelation of the mystery* is ascribed to "the only *wise* God." *God's wisdom reconciles seeming irreconcilables.* So also the very word *wisdom* is again used in the text when elsewhere reference is made to the fact that the very rejection of carnal Israel results, by various links, in the salvation of all of God's people: "By their fall salvation is come to the Gentiles, to provoke them to jealousy . . . that by the mercy shown to y o u [Gentiles] they [Israel] may now obtain mercy. . . . O the depth of the riches and *wisdom* and knowledge of God. How unsearchable are his judgments; how untraceable his ways!" (Rom. 11:11, 31, 33). Accordingly, when in the past certain commentators, in interpreting the expression "iridescent wisdom," have fixed the attention upon various paradoxes such as the following, that God in Christ produces life by means of death, glory by means of shame (the "shame" of the cross), the blessing by means of the curse, power by means of weakness, etc., they were simply following where Scripture itself had led them.

The true dimensions of the term "iridescent wisdom" are, however, much broader than this. There is not a single work of God whether in creation or, as here, in redemption, where that richly variegated wisdom does not manifest itself. It is seen in the church as a whole when it strives earnestly to live to God's glory. It is seen also in every individual believer, drawn out of the darkness into God's marvelous light. We catch glimpses of it *now,* as we study Scripture or as we reflect on the divine providence in our own lives. By the sea of crystal, where at last all things become crystal-clear to us, we shall see it as we have never seen it before, and, filled with rapture, we shall say, "Great and marvelous are thy works, O Lord God Almighty. Righteous and true are thy ways, thou King of the ages" (Rev. 15:3). The words of the Psalmist with reference to God's works in the physical realm will then be applied, with emphasis greater than ever before, also to the *spiritual* realm, namely, "O Lord, how manifold are thy works, *in wisdom* thou hast made them all!" The more the church lives in harmony with its high calling, the more also will the angels be able to see in it God's marvelous wisdom. To make manifest in its life and character the "excellencies" of its Maker-Redeemer, so that the principalities and the authorities may, indeed, see this wisdom is, therefore, part of the church's *Lofty Goal.*

**11.** That God's iridescent wisdom might be made known through the church was **according to the eternal purpose which he formed in Christ Jesus our Lord.** Paul is speaking here about the plan which spans *the ages;* hence, his "eternal purpose," the same purpose which was mentioned also in 1:11. Cf. II Tim. 1:9. It governs the ages in all their continuity and contents. That this purpose centers "in Christ" has been made abundantly clear in chapter 1. Christ is, in fact, the church's *Eternal Foundation.* His very name, fully spelled out here in 3:11, namely, "Christ Jesus our Lord," is essentially the same as that mentioned in 1:2, 3, 17. See on 1:2, but note that the beautiful word of appropriating faith, namely, "our" is added only in 1:3, 17, and in the present passage. There are those who maintain that this very title points to Christ in his historical manifestation here on earth, and, accordingly, that the entire passage deals not with God's purpose in Christ from eternity but rather with the historical realization of that plan. Hence, they interpret the words "which he *formed* (or *made*) in Christ Jesus our Lord" to mean "which he has realized" in him (thus R.S.V.). But although the verb used allows that translation, it is hardly true that the church's *Lofty Goal* of making known God's iridescent wisdom has already been fully realized. Only in glory will it be fulfilled in perfection. And there can be no objection to stating that even from eternity God's plan or purpose centered in him whom we now call "Christ Jesus our Lord." All things considered, therefore, it is best to interpret 3:11 as a very comforting passage, which assures believers that God's ultimate design for the church, namely, that it serve as a school in which the glorious angels may learn more and more about his marvelous wisdom, cannot fail to be realized, resting, as it does, not on the sinking sand of merely human striving but on the impregnable rock of the sovereign and eternal will of the Almighty, a will centered in the Anointed Savior, who is Lord of the entire Church Glorious, yes, *our* Lord. Continued, **12. in whom we have the courage of confident access through faith in him.** Literally, we would have to translate: "in whom we have *the courage and access in confidence.*" But if this be *hendiadys* we obtain the resultant meaning: *courage of confident access.* The three important words here are courage, access, and confidence. The word used for *courage,* namely, *parrēsía,* is very picturesque. It is derived from two Greek words, meaning *all* and *telling;* hence, telling all. The word occurs with great frequency in the New Testament, and in more than one resultant meaning. Light is shed upon its connotation here by such a passage as Phil. 1:20, "by my unfailing *courage* Christ will be magnified in my person," and by Heb. 4:16, "Let us therefore draw near with *courage* ("boldness," A.V., A.R.V.) to the throne of grace." The word *access* has already been explained. See on 2:18. It has been defined as *freedom of approach to the Father, in the confidence that we, Jew and Gentile, have found favor with him.* The third word, *confidence* (same meaning in II Cor. 1:15, but *ground of confidence* in Phil. 3:4), strengthens the idea already present in *access.*

Since, then, Christ Jesus is *ours* and we are *his,* bought with his blood, indwelt by his Spirit, we know that we have free and unrestricted access to the Father. Cf. 2:18. We can and should approach him without restraint, *telling* him *all* our troubles, asking him to help us in *all* our needs. We know that he will welcome us most heartily. Particularly, we should ask him to enable us so to live that the fruits of his grace may be exhibited in us, and the wisdom of God reflected in us, so that the angels may see us as the mirror of God's virtues. Such courage of confident access is possible only "through faith in him," namely, in "Christ Jesus our Lord," the very One "in whom" we were chosen from eternity. God's eternal purpose which cannot fail and the redemption accomplished by Christ Jesus our Lord make such fearless access possible.

13. The apostle concludes this parenthetical paragraph by writing: **Therefore I ask (y o u) not to lose heart over what I am suffering for y o u, which is y o u r glory —.** Meaning: because we have been endowed with this courage of confident access, we should rise above discouragement. Joy in the Lord should fill our hearts at all times, for no one can take from us the

blessings which are ours in Christ Jesus our Lord (see especially verses 6 and 12; cf. 1:3 ff.). In the original we have here a case of abbreviated expression, of which the Bible, and literature in general as well as human speech, is full. See N.T.C. on the Gospel according to John, Vol. I, p. 206. Actually all we have in the Greek text is this: "Therefore I ask not *to lose heart* (literally, *behave badly,* and so *become weary;* cf. II Cor. 4:1, 16; Gal. 6:9; II Thess. 3:13) in my afflictions for y o u," etc. In the abstract various meanings are possible. The main ones are these:

(1) Therefore I ask God that I may not lose heart

(2) Therefore I ask God that y o u may not lose heart

(3) Therefore I ask y o u that y o u may not lose heart

Since nothing in the context suggests God as the One to whom the request is presented, (1) and (2) can be ruled out. Also, another reason for ruling out (1) is that in the situation in which the apostle, a prisoner in Rome, finds himself, it was far more probable that those whom he addressed would lose heart than that he himself would become discouraged. That this is true appears quite clearly from another letter written, perhaps just a little later, during this same imprisonment, namely, Philippians. The church at Philippi seems to have been filled with anxious concern. It was for that very reason that Paul was then going to write, "Now I want y o u to know, brothers, that the things that have happened to me in reality turned out to the advantage of the gospel" (Phil. 1:12). We may well believe, therefore, that also here in Ephesus and surroundings not Paul but those whom he addressed were in danger of losing heart. Accordingly, the third possibility, "Therefore I ask y o u that y o u may not lose heart," is the one which I, along with many others, accept. It is as if the apostle were saying, "What an honor it is for y o u that in the very eyes of God y o u are regarded as being worthy of so much suffering endured by me in y o u r behalf!" (see on verse 1). How precious y o u must be to him! On the "glory" of suffering for Christ's sake see N.T.C. on Philippians, pp. 90, 91.

## Chapter 3

Verses 14–21

Theme: *The Church Glorious*

I *Adoration*
*for its*

*L* ofty Goal

2. To know the love of Christ that surpasses knowledge so as to be filled to all the fulness of God

14 For this reason I bend my knees to the Father, 15 from whom the whole family in heaven and on earth derives its name: the Father's Family, 16 (praying) that according to the riches of his glory he may grant y o u to be strengthened with power through his Spirit in the inner man, 17 that Christ may dwell in y o u r hearts through faith; in order that y o u, being rooted and founded in love, 18 may be strong, together with all the saints, to grasp what is the breadth and length and height and depth, 19 and to know the love of Christ that surpasses knowledge; in order that y o u may be filled to all the fulness of God.

20 Now to him who is able to do infinitely more than all we ask or imagine, according to the power that is at work within us, 21 to him be the glory in the church and in Christ Jesus to all generations forever and ever; Amen.

3:14-21

2. *The Church Should Strive to Know the Love of Christ That Surpasses Knowledge in Order to Be Filled to All the Fulness of God. Paul's Prayer That This Lofty Goal May Be Increasingly Realized. Doxology*

In the preceding paragraph Paul has pointed out that the church of Jew and Gentile must live in harmony with its high calling, so that to the principalities and the authorities in the heavenly places it may display God's iridescent wisdom. How is this end going to be achieved? The answer is given in verses 14-19, which point to the strength-imparting Spirit and the indwelling Christ. These will enable believers to attain to an ever increasing, though necessarily never complete, realization of the second aspect of their *Lofty Goal,* namely, to learn to know the love of Christ in all its dimensions so as to be filled to all the fulness of God.

That the apostle is still writing about The Church Glorious is very clear. In fact, he supplies us with a double description of the concept *church,* calling it, first, "the whole family in heaven and on earth," and afterward, "y o u [Ephesian believers] together with all the saints." Similarly, the fact that here, too, as in verses 1-13, Paul is centering our attention on the church's *Lofty Goal,* the very word "goal" being used by several commentators,[89] appears from the wording: *"in order that* y o u may be enabled to grasp and to know; . . . *in order that* y o u may be filled." And surely no one can quarrel with the adjective *lofty* modifying the noun *goal,* for what could be a loftier purpose or ideal than to know the breadth and length and height and depth of the love of Christ, in order to be filled to all the fulness of God? Now inasmuch as in its own strength the church will never

[89] For example, by Lenski, *op. cit.,* p. 497; and by Simpson, *op. cit.,* p. 82.

be able even to make progress in trying to achieve this objective, the apostle makes this a matter of earnest intercession. He begins by writing, **14, 15. For this reason I bend my knees to the Father, from whom the whole family in heaven and on earth derives its name: the Father's Family.** It is clear that the apostle resumes the sentence begun in 3:1. The meaning of the opening words is therefore *here* as it was *there:* Because blessings so rich have been bestowed upon both Gentile and Jew – reconciliation with God and with one another, and the erection of *one* sanctuary consisting of Jew and Gentile – therefore I bend my knees to the Father. In the intervening verses 2-13 another element, however, has been added to this first reason. Paul has made clear that the Lord has highly favored him by imparting to him the privilege of proclaiming to the Gentiles the good tidings of the unfathomable riches of Christ, and by enabling him to illumine the minds and hearts of all men with respect to the fact that the marvelous mystery, now unveiled, is, on the part of many, being translated into actual day by day living, a fact of amazement and instruction even to angels. Surely, God's wonderful dealings with *him,* Paul, a man in himself so unworthy, have made him all the more confident in prayer. Blessings already received encourage him to ask for even greater ones. Summarizing, we can say, therefore, that what the apostle means when here in verse 14 he writes, "For this reason I bend my knees," is this: It is because God has dealt so kindly with y o u, Ephesians, and with me, Paul, that I have the courage of confident access to the Father in heaven.

The apostle speaks about *bending his knees.* Posture in prayer is never a matter of indifference. The slouching position of the body while one is supposed to be praying is an abomination to the Lord. On the other hand, it is also true that Scripture nowhere prescribes one, and only one, correct posture. Different positions of head, arms, hands, knees, and of the body as a whole, are indicated. All of these are permissible as long as they symbolize different aspects of the worshiper's reverent attitude, and as long as they truly interpret the sentiments of his heart. For a listing of various prayer postures to which Scripture makes reference see N.T.C. on I and II Timothy and Titus, pp. 103 and 104. As to kneeling, in addition to Eph. 3:14 see II Chron. 6:13; Ps. 95:6; Isa. 45:23; Dan. 6:10; Matt. 17:14; Mark 1:40; Luke 22:41; Acts 7:60; 9:40; 20:36; 21:5. This particular posture pictures humility, solemnity, and adoration. It is "to the Father" [90] that this moving supplication, a true pattern of intercessory prayer, is presented. It should be borne in mind, however, that the One addressed is our Father by virtue not only of creation (3:9) but also of redemption. In fact, it is upon this redemptive aspect that the emphasis clearly rests. He is the Father to whom both Jew and Gentile have access *through Christ,* through him alone, *in one*

---

[90] A.V.'s addition "of our Lord Jesus Christ," is not based upon the best textual evidence. It may have been interpolated from 1:3, 17.

*Spirit* (2:18). In this redemptive or soteriological sense he is definitely *not* the Father of all men.

Paul gives a further description of the Father in the words: (I bend my knees) "to the *patéra* (Father) from whom *every* or *all* or *the whole* (or *all the*) [91] *patriá* in heaven and on earth derives its name." The sound-similarity between *patḗr* (here acc. *patéra*) and *patriá* is clearly an intentional play on words. It creates a problem in translation. The other question, as indicated in footnote 91, concerns the translation of the word *pâsa* which in the original precedes *patriá,* whether it should be rendered "every" or "all" or "the whole." The main translations that have been suggested are the following:

(1) *every family* (A.R.V., R.S.V., N.E.B.).

Objection: In a context in which the emphasis from start to finish is on *oneness,* how Jew and Gentile have become *one* organism (2:14-22; 3:6; 4:4-6), an emphasis so strong that the theme of the entire epistle is *The Church Glorious* or *The Unity of All Believers in Christ,* it is as dubious to speak of *every family* as it was in 2:21 to think of *each several building.* Those who, nevertheless, adopt this rendering become entangled in all kinds of questions such as: How many families does Paul have in mind? Do the Jews constitute one family, the Gentiles another? Do the angels form a family all by themselves or must we think of several angelic families: a family of "principalities" and another family of "authorities," etc.?

(2) *all fatherhood* (Phillips, Bruce). Simpson writes that *"Father of all fatherhoods"* is a rendering entitled to strong support (*op. cit.,* p. 79).

Evaluation: This translation has a certain appeal; first, because the play on words (paronomasia) of the original can thus be preserved in the translation, which then becomes, "I bend my knees to *the Father* from whom all *fatherhood* in heaven and on earth derives its name," or something similar; secondly, because it suggests a beautiful and comforting thought, in itself entirely true, namely, that, compared to the heavenly Father's *original* fatherhood, all other fatherhood anywhere in the universe is only *derived* and *secondary, a faint likeness.* If then human fathers love their children so intensely and care for them so generously, how marvelous must be the love and care of the heavenly Father! This thought, in turn, also provides an excellent basis for Paul's confidence that the request which he is about to make will be granted.

There are, nevertheless, two reasons that prevent me from adopting this translation: *a.* nothing in the context has prepared us for a discussion of

---

[91] The omission of the article before πᾶσα does not exclude the rendering "the whole" or "all the." This omission is not unusual with substantives that are viewed either as proper or as abstract nouns; probably the former in the present instance. Cf. footnote 77. Thus Robertson states that in Eph. 3:15 πᾶσα πατρία is "every family," though "all the family" is possible (Gram. N.T., p. 772).

the abstract concept of *fatherhood;* and *b.* the meaning *fatherhood* for *patriá* is foreign to Luke 2:4, "Joseph was of the house and *family* of David"; and to Acts 3:25, "In your seed will all the *families* of the earth be blessed." These are the only other New Testament passages in which the term *patriá* occurs. It is evident that even though it does not necessarily always refer to *family* in the most restricted sense of the term but can also indicate a wider group of persons united by descent from a common ancestor, it always has a concrete connotation. In the references given in M.M., p. 498, and in L.N.T. (A. and G.), p. 642, to contemporary Greek sources it also has the concrete sense.

(3) *the whole family* (A.V., footnote N.E.B.: "his whole family").

Evaluation: I consider this rendering to be correct. It is entirely in harmony with the context. In fact, in words that differ but slightly, the apostle has just told us that all those who believe in Christ, whether they be Jews or Gentiles, now constitute one *household,* a synonym for one *family.* Not only that, but he has even mentioned *the Father's* relation to this household or family. His words were: "For through him we both have our access in one Spirit to *the Father.* So then y o u are no longer strangers and aliens, but y o u are . . . *members of the household of God*" (2:18, 19). In subsequent passages he has re-emphasized this same thought, though by the use of different metaphors (2:20-22; 3:6). He is going to stress it again in 4:1-6. It was, in fact, this very circumstance that filled his heart with great joy.

The only drawback which this translation has is its failure to reproduce the obviously intentional connection between *patēr* (Father) and *patriá* (family), a sound-similarity almost impossible to reproduce in English while still retaining the meaning of the words in the original. Whether to give up the attempt, in which case A.V.'s rendering, or something similar, is still the best that has been offered: "the Father . . . of whom *the whole family* in heaven and earth is named," or else to look with favor upon my solution: "the Father, from whom the whole family in heaven and on earth derives its name: the Father's Family," I leave to anyone's preference. Perhaps someone can suggest a more excellent way.

What is Paul's purpose in attaching this modifier to the words "the Father"? I answer: He probably wishes to indicate that if it be true that the relation between believers and their heavenly Father is so very close that they constitute one family, whose very *name* — hence, existence, essence, character — as "the Father's Family" is derived from his name "Father," then this Father can be trusted to supply every need. See Matt. 7:11; Luke 11:13. This modifier, therefore, far from being inconsequential, furnishes an adequate introduction to the petition which Paul is about to present.

Another point must not be passed by, namely, that, according to this clause, "the family in heaven and on earth," "the Father's Family," is *one.* We speak about the Church Militant on earth and the Church Triumphant in heaven, but these are not two churches. They are *one* church, *one* family. It is in the interest of that *one* church that Christ governs the entire universe (1:22, 23). If even to us who are living in a day of travel by jet, short wave radio transmission, and the automatic relaying of electronic signals by means of synchronous satellites from and to any place on earth, distances seem to vanish, so that places on this planet once considered far apart are now viewed as close together, it should not be too difficult to understand that in the sight of the God who created all things the church of the redeemed in glory and the church of the redeemed on earth constitute *one* family. To be sure, there is nothing in Scripture that warrants the belief that there is *direct* contact between the dead and the living.[92] There *is*, however, indirect contact (Luke 15:7). Besides, the names of *all* believers, whether still on earth or already in heaven, are written in *one* book of life, and engraved on the breastplate of the *one* Highpriest. The Spirit, too, though in different measure, dwells in the hearts of all. All have *one* Father, of whom they are children by adoption (1:5; Rom. 8:15; Gal. 4:5). Christ, being the Son by nature, is not ashamed to recognize these adopted children as his brothers (Heb. 2:11). Every day the praise of the entire church, in heaven and on earth, is directed to *the same* Triune God.

The book of Revelation especially indicates how close are the ties that unite that part of the church which is in heaven with the part that is still on earth. In the early church this glorious truth was not a dead letter. Also in later times some have given beautiful expression to it. Thus, for example, the little girl, one of *seven* children, *two* of whom, however, had died, was certainly right when, according to Wordsworth's famous poem, she continued to maintain, "We are seven." The reader recalls, no doubt, the ending:

"How many are y o u then?" said I,
"If they two are in heaven?"
Quick was the little maid's reply,
"O master, we are seven."

"But they are dead; those two are dead!
Their spirits are in heaven!"
'Twas throwing words away; for still
The little maid would have her will,
And said, "Nay, we are seven!"

When we recite the "Apostles' Creed" and reach the line, "(I believe in) the communion of saints," we will have failed to pour full meaning into this part of our confession unless we understand that we are confessing that

[92] See the chapter devoted to this subject in my book *The Bible on the Life Hereafter*, pp. 62–65.

"we have come to mount Zion, and to the city of the living God, the heavenly Jerusalem, and to the innumerable hosts of angels [a different category of beings but vitally interested in our salvation], to the general assembly and church of the firstborn enrolled in heaven, to God the Judge of all, and to the spirits of just men made perfect" (Heb. 12:22, 23). We will have fallen short unless we cherish the memory of those who at one time were our leaders, reflect on the outcome of their life, and imitate their faith (Heb. 13:7). We will have missed the mark unless we bear in mind and are comforted by the fact that today too the ascended Christ is in the Spirit walking on earth in the midst of the lightbearers (Rev. 1:12, 13); and unless by faith we peer into heaven's opened door (Rev. 4:1), meditate upon the songs of its choirs (Rev. 4, 5, 12, 15, 19), and sense our oneness with all those who have come out of the great tribulation and, having washed their robes in the blood of the Lamb, are living and reigning with Christ in glory (Rev. 7:13-17; 20:4).

As to the intercessory prayer itself, it should be observed that it works its way toward a momentous climax. It is, as it were, a staircase consisting of three steps, a ladder with three rungs; steps or rungs, however, by means of which one is lifted to the very heights of heaven. The three parts of the prayer are readily visible, for the boundaries between them are marked out clearly by the words "in order that" in verses 17 and 19.[93]

**16, 17a.** Paul has introduced his moving trinitarian prayer by saying, "For this reason I bend my knees to the Father, from whom the whole family in heaven and on earth derives its name: the Father's Family," and he continues, **(praying) that according to the riches of his glory he may grant y o u to be strengthened with power through his Spirit in the inner man, that Christ may dwell in y o u r hearts through faith.** God is *glorious* in all his attributes, as has been indicated. See on 1:17. His power (1:19; 3:7) is infinite; his love (1:5; 2:4) is great; his mercy (1:4) and his grace (1:2, 6; 2:7, 8) are rich; his wisdom (3:10) is iridescent; etc. Note particularly such expressions as "the surpassing riches of his grace (expressed) in kindness" (2:7) and compare "the unfathomable riches of Christ" (3:8). In the work of salvation it is never right to stress one attribute at the expense of another.[94] Hodge is right when he states, "It is not his power to the exclusion

[93] In the original this is represented by ἵνα in the *final* sense in these two verses. At the beginning of verse 16 ἵνα is clearly *non-final*.

[94] Is not Lenski guilty of this error when he states, "Omnipotence does not work in the spiritual domain, grace and grace alone does"? (*op.cit.*, p. 418; and cf. pp. 426, 475). On p. 500 this eminent commentator, whose works have been a blessing to many, blames Calvinism — as he does rather frequently — for what he considers an erroneous view. But if "omnipotence does not work in the spiritual domain," would Paul have been saved? Would even a single sinner have been saved? As to the "working of omnipotence in the spiritual domain" see the following New Testament passages (which could easily be supplemented by those from the Old Testament): Acts 1:8; 10:38; Rom. 1:16; 15:13, 19; I Cor. 1:18, 24; 2:4, 5; 4:20; 5:4;

of his mercy, nor his mercy to the exclusion of his power, but it is everything in God that renders him glorious, the proper object of adoration" (*op. cit.*, p. 181). Paul prays therefore that all of God's resplendent attributes may be richly applied to the spiritual progress of those whom he addresses. In particular, he asks that the One who, as 1:19 (cf. 3:7, 20; Col. 1:11) has shown, is himself the Source of power in all its various manifestations, may grant to the Ephesians that, in accordance with the measure of God's glory, they may be strengthened with power through his Spirit in the inner man. This "inner man" is not that which is rational in man as contrasted with man's lower appetites. Paul's terminology is not that of Plato or of the Stoics. On the contrary, the "inner man" is the opposite of the "outer" (or: outward) man. Cf. II Cor. 4:16. The former is hidden from the public gaze. The latter is open to the public. It is in the *hearts* of believers that the principle of a new life has been implanted by the Holy Spirit. See on 3:17. What the writer is praying for is therefore this, that within these hearts such a controlling influence may be exerted that they may be strengthened more and more with Spirit-imparted power. See on 1:19; cf. Acts 1:8. Another way of putting the same thought is this: "that Christ may dwell in y o u r hearts through faith." Wrong is the idea, rather popular among some commentators, that *first,* for a while, the Spirit imparts strength to believers, *after which* there arrives a time when Christ establishes his abode in these now strengthened hearts. Christ and the Spirit cannot be thus separated. When believers have the Spirit within themselves they have Christ within themselves, as is very clear from Rom. 8:9, 10. "In the Spirit" Christ himself inhabits the believers' inner selves. Cf. Gal. 2:20; 3:2. The heart is the mainspring of dispositions as well as of feelings and thoughts (Matt. 15:19; 22:37; Phil. 1:7; I Tim. 1:5). Out of it are the issues of life (Prov. 4:23). Christ's precious indwelling is "through faith," the latter being the hand that accepts God's gifts. Faith is full surrender to God in Christ, so that one expects everything from God and yields everything to him. It works through love (Gal. 5:6).

It is instructive to note that the long list of exhortations (4:1–6:17) by means of which the apostle is about to urge the Ephesians to work out their own salvation (Phil. 2:12) is wedged in between two references to prayer; the first one, here in 3:14-19, being Paul's own prayer; the second in 6:18 ff., being the exhortation unto prayer, in which connection Paul reminds the Ephesians that as he prays for them, they too should pray for him. It is as if the writer were saying: To be sure, believers should strive to reach their goal. They should exert themselves to the utmost. But they should remember at all times that apart from the power of the Holy Spirit – or, stating

---

II Cor. 4:7; 6:7; 12:9; 13:4; Eph. 1:19; 3:16; 6:10; Col. 1:11; II Tim. 1:8; I Peter 1:5; Rev. 19:7; 21:22. Surely, when *the Almighty* reveals his *power,* he reveals his *almighty power,* his *omnipotence!*

it differently, apart from the indwelling of Christ – they are completely powerless. *"With fear and trembling work out* y o u r *own salvation; for it is God who is working within* y o u *both to will and to work for his good pleasure"* (Phil. 2:12, 13). And since so much – in a sense *everything* – depends on God, hence prayer for his strength-imparting power is all important.

The immediate purpose of the strengthening and the indwelling is stated in words which indicate, as it were, the second rung of this prayer-ladder:

**17b-19a. in order that y o u, being rooted and founded in love,[95] may be strong, together with all the saints, to grasp what is the breadth and length and height and depth, and to know the love of Christ that surpasses knowledge.** Since faith works through love, and amounts to nothing without it (I Cor. 13:2), it is easy to see that if *by faith* Christ has established his abiding presence in the heart, believers will be firmly rooted and founded *in love,* a love for God in Christ, for the brothers and sisters in the Lord, for the neighbors, even for enemies. Moreover, this love, in turn, is necessary in order to comprehend Christ's love for those who love him. And in the measure in which the believers' vision of that love which proceeds from Christ expands, their love for him and their ability to grasp his love for them will also increase, etc. Thus the most powerful and blessed chain-reaction in the whole universe is established. It all *began* with God's love in Christ for the Ephesians (1:4, 5; I John 4:19). Like a continuing circle it will *never end.*

The words "rooted and founded" suggest a twofold metaphor: that of *a tree* and that of *a building.* To insure the stability of the tree roots are required, roots that will be in proportion to the spread of the branches. Similarly, as a guarantee for the solidity of a building a foundation is necessary, one that will adequately support the superstructure. Thus firmly rooted the tree, which represents all those who love the Lord, will flourish and bear the indicated fruit. Thus solidly founded the building will continue to grow into a holy sanctuary in the Lord, and will achieve its purpose.

That fruit and purpose is "to grasp what is the breadth and length and height and depth, and to know the love of Christ." Since such *grasping* or *appropriating*[96] and *knowing* can be practised only by those who are rooted and founded in *love,* it is clear that the reference is not to an activity that is purely mental. It is *experiential* knowledge, *heart*-knowledge, which Paul

---

[95] As I see it, the grammatical construction indicates that the phrase "rooted and founded" belongs to the purpose clause introduced by "in order that" at the beginning of verse 18 of the Greek text. The trajection of the particle ἵνα, or, if one prefers, the proleptic placing of the participles, is not unusual. As to the phrase "in love," neither here nor in 1:4, where it also occurs (see p. 78, footnote 18), is the *preceding* clause in need of any additional modifiers.

[96] M.M., p. 328, states that this is Paul's regular use of the verb in active and passive.

has in mind. And since the heart is the very core and center of life and influences all of life's inner activities and outward expressions, what is indicated is a grasping and a knowing with one's entire being, that is, with *all* the "faculties" of heart and mind. Mental appropriation is certainly *included.*

It should not be necessary to point out that when the apostle speaks of being *strong* (exercising great inherent strength; see on 1:19) *to grasp . . .* and *to know,* he does not have two objects in mind but one, namely, the love of Christ. So great is that love that no one will ever be able to appropriate and to know it all by himself alone; hence, "together with all the saints." The saints will tell each other about their discoveries and experiences with respect to it, in the spirit of Ps. 66:16, "Come and hear, all y o u that fear God, and I will declare what he has done for my soul." This activity of getting to know more and more about the love of Christ begins here on earth and will, of course, continue in the life hereafter. The fact that Paul in this very prayer is not forgetting about the church in *heaven* is clear from verse 14. The *Lofty Ideal* is to get to know *thoroughly* Christ's deep affection, self-sacrificing tenderness, passionate sympathy, and marvelous outgoingness. All of these are included in *love* but do not exhaust it. Paul prays that the addressed may appropriate and know this love in all its breadth and length and height and depth! Here, as I see it, the expositor should be on his guard. He should not pluck this expression apart, so that a separate meaning is ascribed to each of these dimensions. What is meant is simply this: Paul prays that the Ephesians (and all believers down through the centuries) may be so earnest and zealous in the pursuit of their objective that they will never get to the point where they will say, "We have arrived. *Now* we know all there is to know about the love of Christ." Just as Abraham was told to look toward heaven and number the stars, so that he might see that numbering them was impossible; and just as we today are being urged by means of a hymn to count our many blessings, and to name them one by one, so that their uncountable multitude may increase our gratitude and astonishment, so also the apostle prays that the addressed may concentrate so intensely and exhaustively on the immensity and glory of Christ's love that they will come to understand *that this love ever surpasses knowledge.* The *finite* heart and mind can never fully grasp or know *infinite* love. Even in the life hereafter God will never say to his redeemed, "Now I have told y o u all there is to be told about this love. I close the book, for the last page has been read." There will always be more and more and still more to tell. And that will be the blessedness of the heavenly life.

This introduces us to the climax. We now reach the top of the ladder: **19b. in order that y o u may be filled to all the fulness of God.** See also on 4:13. In other words, the knowledge just described is transforming in character: "But we all, with unveiled face beholding as in a mirror the glory of the Lord, are transformed into the same image from glory to glory, even as from the Lord, the Spirit" (II Cor. 3:18). To contemplate the glory of Christ's love means to be increasingly transformed into that image. *In one sense* that process of transformation will cease at the moment of death. At the very moment when the soul of the believer enters heaven, a great change will take place, and he, who a moment before was still a sinner, a *saved* sinner, will be a sinner no more, but will behold God's face in righteousness. He will then be absolutely perfect, completely sinless, in every respect obedient to the Father's will (Matt. 6:10; Rev. 21:27). For "all the saints" it will cease, in the sense indicated, at Christ's return. *In another sense,* however, the transformation-process will not cease: growth in such things as knowledge, love, joy, etc., will continue throughout eternity. Such growth is not inconsistent with perfection. Even in the hereafter believers will still be creatures; hence, finite. Man never becomes God. God, however, ever remains infinite. Now when in glory, in a condition of total absence of sin and death, finite individuals are in continuous contact with the Infinite, is it even possible that the finite would not make progress in the matters that have been mentioned? When "the fulness of God" — all of those divine communicable attributes of which God is full: love, wisdom, knowledge, blessedness, etc. — is, as it were, poured into vessels of limited capacity, will not their capacity be increased?[97] To be sure, believers will never be filled *with* the fulness of God in the sense that they would become God. Even the communicable attributes, *in the measure in which they exist in God,* are incommunicable. But what Paul prays is that those addressed may be filled *to* all the fulness of God. Perfection, in other words, also in such matters as knowledge, love, blessedness must ever remain *the goal;* to become more and more like God, *the ultimate ideal.* What Paul is asking, therefore, with special reference, of course, to the church *still on earth,* though the answer to the prayer will *never* cease, is nothing strange, nothing new. It is a request similar to the exhortation of 5:1, "Be therefore imitators of God, as beloved children, and walk in love, *just as* Christ also loved y o u and gave himself up for us, an offering and a sacrifice to God, for a fragrant odor." And again, "It was he who gave some (to be) apostles . . . in order to fully equip the saints for the work of ministry . . . until we all attain to the unity of the faith and of the clear knowledge of the Son of God, to a full-grown man, to the measure of the stature of the fulness of Christ" (4:11-13). Cf. Col. 2:9, 10.

---

[97] On the entire subject of the possibility of progress in the life hereafter, may I once again call the readers' attention to my book *The Bible on the Life Hereafter,* pp. 70–78.

*Doxology*

**20, 21.** When the apostle surveyed God's marvelous mercies whereby, through the supreme sacrifice of his beloved Son, he brought those who were at one time children of wrath into his own family, and gave them "the courage of confident access," the privilege of contemplating in all its glorious dimensions the love of Christ, and the inspiring task of instructing the angels in the mysteries of God's kaleidoscopic wisdom, his soul, lost in wonder, love, and praise, uttered the following sublime doxology: **Now to him who is able to do infinitely more than all we ask or imagine, according to the power that is at work within us, to him be the glory in the church and in Christ Jesus to all generations forever and ever; Amen.** It is immediately clear that this doxology is not only a fitting conclusion to the prayer but also a very appropriate expression of gratitude and praise for all the blessings so generously poured out upon the church, as described in the entire preceding contents of this letter. Besides, it is Paul's way of making known his firm conviction that although in his prayer he has asked much, God is able to grant far more. On this point the apostle, who relished superlatives (see N.T.C. on I and II Timothy and Titus, p. 75), speaks very strongly. Literally he says, "Now to him – that is, to God Triune – who is able to do super-abundantly above all that we ask or imagine (or: think, conceive)," etc. In order to appreciate fully what is implied in these words it should be noted that Paul's reasoning has taken the following steps: *a.* God is able to do all we ask him to do; *b.* he is even able to do all that we dare not ask but merely imagine; *c.* he can do *more* than this; *d. far* more; *e. very far* more. Moreover, the apostle immediately adds that he is not dealing with abstractions. The omnipotence which God reveals in answering prayer is not a figment of the imagination but is *in line with* ("according to") that mighty operation of his power that is already at work "within us." It called us out of darkness and brought us into the light, changed children of wrath into dearly beloved sons and daughters, brought about reconciliation between God and man, and between Jew and Gentile. It is God's infinite might which he exerted when he raised Christ from the dead, and which is now operative in our own, parallel, spiritual resurrection.

Therefore to the One who does not need to over-exert himself in order to fulfil our desires but can do it with ease, "be *the glory* in the church and in Christ Jesus." In other words, may homage and adoration be rendered to God because of the splendor of his amazing attributes – power (1:19, 2:20), wisdom (3:10), mercy (2:4), love (2:4), grace (2:5-8); etc.– manifested in *the church,* which is the body, and in *Christ Jesus,* its exalted head. (On the concept *glory* see N.T.C. on Philippians, pp. 62, 63, footnote 43.)

The apostle's ardent desire is that this praise may endure "to all generations." The word *generation,* in addition to other meanings, has especially two connotations that should be considered in the present connection: *a.* the sum-total of contemporaries (Matt. 17:17); and *b.* the duration of their life on earth; that is, the span of time intervening between the birth of the parents and that of their children. In the present case, as well as in verse 5 above, the latter or chronological sense is indicated, for the phrase "to all generations" is reinforced by "forever and ever." The latter expression means exactly what it says. It refers to *the flow of moments from past to present to future, continuing on and on without ever coming to an end.* Rather strangely it has been defined by some as indicating "the opposite of time," "time without progress," "timeless existence," etc. But as far as creatures and their activities are concerned, the Bible nowhere teaches such timeless existence. The popular notion, also found in some commentaries and in religious poetry, namely, that at death — or according to others, at the moment of Christ's return — believers will enter upon a timeless existence, finds no support in Scripture, not even in Rev. 10:6 when properly interpreted. If in the hereafter believers will acquire *one* divine "incommunicable" attribute, namely, *eternity,* why not the others also, for example "omnipresence"? For more on this see the work mentioned on p. 174, footnote 97.

The blessed activity of which believers have a foretaste even now but which in unalloyed and superabundant grandeur will be their portion in the intermediate state, and far more emphatically in the day of the great consummation, an activity with which the apostle is deeply concerned and for which he yearns in prayer, consists, therefore, in this, that forever and ever the members of the Father's Family ascribe praise and honor to their Maker-Redeemer, whose love, supported by the illimitable power which raised Christ from the dead, will lift their hearts to higher and higher plateaus of inexpressible delight and reverent gratitude. Arrived in glory, their minds unobscured by sin, advance from one pinnacle of spiritual discovery to the next, and then to the next, in an ever ascending series. Their wills, then fully delivered from all the enslaving shackles of willfulness, and invigorated with a constantly growing supply of power, find more and more avenues of rewarding expression. In brief, the salvation in store for God's children resembles the Healing Waters of Ezekiel's vision (Ezek. 47:1-5), which, though when one enters them they are ankle-deep, soon become knee-deep, then come up to the loins, and are finally impassable except by swimming. And because of this constant progress in bliss, the answering progress in praise to God also never ceases, for

"When we've been there ten thousand years,
Bright shining as the sun,
We've no less days to sing God's praise
Than when we first begun."
(John Newton)

When the Holy Spirit inspired the prisoner Paul to write this overpowering doxology, Paul's heart was moved by that same Spirit to express hearty approval by means of the solemn "Amen."

*Summary of Chapter 3*

Paul now turns his attention to the church's *Lofty Goal.* This goal consists of two objects: *a.* to declare God's *wisdom* (1-13); and *b.* to learn more and more about Christ's *love* (14-21). Neither is possible without the other.

Paul arrives at the idea of God's wisdom by the contemplation of the "mystery" which had been revealed to him as to no other. The word *mystery* is used to indicate a truth which would have remained a secret had it not been divinely revealed. In the present instance and frequently when the word mystery is used, Paul is thinking of the fact that, according to God's eternal plan, in connection with the coming of the Messiah and the outpouring of the Spirit the old Jewish theocracy would be completely abolished and in its place would arise a new organism in which Gentiles and Jews would be placed on a footing of perfect equality. See Summary of Chapter 1, No. (7). Says Paul, "To me, the very least of all saints, was this grace given: to proclaim to the Gentiles the good tidings of the unfathomable riches of Christ and to enlighten all on what is the administration of the mystery which for ages has been hidden in God who created all things" (3:8, 9). When the apostle meditated on the fact that this mysterious organism of *a church gathered out of two formerly hostile groups, namely, Jews and Gentiles* was actually being established, and that the instrument which God was using to achieve it was nothing else than a totally unlikely one, namely, *the cross,* object of general derision and ridicule, he saw in this a manifestation of the wisdom of God, that is, of the latter's marvelous power to reconcile seeming irreconcilables, in order to carry out his gracious plan from eternity. By inspiration, he urges that this divine wisdom be made known by the church to all the good angels in heaven. Let the church of both Jews and Gentiles by their very striving to become more and more united for good be a mirror "in which the angels behold the astonishing wisdom of God displayed in a manner unknown to them before" (Calvin).

Not only God's *wisdom,* however, is displayed in the formation of the New Testament church, so is also his *love* in Christ. The apostle utters a prayer that is touching because of its depth of feeling, trinitarian character, and concentration on the love of Christ. He prays that through the indwelling of Christ's Spirit, believers, as it were pooling all their strength, may penetrate ever more deeply into the mysteries of Christ's transforming love, with the purpose of seeing that love in all its dimensions, and learning that it is so rich and marvelous that it can never be fully known.

True *idealism* which ever strives "to be filled to all the fulness of God" is at the same time the most *practical* thing on earth. The more believers, "rooted and founded in love" (otherwise they would not be qualified), make a devotional study of that love of Christ, the more also will they be filled with ardent desire to tell everyone about it. Thus sinners will be won for Christ and God Triune will be glorified. With the thought of the glory of God in his heart and openly expressed Paul closes this chapter.

# Chapter 4:1-16

Theme: *The Church Glorious*

II. *Exhortation*
*describing and urging upon all:*

*O* rganic Unity (amid Diversity) and Growth into Christ

# CHAPTER IV: 1-16

### EPHESIANS

4 1 I, therefore, the prisoner in the Lord, entreat y o u to live lives worthy
of the calling with which y o u were called, 2 with all lowliness and meekness, with longsuffering, enduring one another in love, 3 making every effort to
preserve the unity imparted by the Spirit by means of the bond (consisting in)
peace. 4 (There is) one body and one Spirit, just as also y o u were called in one
hope which y o u r calling brought y o u; 5 one Lord, one faith, one baptism; 6 one
God and Father of all, who (is) over all and through all and in all. 7 But to each
one of us this grace was given within the limits which Christ apportioned. 8 Therefore he says: When he ascended on high he led captive a host of captives, and he
gave gifts to men. 9 — Now this expression, *he ascended,* what can it mean but that
he had (previously) descended into the regions lower than the earth?[98] 10 The
one who descended is himself also the one who ascended higher than all the heavens
in order that he might fill all things — 11 And it was he who gave some (to be)
apostles; and some, prophets; and some, evangelists; and some, pastors and teachers; 12 in order fully to equip the saints for the work of ministry, with a view to
the building up of the body of Christ, 13 until we all attain to the unity of the
faith and of the clear knowledge of the Son of God, to a full-grown man, to the
measure of the stature of the fulness of Christ, 14 so that we may no longer be children tossed to and fro by the waves and whirled around by every gust of doctrine,
by the trickery of men, by (their) talent for deceitful scheming; 15 but adhering
to the truth in love, may grow up in all things into him who is the head, even
Christ, 16 from whom the entire body, harmoniously fitted together and held together by every supporting joint, according to the energy that corresponds to the
capacity of each individual part, brings about bodily growth with a view to its own
upbuilding in love.

---

### 4:1-16

It is clear as daylight and universally admitted that this section, especially in its opening verses, emphasizes unity. This unity, moreover, is not external and mechanical, but internal and organic. It is not superimposed, but, by virtue of the power of the indwelling Christ, proceeds from within the organism of the church. Those, therefore, who in their ecumenical zeal are anxious to erase all denominational boundaries and to create a mam-

---

[98] Or "into the lower regions [literally "parts"] of the earth?" Either translation is possible, with no essential difference in resultant meaning. In favor of "into the regions lower than the earth" is that it would balance "higher than all the heavens" in the next verse.

moth super-church can find no comfort here. On the other hand, neither can those who exaggerate differences and even stand in the way of inter-ecclesiastical co-operation when this can be accomplished without sacrificing any real principle.

The first six verses can be summarized as follows: the church *is* spiritually one; therefore, *let it be* spiritually one! This does not imply any contradiction, the meaning being that believers should "make every effort to preserve the unity imparted by the Spirit by means of the bond (consisting in) peace."

The unity is, however, not such that the individual believer becomes a mere "cog in the wheel." Personal initiative or individual expression, far from being crushed, is encouraged, as verses 7-12, 16, clearly indicate. Also, the oneness is not an end in itself. It is not a superficial desire for *togetherness* in the spirit of the familiar lines:

> "For your friends are my friends, and my friends are your friends; And the more we get together, the happier we'll be."

On the contrary, it is a unity with the purpose of being a blessing to one another, so that the church can be built up, and can thus be a blessing to the world. There is work to be done, as verse 12 clearly shows. And in order to accomplish the tasks assigned, believers should co-operate, each contributing his share to the inner growth of the church. This is all the more necessary because the opponents are very clever (verse 14). It is clear that in this section the idea of *growth* is just as prominent as is that of *unity*. If there be any difference in emphasis I would say the former is even more prominent, especially in verses 12-16. In verse 15 the apostle expresses the idea of growth in these words: ". . . that we, speaking truth in love, *may grow up* in all things into him who is the head, even Christ."

Everything considered, therefore, it would seem that the subtitle *Organic Unity (amid Diversity) and Growth into Christ* supplies the true key to the contents of this section.

1. The apostle begins, saying, **I, therefore, the prisoner in the Lord, entreat y o u to live lives worthy of the calling with which y o u were called.** Paul "the prisoner" (here "in the Lord"; cf. II Tim. 1:8; in Eph. 3:1 and in Philem. 1, 9 "of Christ Jesus," with no essential difference in meaning) has been faithful to his trust, as his very imprisonment, brought about by his loyalty, proves. He, therefore, is all the more justified in entreating the addressed to be likewise faithful, that is, "to live lives worthy of y o u r calling" (cf. Phil. 1:27; Col. 1:10; I Thess. 2:12; III John 6). Let them conduct themselves in harmony with the *responsibilities* which their new relationship to God had imposed upon them and with the *blessings* which this effectual *calling* (for which see on 1:18) had brought them. As to these *responsibilities,* the addressed had been foreordained to sonship (1:5). It is their re-

sponsibility, therefore, to behave in the manner in which adopted children of the heavenly Father could be expected to behave: believing his teachings, trusting his promises, and obeying his will. And as to the *blessings,* these were described in the preceding chapters: election, redemption, sealing, being made alive, being reconciled not only to God but also to those who had formerly been their enemies, having freedom of access to the throne of grace, etc. Surely, a life of gratitude, abounding in good works as its fruit, was in order! It is as if Paul were saying, "If y o u are believers, and wish to be known as such, live as believers." It reminds us of the manner in which Mordecai answered the accusations of those who found fault with him because he refused to obey the king's order to bow down to Haman. He simply answered, "I am a Jew" (implied in Esther 3:4). "Be what y o u are!" says Paul, as it were. He continues this thought by adding: **2, 3. with all lowliness and meekness, with longsuffering, enduring one another in love, making every effort to preserve the unity imparted by the Spirit by means of the bond (consisting in) peace.** The seven-fold description of the Christian life resembles very closely what is found in the twin-letter (see Col. 3:12-15).[99] To avoid repetition may I, accordingly, ask the reader to consult N.T.C. on Colossians and Philemon, pp. 155–160. What is about to be presented is *additional* material, not mere duplication. Though not intended as a complete list of qualities which believers should reveal in their lives, the Ephesian list furnishes a broad characterization of this new disposition and behavior. First mentioned is *lowliness* or *humility.* Having received blessings so great that their true value cannot be expressed in words, it is altogether proper that the recipients be filled with the very basic virtue of lowliness. Note the emphasis: "*all* lowliness and meekness." Humility has been called the first, second, and third essential of the Christian life. The mention of lowliness leads naturally to that of *meekness.* The meek individual is slow to insist on his rights. He realizes that in the sight of God he has no rights at all that are his by nature. All his rights were secured by grace. And although with reference to men he may at times have to insist on his rights (Acts 16:35-40), he does not rashly throw himself into the fray. He would rather "take" wrong than inflict it (I Cor. 6:7). With Abraham he prefers to let Lot have first choice (Gen. 13:7-18), with great reward . . . for Abraham! He exercises *longsuffering.* Emphasis on this virtue was greatly needed in the early church, when believers suffered misunderstanding, harshness, and cruelty from those who did not share their faith. For example, the lot of a Christian wife who was married to an unbeliever was by no means easy. Nevertheless, as long as her husband was willing to live with her in the marriage relationship, the wife must remain with him and try, by means of her God-fearing behavior, to win him for Christ. Thus,

[99] There compassion, kindness, forgiveness, and thankfulness are added to the list of seven characteristics mentioned here in Ephesians.

the grace of longsuffering would be beautifully illustrated in her life. See I Cor. 7:13 and I Peter 3:2. However, not only with respect to "outsiders" must this grace be exhibited, also with reference to fellow-believers. All have their faults and weaknesses. Let every one say to himself, therefore, "In view of the fact that God has been so longsuffering toward me, even though in *his* holy eyes my sins must stand out far more clearly than do my brother's blemishes in *my* eyes, I must surely be patient with my brother."

The mention of longsuffering is followed by that of *endurance* or *forbearance*. Literally the apostle says, combining two virtues, *"enduring* one another in *love."* The person who endures injury tries to pay no attention to it. He *holds himself up,* as the derivation of the word in the original implies, is not shaken up, but continues to keep himself erect and firm. We, too, at times use a somewhat similar expression when we say, "You should *put up* with his ill behavior." However, in saying this *we* do not always mean exactly what the apostle has in mind. We may simply be referring to suffering injury without *open* resentment, though we "boil" within! Paul, however, very aptly combines the forbearance of which he is speaking with the inner disposition of *love.* He everywhere emphasizes this virtue of outgoingness, true and tender affection toward the brother, the neighbor, and even the enemy, the noble endeavor to benefit him and never to harm him in any way. In addition to the Colossian verses to which reference was made earlier, see also Rom. 12:9-21; I Cor. 8:13; 9:22; 10:33; and Gal. 5:22, to select only a few references among the many that could be mentioned. The most complete and strikingly touching chapter on love toward all is I Cor. 13. To be appreciated it should be read, if possible, in the original, and if not possible, at least in several versions!

Now if, by the aid of the Holy Spirit and of prayer, a person truly endeavors so to conduct himself that his life will sparkle with these virtues, *unity,* to which Paul turns next, will be promoted. The spiritual oneness here indicated is an indispensable prerequisite for promoting the health and happiness of the church, for advancing the cause of missions, and for winning the victory over Satan and his allies. It does not come of its own accord but is the result of both effort and prayer; of *effort,* for the apostle says, "making every effort" ("giving diligence," "doing y o u r utmost," cf. II Tim. 2:15), and doing this *constantly* (note the present participle, continuative); and of *prayer,* for he refers to a unity "of the Spirit" (thus literally, but meaning: imparted by the Spirit); hence, the result of earnest prayer (Luke 11:13). It is a oneness of Jew and Gentile, as was emphasized by Paul (2:11-22; 3:6), of lofty purpose (3:10, 18, 19), and of true affection (4:2; 5:1, 2).

This unity is promoted by *peace.* Cf. I Cor. 14:33; II Cor. 13:11; Phil. 4:7; Col. 3:15; II Thess. 3:16; II Tim. 2:22. Here in Ephesians the apostle has already referred to it in 1:2; 2:14, 15, 17; and will refer to it again in

6:15, 23. When there is strife there is disunity. Peace, on the other hand, promotes the perpetuation of unity. Hence, it is, after all, not surprising that Paul writes, "making every effort to preserve the unity imparted by the Spirit by means of the bond ("of," that is, consisting in) peace." This *bond* or *tie that binds believers together* is *peace,* just as in Col. 3:14 it is *love.* This involves no contradiction, for it is exactly love that makes peace possible. Hence, both here in Eph. 4:2, 3 and in Col. 3:14, 15, love and peace are mentioned in close succession. Surely, if it be correct to say that the stability of the roof depends in a sense on the foundation that underlies the entire superstructure, then it is also correct to say that the roof's stability depends on the strength of the walls that immediately uphold it. And since especially in Ephesians the apostle dwells in such detail on the peace established between God and men, resulting in peace between Jews and Gentiles, it is entirely natural that he should *here* speak of *peace* as the bond. Take it in whatever sense one prefers, spiritual peace is ever the gift of love. Unity results.

The exhortation that the addressed may live in love and unity (verses 1-3) is followed by a description of this unity. In this description unity and all those characteristics associated with it are traced first to the Spirit, who had entered into the hearts of the believers; from there back to the Lord (Jesus Christ), whose vicarious sacrifice had made possible the gift of the Spirit; and, finally, to God the Father, who had given his Son and who, together with the Son, was also the Giver or Sender of the Spirit. In close association with the Spirit two other elements of Christian unity are mentioned, making three in all: "one body, one Spirit, one hope." So also, in connection with the Lord, two others, again resulting in a triad: "one Lord, one faith, one baptism." The Father is mentioned all by himself, for the six already named are traceable to him in the sense that whatever is associated with the Spirit and with the Son must, of necessity, also be associated with the Father, for it is he who is "over all and through all and in all." Accordingly, what we have here is a sevenfold description of a threefold unity, a statement of the character of Christian unity and of its trinitarian Source.[100]

4. The first triad is: **(There is) one body and one Spirit, just as also y o u were called in one hope which y o u r calling brought y o u.** The one body is, of course, the church consisting of Jews and Gentiles (2:14-22), the one family in heaven and on earth (3:15). Though in a sense, we are many, yet we are one body in Christ (Rom. 12:5). There is one loaf, one body (I Cor. 10:17). This body or church, moreover, is not an earth-born or

---

[100] I do not believe that there is any call for delving more deeply into the meaning of the number of the elements here mentioned. I find Lenski's numerical symbolism (*op. cit.,* pp. 510, 511) hardly convincing and, at any rate, unnecessary, since we are dealing here with the book of Ephesians, not with the book of Revelation.

man-made institution but a product of the Holy Spirit; hence, "one body and one Spirit." The urgent invitation of the gospel (the *external* call) has been applied to the hearts of the Ephesians by the Holy Spirit, producing the *internal* or *effectual* call. See on 1:18 and 4:1. Their call had brought them hope, a hope firmly grounded in God's promises which cannot fail. It was a hope of receiving the inheritance among the saints in the light (cf: 1:18 with Col. 1:12), as God's gracious reward for a life consecrated to him. The main reason, I believe, why the call had filled them with hope was that the very possession of the Spirit in their hearts was already the first instalment of their inheritance (1:14), and as such a pledge or guarantee of glory to come, a glory arriving not only when soul and body part but also and especially in the great consummation of all things at Christ's return. The fruits (Gal. 5:22, 23) which the indwelling and sanctifying Spirit was bestowing upon them were "firstfruits" (Rom. 8:23), a foretaste of future, ineffable bliss.

The Spirit, in the very process of imparting to the Ephesians the effectual call, also united them, so that they became one spiritual organism: "For by one Spirit we were also baptized into one body, whether we were Jews or Greeks, slaves or free, and we were all made to drink of one Spirit" (I Cor. 12:13; cf. 3:16; 6:19; Rom. 8:9, 11). Just as it is exactly because the human body is pervaded by the spirit that it is *one* and is able to function as a unit, every member in co-operation with all the others, so also it is precisely because the church, Christ's body, is indwelt and influenced throughout by the Holy Spirit that it is a single organism and operates as such.

**5.** Now the second triad: **one Lord, one faith, one baptism.** This Lord is "the Lord Jesus Christ." He is our Lord in the sense that since he bought us we are his. He owns us, loves us, cares for us, and protects us. We recognize his sovereignty, own him as our Deliverer and Ruler, trust, obey, love, and worship him (1:2, 3, 15, 17; 2:21; 3:11, 14; 4:1; etc.: cf. I Cor. 6:13-15, 20; 7:23; 12:3, 5; Phil. 2:11; I Peter 1:18, 19; Rev. 19:16). Whether Jew or Gentile, bond or free, male or female (Gal. 3:28; Col. 3:11), already in heaven or still on earth (Rom. 14:9), we all confess this *one* Lord as ours. We embrace him with *one* faith. What is meant by this one faith? Is it faith in the objective sense, *body of truth, creed* (Gal. 1:23; 6:10; Phil. 1:27 and frequently in the Pastoral Epistles), or is it faith in the subjective sense, *reliance on our Lord Jesus Christ and on his promises?* Among commentators there is great difference of opinion with respect to this question.[101] For

[101] Favoring the objective sense are Westcott and Lenski ("one truth"), though it is only fair to state that the latter does not entirely exclude the subjective meaning. He says, " 'One faith' includes our personal believing, but the stress is on the Christian faith as such, on what constitutes its substance." Simpson refuses to choose. Hodge and Greijdanus accept the theory that the term as here used combines subjective and objective faith. Abbott, Grosheide, Robertson, and Scott favor the subjective sense.

myself, the subjective sense seems to be the one indicated here. It is *one* faith — not historical nor miraculous nor temporary but true and genuine trust — by means of which we embrace the *one* Lord Jesus Christ. It is true that the subjective and the objective cannot be separated: when a person surrenders himself to Christ as his Lord he at the same time also accepts the body of truth with reference to him. Yet this is not the same as saying that the term *faith* is here used in a double sense. The fact that *faith* is mentioned immediately after *Lord* and is immediately followed by *baptism,* all in one very short sentence, would seem to indicate that the triad is a closely knit unit (which was true also with respect to the first triad, mentioned in verse 4). Hence, I agree with Scott, *op. cit.,* p. 204, when he states, "It is better to take the whole sentence as expressive of a single fundamental fact: 'one Lord in whom we all believe and in whose name we have been baptized.' "

With respect to the one baptism Grosheide states, "There is only one baptism which is received by many (perhaps a number of persons simultaneously). All the members of the congregation are baptized in the same manner, and we may well assume, after or in connection with the same sermonic elucidation." By means of baptism the fellowship of believers with their Lord was sealed (Gal. 3:27). "In baptism lies the evidence that all sorts of people (cf. Gal. 3:28), without any discrimination, share in the grace of Christ" (H. N. Ridderbos, *The Epistle of Paul to the Churches of Galatia,* a volume in *New International Commentary on the New Testament,* Grand Rapids, Mich., 1953, p. 147).[102]

**6.** To show the unity within the Trinity as ultimate basis for the unity of the church, the apostle, turning now to the Father, writes, **one God and Father of all, who (is) over all and through all and in all.** The emphasis here, as in 1:3, 17; 2:18; 3:14, 15, is on redemptive Fatherhood. The first person of the divine Trinity is our Father in Jesus Christ. He is "the Father from whom the whole family in heaven and on earth derives its name." To be sure, as our Father he is also our Creator, for he created all things (3:9). This fact makes his Fatherhood in the sphere of redemption stand out even more beautifully. He recreated what he had created, so that we are his in a double sense, and therefore all the more owe him our full devotion. But

---

[102] The question has been asked why Paul makes mention of only one sacrament, namely, baptism. Why does he not also include the Lord's Supper? Lenski, having enumerated several answers which he rejects, states categorically: "The correct answer is that the *Una Sancta* includes also a host of babes and children, none of whom are able to receive the Lord's Supper" (*op. cit.,* p. 514). However, the inclusion of the little ones — and they must be included — does not cancel the fact that the Lord has instituted only *one* true Lord's Supper. Better, therefore, it would seem to me, is Grosheide's observation: "I would remark that when a person does not himself give the reason for omitting a subject it is difficult for anyone else to state what that reason was" (*op. cit.,* p. 63, footnote 7).

that it is on his Fatherhood with reference to the family of believers that the emphasis here falls is clear not only from the fact that this is the prevailing sense in which the term *Father* is used in Ephesians but also from the immediate context. The first person of the Trinity is, accordingly, Father of all,[103] that is, of all those who belong to the family of the faith. Whether they are converts from the Jewish or from the Gentile world makes no difference, just so they are converts. As such he bears a threefold relationship to *all* his children: As Father he is "*over* all," for he exercises control over all. He is, however, also "*through* all," for he blesses us all through Christ our Mediator. And he is "*in* all," for he draws us close to his heart in the Spirit. Thus the three strands are gathered into one, and we perceive that the Spirit about whom verse 4 was centered, and the Lord (Jesus Christ) on whom verse 5 was concentrated, are not to be viewed as separate entities. We worship *one* God (Deut. 6:4), not three gods. Though it is true that Scripture ascribes election especially to the Father, redemption especially to the Son, and sanctification especially to the Spirit, yet in each of these departments all co-operate. The three never work at cross purposes. As has often been remarked, the Father thought our salvation, the Son bought it, the Spirit wrought it. Moreover, the unity amid diversity which pertains to the Trinity is the basis for the essential unity in the midst of the circumstantial variety which characterizes the church, and to which Paul now turns.

7. He writes, **But to each one of us this**[104] **grace was given within the limits which Christ apportioned** (literally, "according to the measure of the gift of Christ"). The apostle has dwelt in detail on the unity of the church. This was necessary, for only when the church recognizes its unity and strives more and more to preserve it, each member co-operating with all the others, will the gospel move mightily forward among the nations, will the church itself rejoice, will Satan tremble, and will the name of God be glorified. However, this *unity* makes allowance for *diversity* of gifts among the many members of the one body. In fact, this very diversity, far from destroying the unity, will, if properly used, promote it. The proper use of the gift, that is, the particular *endowment* (see on 3:2, 7) which in his grace God has bestowed on anyone, implies the following: *a.* that the recipient shall indeed recognize it as a gift, and not as the product of his own skill or ingenuity; *b.* that he view his gift as only one among many and as

---

[103] The entire context clearly indicates that the word πάντων is here not neuter. In the present connection the apostle has not been discussing God's relation to the universe or to nature.

[104] As Paul has previously referred to "the stewardship of God's grace" that had been given to him (3:2) and to "the gift of God's grace" (3:7), the article ἡ before χάρις in 4:7 is altogether natural. I see no reason, therefore, with B D*, etc., to omit it.

limited in extent, a measured gift; and *c.* that he be eager to use it not for his own glory but for the benefit of the entire body, and thus, to God's glory. The best commentary on this verse is what Paul himself writes in I Cor. 12, the entire chapter. In verses 4-6 he states, "Now there are diversities of gifts, but the same Spirit; and there are diversities of service, but the same Lord; and there are diversities of working, but it is the same God who works all in all." And significantly he adds, "But to each is given the manifestation of the Spirit for the common good" (verse 7). It seems that in the early church – as also today – there was a twofold danger: *a.* that those who had received very special endowments might overestimate their importance, give themselves the credit for them, and fail to use them for the benefit of the entire church; and *b.* that those who had not been so richly endowed might lose courage, thinking that they were of no benefit to the church. It was not only Paul who reacted against this real peril; in a slightly different sense so did James even earlier: "Let the brother of low degree glory in his high estate, and the rich in that he is made low" (1:9). The real comfort and glorious lesson for everyone must ever be: "I have received my gift, be it great or small, from Christ himself.[105] I must use it, therefore, as he requires. The Giver will not fail me when I use my gift for the benefit of all."

But is it really true that the Jesus who once walked the earth is now so highly exalted, so glorious, and so richly endowed with authority that he is able to bestow his gifts upon the church and upon its members in lavish quantity? In answer to this question the apostle writes about the ascended Christ and the gifts which he bestowed and is still bestowing. What follows in verses 8-16 is really a unit. However, since the reference to Christ's ascension and its implication is found especially in verses 8-10, this will be studied first of all. Paul writes **8-10. Therefore he says: When he ascended on high he led captive a host of captives, and he gave gifts to men. – Now this expression, *he ascended,* what can it mean but that he had (previously)** [106] **descended into the regions** [107] **lower than the earth? The one who**

[105] I see no good reason to regard τοῦ Χριστοῦ as an objective genitive (Lenski, *op. cit.,* p. 517: "the gift bestowed upon Christ"). Eph. 3:2, 7 as well as I Cor. 12:4-11 all point in the direction of regarding these special gifts as coming *from* Christ and *from* his Spirit. Eph. 4:8 points in the same direction: "he gave gifts to men."

[106] When Codex B and most of the later manuscripts and versions add πρῶτον (first, previously; see A.V.) after "he descended," they probably do this to clarify the text. Though the intention of this addition is to be appreciated, the proposed reading does not have quite sufficient textual support to be adopted. Nevertheless, as a clarification of the meaning of the text the word can be inserted in the translation *between parentheses,* as I have done.

[107] The omission of the word "parts" or "regions" in $p^{46}$ D* G, etc., is of minor significance, as it affects the meaning very slightly, if at all; for in the present context, after "he descended into," the neuter pl. τὰ κατώτερα would still have to be translated "the lower regions (or *parts* or *lands* or something similar)."

**descended is himself also the one who ascended higher than all the heavens in order that he might fill all things —.**

The word "therefore" must here be interpreted to indicate something like "in accordance with this." By direction of the Holy Spirit Paul introduces a passage from the Psalms (Ps. 68:18; LXX 69:19) that has a bearing upon the present subject. He does not intend to quote literally but rather, as occurs so often in such cases, to elucidate a passage by showing how that which in the Psalter was said concerning *God* attained its fulfilment in *Christ.*[108] When we bear in mind the typical character of the old dispensation, the fact that "the Old is by the New explained," so that we do not have two Bibles but one Bible inspired by one original Author, the Holy Spirit, we will not be able to find fault with this method.

The expression "he says" means "God says." This appears rather clearly from the context in such passages as Rom. 9:25; Gal. 3:16, 17; and Heb. 1:5-7; and may be assumed also in such other passages as Rom. 15:10; I Cor. 6:16; II Cor. 6:2; etc.[109] There follows the application of Ps. 68:18 to Christ's ascension and the gifts he bestowed. In A.V. this passage reads as follows: "Thou hast ascended on high, thou hast led captivity captive; thou hast received gifts for men." In A.R.V. the first line is identical; the second reads "thou hast led away captives." This, however, is not a material change, for "captivity" can be interpreted as meaning "a host of captives" (see Judg. 5:12), just as, for example, "the circumcision" means "the circumcized" (Eph. 2:11). The third line is "thou hast received gifts among men." Paul appears to have had in mind the LXX version of the passage, with which, *with respect to the points which require comment,* our English versions agree substantially, though not in every little detail. However, in the apostle's *application* — for, as the passage from the Psalms reads *in Eph. 4:8* it is *applied* rather than literally *quoted* — the words undergo three changes. Two of them, however, are of such minor significance that they can be relegated to a footnote.[110] The one really important change is this, that the passage from which the apostle was borrowing stated that the One who ascended *received* gifts, but the apostle himself in referring to it here says that he *gave* gifts. According to the Old Testament passage God is repre-

---

[108] For other instances in which what is said of *God* in the Old Testament is referred to *Christ* in the New compare Exod. 13:21 with I Cor. 10:4; Isa. 6:1 with John 12:41; and Ps. 102:25-27 with Heb. 1:10-12.

[109] On this see B. B. Warfield, *The Inspiration and Authority of the Bible,* Philadelphia, 1948, pp. 299–348. His refutation of Abbott's contrary contention is interesting and, as I see it, convincing.

[110] Namely, the second person ("thou hast ascended") has been changed to the third ("he ascended"); and the finite verb has been changed into a participle ("having ascended"). As to "thou" or "he," except for the fact that what in the Old Testament applies to God is said here concerning Christ (on which I have already commented) there is no material change. And the change from the finite verb to the participle is merely stylistic.

sented, it would seem, as descending from heaven to wage war against his enemies. He ascends again as Victor, loaded with spoils. What gave Paul the right to apply this *receiving* of gifts to the activity of Christ whereby he *gives* gifts to his church? Ever so many explanations have been offered with which I shall not weary the reader. The one I accept is the following: *Under the guidance of the Holy Spirit the apostle had every right to make this application, for the Victor receives the spoils with a view to giving them away. The giving is implied in the receiving.* When Christ ascended he was not returning to heaven with empty hands. On the contrary, as a result of accomplished mediatorial work he returned *in triumph* to heaven, in the full possession of salvation for his people. These people were, so to speak, in his triumphant procession. They were captives in his train, chained, as it were, to his chariot. There was a vast host of captives. Among them was also Paul, destined, along with the others, to spread abroad the fragrance of the gospel. Thanks be to God! See II Cor. 2:14. Now Christ *received* in order *to give*. He *had earned* in order *to bestow*. He received these captives in order to give them to the kingdom, for kingdom-work. Reasons for adopting this interpretation:

1. The prevailing custom that the victor divides the spoil is recognized also in Scripture. Thus, when Abraham defeated Chedorlaomer and his allies he took booty with the intention of giving it away: to Lot, what he had lost; to Melchizedek, the tithe; to Aner, Eschcol and Mamre, their portion (Gen. 14). Did not David also receive the spoil in order to give it away? (I Sam. 30:26-31). Israel's enemies, too, were in the habit of dividing the spoil, first taking it and then distributing it (Judg. 5:30).

2. Isa. 53:12 says with reference to the coming Messiah, "He will divide the spoil with the strong."

3. According to Acts 2:33 Peter on the day of Pentecost distinctly reminded his audience that "*having received* of the Father the promise of the Holy Spirit, *he* [*Christ*] *has poured out* this which y o u see and hear."

4. The Aramaic Targum on the Psalter and also the Peshitta read, "Thou hast given gifts to men." At the root of this interpretation there must have been a very ancient oral tradition. Now the Targum explained the words of the Psalmist as having reference to Moses, *who received* the law on Sinai *in order to give* it to the people of Israel. All the same, the receiving implied the giving.

5. This explanation suits the present context in which the apostles, prophets, evangelists, etc., are described as *the gifts* of the ascended Christ to the church.

When Paul adds, "Now this expression, *he ascended,* what can it mean but that he had (previously) descended," the logic is not immediately clear. An ascent does not necessarily presuppose a previous descent. The fact, for example, that Elijah ascended to heaven does not mean that he had previously come down from heaven. The solution lies in the fact that Paul is not stating a general law but is speaking about Christ, and is saying that *in his case* ascent implied (previous) descent. This is true, for, as we have seen, Christ's ascension was glorious. He was welcomed back by his Father into heaven (John 20:17; Acts 1:11), and at his entrance into glory all heaven rejoiced (Rev. 12:5, 10). Now *this* ascension whereby he, as Victor over Satan, sin, and death, re-entered heaven in the full merits of his atoning sacrifice would never have been possible had he not first descended from the glories of heaven to earth's shame and suffering. This is simply another way of saying that Christ's exaltation resulted from his humiliation, a humiliation so deep and ineffable that the apostle characterizes it by saying that he "descended into the regions lower than the earth." This expression of verse 9 is in direct contrast with "higher than all the heavens" of verse 10. The two expressions can be understood only when they are viewed in their relation to each other. And they should be so considered for they concern the same person: "The one who descended is himself also the one who ascended higher than all the heavens." Paul is the best commentator of his own words. He furnishes this commentary in Phil. 2:5-11: "He emptied himself . . . and became obedient even to the extent of death; yes, death by a cross. Therefore God raised him to the loftiest heights," etc.[111]

---

[111] Since the interpretation here given of the expression "he descended into the regions lower than the earth" fits the context and is in harmony with Paul's own statement in Philippians, written during the same imprisonment, I comment on other explanations as follows:

(1) The descent refers to Christ's burial or the entrance of his body into Joseph's garden.

Objection: This does not go far enough. The burial is included, to be sure, but only as part of Christ's deep humiliation.

(2) It indicates Christ's descent into the underworld – usually, but not always, conceived of as having occurred during the interval between his death and resurrection – with the purpose variously represented as: *a.* releasing the souls of Old Testament saints from the Limbus Patrum; *b.* proclaiming grace to the lost or to some of them; *c.* taunting Satan with the announcement of his (Christ's) victory, etc. In connection with *c.* it has been remarked that at Christ's arrival the devils were so scared that some of them fell out of hell's window!

Objection: There is nothing in the context either of Ps. 68:18 or of the Ephesian passage to suggest such a descent. Nor is there any hint of it in Phil. 2 or, for that matter, anywhere else in Paul's epistles. According to the Gospels the dying Christ committed his soul to the Father. On the day of the resurrection it was restored to the body from which it had been taken. And as to I Peter 3:19 and 4:6, these passages, too, which cannot now be considered, when contextually interpreted do not teach anything of this nature. It is enough to say that they have reference to preaching to those who, though now dead, were still living on earth when they received God's warnings.

(3) It refers to a descent subsequent to the ascension but before the second coming.

Objection: Leaving out of consideration the rhetorical or figurative use of the verb καταβαίνω in Rom. 10:7, which cannot be used either in defense or refutation

For believers in every age it is certainly a comfort to know that he who ascended higher than all the heavens, an expression that must not be taken in a merely literal sense but in the sense of majesty and exaltation to the Father's right hand so that he reigns over the entire universe and over every creature (1:20-23), is still the same Jesus, filled with the same tender love and sympathetic concern which he showed when on Calvary's cross he descended to regions lower than the earth, that is, to the experience of the nethermost depths, the very agonies of hell (Matt. 27:46). Add to this the equally comforting truth that when he returns on clouds of glory he will still be "this same Jesus" (Acts 1:11), the *one* loving and ruling head of the *one* church. What an incentive to the spirit of *unity* among all the members of the church!

*This Same Jesus*

"This same Jesus!" Oh, how sweetly
  Fall those words upon the ear,
Like a swell of far-off music
  In a night-watch still and drear!

* * *

---

of the theory in question, it is safe to say that nowhere in the New Testament does the verb have this reference. In I Thess. 4:16 it is used in connection with the second coming. The other pertinent passages that speak of Christ's descent occur in the Gospel according to John (3:13; 6:33, 38; 6:41, 42, 50, 51, 58). All of them have reference to Christ's incarnation-descent, even though in John 3:13, as also here in Eph. 4:9, the ascent *is mentioned* before the descent. Note opposite order in Eph. 4:10. There is nothing in the context of Eph. 4:8-10 that points in the direction of a post-ascension descent. Ps. 68:18, which here in Ephesians is applied to Christ's ascension, is also best interpreted as indicating anthropomorphically *a descent* of Jehovah (cf. Hab. 3) *followed by ascent.* "In the Psalm it was Jehovah that ascended, but that was only after he had first descended to earth in behalf of his people from his proper habitation in heaven" (Salmond, *op. cit.,* p. 326).

(4) What we have here is a matter of simple apposition. The right translation is: "He descended into the lower parts, viz. the earth" (Hodge). Calvin favors this interpretation, and so do many other commentators.

Evaluation: This is a very attractive theory. The passages in John's Gospel, to which reference was made under (3), have been appealed to in its support. My hesitancy in accepting it is the objection which I share with many commentators, namely, that if Paul merely wanted to say that Jesus descended to earth he could have stated this in a far more simple manner than by inserting the reference to "the lower regions." Hence, the passages in John's Gospel are not necessarily completely parallel. However, in the final analysis the difference between the view of Calvin, Hodge, etc., and the one which I, along with many others, favor, becomes minimal when this descent to earth is interpreted in its most comprehensive sense, namely, as an *incarnation involving deep humiliation:* "Jesus from his throne on high *came into the world to die.*" Thus Calvin comments as follows on Christ's *descent to the earth:* "And at what time did God descend lower than when Christ *emptied himself* (Phil. 2:7)? If ever there was a time when . . . God ascended gloriously, it was when Christ was raised *from our lowest condition on earth,* and received into heavenly glory." Here the two views, Calvin's and the one I favor, though based on two different renderings of the text, coincide completely!

He, the lonely Man of Sorrows,
'Neath our sin-curse bending low,
By his faithless friends forsaken
In the darkest hours of woe,–
* * *
"This same Jesus!" When the vision
Of that last and awful day
Bursts upon the prostrate spirit,
Like a midnight lightning ray;
* * *
Then, we lift our hearts adoring –
"This same Jesus," loved and known;
Him, our own most gracious Savior,
Seated on the great white throne.
* * *

(Frances Ridley Havergal)

Paul concludes this elaboration on Christ's humiliation and consequent exaltation by adding that his purpose was "that he might fill all things." This has been variously interpreted as meaning:

(1) that he might fulfill all predictions;

(2) that he might accomplish every task that had been assigned to him;

(3) that he might fill the universe with his omnipresence; and

(4) more in detail, that his human nature, including his body, might pass into the full enjoyment and exercise of the divine perfections, and thus become permanently omnipresent, omnipotent, etc.

I reject all these because, as I see it, they are foreign to the present context. This applies very clearly to (1) and (2) about which nothing is said in this context. As to (3), favored by Hodge and others, it is not clear how Christ, by means of his ascension, could become omnipresent. As to his deity he was already omnipresent. And as to his human nature, unless we accept the general proposition that by means of the ascension something peculiar to the divine nature is communicated to *the human nature* – which is *not* the Reformed position – it is hard to see how that human nature could now become omnipresent. And as to (4), the Lutheran position (see Lenski, *op. cit.*, pp. 524, 525), with reference to which, however, there is a difference of opinion among Lutheran theologians, here again the connection between the communication of divine attributes to the human nature, on the one hand, and the gift of apostles, prophets, etc., of which the context speaks, is not immediately clear. Besides, the ascension accounts as found in Luke 24:50-53 and Acts 1:6-11, while clearly describing the transition of Christ, as to his human nature, from one place to another, say nothing at all about any change in Christ's human nature so that it now entered into the full enjoyment and exercise of the divine perfections. Also, it is difficult to see how the human nature can continue its existence when it is fused with the divine.

A better interpretation, it would seem to me, is furnished by the immediate context, both preceding and following, namely, this, that as a result of Christ's descent into Calvary's hell where he made atonement for sin, and of his subsequent resurrection and ascension, which served as evidence that this atonement had been fully accepted, Christ, as the now exalted Mediator, *fills the entire universe with "blessings"* or, if one prefers, with "gifts," the very gifts which he had earned: salvation full and free and the services of those who proclaim it; such as apostles, prophets, evangelists, etc. Here also it is best to let Paul be his own interpreter. He has already called Christ the One "who fills all in all," which has been interpreted to mean, in part, that with a view to his universe-embracing program Christ replenishes the church with his bounteous gifts. See on 1:23. Cf. 1:3; John 1:16; I Cor. 12:5, 28-32. To some of these "gifts" of the ascended Christ Paul now turns his attention, as he continues: **11. And it was he who gave some (to be) apostles; and some, prophets; and some, evangelists; and some, pastors and teachers.** The ascended Savior gave what he had received: men who were to render service to the church in a special way. Before describing each of the groups mentioned in this passage, the following general observations are in order:

1. It is not Paul's intention to furnish us with a complete list of office-bearers, as a comparison with I Cor. 12:28 shows. In the latter passage there is a somewhat similar enumeration but no specific mention of evangelists. The combination "pastors and teachers" is also omitted, but other functionaries, not included in Eph. 4:11, are added. Though there is no scriptural warrant whatever for the tendency to get rid of the idea of "office" and "authority,"[112] for these concepts are clearly implied in Matt. 16:18, 19; John 20:23; Acts 14:23; 20:28; II Cor. 5:3, 4; 10:8; I Tim. 1:18; 3:1, 5; 4:14; 5:17; II Tim. 4:1, 2; Titus 1:5-9; 3:10, nevertheless, "the emphasis in this passage [Eph. 4:11] does not lie on the apostles, prophets, etc. as officers, but as gifts of Christ to his church" (Roels, *op. cit.*, p. 185).

[112] Thus A. Harnack, *The Constitution and Law of the Church*, New York, 1910, p. 5, quotes with approval the words of another: "The rise of ecclesiastical law and the constitution of the Church is an apostasy from the conditions intended by Jesus himself and originally realized." The position of these men – among whom may also be mentioned E. De Witt Burton, C. Von Weizsäcker, F. J. A. Hort, etc. – is that the apostles were not in any sense intended to be ecclesiastical officers but merely bearers of a message; that they were not vested with authority over life and doctrine but merely endowed with special spiritual gifts; or that, if they exercised any authority at all, it was not official but organic, spiritual, ethical. Scott's remark, "As yet there was no official ministry," *op. cit.*, p. 210; and Beare's "the ministry of function alone was known to Paul," *op. cit.*, p. 691, point in the same direction. See the refutation of this idea by O. Linton, *Das Problem der Urkirche in der Neuere Forschung*, Upsala, 1932, p. 71 ff.; and C. B. Bavinck, Art. "Apostel" in *Christelijke Encyclopaedia*, Vol. I, pp. 143–145.

2. The reason why in 4:11 ff. the apostle, whose heart went out to the lost (I Cor. 9:22) does not here stress the *numerical* growth of the church but rather its growth in love and other spiritual qualities, may well have been that the latter is the indispensable prerequisite of the former.

3. In order that the church may be strong it must not only have good leaders (verse 11) but also good, active followers (verse 12). Full salvation cannot be obtained until *all* of God's children obtain it together, a fact which Paul expresses beautifully in II Tim. 4:8, and which here in Ephesians he brings out by his constant use of the word *all* (1:15; 3:18, 19; 6:18).

4. Since here in 4:11 all who serve the church in a special way – not only "apostles, prophets, and evangelists," but also "pastors and teachers" – are designated as Christ's *gifts* to the church, they should be the objects of the love of the entire church. If, when they truly represent Christ, they are rejected, Christ is thereby rejected.

5. And, on the other hand, there is also here an implied admonition for the leaders themselves, namely, that these gifts were not given to them for their own sake but in the interest of Christ's body, the church.

A brief description of the "gifts" here enumerated is as follows:

*a. Apostles,* in the restricted sense of the term, are the Twelve and Paul. They are *the charter-witnesses of Christ's resurrection,* clothed with life-long and church-wide authority over life and doctrine, but introduced here, as already indicated, in order to stress *the service* they render. For a full statement of the characteristics of plenary apostleship see N.T.C. on I and II Timothy and Titus, pp. 50, 51.

*b. Prophets,* again in the restricted sense (for in a broader sense every believer is a prophet), are *the occasional organs of inspiration,* for example, Agabus (Acts 11:28; 21:10, 11). Together with the apostles they are described as being "the church's foundation." See also on 2:20 and 3:5; and see Acts 13:1; 15:32; and 21:9.

*c. Evangelists,* such as Philip (thus designated in Acts 21:8; his activity described in Acts 8:26-40) and Timothy (II Tim. 4:5), are *traveling missionaries,* of lower rank than apostles and prophets. Philip is mentioned first as one of the seven men chosen "to serve tables" (Acts 6:2). Timothy was one of Paul's assistants and representatives. For more about him and about the nature of his work see N.T.C. on I and II Timothy and Titus, pp. 33–39, 156–160, 312, 313. We know that Timothy had been ordained to office (I Tim. 4:14), as was true also with respect to Philip (Acts 6:6). For what office were these men ordained? In the case of Philip it is clear that he was ordained as "deacon," though the term deacon is not used in Acts 6. Must we then assume that when he was used by the Lord for the conversion of the Ethiopian eunuch he was "on his own," as it were, or serving in a different capacity? Similarly, must we take for granted that Timothy served in two separate offices: *a.* as apostolic vicar, and *b.* as evangelist? Is it not more consistent with scriptural data to infer from the account in Acts 6 that *only those* men were to be chosen as deacons who were "full of the Spirit and of wisdom," "full of faith," and that, accordingly, Philip was a *deacon-evangelist?* Are we doing full justice to the office of deacon if this is lost sight of? And does not the case of Timothy also indicate the flexibility of his office? If Timothy, as *evangelist* or *traveling missionary,* can serve the interests of the church best by being Paul's representative, why should he not function as such? Similarly today, instead of multiplying offices, would it not be better to put into practice the full implications of each office and to copy the flexibility of the early church, bearing in mind also that the special charismata of the early church are not ours today? The church of today is not able to produce an apostle like Paul, nor a prophet like Agabus. It is not in need of a Timothy to serve as apostolic delegate, nor of a Philip, addressed by an angel and "caught away" by the Spirit. In common with the early church, however, it does have ministers, elders, and deacons. It also has the Holy Spirit now as then. And it *now* has the complete Bible. Let *all* its offices then be utilized to the full as occasion demands, and in the spirit of true *service.*

*d. Pastors and teachers* are best considered *one* group.[113] Hodge remarks, "There is no evidence in Scripture that there was a set of men authorized to teach but not authorized to exhort. The thing is well nigh impossible" (*op. cit.,* p. 226). I fully agree. What we have here, accordingly, is a designation of *ministers of local congregations,* "teaching elders (or overseers)." By means of expounding the Word these men *shepherd* their flocks. Cf. Acts 20:17, 28; also John 21:15-17. They cannot do so properly without love for Christ.

**12.** The purpose of Christ's gifts to the church is now stated: **in order fully to equip the saints for the work of ministry, with a view to the building up of the body of Christ.** A.V. divides this verse into three separate phrases as follows: "For the perfecting of the saints, for the work of the ministry, for the edifying of the body of Christ." Along this line is also the rendering found in A.R.V. and the one in R.S.V. First, it should be pointed out that the original does not speak about "the work of *the* ministry" but about "the work of ministry," that is, of rendering specific services of various kinds. But even with this change the translation would still be a poor one, for it could easily leave the impression that the saints can be "perfected" without rendering service to each other and to the church. There

[113] The words τοὺς δε are not repeated before διδασκάλους. In itself this non-repetition might not be sufficient to prove that one group is meant, for see p. 141, footnote 74. However, in the present case we have a parallel in I Tim. 5:17b, where mention is made of men who, in addition to exercising supervision over the flock together with the other elders, also labor in the word and in teaching. These shepherds and teachers are *one* group.

should be no comma between the first and second phrases. A better solution, it would seem to me, is that favored by many of the older commentators and more recently by Salmond and by Lenski. These leave out both commas. The resultant idea is that Christ gave some men as apostles, others as prophets, etc., for the purpose of "perfecting" (cf. I Thess. 3:10; Heb. 13:21; I Peter 5:10) or *providing the necessary equipment* for all the saints for the work of ministering to each other so as to build up the body of Christ. I grant the possibility of the correctness of this construction. The meaning then would not differ very substantially from the third main rendering, the one to which I, along with many others, would still give the preference. According to this view of the matter the sentence *does not have two* commas (A.V., etc.) *nor no* commas (Salmond and Lenski) *but one* comma,[114] namely, after the word "ministry." This brings out more clearly that the *immediate* purpose of Christ's gifts is the ministry to be rendered by the entire flock; their *ultimate* purpose is the building up of the body of Christ, namely, the church (see on 1:22, 23).

The important lesson taught here is that not only apostles, prophets, evangelists, and those who are called "pastors and teachers," but the entire church should be engaged in spiritual labor. "The universal priesthood of believers" is stressed here. "Would that all Jehovah's people were prophets!" (Num. 11:29). Church attendance should mean more than "going to hear Rev. A." Unless, with a view to the service, there is adequate preparation, a desire for association, wholehearted *participation,* and the spirit of adoration, there is bound to be Sabbath-desecration. And during the week, too, every member should equip himself to be engaged in a definite "ministry," whether that be imparting comfort to the sick, teaching, neighborhood evangelization, tract distribution, or whatever be the task for which one is especially equipped. The meaning of 4:11, 12 is, moreover, that it is the task of the officers of the church to equip the church for these tasks. To all this it is important to add, however, that "the effectiveness of positive, conscious acts of Christian witness depends to a large extent upon the life of the person giving the witness in those moments not devoted to such witness" (Roels, *op. cit.,* p. 196).

The ideal in view with reference to the building up of the body of Christ is stated in verse 13. **until we all attain to the unity of the faith and of the clear knowledge of the Son of God.** This brings us back again to the spiritual unity demanded in verse 3, and to the "one faith" to which reference was made in verse 5. It also reminds us of 3:19: "in order that y o u may be filled to all the fulness of God." When verse 13 is considered in the light of the preceding verses it becomes clear that what the apostle has in mind is

[114] The theory agrees with N.N.'s punctuation of the Greek text; also with that of Grk. N.T. (A–B–M–W).

this, that the entire church – consisting not only of apostles, prophets, evangelists, "pastors and teachers," but of all others besides – should be faithful to its calling of rendering service, with a view to the upbuilding of the body of Christ, so that true, spiritual unity and growth may be promoted. Note "we all." There is no room in Christ's church for drones, only for busy bees. To the Thessalonians the apostle had said, "For we hear that some among y o u are conducting themselves in a disorderly manner, not busy workers but busybodies" (II Thess. 3:11). Paul sharply rebuked that attitude. It is exactly *unity* that is promoted when all become busily engaged in the affairs of the church and when each member eagerly renders service for which the Lord has equipped him. Thus, it has happened repeatedly that young people began to be imbued with enthusiasm when they engaged in this or that church program. For example, the Board of Home Missions of a certain denomination launches a *S*(ummer) *W*(orkshop) *I*(n) *M*(issions) program. This program requires of the young people who are in it that at different places throughout the country for several weeks during the summer they not only receive special instruction in the aims and methods of missions but also make contact with those who have not been previously reached for Christ. They bring the message, teach, and organize various social and religious activities. They are not afraid to live for a while in a slum district in close and beneficial contact with the community. How the eyes of these young people sparkle upon their return, for they have a story to tell, and are far more aglow with interest in Christ and his church than ever before. Often the contacts made during the summer are continued by means of correspondence and return visits. Also, the Young People's societies and the congregations that have taken part in sponsoring the program, having become thus involved, receive an added blessing when the young witnesses bring their reports. Thus, unity has been promoted, a unity of faith in Christ and of knowledge – not just intellectual but heart-knowledge – of the Lord and Savior, who, because of his majesty and greatness, is here called "the Son of God" (cf. Rom. 1:4; Gal. 2:20; I Thess. 1:10). Thus all believers advance **to a fullgrown man.** The underlying figure is that of a strong, mature, well-built *male* (not just "human being"). In Col. 4:12 this maturity is described as follows: "fully assured in all the will of God." For a detailed tabulation of the meaning of the word *fullgrown* or *mature* see N.T.C. on Phil. 3:15, p. 176, footnote 156. Just as a physically robust man can be pictured as being filled with vibrant strength and without defect, so the spiritually mature individual, which is the ideal for all believers to attain, is without spiritual flaw, filled with goodness, that is, with every Christian virtue that results from faith in, and heart-knowledge of, the Son of God. Continued: **to the measure of the stature of the fulness of Christ.** One could also translate: "to an age-measure marked by the fulness of Christ" (cf. Lenski, *op. cit.*, pp. 532, 536).[115] It does not matter whether the underlying figure is fulness of *age* or fulness of *stature,* for in either case it is a "fulness of *Christ*" that is meant (thus also Grosheide, *op. cit.,* p. 68, footnote 26). It is a fulness of him who completely fulfilled the earthly mission for which he had been *anointed,* and who is willing to impart to those who believe in him salvation full and free.

The question has been asked, Do believers during their present life on earth attain to this "measure of the stature of the fulness of Christ"? According to some they do. Lenski, for example, mentions Paul as one who had attained to it *(op. cit.,* p. 533). The passage itself, however, does not really teach this. To be sure, it should be granted that not all remain "babes" in Christ. A degree – in fact, a high degree – of maturity can be attained even here and now. And the more wholeheartedly all the saints strive to promote it by rendering humble and wholehearted service to one another and to the kingdom in general, the more also the ideal will be realized. Nevertheless, full, spiritual maturity, one that in the highest degree attains to "the measure of the stature of the fulness of Christ," cannot be realized this side of death. Paul himself would be one of the first to admit this. See what he said concerning himself in Rom. 7:14: "I am carnal, sold under sin"; and what he is going to say very shortly after Ephesians had been delivered to its destination: "Brothers, I do not count myself yet to have laid hold. But one thing (I do), forgetting what lies behind (me), and eagerly straining forward to what lies ahead, I am pressing on toward the goal, for the prize of the upward call of God in Christ Jesus" (Phil. 3:14, 15). For the rest, as to degree, time, and possibility of attainment, see on 3:19 where the same subject is discussed.

Marvelous growth in maturity, nevertheless, is certainly obtainable through human effort springing forth from, and sustained from start to finish by, the Holy Spirit. This is clear from the words which follow: **14, 15 . . . so that [116] we may no longer be children tossed to and fro by the waves and whirled around by every gust of doctrine, by the trickery of men, by (their) talent for deceitful scheming; but, adhering to the truth in love, may grow up in all things into him who is the head, even Christ.**

---

[115] The word ἡλικία may refer either to *age* or to *height* or *stature.* Thus, Zacchaeus was small in *stature* (Luke 19:3), Sarah was long past the *age* for conceiving (Heb. 11:11). The man born blind, healed by Christ, had reached the *age* of legal maturity (John 9:21, 23). No one can add a cubit to the length of his *life span* (Matt. 6:27; Luke 12:25). In such passages as Luke 2:52 ("Jesus increased in wisdom and *stature";* but according to others, "in wisdom and *age*") and Eph. 4:13 there is a marked difference of opinion among commentators as to what is meant: *stature* or *age.*

[116] The particle ἵνα clearly has a sub-final sense here. It cannot here mean "in order that." The climax has been reached in verse 13. One does not attain to "the measure of the stature of the fulness of Christ" (verse 13) *in order* not to be tossed, etc., and *in order* to grow (verses 14, 15).

The ideal of full Christian maturity is characterized in verse 14 from its negative aspect; in verse 15 positively. In striving to reach the goal and in advancing in that direction believers are goaded by the desire that they may no longer be like helpless children in a tempest-tossed boat which they cannot manage. Paul knew what it meant to be "driven to and fro" by the waves. While he was writing this, the trip which had brought him to his present Roman imprisonment must have been before him in all its vivid terror (Acts 27:14-44; note especially verse 27). But to be tossed to and fro and whirled around "by every gust of doctrine" is even worse than to experience the dangers of the sea. Just what did the apostle have in mind when he thus admonished the Ephesians? [117] Here we do well to bear in mind two facts: *a.* that most of the addressed were rather recent converts from heathenism; and *b.* that, although we must, therefore, conclude that his description was particularly fitting with respect to them, yet the apostle cannot have been thinking solely of these converts from the Gentile world, for he uses the first person plural, and says, "that *we* may no longer be children tossed to and fro," etc. The fact that heathen in their blindness and superstition are often swayed by the waves and winds of public opinion, believing whatever they have heard last, is vividly illustrated in Luke's account of the experience of Paul and Barnabas at Lystra. First the multitude held Paul to be Hermes, and Barnabas to be Zeus, and was ready to offer sacrifices in their honor. A little later these same people allowed themselves to be persuaded by wicked Jews, and stoned Paul nearly to death (Acts 14:8-20). But even followers of Jesus have much to learn in this respect. A typical example of unsteadfastness, before he became in very deed "a rock," was Simon Peter. In the Gospels he is pictured as a man who is constantly oscillating from one extreme to the other. Now he is seen walking courageously on the waters (Matt. 14:28); a little later he is crying, "Lord, save me" (Matt. 14:30). At one moment he makes a glorious confession (Matt. 16:16). Hardly have the echoes of that wonderful declaration faded, when he begins to rebuke the very Christ whom he has just confessed (Matt. 16:22). He promises to lay down his life for Jesus (John 13:37). A few hours later he is saying again and again, "I am not his disciple" (John 18:17, 25). After Christ's victorious resurrection he lags behind John to the tomb. Arrived, he enters the tomb before John does (John 20:4-6). At Antioch he first casts aside all ideas of racial segregation and eats with the Gentiles. Soon afterward he withdraws completely from the converts of the pagan world (Gal. 2:11, 12).

In addition to his bout with Peter, Paul had had other sad experiences with fluttering and fluctuating mankind. On his first missionary journey John Mark had deserted him (Acts 13:13; 15:38). The Galatians had de-

[117] This has been discussed in a most interesting fashion by J. M. Moffatt, "Three Notes on Ephesians," *Exp.*, Eighth Series, No. 87 (April, 1918), pp. 306–317.

serted the gospel (Gal. 1:6). And at this very time, while Paul was writing his "prison epistles," *some* of the members of the Colossian church must have been in real danger of lending a listening ear to false philosophers. The apostle knows that there is nothing so stabilizing as performing day by day loving service for Christ. No one learns truth faster than he who, with consecrated heart, teaches others. Let the Ephesians, therefore, withdraw their attention from "the trickery of men," and plunge into the work of the kingdom. That is the context here: all the saints, under the leadership of the apostles, prophets, evangelists, "pastors and teachers," united for the work of ministry.

The term "trickery," applied to those who in effect were attempting to lead believers astray, is *kubeia,* from *kúbos,* meaning *cube, die.* Paul is thinking, therefore, of *dice-playing* in which tricks were used in order to win. Hence, the word came to mean *trickery;* here "human trickery," "the talent literally, readiness to do anything for deceitful scheming." Constantly the thoughts and plans of these crafty fellows were directed toward (Greek πρός) "the method of deception." Cf. Col. 2:4, 8, 18, 23; then also Rom. 6:17, 18; II Cor. 2:17; 11:13; Gal. 2:4.

Now error is never overcome by mere negation. Over against the deceitfulness of the errorists the Ephesians should *adhere to the truth,* that is, *practice integrity.*[118] And what *ministry* (see verse 12) can be more noble than that which, while resolutely opposing deceit, setting *truthfulness* "of life and lip" over against it, does all this *in the spirit of love?* There are two great enemies of a successful ministry, whether carried on among believers or among unbelievers. One is departure from truth, compromise with the lie, whether in words or deeds. The other is chilling indifference with respect to the hearts and lives, the troubles and trials, of the people whom one is ostensibly trying to persuade. Paul has the real solution: *the*

---

[118] I agree with the statement of Simpson, "Whether the verb means to *speak* or to *act truly* is hard to decide" (*op. cit.,* p. 99). While some make a point of stressing that ἀληθεύω does not really mean "speaking the truth" but "adhering to the truth" or "living the truth," it remains a fact that the passages referred to in L.N.T. (A. and G.), p. 36, show that "speaking the truth" both here and in Gal. 4:16 is also possible. Thus in Josephus, *Jewish War* III. 322, we read, ". . . thinking that the man might be speaking the truth. . . ." and in his *Life* 132: "Even the inhabitants of Tarichaeae believed that the young men were speaking the truth." The possibility of the correctness of this rendering here in 4:15 must, therefore, be granted. The thought expressed in that case is not so foreign to the context to make it look impossible. On the other hand, there are two reasons why I, nevertheless, would give a slight edge to the rendering "adhering to the truth" or "practicing sincerity." In the first place, if in 4:15 the meaning be "speaking truth," the apostle would be repeating himself in 4:25, where the rendering "speaking truth" leaves no room for doubt. Secondly, the verb used in 4:15 "need not be restricted to truthfulness in speech" (Robinson, *op. cit.,* p. 185); especially not in the present instance where the context would rather seem to point in the direction of *being truthful* or *maintaining truthfulness* over against the deceitfulness of the men who practice trickery and perverse scheming.

*truth* must be practiced *in love* (3:18; 4:2; 5:1, 2), which was exactly what he was constantly doing (II Cor. 2:4; Gal. 4:16, 19; I Thess. 2:7-12); and telling others to do (I Tim. 4:11-13). In fact, *love* (for which see on 4:2) must mark *all* of life. By means of such behavior we will impart a blessing not only to others but to ourselves also, for we will "grow up in all things into him who is the head, even Christ." We must grow up into union with him. The same intimacy of conscious oneness with Christ is stressed in Rom. 6:5, where the idea is expressed that believers are "grown together" with him. Such statements do not in any way obliterate the infinite distinction between Christ and Christians. They do *not* indicate *identity but intimacy.* The distinction between believers and their Lord is clearly enunciated here, for the latter is called "the head," while the former are designated "the entire body." What is meant by growing up into Christ is interpreted by the apostle himself in Phil. 1:21, "For to me to live (is) Christ, and to die (is) gain." In other words:

> "So shall no part of day or night from sacredness be free,
> But all my life, in every step, be fellowship with thee."
> (Horatius Bonar)

**16.** Paul concludes this section by saying, **from whom the entire body, harmoniously fitted together and held together by every supporting joint, according to the energy that corresponds to the capacity of each individual part, brings about bodily growth with a view to its own upbuilding in love.** As *head* Christ causes his *body, the church, to live and to grow* (cf. Col. 2:19). He is its *Organic Head.* As head he also exercises authority over the church; in fact, over all things in the interest of the church (Eph. 1:20-23). He is its *Ruling Head.* It is doubtful whether either of these two ideas is ever completely absent when Christ is called head of the church, though sometimes one connotation and then again the other receives the greater emphasis, as the context indicates. And in such a passage as 5:23, 24 both ideas (*growth* and *guidance*) are brought to the fore. In the present passage (4:16) it is clearly the organic relationship that is stressed. The words reveal a marked resemblance to those found in Col. 2:19: ". . . the head, from whom the entire body, supported and held together by joints and ligaments, grows with a growth (that is) from God." The fact that the human body – which is the underlying figure – is, indeed, "harmoniously fitted together and held together by every supporting joint" is an astounding wonder. It is, however, common knowledge, not refuted by the most up-to-date science. The real message which the apostle is conveying both here in Ephesians and in the Colossian parallel is accordingly this, that to Christ the entire church owes its growth. Just as the human body, when properly supported and held together, experiences normal growth, so also the church, when each of its members supports and maintains loving contact with the others and above all with Christ, will, under the sustaining care of God (or *of Christ,* as here in Ephesians: "Christ, from whom"), proceed from grace to grace and from glory to glory (cf. I Cor. 12). There are, however, two main additions in the Ephesian passage, points not stressed in its Colossian parallel:

1. that the body is fitted together and held together . . . *according to the energy that corresponds to the capacity of each individual part.* Meaning: in the church, too, every spiritually alive member does his part, performing his ministry in accordance with his God-given ability. This is a fine repetition of the thought introduced in all the preceding verses of this section, particularly in verses 7, 12, 13.

2. dropping the underlying figure, that when all the individual "parts" (members) of the church co-operate, the entire church grows spiritually *with a view to its own upbuilding in love.* The love to which reference is made is the same as that mentioned in verse 2; see on that verse. With this marvelous word Paul ends this marvelous section.[119]

### *Seed Thoughts of Ephesians 4:1-16*
(one thought for each verse)

*See Verse*

1. The best missionary method is the truly consecrated life.
2. The qualities which Christ demands of us are those which he himself exemplified.
3. Though peace is indeed a precious gift imparted by the Holy Spirit, it is at the same time the product of human effort.
4. The church is not a man-made institution but the product of the Holy Spirit whose call to repent and to follow Christ in service we should obey. Obedience to that call imparts hope.
5. The one Lord Jesus Christ in whom all Christians believe and in whose name they have all been baptized welds together into *one body* God's children, those still on earth and those already in heaven.
6. Anent the first person of the Holy Trinity, as Father he is *"over all,"* for he exercises control over all. He is, however, also *"through* all," for he blesses us all through Christ our Mediator. And he is *"in* all," for he draws us all close to his heart in the Spirit. Thus we perceive that we worship *one God,* not three gods. It is folly therefore to say, "God is dead but Jesus is still alive." The three are One.
7. A talent is a *gift,* and to no one has Christ imparted every gift. The fact that a person's ability in any direction is a *gift* should keep him hum-

[119] For problems in connection with this comparison of the relation between Christ and his followers, on the one hand, with the human body and its members, on the other, see N.T.C. on Col. 2:19, pp. 128, 129.

ble, for what has he that he has not received? It should also encourage him, for the way to the Giver and his inexhaustible gifts is known.

8. Not only Christ's suffering, death, burial, and resurrection were in our interest; so was also his ascension. He ascended not only to receive glory for himself but also to bestow gifts upon men.
9. The doctrine of Christ's descent into hell on Calvary should be retained. If our Savior did not suffer the torments of hell for us, is he then our Substitute?
10. *Did the descended* Jesus love us with a love so deep and intimate that nothing on earth can compare with it? The *ascended* Christ loves us no less!
11. An apostle was *a gift of Christ to the church.* This was true also with respect to the prophet; and also with respect to an evangelist. Today, too, the man to whom Christ has assigned the task of being "a pastor and teacher" should be so regarded. If, when he truly represents the will of his Sender, he is rejected, those who are guilty of this sin are rejecting the Master himself.
12. It is the duty of the pastor to impress upon everyone under his care the duty and privilege of *lay-ministry.* Only when every member does his part is the body of Christ being built up as it should be.
13. Not only *unity* but also *growth* is demanded of us. The Church's *Organic Unity and Growth* is the theme of this chapter. "Excelsior!" should be our motto. Reaching "the measure of the stature of the fulness of Christ," our aim.
14. The church should emphasize teaching right doctrine.
15. Over against the deceitfulness of the opponent the church should practice truthfulness; always, however, in a context of love.
16. Just as the human body when held together by every supporting joint grows strong, so also the church when it receives the active support of every member, each co-operating according to his ability, will be built up in love.

# Chapter 4:17–6:9

Verses 4:17–5:21

Theme: *The Church Glorious*

II. *Exhortation*
*urging*

*G* lorious Renewal
1. upon all

# CHAPTER IV:17–VI:9

## EPHESIANS

17 This I say, therefore, and testify in the Lord, that y o u should no
longer walk as the Gentiles also walk, in the futility of their mind, 18 being darkened in their understanding, alienated from the life of God because of the ignorance that is in them due to the hardness of their hearts, 19 because they have
become callous and have abandoned themselves to licentiousness for the greedy
practice of every type of impurity. 20 Y o u, however, did not so learn Christ,
21 for surely y o u heard of him and were taught in him, just as it is in Jesus that
truth resides, 22 (having been taught) that with respect to y o u r former manner
of life y o u must put off the old man, which is being corrupted through deceitful
lusts, 23 and must be renewed in the spirit of y o u r minds, 24 and put on the
new man, created after (the likeness of) God in true righteousness and holiness.

25 Therefore, laying aside falsehood, speak truth each (of y o u) with his
neighbor, for we are members of one another. 26 Be angry but do not sin; let not
the sun go down on that angry mood of y o u r s, 27 and do not give the devil a
foothold. 28 Let him who steals steal no longer but rather let him labor, with his
own hands accomplishing what is good, so that he may have something to share
with the needy one. 29 Let no corrupt speech proceed from y o u r mouth, but (only)
such (speech) as is good for edification, as fits the need, that it may impart grace
to the listeners. 30 And do not grieve the Holy Spirit of God in whom y o u were
sealed for the day of redemption. 31 Let all bitterness and anger and wrath and
brawling and slander be put away from y o u, along with all malice. 32 And be
kind to each other, tender-hearted, forgiving one another, just as God in Christ
forgave y o u.

5 1 Be therefore imitators of God, as beloved children, 2 and walk in
love, just as Christ loved y o u and gave himself up for us, an offering and a sacrifice to God, for a fragrant odor.

3 But immorality and impurity of any kind, or greed, let it not even be
mentioned among y o u, as is fitting among saints, 4 also filthiness and silly talk
or wittiness in telling coarse jokes, which things are improper, but rather the expression of thankfulness. 5 For of this y o u can be very sure, that no immoral or
impure person or greedy individual – which is the same as an idolater – has any
inheritance in the kingdom of Christ and of God. 6 Let no one deceive y o u with
empty words; for it is because of these things that the wrath of God comes upon
the sons of disobedience. 7 Therefore do not be their partners, 8 for y o u were
formerly darkness, but now (y o u are) light in the Lord; as children of light ever
walk 9 – for the fruit of light (consists) in all goodness and righteousness and
truth – 10 verifying what is pleasing to the Lord. 11 And do not take any part in
the unfruitful works of darkness but instead even expose them, 12 for the things
done by them in secret it is a shame even to mention. 13 But when all these

(wicked practices) are exposed by the light they are made visible; for everything that is made visible is light. 14 Therefore he says,

"Awake, sleeper,
And arise from the dead,
And Christ will shine on you."

15 Be most careful therefore how y o u walk, not as unwise but as wise,
16 making the most of the opportunity, because the days are evil. 17 Therefore
do not be foolish but understand what (is) the will of the Lord. 18 And do not
get drunk on wine, which is associated with unrestrained living, but be filled with
the Spirit, 19 speaking to one another in psalms and hymns and spiritual songs,
singing and making melody from y o u r heart to the Lord; 20 giving thanks always for all things in the name of the Lord Jesus Christ to (our) God and
Father, 21 subjecting yourselves to each other out of reverence for Christ.

---

4:17–5:21

The theme *renewal* is suggested by 4:23, where Paul tells the Ephesians, "Y o u must be renewed." This renewal, moreover, implies a complete, basic change, a *detachment* from the world which they had formerly served, and an *attachment* to Christ, their newly confessed Lord and Savior. In Paul's own words, it is a *putting* off of the old man and a *putting* on of the new man (4:22, 24). Now the idea of this *Spirit-born total transformation* governs the entire section: 4:17–6:9. Throughout what Paul is saying is, "Be done with the old and adopt the new." He is continually contrasting these two kinds of disposition and behavior. Thus he urges that falsehood be replaced by speaking the truth (4:25); sinful anger, by that which is not sinful (4:26); stealing, by sharing (4:28); corrupt speech, by edifying words (4:29); bitterness, anger, and wrath, by kindness, tenderness and love (4:31–5:2); filthiness and coarse wittiness, by the expression of thankfulness (5:3, 4), etc.

When the *general* admonitions (4:17–5:21) are ended and those *to special groups* (5:22–6:9) are issued, the idea of renewal continues. Husbands must love, not hate, their wives (5:28, 29). Fathers should not provoke their children to anger but should rear them tenderly in the discipline and admonition of the Lord (6:4). Slaves ought to render service not as to men but as to the Lord (6:5-8). Masters must stop threatening and must treat their slaves with consideration (6:9).

Although, to be sure, this renewal is a matter of strenuous, continuous, effort on the part of believers, a process of daily conversion, yet, as already stated, it is throughout a work of the Holy Spirit (4:30; 5:18), for it is only through the Spirit that men are able to put forth the needed effort and to succeed. Hence, it is a transformation or sanctification *full of glory,* nothing less than a change from dismal darkness to glorious light (5:7-14). Accordingly, I cannot find a better sub-title for this section than that of (the Church's) *Glorious Renewal.*

The section that covers the general admonitions has four parts, which may be divided as follows: 4:17-24; 4:25–5:2; 5:3-14; and 5:15-21.

a. 4:17-24

*"Put off the old man. Be renewed. Put on the new man."*

**17.** The paragraph begins as follows: **This I say, therefore, and testify in the Lord, that y o u should no longer walk as the Gentiles also walk.** This "therefore" connects the present paragraph with all that has gone before in 4:1-16. "Because of y o u r high calling, y o u r duty to render service with a view to the building up of Christ's body, no longer conduct yourselves as do the Gentiles." The apostle introduces this admonition with all the authority he is able to summon. He says, "I say and testify." As Bengel has pointed out: when the apostle *admonishes* he does it so that those addressed may act *freely;* when he *encourages,* so that they may act *gladly;* and when he *testifies,* so that they may act *reverently* (with a proper respect for the will of God). Note also "in the Lord." He is speaking and testifying in the sphere of the Lord, with *his* authority, and in the interest of *his* cause. Cf. Acts 20:26; Gal. 5:3; I Thess. 2:12.

They must no longer behave as Gentiles,[120] for they no longer are Gentiles. When this statement is analyzed it becomes clear that two ideas are combined here: *a.* Lay aside y o u r former manner of life (cf. 2:1-3, 12; 4:14, 22); and *b.* do not imitate y o u r present evil environment. With reference to Gentile conduct Paul adds: **in the futility of their mind.** The rendering "vanity" instead of "futility" is not wrong, since the latter is one of the meanings of the former. Nevertheless, inasmuch as "vanity" also has another, very different and yet very common, meaning, namely, *excessive pride, conceit,* "futility" is to be preferred. The apostle emphasizes a very important point, namely, that all those endeavors which the Gentiles put forth in order to attain happiness end in disappointment. Their life is one long series of mocked expectations. It is a pursuing and not achieving, a blossoming and not bearing fruit. Cf. Rom. 8:20. All the rivers run into the sea, but the sea is never filled. The eye is never satisfied with seeing nor the ear with hearing. All this chasing after riches, honor, mirth, etc., is nothing but "a striving after wind" (Eccles. 1:7, 8; 3:9). Their *mind* or *intellect* is fruitless. It produces naught that can satisfy. Continued: **18, 19. being darkened in their understanding, alienated from the life of God because of the ignorance that is in them due to the hardness of their hearts, because they have become callous and have abandoned themselves to licentiousness for the greedy practice of every type of impurity.** In order to see the entire picture of tragic hopelessness, these two verses should be viewed as a unit. It then becomes clear that the futility that characterizes the Gentile mind is a product of darkened understanding and estrangement from the God-given life,

[120] The reading upon which A.V. bases its rendering "not as other Gentiles," is weak.

these two, in turn, resulting from a type of ignorance that is by no means excusable but is due to willful hardening and surrender to unbridled license of every description. *Being darkened* is something that took place in the past but has continuing effect.[121] The "understanding" or power of discursive reasoning had been affected by sin. This understanding is treated here as if it were an eye that had become blind. This darkening, moreover, is far worse than *physical* blindness, for the man who is physically blind knows it and admits it, but the person who is spiritually and morally darkened is blind even to the fact that he is blind (John 9:40, 41). Not only is it true that people of this kind dwell in the darkness, but the darkness dwells in them. They have imbibed it, just as one day they will imbibe ("drink") God's wrath (Rev. 14:10). Contrast these blind eyes with the "enlightened" eyes of believers (2:18). They are, moreover, *alienated* or *estranged*,[122] and this not only from "the commonwealth of Israel" as was pointed out earlier (2:12) but also from "the life of God," that is, from God as the Source of eternal life. This darkening and alienation can be traced to their culpable ignorance, a condition they had brought upon themselves by hardening their hearts against the will of God. At one time, long, long ago their ancestors had had God's *special* revelation, but had rejected it. Many centuries had gone by. And now these distant descendants were suppressing even the light of God's general revelation in nature and conscience with terrible results. The picture, in all its lurid details, is drawn in Rom. 1:18-32; cf. 2:12 and 11:7. The very center of their being, their *hearts*, had become "callous" by their own deliberate action. For "callous" the A.V. and A.R.V. have "past feeling," which is also an excellent rendering, the root meaning of this perfect participle being "having arrived at a condition of freedom from pain," and thus, in general, "having become insensible" with reference here to the divine voice, to God's truth.

Some there are who *over-emphasize* feeling. Their religion never reaches any deeper than the emotions. Their picture is drawn in Matt. 13:5, 6, 20, 21. They are not firmly rooted. They lack conviction. The Gentiles whom Paul here describes as a warning example have followed the exactly opposite course, which, if anything, is even worse. By constantly saying "No" to God's voice in conscience and in the lessons which nature and history had provided, they had at last become hard as stone, dead to all responsiveness to that which is good and uplifting; not, however, dead to *all* feeling and *all* desire. Now there have been many people throughout the course of history who have taken pride in the stifling of *all* feeling. They were ashamed of shedding tears and even of revealing any but the most indifferent reaction

---

[121] That is the sense of the perfect periphrastic. It should not be necessary to remark that ὄντες in verse 18 and οἵτινες in verse 19, masculines, refer to τὰ ἔθνη neuter. This is not at all unusual and is a construction *ad sensum*.

[122] Another perfect participle, construed like *darkened*.

to *any* outside influence. Thus, for example, the Stoic's ideal was release from every emotion ("apatheia"). Again, according to a familiar story, the Spartan youth who had stolen a young fox and had hid it beneath his tunic, allowed the animal to tear out his vitals, without betraying himself by the movement of a muscle. In the camp of the Buddhists the best virtue is passionlessness, and heaven ("Nirvana") has been defined as the cessation of all natural desires. And among the American Indians a captured Iroquois did his level best not to break down under torture, but instead to react to it with perfect equanimity. What we have here, in 4:18, 19, however, is something far worse. The people of whom Paul was writing *did not try to squelch all feeling*. Far from it! They did not oppose *every* type of desire. On the contrary they suppressed only those feelings that are connected with goodness. They were down on all desires that would have brought them into closer harmony with the will of God. By constantly arguing with conscience, stifling its warnings and muffling its bell, they had at last reached the point where conscience could no longer bother them. It was seared (I Tim. 4:2). They *did* have *feeling* and they *did* keep alive *desire,* namely, feeling and desire for evil indulgence. They had abandoned themselves to vice. They *gave themselves up* to it (thus literally, in the original). The result of such base surrender is always this, that, if persisted in, God *gives the sinner up* to suffer the full consequences of his sin, as Exod. 8:15, 32, cf. 9:12; Rom. 1:24, 26, 28 (where the same verb, "give up," is used as here in Eph. 4:19) clearly teach. See also Rev. 22:11. The vice to which they abandoned themselves is called *licentiousness* or "lasciviousness" (see also Rom. 13:13; II Cor. 12:21; Gal. 5:19). The literature of the day was deeply immoral. So corrupt had the Roman world become that somewhat later Origen states that when the people of his day committed adultery and whoredom they did not regard themselves as violating good manners. It has been remarked that it was not lava but lewdness that buried Herculaneum. And the frescoes found amid the ruins of nearby Pompeii show that this city was not any better.

The apostle says that the Gentiles of whom he speaks had abandoned themselves to licentiousness "for the greedy practice [literally: *practice in greed*] of every type of impurity." The greedy person is the one who overreaches. He wishes "to have more than his due." He disregards the rights and feelings of all other people. He goes beyond what is proper and has no respect whatever for any laws of dignity or propriety. Cf. 5:3, 5; Col. 2:5; I Thess. 4:6. By means of his unbridled lust and wanton self-assertion he is digging his own grave. Note particularly: *every type* of impurity. For an enumeration of these types see 4:25-31; 5:3-11, 15, 18; cf. Rom. 1:26-32.

20. In principle, however, the people whom Paul addresses belong to a different category. This had been the case ever since Christ entered into their hearts and lives. Hence, Paul continues: **You, however, did not so**

**learn Christ.** In the original the sentence begins with the word *y o u,* on which, accordingly, great emphasis is placed, as if to say, "Y o u did not learn Christ so as to continue to live as the Gentiles are doing." To learn Christ is more than to learn *about* Christ. Not only had the Ephesians received a body of teaching, namely, about Christ, and not only had they observed in the lives of those who brought it what this doctrine was able to achieve, but in addition, they themselves by an act of Spirit-wrought faith had welcomed this Christ into their hearts. Joyfully they had received the sacrament of holy baptism. And by constant and systematic attendance upon the means of grace, by prayer and answers to prayer, by daily living in accordance with the principles of the truth of the gospel, they had learned Christ, yes, Christ himself in very person.

Paul here presents the appropriation of Christ and of salvation in him as the result of a learning process, a learning with heart and mind. Believers, in other words, are not saved at one stroke. They do not become completely transformed all at once. They learn. There was the basic change wrought by the power of God. This was followed by a constant progress in sanctification, constant but not necessarily uniform. In one person it had been more clearly evident than in another. At one time the progress had been by leaps, but at another time at snail's pace. At times, in all likelihood, there had been reverses, retrogressions. The point which the apostle emphasizes, however, is that whatever had been their degree of advance in learning, they had definitely not learned Christ as an advocate of sin and selfishness, of lewdness and licentiousness. No longer were their minds futile, no longer was their understanding dark. Continued: **21. . . . for surely y o u heard of him and were taught in him.** Justification for this translation – "for surely," where A.V. and A.R.V. have "if so be" – was offered in the explanation of 3:2 where a similar "for surely" occurs. Many of the Ephesians had been taught by Paul himself during his lengthy ministry at Ephesus (Acts 19; 20:17-35). The apostle had been able to reach not only those who were actually living within the city of Ephesus but also people from the surrounding territory. Many had flocked to the city to attend feasts, for business, or for other purposes. Some, no doubt, had gone there for the very purpose of seeing and hearing Paul. But in addition there had been other multitudes, in surrounding cities and villages, who heard the gospel from the lips of those who had received it from Paul (Acts 20:17). It should be borne in mind constantly that this epistle is, in all probability, a letter addressed to a vast multitude of people, many of whom did not live in Ephesus. It was probably a circular letter. See Introduction, pp. 58-61. The addressed, then, had heard of Christ and had been taught not only *about* but *"in"* him; that is, the entire atmosphere had been Christian. Christ, speaking through his ambassadors, was the teacher. He was also the theme. Continued: **just as it is in Jesus that truth resides.** The truth with reference to man's fall into sin, his desperate condition by nature, the salvation procured by Christ, the necessity of faith working through love, principles of Christian conduct, etc.: all these doctrines had Christ as their very center. In Christ's suffering and death by crucifixion the addressed had been able to read how deeply fallen they were, necessitating the death of God's only-begotten Son, a death both painful and shameful. In his triumphant resurrection, ascension, and coronation they had received proof positive that salvation had been achieved. In Christ's constant emphasis upon the fact that men must come to him and rely on him completely, they had been given a lesson in the necessity of faith as appropriating organ of salvation. The Master's marvelous example in humility, self-sacrifice, love, etc. had been given for their instruction. Moreover, had not Jesus himself said, "I am the way and the truth and the life"? (John 14:6). Was not he the very embodiment of the truth, the truth in person? Were not "all the treasures of wisdom and knowledge" hidden in him, hidden in order to be revealed? (Col. 2:3). Was not he the active and living truth, the truth that sets men free (John 8:32; 17:17), the very answer to Pilate's question (John 18:38)?

Verse 21b was parenthetical in character. Continuing now with the main idea expressed in verse 21a: "for surely y o u heard of him and were taught in him," Paul writes: **22-24. (having been taught) that with respect to y o u r former manner of life y o u [123] must put off the old man, which is being corrupted through deceitful lusts, and must be renewed in the spirit of y o u r minds, and put on the new man, created after (the likeness of) God in true righteousness and holiness.**

What the Ephesians had been taught "in Christ" was this, that nothing less than a radical change in their mental outlook and manner of life was necessary, a complete turnabout. Their former manner of life (2:2, 3; 4:17-19; 5:8, 14; cf. Col. 1:21; 2:13; 3:7) must cease. The directive which, from the moment of their vital contact with Christ, was meant to control their entire being in all its manifestations, and to confront them every day and every hour, was curt and crisp: "Put off the old man," that is, "the old nature, whatever y o u are apart from grace" (Col. 3:9; cf. Rom. 6:6), and "Put on the new man," that is, "the new nature, whatever y o u have become, must be, and can become because of grace" (Col. 3:10; cf. Gal. 3:27). It was *a summary formulation* [124] of a tremendously large order. In a sense,

[123] *Because of the parenthetical clause* ("just as it is in Jesus that truth resides," verse 21b) intervening between the main verb "y o u were taught" (verse 21a) and the infinitives governed by it, namely, "to put off" (aorist middle, verse 22), "to put on" (aorist middle, verse 24) and "to be (constantly) renewed" (present passive, verse 23), the subject of these infinitives "y o u" (ὑμᾶς) is written out.

[124] These aorists "to put off" and "to put on" do not indicate that the actions to which they refer are done once for all, at this or that moment in the life of the addressed. They simply *summarize*. They give *a snapshot view*. They do not indicate anything at all with respect to whether putting off the old man and putting on the

they had already put off the old man and put on the new man, namely, when they had given their hearts to Christ, and had professed him openly at the time of their baptism. But *basic* conversion must be followed by *daily* conversion. Even though in principle the believer has become a new creature (or "creation"), he remains a sinner until he dies. The old nature, with which the Ephesians had been on such intimate terms for so many years, is not easy to shed. Getting rid of it is difficult and painful. It amounts, in fact, to a crucifixion (Rom. 6:6). This is true all the more because it is always promising so much. It is being "continually corrupted" through lusts' illusions, those deceptive evil desires[125] with their mighty promises and minimal performances. This corrupting deceptiveness is present, moreover, wherever the old nature is represented, whether in the unbeliever or in the believer. Cain's murder of his brother, a deed which had appeared so attractive when planned, brought nothing but a curse. Absalom's prospective crown, so dazzling at first, resulted in his gruesome death. The vineyard, so luscious and so conveniently located that Ahab, in order to obtain this coveted prize, had not hesitated to sacrifice Naboth's life, brought ruin to the king's household and posterity. The thirty pieces of silver which had shimmered so brightly in Judas' scheming, once in his possession had burned his hands, tortured his soul, and sent the traitor himself scurrying on his way to hanging and to hell. And, not to omit one of God's chosen ones, David, in a moment of weakness, filled with passionate delight in the thought of pleasant days ahead with the object of his lustful yearning, was forced to listen to the words of the Lord which like thunder-bolts fell from the lips of the prophet: "You are the man. The sword will not depart from your house." Truly, the old nature flaunts a golden cup, but upon inspection it is found to contain nothing but filth and abomination (cf. Rev. 17:4). Hence, the Ephesians had been warned most solemnly to put off the old man, to fight him with unrelenting and undiminished vigor in order to divest themselves completely of him.

But while "the old man" is wholly evil, "the new man" is wholly good. He is "created after (the likeness of) God." Cf. Col. 3:10. Other explanatory passages are Eph. 2:10; II Cor. 5:17; Gal. 6:15; and Titus 3:5. Day by day this new creation is advancing "in true righteousness and holiness." The Colossian parallel (3:10) adds "full knowledge." Grace restores what sin has ruinously impaired. God not only *imputes* but also *imparts* righteous-

---

new man takes place in a moment or covers a lifetime. The aorist in John 2:20 refers to an activity that had already lasted forty-six years! Here in Eph. 2:22-24 it is the nature of the indicated actions and the context in which the aorists occur — the fact that they are joined by means of the present durative infinitive referring to the continuing process of mental renewal — that establish the lifelong character of the *putting off* and *putting on*.

[125] With reference to the word ἐπιθυμία see N.T.C. on II Tim. 2:22, especially footnote 146, pp. 271, 272.

ness to the sinner whom he pleases to save. Thus, the believer begins to perform his duties toward his *fellow-men.* But *righteousness* never walks alone. It is always accompanied by *holiness,* so that the regenerated and converted person performs his duties with reference to *God* also. Cf. Luke 1:75; I Thess. 2:10; Titus 1:8. Moreover, the righteousness and holiness which God bestows are *true,*[126] not *deceptive,* as are the lusts spawned by the old nature. They bring life to its true, predestined fulfilment. They satisfy.

As to the figure underlying "putting off" and "putting on," it refers, of course, to what one does with a garment. Frequently such a robe indicates a person's nature or character: either good (Job 29:14; Ps. 132:9; Isa. 11:5; 61:10) or evil (Ps. 73:6; cf. Ps. 35:26; 109:29). How it clings to him! The figure is by no means confined to Scripture. It has become part of general literature. It also occurs in the prayers of God's children: "Disrobe us of ourselves and clothe us with thyself, O Lord."

Both the putting off of the old man and the putting on of the new man are necessary. Some people constantly stress the negative. Their religion is one of don't. Others turn their backs upon every don't, and take peculiar pride in overstressing the positive. Scripture avoids both of these extremes. Ephesians contains many a *do* and many a *don't.* Here in this life both are needed. They are inseparable and point to simultaneous activities. That is what Paul means when he states that the Ephesians had been taught to "put off" the old man and to "put on" the new man. A person can do very little with *one* scissorblade. Twin blades, operating in unison, compose the scissors that will work. He who says "Yes" to Christ is saying "No" to Satan. But though both are necessary, Paul's emphasis throughout is on the positive: "Overcome evil with good" (Rom. 12:21; cf. 13:14). So it is also here in Eph. 4:22-24, for we are taught that the only way in which one can progressively succeed in putting off the old man and putting on the new[127] man is by being renewed in the spirit of one's mind. This renewel is basically an act of God's Spirit powerfully influencing man's *spirit,* here, as also in I Cor. 4:21; Gal. 6:1; and I Peter 3:4, *mental attitude, state of mind, disposition,* with respect to God and spiritual realities.

---

[126] Literally "righteousness and holiness *of the truth*" (according to what is probably the best reading). So also in verse 22 "lusts of the deceit." In view of the presence of the article before *deceit* and before *truth* some deny the adjectival character of these modifiers. The meaning would then become "lusts springing from (the) deceit (or: deception)," and "righteousness and holiness springing from (the) truth." It is doubtful, however, whether there is good ground for this refinement. In any case it is clear that lusts, on the one hand, and righteousness and holiness, on the other, are here contrasted as to their character and value.

[127] In verse 23 note *νέος-ον* as a component element of the verb *renew,* while in verse 24 the adjective that modifies "man" is *καινός-ον*. In Col. 3:10, however, the roles are reversed. Accordingly, though it is true that basically *νέος* indicates *new* as to *time,* while *καινός* refers to *new* as to *quality,* it is obvious that the distinction cannot be pressed either here or in Colossians.

b. 4:25–5:2

*"Do not give the devil a foothold. Be imitators of God."*

25. The apostle now advances from the general to the particular: **Therefore, laying aside falsehood, speak truth each (of y o u) with his neighbor.** That there is a connection between this admonition and the preceding paragraph is clear from the repetition of the word "putting off" or "laying aside" (same verb in the original; cf. verses 22 and 25) and of the reference to "truth" (cf. verse 25 with verses 15, 20, 24). Based upon this evident connection one might interpret Paul's thinking at this point as follows: "In view of the fact that 'in Christ' y o u have been taught to put off the old man and to put on the new man, therefore, put off (or: lay aside) falsehood and speak truth."

One is, however, immediately confronted with a rather incisive difference of opinion among commentators with respect to the translation and meaning of these words. Perhaps the best way to bring out this difference would be to summarize the view of one representative of each of the two opposing theories. The first view is this: What Paul is saying is that since the Ephesians have once for all laid aside falsehood, namely, when they accepted the truth of the gospel, they should now speak truth each with his neighbor. The second is: "There is no need to render 'having put away,' which would seem to imply a separation in time between the two actions [that is, between laying aside falsehood and speaking truth]." [128] Grammatically both renderings – "having put away" and "putting away" (or: "laying aside") – are possible. In favor of the first view it can be argued that the Ephesians had experienced basic conversion. They had, therefore, already decisively repudiated the lie, namely, when they accepted the truth. The meaning of 4:25 could therefore be: "Be consistent. Let y o u r life adorn y o u r confession. Having put away falsehood, now practice the truth." This line of reasoning would also be entirely in harmony with Paul's logic as expressed, for example, in 4:1 ff. and elsewhere.

Nevertheless, although the possibility of the correctness of this theory must be granted, it would seem to me that the opposite view has the best of the argument. Why is it that so very many translators and interpreters have adopted it? *With minor variations* the rendering which I also favor, namely, "Therefore, laying aside falsehood, speak truth each (of y o u) with his neighbor" is that which one will find in A.V., A.R.V., R.S.V., and in substance also in the versions of those who use two imperatives: "Have done

---

[128] The first view is that of Lenski, argued with usual forcefulness, *op. cit.*, pp. 573, 574. He even states, "The participle is . . . aorist, hence not: 'putting away falsehood.' " But surely he must have been aware of the fact that there is also such a thing as *an aorist participle of simultaneous action!* The second view is that of Abbott, *op. cit.*, p. 139.

with falsehood; tell the truth to one another" (Bruce; and cf. Phillips, N.E.B., Williams, Beck, etc.). The reasons, no doubt, are as follows: *a.* it is felt that putting away falsehood and telling the truth are simply two sides of one and the same coin; and *b.* it is also rather apparent that the apostle, on the basis of his previous paragraph, is now beginning to list particular areas in which Christian conduct must reveal itself, one of them being the practice of truthfulness. To most interpreters these facts must have seemed so obvious that in their comments on this passage they do not even discuss the possibility of the opposite view.

Every missionary who has worked for a while with those still living in darkness can testify that not only thinking false thoughts but also definitely telling lies and spreading false rumors is characteristic of the heathen world. For those who had been converted rather recently it must not have been easy to break away from this evil habit. That could well be the reason why Paul, whether directly or indirectly, refers again and again to the necessity of putting a decisive end to the past manner of behavior in this respect, and of adopting an entirely new set of rules. Some, with an appeal to 4:15, 22, 25; 6:14, have even suggested that in and around Ephesus church-members behaved rather dishonestly (see Grosheide, *op. cit.,* p. 69). However that may have been, falsehood and dishonesty are typical of the Gentile way of life (Rom. 1:29) then as now.

The best way to kill the lie is by telling the truth. That is what Paul is actually saying, as by "Speak truth each (of y o u) with his neighbor" he is substantially quoting Zech. 8:16. Especially for those in the congregations addressed who were acquainted with the Old Testament, that is, for the Jewish Christians, the fact that this was a quotation from sacred literature must have added strength to the exhortation. In the opinion of Hodge the word "neighbor," though having the general sense of fellow-man of any creed or nation, here refers to fellow-Christian (*op. cit.,* p. 268); not as if it would be perfectly proper to lie to unbelievers, but because the context demands this interpretation. I believe Hodge is right, the context being: **for we are members of one another.** This recalls 2:13-22; 3:6, 14, 15; 4:1-6, 16, all of which stress the idea that though believers are many, they are also *one,* namely, one body with Christ as head. Lying is not only wrong because it makes light of the intrinsic excellence of the truth, but also because it causes trouble, friction, disunity and sadness in the church. The law of love certainly implies truthfulness.

**26, 27.** The next specific admonition has to do with such matters as anger and resentment: **Be angry but do not sin.** These words recall Ps. 4:4 (LXX: Ps. 4:5), which the apostle is here applying for his own use. The words should not be interpreted separately, as if the sense were, *a.* "Be sure to be angry once in a while"; and *b.* "do not sin." Much less is it true that all anger is here forbidden. Those who, by means of strange reasoning, favor this "interpretation" (?) do so with an appeal to verse 31, but see on that verse. The sense is simply, "Let not y o u r anger be mixed with sin." Anger as such need not be sinful. It is ascribed even to God (I Kings 11:9; II Kings 17:18; Ps. 7:11; 79:5; 80:4, 5; Heb. 12:29), and to Christ (Ps. 2:12; Mark 3:5; John 2:15-17). In fact, the age in which we are living could use a little more "righteous indignation" against sin of every type. Also, the more angry every believer is with his own sins, the better it will be. However, anger, especially with reference to the neighbor, easily degenerates into hatred and resentment. To love *the sinner* while one hates his *sin* requires a goodly supply of grace. The exclamation, "I cannot stand that fellow," is at times uttered even by one church member with reference to another. It is for that reason that the apostle immediately adds: **let not the sun go down on that angry mood** [129] **of y o u r s.** Having spoken about anger, the apostle now turns to that into which anger may easily degenerate, namely, the spirit of resentment, the angry mood, the sullen countenance that is indicative of hatred and of the unforgiving attitude. The day must not end thus. Before another dawns, nay rather, before the sun even sets — which to the Jew meant the end of one day and the beginning of another — genuine forgiveness must not only have filled the heart but must, if at all possible, have come to open expression so that the neighbor has benefited from its blessing. Phillips, though not really translating, does give the sense of the passage when he paraphrases it as follows: "Never go to bed angry." Continued: **. . . and do not give the devil** [130] **a foothold.** Literally, "And do not give a place to the devil." The devil will quickly seize the opportunity of changing our indignation, whether righteous or unrighteous, into a grievance, a grudge, a nursing of wrath, an unwillingness to forgive. Paul was very conscious of the reality, the power, and the deceitfulness of the devil, as 6:10 shows. What he means, therefore, is that *from the very start* the devil must be resisted (James 4:7). No *place* whatsoever must be given to him, no room to enter or even to stand. There must be no yielding to or compromise with him. He must not be given any opportunity to take advantage of our anger for his own sinister purpose.

**28.** From the warning against falsehood and the angry mood the apostle proceeds now to that against stealing. He writes: **Let him who steals steal no longer.** He does not say, "Let him that stole" (A.V.) but "Let him who steals." He is probably referring to people who before their conversion were used to enriching themselves by means of petty larceny, etc., and who were

---

[129] By means of this translation both the sense and the sound-similarity of the words used in the original for "anger" and "angry mood" are preserved.

[130] When *diábolos* is preceded by the article it is definitely *"the devil"* who is indicated. As an adjective it is rendered "slanderous (persons)," hence, "slanderers" (I Tim. 3:11; II Tim. 3:3; Titus 2:3). To avoid misunderstanding, therefore, the rendering "the devil" here in 4:27 is required.

now in danger of falling back into defalcations of various types. But must we then assume that there were thieves in the congregations here addressed? My answer is that at least the danger that some would slip back into this sin was very real. It must not be forgotten that some, perhaps many, of these early converts were slaves. Now lack of trustworthiness in matters material was characteristic of slaves, just as even today "servants" in heathen lands are not always honest, but will snitch things away from their employers when the latter happen not to be looking. According to Philem. 18 – a letter written during this same imprisonment and delivered at about the same time – Paul suspected Onesimus, the runaway slave, of having wronged his master in this respect. And after the release from the present (first Roman) imprisonment Paul was going to write to Titus: "Urge slaves to be submissive in every respect to their own masters . . . *not pilfering, but evincing the utmost trustworthiness*" (Titus 2:9, 10). Is it altogether improbable that even the "converted" slave might, in a moment of weakness, say to himself, "My master has left home. This is my opportunity to take something away from him. After all, he owes me much more, for by what right does he exact all this labor from me? Therefore, when I relieve him of some treasure, I am simply depriving him of that to which he has no right"? But we should not think exclusively of slaves. The sin against which Paul issues his warning was and is today, characteristic of heathenism.

What is Paul's solution? He wants the Ephesians to stop stealing and to practice honesty. But he wants more than that. He realizes that back of this sin of stealing lies a more basic fault, namely, *selfishness*. Hence, he strikes at the very root of the evil, for, by turning the attention of the thief, whether actual or potential, away from himself to the needs of other people, he strives to give him a new interest in life, a new joy. So he writes: **but rather let him labor, with his own hands accomplishing what is good, so that he may have something to share with the needy one.** The thief must stop stealing and begin to do some hard, honest *labor*. Paul uses this word *labor* or *toil* in connection with *manual* labor (I Cor. 4:12; II Tim. 2:6; cf. the noun in I Thess. 1:3; 2:9; II Thess. 3:8); and also in connection with *religious* work (Rom. 16:12 twice; I Cor. 15:10; Gal. 4:11; Phil. 2:16; I Thess. 5:12; I Tim. 4:10; 5:17). Here in 4:28 he has reference to manual labor, as the phrase "with his own hands" indicates. By using his hands in honest work, the worker will be accomplishing something that is good instead of doing that which is bad, contrary to God's law. As to working for a living, Paul himself had set an excellent example. Not only did he perform an amount of religious labor, of the highest quality, that is almost beyond belief, but in addition he at times even worked with his own hands in order to supply his own needs and those of others. He was able to say to the Thessalonians, "For y o u remember, brothers, our toil and hardship: by night and by day (we were ) working at a trade (or: "working for a living"), in order not to be a burden to any of y o u while we proclaimed to y o u the gospel of God" (I Thess. 2:9; cf. Acts 20:33, 34). For a detailed account of Paul's teaching with respect to *work* and receiving remuneration for it, see N.T.C. on I and II Thessalonians, pp. 65, 66, 201, 202.

Paul stresses the fact that the laborer should think not only of himself but also of his brother, especially of the one who is in need. The apostle himself was a man of tender and far-reaching sympathies (Gal. 6:10). He was "eager to help the poor" (Gal. 2:10). And he actually helped them! In fact, the very missionary tour which had resulted in his present imprisonment had been a benefit-journey in the interest of the Jerusalem poor. He had been gathering funds for the needy in that city. These needy ones were very dear to him, and by encouraging even those churches whose membership was drawn mostly from the Gentile world to extend a helping hand he was at the same time trying to do his part in welding the various churches into a fellowship of love and mutual helpfulness (Acts 24:17; Rom. 15:26; I Cor. 16:1-9; II Cor. 8; 9). In all this he was but following the example of his Lord and Savior, who while still on earth, spoke of the work of mercy again and again and whose pitying heart was deeply moved by the plight of the poor (Matt. 5:7; 19:21; 25:35, 36; Luke 4:18; 6:20; 14:13, 14; 16:19-31; John 13:29).

**29.** See also on 5:4. From a warning against the improper attitude toward material things Paul proceeds to an admonition against the improper use of the tongue, also in this case setting the positive over against the negative, in the spirit of Rom. 12:21, "Overcome evil with good." He writes: **Let no corrupt speech proceed from y o u r mouth.** Corrupt speech is that which is putrid, rotten; hence also corrupting, defiling, injurious (Matt. 15:18). We may well assume that for many years these rather recent converts to the Christian faith had been living in an impure environment, where foul conversation, at feasts and other social gatherings and parties, had been the stock in trade of everyone present. The change from this toxic environment to the pure and wholesome atmosphere of Christian fellowship must have been nothing short of revolutionary. Even believers who are well advanced in sanctification have at times complained about the fact that it was difficult for them to cleanse their minds entirely from the words and melody of this or that scurrilous drinking song. They hated it, fought against it, were sure at last that they had expelled it forever from their thoughts, and then suddenly there it was again, ready to plague and torture them by means of its reappearance. Thus also certain vile phrases or catch-words, sometimes even profanity, all too common in the pre-conversion period of life, have the habit in unguarded moments to barge right in and to befoul the atmosphere. Think of Simon Peter who, although a disciple of the Lord, "began to curse and to swear" when he thought that his life was in danger (Matt. 26:74).

Here, too, the only remedy, in addition to prayer, is to fill mind and heart with that which is pure and holy, in the spirit of Gal. 5:22 and Phil. 4:8, 9. Accordingly, Paul continues: . . . **but (only) such (speech) as is good for edification,** that is, for "building up the body of Christ" (4:12), **as fits the need** (literally, "edification of the necessity," meaning: edification required by a concrete or specific need), **that it may impart grace to the listeners,** that is, that it may spiritually benefit them. This recalls Col. 4:6, "Let y o u r speech always be gracious, seasoned with salt, so that y o u may know how to answer each individual." See also Col. 3:16.

We notice an interesting parallel between verses 25, 28, and 29. In each case the apostle urges the addressed *to be a blessing* for those with whom they have daily contact. Merely *refraining from* falsehood, stealing, and corrupt speech will never do. Christianity is not a mere "don't" religion, and believers must not be content to be mere zeros. Instead, they should copy the example of their Master, whose words were so filled with grace that the multitudes were amazed (Luke 4:22). "A word in due season, how good it is!" (Prov. 15:23).

**30.** When the apostle warns against ill behavior and urges Christian conduct upon all the addressed, he is never forgetting about all the "interested" parties. He has already mentioned the neighbor, the devil, the needy one, and the listeners (verses 25, 27, 28, and 29). It does not surprise us, therefore, that he now refers to one more interested party, *most interested indeed,* namely, the Holy Spirit. He writes: **And do not grieve the Holy Spirit of God in whom y o u were sealed for the day of redemption.** It is said at times that the church has failed to do full justice to the doctrine of the Holy Spirit; that it has neglected to bestow upon him the attention given to the Father and to the Son. There may be truth in this. As for Paul, however, he has no share in this blame. The term "the Holy Spirit" occurs about thirty times in his epistles, if we include such synonymous appellatives as "Spirit of God," "Spirit of Jesus Christ," etc. In addition I have counted at least seventy instances in which I, for one, would interpret the term *pneúma* (occurring without the adjective "holy") as referring to the third person of the Holy Trinity. On that subject, however, there is some difference of opinion among commentators. Be that as it may, the epistle to the Ephesians mentions the Holy Spirit again and again, using the very term (1:13; 4:30) or simply the designation: "the Spirit" (1:17; 2:18, 22; 3:5, 16; 4:3, 4; 5:18; 6:17, 18). In most of these cases there is general agreement that the reference is to the Paraclete.

The reason for this frequency of occurrence is obvious: Paul wishes to impress upon us that apart from God we cannot be saved; that is, that whatever good there is in us has its origin in the Holy Spirit. He both imparts life and sustains it. He causes it to develop and to reach its ultimate destination. It is he, therefore, who is the Author of every Christian virtue, every good fruit. Hence, whenever the believer pollutes his soul by any deceitful, vengeful, covetous, or filthy thought or suggestion, he is *grieving* the Holy Spirit. This is all the more true because it is the Spirit that dwells within the hearts of God's children, making them his temple, his sanctuary (2:22; I Cor. 3:16, 17; 6:19). By means of every evil imagination, cogitation, or motivation that indwelling and sanctifying Spirit is therefore, as it were, cut to the heart. Besides, not only does the Spirit *save* us but he also fills us with the joy, the assurance, of salvation; for, as was made clear earlier, and as is repeated in substance here in 4:30, it was "in" him ("in connection with," hence also "by means of," him) that we were "*sealed* for the day of redemption," that great day of the consummation of all things, when our deliverance from the effects of sin will be completed. It is the day of Christ's return, when our lowly body, refashioned so that it will have a form like Christ's glorious body, will rejoin our redeemed soul in order that in soul and body the entire victorious multitude may inhabit the new heaven and earth to glorify God forever and ever. The very meditation on the fulfilment of this hope should have a purifying effect on us (I John 3:2, 3). For further explanation see on 1:13, 14; cf. Luke 21:28; Rom. 8:23. Hence, reversion to pagan attitudes and practices is a sign of base ingratitude. How this must *grieve* the indwelling Spirit! We may call this a highly anthropomorphic expression, and so it is, both here and in Isa. 63:10 from which it is borrowed. It is, however, in a sense, a most comforting anthropomorphism, for it cannot fail to remind us of "the love of the Spirit" (Rom. 15:30), who "yearns for us even unto jealous envy" (James 4:5). That is also the context in Isaiah. Read Isa. 63:10 in connection with the verse which precedes it. To be sure, "grieving the Spirit" may not be as strong a term as "resisting" the Spirit (Acts 7:51); which, in turn, is not as trenchant as "quenching the Spirit" (I Thess. 5:19). Nevertheless, one step in the wrong direction easily leads to the next. Let the Ephesians, and all those down the centuries for whom the epistle was intended, take this to heart! Note also with what emphasis the Comforter's full name is spelled out: "the Holy Spirit of God," or, even more literally, "the Spirit, the Holy One, of God," with special emphasis on his holiness. The stress is both on his majesty and on his sanctifying power. He is "holy" and this not only as being spotlessly sinless in himself, but also as the very Source of holiness for all those in whose hearts he deigns to dwell!

**31.** Paul now returns once more to the sins of the tongue (cf. verses 25 and 29 above). Six specific items are mentioned, as he continues: **Let all bitterness and anger and wrath and brawling and slander be put away from y o u, along with all malice.** *Bitterness* is the disposition of the person with a tongue sharp as an arrow, keen as a razor. He resents his neighbor, and so he "needles" him, is ever ready to "fly off the handle" with a reply that bites or stings. *Anger* or *fury* (Latin: *furor*), is a strong feeling of antagonism which is expressed in the tumultuous outburst, the hot retort. As here used, occurring in the evil company of words like *bitterness* and *brawling* (contrary to its use in verse 26), it is potential murder (Matt. 5:21, 22). *Wrath* (Latin: *ira*) is settled indignation, when the heart is like a roaring furnace. *Brawling* (cf. Acts 23:9) is the violent outburst of the person who has completely lost his temper and begins to yell at others. *Slander* or *reviling* is abusive speech, whether directed against God or against man.[131] This catalogue of the evil use of the tongue is summarized in the words "along with all malice." *Malice* is not merely "mischief" but, in general, the evil inclination of the mind, the perversity or baseness of disposition that even takes delight in inflicting hurt or injury on one's fellowmen. "Let all of these things be put away from y o u," says Paul by the inspiration of the Holy Spirit.

32. Now, in the final analysis, the putting away of the aforementioned evil dispositions, words, and actions can be accomplished only by the acquisition and development of the opposite virtues. Accordingly, turning once more to positive exhortations, the apostle states: **And be kind to each other, tender-hearted.** This may be compared with Col. 3:12, 13: "Put on, therefore, as God's elect, holy and beloved, a heart of compassion, kindness . . . , forgiving each other if anyone have a complaint against anyone. Just as the Lord has forgiven y o u, so do y o u also." *Kindness* is Spirit-imparted *goodness* of heart, the very opposite of the *malice* or *badness* mentioned in verse 31. The early Christians by means of kindness commended themselves to others (II Cor. 6:6). God, too, is kind (Rom. 2:4; cf. 11:22), and we are admonished to become like him in this respect (Luke 6:35). When the kind person hears a piece of malicious gossip, he does not run to the telephone to let others in on the delectable tidbit. When someone's faults are pointed out to him, he tries, if he can at all do so in honesty, to offset these failings by pointing out the criticized individual's good qualities. Kindness marks the man who has taken to heart I Cor. 13:4. *Tenderheartedness* (cf. I Peter 3:8 and "the heart of compassion" of Col. 3:12) indicates a very deep feeling, "a yearning with the deeply-felt affection of Christ Jesus."[132] Paul adds: **forgiving one another, just as God in Christ forgave y o u.** Colossians says, "just as *the Lord*"; Ephesians, "just as *God in Christ*." There is no essential

[131] The Greek word used is *blasphemy*. But in Greek this word has a somewhat broader meaning than in English. While in our language it refers to abusive language with respect to God or things religious, that is, to *defiant irreverence*, in the original it refers to insults directed either against God or against men. In the present instance, as the context indicates, the latter is clearly meant: scornful and insolent language directed against a neighbor, slander, defamation, detraction.

[132] The tenderhearted person has *"good* or *strong bowels"* that is, those that are the seat of, or affected by, deep and powerful feelings of love and pity. That indicates the derivation of the word here used in the original. As to the problem in connection with this use of the term "bowels" see N.T.C. on Philippians, p. 58, footnote 39.

difference. Father, Son, and Holy Spirit are one. They co-operate in all of these activities that concern our salvation. To forgive "just as God in Christ" forgave means: just as freely, generously, wholeheartedly, spontaneously, and eagerly. For a justification of this interpretation see such passages as Matt. 18:21-27, 35 and Luke 23:34. Moreover, all the injuries that *we* have ever suffered because of the ill-will of our fellow-men can never be compared with the abuse *he,* the sinless One, endured: being spit upon, maligned, crowned with thorns, crucified. Yet he forgave! In doing this he left us *an example* (I Peter 2:21-25).

But he did more than this. He also left us a *motive* for exercising forgiveness. Having been forgiven so much, should not we forgive? See again Matt. 18:21-35. That example and that motive, however, relate to more than our duty *to forgive.* They touch the entire broad area of *love,* of which the exercise of forgiveness is only one manifestation, though a very important one. In *every* area of life love should manifest itself, the love patterned after, and motivated by, God's love in Christ. Hence, Paul continues: **5:1, 2.**[133] **Be therefore imitators of God, as beloved children.** Again and again Jesus and the apostles emphasized that believers should strive to be imitators of God. Now to people who are living in an age which proudly proclaims, "*We* have conquered space," and which drags God down to the level of a benign Santa Claus, it may not seem at all outrageous to strive to *imitate* God. But if, by the grace of the really living God, the words, "Be still and know that I am God!" have retained some meaning for us, this crisp command to imitate him may baffle us. We stand in awe before his majesty. How can we imitate him whom we cannot even fathom? With Zophar we are inclined to say, "Canst thou by searching find out God? Canst thou find out the Almighty to perfection? It is high as heaven; what canst thou do? Deeper than Sheol; what canst thou know?" (Job 11:7, 8). With Isaiah we see the Lord sitting upon a throne, high and lifted up, and we hear the voices of the flying seraphim, as they cover their faces and their

---

[133] Whether with Lenski, etc., we should begin an entirely new section here, to coincide with the chapter-division, on the basis of the circumstance that Paul's "therefore" often introduces something new (4:1, 17; 5:15; and so also 5:1), or should rather, with Bruce, Hodge, Scott, and many others, include 5:1, 2 with the preceding verses (so that, for example, 4:25–5:2 would form one paragraph), is largely a matter of choice. A good argument can be advanced for either position. The presence of "therefore" in 5:1 is not conclusive for the former of these two positions, for that word by no means always introduces a new paragraph (see 5:7). Also, why should it be necessary to accept a wide gap between 4:32 and 5:1, but an easy transition between 5:2 and 5:3? The new thought introduced in 5:1 is, after all, a logical conclusion and further development of that expressed in 4:32. Simpson remarks, "There is no real break here" (*op. cit.,* p. 114). But with respect to 5:3 Grosheide states, "With the mention of *immorality* the apostle arrives at an entirely new subject." One good way to treat 5:1, 2 may well be that followed by several exegetes, namely, to regard it as a sub-paragraph within the paragraph 4:25–5:2.

feet, and are crying continually, "Holy, holy, holy is Jehovah of hosts; the fulness of the earth is his glory." And we, too, answer, "Woe is me! for I am undone; because I am a man of unclean lips . . . for my eyes have seen the King, Jehovah of hosts" (Isa. 6:1-5). Rather than even faintly to imagine that we, creatures of the dust, would ever be able *to imitate God,* we feel like falling down upon our knees and saying, with Simon Peter, "Depart from me; for I am a sinful man, O Lord" (Luke 5:8). And we understand why John, when similarly overcome, said, "When I saw him, I fell at his feet as one dead" (Rev. 1:17).

It is only in that spirit of awe and humble reverence that we can properly study this glorious theme of "the imitation of God." It is only then that the Lord will lay his right hand upon us and say, "Fear not!" Obedience to the command to imitate him is, after all, possible. This is true for the following reasons: *a.* we are created as his image; *b.* his enabling Spirit dwells within us; and *c.* by his regenerating and transforming grace we have become his *children,* that is, *imitators.* To be sure, we cannot imitate God by creating a universe and caring for it day by day, or by devising a method of satisfying the demands of justice and of mercy in saving men from the pit into which they have cast themselves, or by raising the dead, or by creating a new heaven and earth. *But in our own finite way we can and must imitate him; that is, we must copy his love.*

It is amazing how often Jesus and the apostles emphasized that believers should strive to be imitators of *God* (Matt. 5:43-48; Luke 6:35; I John 4:10, 11), and of *Christ,* which essentially amounts to the same thing (John 13:34; 15:12; Rom. 15:2, 3, 7; II Cor. 8:7-9; Phil. 2:3-8; Eph. 5:25; Col. 3:13; I Peter 2:21-24; I John 3:16; a list of passages by no means complete). By adding that those addressed should do so as *children,* the idea is greatly strengthened, as if to say, "Are not children great imitators, and are not y o u God's children?" Moreover, the modifier "beloved" adds even more weight to this admonition, for, other things being equal, it is exactly *the child who is the object of love* that will be the most eager imitator of those who love him. Paul adds: **and walk in love,** that is, let love be the very tenor of y o u r life. Let it characterize all y o u r thoughts, words, and deeds. For *walking* see also 2:10; 4:1, 17; 5:8, 15. Continued: **just as Christ loved y o u.** Not just anything which men may wish to dignify with the name "love" should be the pattern for our thought and conduct, but very distinctly Christ's own purposeful, self-sacrificing love must be our example. And, to be even more specific, there is added: **and gave himself up for**[134] **us.** Here

[134] In connection with the preposition ὑπέρ two extremes must be avoided: *a.* to say that ὑπέρ = ἀντί. Though, on the basis of the occurrence of ὑπέρ in such passages as Gal. 2:20; 3:13 and in ancient letters in which one individual signs *for* another, this absolute identity of meaning has been maintained, it is extremely doubtful whether the two prepositions *as such* ever have *exactly* the same force. Moreover, we do not need Eph. 5:2 to prove the substitutionary atonement. Matt.

it must not escape our attention that when Paul urges the addressed to imitate *God* he, in one and the same breath, illustrates this love of *God* by directing our attention to that which *Christ* had done for us. This surely indicates not only that Father and Son are the same in essence but also that what the Father does he does in connection with the Son (4:32) and that neither loves us less than the other.

In his great love Christ *gave himself up,* surrendering himself willingly, to his enemies, and thus to his Father. This surrender is genuine. It was not forced upon him (John 10:11, 15). Among those for whom Christ had thus yielded himself as an offering for sin was also the great persecutor Paul. The thought of Christ's great love grips him to the extent that he changes the pronouns, so that *y o u* ("just as Christ loved y o u") now becomes *us* ("and gave himself up for us"). The apostle never writes in the abstract. Compare Gal. 2:20: "the Son of God who loved *me,* and gave himself up *for me.*" See also Gal. 1:16. It is this spirit of giving oneself sacrificially and voluntarily which believers are urged to imitate.

The voluntary self-sacrifice of Christ during the entire period of his humiliation and especially on the cross is here called **an offering and a sacrifice** [135] **to God.** It was an *offering* for he willingly *brought* it (Isa. 53:10). It was a *sacrifice,* and as such could well remind one of the *fumes* rising from the altar when the burnt-offering was consumed whole, symbolizing *entire surrender to God.* But though the word used in the original does not always

---

20:28; Mark 10:45; John 1:29; Acts 20:28; I Cor. 6:20; Eph. 1:7; Heb. 9:28; I Peter 1:18, 19; 2:24 teach this clearly enough, especially when interpreted in the light of Exod. 12:13; Lev. 1:4; 16:20-22; 17:11; and Isa. 53. To be avoided also, however, is *b.* to deny that, in the light of all of Scripture, ὑπέρ, as here used, *implies* Christ's substitutionary death. The vicarious death of Christ is certainly *implied* here, for, according to the doctrine of Scripture throughout, in what other way could Christ have died *for* us — that is, *for our benefit, in our interest* — than by dying *in our stead?*

[135] The word προσφορά is very general in meaning. It might include peace, meal, and drink offerings such as were offered by (or *for*) those who wished to be released of a temporary Nazirite vow (Acts 21:26). It could also refer to alms or gifts to the poor, of whatever character (Acts 24:17), or even to the offering up of the Gentiles, now Christians, to God (Rom. 15:16). In Heb. 10:10, 14 it refers to Christ's offering of himself for sin, once for all.

The word θυσία, too, is very comprehensive in connotation. Its association with bloody sacrifices or with the altar upon which these are offered is common (Mark 12:33; Luke 2:24; Luke 13:1; Acts 7:42; I Cor. 10:18). Thus, it also suits Christ's bloody self-sacrifice upon the cross (Heb. 7:27; 10:12; cf. 10:27). But its use is not limited to bloody offerings or to anything that is consumed on the altar. Abel's offering was associated with blood; not that of Cain. Yet the same word θυσία refers to both of these offerings or sacrifices (Heb. 11:4). This is also the word used to describe the gift which Paul received from the Philippians by the hand of Epaphroditus (Phil. 4:18). In Phil. 2:17; Heb. 13:15, 16; and I Peter 2:5 the word is used in a definitely figurative sense. Christian life and conduct, springing from faith, the sacrifice of praise, goodness and generosity, all such things, when offered to God in the proper spirit of humility and gratitude, are *sacrifices.*

refer to sacrifices consumed on the altar but may also have a more general reference (for which see footnote 135), we learn from other passages of Scripture (e.g., Matt. 26:36-46; 27:45, 46; II Cor. 5:21; cf. Isa. 53) that as to his human nature Christ was indeed consumed by the wrath of God in the sense that "the weight of our sins and of the wrath of God pressed out of him the bloody sweat in the garden" and caused him to suffer "the deepest reproach and anguish of hell, in body and soul, on the tree of the cross, when he cried out with a loud voice: My God, my God, why hast thou forsaken me." Thus he had accomplished his task and had fulfilled the prophecies, with special reference now to Ps. 40:6 (LXX: Ps. 39:7, 8). In that passage the same two words, *offering* and *sacrifice,* are used, but now in reverse order, *sacrifice* and *offering,* in connection with the Messiah's offering of himself to God: *"Sacrifice and offering* thou hast no delight in . . . . Then said I, Lo, I am come; in the roll of the book it is written of me." By the author of the epistle to the Hebrews that passage is appropriately applied to Christ and his self-sacrifice (Heb. 10:5-7). In connection, then, with this offering and sacrifice to God, as an example and motive for us, Paul adds: **for a fragrant odor;** literally, "an odor of a sweet smell." Cf. Exod. 29:18; Ezek. 20:41; Phil. 4:18. The meaning is that this offering and sacrifice *was* – and *is* in our case, when we imitate the spirit in which Christ presented it – well-pleasing to God. Every deed done out of love and gratitude to God, whether it be Abel's (Gen. 4:4), or Noah's (Gen. 8:21), or that of the Israelites of old (Lev. 1:9, 13, 17) or that of new dispensation believers who dedicate themselves to God (II Cor. 2:15, 16), pleases God. Unique among them all is *Christ's* self-sacrifice. Yet, the latter's spirit must be reflected every day and every hour in the hearts and lives of his followers,[136] for a fragrant odor.

c. 5:3-14

*"You were formerly darkness, but now you are light in the Lord; as children of light ever walk."*

The Glorious Renewal of which Paul is speaking in this entire section (4:17–6:9) calls for self-sacrifice instead of self-indulgence. Since in the preceding verses great emphasis was placed on *self-sacrifice* in imitation of Christ, the attention is now shifted to its very opposite: *self-indulgence.* Stating it differently, the admonition to "walk in love" is followed here by the condemnation of love's perversion. Paul minces no words as he proceeds: **3. But immorality and impurity of any kind, or greed, let it not even be mentioned among you.** The list of vices which begins here may be compared with similar ones in Paul's other epistles (Rom. 1:18-32; I Cor. 5:9-11; 6:9, 10; Gal. 5:19-21; Col. 3:5-9; I Thess. 4:3-7; I Tim. 1:9, 10; II Tim. 3:2-5;

---

[136] On the imitation of Christ see also Willis P. De Boer, *The Imitation of Paul, An Exegetical Study,* doctoral dissertation submitted to the Free University of Amsterdam; Kampen, 1962.

and Titus 3:3). Christ, he alone, supplies the *example, motive,* and *power* to overcome them. Verse 3 centers around sexual perversion of every description. Though *immorality* (cf. Matt. 5:32; 15:19; 19:19; John 8:41; I Thess. 4:3) refers basically to unlawful sexual intercourse, it probably includes illicit, clandestine relationships of every description. Evil in the sexual realm was, and is today, a characteristic feature of paganism. It is often closely associated with idolatry. That even those who had turned to Christ had not thoroughly shaken off this sin is clear from I Cor. 5:1 ff. Is it also implied in the present epistle: 5:27? *Impurity* or *uncleanness,* not only in deeds but also in words, thoughts, intents of the heart, desires, and passions, is here condemned. The phrase "of any kind" covers a very large territory! For *greed* (cf. 4:19) the apostle uses a word which means *over-reaching.* Greed is *selfishness.* It characterizes the money-grubber. Nevertheless, in the present connection, because of its close association with *immorality* and *impurity,* it may well apply especially to ravenous self-assertion in matters of sex, at the expense of others: the going beyond what is proper and defrauding the brother (cf. I Thess. 4:6 where the related verb is used in a similar connection). "Let it not even be mentioned among y o u," says Paul, meaning: so far should y o u be removed from the sin of this type that the very suspicion of its existence among y o u should be banished once and for all. He cannot have meant that sex must never be discussed, and that warnings with respect to the evil of immorality and its attendant sins must never be heard, for he himself is at this very moment discussing it and issuing such a warning. With respect to the desirable absence of transgression in this area Paul adds: **as is fitting among saints.** Are not "saints" (cf. 1:1) those who have been set apart by God to be his very own? Have they not, by the power of the sanctifying Spirit, dedicated themselves completely to their Lord; hence also to a new walk of life?

4. Among the sins that should not even require mention are **also filthiness and silly talk or wittiness in telling coarse jokes.** *Filthiness* or *shamefulness* covers more than "shameful language" (Col. 3:8). It includes *any* thought, imagination, desire, word, or deed of which a believer who is sensitive to the demands of God's holy law and who views himself as living constantly in his presence would be ashamed. *Silly talk* is the kind of conversation one could expect to hear from the lips of a fool or of a drunkard. The next term is hard to translate. Judged on the basis of its derivation it is very innocent, for it means literally "that which turns easily." The closest to it as to etymological significance would be *versatility;* for this, too, has reference to turning easily. The versatile person is able to turn with ease from one subject to another, being at home in all of them. Similarly, the word which the apostle employs was often used in a favorable sense, to indicate the nimble-witted individual. However, it is also possible for certain speakers *to move very easily* into the mire of unbecoming expressions. They seem to have a garbage

can type of mind, and every serious topic of conversation reminds them of an off-color jest or anecdote. The word used in 5:4 has therefore come to mean *coarse jesting, wittiness in telling coarse jokes.* There need be nothing wrong with a joke. Good humor is what everybody needs. But the kind to which Paul refers should be thoroughly avoided. Regarding such practices the apostle adds: **which things are improper.** They are improper because they are *not worthy of the calling with which believers were called.* See on 4:1. What, then, is the remedy for the vices mentioned? The apostle answers this question by stating: **but rather the expression of thankfulness.** See further on 5:20. When mind and heart are centered on "all things bright and beautiful" which God grants to us and still has in store for us, the interest in squalid indecency will vanish. So the apostle places *thankfulness* over against *wittiness.* This translation not only gives the sense but preserves, to some extent, the wordplay of the original (*eucharistía* over against *eutrapelía*). *Clarion praise* should be substituted for the *clever* (but vulgar) *phrase.* Continued: **5. For of this y o u can be very sure, that no immoral or impure person or greedy individual – which is the same as an idolater – has any inheritance in the kingdom of Christ and of God.** The apostle wishes to emphasize this very important point, namely, that *immorality* and *salvation* are opposites. Hence, he says what literally could almost be translated, "For this y o u know, knowing." However, since in the original the finite verb and the participle which follows it are not forms of the same word, a better *literal* rendering would be, "For this y o u know, recognizing." Many translators and interpreters, though differing in their views of this expression, have, however, felt that the reason why the apostle makes use of these *two* words where ordinarily *one* would have sufficed is that he wished to lay special stress on what he is about to say. If we accept this position, the rendering would be: "For of this y o u can be very sure." [137] The fact of which the Ephesians can be very sure is this, that no one who practices the sins mentioned in verse 3 (and elaborated in verse 4) has any

---

[137] With Robertson, *Word Pictures,* Vol. IV, p. 542, I regard ἴστε to be not imperative but present indicative. His rendering is, "Y o u know recognizing by your own experience." Implied in this translation is the fact that basically the finite verb refers to a knowledge by intuition or by reflection, the participle to a knowledge by observation and/or experience. Hodge (*op. cit.,* p. 285) believed that the finite verb referred to what Paul had said in verse 3, the participle to what follows it in verse 5. Though this separation may appear somewhat unnatural, yet the very wording of verse 5 proves that Paul reverts to what he had said in verse 3. Still others refer to the familiar Hebrew idiom according to which two forms of the same word occurring in immediate sequence strengthen the idea that is being expressed: Thus, "dying thou shalt die" means "thou shalt surely die"; cf. "blessing I will bless" and "multiplying I will multiply." However, the idiom used here in 5:5 is not *exactly* the same, since the finite verb and the participle are forms of *different* verbs. As many translators see it, the combination of the two Greek forms so closely related in meaning could still convey an emphasis similar to that of the Hebrew idiom. If not, then Robertson's more literal rendering must be regarded as correct.

inheritance in the kingdom of Christ and of God. One of these sinful practices is greed. That calling a person "a greedy individual" is the same as calling him "an idolater" (cf. Col. 3:5) is clear even on the surface, for such a person is worshiping someone else than the true and living God. That someone else is *himself*. He has made of himself an idol and is therefore an idolater. To a Jew, like Paul and some of the Ephesians, there was no greater sin than that of idolatry (cf. I John 5:21).

Though conditions among those addressed cannot have been very bad morally or spiritually – for Paul praises the Ephesian believers in no uncertain terms (1:15) and has nothing to say by way of direct adverse criticism –, yet the impression is left that there was still considerable room for improvement. The danger of falling into the errors of licentious gnosticism was never far removed. This seems to have been especially the case in Asia Minor. A few years later, during his second Roman imprisonment, Paul was going to remind Timothy of this peril (II Tim. 3:1-9). Timothy was probably carrying on a ministry at Ephesus at that time. John, too, writing to people in this same region, would have to combat this nefarious error (I John 3:4-10; Rev. 2:6, 14, 15, 20). See also II Peter 2:12-19 and Jude 4, 8, 11, and 19.

With a pastor's loving heart, therefore, Paul issues his warning. No one who continues to practice the pagan vices, whether because he is following old habit and the course of least resistance or else because he has adopted a reasoned excuse (Rom. 6:1), has a share in the one and only kingdom, namely, that of Christ and of God. Cf. Rev. 21:27; 22:15. It is, of course, impossible to speak about the kingdom of Christ without speaking about the kingdom of God. In principle this kingdom is already present in the hearts and lives of God's children. One day it will be theirs in full measure (1:18; 3:6). See N.T.C. on Colossians and Philemon, pp. 63, 64, especially footnote 47. Continued: **6. Let no one deceive y o u with empty words.** Cf. Col. 2:4, 8; I Tim. 2:14; James 1:26. "Empty" words are those that are void of truth and filled with error. When heeded they will prove the sinner's downfall: **for it is because of these things that the wrath of God comes upon the sons of disobedience.** Cf. Col. 3:6. By means of what has been called "a prophetic present tense" (cf. John 4:21; 14:3) Paul stresses the fact that the coming of the wrath of God, to be visited upon those who live in the sins mentioned in verses 3-5 and who listen to empty words assuring them that all is well, is so certain that it is as if that wrath had already arrived, and *in principle* it actually has arrived. These sinister practices attract God's displeasure like a fully lit up enemy target attracts bombs. The wrath spoken of here, though in a sense already present, is also ever on the way, until on the day of the great consummation of all things it will be fully revealed (cf. John 3:36; Rom. 2:5-11; II Thess. 1:8-10; Rev. 14:9-12), for "sons of disobedience" are "children of wrath" (see on 2:2).

It should not escape our attention, however, that even this stern warning has repentance as its object, as the tender admonition which immediately follows in verses 7 and 8 clearly shows. See also verses 10, 14-17; and cf. Rev. 2:16, 21, 22; 3:19; 9:20, 21. As a father pleads with his children whom he dearly loves, so this prisoner of Christ Jesus, a hero of the faith who is facing the possibility of a death sentence and therefore weighs every word, continues: **7. Therefore do not be their partners,** "fellow-sharers" (cf. 3:6) in their sin, their guilt, and their everlasting punishment. Cf. II Cor. 6:4-18. Meaning: in the light of God's marvelous love and mercy in Christ, the upward call that was extended to y o u, y o u r own profession of faith, and the wrath of God coming upon the sons of disobedience, think on y o u r way, walk in paths of light and be done forever with the works of darkness. Continued: **8. for y o u were formerly darkness.** In earlier days (2:1-3, 11, 12; 4:14, 17) the Ephesians had been darkness. Cf. 4:18, "darkened in their understanding, alienated from the life of God," etc. Not only had they been *in* darkness as in an evil environment, but they themselves had been part of that realm. *The darkness had been in them,* namely, the darkness of lack of the true knowledge of God (II Cor. 4:4, 6), depravity (Acts 26:18), and despondency (Isa. 9:1, 2). Continued: **but now (y o u are) light in the Lord.** Now they belong to the realm of light, for they now have the true knowledge of God (Ps. 36:9), righteousness and holiness (Eph. 4:24), happiness (Ps. 97:11; Isa. 9:1-7). It is only "in the Lord," that is, in vital connection with him, that they are now light. Moreover, since now they are light, they have also become light-transmitters: from them light radiates forth to all those with whom they come into contact. Ever since Jesus, "the light of the world" (John 8:12), entered their hearts (II Cor. 4:6), they, too, in their own small way, had become "the light of the world" (Matt. 5:14). In their entire conduct they reflect Christ, as the moon reflects the sun. Hence, **as children of light ever walk.** Here is another and beautiful Semitism: they are now, by God's grace, the very offspring of him who is the light. No longer are they "children of wrath" (2:3) or "sons of disobedience" (2:2; 5:6), but "children of light." Then let them be consistent. Let them in their daily life *be and constantly remain* true to what in principle they have become. Let them walk and keep on walking as children of light; that is, let the true knowledge of God and of his will be their standard constantly; let righteousness and holiness characterize all their attitudes, words, and actions; and let the joy of salvation be the very tenor of their lives. On "walking" see also 2:10; 4:1, 17; 5:2, 15. That this is what they are and how they should walk is evident, as the apostle brings out in a parenthetical statement: **9. — for the fruit of light [138] (consists) in all goodness and righteousness and truth —.** How does

[138] The variant "fruit of the Spirit," though supported not only by many late and definitely inferior manuscripts but even by the valuable p[46], is probably an assimilation to Gal. 5:22.

one know whether or not he is walking as a child of light? The answer is that light bears fruit, and this fruit will supply the needed evidence (Matt. 5:16; 7:20). The *qualities* of heart and life from which good works proceed are to be considered light, fruit. Paul mentions *all goodness,* a very general term, the opposite of "all malice" (4:31). Such goodness is Spirit-created moral and spiritual excellence of every description. Another way of looking at this goodness is to call it *righteousness,* the joy in doing what is right in the eyes of God, walking the straight path and never deviating from it. And still another description is *truth:* integrity, reliability, over against the sham, falseness, and hypocrisy that characterized the old way of life in which the Ephesians had formerly walked (4:14, 25; 5:6).

Returning now to the main clause of verse 8b, "As children of light ever walk," Paul adds: **10. verifying what is pleasing to the Lord.** Meaning: by walking constantly as children of light, and thus producing the fruit of light, y o u will, by y o u r very attitudes and action, be *verifying or proving*[139] what is pleasing to the Lord. That is Paul's glorious answer to the question, "How can I know whether I am really a child of God, one with whom God is pleased?" The answer amounts to this: "Do not worry or speculate or philosophize or argue. Just go right ahead and do the will of God as he has revealed it. The proof or evidence for which y o u are looking will then be abundantly supplied to y o u. Y o u will have the verification in y o u r heart. The assurance or peace will be distilled into y o u r life as the dewdrops are distilled and impearled upon the leaves." This is Scripture's answer throughout (Rom. 8:16; 12:1, 2; II Cor. 5:9; Phil. 4:6, 7, 18; Col. 1:10; and II Peter 1:5-11). Since Jesus as the world's light, was ever walking in the light and doing the will of his Father (John 4:34; 5:30; 6:38), it is not at all surprising that more than once he was given the assurance that the Father *was pleased* with him (Matt. 3:17; 17:5; cf. 12:18). And, although in the present life we, his followers, should not expect to hear what he heard, namely, an audible voice from heaven, the Holy Spirit will nevertheless impart that assurance also to us when we walk in the light.

Another tender warning, the negative side of what in verses 8-10 was expressed in positive terms, follows, an admonition which recalls verse 7. Paul lovingly pleads: **11. And do not take any part in the unfruitful works of darkness.** By works of darkness are meant such things as immorality, impurity, greed, filthiness, silly talk, etc. (5:3, 4), and also those mentioned in 4:25-32; briefly, *any and all* works belonging to the realm of depravity and inspired by its prince. Such works are called *unfruitful.* They are sterile

---

[139] The verb δοκιμάζω has various meanings: *a. to put to the test, examine* (I Cor. 11:28; II Cor. 13:5); *b. to prove or verify* by means of testing (I Cor. 3:13; I Peter 1:7); and *c. to approve* (I Cor. 16:3). Here the second meaning best suits the context.

in the sense that they do not glorify God, do not win the neighbor for Christ, and do not bring inner peace or satisfaction. Note that Paul recognizes no twilight zone. Although according to Scripture there are degrees of sinfulness and also degrees of holiness, nevertheless, there is no region of the shades. A person is either a believer or an unbeliever. Works belong either to the light or to darkness. Those who have sworn allegiance to the Ruler of the realm of light *must take no part whatever* in the empty, futile, thoroughly disappointing, works of darkness.

Does this mean now that the Ephesians should withdraw themselves from the men of the world; that they should become hermits and move as far as possible away from wicked men? Not at all! Though they are not *of* the world, yet they are *in* the world and have a mission to fulfil. Says Paul: **but instead even expose**[140] **them,** that is, these unfruitful works of darkness. Those who belong to the realm of light cannot be neutral with respect to the work of darkness. Compromise, too, is definitely ruled out. For example, when God says, "Worship me alone," and another says, "Worship idols," it will not do to try to worship Jehovah under the symbolism of images which are on the way to becoming idols. The sin of Jeroboam was an abomination to Jehovah (I Kings 12:25-33). Sin must be *exposed.* One is not being "nice" to a wicked man by endeavoring to make him feel what a fine fellow he is. The cancerous tumor must be removed, not humored. It is not really an act of love to smooth things over as if the terrible evil committed by those still living in the realm of darkness is not so bad after all. With respect to this Paul continues: **12. for the things done by them in secret it is a shame even to mention.**

But if one feels ashamed even to mention the horrible deeds of those who live in darkness, how then can he expose these deeds? Lenski's answer is, "To state them in our reproof is shameful not for us who make the statement in reproof, but for those who engage in these works" (*op. cit.,* p. 609). This explanation, however, impresses me as being unnatural. I wonder whether any unbiased reader of Scripture would ever have drawn that conclusion. When the apostle tells the Ephesians *to expose* the works of darkness, does he not mean that *they* (and all others for whom the letter was intended throughout the course of history) should expose them? So when he now adds in one breath that it is a shame *even to mention* these secret practices, is not the obvious meaning: "*Y o u* should expose them, for they are so very wicked, that *for anyone* even to mention them is shameful"? But how were they able to expose them and yet not mention them? The answer which is clear from the entire context is that by means of a life of

[140] For a discussion of the verb ἐλέγχω and a tabulation of its seventeen New Testament occurrences see N.T.C. on the Gospel according to John, Vol. II, pp. 324, 325, footnote 200.

goodness and righteousness and truth (verse 9) they must reveal what a vast contrast there is between the works of those who walk in the light and the works of those who walk in darkness. There are sins so altogether repulsive that it is better by far never to mention them. Conditions in the pagan world of Asia Minor seem to have been particularly bad. Roland Allen, in his work, *Missionary Methods: St. Paul's or Ours?*, London, third edition, 1953, p. 49, remarks, "If the moral atmosphere of Greece was bad, in Asia Minor it was even worse." Continued: **13. But when all these (wicked practices) are exposed by the light**[141] **they are made visible.** Meaning: when, *by means of contrast with the conduct of believers as "children of light,"* the terrible deeds of wickedness that mark "the sons of disobedience" are thus exposed, these horrible practices are shown up for what they really are. That this is true is shown by the rule expressed in the following statement: **for everything that is made visible is light;** that is, *whatever*, whether attitudes, words, practices, etc., is made manifest by having been thus contrasted loses its hidden character, takes on the nature of light, and is seen for what it really is.

In verses 11-13 the emphasis has been on *deeds* rather than on the *doers*. It was the deeds that were exposed. However, it is readily understandable that when wicked men's evil deeds are thus laid bare, the doers are indirectly reproved. They are made to see how great their sins and miseries are; hence, how desperately they need a radical change of life. The transition to the next line is therefore very natural: **14. Therefore he says:**

> **"Awake, sleeper,**
> **And arise from the dead,**
> **And Christ will shine on you."**

There is no sound reason here to interpret "he says" in any other way than in 4:8; hence, "God says," for the apostle is obviously referring to these words as authoritative. What is their source? Among the many answers given the two most popular ones are: *a.* Isa. 60:1 (and perhaps certain somewhat similar passages, as Isa. 9:2; 26:19; 52:1) ; *b.* an early Christian hymn. As to the first, favored by Calvin, Findlay, Hodge, and others, today it seems to be in style to dismiss this at once with the remark that there is no, or only very slight, similarity between Eph. 5:14 and Isa. 60:1. For myself, the more I study Isa. 60:1 in the light of its own context the more I begin to see certain resemblances. It is perhaps instructive to place the two passages alongside of each other:

---

[141] As I see it the phrase *ὑπὸ τοῦ φωτός* modifies the immediately preceding *ἐλεγχόμενα*, just as in verse 12 the parallel phrase *ὑπ' αὐτῶν* should be construed with the similarly immediately preceding *γινόμενα*.

| Isa. 60:1 | Eph. 5:14 |
| --- | --- |
| Arise, shine; | Awake, sleeper, |
| For your light has come, | And arise from the dead, |
| And the glory of Jehovah has risen upon you. | And Christ will shine on you. |

1. In the context of the Isaiah passage the daughter of Zion is represented as forsaken, her land as desolate (Isa. 62:4). We read about captives and prisoners (Isa. 61:1). Also the Ephesian passage presupposes a condition of wretchedness, the sleep of death which *has* or *had* befallen the one addressed.

2. In both passages the one who is pictured as lying down in sleep or death is commanded to arise. Cf. Rom. 13:11; I Thess. 5:6.

3. In both the one addressed receives encouragement.

4. The substance of this encouragement is the same in both cases, namely, that light will be imparted to the one who heretofore has been in darkness.

5. In Isaiah the One who imparts this light is *Jehovah,* in a context which by Jesus himself was interpreted as referring to himself. Cf. Isa. 61:1, 2a with Luke 4:16-21. See also footnote 108. In Ephesians it is *Christ* who shines upon the formerly wretched one.

6. In Isaiah 40–66 deliverance from the *Babylonian* captivity through Jehovah's anointed Cyrus (see especially chapters 40–48) seems to be a symbol of deliverance from *spiritual* captivity through the gloriously anointed "Servant of Jehovah" (see especially chapters 49–57). Chapters 58–66, in which 60:1 occurs, speak of the glory of redeemed Zion. It is not impossible, therefore, that the early church of the new dispensation saw Christ in this passage (Isa. 60:1) as the One who causes the light of salvation to shine forth upon those who arise from their death-sleep of sin. If Jesus was able to interpret a passage from chapter 61 as referring to himself, as has just been indicated (see under 5.), why should it be impossible to explain or at least apply a passage from the immediately preceding chapter similarly?

It is my conviction, therefore, that the theory according to which, either directly or indirectly, the Ephesian passage has its root in Isa. 60:1 must not be readily dismissed as if it were entirely out of the question. There may not be sufficient reason to consider the connection between the two passages to have been definitely established, but there *certainly* is no ground whatever for rejecting even the possibility of this connection.

Even so, however, there could be an element of truth in theory *b.* It is conceivable that though Eph 5:14 is in the final analysis rooted in Isa. 60:1, the form in which the latter passage is here reproduced by Paul was that of lines from an early Christian hymn. The hymn, in other words, may have been based on the Isaiah passage. It is clear at any rate that when Paul was writing what is now called the fifth chapter of Ephesians he had *hymns* in mind, for he mentions them only a few verses later, namely, in 5:19. Now if Eph. 5:14 was taken from a hymn, was it an Easter hymn, according to which the commemoration of Christ's physical resurrection reminded the one addressed to live a life in harmony with his *spiritual* resurrection, the two resurrections being related to each other as cause and effect? Or was it perhaps a song chanted in connection with the baptism of those who professed to have been awakened out of their sleep and to have been raised from the dead when they accepted Christ, and who were by means of this hymn urged to die more fully and constantly to "the old man" and increasingly day by day to put on "the new man"? We must confess that no one really knows for sure either the origin of these lines or the extent and manner of their use in the early church. What is certain, however, is the fact that they do not seem out of place in the present context. They apply to the man who is still living in paganism. When the wicked deeds of such a person have been exposed, the only way of escape must be clearly pointed out to him, so that he may wake up out of his sleep, may arise from the dead (cf. Luke 15:32) and Christ may shine on him.

In the light, however, of the entire preceding context (see especially verses 3-11) it is clear that the apostle has in mind not only the pagan but *also and especially* the convert. Paul's aim is to show that he who has renounced the wicked ways of the world should live a life consistent with his new standing. Therefore, instead of any longer taking part in the unfruitful works of darkness, he should emerge *completely* from his sleep and arise and withdraw *in every respect* from the wicked ways of the company of the spiritually dead. The blessed result will be that Christ will shine upon him. That would seem to be the meaning of the passage.

This, however, introduces another question. Do not these lines which the apostle is quoting with approval reverse the proper order of the elements in the process of becoming saved? Do they not seem to teach that it is man who turns to God before God turns to man? The sinner, so it would seem, is urged to wake up out of his spiritual sleep, and to arise from the dead (implying a resurrection from his death in sin), and only then will Christ shine upon him. The answer is: *a.* There is a long list of passages, both Old and New Testament, to which the same objection, if valid, would apply (for example, Deut. 4:29; 30:1-10; Ps. 50:14, 15; 55:16; Isa. 55:6, 7; Jer. 18:5-10; Matt. 11:28-30; Acts 16:31; Rev. 3:20). *b.* These passages stress human responsibility. *c.* None of them teaches that man is able, *in his own power,* to wake up or to arise from the dead. He can do this only by means of the grace of God and the power of the Holy Spirit. The very fact that he is called upon to arise *from the dead* implies this (see what was said about this in the interpretation of 2:1-9). In the process of becoming saved God always takes the lead. No one is able to become converted unless God first regenerates him. Also, after basic conversion has taken place there is never a moment in a person's life when he can do anything of spiritual value apart from his Lord. *d.* Christ, however, is not only the *Alpha* (beginning) of his salvation; he is also the *Omega* (the end); that is, he is not only salvation's *Originator;* he is also its *Rewarder.* Hence, when by divine grace and power the sinner puts off the old nature and puts on the new, when more and more he awakens and arises from the dead, the light from Christ shines upon him, illumining his entire life with tender, marvelous, mellow radiance, the radiance of the Savior's loving presence. It is thus that "the path of the righteous is as the dawning light that shines more and more unto the perfect day" (Prov. 4:18).

d. 5:15-21

*"Do not get drunk on wine, but be filled with the Spirit."*

Continuing his tender admonitions with respect to the church's Glorious Renewal Paul writes: **15. Be most careful therefore how y o u walk.**[142] Here again, in complete harmony with what has gone before, we are shown how very necessary it is for believers to show in every way and at all times that they have repudiated their old nature and have embraced the new and godly life. That is the only effective way of verifying one's own state of salvation, exposing the unfruitful works of darkness, calling the workers to repentance, and doing all this to the glory of God. Continued: **not as unwise but as wise.** Cf. 1:8, 17; Col. 1:9, 28; 3:16; 4:5. The unwise are those who, having no insight into things that pertain to God and salvation, are not aiming to reach the highest goal and therefore do not know and do not even care to know what are the best means to reach it. They regard as very important what is in reality of minor value or may even be harmful, and they do not appreciate what is indispensable. They conduct themselves accordingly. Those who are wise, on the other hand, have the proper insight and walk in harmony with it. They also make a judicious use of their time. In that trend Paul continues: **16. making the most of the opportunity.** They should not wait for opportunity to fall into their laps but should *buy it up,* not counting the cost. In the light of the entire context the opportunity referred to is that of showing by means of their life and conduct the power

[142] Should we read, "Look therefore *how carefully* y o u are walking"? Or rather, "Look therefore *carefully how* y o u walk"? In other words, is the correct reading πῶς ἀκριβῶς or is it ἀκριβῶς πῶς? A good case can be presented in defense of either. For myself I like Foulkes' reasoning in favor of the second reading. He writes, "This is a command that is essentially more likely to come from Paul's pen than that they should walk 'precisely' or 'strictly'. Paul could well use this word in its superlative form of his former life as a Pharisee (Acts 26:5), but to use it of the Christian life would have conveyed too much of a suggestion of renewed legalism" (*The Epistle of Paul to the Ephesians, An Introduction and Commentary,* Grand Rapids, Mich., 1963, p. 149). Either way, however, the emphasis is on the importance of Christian conduct.

and glory of the gospel, thus exposing evil, abounding in good works, obtaining assurance of salvation for themselves, strengthening the fellowship, winning the neighbor for Christ, and through it all glorifying God. The opportunity missed will never return. Let it therefore be used *to the full*. Read Mark 1:21-34 and see how much work Jesus was able to crowd into a single day, and what he did very early the next morning (Mark 1:35). Paul adds: **because the days are evil.** A single glance at the preceding context (see especially 4:14, 17-19, 25-31; 5:3-7, 10-12; cf. Rom. 1:18-32) will show how indescribably evil were the days when this letter was written. Similar admonitions are found in Rom. 13:11-14; I Cor. 7:29; II Cor. 6:14-18; Gal. 6:9, 10; and Col. 4:5. Continued: **17. Therefore do not be foolish but understand what (is) the will of the Lord.** The admonition of verse 15 – "not as unwise" – is repeated in slightly different language. The Ephesians must not be "without reflection or understanding." They must not show "want of sense," which amounts to saying that they must not be foolish. The connective "therefore" in the light of the preceding context may be interpreted as meaning: because the danger is so great, the wickedness so appalling, the opportunity so precious, and because constant watchfulness, earnest effort, and unwavering zeal are so necessary, do not be absurd. On the contrary, understand what is the will of the Lord, that is, of the Lord Jesus Christ. See 2:21; 4:1; 5:10. Do not depend on y o u r own acumen. Do not regard the advice of other people as the ultimate touchstone of the truth. Let the will of y o u r Lord as he has revealed it by means of his own word and example and by the mouth of his chosen messengers be y o u r standard and guide. See 5:10; cf. Rom. 12:2; I Peter 2:21.

One outstanding manifestation of "want of sense" is *drunkenness*. Its antidote, being "filled with the Spirit," indicates a far better avenue to true *understanding*. Hence, there is a double connection between verses 17 and 18. Paul writes: **18. And do not get drunk on wine, which is associated with unrestrained living, but be filled with the Spirit.** There are times when exhilaration of heart and mind is entirely proper. Scripture makes mention of shouting for joy (Ps. 5:11; 32:11; 35:27; etc.), fulness of joy (Ps. 16:11), good tidings of great joy (Luke 2:10), joy unspeakable and full of glory (I Peter 1:8). Exhilaration is wrong, however, when the method of inducing it is wrong. Thus it is improper to seek excitement from the excessive use of wine. It is the *abuse* of wine that is forbidden, not the *use* (I Tim. 5:23). That such abuse was a real danger in the early church, as it certainly is also today, appears from such restrictions as the following: "The overseer therefore must be above reproach . . . not (one who lingers) beside (his) wine" (I Tim. 3:3; cf. Titus 1:7); "Deacons similarly (must be) dignified, not . . . addicted to much wine" (I Tim. 3:8); and "Urge aged women similarly (to be) reverent in demeanor . . . not enslaved to much wine" (Titus 2:3).

Intoxication is not the effective remedy for the cares and worries of this life. The so-called "uplift" it provides is not real. It is the devil's poor substitute for the "joy unspeakable and full of glory" which God provides. Satan is ever substituting the bad for the good. Has he not been called "the ape of God"? Getting drunk on wine is "associated with unrestrained living" or "dissolute behavior," "recklessness" (Titus 1:6; I Peter 4:4). It marks the person who, if he so continues, *cannot be saved.*[143] But he need not so continue. The prodigal son of the unforgettable parable lived *recklessly* (an adverb cognate with the noun *recklessness* or *unrestrained living* occurring here in Eph. 5:18). *Extravagance* and *lack of self-control* were combined in his behavior, just as in all likelihood they are combined in the meaning of the word "unrestrained living" used in this passage from Paul's letter to the Ephesians. Nevertheless, there was salvation for him when he repented. Let anyone who may read this take courage (Isa. 1:18; Ezek. 33:11; I John 1:9).

The real remedy for sinful inebriation is pointed out by Paul. The Ephesians are urged to seek a higher, far better, source of exhilaration. Instead of *getting drunk* let them *be filled.* Instead of getting drunk on *wine* let them be filled with *the Spirit.* Note the double contrast. Although it is true that the apostle makes use of a word, namely, *pneúma,* which in the translation should at times be spelled *with,* at other times *without,* a capital letter (hence "Spirit" or "spirit"), it should be capitalized in this instance, as is often the case. Paul was undoubtedly thinking of the third person of the Holy Trinity, the Holy Spirit. Evidence in support of this view: *a.* the expression "filled with" or "full of" the *pneúma,* when the reference is to the Holy Spirit, is very common in Scripture (Luke 1:15, 41, 67; 4:1; Acts 2:4; 4:8, 31; 6:3; 7:55; 9:17; 13:9); [144] and *b.* the very contrast here in 5:18 between getting drunk on wine and being filled with the *pneúma* occurs also, though in a slightly different form, in Acts 2:4, 13, where the reference can only be to the Holy Spirit.[145]

---

[143] There are those who point out that etymologically ἀσωτία describes *the condition of the person who cannot be saved.* But here one would have to determine first of all what the word *saved* actually means in such a case. And even if this were determined, it would still remain true that, although derivations and word histories are instructive and do shed some light on meanings, *actual use of a word in a given context* is far more important. When, accordingly, I state that the person in question, if he so continues, *cannot be saved,* this conclusion is based not on etymology, nor on semantics, but on clear scriptural teaching (I Cor. 6:9, 10).

[144] The fact that here, in 5:18, by way of exception, we read ἐν πνεύματι does not invalidate this conclusion. The preposition ἐν covers a very wide area, especially in Koine Greek, in this case an area probably even broadened by the influence of Hebrew *b^e^,* either directly, or indirectly via the LXX. Also, the suggestion that in the present case the unusual phrase was selected in order to convey the fact that the Holy Spirit is not only the agent *by* whom believers are filled but also the One *in* whom they are filled must not be lightly dismissed.

[145] This rather generally accepted view as to the reference here in 5:18 to the Holy Spirit must therefore be maintained over against Lenski who calls it "impossible" (*op. cit.,* p. 619).

By the ancients, moreover, an overdose of wine was often used not only to rid oneself of care and to gain a sense of mirth but also to induce communion with the gods and, by means of this communion, to receive ecstatic knowledge, not otherwise obtainable. Such foolishness, often associated with Dionysiac orgies, is by the apostle contrasted with the serene ecstasy and sweet fellowship with Christ which he himself was experiencing in the Spirit when he wrote this letter to the Ephesians (see on 1:3; 3:20). What he is saying therefore is this: getting drunk on wine leads to nothing better than debauchery, will not place y o u in possession of worthwhile pleasure, usable knowledge, and perfect contentment. It will not help y o u but hurt y o u. It leaves a bad taste and produces no end of woe (cf. Prov. 23:29-32). On the other hand, being filled with the Spirit will enrich y o u with the precious treasures of lasting joy, deep insight, and inner satisfaction. *It will sharpen y o u r faculties for the perception of the divine will.* Note the immediate context, verse 17. So, "do not get drunk on wine, but be filled with the Spirit." [146]

Being thus filled with the Spirit believers will not only be enlightened and joyful but will also give jubilant expression to their refreshing knowledge of the will of God. They will reveal their discoveries and their feelings of gratitude. Hence Paul continues: **19. speaking to one another in psalms and hymns and spiritual songs.** The term *psalms* in all probability has reference, at least mainly, to the Old Testament Psalter; *hymns,* mainly to New Testament songs of praise to God and to Christ (verse 14 above, in which Christ is praised as the Source of light, containing perhaps lines from one of these hymns); and finally, *spiritual songs,* mainly to sacred lyrics dwelling on themes other than direct praise to God or to Christ. There may, however, be some overlapping in the meaning of these three terms as used here by Paul.

The point to note is that by means of these psalms, hymns, and spiritual songs, Spirit-filled believers must *speak to each other.*[147] They are not merely *reciting* what they have committed to memory. "Daughter, do *you* know that *your* Redeemer lives?" said the director to the soloist. After an affirmative answer he continued, "Then sing it again, and this time *tell us* about it." She did, and there were tears of joy and thanksgiving in every eye. Continued: **singing and making melody from y o u r heart to the Lord.** The idea of some [148] that in the two parts of this one verse the apostle has reference to two kinds of singing: *a.* audible ("speaking") and *b.* inaudible ("in the stillness of the heart"), must be dismissed. If that had been his intention,

---

[146] On this passage see also J. M. Moffatt, "Three Notes on Ephesians," *Exp,* Eighth Series, No. 87 (April, 1918), pp. 306–317.

[147] The reflexive ἑαυτοῖς is here used as a reciprocal as was the case in 4:32; hence, not "for yourselves" (Lenski) nor "to yourselves" (A.V.), but "to one another." See N.T.C. on Colossians and Philemon, p. 161, footnote 137.

[148] See Salmond, *op. cit.,* p. 364.

he would have inserted the conjunction *and* or *and also* between the two parts. The two are clearly parallel. The second explains and completes the first: when believers get together they should not be having wild parties but should edify each other, speaking to one another in Christian song, and doing so *from the heart, to the* praise and honor of their blessed *Lord.* They should make music with the voice ("singing") or in any proper way whatever, whether with voice or instrument ("making melody"). Cf. Rom. 15:9; I Cor. 14:15; James 5:13. For further details of interpretation see N.T.C. on Colossians and Philemon, pp. 160–163 where a closely similar passage (Col. 3:16) is discussed more at length.

By means of psalms, hymns, and spiritual songs believers reveal their *gratitude* to God. On this theme Paul now enlarges as follows: **20. giving thanks always for all things in the name of our Lord Jesus Christ to (our) God and Father.** See what has been said about this passage earlier, on p. 45. In addition, the following:

### *Proper Thanksgiving*

1. *What is it?*

Thanksgiving is grateful acknowledgment of benefits received. It presupposes that the person who engages in this activity recognizes three things: *a.* that the blessings which he enjoys *were bestowed upon himself,* so that in all honesty he cannot give *himself* the credit for them; *b. that he is totally unworthy* of them; and *c.* that they are *great and manifold.*

Paul has mentioned the giving of thanks once before in this chapter (5:4). He refers to it again and again in his epistles. So important does he regard it that he wants believers to be "overflowing with thanksgiving" (Col. 2:7). Gratitude is that which completes the circle whereby blessings that drop down into the hearts and lives of believers return to the Giver in the form of unending, loving, and spontaneous adoration. Properly pursued, such giving of thanks is a self-perpetuating attitude and activity, for it implies a review of blessings received. Naturally, such a review, the purposeful concentration of attention upon benefits, causes them to stand out more clearly, resulting in increased thanksgiving. The expression of gratitude is therefore a most blessed response to favors undeserved. While it lasts, worries tend to disappear, complaints vanish, courage to face the future is increased, virtuous resolutions are formed, peace is experienced, and God is glorified.

2. *When must it take place?*

The apostle says, "always." It is proper to give thanks *after* the blessing has been received, that is, when the situation that caused alarm has passed and quiet has been restored, as did the Israelites *after* their passage through the Red Sea (Exod. 15); as did the author of Ps. 116 *after* the Lord had heard his prayer; and as one day the glorious multitude will do on the shores of the sea of crystal (Rev. 15). It is also proper to give thanks *in the very midst* of distress, as did Jonah when he was in "the fish's belly" (Jonah 2:1, 9). It is even proper to sing songs of praise and thanksgiving *before* the battle has commenced, as Jehoshaphat ordered (II Chron. 20:21). *Always* believers can and should give thanks because there is never a moment when they are not under the watchful eye of Jehovah whose very name indicates that his mercies are unchangeable and will never fail.

3. *For what must thanks be given?*

Paul answers, "for all things." Hence, gratitude must be felt and expressed for blessings physical and spiritual; "ordinary" and extraordinary; past, present, and future (the latter, because they are included in an infallible promise); and even for things withheld and for things received. It should be constantly borne in mind that the one who, under the guidance of the Spirit, issued this admonition was himself a prisoner while he so commanded. But *in spite of* his chain, nay rather *for* his chain, he thanked God (Phil. 1:12-14). He was able to "take pleasure in weaknesses, injuries, hardships, and frustrations" (II Cor. 12:10). Again and again during this imprisonment Paul thanks God and exhorts those whom he addresses to be thankful also (Eph. 1:16; 5:4, 20; Phil. 1:3, 12-21; Col. 1:3, 12; 2:4; 3:17; 4:2; Philem. 4). This may seem very strange. It is, however, entirely consistent with the rest of Paul's teachings, for it harmonizes beautifully with the assurance that "to them that love God *all things* work together for good" and that "in all these things we are more than conquerors through him that loved us" with a love from which we can never be separated (Rom. 8:28-39).

4. *How must thanks be given?*

The answer is "in the name of our Lord Jesus Christ," because it was he who earned all these blessings for us, so that we receive them all "together with him" (Rom. 8:32). It is also he who will purify our petitions and thanksgivings and, thus purified, will present them, together with his own intercession, before the countenance of the Father.

5. *To whom must it be offered?*

The answer is "to (our) God and Father." There are those who never give thanks at all. Like the rich fool in the parable that is recorded in Luke 12:16-21 they seem to give themselves the credit for everything they possess or have accomplished. There are others, however, who sense their obligations *to their neighbors.* They recognize *secondary causes,* but never the *First Cause* (Rom. 1:21). Since, however, the Ephesians knew that all their blessings were constantly coming from God, the God who in Christ Jesus is their Father, and since they also were aware of the fact that they constituted part of "the Father's Family" (see on 3:14, 15), so that every benefit which they had received, were now receiving, or would still receive, proceeded from his love, they must have been able to understand the reasonableness of the exhortation that to this God and Father of theirs they should ascribe constant thanksgiving and praise.

Having exhorted the Ephesians with respect to their duty to God, Paul very logically concludes this section by admonishing them in regard to their obligation toward each other. He does this in words which at the same time form an excellent transition to the thoughts with which he will be occupied in the next paragraph.[149]

Paul has been urging the Ephesians to express their thanksgiving to God by means of psalms, hymns, and spiritual songs. Now in order that this may be done successfully two things are necessary: *a.* that the thanksgiving and praise be addressed in the proper manner to the proper person, and *b.* that there be harmony among the singers. In a choir every singer must know his place so that his voice may blend with that of others. In an orchestra there must be no discord. Hence, Paul states: **21. subjecting yourselves** [150] **to each other out of reverence for Christ.**[151] Again and again our Lord, while on earth, emphasized this very thought, namely, that each disciple should be willing to be the least (Matt. 18:1-4; 20:28) and to wash the other disciples' feet (John 13:1-17). Substantially the same thought is also expressed in Rom. 12:10: "in honor preferring one another" and in Phil. 2:3: "(doing) nothing from selfish ambition or from empty conceit, but in humble-mindedness each counting the other better than himself." Cf. I Peter 5:5. *Affection* for one another, *humility,* and a *willingness to cooperate* with other members of the body are the graces that are implied here in Eph. 5:21. The thought of the passage recalls what the apostle had said

---

[149] With A.R.V. and Lenski I include this verse in the present section, contrary to the paragraphing found in R.S.V., Hodge, etc. The reasons given by Lenski for so doing are mine also, namely, *a.* the sentence simply continues, with durative present participle similar to those that precede; *b.* the mention of mutual subjection here in verse 21 differs from subjection of wives to husbands, children to parents, and slaves to masters, discussed in the next section; and *c.* a new subject begins with verse 22: table of household duties.

It is necessary to add, however, that the relation between verse 21 and those that follow is close, since in both cases the matter of willingness to subject oneself is discussed. In fact verse 22 borrows its implied predicate from verse 21. Note how N.E.B., probably to indicate the transitional nature of verse 21, makes of it a little paragraph all by itself.

[150] The simplest construction would be to regard all these five present participles – speaking, singing, making melody, giving thanks, and subjecting (yourselves) – as governed by "be filled with the Spirit" (5:18). So construed, all of them have the force of present imperatives. When one is filled with the Spirit he will wish to engage in the activities indicated by the participles. A hostile attitude toward these activities, or an attempt at unconcern or so-called neutrality, shows that the individual to whom this would apply is not Spirit-indwelt.

[151] The better manuscripts read Χριστοῦ, not θεοῦ on which A.V. "in the fear of God" is based.

earlier in this same letter: "with all lowliness and meekness, with long-suffering, enduring one another in love, making every effort to preserve the unity imparted by the Spirit by means of the bond (consisting in) peace" (4:2, 3). Paul knew by experience what would happen in a church when this rule is disobeyed (I Cor. 1:11, 12; 3:1-9; 11:17-22; 14:26-33). He therefore stresses the fact that "out of reverence for Christ," that is, with a conscious regard for his clearly revealed will, every member of the body should be willing to recognize the rights, needs, and wishes of the others. Thus believers will be able to present a united front to the world, the blessing of true Christian fellowship will be promoted, and God in Christ will be glorified.

# Chapter 4:17–6:9

Verses 5:22–6:9

Theme: *The Church Glorious*

II. *Exhortation*
*urging*

*G* lorious Renewal
2. upon special groups

22 Wives, (be subject) to y o u r own husbands as to the Lord, 23 for the husband is head of the wife as also Christ is head of the church, he himself (being) the Savior of the body. 24 Then, just as the church is subject to Christ so also wives (should be subject) to their husbands in everything. 25 Husbands, love y o u r wives just as also Christ loved the church and gave himself up for her; 26 that he might sanctify her, cleansing her by the washing of water in connection with the spoken word; 27 in order that he might present the church to himself brilliant in purity, having no spot or wrinkle or any such thing, but that she might be holy and faultless. 28 That is the way husbands also ought to love their own wives as their own bodies. He who loves his own wife loves himself; 29 for no one ever hated his own flesh; on the contrary, he nourishes it and cherishes it, just as also Christ (does) the church, 30 because we are members of his body. 31 "Therefore shall a man leave his father and mother, and shall cleave to his wife; and the two shall become one flesh." 32 This mystery is great, but I am speaking with reference to Christ and the church. 33 Nevertheless, let each one of y o u also love his own wife as himself, and let the wife see to it that she respects her husband.

6 1 Children, obey y o u r parents in the Lord, for this is right. 2 "Honor your father and your mother," which is a commandment of foremost significance, with a promise attached: 3 "that it may be well with you" and that y o u may be on earth a long time. 4 and fathers, do not provoke y o u r children to anger but rear them tenderly in the discipline and admonition of the Lord. 5 Slaves, be obedient to those who according to the flesh are y o u r masters, with fear and trembling, in the sincerity of y o u r heart, as to Christ, 6 not in the way of eye-service as men-pleasers, but as slaves of Christ, doing the will of God from the heart, 7 with ready mind rendering service as to the Lord and not to men, 8 knowing that whatever good each one does this he will receive back from the Lord, whether (he be) slave or free. 9 And masters, do the same things for them, and stop threatening, knowing that (he who is) both their master and y o u r s is in the heavens, and there is no partiality with him.

5:22–6:9

As indicated previously (see p. 208) the theme Glorious Renewal is here continued but is now applied to special groups; as follows: wives and their husbands (5:22-33); children and their parents (6:1-4); and slaves and their masters (6:5-9).

a. 5:22-33

*"Wives, be subject to y o u r own husbands.*
*Husbands, love y o u r wives."*

**22. Wives, (be subject)** [152] **to y o u r own husbands as to the Lord.** Some of the material found in 5:22–6:9 parallels Col. 3:18–4:1. Wherever it does,

[152] The verb is undoubtedly to be supplied from the preceding verse (cf. same verb in Col. 3:18).

I refer the reader to N.T.C. on Colossians and Philemon, pp. 167–177, for *details* of exegesis. This will leave more room for expatiating in the present Commentary on those Ephesian passages that are not found in Colossians.

No institution on earth is more sacred than that of the family. None is more basic. As is the moral and religious atmosphere in the family, so will it be in the church, the nation, and society in general. Now in his kindness toward womanhood, the Lord, fully realizing that within the family much of the care of children will rest on the wife, has been pleased not to overburden her. Hence, he placed *ultimate* responsibility with respect to the household upon the shoulders of her husband, in keeping with the latter's creational endowment. So here, through his servant, the apostle Paul, the Lord assigns to the wife the duty of obeying her husband. This obedience must be a voluntary submission on her part, and that only to *her own* husband, not to *every man*. What will make this obedience easier, moreover, is that she is asked to render it "as to the Lord," that is, as part of her obedience to him, the very One who died for her. Continued: **23. for the husband is head of the wife.** A home without a head is an invitation to chaos. It spells derangement and disaster worse even than that which results when a nation is without a ruler or an army without a commander. For excellent reasons (see I Tim. 2:13, 14) it has pleased God to assign to the husband the task of being the head of the wife, hence also of the family. This headship, moreover, implies more than rulership, as is clear from the words which follow, namely, **as also Christ is head of the church, he himself (being) the Savior of the body.** This statement may come as a surprise to those who have been used to place undue stress on a husband's *authority* over his wife. To be sure, he has that authority and should exercise it, but never in a domineering manner. The comparison with Christ as head of the church (cf. 1:22; 4:15; Col. 1:18) reveals in what sense the husband is the wife's head. He is her head *as being vitally interested in her welfare.* He is her *protector. His pattern is Christ who, as head of the church, is its Savior!* What Paul is saying, therefore, amounts to this: the wife should voluntarily submit herself to her husband whom God has appointed as her head. She should recognize that, in his capacity as her head, her husband is so closely united to her and so deeply concerned about her welfare that his relation to her is patterned after the sacrificial interest of Christ in his church, which he purchased with his own blood! One is reminded of those many Old Testament passages in which Jehovah's love for his people is vividly portrayed. There is, for example, the story of Hosea's unfailing tenderness toward his wife Gomer. Though the latter was not true to him, went after other "lovers," and conceived "children of whoredom," nevertheless Hosea, instead of rejecting her, slips away to the haunt of shame, buys her back for fifteen pieces of silver and a homer and a half of barley, and mercifully restores her to her former position of honor (Hos. 1–3;

11:8; 14:4). For similar passages describing the Husband's (Jehovah's) marvelous reclaiming love see Isa. 54:1-8; 62:3-5; Jer. 3:6-18; 31:31-34. Let the wife, therefore, obey her husband who loves her so very, very much! And let her bear in mind that by being obedient to her husband she is being obedient to her Lord.

Not everyone accepts this interpretation of the passage. In addition to those who interpret the clause, "he himself (being) the Savior of the body" as a direct reference *not* to Christ but to *the husband* as being the defender of the wife (in which case the translation becomes *savior,* not *Savior*), an interpretation so completely out of line with the immediately preceding words that it deserves no further comment, there are also those who believe that the reference to Christ as the church's Savior is a kind of *aside,* or else expresses "a relation which Christ bears to the church which finds no analogy in that of the husband to the wife" (Hodge, *op. cit.,* p. 313). Just why the apostle would have inserted this clause if it had nothing to do with the subject is not explained. Calvin, on the other hand, in commenting on the words, "And he is the Savior [or "savior"] of the body," makes the following very apt remark, "The pronoun *he* is supposed by some to refer to *Christ;* and by others to *the husband.* It applies more naturally, in my opinion, to Christ, but still with a view to the present subject. In this point, as well as in others the resemblance ought to hold." Incidentally, I might call attention to the fact that in Calvin's own case the resemblance between *a.* Christ's love and care for his church and *b.* Calvin's love and care for Idelette certainly held. Contrary to the opinion of many who are ever picturing John Calvin as a stern, autocratic individual, here was a man who loved his wife very tenderly; while she, in turn loved and obeyed him with the same complete devotion.[153] Says P. Schaff, in commenting on Calvin's character, and in particular on the relation between Calvin and his wife, "Nothing can be more unjust than the charge that Calvin was cold and unsympathetic" (*History of the Christian Church,* New York, 1923, Vol. VII, p. 417).

Paul summarizes the contents of verses 22 and 23 as follows: **24. Then,**[154]

---

[153] Read Edna Gerstner's *Idelette,* Grand Rapids, Mich., 1963. This is a biographical novel rich in authentic detail. Cf. L. Penning, *Life and Times of Calvin,* translated by B. S. Berrington, London, 1912, pp. 145–148.

[154] The interpretation of ἀλλά as if it is always adversative has led to many wrong interpretations, one of them being that the apostle meant to say, "*But* even though the relation of Christ to the church is unique, for he is the Savior of the body and as such cannot be imitated, *nevertheless* wives should be subject to their husbands," etc. What is forgotten is the fact that ἀλλά has other meanings besides *but, yet, nevertheless.* I agree with Grosheide when he states that in the present instance ἀλλά *summarizes* (*op. cit.,* p. 87). This view is also in line with L.N.T. (A. and G.), p. 38, which interprets the meaning of the particle as used here in 5:24 to be *now, then;* meaning No. 6. It is true that there is a sense in which the act whereby Christ saved the church cannot be imitated, as has been explained in detail in my comments on 5:1. There is, however, also a sense in which Christ's

**just as the church is subject to Christ so also wives (should be subject) to their husbands in everything.** The submission of the church to Christ is voluntary, wholehearted, sincere, enthusiastic. It is a submission prompted not only by a conviction, "This is right and proper because God demands it," but also by love in return for Christ's love (I John 4:19). Let the same be true with respect to the submission of wives to their husbands. Moreover, that obedience must not be partial, so that the wife obeys her husband when the latter's wishes happen to coincide with her own, but complete: "in everything." This little phrase must, however, not be interpreted as if it meant *"absolutely everything."* If the husband should demand her to do things contrary to the moral and spiritual principles established by God himself, submission would be wrong (Acts 5:29; cf. 4:19, 20). With this exception, however, her obedience should be complete.

The admonition addressed to *husbands* begins as follows: **25. Husbands, love y o u r wives, just as also Christ loved the church and gave himself up for her.** The love required must be deep-seated, thorough-going, intelligent and purposeful, a love in which the entire personality – not only the emotions but also the mind and the will – expresses itself.[155] The main characteristic of this love, however, is that it is spontaneous and self-sacrificing, for it is compared to the love of Christ whereby he *gave himself up* for the church. More excellent love than that is inconceivable (John 10:11-15; 15:13; I John 3:16). See also on 5:2.

When a believing husband loves his wife in this fashion obedience from the side of his believing wife will be easy. Illustration taken from life: "My husband loves me so thoroughly and is so good to me that I jump at the opportunity to obey him." That was putting it beautifully!

Christ loved the church and gave himself up for her, **26. that he might sanctify her,** separating her unto God and to his service, that *positively;* and *negatively:* **cleansing her,** that is, delivering her from sin's guilt and pollution (Heb. 9:22, 23; 10:29), this two-fold process (sanctifying and cleansing) of necessity occurring simultaneously and not finished until death.[156] Con-

---

sacrificial love can and should serve as an example. To be sure, *John* 3:16 is true, but so is *I John* 3:16! To deny this, as happens so frequently, even in the name of Calvinism, is a superimposition of doctrine on exegesis with which John Calvin himself would never have agreed, as is indicated by his own comments on this passage.

[155] I base this interpretation not so much on the use of ἀγαπάω instead of φιλέω here in 5:25, as on the manner in which the love that is required of husbands is here described, namely, as a love patterned after that of Christ for his church. As to the verb ἀγαπάω itself in comparison with φιλέω, Paul uses the latter only twice (I Cor. 16:22 and Titus 3:15). He uses ἀγαπάω more than thirty times. Evidently the verb ἀγαπάω, though in most cases (as here) retaining its full distinctive meaning, is beginning to push out the verb φιλέω, by absorbing some of its contents. A clear distinction is not always demonstrable. See N.T.C. on the Gospel according to John, Vol. II, pp. 494–500.

[156] The fact that the aorist active subjunctive ἁγιάσῃ is followed by the aorist active participle καθαρίσας does not necessarily mean that Christ by his death first cleansed

tinued: **by the washing of water.** As to the first noun, here, as in Titus 3:5, the only other occurrence of this word in the New Testament, the right translation is in all probability *washing,* rather than *laver* or *basin for washing.*[157] But while Titus 3:5 (on which see N.T.C. on I and II Timothy and Titus, pp. 391, 392) speaks of "a washing *of regeneration* and renewing by the Holy Spirit," the Ephesian passage mentions the washing *of water* **in connection with the spoken word.** Though the two passages are certainly closely related, they are not identical. This "washing of (or: "with") water" here in Eph. 2:26 can hardly have reference to anything else than to baptism. So much should be clear. However, does this mean that the rite *as such* purifies and sanctifies? If so I would have to retract everything I said a moment ago with reference to sanctifying and cleansing being two aspects of a lifelong process. The meaning then would simply be this: "Christ loved the church and gave himself up for her in order that he might *by means of the rite of baptism with water* sanctify and cleanse her." An outward rite would then impart an inward grace. An enormous significance would thus be assigned to baptism with water! That external rite would take care of just about everything. Having been baptized, little else would be needed. The death of Christ would have occurred in order to bring about that *one* and only necessary experience, so that thereby the person who undergoes it might be saved for all eternity. Not many would endorse such an extreme view. But let us guard ourselves also against moving too far in that general direction.[158]

---

his people and that he then subsequently sanctifies them. The aorist as such can refer to either antecedent or simultaneous action. In the present instance it is hard to construe this participle in the former sense. The fact that verb and participle are aorists, moreover, does not in any way indicate the amount of time involved, whether it be short or long. Although it is true that justification takes place once for all, while sanctification is a continuous process, the present passage does not in any way prove that the participle *cleansing* refers exclusively to *justification,* while the verb *sanctify* refers exclusively to *sanctification.* The distinction is probably simply between the *negative* and the *positive* aspects of the operation of the Holy Spirit in the hearts and lives of God's children.

[157] Simpson, who made a special study of this word, points out that ὁ λουτήρ, not τὸ λουτρόν, is the LXX vocable for the laver of Judaism, and that λουτρόν, both in Attic and Hellenistic Greek, as often signifies the act of washing as the vessel or the locality of ablution. See his work, *The Pastoral Epistles,* London, 1954, pp. 114 ff.

[158] It is interesting to read Lenski's very positively expressed views regarding this matter, *op. cit.,* pp. 632–635. He stresses the fact that Paul is referring to baptism with "actual water," "most definite water." He further emphasizes that this baptism with water is "a washing of regeneration in the Holy Spirit" (Titus 3:5), and that the phrase "in connection with the spoken word" unquestionably refers to *the baptismal formula* as spoken by the administrant. As to the statement by Robertson, namely, "Neither there [I Cor. 6:11] nor here [Eph. 5:26] does Paul mean that the cleansing or sanctification took place in the bath save in a symbolic fashion," he remarks, "The plainest Greek is not proof against dogmatic prejudice, — a warning to all exegetes." The warning in connection with the dogmatic prejudice should certainly be taken to heart by all of us. Was it taken fully to heart by Lenski?

It is not the rite of baptism with water that saves. It is "the washing of water *in connection with the spoken word*" that is used as means of sanctification and cleansing. And there is nothing in the context that would indicate that this "spoken word" is to be restricted to the baptismal formula. Let Paul be his own interpreter. In the very next chapter (6:17) he tells the Ephesians, "And take . . . the sword of the Spirit which is *the spoken word of God.*" He surely cannot have meant that this sword of the Spirit which believers must wield is nothing else than the baptismal formula! It is, of course, *the gospel, the entire Word of God.* Compare Christ's petition, *"Sanctify them in the truth; thy word is truth"* (John 17:17). Hence, in connection with the present passage (5:26) the interpretation must be that when the meaning of baptism is explained to, understood by, and through the operation of the Holy Spirit applied to the minds and hearts of those who are baptized – and, of course, this takes place throughout life – the purpose of Christ's death is accomplished and believers are sanctified and cleansed. Baptism, to be sure, is important. It is a marvelous blessing. It is not only *a symbol* but also *a seal, a picture* and a definite *assurance* of the fact that God's gracious promise of salvation will certainly be realized in the life of the baptized individual who trusts in him. By means of this precious sacrament the gracious invitation to full surrender is made *very vivid* and *very personal.* But it has no saving efficacy apart from the word applied to the heart by the Spirit. Cf. John 3:5; Rom. 10:8; I Peter 1:25. It is exactly as Calvin, commenting on this passage, says: "If *the word* is taken away, the whole power of the sacraments is gone. What else are the sacraments but seals of the word? . . . By *the word* is here meant the promise, which explains the value and use of signs."

The *immediate* purpose of Christ's self-abasement (verse 25b) having been stated in verse 26, Paul now (in verse 27) indicates the *ultimate* purpose; or, expressing it differently, he shows to what end Christ sanctified and cleansed the church: **27. in order that he might present the church to himself brilliant in purity.** The church is even now *in essence* "Christ's bride." However, as such she has not yet been made manifest in all her beauty. The wedding is a matter of the future.

In order to understand the present passage it is necessary to review the marriage customs implied in Scripture. First, there was *the betrothal.* This was considered more binding than "engagement" with us. The terms of the marriage are accepted in the presence of witnesses and God's blessing is pronounced upon the union. From this day groom and bride are *legally* husband and wife (II Cor. 11:12). Next comes *the interval* between betrothal and the wedding-feast. The groom may have selected this period to pay the dowry to the father of the bride, that is, if this had not already been done (Gen. 34:12). Then there is *the preparation* and *procession* with a view to the wedding feast. The bride prepares and adorns herself. The groom also arrays himself in his best attire, and, accompanied by his friends, who sing and bear torches, proceeds to the home of the betrothed. *He receives the bride* and conveys her, with a returning procession, to the place where the wedding-feast will be held. Finally, the great event arrives: *the wedding-feast* itself, including *the wedding-banquet.* The festivities may last seven or even twice seven days (Matt. 22:1-14).

Now Scripture again and again compares the love-relationship between Jehovah and his people, or between Christ and his church, to a bridegroom and his bride (Ps. 45; Isa. 50:1; 54:1-8; 62:3-5; Jer. 2:32; 3:6-18; 31:31-34; Hos. 1–3; 11:8; 14:4; Matt. 9:15; John 3:29; II Cor. 11:2; Rev. 19:7; 21:2, 9). The church is betrothed to Christ. Christ has paid the dowry for her. He has bought the one who *is* essentially – *is to be* eschatologically – his bride:

> "From heaven he came and sought her
> To be his holy bride;
> With his own blood he bought her,
> And for her life he died."
>
> Samuel J. Stone, lines taken
> from the hymn, "The Church's
> One Foundation."

The "interval" of relative separation has arrived. It refers to this entire dispensation between Christ's ascension to heaven and his coming again. Now it is during this period that the bride must make herself ready. She will array herself in fine linen, glistening and pure. See Rev. 19:8 for metaphorical meaning. However, Paul looks at this preparation of the bride from the divine point of view. *It is the bridegroom himself, even Christ, who here in 5:27 is described as preparing the one who one day will be manifested as his bride, so that she will be "brilliant in purity."* The *presentation* here referred to must be viewed as definitely eschatological, that is, as referring to the great consummation when Jesus returns upon clouds of glory. Not only is it true that "the wife of the Lamb" *makes herself* ready (Rev. 19:7), and not only with a view to the future do God's duly appointed servants perform a function in this respect (II Cor. 11:2; Phil. 1:10; 2:16; Col. 1:28; I Thess. 2:19, 20; I John 2:28), but Christ himself readies her in order to present her to himself. The point stressed is, of course, that she, the church, can do nothing in her own power. She owes all her beauty to him, the bridegroom. It is for that very reason that when she is at last manifested in full view she is seen to be so brilliant in purity, that she answers the description as here given, namely, **having no spot or wrinkle or any such thing, but that she might be holy and faultless.** The word "spot" is in the New Testament confined to this passage and II Peter 2:13. In the latter passage the word used in the original has been rendered "spots" (A.V.,

A.R.V.), and "blots" (R.S.V.). It there refers to *persons.* M.M., p. 584, quotes a passage in which it is applied similarly and can be translated "dregs" ("the dregs of humanity from the city"). The word "wrinkle" is in the New Testament found only here in 5:27. It occurs neither in the Septuagint nor in the Apocrypha, but is otherwise not uncommon. It is useless to try to distinguish between the resultant reference or metaphorical sense of these two words. The combination of the two in the present passage simply *stresses* the fact that when in the day of days the victorious Lord of lords and King of kings presents the church to himself she will have *no moral or spiritual stain whatever.* The Bridegroom, *because of his great love for his bride* (note connection between verses 27 and 28) is going to present her *to himself* "holy and faultless" (see 1:4 for explanation). To be sure, he performs this deed of *joyful public acknowledgment* with a view to himself, that *he* may therein rejoice and be glorified, for salvation never ends in man, always in God. Nevertheless, is not this marvelous welcome which the bride will receive also *her* supreme honor? Does it not indicate that she is and will forever remain the object of his everlasting delight? Cf. Zeph. 3:17. **28. That is the way husbands also ought to love their own wives as their own bodies;** not meaning: they should love their own wives just as they love their own bodies, but they should love their own wives, as being their own bodies. The husband is the head of the wife, as Christ is the head of the church. Hence, as the church is Christ's body, so the wife is in a sense the husband's body. Thus intimately are the two united. Therefore, husbands should love their wives. The thought of verse 25 is repeated here and strengthened. In the light of the immediately preceding context (verses 26 and 27) the thought now expressed is that not only should husbands love their wives with self-sacrificing love, a love patterned after that of Christ for his church, but also, in so doing, they should help their wives to make progress in sanctification. A large order, indeed! Husbands should love their wives for what they are and should also love them sufficiently to help them to become what they should be. **He who loves his own wife loves himself,** for, as already implied in the preceding statement, the wife is part of him, that is, has become intimately united with him. See on verse 31. Paul is already thinking of the words of Gen. 2:24 which he is going to quote a little later. Now if this fact, namely, that the wife is the husband's body, has been grasped, then the husband will indeed love his wife. **29. for no one ever hated his own flesh,** that is, his own body; **on the contrary, he nourishes it,** supplies it with food, etc., **and cherishes it.** For *nourishing* see also on 6:4; for *cherishing,* I Thess. 2:7. Each of these words in its own right, and even more, in combination with the other, indicates the attention that is paid to the body. Paul is, however, not thinking only of supplying the body with barely enough food, clothing and shelter to enable it to eke out a mere existence; he refers instead to the bounteous, elaborate, unremitting, and sympathetic care we bestow on our bodies. Continued: **just as also Christ (does) the church, 30. because we are members of his body.**[159] There is never a moment that Christ does not tenderly watch over his body, the church. We are under his constant surveillance. His eyes are constantly upon us, from the beginning of the year even to the end of the year (cf. Deut. 11:12). Therefore we cast all our anxiety upon him, convinced that we are his personal concern (I Peter 5:7), the objects of his *very special* providence.

It is striking that the apostle, who has been referring to Christ as the head and to the church as his body (see especially verses 23 and 29) and who, by clear implication, has described him as the bridegroom and the church as the bride (verse 27), now suddenly refers to *the individual members* of that body, and even more strikingly, though not at all contrary to his custom, *includes himself: "we* are members of his body" (cf. Rom. 12:5). The reason must be that Paul, *the prisoner* – this must never be lost sight of – is deeply touched by this marvelous fact that his own life, too, is dear to the heart of him who is enthroned in heavenly majesty; and, adds Paul, as it were, so are the lives of *all* believers. Paul loved them all and was never able to think of himself alone (II Tim. 4:8). It soothes the apostle to reflect on the truth that "Christ leaves us not when the storm is high, and we have comfort for he is nigh." Therefore, also, thus is his argument, we as members of his body, urged on by his example and enabled by his Spirit, should do to others as Christ does to us. And since Christ as our head, so assiduously cares for us, members of his body, let husbands take this to heart and let them strive to emulate Christ in the loving attention which they focus upon *their* bodies, that is, upon their wives. This, moreover, is in harmony with the divine command[160] recorded in Gen. 2:24, an ordinance that has been in the background of Paul's thinking all the while and which he now finally quotes, almost exactly[161] according to the Septuagint (Greek) translation of

---

[159] Although Hodge, Simpson and others favor the retention of the words "of his flesh and of his bones" (A.V.), the latter claiming that they have "strong MSS. support," and the former that "they are required by the context," I cannot join their company. The external evidence for their retention does not impress me as being nearly as strong as is that for their omission, and since in the present paragraph the oneness of Christ and his church has been stressed over and over, I do not see that anything is lost when they are left out.

[160] As G. Ch. Aalders has pointed out in his commentary *Het Boek Genesis* (a volume in *Korte Verklaring der Heilige Schrift*), Kampen, 1949, Vol. I, p. 127, this is indeed a divine command or ordinance. If those were right who are of the opinion that the Genesis passage (whether ascribed to Adam or to Moses) merely indicates what usually happens, or prophetically, what will generally happen, namely, that a man will leave his father and his mother, etc., the Lord would not have appealed to it as to an ordinance of God (Matt. 19:5, 6).

[161] The phrase ἀντὶ τοῦτο, with which the passage opens here in Eph. 5:31 and which has been interpreted variously, should really present no difficulty. It represents the Hebrew *'al-kēn* = "therefore." The Septuagint has **ἕνεκεν τοῦτου**: *on account*

the Hebrew passage: **31. "Therefore shall a man leave his father and his mother and shall cleave to his wife."** The word "therefore" does not connect with anything here in 5:31. It belongs to the Genesis context. Adam rejoiced when he received Eve from the hand of Jehovah God. He gave expression to his joy and to his faith by saying, "This, indeed, is bone of my bones and flesh of my flesh! She shall be called *Ishshah* (Woman), because she was taken out of *Ish* (Man)" (Gen. 2:23). There follows: "Therefore shall a man leave his father and his mother," etc. The reasoning in Genesis is accordingly on this order: since, by virtue of creation, the bond between husband and wife is stronger than any other human relationship, surpassing even that between parents and children, therefore it is ordained that a man shall leave his father and his mother and shall cleave to his wife. God mercifully bases his *marriage ordinance* upon man's own natural inclination, the strong bent or desire with which the Almighty himself endowed him. Quotation continued: **"and the two shall become one flesh."** Whatever else this may mean as to oneness in mind, heart, purpose, etc., basically, as the very words (*cleave, flesh*) in their combination imply, the reference is to sexual union. Cf. I Cor. 6:16. In a very real sense, therefore, the two are no longer two but one. When we consider the fact that this intimate conjugal act is here placed in a context of love so deep, so self-sacrificing, so tender and pure that it (this love) is patterned after that of Christ for his church, it will be clear that no more noble description of the relation of a husband to his wife has ever been presented or is even possible. Incidentally, we are also shown here that consistent Christian living touches every phase of life, not excluding sex. The chain of our conduct as believers is as strong as is its weakest link. Note also, that according to this passage *the two* – not the three, four, five, or six – become *one* flesh. Cf. Matt. 19:5, 6. All adultery and promiscuity, by whatever fancy name it may be called, is here condemned. Cf. Matt. 5:32; Rom. 7:1-3.

Paul adds: **32. This mystery is great, but I am speaking with reference to Christ and the church.** In a footnote I list various explanations of this passage which I cannot accept.[162] Unless the context is kept in view a cor-

---

*of this,* but the meaning is the same. See my doctoral dissertation *The Meaning of the Preposition ἀντί in the New Testament,* 1948, p. 93.

[162] The following are just a few of the many that have been offered. The mystery is: God's purpose to unite all things in Christ, the oneness of believers with Christ, the fact that two can become one, the mysterious attraction of male for female and vice versa, the *sacrament* of marriage. The Roman Catholic view is in line with the rendering found in the Vulgate: *sacramentum hoc magnum est.* Calvin comments: "They have no ground for such an assertion [that marriage is a sacrament], unless it be that they have been deceived by the doubtful signification of a Latin word, or rather, by their ignorance of the Greek language. If the simple fact had been observed that *Mystery* is the word used by Paul, a mistake would never have occurred. We see the hammer and anvil by which they fabricate this sacrament. . . . This blunder arose from the greatest ignorance." And it is true, indeed, that if in

rect interpretation will be impossible. Paul has just now spoken about the marriage ordinance, in accordance with which *two* people become so intimately united that in a sense they become *one*. *"This mystery* is great," he says. He must, therefore, be referring to marriage. However, he makes very clear that he is not thinking of marriage *in and by itself*. He definitely mentions once more the link between it and the Christ-church relationship. Accordingly, I can find no better answer to the question, "What is meant here by *the mystery,* that is, by *the secret that would have remained hidden had it not been revealed?"* than the one given by Robertson in his *Word Pictures,* Vol. IV, p. 547: "Clearly Paul means to say that the comparison of marriage to the union of Christ and the church is the mystery." The union of Christ with the church, so that, from the sweep of eternal delight in the presence of his Father, God's only begotten Son plunged himself into the *dreadful darkness and awful anguish of Calvary* in order to save his *rebellious people,* gathered from among all the nations, and even to dwell in their hearts through his Spirit and at last to present *them* – even these utterly undeserving ones – to himself as his own bride, with whom he becomes united in such intimate fellowship that no earthly metaphor can ever do justice to it, *this* even in and by itself is a mystery. Cf. 3:4-6; Col. 1:26, 27. But the fact that this marvelous love, this blissful Christ-church relationship, is actually reflected here on earth in the union of a husband and his wife, so that by the strength of the former bond (Christ-church), the latter (husband-wife) is now able to function most gloriously, bringing supreme happiness to the marriage-partners, blessing to mankind, and glory to God *that,* indeed, is the Mystery Supreme!

This idea of marriage should never be lost sight of by those who have been united in Christian matrimony. Every day the husband should ask himself, "Does my love for my wife reveal the marks of Christ's love for his church?" That high ideal must never be relinquished. A step toward its realization is mentioned in the words: **33. Nevertheless, let each one of y o u also love his own wife as himself.** Note: "his own" wife, not someone else; "each one," there is no room for exceptions; "as himself," no less; "constantly" (implied in the present, durative imperative), not off and on. And as far as the wife is concerned: **and let the wife see to it that she respects her husband** (see on verse 22). The rendering "respects" is probably the best one. In our English language "fear" (A.R.V.) is somewhat ambiguous. Though it may not be a *wrong* translation, for the verb *fear* can be employed in the sense of reverencing (A.V. "reverence"), nevertheless since, because of popular usage this word so easily conjures up visions of awe, dread, and fright, and since "There is no fear in love; but perfect love

---

order to be a *sacrament* a custom must have been instituted by Christ and if it must be "a visible sign of invisible grace" (Augustine), then marriage cannot properly be called a sacrament.

casts out fear" (I John 4:18), it is probably better to use the word "respects" (R.S.V.). Let, therefore, the wife see to it that she "pays her husband all respect" (N.E.B.).

b. 6:1-4

*"Children, obey y o u r parents.*
*Fathers, rear them tenderly."*

**6:1. Children, obey y o u r parents.** Compare the following passages: Exod. 20:12; 21:15-17; Lev. 20:9; Deut. 5:16; 21:8; Prov. 1:8; 6:20; 30:17; Mal. 1:6; Matt. 15:4-6; 19:19; Mark 7:10-13; 10:19; 18:20; Col. 3:20. The apostle assumes that among those who will be listening when this letter is read to the various congregations the children will not be lacking. They are included in God's covenant (Gen. 17:7; Acts 2:38, 39), and Jesus loves them (Mark 10:13-16). Were Paul to be present with us today he would be shocked at the spectacle of children attending the Sunday School and then going home just before the regular worship service. He has a word addressed directly and specifically to the children. The implication is clear that also today sermons should be such that even the children can understand and enjoy them, at least to some extent, varying with age, etc., and at times the pastor should direct his attention *especially to* them.

What the apostle tells the children is that they should obey their parents. This obedience, moreover, should flow not only from the feeling of love, gratitude, and esteem for their parents, though these motivations are very important, but also and especially from reverence for the Lord Jesus Christ. Paul says that it should be an obedience **in the Lord,** and he adds, **for this** obedience **is right.** The proper attitude of the child in obeying his parents must therefore be this: I must obey my parents because the Lord bids me to do so. What he says is *right* for the simple reason that *he* says it! It is he who determines what is right and what is wrong. Hence, when I obey my parents I am obeying and pleasing *my Lord.* When I disobey them I am disobeying and displeasing *him.* It is true that, in so ordering, God – or, if one prefers, Christ – shows his wisdom and love. Under God, these children owe their very existence to their parents. The parents, moreover, are older, have had more experience, know more, and as a rule are wiser. Also, when conditions are normal, until the time of marriage no one *loves* these children more intensely than do their parents. And even after the parent-child relationship has been replaced by the (in a sense) even closer bond of husband-wife, the parents, if still alive, continue to love their children no less than before.

Paul's emphasis on the fact that such obedience is right is strengthened by a reference to an express divine command: **2, 3. "Honor your father and your mother," which is a commandment of foremost significance, with a promise attached: "that it may be well with you" and that you may be on**

**earth a long time.** The apostle shows what an excellent pedagogue he is, for just as even today *the ten commandments* are among those portions of Scripture which children learn by heart in their early youth, so – and probably even more so – was this true in Israel. And may we not also believe that even the children in formerly *Gentile* families were soon taught the decalogue, so that their sense of guilt and instant need of the Savior might be sharpened and their gratitude to God for salvation received might find adequate expression in consecrated conduct? [163]

The quotation is from Exod. 20:12 and Deut. 5:16, the first part of it literally according to the Septuagint. *To honor* father and mother means more than *to obey* them, especially if this obedience is interpreted in a merely outward sense. It is the inner attitude of the child toward his parents that comes to the fore in the requirement that he *honor* them. All selfish obedience or reluctant obedience or obedience under terror is immediately ruled out. To honor implies to love, to regard highly, to show the spirit of respect and consideration. This honor is to be shown to *both* of the parents, for as far as the child is concerned they are equal in authority. What follows, namely, "which is the first commandment with promise" (A.V., A.R.V., and very similarly also R.S.V., N.E.B., Phillips, Moffatt, Weymouth, Berkeley) has led to much difficulty, in view of the fact that an earlier commandment, regarded by some as the first and by others as the second, also has a promise attached to it: "showing lovingkindness to thousands of them that love me and keep my commandments" (Exod. 20:6). Surely that promise *precedes* the one that accompanies the commandment to honor father and mother. How then can Paul say that the latter is *the first* commandment with a promise? Some proposed solutions:

1. Paul means: the first commandment of the second table of the law. Objection: The division into tables is not always the same. Besides, the Jews generally regarded the commandment to honor father and mother as belonging to the first table.

2. It was the first commandment that spoke to the heart of the child, the first one which had special meaning for him. Objection: The text does not read: "the first commandment *for the child*" but ". . . *with a promise.*"

3. It was actually the first commandment with a promise, for the earlier

[163] In the teaching of Jesus there is constant reference to the ten commandments either as a group or singly (Matt. 5:27-32; 15:4-6; 19:18, 19; 22:37-40; Mark 10:19; 12:28-31; Luke 18:20; and perhaps John 4:24). Paul, too, refers to one or more of them not only here in Eph. 6:2, 3, but also in Rom. 7:7-12; 13:8-10; Gal. 5:14, but never as a means to be saved. *The Didache,* which has been ascribed to the period A.D. 120–180, opens with a summary of the law and in its second chapter mentions several of its commandments. See also the so-called *Letter of Barnabas,* chapters 15 and 19. It seems that not only did the Jews diligently teach the commandments to their children and to Gentile proselytes but that these commandments also figured prominently in *Christian* instruction, although, of course, the *purpose* of this teaching differed widely in the two camps.

promise (Exod. 20:6) is of a general nature. It is a promise to all who love God and keep his commandments. Objection: Though the general nature of that earlier promise must be granted, it remains true that it was attached to *the second* (or *first,* whichever way one prefers to count) commandment, so that the commandment that children honor their parents was not *the first* with an attached promise.

4. It was *the most important commandment* of the entire decalogue, *the first,* therefore, *in rank,* though not in order of enumeration. Evaluation: I believe this comes close to the truth, though it is still erroneous. Is not *the first* commandment, "Thou shalt have no other gods before me," at least as important as is *the fifth* (or *fourth*)?

There is, however, another solution which I personally accept as the right one. We arrive at it by bearing in mind two things: *a.* that the word generally translated *first* may indicate *rank* as well as numerical sequence. Thus, when a scribe asked Jesus, "Which commandment is *the first* of all?" he did not mean, "Which commandment *is mentioned first?*" but *"Which is first in importance?"* And *b.* the original does not read *"the* first commandment"; it reads, *"a* commandment first," that is, "commandment of foremost significance," not necessarily *the* most important of all.

In what sense is it true that this commandment is *one of extraordinary significance,* being so important, in fact, that in Lev. 19:1 ff. the list of commandments under the general heading, "You shall be holy, for I Jehovah your God am holy" opens with this one? The answer is found in the promise that is attached to it, namely, "that it may be well with you and that you may be on earth a long time." Notice the slight change in the wording from what is found in Exod. 20:12 and Deut. 5:16. Paul, by divine inspiration, lifts the promise out of its old, theocratic form. He speaks not of living long "in the land which God has given you" but of *being on the earth a long time*. The promise "that it may be well with you" (Deut. 5:16) is, however, retained. When the objection is raised that in spite of this promise many disobedient children prosper and become very old, while many obedient children die early, the answer is that the principle here expressed is, nevertheless, entirely valid. To be sure, obedience or disobedience to parents is not the only factor that determines a person's span of life, but it is an important factor. Disobedience to godly parents indicates an undisciplined life. It leads to vice and dissipation. This, in turn, *all other things being equal,* shortens life. For example, when a devout father warns his son against the evil of chain-smoking, addiction to alcohol, sins pertaining to sex, etc., and the son disregards his advice, he is following a course that does not as a rule lead to long life on the earth. In addition it should be borne in mind that though a disobedient child may live on and on and become a centenarian, as long as he continues in his wickedness *it will not be well with him*. He will have no peace! Living, as we do, in an age in which such matters as self-discipline and respect for authority are frowned upon, it is well to take to heart what is taught here in 6:2, 3. Undisciplined children spell ruin for the nation, the church, and society! The promise of God to reward obedience still holds.

Not only to wives, children, and slaves are these admonitions directed, however. Also to husbands, parents, and masters. *Glorious Renewal* must be experienced by all. So Paul, having addressed the children, turns now to the parents, and in particular to the fathers, though with application also to the mothers. **4. And fathers, do not provoke y o u r children to anger.** Note the fairness of these admonitions. The duty of wives is not stressed at the expense of that of husbands, nor that of slaves to the neglect of that of masters. So also here: the admonition addressed to fathers follows hard upon that directed to children. Although it is true that the word "fathers" at times includes "mothers" (Heb. 11:23), just as "brothers" may include "sisters," and that the directive here given certainly *applies also* to mothers, nevertheless it would hardly be correct in the present passage to substitute the word "parents" for "fathers." The fact that in verse 1 Paul employs the more usual word for *parents* seems to indicate that here in verse 4 *fathers* means just that. The reasons why the apostle addresses himself *especially* to them could well be *a.* because upon them as heads of their respective families the chief responsibility for the education of the children rests; and *b.* perhaps also because they, in certain instances even more than the mothers, are in need of the admonition here conveyed.

The parallel passage (Col. 3:21) has: "Fathers, do not exasperate y o u r children," meaning: "Do not embitter them or stir them up." There is very little essential difference between that and "Do not provoke y o u r children to anger." The cognate noun is "angry mood" (4:26). Some ways in which parents may become guilty of this error in bringing up their children:

1. *By over-protection.* The fathers – and mothers too – are so fearful that harm may befall their darlings that they fence them in from every direction: "Do not do this and do not do that. Do not go here and do not go there," until this process of pampering arrives at a point where we can almost imagine them to advise their offspring, "Do not venture into the water until you have learned to swim." Yet swim they must! To be sure, children should be warned against great dangers. On the other hand, a modicum of risk-taking is necessary for their physical, moral, and spiritual development. If the little bird remains in the safety of its nest it will never learn to fly. Besides, the over-protective attitude has the tendency of depriving the children of confidence and of instilling in them the angry mood, especially when they compare themselves with other children who are not receiving this special treatment.

2. *By favoritism.* Isaac favored Esau above Jacob. Rebekah preferred Jacob (Gen. 25:28). The sad results of such partiality are well known.

3. *By discouragement.* Example taken from life: "Dad, I am going to study hard and become a doctor," or perhaps a lawyer, teacher, mechanic, minister, or whatever it was the boy had in mind. Dad's answer: "You might as well forget about that. That will never happen anyway."

4. *By failure to make allowance for the fact that the child is growing up, has a right to have ideas of his own, and need not be an exact copy of his father to be a success.*

5. *By neglect.* In the quarrel between David and his son Absalom was the fault *entirely* on Absalom's side? Was not David also partly to blame because he neglected his son? (II Sam. 14:13, 28).

6. *By bitter words and outright physical cruelty.* Here is a father who loves to throw his weight around and to make use of his superior strength. Scolding his children and inflicting severe physical punishment has become a habit with him. Court records are filled with cases of unbelievable cruelty to boys and girls, including babes.

Paul places the positive over against the negative by continuing: **but rear them tenderly.** Fathers – mothers too – must provide their children with food, not only physical but also mental and spiritual. They must *nourish* them (see on 5:29), *rear them tenderly.*[164] "Let them be fondly cherished" (Calvin). However, this does not exclude *firmness:* **in the discipline and admonition of the Lord.** In Heb. 12:11 this word "discipline" refers to "chastening," which, though at the time when it is administered may not be pleasant, is appreciated afterward and produces excellent fruit. Cf. I Cor. 11:32; II Cor. 6:9; II Tim. 2:25. In II Tim. 3:16 this "discipline" is the "*training* in righteousness." "Discipline," accordingly, may be described as training by means of rules and regulations, rewards, and when necessary, punishments. It refers primarily to *what is done to the child.*

The meaning of the word rendered "admonition" appears from I Cor. 10:11, "These things were written for our *admonition,*" and from Titus 3:10, "After the first and second *warning* (or: admonition) have nothing to do with a factious person." "Admonition" is therefore prevailingly training by means of the spoken word, whether that word be teaching, warning, or encouragement. It refers primarily to *what is said to the child.* "Admonition" would seem to be somewhat milder than "discipline." Nevertheless, it must be earnest, not just a feeble observation such as, "No, my sons; it is not a good report that I hear" (I Sam. 2:24). In fact, it is distinctly reported that Eli "did not admonish them [his sons]" (I Sam. 3:13).[165]

All of this discipline and admonition must be "of the Lord." That should

---

[164] Since ἐκτρέφετε is used here as the antonym of *provoke to anger,* full justice should be done to its prefix; hence, *love* must replace *anger.* The children should be reared *tenderly.*

[165] See Trench, *Synonyms of the New Testament,* paragraph xxxii, an excellent treatment of the two terms παιδεία and νουθεσία.

be its *quality*. It should amount to *Christian* training, therefore, and this in its most comprehensive sense, certainly including giving the child a noble *example* of Christian life and conduct. The entire atmosphere in which the training is given must be such that the Lord can place the stamp of his approval upon it.

It is improper, in this connection, to overlook the fact that according to this passage (and cf. Deut. 6:7) not the state or society in general or even the church is *primarily* responsible for the training of the youth, though all of them have a vital interest in it and also a measure of responsibility with respect to it. But *under God* the child *belongs* first of all and most of all to the parents. It is they who should see to it that as far as they can help it those agencies that exert the most potent influence upon the child's rearing are definitely Christian. *The very heart* of Christian nurture is this: to bring *the heart* of the child to *the heart* of his Savior.[166]

c. 6:5-9

*"Slaves, obey y o u r masters. Masters, stop threatening."*

A rather detailed account of *Scripture on Slavery* will be found in N.T.C. on Colossians and Philemon, pp. 233–237. 5. **Slaves, be obedient to those who according to the flesh are y o u r masters.** Paul does not advocate the immediate, outright emancipation of the slaves. He took the social structure as he found it and endeavored by peaceful means to change it into its opposite. His rule amounted to this: Let the slave wholeheartedly obey his master, and let the master be kind to his slave. Thus the ill-will, dishonesty, and laziness of the slave would be replaced by willing service, integrity, and industry; the cruelty and brutality of the master, by considerateness and love. Slavery would be abolished *from within,* and a gloriously transformed society would replace the old. "Be obedient" is the same command used with reference to *children* in verse 1. There is comfort in the words "masters *according to the flesh,*" for it implies: "Y o u have another Master, who watches over y o u, is just and merciful to y o u in all his dealings, and to whom both y o u and y o u r earthly masters are responsible." Continued: **with fear and trembling.** Cf. II Cor. 7:15. Must they be filled with this spirit because they are slaves? No, "fear and trembling" befits anyone to whom the Lord has assigned a task (Phil. 2:12), Paul himself not excluded (I Cor. 2:3). It does not mean that slaves must approve of tyrannical methods or that they must melt with fear before their masters. It does mean, however, that they should be filled with conscientious solicitude when they recognize the real nature of their assignment, namely, so to conduct themselves toward their masters that the latter whether they be believers or not, will be able

166 For a discussion of the subject *Principles and Methods of Education in Israel: Background for the Understanding of II Tim. 3:15* see N.T.C. on I and II Timothy and Titus, pp. 296–301. A brief bibliography is included in footnote 160 on p. 299.

to see what the Christian faith accomplishes within the hearts of all who practice it, not excluding slaves. This implies, of course, that slaves will recognize their own inadequacy and ask the Lord to help them to realize this high purpose. Continued: **in the sincerity of y o u r heart;** or "with singleness of heart." That is, with an undivided mind, with integrity and uprightness (cf. I Chron. 29:17). This obedience should be rendered **as to Christ,** that is, fully realizing that they are actually rendering it to their heavenly Master, the Lord Jesus Christ. Hence, **6. not in the way of eye-service as men-pleasers, but as slaves of Christ, doing the will of God from the heart.** They must not obey simply to catch the eye of their masters for selfish purposes. They should not seek to please men with the ulterior motive of seeking profit for themselves. The apostle means, therefore: "Fill y o u r service with the energy and the enthusiasm with which y o u would fill it were it done for Christ, *for it really is being done for Christ.* It is to him that y o u belong. Take then that service of y o u r s and lift it to a higher plain. Do the will of God from the heart, with all enthusiasm. And remember that y o u have nothing to be ashamed of. Y o u r Lord himself was also a servant, even *the Servant of Jehovah.* It was he who girded himself with a towel and washed the feet of his disciples (John 13:1-20). It was also he who said, 'For the Son of man also came not to be ministered to (or: to be served) but to minister (or: to serve), and to give his life a ransom for many' (Mark 10:45). And it was he who 'emptied himself, as he took on the form of a servant . . . humbled himself and became obedient even to the extent of death, yes, death by a cross' (Phil. 2:7, 8)." Continued: **7. with ready mind rendering service as to the Lord and not to men.** In spirit people really cease to be slaves as soon as they begin to work for the Lord and are no longer working *primarily* for men. Beyond their master they see their Master. Illustration: when the man who was conveying a load of bricks on his wheel-barrow was asked what he was doing, his answer was, "I am building a cathedral for the Lord." With that thought in mind he was putting his whole soul into his job. Paul ends his admonition to slaves by writing: **8. knowing that whatever good each one does this he will receive back from the Lord, whether (he be) slave or free.** With God there is no partiality (Lev. 19:15; Mal. 2:9; Acts 10:34; Col. 3:25; James 2:1). This is brought out very forcefully, for literally the apostle says, "knowing that *each one* [note forward position of "each one" for emphasis] whatever he does (that is) good, this he will receive back from the Lord, whether slave, whether free." It is the intrinsic good that was done that will matter in the day of judgment. And that intrinsic good is not determined by the social position of the doer, whether he was a master or a slave. Matt. 25:31-46 brings this out beautifully. *It is the nature of the deed that determines the reward.* And in that "nature" *the motivation* is, of course, included. Not only *what* one has said or has done is important but also, and especially, why he said or did it. Did his deeds prove that he really meant what he said? (Matt. 7:21-23).

Only the good is mentioned here. Both good and bad are spoken of in Eccles. 12:14; Col. 3:25; and II Cor. 5:10. Reason for the difference? We simply do not know. There may be truth in the answer of those who say that *only good* was mentioned here for the greater encouragement of the Ephesians. It is certain, at any rate, that no good deed is ever done in vain. "There's but one life [on this earth]; 'tWill soon be past. Only what's done for Christ will last." That God Triune, or that the Lord Jesus Christ in his capacity as Judge, will reward the services that were rendered in love and obedience to him, is clear from many a Scripture passage: Gen. 15:1; Ruth 2:12; Ps. 19:11; 58:11; Isa. 40:10, 11; 62:11; Jer. 31:16; Matt. 5:12; 6:4; 25 (the entire chapter); Luke 6:35; 12:37, 38; I Peter 1:17; II John 8; and Rev. 2:7, 10, 11, 17, 23, 26-28; 3:4, 5, 9-12, 20, 21; 22:12. This reward is entirely of grace, not of merit. Just as by reason of sin all *men* stand condemned before God (Rom. 3:22, 23), so also by reason of grace all *believers,* whether slave or free, receive a reward for the good they have done.

Among those to whom this letter was addressed there were probably not many "slave-owners." Cf. I Cor. 1:26-28. Yet, there were some. In fact, the same messenger who delivered this letter to its destination also delivered another letter, one addressed to a "slaveowner," namely, Philemon. This was on the same trip when the Colossians, too, received their epistle. To the masters, therefore, a word must also be addressed, but as these were relatively few in number, and as even that part of the admonition that had been addressed to the slaves was full of implied significance also for their masters, the exhortation directed specifically to the latter could be brief: **9. And masters, do the same things for them.** Co-operation must be a two-way street. It must be shown by both groups: masters and slaves. So, in effect Paul is saying to the masters: "Promote the welfare of y o u r slaves as y o u expect them to promote y o u r s. Show the same interest in them and in their affairs as y o u hope they will show in y o u and y o u r affairs." Continued: **and stop threatening.** In other words, "Let y o u r approach be positive, not negative." Hence, not, "Unless you do this, I will do that to you," but rather, "Because you are a good and faithful servant, I will give you a generous reward." Before threatening, the slave stood helpless. He had no means of defending himself, not even, generally speaking, before the law. But as a believer he did have a real Defender. Hence, the apostle directs the attention of the masters to this fact, saying: **knowing that (he who is) both their master and y o u r s is in the heavens, and there is no partiality with him.** See James 5. Because of all that has already been said on this subject of impartiality (see on verse 8), no further comment is necessary.

*Summary of Chapter 4:17–6:9*

This section consists of two main divisions. In the first (4:17–5:21) the admonitions are addressed to the entire church; in the second (5:22–6:9), to the different members of the family: wives, husbands; children, fathers; slaves, masters. The general theme is (The Church's) *Glorious Renewal.* This renewal or transformation has the following characteristics:

(1) As already indicated, it has reference to the church in general, but also to the individual member.

(2) It is both negative ("Put off the old man") and positive ("Put on the new man"). For the first see 4:17, 22, 25a; etc.; for the second, 4:23, 24, 25b, 28b, 32; 5:1, 2; etc. *It stresses the positive* in the sense that evil must be overcome with good (5:18-21).

(3) It opposes self-indulgence (5:3-7, 18a) and encourages self-sacrifice (5:2, 25).

(4) Its Author is the Holy Spirit (4:30; 5:18) but it fully recognizes the role of human responsibility (in all the admonitions).

(5) It relates to *the past* (break with it, 4:17, 22), *the present* (be what y o u are, 5:8), and *the future* (the inheritance *or* the experience of God's wrath, what will it be? 5:5, 6).

(6) It combats specific sins: immorality, greed, falsehood, wrath, dishonesty, corrupt speech, slander, malice, drunkenness, etc. (4:25-31; 5:18; etc.) but also the underlying evil nature (4:17, 22). Similarly, it recommends specific virtues: truthfulness, industry, generosity, gracious speech, kindness, tenderheartedness, the forgiving disposition, love, thankfulness, righteousness (4:25b, 28b, 29b, 32; 5:2, 4b, 9) but also the basic godly nature (4:23, 24).

(7) It is fair to all and believes in the principle of reciprocity in human (and especially in family) relationships (5:22–6:9).

(8) It derives its example, motive, and strength from Christ (4:32; 5:2, 23, 24).

(9) It banishes the darkness and welcomes the light (5:7-14).

(10) It is gladdening, for it causes the one who experiences it to break forth into cheerful thanksgiving, into the singing of psalms, hymns, and spiritual songs, and into making melody from the heart to the Lord.

# Chapter 6:10–24

Theme: *The Church Glorious*
II. *Exhortation*
*urging all to put on*
*the Church's God-given*

*E* ffective Armor. Conclusion.

# CHAPTER VI:10-24

**EPHESIANS**

---

10 Finally, find y o u r (source of) power in the Lord and in the strength
of his might. 11 Put on the full armor of God in order that y o u may be
able to stand firm against the crafty methods of the devil. 12 For not against flesh
and blood is our wrestling but against the principalities, against the authorities,
against the world-rulers of this darkness, against the spiritual forces of evil in the
heavenly places. 13 Therefore take up the full armor of God in order that y o u
may be able to stand y o u r ground in the day of evil, and having done everything, to stand firm. 14 Stand firm therefore, having fastened the belt of truth
around y o u r waist, and having put on the breastplate of righteousness, 15 and
having shod y o u r feet with readiness derived from the gospel of peace, 16 and
in addition to everything else, having taken up the shield of faith, by means of
which y o u will be able to extinguish all the flaming missiles of the evil one;
17 and take the helmet of salvation, and the sword of the Spirit which is the
spoken word of God, 18 by means of all prayer and supplication, praying at all
times in the Spirit, and with a view to this, being on the alert in all perseverance
and supplication, for all the saints; 19 and (praying) for me, that when I open
my mouth I may be given a message, so that I may make known courageously the
mystery of the gospel, 20 for which I am an ambassador in a chain, that when
I proclaim it I may speak with courage as I ought to speak.

21 But in order that y o u also may know my affairs, how I am getting
along, Tychicus the beloved brother and faithful minister in the Lord, will make
them all known to y o u, 22 whom I am sending to y o u for this very purpose, that
y o u may know our circumstances and that he may strengthen y o u r hearts. 23
Peace (be) to the brothers, and love with faith, from God the Father and the Lord
Jesus Christ. 24 Grace (be) with all those who love our Lord Jesus Christ with (a
love) imperishable.

---

### 6:10-20

#### 1. *"Put on the full armor of God"*

The church's
*E* ternal Foundation
*U* niversal Scope
*L* ofty Goal
*O* rganic Unity and Growth, and
*G* lorious Renewal
having now been set forth, there remains the exhortation that believers arm themselves with the church's God-given
*E* ffective Armor. This is followed by the Conclusion to the entire let-

ter: a warm recommendation of the letter's bearer and an equally warm and unique benediction.

In all the preceding sections Paul has described salvation as being, on the one hand, the product of God's sovereign grace, on the other hand the promised reward of human effort, the latter being made possible from start to finish by the former. These two elements — divine grace and human responsibility — are again most beautifully combined in this closing section. *Man* must equip himself with a full suit of arms, that is, it is he who must *put it on.* It is also *he, he alone,* who must *use* this entire panoply. Nevertheless, the weapons are called "the full armor *of God.*" It is *God* who has forged them. It is *God* who gives them. Not for one single moment is man able to employ them effectively except by *the power of God.*

But what is it that makes the taking up of this formidable armor absolutely necessary, so essential that salvation is impossible without it? The answer is that the church has an enemy hell-bent on its destruction. So Paul begins this remarkable concluding exhortation with respect to the church's Effective Armor by saying: **10. Finally,**[167] **find y o u r (source of) power**[168] **in the Lord and in the strength of his might.** It is the exercise or manifestation of the might of the Lord that is the source of power for believers.[169] Apart from Christ Christians can accomplish nothing at all (John 15:1-5). They are like branches severed from the vine. On the other hand, in close fellowship with their Lord they can do whatever they need to do: "I can do all things in him who infuses strength into me" (Phil. 4:13; cf. II Cor. 12:9, 10; I Tim. 1:12). The reason is that the might of the Lord is infinite. By his strength God not only created the heavens and the earth, caused the mountains to tremble, the rocks to melt, Jordan to be driven back, the cedars of Lebanon to be broken in pieces, and the forests to be stripped bare, but specifically, as already emphasized in the *Ephesian* context, by his strength he caused *a. the Savior to arise from the dead (1:20)* and *b. his chosen ones to be made alive from their death in trespasses and sins (2:1).* It is, therefore, as if Paul were saying: "When I urge y o u to find y o u r source of power in the Lord and in the strength of his might, I am not making an unreasonable request, for y o u yourselves know that his omnipotence has been revealed *by these two marvelous deeds.* Hence, we are not

[167] In view of the present context there is only a minimal difference in meaning between τοῦ λοιποῦ ("in respect of the rest") and τὸ λοιπόν ("as for the rest"). Either reading may here be rendered "finally." Thus also N.T.L. (A. and G.), p. 481; Lenski, *op. cit.,* p. 657; and Robertson, *Word Pictures,* Vol. 4, p. 549. Contrast Simpson, *op. cit.,* p. 142.

[168] The question whether this present imperative should be construed as middle or as passive (cf. Acts 9:22; Rom. 4:20; II Tim. 2:1) is academic since the former "strengthen yourselves" or the latter "be strengthened" coalesce because of the modifier "in the Lord."

[169] For the meaning of the nouns δύναμις (implied in the verb ἐνδυναμοῦσθε), κράτος, and ἰσχύς see on 1:19.

dealing with abstractions but with *the power of God demonstrated in human history*. You are aware, therefore, of the fact that when you ask him to strengthen you, he will certainly hear you, for he is able to do infinitely more than all we ask or imagine" (3:20).

Paul continues: **11. Put on the full armor of God in order that you may be able to stand firm against the crafty methods of the devil.** The question might be asked, "In view of the fact that by means of the two marvelous deeds mentioned above it has become clear that the power of God in Christ is *infinitely superior* to that of Satan and his allies, need we be so concerned about the onslaught of the prince of evil?" The answer is: "Assurance of this superiority, however, does not diminish the seriousness of any given conflict on any 'evil day' nor give certain assurance of victory in any particular battle" (Roels, *op. cit.*, p. 216). I find myself in complete agreement with the words quoted, and wish only to add that, looked at from the angle of man's responsibility, it is even possible to say that not only this or that particular battle but the entire war will be lost unless we exert ourselves. It is true that the counsel of God from eternity will never fail, but it is just as true that in that plan of God from eternity it was decided that victory will be given to those who overcome (Rev. 2:7, 11, 17, etc.). Overcomers are conquerors, and in order to conquer one must fight!

Moreover, the war must be waged *strenuously*, for the foe is none other than *ho diábolos*, that is, the devil (Matt. 4:1, 5, 8, 11; John 8:44; I Peter 5:8; Jude 9; Rev. 2:10; 12:9; 20:2). It is clear that the apostle believed in the existence of a personal prince of evil. Paul was writing to people most of whom before their rather recent conversion to the Christian faith had been in great fear of evil spirits, as is true also today among pagans. It is almost impossible to appreciate how widespread, haunting, and overwhelming is this dread of demons which one encounters throughout heathendom. How did Paul counteract this fear? Did he say what many are saying today, namely, "The world of evil spirits is one huge untruth, a mere figment of the imagination"? He did not. Instead, without accepting paganism's demonology or animism, he, nevertheless, emphasizes the great and sinister influence of Satan. So do the other inspired writers. What they all say in describing the power of the devil can be summarized somewhat as follows: Having been cast out of heaven, he is filled with fury and envy. His malevolence is directed against God and his people. His purpose is, therefore, to dethrone his great Enemy, and to cast all God's people – in fact, *all* people – into hell. He walks about as a roaring lion seeking whom he may devour. He has a powerful, well-organized army (as will be shown in a moment), and has established an outpost within the very hearts of those whom he aims to destroy.

Also, his *methods*, says Paul, are *crafty* (see on 4:14). They are the schemes *of the deceiver*. Of this fact believers are not ignorant (II Cor. 2:11).

Now this expression "crafty methods" will be no more than a hollow sound unless we give scriptural content to it. Some of these clever ruses and vicious stratagems are the following: mixing error with just enough truth to make it appear plausible (Gen. 3:4, 5, 22), quoting (really misquoting!) Scripture (Matt. 4:6), masquerading as an angel of light (II Cor. 11:14) and causing his "ministers" to do likewise so that they "fashion themselves as apostles of Christ" (II Cor. 11:13), aping God (II Thess. 2:1-4, 9), strengthening people in their belief that he does not even exist (Acts 20:22), entering places where he is not expected to enter (Matt. 24:15; II Thess. 2:4), and above everything else promising people that good can be attained through wrongdoing (Luke 4:6, 7).

In view of all this, therefore, it is clear why, in the name of his Sender, the apostle issues the mobilization order: "Put on the full armor of God." Leave nothing out. Y o u will need every weapon. Do not try to advance against the devil and his host with equipage from y o u r own arsenal. Rather, say with David, "I cannot go with these, for I have not proved them" (I Sam. 17:39). Such weapons as trusting in human merits, in one's own erudition or mental acumen, in seclusion from the world, in the invocation of saints and of angels, in the theory that sin, sickness, and Satan do not exist, etc. will not avail in "the evil day." Therefore, "put on the full armor *of God,* forged by him and furnished by him. Put it on, equip yourselves with it so that y o u may be able *to stand,* not *to stand idle* but in the battle *to stand firm, to hold y o u r ground* against the devil's crafty methods." Continued:

**12. For not against flesh and blood is our wrestling but against the principalities, against the authorities, against the world-rulers of this darkness, against the spiritual forces of evil in the heavenly places.** The reason for the urgent character of the admonition is that we are not fighting against "flesh and blood,"[170] that is, against mere, frail men (Gal. 1:16), with all their physical and mental infirmities (respectively I Cor. 15:50 and Matt. 16:17). On the contrary it is against an innumerable supermundane host of evil spirits: the devil himself and all the demons under his control, that we are waging warfare. These fallen angels are here characterized as "principalities" and "authorities" (on which see 1:21 and N.T.C. on Col. 1:6); as "the world-rulers of this darkness," that is, as those who — under the permissive providence of God — are in tyrannical control of the world of ignorance, sin, and sadness; and as "the spiritual forces of evil *in the heavenly places,*" that is, in the supermundane realm. The term, "heavenly places," although *everywhere,* including here, referring to what may be called in a very broad sense "the celestial sphere" cannot have *precisely the same* meaning here as elsewhere. While in the remaining Ephesian passages it

[170] Literally here and in Heb. 2:14 "blood and flesh," but it is futile to search for any important difference in meaning between this word order and the reverse in Matt. 16:17; I Cor. 15:50; and Gal. 1:16.

indicates the heaven whence blessings descend (1:3), where Christ sits enthroned at the Father's right hand (1:20), where the redeemed are seated with Christ (2:6), and where the good angels have their abode (3:10), it must *here* (6:12) refer to the region above the earth but below the heaven of the redeemed; in other words, it must here indicate what in 2:2 is called "the domain of the air." Inasmuch as the reference is to "the world-rulers of this darkness" with whom believers must *contend,* this alteration in the application of the term should not cause any difficulty. See further on 2:2.

When the apostle implies that with "the full armor of God," including such weapons as *shield* and *sword* (verses 16, 17), we must "wrestle" against the innumerable spiritual host, he must not be accused of inconsistency, as if he started out with the idea of believers opposing the foe on the field of battle, and then quickly changed the scenery from that of the battle-field to that of the gymnasium. The true explanation is probably far more simple: the apostle means that *the battle* is such a violent hand-to-hand encounter that *in that respect* it amounts to *wrestling.* If this is a mixed metaphor it is not inconsistent.

Now it is because of this very intense and personal nature of the warfare against the devil and all his minions that Paul repeats and also develops the thought already expressed in verse 11, by saying: **13. Therefore take up the full armor of God.** The language used here is very incisive. The command is curt and crisp, as if to say, "Do not allow the enemy to find y o u defenseless. Take up y o u r armor. Do so at once, without any hesitancy or waste of time. And remember: take up the *full* panoply!"[171] The purpose is: **in order that y o u may be able to stand y o u r ground in the day of evil,** that is, in the day of severe trial, the critical moments in y o u r lives when the devil and his sinister underlings will assault y o u most vehemently (cf. Ps. 41:2; 49:5). And inasmuch as one never knows when these crises will occur, the clear implication is: be ready *always.*

We must be careful, however, not to infer from this that Christians are pictured here as sitting back, as it were, waiting in the shelter of their fortress for Satan's attack. The context (see on verses 17 and 19) does not allow this rather common interpretation. The "standing" of which Paul speaks (verses 11, 14) is not that of a brick wall that is waiting passively, as it were, for the assault of the battering ram. The soldiers referred to here are drawn up in battle array and rushing into the fight. They are both defending themselves and attacking. Only when they make full use of God's armor will they be able to "stand their ground," that is, to withstand the foe, stand up against[172] him, repulse his onrush and even gain ground, for the sentence

---

[171] The urgency of the command appears from the five aorists that are used in this one sentence.

[172] ἀντιστῆναι from ἀνθίστημι, an ἀντί-compound, occurring also in the following passages: Matt. 5:39; Luke 21:15; Acts 6:10; 13:8; Rom. 9:19; 13:2; Gal. 2; 11;

continues: **and having done everything, to stand firm.** The assumption is that they *will have accomplished thoroughly* — will have carried through to the end, as implied in the original — marvelous things. Resisting the devil, standing up against him, has this comforting result that, at least for the moment, the devil will flee (James 4:7; cf. Matt. 10:22).

To give even more substance to the character and the necessity of this battle against the devil and his hosts, this intense and vehement struggle, see what it meant in the life and labors of Paul himself. For him it had been, and/or was even now, a fight against Satan-inspired Jewish and pagan vice and violence; against Judaism among the Galatians and others; against fanaticism among the Thessalonians; against contention, fornication, and litigation among the Corinthians; against incipient Gnosticism among the Ephesians and far more among the Colossians; against fightings without and fears within; and last but not least, against the law of sin and death operating within his own heart.

It may be regarded as a trite saying, but it is true nevertheless, that the best defense is an offense. All of Paul's missionary journeys may be regarded as manifestations of offensive warfare. Paul was invading the territory which heretofore had been the devil's own, for "the whole world lieth in the evil one" (I John 5:19). The reason he had made these incursions into the hostile territory, and was going to make even more, was that the devil had something that was earnestly desired by the apostle, namely, the souls of men. Paul wanted them in order to present them to God. He yearned with all his heart to be used as God's agent in bringing about the rescue of men from the realm of darkness and their transfer into the kingdom of light. Whenever he refers to this subject he uses language that is expressive of deep feeling (Rom. 1:13; 10:1; I Cor. 9:22; 10:33; etc.). Paul loved ardently!

We see, therefore, that in order properly to interpret what the apostle meant by this battle it must be borne in mind that the church and Satan are on a collision course. They are rushing at each other. They clash!

With all this by way of introduction, showing why believers must by all means be fully equipped for battle against the forces of evil, their suit of armor is now described. In order to do this the apostle makes use of six metaphors derived from the armor of the Roman hoplite, the heavily armed Roman legionary going forth to battle. To be sure, there is also a seventh weapon, the climax of them all. However, that seventh one stands in a place all by itself. It is not indicated by any figure or metaphor. To do jus-

---

II Tim. 3:8; 4:15; James 4:7; and I Peter 5:9. While in all of these passages it means *to resist*, in some it implies *to resist successfully* (Luke 21:15; Acts 6:10; Rom. 9:19). In the present instance (Eph. 6:13) the successful character of the resistance is brought out especially in the words: "and having done everything, to stand firm." See also footnote 161.

tice to the six one should see the entire picture all at once. Hence, verses 14-17 are printed together here:

**14-17. Stand firm therefore,**

*a.* **having fastened the belt of truth around y o u r waist,**

*b.* **and having put on the breastplate of righteousness,**

*c.* **and having shod y o u r feet with readiness derived from the gospel of peace,**

*d.* **and in addition to everything else, having taken up the shield of faith, by means of which y o u will be able to extinguish all the flaming missiles of the evil one;**

*e.* **and take the helmet of salvation,**

*f.* **and the sword of the Spirit which is the spoken word of God.**

When the question is asked, "What was the source of this imagery?" the answer is anything but unanimous. Some are of the opinion that *the Roman guard* to which Paul was attached by means of a "chain" or handcuff (verse 20) naturally suggested the various pieces of the panoply of which mention is made here. But it is hard to believe that a guard inside a prison would be holding the huge shield of which mention is made in verse 16. *The lightly armed fighter,* equipped with bow and arrows, will not do either as a basis for the symbolism we find here. As to *the Roman warrior,* the Greek historian Polybius describes him as having a shield, sword, two javelins, a helmet, greaves, and heart-guard or something more elaborate to replace it. It is evident at once that Paul mentions neither greaves nor javelins. On the other hand, he does mention the girdle or belt and, by implication, the shoes. Perhaps the best answer to the question as to source would seem to lie in this general direction: the apostle is thinking of the heavily armed Roman soldier, but in the use of his metaphors is being constantly influenced by such Old Testament passages as Isa. 11:5; 49:2; 59:17; etc., passages which he does not slavishly copy but modifies for his own purpose. Also, it must be borne in mind that much earlier than this Paul had already made use of somewhat similar language: "But since we belong to the day, let us be sober, putting on a breastplate of faith and love, and for a helmet (the) hope of salvation" (I Thess. 5:8). Cf. I Cor. 9:7; II Cor. 6:7. Later he was going to write II Tim. 2:3, 4. After all, the imagery found here in Eph. 6:14-17 would naturally suggest itself to a battle-scarred veteran like Paul.

When we study the various pieces of the panoply there is one item that must not be left unmentioned, namely, the (by and large) natural order in which the various pieces are mentioned: the soldier would first of all fasten his *belt,* next put on his *breastplate,* then his *sandals.* Also, having taken his shield with his left hand and now holding it, he could not very well follow up this action immediately by taking his sword with his right hand, not sheathing it but *holding* it in readiness for immediate use, for in that case he would have no hand left with which to take the helmet. Hence, the order is *shield, helmet, sword.* This, to be sure, was not the only possible sequence, and may not even have been the actual order in which a soldier would equip himself. The order: helmet, sword, and shield suggests itself. But possibly in order to work his way toward a climax Paul mentions first those weapons which in physical warfare are considered defensive, and saves the sword, as the most emphatically and obviously offensive weapon, to the very last.

Now before setting out to do battle with as formidable a foe as the devil and all his host, one may well ask the question: *"Do I really want to fight him at all? Am I sincere about this spiritual warfare?"* Hence, Paul says, "Stand firm, therefore, having fastened the belt of truth around your waist." The girdle or belt, in physical warfare, was fastened or buckled around the short tunic worn by the soldier. Thus his limbs were braced up for action. Both breastplate and sword (the latter when not in use) were subsequently attached to this cincture. The belt, therefore, was very important. It was basic. So also in spiritual warfare *truthfulness* – which Paul has been stressing right along over against the *deceitfulness* that characterizes the man of the world (4:15, 25; 5:6, 9) – is the basic quality needed by the warrior. By this truthfulness is meant *sincerity of mind and heart,* removal of all guile and hypocrisy. There must be "truth in the inward parts" (Ps. 51:6).[173] "Whosoever is fearful and trembling, let him return home" (Judg. 7:3). And more than two-thirds of the army went home! In the battle against Satan and his armies there is no room for Demas! Sincerity is a mighty weapon, and this not only defensively. All other things being equal, the sincere person is far more likely to be a blessing to all those with whom he comes in contact than is the hypocrite.

The second question is: *"Am I living the kind of life that enables me to engage in this conflict?"* Have I put on "the breastplate of righteousness"? Cf. Isa. 59:17. In the underlying figure the breastplate has been described as the armor that covered the body from neck to thighs. It consisted of two parts, one covering the front, the other the back (cf. I Sam. 17:5, 38; I Kings 22:34; II Chron. 26:14; Neh. 4:16). Spiritually the breastplate is *the devout and holy life, moral rectitude* (Rom. 6:13; 14:17). It will be recalled that in I Thess. 5:8 Paul speaks of "the breastplate of faith and love." In both of the previous Ephesian instances the word "righteousness" was employed in an ethical sense (4:24; 5:9). And in II Cor. 6:7 Paul mentions "the armor of righteousness on the right hand and on the left," that is, such armor as enables one to meet attack from any quarter. This occurs in a context in which purity, kindness, etc. are also mentioned. In addition it should be borne in mind that the apostle in this very epistle has been plac-

[173] Along this line the figure is interpreted by Calvin, Erdman, Greijdanus, Salmond, Scott, and others.

ing great stress on the necessity of living lives worthy of the calling with which believers were called (4:1). Apart from such a life the would-be Christian has *no defense* against Satan's accusations. He has no assurance of salvation. And he also lacks the power to attack, for the testimony of the lips will be ineffective, the neighbor will not be won for Christ, and the evil one will not be vanquished. On the other hand, when *righteousness* in conduct is present, what a mighty weapon for defense and offense it becomes! [174]

*"Am I prepared to fight?"* is the next question. In other words, Have I shod my feet with "readiness derived from the gospel of peace"? The meaning of this expression has been much debated. Nevertheless, the following facts must be admitted: *a.* In order to promote facility of motion over all kinds of roads Roman soldiers were in the habit of putting on "shoes thickly studded with sharp nails" (Josephus, *Jewish Wars* VI. i. 8). Thus, one important reason for Julius Caesar's success as a general was the fact that his men wore military shoes that made it possible for them to cover long distances in such short periods that again and again the enemies were caught off guard, having deceived themselves into thinking that they still had plenty of time to prepare an adequate defense. In the victories won by Alexander the Great this same factor had played an important role. Accordingly, proper footwear spells readiness. *b.* A person who experiences within his own heart the peace of God that passes all understanding, the very peace which the gospel proclaims, has been delivered of a great burden. The conviction of being reconciled with God through the blood of Christ gives him the courage and the zeal to fight the good fight. If *the gospel,* accepted by faith, had not given him this peace, how could he be prepared to engage in this battle? *c.* The fact that this *readiness* is actually *derived from the gospel whose message or content is peace* is clear from such passages as 2:15, 17; cf. Rom. 5:1. The expression "having shod y o u r feet with readiness derived from the gospel of peace" makes good sense, therefore. Here again the believer has a twofold weapon, defensive and offensive.

*"Am I able to defend myself against Satan's attack?"* Prominent among the weapons of defense were *the shield* for the protection of the body (especially the heart, lungs, and other vital organs) and *the helmet* for the protection of the head. As to the shield, the one to which reference is made here measured four feet in length by two and one half feet in breadth and was oblong in shape and covered with leather. It was a kind of "door" for protection against enemy-missiles dipped in pitch or similar material and

---

[174] This explanation is favored by Calvin, Erdman, Salmond, Westcott, etc. Lenski, on the other hand, rejects it, and interprets the figure as having reference to imputed righteousness, *op. cit.,* p. 667. It is true, of course, that imputed and imparted righteousness can never be separated. They can, however, be distinguished. For the reasons given the reference here in 6:14 is to *imparted* righteousness.

set on fire before being discharged. When these darts collided with the shields their points were blunted, their flames extinguished. Similarly the exercise of genuine God-given faith enables one "to extinguish all the flaming missiles of the evil one." In the devil's quiver there are all kinds of fiery bolts. Paul mentions "tribulation, anguish, persecution, famine," etc. Some of these missiles enkindle doubt, others lust, greed, vanity, envy, etc. Only by looking away from self to God Triune, placing one's trust in him for life, death, and eternity, relying on his word of revelation and promise, is it possible to repel this shower of flaming arrows. Things looked thoroughly hopeless to Jairus when his servants arrived with the announcement, "Your daughter is dead, do not bother the Teacher any more." But Jesus answered, "Fear not, only believe" (Luke 8:49, 50). But faith is more than a weapon of defense. It is also "the victory that overcomes the world" (I John 5:4).[175] Surely, this shield must be taken up "in addition to everything else."

"And take the helmet of salvation," says Paul, borrowing this metaphor from Isa. 59:17. However, Paul applies the figure differently, for in Isaiah it is Jehovah who wears this helmet, but here in Ephesians believers are called upon to receive it. In I Thess. 5:8 the apostle had identified the helmet with "the hope of salvation," here with salvation itself. The difference is perhaps not as important as it may seem, since salvation is both a present possession and an inheritance not yet fully acquired in this life; hence, the object of firmly anchored hope.

"Take it," says Paul. The verb might also be translated: *accept* (it). Just as a helmet is *accepted* by the soldier out of the hand of the officer in charge of supply and distribution, so salvation and all that pertains to it, including even the faith whereby we accept it (2:8), is God's free gift. The helmet of iron and brass (I Sam. 17:5, 38; II Chron. 26:14; cf. I Macc. 6:35) afforded a measure of protection for the head, as did the breastplate for the heart, etc. In the Herodian period Greek and Roman helmets both of leather and brass were used extensively. It is easy to see that for the Christian salvation is indeed a weapon of *defense.* Were it not for the fact that in the midst of hardship and persecution the assurance of salvation both present and future dwells in his heart he might easily give up the fight. It is exactly this precious treasure that fortifies him with strength to continue the fight, for *as to himself* he knows that what God has begun in him will be carried on to completion (Ps. 138:8; Phil. 1:6). *As to the neighbor* whom the helmeted believer is trying to rescue from the power of darkness, God's word will never return to him void but will accomplish that which he pleases (Isa. 55:11). Hence, the Christian soldier continues the fight, with "blessed as-

[175] While by far the most commentators view this shield as a symbol of faith in action, which, as I see it, is the correct explanation, Lenski places the emphasis on "the objective content of faith" (*op. cit.,* p. 671).

surance" clearly evident in his looks and entire demeanor and with a testimony upon his lips. It is clear therefore that also the helmet as Paul here interprets it (= salvation) is not only a piece of *defensive* armor. Do not the *songs* of salvation, considered as an essential part of salvation, constitute a mighty weapon in the believers' *offensive* as well as defensive armor?

The final question is, *"Have I learned the art of offensive warfare?"* We have been studying those weapons that are generally included under the heading *defensive armor.* We have seen, however, that though in physical warfare this description may be entirely adequate, in spiritual combat it hardly reaches far enough. Even *truthfulness* or *integrity* — the belt — is not exclusively defensive. *It captivates! Righteousness* — the breastplate — not only serves as a protection; it also wins the neighbor for Christ, that God may be glorified (Matt. 5:16). The *peace* that provides *readiness* for the spiritual battle — the *shoes* — furnishes both time and energy for invading the enemy's domain and robbing him of the spoils he has taken. *Faith* — the shield — overcomes the world, recapturing the lost. And *salvation* — the helmet — sings its way into the enemy's prison-camp, setting the prisoners free. But although all this is undoubtedly true, nevertheless, *the most conspicuously offensive weapon,* offensive both in physical and spiritual combat, is certainly the sword. Says Paul: " (and take) the sword of the Spirit which [176] is the word of God."

The underlying figure is that of *the short sword,* the one carried and wielded by the heavily armed Roman soldier.[177] With it he not only defended himself, but sallied forth into the ranks of the enemy and won victories. As has already been indicated (see on 5:26), *this sword is the gospel* (cf. I Peter 1:25), *God's utterance;* if you wish, *the Bible, the entire Word of God.* First it was spoken by him, and now his servants proclaim it to others. *As long as what they proclaim is really in harmony with God's special revelation as it was subsequently deposited in written or printed form in what we now call the Bible it remains the very sword here referred to.* Even the least deviation from the word as originally given is, of course, the word of man, not of God. Errors in transcription or translation, in doctrine or in ethics, no matter how enthusiastically these may be defended from the pulpit, are no part of "the spoken (or: uttered) word." It is this word that "stands forever" (Isa. 40:8), and cannot be defeated. The hammers that would destroy it will be broken. The anvil remains.

This spoken word is called "the sword *of the Spirit*" because it is given by the Spirit (II Tim. 3:16; II Peter 1:21) and perhaps also because by the Spirit it is applied to the heart. Soldiers for Christ handle the word, heed

---

[176] The neuter ὅ may be due to the influence of ῥῆμα, which is stressed.

[177] This μάχαιρα is distinguished from the ῥομφαία (Luke 2:35; Rev. 1:16; 2:12, 16; 6:8; 19:15, 21). The latter is the heavy great-sword that proceeded out of Christ's mouth as John saw him in a vision on Patmos.

it, hide it in their hearts, and hold it forth among the nations. The sword, thus wielded, is "living and active, sharper than any two-edged sword, piercing even to the dividing of soul and spirit, of joints and marrow, and quick to discern the thoughts and intentions of the heart" (Heb. 4:12).[178] By using this powerful sword Paul and his associates had won amazing victories. And any victory that is being won today either at home or abroad is the result of the wielding of this sword. *God is not dead!* He lives and speaks in and through his message.

It is by means of it that man's state of guilt before God is revealed, his sinful condition exposed. Through it, too, when applied to the heart by the Spirit, man is led to the Savior from sin, and to thanksgiving and praise. Through it doubts are dispelled, fears driven away, assurance of salvation given, and Satan put to flight. When Jesus was tempted he answered every word of the devil by an appeal to the written Word of God!

### *The Four "All's"* [179] *of Prayer*

The *word of God directed to men* (verse 17) is very powerful indeed, especially when it is in close association with *the word of men directed to God* (verses 18-20), not as if God and men were equal partners but because the word of men directed to God is Spirit-given, Spirit-guided ("in the Spirit"). Paul writes:

**18. by means of all prayer and supplication,**
**praying at all times in the Spirit,**
**and with a view to this, being on the alert in all perseverance and supplication,**
**for all the saints.**

In his own power the soldier can do nothing against so great a foe. Hence, as he takes and puts on each piece of his armor and as he makes use of it in the battle he must pray for God's blessing.

1. *The Variety of Prayer: "all* prayer and supplication"

The apostle makes a special point of it that the soldier's communion with his General – the believer's fellowship with his God – should not be of just one kind. Some people are always asking for things. Their entire prayer-life consists of that. But *prayer* – the first word is very general – should include not only cries for help but also confession of sin, profession of faith, adoration, thanksgiving, intercession. Moreover, prayer-life should be definite, not just "O Lord, bless all that awaits thy blessing," which is a big order, but "supplication" or "petition" for the fulfilment of definite

---

[178] In this passage the *"word"* is λόγος, not ῥῆμα, but the central thought is the same for either, for the two terms are coextensive.

[179] The word πᾶς ("all") is used four times in verse 18: πάσης, παντί, πάσῃ, and πάντων, four different forms.

needs, a request for specific benefits. This means that the man who prays should become acquainted with concrete situations all over, at least not limited to his own contracted horizon, situations in connection with which help is needed. He should set aside, perhaps, *today* to stress this need, *tomorrow* to remember another.

2. *The "when" and the "where" of Prayer:* "at *all* times . . . in the Spirit."

Prayer in time of "great calamity" or "catastrophe" has long been in vogue. For many people, however, "Thanksgiving Day" comes just once a year. It is the day set aside by the national government. The apostle admonishes the addressed to take hold on God "at every occasion." "In *all* thy ways acknowledge him" (Prov. 3:6).

As to the "where" of prayer, it is not to be confined either to "Jerusalem" or to "this mountain" but should always be "in (the sphere of) the Spirit," that is, "with his help" and "in harmony with his will" as revealed in the Word which he inspired.

3. *The Manner of Prayer:* "being on the alert in *all* perseverance and supplication." Cf. Col. 4:2.

Those who are not "alert" but listless and indifferent to what is going on in their homes, in the streets of their city, in their state or province, in their country, in their church, in their denomination, or in the world at large will have a very restricted prayer-life. Those who do not know the will of God because they devote so little time to the study of the Word will fail to harvest the fruits of prayer. Those who do not know the promises cannot be expected to "go to the deeps of God's promise" in their devotions. They will not partake of a deep and satisfying communion with God. Consequently, they will perhaps pray now and then only. There will be no "perseverance" and little "supplication" (petition for definite benefits).

4. *The Indirect Objects of Prayer:* "for *all* the saints"

Christ during his sojourn on earth evaluated intercessory prayer ("prayer for others") very highly, as is shown by many incidents (Matt. 9:18-26; 15:21-28; 17:14-21; etc.). So did Paul. The heart of our Great Intercessor who not only intercedes for us but actually *lives in order to do so* (Heb. 7:25) is deeply touched by such petitions! Thus the fellowship of saints is kept alive and real.

In this fellowship of prayer the Jewish convert must not forget the Gentile convert, the old must not ignore the young, the free must not neglect those in bondage, nor vice versa. It must be prayer "for *all* the saints." With God there is no partiality.

Up to this point the apostle has said very little about his own physical circumstances. He is not a complainer. He has made brief mention of the fact that he was writing as a prisoner (3:1; 4:1), and has also urged the

Ephesians "not to lose heart" over what he was suffering for them (3:13). But that was all; and even in the given passages he was thinking not of himself so much as of the welfare of those addressed.

Now at last he for one brief moment centers the attention on himself, his own needs, and asks that when prayer is made "for all the saints," he, too, may be remembered in a special way. Notice, however, how nobly he expresses himself: **19. and (praying) for me, that when I open my mouth I may be given a message, so that I may make known courageously the mystery of the gospel.** Cf. Col. 4:2, 3. Even the requested prayer for himself is in reality to be a petition for the progress of the gospel! Paul knew that the Lord had chosen him to be a prominent leader. As such, a heavy load of responsibility rested on his shoulders! Yet, he was aware of his own weakness, of the fact that he stood in need of divine strength and guidance every moment. So, as he had done on other occasions (Rom. 15:30; I Thess. 5:25; II Thess. 3:1, 22) and was doing now also in another letter (Col. 4:3), he asks that those whom he addresses will remember him in their prayers. He does not ask, however, that they may pray for his release from prison. What he does ask is that they may invoke God's blessing upon him as an effective witness for Christ. "Ask God to give me two things," he says, as it were: *a. "a message* when I open my mouth" (Matt. 10:19), and *b. "courage* at all times to deliver that message in a worthy manner" (cf. Acts 4:13). In his zeal for the salvation of sinners to the glory of God the apostle considered even his present difficult circumstances to be an opportunity to tell everyone – the constantly changing guards, the visitors, the Roman tribunal in case he should (or should *again*) be summoned to appear before it – "the mystery of the gospel" (= "the mystery concerning Christ," Col. 4:3), the blessed truth which would have remained a secret had not God revealed it, namely, that in Christ there is salvation full and free for *everyone* who embraces him by faith, even for both Jew and Gentile on a basis of perfect equality. Cf. 3:3, 4, 9; Rom. 16:25; Col. 1:26, 27; 2:2; 4:3; I Tim. 3:9, 16. Continued: **20. for which I am an ambassador in a chain.** The fact that when Paul arrived in Rome he, by a chain at the wrist, was fastened to a Roman guard is implied in Acts 28:20. Though his first Roman imprisonment, during which Colossians, Philemon, Ephesians, and Philippians were written, seems never to have been as harsh and severe as his second was going to be, he was a "prisoner," nevertheless. (For the first imprisonment compare 3:1; 4:1; with Acts 28:16, 30. For the second imprisonment see II Tim. 1:12; 2:3, 10; 4:6-8, 14-16).

His imprisonment, however, is not a shame. It is an honor; for whatever men may think, the truth of the matter is that he is, and is conscious of being, *an ambassador*[180] *in a chain.* What a paradox! Is not an *ambassador*

---

[180] The verb used is πρεσβεύω, meaning: "I am a πρεσβευτής, an ambassador." This word πρεσβευτής must not be confused with πρεσβύτης, old man (Philem. 9).

supposed to be *free?* But here is an official representative of him who is King of kings and Lord of lords, and *this* ambassador is chained! May he never forget whom he represents. Therefore, whenever he proclaims the glorious *mystery of the gospel* may he do so in a manner befitting his high office. "Pray," says he, **that when I proclaim it I may speak with courage as I ought to speak;** virtually repeating, for the sake of emphasis, what he has said in the preceding verse.

On this high level Paul ends the main part of his epistle. He has been setting forth "the benefits divine which we in Christ possess." As an ambassador equipped with this message he is writing, both *defending and attacking,* both *reacting against* anyone who might wish to oppose his Sender's gospel *and* at the same time *taking the initiative* and with his message invading the enemy's territory. Does not this passage (6:19, 20) shed light on the manner in which the immediately preceding "whole armor of God" should be interpreted, that is, as indicating *a panoply that is both defensive and offensive?* It is as if we can hear the apostle making his appeal and saying:

"On Christ's behalf, therefore, we are ambassadors, seeing that God is entreating through us. We implore (y o u) on behalf of Christ, be reconciled to God! Him who knew no sin he made (to be) sin on our behalf that we might become God's righteousness in him."

6:21-24

2. *Conclusion*

The item of information contained in verses 21 and 22, including a warm recommendation of Tychicus, the bearer of these letters (Colossians, Philemon, Ephesians), is almost identical with Col. 4:7, 8. The slight differences can be seen by comparing the parallel passages in Ephesians and Colossians on p. 25. If Colossians (right column) was written before Ephesians (left column), as I have assumed, then the word "also" (in "that y o u *also* may know my affairs") here in Eph. 6:21 can be explained as meaning: "y o u as well as the Colossians." The entire passage in Ephesians is as follows: **21, 22. But in order that y o u also may know my affairs, how I am getting along, Tychicus, the beloved brother and faithful minister in the Lord, will make them all known to y o u, whom I am sending to y o u for this very purpose, that y o u may know our circumstances and that he may strengthen y o u r hearts.**

Tychicus [181] was one of Paul's intimate friends and highly valued envoys. He hailed from the province of Asia, and had accompanied the apostle when

[181] For the meaning of the name see N.T.C. on Philippians, pp. 138, 139, footnote 116, where the explanation of many other personal names is also given. For more on Tychicus, e.g., his relation to Paul after the latter's first Roman imprisonment, see N.T.C. on Titus 3:12 and on II Tim. 4:12.

at the close of the third missionary journey the latter was returning from Greece through Macedonia and then across into Asia Minor and so to Jerusalem on a charitable mission (Acts 20:4); that is, on that trip Tychicus had traveled in advance of Paul from Macedonia to Troas, and had been waiting for the apostle in that city. And now, some four years later, having spent some time with Paul in Rome during the latter's first Roman imprisonment, Tychicus had been commissioned by the apostle to carry these letters to their destination, as is clear from the present passage, from its parallel in Colossians, and from a comparison of Col. 4:9 with Philem. 1, 8-22. It stands to reason that Tychicus, having just now spent some time with Paul and being a "beloved brother" – a member of the Father's Family, along with all believers – and "faithful minister in the Lord" – Christ's special servant, loyal to his Master in every respect –, would be the right person, as he traveled from church to church, to supply all the necessary information about Paul and his companions and fellow-Christians in Rome. Besides, paper was not as plentiful and cheap as it is today, the circumstances under which Paul had to dictate his letters were not altogether favorable, and certain things are better *said* than *written,* especially in a letter intended for a wide circle of readers (which was true also of Colossians, as Col. 4:16 indicates, though probably in a more limited way). The oral message which Tychicus will bring will be not only *informative,* however, but also *consolatory.* Hence, Paul writes: "that you may know our circumstances and that he may strengthen your hearts," the latter, no doubt, by stilling their fears (see on 3:13; cf. Phil. 1:12-14) and by supplying the "atmosphere" of consolation and spiritual strengthening based on the promises of God. The most substantial consolation of all would be the very letter of Paul which Tychicus would deliver.

The closing benediction follows: 23. **Peace (be) to the brothers, and love with faith, from God the Father and the Lord Jesus Christ.** Peace, love, and faith are among the themes most often referred to in this epistle. For *peace* see 1:2; 2:14, 15, 17; 4:3; and 6:15; for *love* among the brothers or within the community (including the love of a husband for his wife) see 1:15; 4:2, 15, 16; 5:25, 28, 33; in a more general sense: 3:17; 5:2a; for the love of God in Christ for believers: 1:4; 2:4; 3:19; 5:2b; and for *faith* see 1:15; 2:8; 3:12, 17; 4:5, 13; 6:16. These were the very qualities that needed to be emphasized in that day and age. Is not the same true also today?

The *peace* of which the apostle is thinking is harmony among brothers. Nevertheless, it cannot exist unless through faith in Christ and his atoning sacrifice it has been established first of all in the heart of individual believers. It is impossible to separate these two. *Love,* too, though here again emphatically that among brothers, cannot be separated from the love toward God in Christ; both of these resulting from the love of God in Christ for those who are his own. *Faith* means trusting in God Triune who has revealed himself to the church in Jesus Christ. It is the gift of God (2:8). Verse 24 adds *grace.*

There are those who lay special stress on what they believe to be "the reverse order" in which these items are here mentioned. As they see it, in this enumeration the effect precedes the cause, the "proper" order being: first *grace,* because it is that divine attribute to which man owes everything; next *faith,* because it is the fruit of grace; and finally *peace and love,* as twin children of faith. I have no objection whatever against this representation as long as it makes allowance for an important qualification. To be sure, God's grace is basic. None of the others can ever begin to approach it as the cause or producer of every virtuous quality or activity in man. Yet, the relationship between the items here mentioned is richer and more bountiful by far than the simple sequence: grace → faith ↗ peace & ↘ love indicates. Each quality, as soon as it is present, reacts upon the others and enriches them. The more a person exercises his faith in the Lord Jesus Christ, the more also the work of divine grace will blossom forth in his life; and so also with the others. Love has been described as faith's fruit, but it also enriches faith; etc. All these qualities, attitudes, and activities proceed from "God the Father," who is their Source, and "the Lord Jesus Christ" (see on 1:17) who by the shedding of his blood merited them as gifts for his children. The perfect equality of Father and Son is again clearly evident: *one* preposition ("from") precedes both. Continued: **24. Grace (be) with all those who love our Lord Jesus Christ with (a love) imperishable.** It has been pointed out that in verse 23 the love to which reference is made is "emphatically that among brothers." Here in verse 24 it is the love for *the Lord Jesus Christ* that is stressed. Grace was the root of this love. The enrichment of grace is the fruit of the love that has the Savior as its object. Once this love for Christ is present in the heart it can never vanish for it is a divine endowment. Literally, the apostle says, "Grace" – that is, *the* very grace to which he has referred so often (see especially 2:5-8) – " (be) with all those loving our Lord Jesus Christ *in imperishability.*" For *imperishability* or *incorruptibility* see also Rom. 2:7; I Cor. 15:42, 50, 53, 54; II Tim. 1:10. It is, however, not in conflict with good grammar to construe this last phrase as an adverb; hence, "imperishably." As to what it modifies it surely seems more natural that it would belong to the nearby *loving* than to anything more remote. In harmony with many interpreters, therefore, and also with most translators, I, therefore, translate as follows: "those loving imperishably," which is the same as saying, "Grace (be) with all those who love our Lord Jesus Christ with a love which, once present, can never perish."

*Seed Thoughts of Ephesians 6:10-24*

(one thought for each verse)

See Verse

10. The exhortation to find one's source of power in the Lord is reasonable, for the Lord has demonstrated his power again and again both in nature and in grace and is still doing this.
11. The omission of a single piece of armor is dangerous, for the devil will soon discover a person's Achilles' heel.
12. Denial of the existence and activity of a personal devil and his well-organized hosts is becoming more foolish every day.
13. In order to stand your ground in the day of evil or crisis, stand your ground *today!*
14. A sincere resolve to fight Satan in the strength of the Lord, coupled with right conduct, points the way to victory. Make full use therefore of the God-given *effective Armor.*
15. It is the guilt-eased heart that makes the feet nimble.
16. Against Sinai's lightnings, hell's rage, and the atheist's ridicule the firm grip of faith in God and his promise always wins.
17. Assurance of salvation is contagious: almost everyone likes to listen to the martial music of an army marching on to victory. The word of God is mightier than any two-edged sword.
18. If prayer-life is weak, is it because you have not done justice to the four "all's" mentioned in this verse?
19. There is great power in intercessory prayer.
20. Some take special pride in speaking "bluntly." It is far better to ask for grace to speak "courageously."
21. Believers take a keen interest in each other's welfare.
22. Giving out information may be perfectly proper, particularly when the purpose is to strengthen the hearts of the listeners.
23. The peace that passes all understanding, the love that is the greatest of the three greatest, and the faith that overcomes the world, these three precious treasures *are given away* to anyone who sincerely requests them of God the Father and the Lord Jesus Christ.
24. The gifts of God's grace are imperishable.

# General Bibliography

For other titles see List of Abbreviations at the beginning of this volume.


Aalders, G. Ch., *Het Boek Genesis* (*Korte Verklaring der Heilige Schrift*), Kampen, 1949, Vol. I.

Abbott, T. K., *The Epistles to the Ephesians and to the Colossians* (*International Critical Commentary*), New York, 1916.

Allan, J. A., *The Epistle to the Ephesians* (*Torch Bible Commentaries*), London, 1959.

Allen, R., *Missionary Methods: St. Paul's or Ours?*, London, 1953.

Ante-Nicene Fathers, ten volumes, reprint, Grand Rapids, 1950, for references to Clement of Alexandria, Irenaeus, Justin Martyr, Origen, Tertullian, etc.

Barclay, W., *The Letters to the Galatians and Ephesians* (*The Daily Study Bible*), Philadelphia, 1958.

Barnes, A., *Notes on the New Testament, Ephesians, Philippians and Colossians,* reprint Grand Rapids, 1949.

Barnette, H., "One Way of Life: Personal and Social," *RE*, Vol. 60, No. 4 (Fall 1963), pp. 414–429.

Barry, A., *The Epistles to the Ephesians, Philippians, and Colossians* (C. J. Ellicott's *New Testament Commentary for English Readers*), New York, 1896.

Barth, K., "Gottes Gnadenwahl," *Die Lehre Von Gott, Die Kirchliche Dogmatik,* II/2, 3e. Auflage, Zürich, 1948.

Barth, M., "Conversion and Conversation," *Int*, Vol. 17, No. 1 (Jan. 1963), pp. 3–24.

Bartlett, W., "The Saints at Ephesus," *Exp, Eighth Series,* No. 107 (Nov. 1919), pp. 327–341.

Bavinck, C. B., Art. "Apostel" in *Christelijke Encyclopaedia,* Vol. I, pp. 143–145.

Bavinck, H., *Gereformeerde Dogmatiek,* Vol. II, *Over God;* English translation, *The Doctrine of God,* translated by W. Hendriksen, Grand Rapids, 1955.

Beare, F. W., *The Epistle to the Ephesians* (*Interpreter's Bible,* Vol. X), New York and Nashville, 1953.

Benoit, P., *La Sainte Bible traduite en français sous la direction de l'École Biblique de Jerusalem,* 1949.

Berkhof, L., *New Testament Introduction,* Grand Rapids, 1916.

Berkhof, L., *Systematic Theology,* Grand Rapids, 1949.

Berkouwer, G. C., *De Triomf der Genade in de Theologie van Karl Barth,* Kampen, 1954.

Bible, Holy, In addition to references to Bible-versions other than English, there are references to the following English translations: A.V., A.R.V., R.S.V., N.E.B., N.A.S.B. (N.T.), Amplified New Testament, Beck, Berkeley, Goodspeed, Moffatt, Phillips, Weymouth, Williams. These are *references.* The *translation* which is found in N.T.C. and followed in the exegesis is the author's own.

Bowman, J. W., "The Epistle to the Ephesians," *Int,* Vol. 8 (April 1954), pp. 188–205.

Braune, K., *The Epistle of Paul to the Ephesians* (*Lange's Commentary on the Holy Scriptures*), republished, Grand Rapids, no date.

Brown, R., "Ephesians among the Letters of Paul," *RE,* LX, No. 4 (Fall 1963), pp. 372–379.

Bruce, F. F., *The Epistle to the Ephesians, A Verse-by-Verse Exposition,* London, 1961.

## EPHESIANS


Bruce, F. F., *The Letters of Paul, An Expanded Paraphrase,* Grand Rapids, 1965.

Cable, J. H., *The Fulness of God,* Chicago, 1945.

Calvin, John, *Institutes of the Christian Religion* (translated by John Allen, Philadelphia, 1928), Vol. I.

Calvin, John, *Commentarius In Epistolam Pauli Ad Ephesios* (*Corpus Reformatorum,* Vol. LXXX), Brunsvigae, 1895; English Translation (*Calvin's Commentaries*) Grand Rapids, 1948.

Chafer, L. S., *The Ephesian Letter,* New York, 1935.

Colwell, E. C., "Biblical Criticism: Lower and Higher," *JBL* (March 1948), p. 4.

Conybeare, W. J., and Howson, J. S., *The Life and Epistles of St. Paul,* Grand Rapids, 1949.

Coutts, J., "Ephesians I.3-14 and I Peter I.3-12," *NTSt,* Vol. 3, No. 2 (Jan. 1957), pp. 115–127.

Dale, R. W., *The Epistle to the Ephesians,* 1961.

Dalmer, J., "Bemerkungen zu I Kor. 10.3-4 und Eph. 4.8-10," *TSK,* 63 (1890), pp. 569–592.

De Boer, W. P., *The Imitation of Paul, An Exegetical Study,* doctoral dissertation, Kampen, 1962.

Deissmann, A., *Light from the Ancient East* (translated by L. R. M. Strachan), New York, 1927.

Dibelius, M., *An die Kolosser, Epheser, an Philemon* (Lietzmann's *Handbuch zum Neuen Testament*), 3rd edition, revised by H. Greeven, Tübingen, 1953.

Erdman, C. F., *The Epistle of Paul to the Ephesians,* Philadelphia, 1931.

Filson, F. V., "Ephesus and the New Testament," *The Biblical Archaeologist Reader,* 2 (edited by D. N. Freedman and E. F. Campbell, Jr.), New York, 1964, pp. 343–352.

Findlay, G. G., *The Epistle to the Ephesians,* New York, 1931. This is also included in *The Expositor's Bible,* Vol. VI, pp. 1–108.

Foulkes, F., *The Epistle of Paul to the Ephesians* (*The Tyndale New Testament Commentaries*), Grand Rapids, 1963.

Gerstner, E., *Idelette,* Grand Rapids, 1963.

Gerstner, J. H., *The Epistle to the Ephesians* (*Shield Bible Study Series*), Grand Rapids, 1958.

Goodspeed, E. J., *New Solutions to New Testament Problems,* Chicago, 1927.

Goodspeed, E. J., *The Meaning of Ephesians,* Chicago, 1933.

Goodspeed, E. J., *New Chapters in New Testament Study,* New York, 1937.

Goodspeed, E. J., *The Key to Ephesians,* Chicago, 1956.

Greijdanus, S., *Bizondere Canoniek,* Kampen, 1949, two volumes.

Grosheide, F. W., *De Brief Van Paulus Aan De Efeziërs* (*Commentaar op het Nieuwe Testament*), Kampen, 1960.

Harnack, A., *The Constitution and Law of the Church,* New York, 1910.

Hendriksen, W., *The Meaning of the Preposition ἀντί in the New Testament,* doctoral dissertation, Princeton, 1948.

Hendriksen, W., *Bible Survey,* Grand Rapids, 1961.

Hendriksen, W., *More Than Conquerors, An Interpretation of the Book of Revelation,* Grand Rapids, 1963.

Hendriksen, W., *The Bible on the Life Hereafter,* Grand Rapids, 1963.

Hodge, C., *A Commentary on the Epistle to the Ephesians,* Grand Rapids, 1954.

Hoekstra, S., "Vergelijking van de Brieven aan de Efeziërs en de Colossers, vooral uit het Oogpunt van Beider Leerstelligen Inhoud," *TT* (1868), pp. 562–599.

Hogarth, D. J., *The Archaic Artemisia,* 1908.

## EPHESIANS


Holtzmann, H. J., *Kritik der Epheser und Kolosserbriefe,* 1872.

Hort, F. J. A., *Prologomena to St. Paul's Epistles to the Romans and the Ephesians,* London, 1895.

Iliffe, J. F., "The ΘΑΝΑΤΟΣ Inscription from Herod's Temple: Fragments of a Second Copy," *Quarterly of Department of Antiquities in Palestine* VI (1938), pp. 1 ff.

King, A. C., "Ephesians in the Light of Form Criticism," *ET,* 63 (1951–1952), pp. 273–276.

Klooster, F. H., *The Significance of Barth's Theology: An Appraisal with Special Reference to Election and Reconciliation,* Grand Rapids, 1961.

Knox, W. L., *St. Paul and the Church of the Gentiles,* Cambridge, 1939.

Kuyper, A., Sr., *De Gemeene Gratie,* three volumes, Kampen, no date.

Kuyper, A., Sr., *Het Werk van den Heiligen Geest,* Kampen, 1927.

Lenski, R. C. H., *Interpretation of St. Paul's Epistles to the Galatians, to the Ephesians, and to the Philippians,* Columbus, Ohio, 1937.

Lightfoot, J. B., *Saint Paul's Epistle to the Colossians and to Philemon,* reprint of 1879 edition, Grand Rapids.

Lightfoot, J. B., *Notes on the Epistles of St. Paul,* London, 1895. This volume contains notes on the Greek text of Eph. 1:1-14.

Linton, O., *Das Problem der Urkirche in der Neuere Forschung,* Upsala, 1932.

Lock, W., *St. Paul's Epistle to the Ephesians* (*Westminster Commentaries*), London, 1929.

*Loeb Classical Library,* New York (various dates), for Eusebius, Herodotus, Josephus, Philo, Plato, Pliny, Plutarch, Strabo, Xenophon, etc.

Mackay, J. A., *God's Order, The Ephesian Letter and This Present Time,* New York, 1957.

Mackay, J. R., "Paul's Great Doxology," *EQ,* Vol. 2 (1930), pp. 150–161.

McNicol, J., "The Spiritual Blessings of the Epistle to the Ephesians," EQ, Vol. 9 (1937), pp. 64–73.

Metzger, B. M., "Paul's Vision of the Church; A Study of the Ephesian Letter," *TTod,* 6 (1949–1950), pp. 49–63.

Mitton, C. L., "Unsolved New Testament Problems: E. J. Goodspeed's Theory Regarding the Origin of Ephesians," *ET* 59 (1947–1948), pp. 323–327; and *ET* 60 (1948–1949), pp. 320–321.

Mitton, C. L., *The Epistle to the Ephesians; Its Authorship, Origin, and Purpose,* Oxford, 1951.

Mitton, C. L., *The Formation of the Pauline Corpus of Letters,* London, 1955.

Mitton, C. L., "Important Hypotheses Reconsidered; VII. The Authorship of the Epistle to the Ephesians," *ET,* 67 (1955–1956), pp. 195–198.

Moffatt, J., *Introduction to the Literature of the New Testament,* New York, 1918.

Moffatt, J., "Three Notes on Ephesians," *Exp,* Eighth Series, No. 87 (April 1918), pp. 306–317.

Moule, H. C. G., *Ephesian Studies,* New York, 1900.

Murray, J., *Christian Baptism,* Philadelphia, 1952.

Mussner, F., *Christus, Das All und die Kirche,* Trierer Theologische Studien, V, Trier, 1955.

Niebuhr, R., *Man's Nature and His Communities: Essays on the Dynamics and Enigmas of Man's Personal and Social Existence,* New York, 1965.

Ockenga, H. J., *Faithful in Christ Jesus, Preaching in Ephesians,* New York, 1948.

Parvis, M. M., "Ephesus in the Early Christian Era," *The Biblical Archaeologist*

*Reader,* 2 (edited by D. N. Freedman and E. F. Campbell, Jr.), New York, 1964, pp. 331–343.

Paulus, H. E. G., *Philologisch-kritischer Kommentar über das Neue Testament,* Lübeck, 1800.

Peake, A. S., *Critical Introduction to the New Testament,* 1909.

Penning, L., *Life and Times of Calvin,* translated by B. S. Berrington, London, 1912.

Percy, E., *Die Probleme der Kolosser- und Epheserbriefe,* Lund, 1946.

Piper, O. A., "Praise of God and Thanksgiving," *Int,* Vol. 8, No. 1 (Jan. 1954), pp. 3–20.

Ramsay, W. M., *The Letters to the Seven Churches of Asia,* 1904.

Ridderbos, H. N., *The Epistle of Paul to the Churches of Galatia* (*New International Commentary on the New Testament*), Grand Rapids, 1953.

Robertson, A. T., *Word Pictures in the New Testament,* New York and London, 1931, Vol. IV, on Ephesians, pp. 514–552.

Robinson, J. A., "The Church as the Fulfilment of the Christ: a Note on Ephesians 1:23," *Exp.,* 5th series, 57 (1898), pp. 241–259.

Robinson, J. A., *St. Paul's Epistle to the Ephesians,* London, 1907.

Roels, E. D., *God's Mission, The Epistle to the Ephesians in Mission Perspective,* doctoral dissertation, Franeker, 1962.

Salmond, S. D. F., *The Epistle to the Ephesians* (*The Expositor's Greek Testament,* Vol. Three), Grand Rapids, no date.

Sanders, E. P., "Literary Dependence in Colossians," *JBL* (March 1966), pp. 28–45.

Schaff, P., *History of the Christian Church,* New York, 1923, Vol. VII.

Schille, "Liturgisches Gut im Epheserbrief," doctoral dissertation, Göttingen, 1952.

Scott, E. F., *The Epistles of Paul to the Colossians, to Philemon, and to the Ephesians* (*Moffatt Commentary*), New York, 1930.

Simpson, E. K., *The Pastoral Epistles,* London, 1954.

Simpson, E. K., *Commentary on the Epistle to the Ephesians* (*New International Commentary on the New Testament*), Grand Rapids, 1957.

Smalley, S. S., "The Eschatology of Ephesians," *EQ,* Vol. 28, No. 3 (July–September, 1956), pp. 152–157.

Stewart, J. S., *A Man in Christ, The Vital Elements of St. Paul's Religion,* New York and London, no date.

Streeter, B. H., *The Primitive Church,* New York, 1929.

Summers, R., "One Message – Redemption," *RE,* Vol. 60 (Fall 1963), pp. 380–398.

Talbot, L. T., *Lectures on Ephesians,* Wheaton, Ill., 1937.

Thiessen, H. C., *Introduction to the New Testament,* Grand Rapids, 1943.

Trench, R. C., *Synonyms of the New Testament,* edition Grand Rapids, 1948.

Van Leeuwen, J. A. C., *Paulus' Zendbrieven aan Efeze, Colosse, Filemon, en Thessalonika* (*Kommentaar op het Nieuwe Testament*), Amsterdam, 1926.

Van Til, C., *The New Modernism: an appraisal of the theology of Barth and Brunner,* Philadelphia, 1946.

Van Til, C., *Has Karl Barth Become Orthodox?,* Philadelphia, 1954.

Ward, W. E., "One Body – the Church," *RE,* Vol. 60, No. 4 (Fall 1963), pp. 398–413.

Warfield, B. B., *The Inspiration and Authority of the Bible,* Philadelphia, 1948.

Westcott, B. F., *Saint Paul's Epistle to the Ephesians,* London, 1906.

Whitaker, G. H., "The Chief Cornerstone," *Exp,* 8th series (1921), pp. 470–472.

Wood, J. T., *Discoveries at Ephesus,* 1877.

Wright, G. E., *Biblical Archaeology,* London and Philadelphia, 1957.

Zahn, Th., *Einleitung in das Neue Testament,* 1897–1900.